The Cambridge History of
Literary Criticism

VOLUME 5

Romanticism

This latest volume in the celebrated *Cambridge History of Literary Criticism* surveys literary criticism of the Romantic period, chiefly in Europe. Its seventeen chapters are by internationally respected academics and explore a range of key topics and themes. The book is designed to help readers locate essential information and to develop approaches and viewpoints for a deeper understanding of issues discussed by Romantic critics or those that were fundamental to their works. Primary and secondary bibliographies provide a guide for further research.

The coverage of the book, focussing on themes and genres but drawing in discussion of the key authors, will ensure that it becomes a standard reference work on the period c.1780–c.1830. These remain in many ways the formative years for modern Anglo–American as well as European literary history.

Marshall Brown is Professor of English and Comparative Literature at the University of Washington. He is the author of *The shape of German Romanticism*; *Preromanticism*; and *Turning points: essays in the history of cultural expressions*. In addition, he has published widely in such journals as *PMLA*; *Critical inquiry*; *ELH*; *Studies in Romanticism*; *European Romantic review*; *Comparative literature*; *The eighteenth century: theory and interpretation*; *German quarterly*; and *Italian quarterly*. Marshall Brown is editor of *Modern language quarterly: a journal of literary history*.

The Cambridge History of
Literary Criticism

The Cambridge History of Literary Criticism will provide a comprehensive historical account of Western literary criticism from classical antiquity to the present day, dealing with both literary theory and critical practice. The History is intended as an authoritative work of reference and exposition, but more than a mere chronicle of facts. While remaining broadly non-partisan it addresses, where appropriate, controversial issues of current critical debate without evasion or false pretences of neutrality. Each volume is a self-contained unit designed to be used independently as well as in conjunction with the others in the series. Substantial bibliographic material in each volume provides the foundation for further study of the subjects in question.

VOLUMES PUBLISHED

Volume 1: *Classical Criticism*, edited by George A. Kennedy
Volume 3: *The Renaissance*, edited by Glyn P. Norton
Volume 4: *The Eighteenth Century*, edited by H. B. Nisbet and Claude Rawson
Volume 5: *Romanticism*, edited by Marshall Brown
Volume 7: *The Twentieth Century: Modernism and the New Criticism*,
edited by A. Walton Litz, Luke Menand and Lawrence Rainey
Volume 8: *From Formalism to Poststructuralism*, edited by Raman Selden

OTHER VOLUMES IN PREPARATION

Volume 2: *The Middle Ages*, edited by Alastair Minnis
Volume 6: *The Nineteenth Century*
Volume 9: *Twentieth-Century Historical, Philosophical and Psychological Perspectives*, edited by Christa Knellwolf and Christopher Norris

FOUNDING EDITORS
Professor H. B. Nisbet
University of Cambridge

Professor Claude Rawson
Yale University

The contribution of H. B. Nisbet and Claude Rawson in helping to specify and approve the shape of Volume 5, and in advising on early drafts of the contributions, is gratefully acknowledged.

The Cambridge History of
Literary Criticism

VOLUME 5
Romanticism

Edited by

MARSHALL BROWN

 CAMBRIDGE
UNIVERSITY PRESS

PUBLISHED BY THE PRESS SYNDICATE OF THE UNIVERSITY OF CAMBRIDGE
The Pitt Building, Trumpington Street, Cambridge CB2 1RP, United Kingdom

CAMBRIDGE UNIVERSITY PRESS
The Edinburgh Building, Cambridge CB2 2RU, UK   http://www.cup.cam.ac.uk
40 West 20th Street, New York, NY 10011-4211, USA   http://www.cup.org
10 Stamford Road, Oakleigh, Melbourne 3166, Australia

© Cambridge University Press 2000

First published 2000

Printed in the United Kingdom at the University Press, Cambridge

Typeset in 10/12pt Sabon   [GC]

A catalogue record for this book is available from the British Library

ISBN 0 521 30010 X hardback

To the memory of
Ernst Behler

Contents

Contributors

Jonathan Arac is Professor of English at the University of Pittsburgh and a member of the *Boundary 2* editorial collective. He is author of *Commissioned spirits* (1979), *Critical genealogies* (1987) and *'Huckleberry Finn' as idol and target* (1997), and he has edited five volumes of original essays, including *Postmodernism and politics* (1986). His contribution to this volume relates closely to his book in progress, to be published by Duke University Press, entitled *Impure worlds*.

Joel Black is Associate Professor of Comparative Literature at the University of Georgia. He is the author of *The aesthetics of murder: a study in Romantic literature and contemporary culture* (1991) and essays on De Quincey, Foucault, Pynchon and Gaddis. He is currently working on studies of contemporary film, Wilde's aesthetics and Freudian science.

Marshall Brown is Professor of English and Comparative Literature and Adjunct Professor of Music and German at the University of Washington, where he edits *Modern language quarterly: a journal of literary history*. He has written *The shape of German Romanticism* (1979), *Preromanticism* (1991) and *Turning points: essays in the history of cultural expressions* (1997), and edited *La via al sublime* (1987, with Giovanna Franci and Vita Fortunati), *The uses of literary history* (1996) and *Eighteenth-century literary history: an MLQ reader* (1999). His next book will be *The gothic text*.

Alfredo De Paz is Professor of the Methodology of Art Criticism at the University of Bologna (Italy). He has written many essays and theoretical and historical books on the art and culture of the nineteenth and twentieth centuries. For many years he has been engaged in interpreting European Romanticism in a contemporary and postmodern perspective. His publications include *Sociologia e critica delle arti* (1980), *La rivoluzione romantica* (1984), *Goya: arte e condizione umana* (1990), *Il romanticismo e la pittura: natura, simbolo, storia* (1992), *Europa romantica: fondamenti e paradigmi della sensibilità moderna* (1994), *Géricault: la febbre dell'arte e della vita* (1997).

Paul H. Fry is William Lampson Professor of English and Master of Ezra Stiles College at Yale University. He is the author of *The poet's calling in the English ode* (1980), *The reach of criticism* (1984), *William Empson: prophet against sacrifice* (1990) and *A defense of poetry* (1994), and editor of *The rime of the Ancient Mariner: case studies in contemporary criticism* (1998), together with numerous articles on Romanticism, the history of criticism (including an article on I. A. Richards for the present series) and literary theory. He is writing a book on Wordsworth.

Gary Handwerk is Professor of English and Comparative Literature and chairman of the Department of Comparative Literature at the University of Washington. He is the author of *Irony and ethics in narrative: from Schlegel to Lacan* and translator of *Human, all too human* for *The complete works of Nietzsche*. He has published articles on nineteenth- and twentieth-century narrative and, most recently, articles on several of William Godwin's novels and on Romantic conceptions of history. He is currently at work on new editions of *Caleb Williams* and *Fleetwood*.

Theresa M. Kelley is Marjorie an Lorin Tiefenthaler Professor of English at the University of Wisconsin. She has published essays on eighteenth-century aesthetics, the sister arts, Romantic poets, rhetoric and art, and participates in an exchange on Romanticism and Philosophy for *Praxis*, the on-line journal of Romantic Circles on the Web. She is the author of *Wordsworth's revisionary aesthetics* (1988) and *Reinventing allegory* (1995) and co-editor with Paula Feldman of *Romantic women writers: voices and counter-voices* (1995). Her current projects include a study of the role of botany and botanical illustration in Romantic culture and an investigation of Staël's writing on passion and reason.

Jon Klancher, Professor of English at Carnegie Mellon University, is the author of *The making of English reading audiences, 1791–1832* (1987) and articles on Coleridge, Godwin, Bakhtin, Romantic criticism and the French Revolution and other topics. He is currently writing a study of disciplinary formation and the institutional contexts of cultural criticism, political debate and literary theory in the Romantic age.

Herbert Lindenberger is Avalon Foundation Professor of Humanities in Comparative Literature and English at Stanford University, where he also founded and chaired Comparative Literature. His books include *On Wordsworth's 'Prelude'* (1963), *Georg Büchner* (1964), *Georg Trakl* (1971), *Historical drama: the relation of literature and reality* (1975), *Saul's fall: a critical fiction* (1979), *Opera: the extravagant art* (1984), *The history in literature* (1990) and, most recently, *Opera in history: from Monteverdi to Cage* (1998). He has held Fulbright, Guggenheim and

National Endowment for the Humanities fellowships. During 1997 he served as president of the Modern Language Association. He is currently working on a larger study of the interrelationship of the arts that will expand the essay in the present volume.

Kurt Mueller-Vollmer is Professor of German Studies and Humanities, emeritus, at Stanford University and guest associate with the Center for Advanced Study in the Internationality of National Literatures at the University of Göttingen (Germany). He has published widely in the areas of Romanticism, German–American cultural relations, hermeneutics and literary theory, language theory, and translation studies and on the work of Wilhelm von Humboldt. His book publications include *Toward a phenomenological theory of literature* (1963), *Poesie und Einbildungskraft: zur Dichtungstheorie Wilhelm von Humboldts* (1967), *The hermeneutics reader* (1985, 1988, 1991, 1994) and *Wilhelm von Humboldts Sprachwissenschaft* (1991). He has edited (with M. Irmscher) *Translating literatures, translating cultures: new vistas and approaches in literary studies* (1998) and is editor in chief of the critical edition of Wilhelm von Humboldt's *Writings on linguistics*.

David Perkins is Marquand Professor of English and American Literature, emeritus, at Harvard University, where he served in the departments of English, Literature and Comparative Literature. He is the author of numerous books and articles on English Romanticism, modern poetry and problems and theories of literary history.

Tilottama Rajan is Professor of English, director of the Centre for Theory at the University of Western Ontario, and founder of the North American Society for the Study of Romanticism. She is the author of *Dark interpreter: the discourse of Romanticism* (1980) and *The supplement of reading: figures of understanding in Romantic literature* (1990) and coeditor of *Intersections: nineteenth-century philosophy and contemporary theory* (1995) and *Romanticism, history, and the possibilities of genre: reforming literature 1789–1837* (1998). Her current project is a study of relationships between phenomenology, deconstruction and poststructuralism.

Albert Sbragia is Associate Professor of Italian at the University of Washington and director of the Cinema Studies Program. Publications include *Carlo Emilio Gadda and the modern macaronic* (1996) and essays on Gadda, Calvino, Svevo and the nineteenth-century Italian novel. He is the translator of Franco Moretti's *The way of the world: the Bildungsroman in European civilization* (1987).

Helmut J. Schneider is Professor and chairman of the department of German at the University of Bonn (Germany). He formerly taught German and Comparative Literature at the University of California, Irvine, and the University of California, Davis. He has worked extensively on the history of pastoral poetry, the German idyll and landscape and utopia. He is the author of *Bürgerliche Idylle: Studien zu einer literarischen Gattung des 18. Jahrhunderts am Beispiel von Johann Heinrich Voss* (1975) as well as articles on landscape aesthetics, Lessing, Kleist and modern authors, and has edited three anthologies: *Idyllen der Deutschen* (1978), *Deutsche Landschaften* (1981), and *Deutsche Idyllentheorien im 18. Jahrhundert* (1988).

E. S. Shaffer, F. B. A., is Senior Research Fellow and Director of the Research Project on the Reception of British Authors in Europe at the School of Advanced Study, University of London. She was visiting Fellow of All Souls College, Oxford, in 1996. She is the author of *'Kubla Khan' and The Fall of Jerusalem: the mythological school in Biblical criticism and secular literature 1770–1880* (1975), and has published widely on English and German Romantic thought, including 'The hermeneutic community: Coleridge and Schleiermacher' in *The Coleridge connection* (1990) and 'Romantic philosophy and the organization of the disciplines' in *Romanticism and the sciences* (1990). Other books include *Erewhons of the eye: Samuel Butler as painter, photographer and art critic* (1988); she edited and introduced George Eliot, *Middlemarch* (1991), and *Literature and science: the third culture* (1998). She is editor of *Comparative criticism*, an annual journal of which volume 20 is 'Philosophical dialogues' (1998). She is working on a book on Coleridge's literary theory.

David Simpson is Professor and G. B. Needham Fellow in English at the University of California, Davis. He has written many books on Romanticism and other fields, of which the most recent are *The academic postmodern and the rule of literature: a report on half-knowledge* (1995) and *Romanticism, nationalism and the revolt against theory* (1993). He edited *German aesthetic and literary criticism: Kant to Hegel* (1984) and *The origins of modern critical thought: Lessing to Hegel* (1988), both published by Cambridge University Press. He is currently at work on a book titled *Situatedness: or, why we keep saying where we're coming from*.

David Wellbery is William Kurrelmeyer Professor of German at Johns Hopkins University. He is the author of *Lessing's 'Laocoön': semiotics and aesthetics in the age of reason* (1984), *The specular moment: Goethe's early lyric and the beginnings of Romanticism* (1996) and *Neo-retorica e desconstrução* (1998). He has edited several books and published numerous essays on literary theory and on German literature from the eighteenth century to the present. He is currently writing a book on Schopenhauer and modernism.

Introduction

MARSHALL BROWN

Many of the presuppositions and practices that prevail in contemporary aesthetics and literary criticism originate in writings from the Romantic decades.[1] So do several positions to which the contemporary climate is hostile. Hence Romanticism is often regarded as the root of contemporary attitudes – the beginning of Modernism which, conversely, is viewed as late Romanticism – and likewise, not infrequently, as the source of the troubles from which we are now at last freeing ourselves. Obviously, no period of the past has a monopolistic claim to be the origin of the modern (or the postmodern); nor do Modernism and postmodernism begin in and as anything other than themselves, whatever elements in the past may have inspired them. Still, it is generally agreed that the writing about literature from the period between 1780 and 1830 has a special bearing on the present.

Increasingly since the Romantic era literary criticism has been concerned not just with works but with writers and readers. When Wordsworth's Preface to *Lyrical ballads* defines the poet as 'a man speaking to men', he is, to be sure, making a point about the democratization of letters ('man'=common man) and missing one about the situation of women and women writers; both of these issues are discussed in this volume. But he is also making a novel statement about the communicative value of literature. The writer does not just provide moral exempla and frame a golden world; literature is there to be read and understood. One important new strand of Romantic criticism thus turns its attention to hermeneutics and interpretation: how do readers grasp what authors are saying? Criticism

---

[1] Our volume, entitled *Romanticism*, aims to represent the range of writing remaining of interest and influence from the years between about 1780 and 1830. In the German arena it remains common to label some of the writings Romantic and others (particularly in connection with Goethe, Schiller and Humboldt) Classic. In the Latin countries and in the United States the label Romantic often gets applied to writers contemporary with the British Victorians and the German Biedermeier; their Romanticisms will be covered chiefly in volume 6 of this series, while some early figures, especially Rousseau, primarily appear in volume 4. In *Romanticism and gender*, New York: Routledge, 1993, Anne Mellor has argued cogently against lumping all the writings of these decades under a single label. Names remain useful hooks, but our aim has been to represent in their variety the writings of a period, not a movement.

grows at once (though not always in the same writers) more psychological and more technical, two functions often joined in Romantic rhetorical theory and in its deconstructive avatars. And criticism also grows more sociological, as the need to define a readership is increasingly felt. Earlier genre criticism concerned the laws of composition of different types of writing; now it also considers their different purposes and audiences.

Wordsworth's poet, however, speaks *to* men, not *with* them. Alongside the reader's part, the situation of the poet is at issue in much Romantic criticism. No longer the inspired representatives of divine order, and not yet Arnoldian pedagogues, Romantic authors have their own, multiple versions of authority. One might glance back to the threshold of Romanticism, where ancient erudition had breathed a newly personal spirit in Laurence Sterne's whimsical invocation, 'Read, read, read, read, my unlearned reader! read' (*Tristram Shandy* III.36). At the same moment Samuel Johnson's Imlac had called the poet 'the interpreter of nature, and the legislator of mankind, and . . . a being superiour to time and place' (*Rasselas*, ch. 10). Imlac, of course, is a little loony, until brought down to earth by confronting the seriously disordered imagination of an astronomer who madly thinks he rules the heavens. Such are the figures who serve as equivocal models for Percy Shelley's paean to poets as 'hierophants' and 'legislators of the world' (conclusion of 'Defence of poetry'). But if Shelley's 'world' Romantically ups the ante from Imlac's social pretensions to the astronomer's universal ones, he simultaneously deflates them with the pathos of his negations: his poets are 'hierophants of an *unapprehended* vision' and '*unacknowledged* legislators' (my italics).[2] Ever since Plato, poetry was constitutionally on the defensive; in the Romantic period it became – to use what was then still a new sense of the word – nervous.

The last epigone of the platonic poet with his divine frenzy was the preromantic figure of the genius. In early Herder and other writers of the German *Sturm-und-Drang* movement we frequently find poets credited

---

[2] Earl Wasserman's unashamedly high-toned, neoplatonic reading of Shelley's 'Defence' bypasses the 'unacknowledged' and even contrives to neutralize it, claiming that 'the poetic transaction involves only the poet and his poem, not an audience' (*Shelley: a critical reading*, Baltimore, MD: The Johns Hopkins University Press, 1971, p. 220). Yet earlier, in a paragraph buttressed by a hefty quotation from the 'Defence', Wasserman says that the 'end' of *The Cenci* 'is a creative moral insight by the audience, an insight to which the play can only provoke and guide the audience by a true representation of human nature' (p. 102). For a more cautious, more explicitly proto-Arnoldian reading along similar lines, arguing that the 'actual and constantly operative power of poetry . . . is unacknowledged because it is unnoticed by everyone, including the poets themselves', see Paul H. Fry, *The reach of criticism: method and perception in literary theory*, New Haven, CT: Yale University Press, 1983, p. 161. Of course, the stature of 'the poets themselves', on this account, remains in question.

with liberated genius, sometimes even in the untranslatable compound form of the *Kraftgenie*. Kant codified Imlac-like yearnings and proto-Shelleyan nostalgia when he influentially defined genius as 'the talent (gift of nature) which gives the rule to art' (*Critique of judgment*, § 46). But he balanced praise with disparagement of *Sturm-und-Drang* excesses by insisting on taste and craft as other essentials: when out of place or out of line, genius is 'totally laughable' ('vollends lächerlich', § 47). As poets started going mad for real, the evidence began to come in, and the reports on Collins, Cowper and Clare, Sade, Hölderlin and even Blake were far from encouraging. Nor did the suicidal fraud of Chatterton or the obstinate one of Macpherson help the neoplatonic cause. In 'Resolution and independence' Wordsworth moralizes 'Chatterton, the marvellous Boy', and the tipsy Robert Burns with the famous lines, 'We Poets in our youth begin in gladness; / But thereof come in the end despondency and madness'. And while Keats dedicated *Endymion* to Chatterton's memory, the mood is far from exalted when his Epistle 'To George Felton Mathew' sequentially evokes Chatterton, 'that warm-hearted Shakespeare', 'Milton's blindness', and 'those who strove with the bright golden wing / Of genius, to flap away each sting / Thrown by the pitiless world'. Increasingly, it was the psychology of poetic genius and not its authority that came up for discussion. Generally, of course, if not in Keats's list, Shakespeare stood out from all competitors; the Romantic encounters with Shakespeare therefore became a crucial final reckoning with doctrines of legitimizing inspiration, preceding the Icarian swoops and swoons of Baudelaire and Tennyson and the obsessive ivory-tower perfectionism of the symbolists.

Often in Romantic criticism the struggles of readers to understand and of writers to be understood and the anxiety of creators to measure up were counterbalanced by an increasing emancipation and exaltation of art. The old moral imperatives had faded into the social graces of eighteenth-century taste and had been degraded even further in attacks such as Rousseau's on the frivolousness of aesthetic spectacle. The latest defence of poesy, particularly associated with Kant and Schiller, was to value play itself as a humanizing and elevating moral value. Art becomes not the representative of religion but its propaedeutic (Hegel) or even its substitute (Schelling and his followers). High and low come together in the more dizzying tributes to Romantic irony. From the varieties of Romantic-era criticism can be derived both the elitist formalism of the modernists and the anti-elitist high jinx of postmodernists, though both tend to strip Romantic motifs of their sublime, metaphysical or transcendental dimensions.

Finally, critics in the Romantic era became self-conscious about their position in time and space. Even in its turn to antiquity, the Renaissance had present ends in mind.[3] With Herder's historicism as both symptom and cause, Romantics worried about their historical role and studied poetry in its historical unfolding. They also used poetics to project destinies: utopia becomes an aesthetic realm lodged in the distant future. Nor – though the connections are often overlooked – was Romantic situational thinking limited to temporality. It becomes geographical in the increasing nationalism of European culture of the period, leading to a growing divergence among the various European literary traditions. It becomes sociological in the burgeoning interest in folksong and, more generally, in writing for and by the lower classes (in verse chiefly) and the middle classes (in the novel). Situational thinking likewise motivates the growing, if still incipient and uneven attention to women as writers and readers of literature. It renders discussions of literature and the other arts richer and less judgemental than in earlier periods. And, finally, it regulates the complex use of nature as model, goal and nostalgic absence in so much Romantic criticism.

Such, in a quick conspectus, are the motifs that the following chapters pursue. We chose to request substantial essays investigating large areas of Romantic period writing. Other surveys focus more than ours does on digesting facts including, particularly, the tenets of individual authors. We preferred to let our chapters model how Romantics thought through and debated larger issues. The chapters are real essays, informational in their base, but ultimately more concerned with showing how Romantic ideas work and how contemporary critics may investigate and use them. A particular challenge for all our authors was to pursue their topics on an international basis and to show the coherence remaining as national traditions diverge. German abstraction can seem airless to British Romanticists, British empiricism can seem pedestrian to philosophical minds, and the French, in this period, can seem parochial or insubstantial to both; one aim of our volume has been to show how each tradition can animate and illuminate the others.

Because we wanted a volume that would be useful today and to an Anglophone readership, we have not tried to represent all facets of literary criticism from our period equally. Survivals from earlier eras are vital to a balanced view of our decades. It should be remembered that Hugh Blair's *Lectures on rhetoric and belles lettres* were far more often printed and more widely read than the Preface to *Lyrical ballads*. But choices had to be made, and in a book designed for contemporary readers we preferred

---

[3] See Daniel Javitch's fine recent demonstration that even the Aristotle revival envisioned using Ancient means for Modern ends: 'The emergence of poetic genre theory in the sixteenth century', *Modern language quarterly* 59 (1998), pp. 139–69.

Wordsworth.[4] Similarly, topics that seemed of more local importance have been left for specialized works, where discussions can readily be found. Thus, in connection with stylistics, the extensive German discussions about the proper use of classical metres, Kleist's fascinating hints about prose, and even Wordsworth's dissection of poetic diction and metre were set aside in favour of less technical, more overtly conceptual and ideological issues of rhetoric that have been much debated in criticism of recent decades. A number of issues and figures straddle the eighteenth-century and Romantic volumes: more systematic synopses of Kant and Schiller and of the sublime, the beautiful and the picturesque will be found in volume 4, where they synthesize earlier lines of thinking, whereas in our volume they appear in connection with distinctive sallies of innovation. Conversely, Fielding's theory of the novel was, in its day, eccentric in both form and substance, and it is treated more fully here in connection with the German theories of the novel that take up where Fielding leaves off.

*

The 'we' I have used in this introduction is a real but not a happy one. The original plan for the volume was Ernst Behler's, to which I contributed only a few refinements, and it was to have been his and my responsibility jointly. As editor, essayist, teacher, administrator, colleague and human being, Ernst was a force of nature. He died, suddenly and at the pinnacle of his career, before he could write his chapter or introduction, let alone see the volume through. It is in sadness, not joy, that I have dedicated it to his memory.

After Ernst, my largest gratitude is to the contributors. Those who finished early and waited patiently and those who persisted long with tough assignments are equally in the debt of all of us. Special thanks are due to two who coped splendidly with speedy fulfilments of late commissions: Theresa Kelley for her chapter on women in Romantic criticism, and David Simpson for the chapter on philosophy, replacing the one it was not given to Ernst to write. Eric Schaad laboured countless hours checking quotes and citations and supplementing bibliographies; one could not wish for a more meticulous and responsive co-worker. A Cambridge University Press sandwich, Josie Dixon between two slices of Kevin Taylor, waited when waiting was necessary, responded immediately when

---

[4] For an impressively thorough and informative study of a slice of what was actually written and read in the Romantic period, see Friedrich Sengle, *Biedermeierzeit: deutsche Literatur im Spannungsfeld zwischen Restauration und Revolution 1815–48*, 3 vols., Stuttgart: Metzler, 1971–80, vol. 1. I am not aware of comparable studies for other decades and countries.

questions arose and generally kept me in line. A sabbatical from the University of Washington and a fellowship from the Woodrow Wilson International Center for Scholars, while targeted for another project, helped a lot with this one. For once, Jane did not help much, but she was always there when wanted and constantly in my thoughts.

I

Classical standards in the period

PAUL H. FRY

If this topic should seem either too piecemeal or too self-evident to include in a general volume on romantic criticism, it may help to recall that for René Wellek the status of neoclassical criticism among the Romantics is the crucial issue that makes the second volume of his *History of modern criticism* possible: 'I think we must recognize that we can speak of a general European Romantic movement only if we take a wide over-all view and consider simply the general rejection of the neoclassical creed as a common denominator.'[1] But possibly this claim only deepens suspicion. Arthur Lovejoy had famously argued that no criterion of any kind was common to all Romanticisms, and Wellek, who wrote his equally famous rebuttal of Lovejoy while at work on volume two, would have been especially eager at that time to uphold the legitimacy of broad period definitions.[2] Can the exceptions, we may ask – Byron and Chateaubriand, for example – ever be acceptably rationalized from any standpoint, not just Lovejoy's?

Nevertheless, whatever one might feel moved to say on other occasions, this is clearly not the place for the postmodern insistence that only an atomism vastly exceeding even Lovejoy's can do justice to the complexity of literary history (and in any case, Musset had already said that about 'Romanticism' in 1824![3]). One must do what one can, aided in this case by the easily overlooked precision of Wellek's claim: we can try at first to agree, tentatively, that what the spirit of the Romantic age rejects is the neoclassical, not necessarily the Classical or the texts of antiquity, and proceed from there. It may finally be possible to show, however, that there is something even more telling, more truly characteristic and self-defining, albeit more varied, about the Romantic reception of Classical antiquity itself.

[1] René Wellek, *A history of modern criticism: 1750–1950*, vol. II: *The Romantic age*, New Haven, CT: Yale University Press, 1955, p. 2.
[2] See Arthur Lovejoy, 'On the discrimination of Romanticisms' (1924), and René Wellek, 'The concept of "Romanticism" in literary history: the term "Romantic" and its derivatives', 1949, conveniently anthologized in *Romanticism: points of view*, Robert F. Gleckner and Gerald E. Enscoe (eds.), Englewood Cliffs, NJ: Prentice-Hall, 1970.
[3] Lovejoy approvingly cites Alfred de Musset's *Lettres de Dupuis et Cotonet* as the '*reductio ad absurdum* of efforts to define romanticism' (*Romanticism*, Gleckner and Enscoe (eds.), p. 66n.).

By 'Neoclassical' in this contrastive context we conventionally under-stand the domination of taste by Opitz and Gottsched in Germany, Boileau in France and Pope together with other verse essayists on criti-cism like Roscommon in England (it has been wittily observed that the neoclassical is the moment when poetry and criticism are one). The differ-ence between the neoclassical and the Classical is for the most part self-explanatory (as between Pope and Homer, or even between Pope and Virgil), but much harder to maintain, as we shall see, when one considers the reception of the Classical texts of criticism – Horace obviously, but also Longinus, who was popularized by Boileau, and Aristotle most prob-lematically of all. When Wordsworth so disturbingly says, 'Aristotle, I have been told . . .', then misunderstands what he has been 'told'[4] while purporting to agree with it, even though the Preface to *Lyrical ballads* taken as a whole is the most radically anti-Aristotelian piece of critical speculation one could imagine, our perplexity is not just focussed on the sociohistorical interest that attaches to Wordsworth's alleged ignorance (and cheerful willingness to confess it) against the backdrop of earlier lit-erary institutions, but also on the simple question what is meant by 'Aris-totle': is this the neoclassical Stagyrite or is it the ancient sage who upholds the honour of poetry against the attack of Plato? And how significant can it be that Wordsworth seems in this place to have the latter figure in mind, since elsewhere he seems certainly to anticipate the modern consensus that Plato is proto-romantic while Aristotle is proto-neoclassical?[5]

Taking it as given, however, that in most cases we know what is meant by the Neoclassical, all will agree that the clearest instance of the 'Romantic' rejection of this 'creed', uttered in the name of the classical Apollo, can be found in Keats's 'Sleep and poetry' (1817), where a diatribe against poets who 'sway'd about upon a rocking horse, / And thought it Pegasus' con-cludes as follows:

> A thousand handicraftsmen wore the mask
> Of Poesy. Ill-fated, impious race!
> That blasphemed the bright Lyrist to his face,
> And did not know it, – no, they went about,
> Holding a poor, decrepid standard out

---

[4] William Wordsworth, 'Preface to *Lyrical ballads*', in *Wordsworth: poetical works*, Thomas Hutchinson (ed.), Ernest de Selincourt (rev. edn), London: Oxford University Press, 1974, p. 737.

[5] 'The English', Wordsworth is said to have remarked in conversation, 'with their devotion to Aristotle, have but half the truth; a sound philosophy must contain both Plato and Aris-totle.' Cited from *Old friends: memories of old friends, being extracts from the journals and letters of Caroline Fox*, Horace N. Pym (ed.) (1884) in *The critical opinions of William Wordsworth*, Markham L. Peacock, Jr (ed.), Baltimore, MD: The Johns Hopkins Univer-sity Press, 1950, p. 76.

Mark'd with most flimsy mottos, and in large
The name of one Boileau![6]

Even here qualifications are in order. By 1819 Keats himself was reading (and imitating here and there in *Lamia*) the poetry of Dryden. Hence even though there was a widespread tendency to follow Johnson in considering Dryden a more dynamic poet than Pope (just as Homer and Shakespeare were thought more dynamic than Virgil and Jonson), it must be granted nonetheless that within the space of two years Keats's taste had become more catholic. Also, this is the very passage which more than anything else earned Keats the scorn of the 'Romantic' Byron.

Still and all, the passage remains exemplary: the contempt for rules presumed – *qua* rules – to be mechanical and arbitrarily superimposed is after all an undeniable hallmark of Romanticism. Many Romantic texts could be cited in which the decline from the Classical to the neoclassical is seen precisely as the transformation of the normative from internal necessity to external constraint. And undoubtedly among the English Romantics, always with the loud exception of Byron and likewise excluding such contemporaries as the verse essayist on criticism William Gifford, the poetry of Pope was considered competent at best and even subject to the question – first raised in a more defensive spirit by Johnson – whether indeed it was poetry at all.[7] The arch-villain was Pope's Homer. It must come as a shock to any reader of Keats's sonnet on Chapman's Homer that he had already read Pope's Homer, which 'made no impression on him'[8]; and we have also Wordsworth's belief (appearing in an 1808 letter to Scott encouraging Scott's edition of Dryden and therefore saying whatever could be said *in favour* of Dryden and his period) that '[I]t will require yet half a century completely to carry off the poison of Pope's Homer'.[9]

In the English tradition it is hard to point to a time when the Neoclassical, or 'pseudo-classical',[10] was not already under attack. Sir William Temple's *Essay of poetry* (1690) is a case in point, with its indictment of the 'Moderns' for being too lapidary in matters of style and diction; and the increasingly Longinian element I have elsewhere identified in Dryden's

---

[6] John Keats, *The poems of John Keats*, ed. Jack Stillinger, Cambridge, MA: Harvard University Press, 1978, p. 74.

[7] For argument that this was a received idea, imposed merely by the hegemony of Wartonian literary history and not fully consistent with the actual continuity of certain romantic and neoclassical tenets, see Robert Griffin, *Wordsworth's Pope: a study in literary historiography*, Cambridge University Press, 1995, *passim*.

[8] Gilbert Highet, *The Classical tradition: Greek and Roman influences on Western literature*, New York: Oxford University Press, 1957, p. 416.

[9] *The letters of William and Dorothy Wordsworth: the middle years*, Part I: 1806–1811, Ernest de Selincourt (ed.), Mary Moorman (rev.), Oxford: Clarendon Press, 1969, p. 191.

[10] The expression, referring to Opitz, is L. A. Willoughby's: *The Romantic movement in Germany*, New York: Russell & Russell, 1966, p. 7.

late prefaces[11] is an advance critique of any dogged adherence to regularity – the sort of thing expressed most woodenly, for example, by the 'Modern' Charles Gildon among Dryden's near contemporaries. As Walter Jackson Bate put it, 'the Moderns in general felt, not that the Ancients were too bound by rules, but that they were not correct enough in their observance of them'.[12] But the Moderns never got the better of any exchange of opinion even in their own time, and it remains the case that the strictly neoclassical in England is to a large extent a straw man. This is not to say that the Restoration and Queen Anne ethos was always already preromantic. Certain invariants can be pointed to, such as the fact that throughout this period – as it was commonplace to complain by the time of Mme de Staël, for example – critical analysis and even textual emendation was always aimed at 'faults' rather than 'beauties', suggesting a completely unshaken faith in the juridical power of standards, if not perhaps always exactly the same ones. By the same token it is telling, I think, that Bishop Thomas Warburton's treatise on the origin of language, *The divine legation of Moses* (1741), shies away from the idea (typified in Herder and Rousseau a generation later and still current in Shelley) that the language directly emergent from prelinguistic rude noises was chiefly poetic metaphor. Any extravagance of figure in primitive language was owing rather, Warburton argued, to 'rusticity of conception',[13] and speakers advanced towards a civilized indulgence in metaphor only through a succession of stages. And again, it is unwise to assume that Pope's brave disorder producing a grace beyond the reach of art is an endorsement of anything approaching what was later considered sublime, although the nod to Longinus is clear enough. 'Grace' evokes *'gratia'*, the *'je ne sais quoi'*, a safety-valve for latitude invoked throughout the seventeenth century, rather than the sublime, which plays an equivalent role in the eighteenth.[14]

But if even these exceptions serve in some measure to demonstrate that the neoclassical was never more than a tendency in the history of English taste, that is after all what has long been thought. If Pope's Longinus

---

[11] Paul H. Fry, *The reach of criticism: method and perception in literary theory*, New Haven, CT: Yale University Press, 1983, pp. 87–124; Fry, 'Dryden's earliest allusion to Longinus', *ELN* 19 (1981), 22–4.

[12] Bate, *From Classic to Romantic: premises of taste in eighteenth-century England*, New York: Harper, 1946, p. 32.

[13] Quoted by René Wellek, *The rise of English literary history*, Chapel Hill, NC: University of North Carolina Press, 1941, p. 88. The striking verbal anticipation serves precisely to show that no doctrine could invert the values of Wordsworth more completely.

[14] See Samuel Holt Monk, ' "A Grace beyond the reach of Art" ', *Journal of the history of ideas* 5 (1944), pp. 131–50. I think I was wrong to suggest in *The reach of criticism* (p. 83) that this concept looks forward to Hazlitt's *gusto*. Hazlitt looks back rather to the Renaissance emphasis on *energeia*, I now feel – a doctrine which has relatively little to do with *sprezzatura*, etc.

is scarcely that of, say, John Dennis ('Sir Tremendous Longinus'), he is perhaps still more recognizable in Pope (if only as an alter ego in *Peri Bathous*) than he is in Boileau, even though the latter published his translation and commentary on Longinus together with his own *Art poétique* in 1674. Boileau's main emphasis falls on what Longinus has to say about harmony and rhythm (*synthesis*), chiefly in chapter 39 of the *Peri Hupsous*, and very little on those formally disruptive verbal devices, such as scrambled or disconnected word order, which chiefly influenced English taste. As Bate argues (*Classic to Romantic*, p. 170), and as Robert Southey boasted in *Specimens of the later English poets* (1807) while disparaging neoclassicism, the English had a great literary Renaissance to look back upon.[15] Its benchmark was the irregular Shakespeare rather than the elegant Racine (a famous debate that Stendhal was the first French writer to decide in favour of the English). The Germans of the early eighteenth century, meanwhile, had only Baroque models to imagine themselves capable of polishing. However, the Germans themselves began a retreat from the neoclassical norm when the Swiss critics Bodmer and Breitinger drew on Addison to introduce a taste for English poetry in the tradition of Milton, resulting in a degree of preromantic sentiment, from Haller to Klopstock, that can well be compared with what happened in England between Thomson and Cowper.

It is a question, in fact, and one which harbours much of what remains to be said on this topic, whether the 'Romantic' view of the neoclassical is not really rather at bottom 'preromantic', precisely because the distinction between the neoclassical and the Classical was not really available until the German theorists of the 1790s began to articulate a notion of the Romantic understood in contrast with a frame of mind to be respected, not disparaged – namely, the Classical. And once the cordiality toward Classicism in Schiller, Goethe, the Schlegels and Hegel emerged, in tandem with English neohellenism and the pervasive contrast everywhere between Greece and Rome (of which more below), the neoclassical tended to become, apart from the jejune truculence of Keats, not just a straw man but a dead horse.

A few remarks on the reception of Longinus may make this clearer, while showing that the issue is not just a matter of contrasting Greece and Rome. The authority of Longinus was highest, and perhaps equally high, both in the neoclassical moment and in the preromantic reaction against it; yet before this period, in the Renaissance to which the Romantics looked back in overlooking the Age of Pope, and likewise after this period in the age of Romanticism itself, Longinus is scarcely heard of. It is important

---

[15] See Southey, ed., *Specimens of the later English poets*, 3 vols., London: Longman, 1807, I: xxiii–xxxi.

to see the implications of this fact. An obscure English translation of Longinus in the early seventeenth century by Thomas Hall went unread (Milton mentions Longinus in *Of education*, but we strongly suspect that he had not read him), and only Boileau's French version began the vogue which was sustained by Leonard Welsted's translation of 1712. And then, as the century reaches its close, Longinus is still mentioned from time to time by the first major Romantic writers and their successors, but he has obviously ceased to matter.

This is not hard to explain. Somewhat resembling the revisionary readers of Longinus in recent times (Thomas Weiskel, Neil Hertz and the present writer, for example), the critics and poets who took Longinus seriously understood the 'sublime' (or lofty, or elevated) as an effect of rhetoric serving to broaden and diversify the possibilities of an exercise, verse-writing, which remained at bottom, after Aristotle, a *techne*, or craft. This is not quite the view of poetry either before or after this period, times when psychological forces that are not exclusively formal are more broadly acknowledged – as indeed they are, it should be said, in the text of Longinus itself. Both *enargeia* – as I have said – and *energeia* matter greatly to the Renaissance; and in the later eighteenth century, when the sublime becomes increasingly psychological in successive analyses from Burke to Kant, no longer residing either in the external world or in the texture of language but standing disclosed as nothing other than the power of mind itself, it comes to be replaced by another term, 'imagination', which then becomes the place-holder indicating the value of the meta-formal in the period that contrasts its own achievement with the Classical rather than the neoclassical. Wordsworth in a letter of 1825 sums up what has happened by emphasizing that an interest in Longinus, binding the neoclassical and the preromantic together, must at bottom be an interest in rhetoric:

one is surprised that it should have been supposed for a moment, that *Longinus* writes upon the Sublime, even in our vague and popular sense of the word – What is there in Sappho's ode that has any affinity with the sublimity of Ezekiel or Isaiah, or even Homer or Eschylus? Longinus treats of animated, impassioned, energetic or if you will, elevated writing – of these, abundant instances are to be found in Eschylus and Homer – but nothing would be easier than to show, both by positive and negative proof, that his *hupsous* when translated sublimity deceives the english Reader, by substituting an etymology for a translation. Much of what I observe you call sublime, *I* should call grand or dignified.[16]

Perhaps this evidence of a certain critical distance from preromanticism in the period succeeding it will indicate in part why the neoclassical can

---

[16] *The letters of William and Dorothy Wordsworth: the later years, part 1: 1821–1828,* Ernest de Selincourt (ed.), Alan G. Hill (rev.), Oxford: Clarendon Press, 1978, p. 335.

appear to be rehabilitated in extraordinary cases like that of Byron, whose 1821 controversy with William Lisle Bowles about the value of Pope's poetry shows him to have outgrown, or in any case survived beyond, the literary historiography of the Wartons in which the much older Bowles is still completely entangled. Bowles in his biography of Pope disparages Pope's anthropocentrism (viewed implicitly as irreligious) and his failure to appreciate the sublimity of the natural world. Byron retorts, in a series of letters to his publisher intended for circulation, that all landscape is barren without the traces of human history, and he is able to do so because he can spontaneously suppose, in the aftermath of Kant on the sublime rather than the Wartons on the Spenserian tradition, that the sublime is located in the human mind and not in the inhuman world. He can take the lawlessness of imagination, of Renaissance overreaching, for granted, thus freeing himself to reconsider whether or not the technical and moral legacy of Pope's poetry is not after all superior to its preromantic alternatives – including, as he misreads it, the 'lake poetry' of Wordsworth and his generation. But the author of *Don Juan* II–III, with its evocation of a knowingly lost idyll, is finally closer to the neohellenism of Shelley and Keats than the neoclassicism of Pope. Byron's is the Romantic distance from lost harmony, not the preromantic distance from cultural artifice. A. W. Schlegel is reputed to have said of Herder that 'his researches on the subject of popular and legendary poetry seem to have led him to the conclusion that the Muse can only be successfully cultivated by her rudest votaries',[17] and here again one sees the contrast between the preromantic backlash against any and all refinement (with all the Wertherism of *Sturm und Drang* rejecting even the archaic vigour of Homer in favour of Ossian) and the cordial dialogue of the generation called Romantic, here in the voice of Schlegel, with Classicism.

All of which is merely to endorse, in some measure, the commonplace revision of a commonplace: the Romantic reaction against Classical standards should not be exaggerated. But we should also be cautious not to assert, as John O. Hayden does, that it has been exaggerated in the past. In attacking M. H. Abrams's canonical analysis of the shift from mimetic to 'expressive' critical standards in *The mirror and the lamp*, Hayden argues that the 'Romantics' (i.e., presumably, Coleridge read a certain way rather than Wordsworth read a certain way) were interested not in the expressive but rather in 'creative theory', which he then commandeers for mimesis in order to extend the influence of Aristotle through the Romantic period.[18] But a lamp shines *on* something; Abrams actually

---

[17] H. G. Fiedler (ed.), A. W. *Schlegel's lectures on German literature from Gottsched to Goethe* (1833 notes by George Toynbee), Oxford: Basil Blackwell, 1944, p. 35.

[18] John O. Hayden, *Polestar of the ancients: the Aristotelian tradition in Classical and English literary criticism*, Newark, DE: University of Delaware Press, 1979, esp. pp. 168–9.

drives no such wedge between the expressive and the creative, hence leaves far less room for disagreement than Hayden believes.

No one has ever wanted to claim, *pace* Hayden, that the Romantics abandoned Aristotle – although it will be necessary to show in what follows that they distanced themselves from him. The traditional claim has always been, rather, that they reinterpret him (as an organicist rather than a mechanist) and in some cases, as hierophants of the fragmentary, disagree with his emphasis on teleological unity. Again, to be sure, Wordsworth's willingness to admit, or pretend, that he had never read the *Poetics* makes for an interesting chapter in the history of changing cultural institutions. While it is fair enough to point out, with Gilbert Highet, that 'Shelley knew more Greek than Pope. Goethe knew more Greek than Klopstock' (*The Classical tradition*, p. 355), it is still more relevant to remember, with John Hodgson, that 'the proportion and probably the absolute number of readers, at least, who did not require translations of . . . Classical authors was rapidly decreasing' in the time of Wordsworth.[19] However great or small the Romantic turn away from Classical standards may have been, what is much less open to dispute is simply that the knowledge of Classical standards was diminishing as the demographics of literacy changed – and that this was one reason why young writers like Keats (and apparently Wordsworth) could emphasize originary strength more boldly than was hitherto imaginable. When Edward Young calls for 'Original Composition' in 1759, he knows that educated persons answering to the name of poet will need to suppress their intimacy with ancient writings in order not to imitate them. For a Wordsworth or a Keats the effort of suppression – at least of ancient poets and, still more, of ancient critics – need not have been as exhausting.

Perhaps the safest thing to say about the paradigm aspect of the Romantic attitude toward Classical standards is that, in contrast with the preromantic attitude, it is highly unstable. Friedrich and August Wilhelm Schlegel are thought to be largely in agreement about the Classical tradition, for example (and it was Friedrich who began, like Nietzsche, as a Classical philologist); yet whereas Friedrich could criticize Goethe for the neoclassicism of the *Propyläen*, his brother could adopt the supremely neoclassical tactic of criticizing Aristotle for generic laxity in judging epic by the rules of tragedy. Alongside the volatility of such views there is the instinct for compromise which seems aimed precisely at discouraging the penchant for extremes. Thus one finds Friedrich Schlegel saying things like 'It is equally fatal for the mind to have a system, and to have none. One will simply have to decide to combine the two'; or again: 'All Romantic studies

---

[19] John Hodgson, ' "Was it for this . . . ?": Wordsworth's Virgilian questionings', *Texas studies in literature and language* 33 (1991), p. 133.

should be made Classical; all Classical studies should be made Romantic.'[20] Just so, in Wellek's words, Madame de Staël in *De l'Allemagne* wants 'German literature more regular, more tasteful, and French literature less circumscribed by rigid conventions, freer to indulge in flights of imagination' (*History of modern criticism*, II, 229).

Responsibility for this sort of balancing act, with its faith in the efficacy of dialectics, can be traced perhaps most directly to Friedrich Schiller's letters *On the aesthetic education of man* (1795), with its terms traceable in turn to Kant's *Critique of judgement* (1790). In Schiller's text notions of 'system' and 'the classical' are aligned with the *Formtrieb* of categorical reason (but also with the idolization of reason in the French Revolution), while the asystematic and the Romantic lean toward the *Stofftrieb*, the sensuous empiricism, of the understanding (allegorizing the baser instincts that inspired the French Revolution). 'Aesthetic education', which for Schiller as for Goethe is nothing other than the neutralization of revolutionary instincts by flexibility of mind (Schiller's *Spieltrieb*), leads to compromise formations that precisely and fully anticipate the Romantic cordiality toward the Classical. For example: 'The important thing . . . is to dissociate caprice from the physical and freedom from the moral character; to make the first conformable with law, the second dependent on impressions.'[21] In the ultimate formulations of the contrast between *Klassik* and *Romantik*, as we shall see, the physical and the moral tend to change places, each remaining in a state of estrangement from the other, but the lines once drawn remain unchanged; and the ensuing state of dialectical interdependency is what keeps the romantic in German thought from being viewed progressively at any time as an advance over some prior perspective.

The Romantic outlook, then, was thought in a sense to be necessary, an emergent historical determination, yet no one until Stendhal, the first who willingly called himself a Romantic, was prepared to assert that it was necessarily better than the Classical outlook. Indeed, starting from Schiller's sense (in *On naive and sentimental poetry*, 1795) that the only belated options of the 'sentimental' poet are the alienated and unheroic genres of idyll, elegy, and satire, and continuing right through to Hegel's 'unhappy consciousness', Romanticism is understood as an almost foolish crisis of estrangement, an extreme deracination of the ideal from the ground of reality. In certain passages of these writers, T. E. Hulme's caricature of Romanticism a century later is already in place; it 'flies away into

---

[20] Both aphorisms are quoted by Ernst Behler in important articles on this topic – the former in 'Problems of origin in literary history', *Theoretical issues in literary history*, David Perkins (ed.), Cambridge, MA: Harvard University Press, 1991, p. 15; and the latter in 'The origins of Romantic literary theory', *Colloquia Germanica* 2 (1968), 121.
[21] Friedrich Schiller, *On the aesthetic education of man*, Reginald Snell (trans.), New York: Ungar, 1965, p. 30.

the circumambient gas'.[22] Many of the writers we call Romantic in fact see
themselves not as Romantic but as postromantic, very much on analogy
with our own self-conception as postmodern; they look back to the period
from Dante to Shakespeare and Cervantes as Romantic, just as Hegel in
the *Phenomenology of mind* identifies unhappy consciousness not with
any contemporary state of things but with the emergence of Christianity.
To this issue I shall return in conclusion.

The very fact that these writers see themselves as being in a position
to perform comparative analysis shows them standing, or professing
to stand, outside and above any fixed viewpoint, distanced perhaps from
any fully authentic voice but possessed thereby of the quality that Byron
according to Lady Blessington called *mobilité*,[23] that Keats called negative capability and Hazlitt gusto – and that Friedrich Schlegel twenty years
earlier called irony. (It was not until 1811 that Coleridge introduced the
classic–romantic distinction in England, and several more years passed
before Staël's English sojourn and John Black's translation of A. W.
Schlegel's lectures made the terms familiar. In his letters to Goethe of this
period Byron asks him what he makes of the distinction. Perhaps this is
why it took so much longer for volatility of perspective to become a feature of English Romantic thinking.) Although Friedrich Schlegel called the
novels of Jean Paul Richter 'the only romantic products of an unromantic
age',[24] Jean Paul's work seems to us rather to be very much of its moment;
and it is strange likewise to us that Stendhal was willing to call himself
Romantic in *Racine and Shakespeare* yet seems to embody, in his novels,
precisely that mercuric instability of viewpoint (one finds it also in Kleist
and in Goethe's *Elective Affinities*) which for sheer mobility exceeds even
the play of dialectic in, say, Byron or Pushkin or Heine – and is more
subtle also than the 'dialogism' or 'novelization' of poetic genres that the
Bakhtinian approach to this period so obviously adopts from Friedrich
Schlegel.

It will not have escaped the reader's attention that in some respects on
the present view it would be appropriate to fold the important poetry and
criticism of Wordsworth back into the preromantic. Blake, who reads
even Wordsworth as a pernicious classicist 'hired', like Reynolds, 'to
depress art',[25] but is perhaps also best viewed as himself preromantic just
for that reason, constitutes another broad exception. Most of the writers

[22] T. E. Hulme, 'Romanticism and Classicism' in *Criticism: the major texts*, Walter J. Bate
(ed.), New York: Harcourt, 1970, p. 566.
[23] Marguerite, Countess of Blessington, *Conversations of Lord Byron with the Countess of
Blessington*, London: R. Bentley, 1834, p. 67.
[24] Friedrich Schlegel, *Dialogue on poetry and literary aphorisms*, Ernst Behler and Roman
Struc (trans.), Philadelphia, PA: University of Pennsylvania Press, 1968, p. 95.
[25] William Blake, *The poetry and prose of William Blake*, David V. Erdman (ed.), Garden
City, NY: Doubleday, 1970, p. 625.

who are considered Romantic, however, but who consider themselves to be poised, or trapped, somewhere between the Romantic and the Classical, do fully realize that the Classical for better or worse is a historically delimited moment that can only be reentered by completely artificial means. I do not feel that Todorov sufficiently recognizes the self-consciousness of this period when he writes, albeit instructively:

One is already romantic if one writes the history of the passage from the classics to the romantics; or is still classical if one perceives the two as simple variants of a unique essence. Whatever solution is chosen, the writer adopts the viewpoint proper to one of these periods in order to judge – and distort – the other.[26]

I would say that it is not distortion but nostalgia that one encounters in this moment. Part of the fate, the historical determinism, experienced by the writers of the period called Romantic, was the sense of historical determination itself – the historicism with which the rise of responsible philology had imbued them. Historicism distanced them from the Classical in two ways: it made the cultural aspect of what Keats called the grand march of intellect seem irreversible without necessarily seeming progressive ('Why the Arts are not progressive' was not just Hazlitt's theme); and it introduced a sense of the relativity of values that was itself in conflict with the universality of classical standards. Anyone who valued the Classical as a contrastive term, in other words, was in some measure anticlassical. (The same is true, incidentally, of the 'traditional', the vanishing social ideal which occasions the pathos both of Scott's historical fiction and of Balzac's *Comédie humaine*.) The implications of the relative view, ordinarily expressed as ambivalence, are for the first time embraced in behalf of the Romantic by Stendhal in *Racine and Shakespeare*: romanticism, he says, is 'the art of giving to the people literary works which in the present state of their customs and beliefs are capable of giving the most pleasure possible', while 'classicism, on the contrary, gives them the literature which yielded the most pleasure possible to their great-grandparents'.[27] Yet it is Stendhal's very celebration which announces, in turn, the coming obsolescence of the Romantic. The absence of this sort of covert historicist caveat in the rebellious literary manifestoes of the early twentieth century may serve usefully to indicate the way in which

---

[26] Tzvetan Todorov, *Theories of the symbol*, Caroline Porter (trans.), Ithaca, NY: Cornell University Press, 1982, p. 289. Quoted in a similar context by Thomas Vogler, 'Romanticism and literary periods: the future of the past', *New German critique* 38 (1986), p. 133.

[27] 'Le *romantisme* est l'art de présenter aux peuples les œuvres littéraires qui, dans l'état actuel de leurs habitudes et de leurs croyances, sont susceptibles de leur donner le plus de plaisir possible. Le *classicisme*, au contraire, leur présente la littérature qui donnait le plus grand plaisir à leurs arrière-grands-pères.' Stendhal (Henri Beyle), *Racine et Shakespeare*, Henri Martineau (ed.), Paris: Le Divan, 1928, p. 43.

Modernism, unlike romanticism, attempted to reenter the timeless classical paradise by artificial means.

By way of penance for having ventured a generalization about
Wordsworth in this context which in most ways will seem intelligible
enough (the 'real language of men' and 'the beautiful and permanent
forms of nature' can scarcely be thought subject to change (Preface,
Wordsworth, p. 735), yet there is very little that is Classical, or even cog-
nizant of the Classical, about the way in which they are conceived), I must
now confess that perhaps the fullest and most interesting historicist contrast between Classical objectivity and Romantic subjectivity is to be
found in Wordsworth himself – in the fascinating and too often overlooked
'Letter to a friend of Burns':

> Our business is with [the books of classical writers], – to understand and to
> enjoy them. And, of poets more especially, it is true – that, if their works be
> good, they contain within themselves all that is necessary to their being
> comprehended and relished. It should seem that the ancients thought in this
> manner; for of the eminent Greek and Roman poets, few and scanty memorials
> were . . . ever prepared; and fewer still are preserved. It is delightful to read
> what, in the happy exercise of his own genius, Horace chooses to communicate
> of himself and his friends; but I confess I am not so much a lover of knowledge,
> independent of its quality, as to make it likely that it would much rejoice me,
> were I to hear that records of the Sabine poet and his contemporaries, composed
> upon the Boswellian plan, had been unearthed among the ruins of Herculaneum
> . . . Far otherwise is it with that class of poets, the principal charm of whose
> writings depends upon the familiar knowledge which they convey of the
> personal feelings of their authors. This is eminently the case with the effusions
> of Burns'.[28]

And, the reader exclaims somewhat unwarily, with the relentlessly
autobiographical effusions of Wordsworth! There is in Wordsworth the
disclaimer, to be sure, that such feelings are valueless if they are not common to all, the poet being 'a man speaking to men' (Preface, *Wordsworth*,
p. 737), and we know that Wordsworth might not have extended such a
disclaimer to at least some of the feelings of Burns (hence the hint of
condescension in the special pleading he thinks Burns deserves); but
nevertheless, the historicism Wordsworth recommends in this passage is
after all more radical than most modern readers, reading as 'theorists',
formalist or psychoanalytic, would care to espouse. It is as though we were
enjoined, in keeping with Wordsworth's tone, to read the works of one
period in the spirit of a rigorous anti-intentionalist and the works of
another in the spirit of a gossip columnist; and, surprisingly in that the
opinions are Wordsworth's, we cannot deny, no matter which reading

---

[28] *The prose works of William Wordsworth*, 3 vols., A. B. Grosart (ed.), rev. edn, New York:
AMS Press, 1967, II: 11–12.

practice more closely resembles our own, that it is the former on which he confers more dignity.

There is one issue that at least arguably restores stability to the relationship between the Romantic and the Classical; and to that issue – again – I shall turn in conclusion. In the meantime, however, there is more to be said about the instability I have emphasized in contrast with the much more paradigmatic preromantic reception of the neoclassical. As a case in point, yielding little but confusion at least on first view, consider the effect on Homer's reputation of Friedrich August Wolf's pioneering *Prolegomena ad Homerum* (1795), the first work of scholarship to argue authoritatively for the multiple and anonymous authorship of the *Iliad* and the *Odyssey*. Before Wolf, a consensus had been building about Homer: he was a splendidly 'regular' poet, exercising a command over the three unities that exceeded even Aristotle's grasp of the matter (this is the view of Gildon and others); but he was also, in contrast with Virgil, endowed with 'genius', and the character of his writing was 'rapid', 'impetuous', 'nervous' and bursting with energy (this is already the view of Dryden and Pope, and is rarely challenged in the ensuing decades). Here again the neoclassical and the preromantic are fixed in relation to one another, often in this case even without conflict, although there were many in the 'Augustan' age who preferred Virgil (whose *lacrimae rerum* were not romanticized until the late nineteenth century), and many in the later period who preferred Homer insofar as he himself was not considered too neoclassical for the taste of *Sturm und Drang*. All of these commonplaces, which are gathered together by Johnson among the maxims of his Dick Minim the Critick in the *Idler*, persisted throughout the period when a growing, increasingly historicist understanding of Homer was being achieved, prior to Wolf, by Thomas Blackwell (*Enquiry into the life and writings of Homer*, 1735) and Robert Wood (*Essay on the original genius and writings of Homer*, 1769).

One effect of Wolf's book was somewhat to diminish the reputation of Homer at just the time when one might have expected it to flourish – and when, indeed, he continued frequently to be compared with Shakespeare. (Schiller contemporaneously with Wolf somewhat equivocally celebrates Homer as the lone exemplar of the Naive Poet, but this is already perhaps part of the complication I wish to emphasize.) The fact is, Homer simply was not mentioned or thought about as often as he was before the 1790s. Keats's awed fascination in his sonnet of 1816 should be read in part as a not wholly convincing protest against the dominance of the epic tradition by Milton in the preceding period.[29] For reasons famously enunciated by

---

[29] See my reading of this sonnet in *A defense of poetry: reflections on the occasion of writing*, Stanford, CA: Stanford University Press, 1995, pp. 147–52.

Milton's Satan and echoed by Romantic practice, the mind had come to be 'its own place', supplanting the outward shows of human events, and Milton replaced Homer in the same way that the imagination replaced rhetorical and scenic sublimity. Undoubtedly the role of Milton was much greater in England than in Germany (although it had been Milton mediated by Addison who had altered German taste at an earlier period), but there too Homer appears to have lost ground.

Perhaps the most important reason for these changes will emerge, again, in the context of my concluding remarks, but I think Wolf has something to do with it as well. 'Literary men', says Highet, 'found Wolf's book discouraging' (*The Classical tradition*, p. 385), and he points to Goethe's 'Homer wider Homer' as a sign of their frustration.[30] It is true, as Ernst Behler remarks, that to 'dissolve an individual author into a collective entity governed by a "popular spirit" or a "spirit of the age" was not unusual during the Romantic period: the Song of the Nibelungen, Shakespeare's dramas, and the fairy tales collected by the Grimm brothers come to mind' ('Problems of origin', p. 18). And no doubt this tendency is not unrelated to the – again anti-classical – preoccupation with the fragment first theorized by the Jena circle. But at the same time, the decomposition of Homer posed a severe challenge to ideas of original genius and organic unity. If in the latter case various theories of the symbol could mediate the fragmentary and the holistic, it was more difficult to explain (by reading Plato, for example, without the help of neoplatonic revisionism) how 'genius' could remain a plausibly originary concept when separated from what Coleridge called 'the shaping spirit of imagination' ('Dejection: an ode', 1802). One can see this issue vexing much of Coleridge's poetry around the time that saw the publication of Wolf's treatise: the 'one all-conscious Spirit, which informs / With absolute ubiquity of thought / . . . All his involvéd Monads' ('The destiny of nations', 1796, lines 44–7) is one such effort, as is 'what if all of animated nature / Be but organic Harps diversely fram'd' ('The eolian harp', 1795). 'But where', wrote Fichte to Friedrich Schlegel in 1800, 'did the source for the first artist, who had nothing before himself, come from?'[31]

That poems hitherto considered to be works of genius, in sum, could still impress themselves upon the reader in all their apparent self-sufficiency meant finally either that doctrines of creative genius were not at the heart of the matter after all (confirming the mimetic standards of Classicism) or that these poems were not quite as pluperfect as they had been held to be (further eroding the authority of ancient standards). It is again

---

[30] Goethe fears that 'you cannot establish that there is a Homer before Homer' in 'On German architecture', *Essays on art and literature*, John Gearey (ed.), Ellen and Ernest von Nordhoff (trans.), New York: Suhrkamp, 1986, p. 8.

[31] Quoted in Behler, 'Problems of origin', p. 14.

Wordsworth, this time the older Wordsworth writing to Henry Nelson Coleridge in 1830, who manages to combine these views while reflecting the sea-change in Homer's reputation most fully: 'the books of the Iliad were never intended to make one Poem, and . . . The Odyssey is not the work of the same man or exactly of the same age. [Homer is] second only to Shakespeare, . . . But at the same time I cannot think but that you in some points overrate the Homeric Poems, especially the manners' (*Letters: the later years, part II*, pp. 318–19). There are two different and seemingly contradictory tendencies at work in this passage, conspiring to a single end. First, the denial that original genius belongs to any single author plainly reduces the value of the work; yet at the same time the work's putative loss of unity seems to recall to mind the classical standard of unity which has less to do with creativity than with such imitative considerations as 'manners'. That both these tendencies are nevertheless characteristically Romantic – together with the historicism implicit in the by then widespread belief that the *Odyssey* is a later poem – can be demonstrated by contrasting them with their preromantic equivalents: whereas Wordsworth's Homer is not Classical enough because the knowledge that 'he' is without creative unity apparently colours the question of mimetic unity in the Homeric poems as well, the Homer of Goethe's Werther, by contrast, is too Classical because he is too closely linked to notions of calm and noble simplicity made fashionable by Winckelmann. Ossian is the truer voice of feeling for Werther even though, or perhaps because, very few admirers of the Ossianic poems believed Macpherson's claim that Ossian was a single author.

The history of Virgil's reputation throughout this period is less complex and varied. He was despised as a courtier in radical moods (by Hugo in exile, for example) and praised with lukewarmth on more dispassionate occasions as a 'moon of Homer' (by Hugo in the Preface to *Cromwell*[32]), while running beneath it all was an admiration for Virgil's sheer talent as a poet that was difficult to express except in the sincere but only faintly perceptible flattery of imitation. The Virgilian – and Horatian – georgic conventions of stationing the scene and the viewer's movement through the scene (*Iam . . . Iam.*) that are so much a part of preromantic loco-descriptive and *Spaziergang* poetry can still be felt in Keats's 'To autumn' ('And . . . And . . . And now'); and in general it is this side of Virgil (his pathos, again, not yet having become focal) that Romanticism exploits. As Bruce Graver summarizes the matter, 'Virgilian didacticism becomes Wordsworthian description'.[33] In speaking of Milton as Wordsworth's precursor, it is well to remember, as Graver reminds us ('Wordsworth's

[32] Victor Hugo, Préface to *Cromwell*, Paris: Larousse, 1949, p. 40.
[33] Graver, 'Wordsworth's georgic beginnings', *Texas studies in literature and language* 33 (1991), p. 146.

georgic beginnings', 154), that Wordsworth considered Milton to have formed his blank verse on the model of Virgil's hexameters.

Most obviously, though, it remains to ask how and to what extent Romantic taste altered the authority of ancient literary criticism. The somewhat surprising eclipse of Longinus I have discussed; but then Longinus's influence had not been as venerable as that of Horace and Aristotle: ancient, yes, but only recently canonized, with the result that in important ways other oft-cited names such as Scaliger, Heinsius and Corneille could easily seem better established. The Horace of the odes was never wholly out of favour (Wordsworth nearly always spoke well of him, for example), but the didactic Horace, especially the author of the *De arte poetica*, almost entirely ceased to matter as an arbiter even though many Horatian snippets remained in the language as nearly anonymous idioms and proverbs. Horace's fate in this regard is simply that of neoclassicism, and perhaps more broadly (outside of France) the fate of Roman culture in general. That there were almost literally two Horaces in the Romantic period can be found reflected in the remarkable wording of Shelley's Preface to *The revolt of Islam* (where incidentally Longinus is, again, a *mere* critic, hardly the patron saint of preromanticism): 'Longinus could not have been a contemporary of Homer, nor Boileau of Horace.'[34] Here the analogy can only hold if Horace the critic and direct precursor of Boileau has been so completely forgotten that the momentary confusion felt by a modern reader simply doesn't enter Shelley's mind.[35]

I have already outlined the traditional approach to the Romantic reception of Aristotle: either he simply fades, partially, from view, or he is recuperated, no longer the guardian of 'regularity', as a theorist of organic form. This is the Aristotle of Wordsworth and Coleridge, respectively. Aristotle's fate in Wordsworth's Preface we have witnessed; but in fact he makes a livelier appearance in the 'Intimations ode', a programmatically platonic poem based on the tenth book of the *Republic* (not just the Myth of Er but also the attack on poets), in which Aristotle is challenged as it were in advance from the standpoint of Plato's critique of imitation as chameleonic role-playing:

> And with new joy and pride
> The little Actor cons another part;
> Filling from time to time the 'humorous stage'
> With all the Persons, down to palsied Age,

---

[34] *The complete poetical works of Percy Bysshe Shelley*, 2 vols., Neville Rogers (ed.), Oxford: Clarendon, 1975, II: 104.

[35] In a unique study of this topic, *The influence of Horace on the chief poets of the nineteenth century*, New Haven, CT: Yale University Press, 1916, Mary Rebecca Thayer argues that in this passage Shelley 'deliberately disregards Horace as a literary critic' (p. 41), but I think Shelley simply forgets that anyone might consider Horace a literary critic.

>That Life brings with her in her equipage;
>As if his whole vocation
>Were endless imitation. (101–7)

The quotation entailing the theory of Humours is from Samuel Daniel, but is coloured, I think, by the slight forward anachronism of Jonson's usage and that of his successors, thus reinforcing the neoclassicism of the role played by Aristotle – advocate of role-playing for six-year-olds – in contrast with the visionary oneness of the antitheatrical platonist infant. The most important engagement with Aristotle in the Preface is not 'Aristotle, I have been told', after all, but the claim made for the *Lyrical ballads* themselves that 'the feeling therein developed gives importance to the action and situation, not the action and situation to the feeling' (Preface, *Wordsworth*, p. 735). This makes *dianoia* (thought) with some admixture of *ethe* (character or role) paramount in importance over *praxis* (action), whereas Aristotle had listed these elements of poetic composition in the opposite order. This is indeed what is revolutionary about Wordsworth's treatment of the traditional ballad (in some measure qualifying Robert Mayo's well-known demonstration that the poems in this volume were characteristic of their time); and there is no passage that more clearly illustrates what we conventionally call the romantic turn toward subjectivity. The 'Prospectus to *The Recluse*', making 'the Mind of Man – / My haunt, and the main region of my song' (*Wordsworth*, p. 590), performs the same service for epic.

Organicism, so important to Herder, to Goethe's *Pflanzenlehre*, and to the Schlegels, only appears fully formed, Wellek argues, in Coleridge and Hugo outside of Germany (*History of modern criticism*, II, p. 3). It is this strain in Romanticism that has attracted the most dialectically inclined scholars, from Orsini to McFarland, who have typically been Coleridgians. Wellek himself distinguishes between emotive Romanticism, plainly associated with Wordsworth, from which little of theoretical value can be expected, and 'the establishment of a dialectical and symbolist view of poetry', the foundational credo of which is Coleridge's definition of the Symbol in *The statesman's manual*, together with the apotheosis of the imagination as 'esemplastic power'. Now, in all such thinking at this period it must be admitted that the influence of Aristotle is largely implicit – a symptom, it might be retorted, of his fading from view rather than of his reinterpretation. But however much or little Coleridge the literary theorist may have had Aristotle continuously in mind, the organicist *Poetics* which emerged in the seminal modern translation and commentary by S. H. Butcher (1894) and which continued to hold sway throughout the floruit of the New Criticism and of Wellek himself, is really quite inconceivable without the mediatory influence of Coleridge.

The key passages are the ones in which Aristotle insists that the 'parts' of a tragedy have a necessary order that cannot be rearranged, and says also that you cannot have an animal (*zoon*) that is too long or short. Although it seems quite obvious to recent commentators that the interdict against exchanging parts is grossly macroscopic (you cannot have your exodos before your parodos, for example, but you can put a metaphor anywhere you like as long as there are not too many), and that the passage allegedly concerning organic animal life is actually about a *schema* or blueprint of an animal, this was by no means obvious to the disciples of Butcher. They thought such passages were redolent of Coleridgian thinking. But the only place in Coleridge where Aristotle actually surfaces in this context, chapter 17 of the *Biographia literaria*, may be said perhaps to give comfort to both sides. The footnote, which says among other things that 'Aristotle has . . . required of the poet an involution of the universal in the individual', can be said to have given rise to the organicist revision; but the footnote is written to warn the reader away from believing that the main text, which says in Aristotle's name that 'the persons of poetry must be clothed with generic attributes', is covertly neoclassical: 'Say not that I am recommending abstractions.'[36] And yet, if one places this passage in its entirety (poetry is ideal, it admits no accidents, and so on) alongside Johnson's rescue of Shakespeare from the strictures of Rymer and Voltaire ('His story requires Romans or kings, but he thinks only on men'[37]), there is no doubt that it is Coleridge who is the more 'neoclassical', the more high-mimetic, of the two.

It is possible to make too much of this. Not just Johnson, whose argument against the Unities was borrowed by Stendhal, but Lessing, Diderot and others had produced relatively low-mimetic revisions of Aristotle in order to reflect the new fashion for a *drame bourgeois* – or, in Johnson's case, simply to accommodate the spectator's legitimate craving for novelty ('all pleasure consists in variety'), and perhaps also to support his own taste for the novels of Richardson. Coleridge may well have felt that these doctrines of imitation were simply unphilosophical, or worse, reflective of the empiricist drift towards Associationism against which Aristotle's *De anima* is invoked as a safeguard earlier in the *Biographia* (ch. 5). Still and all, if this is the case then it is not in fact Aristotle from whom Coleridge chiefly derives his undoubted emphasis on organic form in many other places; and it cannot be said unreservedly therefore that there is a 'Romantic' Aristotle until the end of the nineteenth century (when a Romantic Virgil also emerges), owing largely to the influence of Coleridge but owing very little to his imputed Aristotelianism.

[36] Samuel Taylor Coleridge, *Biographia literaria*, George Watson (ed.), New York: Everyman, 1971, p. 191.
[37] Johnson, 'Preface to *Shakespeare*', in *Criticism: the major texts*, Bate (ed.), p. 210.

And so I think it fair to say after all, without much qualification, that the authority of Aristotle weakens in the Romantic period together with that of Longinus and Horace. The two Greeks were read through the eyes of an earlier generation, but without that generation's enthusiasm; and this made them seem Roman (perhaps also because they were read frequently in Latin if not in modern languages). The neoclassical filter through which their views were strained and which also produced their forbidding image as arbiters and legislators was rarely if ever set aside. Thus Aristotle and Longinus could benefit little from neohellenism and from the increasingly generalized and graecophile contrasts between Greece and Rome. 'It was the claim of the romanticists', writes Harry Levin, 'that their school had purified the Greek tradition by repudiating Rome . . . [And] gradually the formalistic and pedantic elements came to be identified with Latin culture'.[38] And yet from Rome – as in Dante – there arose the very phenomenon that finally estranged the Romantic generation most conclusively from the Classical, and more particularly from the earthbound idyll that was Greece: namely, Christianity. This progression was so clear to Madame de Staël that she reversed the usual evaluative contrast between Greece and Rome and insisted that, with its more refined customs and elegant manners, Rome actually represented a step forward toward the emergence of Christianity – with its improvement in the position of women.

The 'atheist' Shelley too insists in his 'Defence of poetry' that the age of chivalry with its Christian backdrop marks a step forward in the treatment of women. Strange as it may seem to modern ears that placing women on a pedestal answered somehow to a feminist impulse, that is how Shelley and his contemporaries read Dante. Goethe's early modern Faust shares the salvation of Dante's Pilgrim ('Das Ewig-Weibliche / Zieht uns hinan'), and even Mary Wollstonecraft's *Vindication of the rights of women*, with its thesis that women should be better educated to be better companions for men, seems poorly situated for discerning the condescension of this exaltation. 'Homage for genuine female worth' was part of the Christian and northern Romantic spirit, thought A. W. Schlegel.[39] It was not Gretchen or Beatrice, though, but the Virgin with whom they intercede who accords this new, and newly glamorous, role to women at the historical moment in question – and who is also the key factor stabilizing the Classic–Romantic dialectic we have been studying. Just as Dante parts company with Virgil at the utmost height of Purgatory in order to transcend earthly imperfection, so Romanticism somewhat sadly consigns the earthly finitude even of the most idyllic Classical moment to the irreversibility of

---

[38] Levin, *The broken column: a study in Romantic Hellenism*, Cambridge, MA: Harvard University Press, 1931, p. 20.

[39] August Wilhelm Schlegel, *A course of lectures on dramatic art and literature*, John Black (trans.), London: Bohn, 1846, p. 25.

the past. Hence, also, the subordination of Homer to Milton, who repeatedly expels the Classical gods, always with evident reluctance.

The alignment of Romanticism with Christianity is perhaps most obvious in France and Germany: Madame de Staël's insistence that Romantic poetry 'owes its birth to the union of chivalry and Christianity'[40] corresponds to *Le génie du christianisme*, in which Chateaubriand interestingly says that 'only with Christianity does there come a feeling for landscape in itself, apart from man'; while the increasingly devout Catholicism of the brothers Schlegel seems simply to confirm Hegel's scheme, in which Romanticism is a late recrudescence, mediated by 'Scepticism', of that Unhappy Consciousness estranged from Spirit which in its essence is Christianity. Perhaps the definitive pronouncement against the classical in this respect is that of A. W. Schlegel in his *Lectures on dramatic art and literature*: 'But however highly the Greeks may have succeeded in the Beautiful, and even in the Moral, we cannot concede any higher character to their civilization than that of refined and ennobled sensuality' (*A course of lectures*, p. 24). But the English too came around to these views. Hazlitt accepts Schlegel's terms, including his distinction between a Doric temple and Westminster Abbey; and Coleridge for his part likewise identifies Romanticism with the emergence of Christianity, its Christian characteristics being 'its realism, its picturesque qualities [here is the "gothic" element], its diversity and complexity, its striving toward the infinite, its subjectivity, and its imagination'.[41]

The apparently more secular mythopoetic strain even of the neohellenist English Romantics rests on a comparable structure. 'The late remorse of love' is Byron's revision of the classical Nemesis in the Forgiveness Curse he hurls from the Coliseum (*Childe Harold* IV, with Byron's 'nympholepsy' theme culminating here in the story of Numa and Egeria), and a similar revocation of a curse in Shelley inspires *das Ewig-Weibliche* (Asia, the spirit of love) to unbind the Prometheus of Aeschylus. The whole burden of the classical idyll in *Don Juan* II is its bittersweetness – its fragility, finitude, and blindness; while in 'Defence of poetry' Shelley, in announcing that 'the great secret of morals is love'[42] introduces the binding ingredient that enables the perception of similitude in dissimilitude called metaphor, an ingredient that must first have emerged, in the logic of Shelley's historiography, when chivalry introduced amorous idealism. Keats would appear to constitute a partial exception here, at least insofar as he can be said to chant a 'poetry of

---

[40] Baroness de Staël-Holstein, *Germany*, 2 vols., London: John Murray, 1814, I: 304.
[41] Herbert Weisinger, 'English treatment of the Classic–Romantic problem', *Modern language quarterly* 7 (1946), p. 482.
[42] Percy Bysshe Shelley, *Shelley's poetry and prose*, Donald Reiman and Sharon B. Powers (eds.), New York: Norton, 1982, p. 487.

earth' ('On the grasshopper and the cricket') that owes little to anything but a powerfully naturalistic reading of the early Wordsworth and to an idiosyncratically unqualified embrace of the Classical by way of Lemprière's *Dictionary*. But even in Keats the characteristic tensions persist. The too obviously mechanical synthesis of Cynthia and the Indian Maid at the end of *Endymion* is no doubt meant to rebuke the unhappy consciousness of the poet–idealist who turns his back on an Arab Maiden in Shelley's *Alastor*, but it remains a clumsy manœuvre that leaves Peona for one in an unpromising state of bewilderment – and if in a later and more graceful effort the casement is left ope at night to restore the Warm Love to Psyche, Cupid has nevertheless not yet appeared. The complete failure of Thea in the mediatory role in the first *Hyperion*, together with the substitution of the grimly forbidding Moneta for Thea in the second, should not prevent us from seeing that in fact everywhere in Keats's mythopoetic work the structure of feminine intercession remains intact, a structure that is carried forward from the mariolatry of early Christianity.

This then is the most decisive Romantic departure from the Classical. 'Love' had long been understood as a 'modern' improvement on the Classical (as in Racine and Corneille, or in the 'heroic dramas' introduced by Dryden and Davenant), but the pathos of neoclassical love was more likely to be destructive than redemptive. The salvific immanence of the feminine differs likewise from the Classical invocation of the muse precisely in that the Nine after all never really 'descend'. The poet calls on one of them simply in order to designate a generic expectation and then gets on with his business. Classical heroines too have a different niche. *The aeneid*, Dante's model in so many other respects, offers the point of contrast: Aeneas is not led forth by Creusa but leads her, hence loses her; he is led astray by Dido and has no relation at all to the demure Lavinia, whose romantic adoration by Turnus is of no more use to him than the evasive tactics of his sister Juturna. Venus, meanwhile, playing the role of Athena in *The odyssey*, belongs in the trickster–companion tradition that Classical mythopoeisis appears to share with the folklore of yet more ancient cultures rather than with early Christianity. Pretty clearly, the price women pay for their ennoblement by Romanticism is the loss of cleverness and personality. If in Classical comedy the heroine tended to be resourceful and the hero faceless, in the metaphysical comedies of Christianity and Romanticism the opposite tendency emerges – in Mary Shelley's *Frankenstein* as much as anywhere else. Whereas the Classical goddess (who could as easily be a god like Hermes) either helps or hinders, the Romantic mediatrix either inspires self-help (most painfully in the case of Keats's Moneta) or fails to do so.

Having thus isolated a constant thread running through the Romantic turn from Classicism, it remains for me to ask in conclusion whether the

self-definitions of Romanticism – and more particularly the very word
itself – reflect its consonance with early Christianity. Remembering the
reluctance of the Romantics to call themselves Romantic, even as they
acknowledge their part in the estrangement from the Classical, we should
not be surprised to find the word consistently linked to medieval and early
modern developments. It comes, depending on the account, either from
'romance', the mixture of Latin with modern languages, or from *roman*,
the novel, which mixes the Classical genres into the *genus universale* celebrated in Friedrich Schlegel's *Dialogue on the novel*. In either mixture, what
comes into prominence is the fragment. The preponderance of deliberately or inadvertently unfinished texts during this period is the formal
corollary of certain themes: the feeling of estrangement from – among
other things – the wholeness of the Classical outlook, together with the
feeling that language can exist at best only in a synecdochic relation to
the infinite, like Coleridge's 'symbol', and at worst only as a scrap or shard
the very inadequacy of which proclaims the infinite as absence. The last
word, then, to which I have already alluded, may be given to Blake. When
Wordsworth wrote of how 'exquisitely the individual Mind / . . . To the
external World / Is fitted', and vice versa, Blake responded, in his famous
marginalium, 'You shall not bring me down to believe such fitting & fitted
I know better & Please your Lordship' (*Poetry and prose*, p. 656). In
Blake's eyes Wordsworth's naturalism makes a classicist of him, and
aligns his view of mind and world to the aristocratic habits of perception
that had for so long claimed the harmoniousness of classical study as a private fiefdom. A glance at Wordsworth's Preface alone, where aristocratic
habits of diction are rejected, and where even Aristotle is treated as a
stranger, may convince us that Blake is wrong. But the example shows
perhaps as clearly as any the distance that Romanticism has travelled from
Classical standards.

2

Innovation and modernity

ALFREDO DE PAZ

Translated by Albert Sbragia

In this essay I would like to discuss the inaugural and modern dimensions of literary and artistic Romantic criticism in Europe. It is useful to begin, however, with a few general observations on the Enlightenment, and, first of all, with the fact that in this period reason was engaged in a critique of the world and of itself, thereby transforming traditional rationalism and its atemporal, geometric qualities. *Modernity* has its origins in this new orientation of reason and criticism, that is to say, in the emergence and diffusion of critical reason in every sphere.

Criticism becomes, therefore, the distinctive trait of modernity. Modernity begins as a critique, expressed through the principles of reason, philosophy, religion, morality, law, history, economics and politics. From this same critique arise the fundamental concepts and cardinal ideas of modernity, above all, progress, evolution, revolution, liberty, democracy, science and technology.

Criticism manifested itself in numerous ways and domains, first and foremost in the critique of Reason itself, in reason's renunciation of the grandiose constructs which identified it with the good, with being and with truth. Reason likewise ceased to be the home of the idea and became instead a journey, an investigative methodology based on scientific and empirical principles. Criticism also expressed itself as the critique of metaphysics and of its truths impervious to change. But it *likewise* became the critique of the certainties of traditional values, institutions and beliefs. With Rousseau, Laclos and Sade, to mention a few emblematic names, criticism expressed itself as the critique of habits and customs. It became a reflection on the passions, feelings, and sexuality, often a considerably transgressive reflection in the more or less explicit awareness that the 'freedom to say all' constitutes one of the fundamental presuppositions in order for individuals to master their own destinies. With Edward Gibbon and Montesquieu, criticism became 'historical criticism'. *The history of the decline and fall of the Roman Empire*, conceived between 1776 and 1788, is one of the first attempts at a 'scientific history', while Montesquieu, albeit from a liberal perspective, was the first to have shown the interdependence of every aspect of social life – juridical, economic, moral, religious – without trying to include this 'totality' in a fixed system. But criticism also meant the discovery of the 'other', of the 'different', from an ethnic and cultural point of view. And it meant a change of perspective in the natural sciences, astronomy, geography, biology.

In the end, criticism became history. It produced the great revolutions of modernity which drew their inspiration from seventeenth-century thought, in particular, the French Revolution and the revolutions of independence of Spain's and Portugal's American dominions.

Enlightenment critical thought can be placed then at the origins of modernity. Yet Romanticism too is to be located squarely at these origins, even if the Romantic origins of the modern are both continuative and antagonistic with respect to those of the Enlightenment. That is to say, Romanticism's relationship with modernity is, simultaneously, one of affinity and antagonism. An offspring of the critical age, and therefore of the Enlightenment, Romanticism saw itself as a sort of grand transformation of letters, the arts, imagination, sensitivity, taste and ideas. In this sense, Romanticism can be considered, metaphorically, a 'rebellious child'. Its principal task was to foreground the *critique of critical reason* by opposing itself both to *Christian time* (an *historical and mortal time* to which is adjoined the *supernatural time* of eternity) and to *utopic, Enlightenment time*. It pits the *instantaneous time of the passions, love and blood* equally against origins, succession, and utopian fantasy. Thus despite its Enlightenment roots, it represents likewise, as Octavio Paz has suggested, a *negation of enlightened modernity* (*La otra voz: poesía y fin de siglo*). Romanticism can be understood then as *a negation of modernity but within modernity*, or, in other words, as a *modern negation of modernity*.

The Enlightenment criticized the alienation of confused thought, the temptations of sentiment and of the imagination, not to mention the abdication of reason to the unbridled expressions of fantasy. Romanticism, in its turn, as Georges Gusdorf has suggested, forcefully denounced another and perhaps, from our own viewpoint, more dangerous type of alienation, the alienation of a clear and distinct consciousness that is the prisoner of those objective proofs that separate it from the fundamental exigencies of existence (*Fondements du savoir romantique*). From the Romantic point of view, as Gusdorf points out, the certainties of the intellect are no more than a spider's web spun in the void, a veil of illusion destined to drift away from authentic existence at the risk of God and oneself. As we read in Ugo Foscolo's *Le ultime lettere di Jacopo Ortis* (*The last letters of Jacopo Ortis*), Douglas Radcliff-Umstead (trans.): 'What is man if you abandon him to his cold, calculating Reason? Vicious, basely vicious' (1 November 1797, *Ultime lettere*, p. 31).

It must be understood, however, that the struggle of the Romantics was not against reason, but a struggle in the name of a larger and higher reason, one in harmony with the real complexity of human beings. The Enlightenment thought it had discovered the definitive formulas of a truth on the march that would achieve completion in a short time. The French Revolution had provided the occasion, a legitimate one in some aspects, to render reason unto Reason, to give it the force of law in terms of constitutions, codes and regulations. But the course of history was to shatter these attempts to petrify the mind of man. The most original postromantic modern thinkers – in particular Schopenhauer, Kierkegaard and Nietzsche – expressed, each in his own way, an explicit critique of an epoch and a culture which had been blinded by the objectivity and illusory 'truths' of progress, the foremost effect of which had been the destruction of the individual in the anonymous and pseudo-democratic mediocrity of mass society.

The above considerations, I believe, help us to understand in a more adequate theoretical manner the problem of Romantic criticism and its relationship with modernity. René Wellek has suggested, appropriately, that 'one can speak of a Romantic movement in criticism in two very different senses: in a wider sense it was a revolt against neoclassicism, which meant a rejection of Latin tradition and the adoption of a view of poetry centred on the expression and communication of emotion. It arose in the eighteenth century and forms a wide stream flooding all countries of the West. In a narrower sense, we can speak of Romantic criticism as the establishment of a dialectical and symbolistic view of poetry' (*A history of modern criticism*, II, 3). Yet Romantic criticism – as Lacoue-Labarthe and Nancy have shown – regards both totalities and simple, direct and essential characteristics, even when the latter point toward openness rather than closure. In place of a traditional, rationalistic critical explanation of already given, beautiful things, Romanticism, especially German Romanticism, substituted a critique of art. The Romantic approach assumes the guise of a paradox: it is not so much because there is *art* that there is *criticism*, but rather it is to the degree that there is criticism that there is art (see Philippe Lacoue-Labarthe and Jean-Luc Lang Nancy, *L'absolu littéraire*).

Before we turn to an examination of the various critical positions themselves, it should be noted that with the approach of the Romantic age there emerges an impatience with authority and a denunciation of rules in the name of feeling. One sees this growing awareness best in the most restless and sensitive minds of the Enlightenment period. The abbot Jean-Baptiste Du Bos, for example, affirmed in his 1734 *Réflections sur la poésie et la peinture* that 'the first aim of painting is to move us. A work that produces great emotion must be accounted altogether excellent . . . A work can be of inferior value without violating the rules, just as a work full of violations with regard to the rules can be a work of great value.' This preeminence of sensibility and feeling erupted fully with the *Sturm und Drang*, the most salient manifestation of European preromanticism, the greatest thinker of which was Jean-Jacques Rousseau. And in Goethe's *Sorrows of young Werther*, one finds assertions like the following: 'Say what you will of rules, they destroy the genuine feeling of Nature and its true expression' (May 26, p. 11). In a way that is at times extreme, but of an extremism born from a passion for all forms of creativity, the preromantics and later the Romantics were aware that aesthetic rules, like civil laws, allow one to avoid chaos, but are also devoid of creative force. At most, these rules make possible honest but banal creations. In this way, the academic idea of scholastic works subject to a canonical style was succeeded by the revolutionary idea of personal and original works, part of the denunciation of established authority which was spreading in artistic as well as in political circles.

The Romantic age is marked by the idea that there is no one model of Beauty and that there exist relationships between literary works and the customs, institutions and genius of different peoples. This idea is found in various forms, in France, in the thought of Madame de Staël and Chateaubriand, in Italy, in that of Alessandro Manzoni. It is an idea which issues forth from eighteenth-century thought, and it allows criticism to find, in the nineteenth century, surer paths and more fruitful methods.

The title of Madame de Staël's 1800 work, *De la littérature considerée dans ses rapports avec les institutions sociales*, is eloquent enough. Staël proposed, according to her own words, to examine the influence of religion, custom and law on literature, and the influence of literature on religion, custom and law. This idea of the relationships existing amongst the different manifestations of the social activity of a people was not new. After the 'moderns', and Jean-Baptiste Du Bos, it had already been applied to literature. Madame de Staël also borrows the idea of the unlimited progress of the human spirit and its creations, but the consequences of these principles never before had been carried so far.

Madame de Staël conceives of literature as something dynamic, subject to the variations of habits and politics. Criticism's role, as a consequence, can no longer be one of establishing dogmas. Its mission, according to Staël, is the animated description of masterpieces. Arising from the works themselves, criticism draws out their beauty in harmony with the authentic spirit of art. Moreover, the critical work, through passion and admiration, attempts to initiate the reader in the fruition of this revelation, which is constituted precisely by beauty. The critic, then, will need not only his own specific geniality to lift him to the heights of the masterpiece, that is to say, to the heights of the greatest spirits, but also an eloquence full of flight which will let his own readers grasp the beautiful things he has discovered. He should possess a sort of interpretative rhetoric not devoid of that 'apotheosis of feeling', which, according to Staël, characterizes 'modern poetry'. More than a judge of bad authors that one would do best to ignore, the critic must become an initiator whose influence would be beneficial to those authors themselves. Those authors should find in the critic an appraiser of their more genial qualities who is able to stimulate and encourage them. From Staël's point of view, without a reform of criticism, no authentic literary reform is possible.

Published two years after Madame de Staël's book in 1802, François René de Chateaubriand's *Génie du christianisme* was an equally important event. In his desire to demonstrate that the Christian religion had not been harmful to the progress of arts and letters, as some had argued, but had favoured it, Chateaubriand was likewise compelled to establish links between literature and religion. Nor was this idea new. In the course of the *querelle des anciens et des modernes*, the argument was often advanced that the superiority of the Moderns derived from the superiority of their religion in relation to that of pagan antiquity. Chateaubriand, however, fully and systematically exploits this idea and, most importantly, enriches it through his own talent. This is truly why he is so important for the history of criticism. We are no longer dealing with the criticism of a man of letters who judges those who belong to his own generation and those of previous generations, but, on the contrary, with a man of genius who perceives genius because it meets his own standard. We are no longer in the presence of a criticism of faults, a cavilling and at times petty examination of works of the spirit, but rather, in Chateaubriand's own words, of a 'criticism of beautiful things'.

As for Alessandro Manzoni, it can be said that as a novelist and poet he is not only one of the 'beacons' of Italian literary Romanticism (together with Ugo Foscolo and Giacomo Leopardi), but that he is also a first-rate critic. The core principle of his poetics and critical judgments is that poetry (literature) must represent the true. This principle is articulated most convincingly in his *Lettre à Monsieur Chauvet sur l'unité de temps et de lieu dans la tragédie* (1823), in which Manzoni affirms that the task of poetry is to complete history through the intuition and representation of the interior life of historical characters of whom history records only their actions.[1] Fidelity to the true is the foundation of Manzoni's critique of the rule of the three unities of time, place and action. The observance of this rule can generate unlikelihood and falsity, as demonstrated by his acute

---

[1] In May of 1820 the French poet and man of letters Jean-Jacques Victor Chauvet published in the journal *Lycée français* an analysis of Manzoni's *Conte di Carmagnola*, which had appeared in January of the same year. In addition to his positive comments, Chauvet declared that Manzoni's work was weakened by not respecting the two unities of time and place, the validity of which he supported not with the usual argument of verisimilitude, but in regard to the work's unity of action, or, in other words, the organic unity of the work of art. In his letter–essay of response, Manzoni counters analytically and with passion Chauvet's objections.

analyses of dramatic works, including his splendid comparison of Shakespeare's *Othello* and Voltaire's *Zaïre* in the letter to Chauvet.[2] According to Manzoni, the observance of the rule of the three unities is also responsible for the supremacy in theatre, especially in French theatre, given to amorous passion, a supremacy which explains the moral condemnation of the theatre by writers such as Bossuet and Rousseau. To this theatrical system, which makes the viewer participate in the passions of the characters, with negative ethical effects, Manzoni opposes another, which he calls the 'historical' system. The historical system is free from any hindrance of arbitrary rules and is able to depict circumstances and sentiments in their objective and integral reality, thereby generating positive moral effects. This different theatre takes Shakespeare as its model and symbol, whom Manzoni considers, together with Virgil, to be one of humankind's greatest poets, especially in his ability to instil his poetry with ethical urgency. In Manzoni's criticism, aesthetic judgment and moral judgment always coincide as the consequence of his principle that the knowledge of the true is man's fundamental concern, and its faithful portrayal is in itself an education (*Scritti*).

Early German Romanticism had already helped to give to the idea of criticism a statute of special importance. This is especially true in the case of Friedrich Schlegel, who offered the following judgment of criticism: 'Poetry can only be criticized by way of poetry. A critical judgment of an artistic production has no civil rights in the realm of art if it isn't itself a work of art' (Critical fragment 117 in *Philosophical fragments*, p. 14). Of course, Schlegel did not maintain that a book review possessed the same beauty or value as a poem by Goethe (whom he admired more than Shakespeare, Dante or Cervantes). He did believe, however, that an authentically inspired piece of criticism should contain the same richness as many literary works. When Schlegel wrote his review of Goethe's *Wilhelm Meister*, he stated, implicitly, what can be a novel and what was lacking in the run-of-the-mill novels of his time. For Schlegel, criticism is constructive, and, in a certain sense, autonomous, but above all, it is not 'outside of art', so that it is possible to affirm that 'a critical sketch is a critical work of art' (*Athenaeum* fragment 439).

After the 'heroic' years of 'first Romanticism', two other texts by Schlegel are useful in order to 'define' his critical personality.

The first is *Geschichte der alten und neuen Literatur* (*History of ancient and modern literature*), emblematic in its linkage of 'criticism' and 'history',

[2] According to Manzoni, Voltaire, because he is restricted by the unities of time and place, has no choice but to force the situation which leads the protagonist to his crime in an unnatural way. In Shakespeare's work, on the contrary, the affair takes place over a period of time necessary to its natural development, thereby reaching its climactic catastrophe in a natural and likely fashion.

'critical interpretation' and the 'totality of the historical process'. The book consists of a series of lectures given by Schlegel in Vienna in 1812, and it is, without a doubt, one of the first examples of literary history in the modern sense of the word. In the first place, the canon of great works established by Schlegel's 'lessons' remains, in its essence, the accepted canon of contemporary historiography. His most important innovation, however, can be found at the methodological level. Schlegel attempts to join a critical approach that is respectful of the poetic particularities of individual works with a totalizing historical approach aimed at understanding literature as a universal totality that develops in a historical evolution.

Schlegel's second text takes as its argument art criticism itself, in particular painting, and it incorporates various texts that are inscribed temporally and ideally in Schlegel's conversion to Catholicism. Whence the title, *Ansichten und Ideen von der christlichen Kunst* (*Opinions and ideas on Christian art*, 1822–5), which Schlegel himself gives to the collection of his texts, when, in the 1820s, he unites them in the preparation of his complete works. Schlegel's intent in these critical–artistic reflections is to define the principles of early Italian and German Christian painting, and of gothic architecture. He then contrasts these to the intellectualism – a principle decadence in art from the Renaissance on – that was responsible, in his own time, for the contrived affectations of Mengs's neoclassicism and of contemporary French painting. For Schlegel, art could revive only by joining itself to religious feeling as the final result of the free, idealist development of the spirit. It was by means of this feeling, expressed in Christian doctrine, that the works of the medieval painters had risen to an exalted symbolic meaning incorporating within itself, in a totalizing and harmonious fashion, everything that was fragmented subsequently into autonomous artistic genres, such as landscape painting, portraiture and the still life. The original plenitude is still present in the major Renaissance artists, such as Correggio, Leonardo da Vinci and Raphael. But Raphael himself reaches this plenitude not so much in his celebrated late masterpieces as in the works of his middle period, in which diverse stylistic contributions are revived with an intense coherence of purpose.

Furthermore, Schlegel argues, while sculpture, which reached its apex with the Greeks, remains linked to a physical dimension, painting, in its ability to adapt itself to the infinite phenomenology of the manifestations of life, is the true art of the spirit. In Schlegel's view, the painter can find guidance in poetry, the only art able to mediate all the others, yet he must remember that he is a poet not of words, but of colours. The art of complete spiritual freedom released from practical necessity, and the ideal means of union with the divine, painting can have a vast representational range only if it is able to let the spiritual element prevail over naturalistic and sensible ones. From this viewpoint, for Schlegel, it was not so much Italian painting but rather early German painting – that of the Van Eycks, Dürer, Holbein – which remained faithful to the Christian ideal, since it was immune to classical imitation and, despite reciprocal influences among the various schools, individually national. Modern painters, for their part, will be able to free themselves from classicizing rhetoric by taking Romantic poetry as their guide. Even with this, it is only by returning to the religious source of feeling, as had the early painters, that modern painters will arrive at 'Christian beauty'. For Christian beauty, contrary to Classical beauty (which is attracted primarily to sensible and sensual components), is characterized by its aspiration to the divine in its diverse forms of consuming, nostalgic tension, or those of faith and love.

Schlegel's experience leads us more generally to the conceptions of criticism of German Romanticism overall. We can better appreciate these in reference to Walter Benjamin's interpretation in his 1918 *Der Begriff der Kunstkritik in der deutschen Romantik* (*The concept of criticism in German Romanticism*), which will serve as a guideline for my own interpretation, before I turn to the main features of Hegel's aesthetics and 'critical method'.

According to Benjamin, criticism is the method of reflection that takes art as its object. In other words, criticism is the cognitive modality specific to art, both as idea, and as product. 'The task for the criticism of art', Benjamin writes, 'is knowledge in the medium of reflection that is art. All the laws that hold generally for the knowledge of objects in the medium of reflection also hold for the criticism of art' (Benjamin, 'Concept of criticism', p. 151). As with reflection, criticism cannot be seen as the taking of a position extraneous to its object. It is not a question of a *judgement* on the work. In fact, it is only from Romanticism onwards that the term 'art critic' (*Kunstkritiker*) definitively establishes itself *vis-à-vis* the older term 'art judge' (*Kunstrichter*).

The Romantics refuse Enlightenment rationalism's sceptical dogmatism of judgment from without. They refuse what Benjamin calls 'the idea of sitting in judgment over artworks' (p. 143). But they also refuse the dogmatism of certain theories inspired by the *Sturm und Drang* which see in art an acritical product of the artist's creative power and subjectivity. Freedom from heteronomous doctrines and the establishment of an idea of criticism internal to the artistic experience are the mainstays of Romantic aesthetic theory. Kant's inquiry paved the way in the affirmation of the *autonomy* of the powers and *critique* of reason. 'The subject of reflection', Benjamin points out, 'is, at bottom, the artistic entity itself, and the experiment consists not in any reflecting *on* an entity, which could not essentially alter it as Romantic criticism intends, but in the unfolding of reflection – that is, for the Romantics, the unfolding of spirit – *in* an entity' (p. 151).

Rules of the Beautiful have nothing to do with criticism. The work's law coincides with its form. Only the work prescribes and imposes the means of its knowability and its growth in the hands of its user–critic. To critique is an act of reflection on the work: it means to potentiate it, to raise it to a higher level of consciousness. In his 1797–8 *Fragmente und Studien*, Novalis calls this process *Romantisieren*: 'Romantisieren ist nichts, als eine qualitative Potenzierung' (Novalis, *Werke*, p. 384). The reader purifies the work, shapes it, elevates different parts of it by giving them new meanings. Only if it generates other *forms* and connections is the work a form of art. This process of raising the work, into previously unexplored aspects, reminds us of Benjamin's theory of translation: 'Thus translation, ironically, transplants the original into a more definitive linguistic realm since it can no longer be displaced by a secondary rendering. The original can only be raised there anew and at other points of time' (Benjamin *Illuminations*, p. 75). Such observations are more interesting still if we recall how Novalis himself had compared translations to criticism, arguing that some translations, which he calls 'mythic', complete the original work: 'Translation is either grammatical or modifying or mythic. Mythic translations are those in the highest style. They represent the pure and complete character of the individual work of art. They do not give us the real work, but its ideal' (Novalis, *Werke*, p. 337).[3]

The critical completion is not only internal to the individual work of art, it is also internal to art as a medium. The reflective potentiation is an immersion into the totality of art, and it places the work in connection with every other formed or developing product. '[C]riticism is therefore the medium in which the restriction of the individual work refers methodically to the infinitude of art and finally [*endlich*] is transformed into that infinitude [*Unendlichkeit*]' (Benjamin, *Concept of criticism*, p. 152). The work shades off into the idea of art. The methodical connecting of the work by means of and in the reflective medium can be explained through the theory of the work as form.

Benjamin formulates three fundamental consequences of this theory of criticism for the evaluation of works: the implicit nature of critical judgment, the impossibility of a scale of positive values, and, finally, the uncriticizability of the bad. (1) The first principle states that the judgment of a work must never be explicit, but is always implicit in the fact itself of its Romantic critique: 'For the value of a work depends solely on whether it makes its immanent critique possible or not . . . The criticizability of a work demonstrates on its own the positive value judgment made concerning it; and this judgment can be rendered not through an isolated inquiry

---

[3] Novalis's thoughts here are part of his *Vermischte Bemerkungen* (the original version of *Blütenstaub*) conceived in 1797–8.

but only by the fact of critique itself' (pp. 159–60). (2) As concerns the second principle, the impossibility of a scale of positive values, we can say, with Benjamin, that the implicit evaluation of works of art in Romantic criticism is noteworthy precisely because it does not dispose of any scale of values: 'If a work can be criticized, then it is a work of art; otherwise it is not – and although a mean between these two cases is unthinkable, no criterion of the difference in value among true works of art may be contrived either' (p. 160). (3) As concerns the third principle, the uncriticizability of the inferior work, in it, Benjamin states, 'we see one of the hallmarks of the Romantic conception of art and of its criticism' (*Ibid.*). Schlegel expressed it most clearly, according to Benjamin, in the conclusion to his essay on Lessing: 'True criticism can . . . take no notice of works that contribute nothing to the development of art . . . indeed, in accordance with this, there can be no true criticism of what does not stand in relation to that organism of cultivation and of genius, of what does not authentically exist for the whole and in the whole' (Schlegel, *Jugendschriften*, II: 423; quoted in Benjamin, *Concept of criticism*, p. 160). And Benjamin emphasizes that the 'Romantic *terminus technicus* for the posture that corresponds to the axiom of the uncriticizability of the bad – not only in art, but in all realms of intellectual life – is "annihilate". It designates the indirect refutation of the nugatory through silence, through ironic praise, or through the high praise of the good. The mediacy of irony is, in Schlegel's mind, the only mode in which criticism can directly confront the nugatory' (Benjamin, 'Concept of criticism', 160).

Benjamin also engages a problem that is of primary importance not only as concerns Romantic culture, but for our own as well: the problem of subjectivity and objective knowledge in relation to criticism as an interpretative practice. 'Criticism, which for the contemporary understanding is the most subjective of things, for the Romantics was the regulator of all subjectivity, contingency and arbitrariness in the genesis of the work. Whereas in contemporary conceptions criticism is compounded of objective knowledge and the evaluation of the work, the distinctive element of the Romantic concept of criticism lies in its freedom from any special subjective estimation of the work in a judgment of taste' (pp. 160–1). The result, from Benjamin's point of view, is that evaluation is immanent to the objective inquiry and knowledge of the work. 'The critic does not pass judgment on the work; rather, art itself passes judgment, either by taking up the work in the medium of criticism or by rejecting it and thereby appraising it as beneath all criticism. Criticism should, by the choice of what it treats, arrive at the finest selection among works. Its objective intention is not expressed in its theory alone. If, in aesthetic matters, the persisting historical validity of assessments provides a clue to what one can sensibly call their objectivity, then at least the validity of the critical judgments of Romanticism has been confirmed' (p. 161).

The artistic form must expose itself to the suppression of the limit. To find completion in its critique it must let its closed perfection be destroyed. Destruction is the *conditio sine qua non* of the work's existence, of its passage into the limitless continuum of forms. Annulment prepares duration. The admission of the work into the medium dissolves its contours and transforms it into a moment in the overall life of art. It connotes the work *temporally*, i.e., the work loses its appearance of ahistoricity which it derived from its isolation, from its presumption of self-sufficiency. The system of art *is* in that it *becomes*: all knowledge is metamorphosis. The German term *Darstellung*, translated as 'exposition', also has the meaning of 'chemical preparation'. Criticism is a sort of alchemical intervention that irreversibly changes the quality of the work. When the work is introduced into the medium of forms – that is, into the temporal and historical continuum – its artistic depth is ascertained, its ability to endure.

The nineteenth century – the 'century of Romanticism' – was the century of History. The Classical thinkers established universal principles and reasoned upon these principles which they considered to be certain. The spirit of the nineteenth century, instead, is that of becoming. Ideas are valid in their time and place of apparition, but not for all nor forever. The same is true for artistic forms. Each truth, each doctrine and each work has a relative value. They can be adequately understood in relation to the place they occupy in space and time. Works of art become in this way historical symbols, or, more simply, documents.

At the aesthetic level, Hegel provided a schematic, but surprising and suggestive version of this philosophy of becoming. Hegel's key work in this regard is his *Aesthetics*, a series of lectures he gave in Berlin from 1817–29 which were published in 1835 after his death. His general method is dialectical, so that ideas appear in triads. Thesis attracts antithesis and the opposites are united at the superior level of synthesis. Hegel applies this dialectic to aesthetics. The core of the *Aesthetics* is its second part in which Hegel, for whom artistic form is basically the primary expression of the idea, shows how art has been successively symbolic, classical and romantic.

The first period is that of *symbolism*, mythology, oriental art, and, on the level of the systematic classification of the arts, architecture. In it the relationship between the idea and the sensible form is sought, but not yet achieved. Symbolic art is characterized by the fact that in it the idea is in search of its true artistic expression, which is still in itself abstract and indeterminate and does not have an adequate criterion in order to manifest itself harmoniously in the sensible world. As a result, in its effort to penetrate into concrete existence, symbolic art cannot reach an agreement or perfect identification between meaning and form, but only a symbolic expression which still betrays this inadequacy. The symbol, in fact, is that natural reality which tends to represent a signified in only an abstract and ambiguous way. Thus, for example, the lion may represent a lion itself or strength, of which it is a symbol. It is only in the human figure, however, that the idea can find an expression that has managed to see itself as a free and infinite subjectivity.

The second period is that of *Classical art*, that is to say, of Greek art and of *sculpture*. It is the age in which the work becomes the action of the Ideal, and achieves, in a resolute fashion, the unity of Idea and Form. Classical art is the art which flourished in the Greco–Roman era and is marked by a perfect and unrepeatable equilibrium between form and content, between the external and the internal, as is demonstrated by the solemn tranquillity of its marble sculptures of heroes and gods. By means of this general characterization, Hegel views ancient art in its aspect of harmony and catharsis, although he is not insensitive to the non-Apollonian elements of this art, especially those of Greek tragedy. The emergence of subjectivity in the wake of the affirmation of Christianity signals the twilight of classical art and the emergence of the new art which Hegel calls 'Romantic art'.

The third period is that of Romanticism. It can be identified with modern art, and, at the level of the systematic classification of the arts, with *painting*, *music* and *poetry*. It is the era in which the infinity of the idea can be realized only in the finitude of intuition, in that changeability which, at every moment, tends to dissolve each concrete form. Classical art's unity of Idea and Form, which had taken the place of the inadequacy between the limited expression and infinite content of symbolic art, can no longer find its proper fulfilment in modern Romantic art. The Romantic arts no longer offer that Classical, harmonious balance between the visible and the absolute. Since it is no longer possible to represent the absolute in an immediately visible form, the Romantic arts return to an invisible absolute. What results is imbalance and decline, in the sense that content, as the subjectivity of the idea, exceeds form and requires, as a consequence, higher forms to express itself that cannot be reduced to sensible and finite objects. The idea becomes conscious of itself and we reach, according to the Hegelian view, 'the death of art'. This expression should not be understood, however, to mean the disappearance of art itself, since, in the Absolute, spirit, art, religion and philosophy coexist eternally. The 'death of art' can, instead, be understood in a double way. On the one hand, art is no longer, in modernity, the adequate expression of the absolute Spirit, an adequacy which philosophical and scientific categories and concepts do possess. On the other hand, art has a new identity, one which we could define as anticlassical, conforming ideally to the Modern era with respect to a different, preceding (i.e., Classical) identity, that of the eclipsed, Preromantic epochs.

According to Hegel, art in its ultimate destination, as the creator of 'beauty', as the sensible apparition of the idea, is something which for us belongs to the past. In a famous passage in his *Aesthetics*, Hegel affirms:

> But while on the one hand we give this high position to art, it is on the other hand just as necessary to remember that neither in content nor in form is art the highest and absolute mode of bringing to our minds the true interests of the spirit . . .
>
> [I]t is certainly the case that art no longer affords that satisfaction of spiritual needs which earlier ages and nations sought in it, and found in it alone, a satisfaction that, at least on the part of religion, was most intimately linked with art. The beautiful days of Greek art, like the golden age of the later Middle Ages, are gone. The development of reflection in our life today has made it a need of ours, in relation to both our will and judgement, to cling to general considerations and to regulate the particular by them, with the result that universal forms, laws, duties, rights, maxims, prevail as determining reasons and are the chief regulator. But for artistic interest and production we demand in general rather a quality of life in which the universal is not present in the form of law and maxim, but which gives the impression of being one with the senses and the feelings, just as the universal and the rational is contained in the imagination by being brought into unity with a concrete sensuous appearance. Consequently the conditions of our present time are not favourable to art. It is not, as might be supposed, merely that the practising artist himself is infected by the loud voice of reflection all around him and by the opinions and judgements on art that have become customary everywhere, so that he is misled into introducing more thoughts into his work; the point is that our whole spiritual culture is of such a kind that he himself stands within the world of reflection and its relations, and could not by any act of will and decision abstract himself from it; nor could he by special education or removal from the relations of life contrive and organize a special solitude to replace what he has lost.
>
> In all these respects art, considered in its highest vocation, is and remains for us a thing of the past. Thereby it has lost for us genuine truth and life, and has rather been transferred into our *ideas* instead of maintaining its earlier necessity in reality and occupying its higher place.   (Hegel, *Aesthetics*, I: 9–11)

Hegel maintained that art would end up exiting from the scene since human consciousness, at the impulse of history, would demand higher forms than those offered by art in order to arrive at the recognition of 'truth'. He advanced the idea that rational thought, religion and philosophy – i.e., the higher activities of the Spirit – would replace art in its role as the messenger of truth, and that art itself would explicitly reveal its own decadence by becoming evermore anarchic and individualistic. This is the origin of that movement Hegel sees as typical of the culture of his own age but which, *mutatis mutandis*, is also valid for the coming modernity, namely, the movement from art to the 'philosophy' or science of art. It is the movement from artistic creation to the reflection on art, from making art to the interrogation of the meaning, significance and values of art itself, from artistic creation to criticism as the hermeneutic search for meanings within and through works, but also beyond the material reality of those works:

What is now aroused in us by works of art is not just immediate enjoyment
but our judgement also, since we subject to our intellectual consideration
(i) the content of art, and (ii) the work of art's means of presentation, and the
appropriateness or inappropriateness of both to one another. The *philosophy* of
art is therefore a greater need in our day than it was in days when art by itself as
art yielded full satisfaction. Art invites us to intellectual consideration, and that
not for the purpose of creating art again, but for knowing philosophically what
art is.
                                                                                    (p. 11)

Is not this 'philosophy of art' of which Hegel speaks the critical activity itself? If this is the case, the Hegelian conception becomes a fundamental reference point in the awareness of a central role of criticism within modern aesthetics and the modern theory of art in its evolution from Romanticism to the historical avant-gardes and beyond.

Together with the articulation of these problems of a theoretical and speculative nature, does Hegelian aesthetics generate a specific critical methodology? Even though Hegel did not formulate a critical method, a close reading of his *Aesthetics* reveals the emergence of two new criteria: historicity and originality.

As concerns the criterion of historicity, it should be stressed that Hegel understood that different styles are not more or less felicitous in relation to a perfect expression, but that each is the adequate expression of a moment of art and a moment of history. Artistic production, in this way, appears linked to history, and individual works offer themselves as moments of the Spirit. From the Hegelian viewpoint, artistic works thus situated in the historical process are not devalued to the rank of figurative documents or illustrations. If works of art acquire their full meaning only in relationship to their own time and environment, it is not as secondary products of a society, but in reference to other equally situated works. They acquire meaning and value to the degree to which they occupy their place in an irreversible evolution. It could be said that it is not history that explains art, but art, the testimony of a sought after and constructed thought, that adds a meaning to history. This reference to a general evolution of art that legitimates or condemns a work according to its geographical and chronological coordinates can be called the criterion of historicity.

Concerning the criterion of originality, we can say that Hegel overturned the established relationship between thought and art. Instead of seeing in works of art the reflection of a discursive thought of a religious or a philosophical nature, Hegel forcefully posited the primordial and auto-nomous nature of art. Art is not a secondary activity; it is a phenomenon of essential creation, an original state of thought.

Masterpieces are not so much reflections or games, but rather the expres-sion of the innermost feelings of the species. The work has significance in itself. It is the more expressive the more its realization is new and original. The novelty of the artistic model replaces conformity to the rules of a school.

I turn now in conclusion to the thought of the French poet Charles Baudelaire. Baudelaire's critical perspective or methodology constitutes an ideal bridge between Romanticism and Symbolism, and, therefore, between Romanticism and the historical avant-gardes, especially surreal-ism. Baudelaire becomes the prophet of that fully achieved modernity of which the Romantics had been the initiators.

Let me begin by noting that in Baudelaire's creative experience, critical activity and poetic activity are in constant correlation. Just as there is no poetry that is not at the same time a critique of life and of existence, a dif-ferent vision of their values, there is no authentic criticism that is not at the same time poetry, a common 'way of feeling'. One of the foundations of Baudelaire's 'critical methodology' lies in this Romantic awareness of the impossibility of separating criticism and poetry, passion and reason, criticism and metaphysics: 'It would be a miracle if a critic became a poet, and it is impossible for a poet not to contain within himself a critic' (Baudelaire, *Selected essays*, p. 208). And the same exigency has often reappeared in some of the greatest intellectual experiences of the West, those of Walter Benjamin and Paul Eluard for instance, to name only two. In his 'Salon du 1846', Baudelaire reveals his general awareness that 'pas-sion . . . exalts reason to new heights', and he is more specifically aware that 'criticism invariably borders on metaphysics' (*Selected essays*, p. 39). The result is that the 'best criticism' is 'that which is amusing and poetic; not a cold, mathematical criticism which, under the pretext of explain-ing everything, shows neither hate nor love, and deliberately divests itself of every kind of temperament, but – since a beautiful picture is nature reflected by an artist – the best criticism will be the reflection of that picture by an intelligent and sensitive mind. Thus the best criticism of a picture may well be a sonnet or an elegy' (p. 38).

It is precisely in view of this anticipated relationship between 'criticism' and 'poetry' that one can understand Baudelaire's polemic against all 'sys-tems'. The 'praise of feeling' as opposed to the 'systematic spirit' is beauti-fully enunciated by Baudelaire in his 'Exposition Universelle, 1855', in which he points out that, among other things,

a system is a kind of damnation which forces us to a perpetual recantation;
it is always necessary to invent another, and the exertion required is a cruel
punishment . . . To escape the horror of these philosophical apostasies,
I proudly resigned myself to modesty: I was content to feel; I sought refuge in
an impeccable naïveté . . . Everyone can easily understand that if the men whose
task it is to express the beautiful were to conform to the rules of narrow-minded
professors, beauty itself would disappear from the earth, since all types, all ideas,
all sensations would be fused into a vast, monotonous, impersonal unity, as
immense as boredom and as nothingness. Variety, the *sine qua non* of life, would
be effaced from life. So true is it that in the multiple productions of art there is
something always new which will forever escape the rules and the analyses of the
school!
                                                      (*Selected essays*, p. 81)

Criticism, for Baudelaire, was the privileged path for the quest and invention of that modernity of which *Les fleurs du mal* and the *Petits poèmes en
prose* were to become the living proof at the level of creative language.

Baudelaire always admired and personally laid claim to many of the
qualities and principles of Romanticism, above all because there existed a
true psychological and emotional affinity between him and the Romantics.
The most characteristic traits of the Romantic soul, such as melancholy,
rebellion, the sense of mystery and the infinite, can all be found, in different degrees of intensity, in Baudelaire's temperament. Samuel Cramer, the
hero of the poet's only short story, the 1847 'La Fanfarlo', provides us
with a fairly accurate image of the psychological profile of his author. The
story begins in fact with a description of the hero as being of 'a murky
nature streaked with bright flashes of lightning – at once both lazy and
enterprising – a prolific producer of intricate plans and laughable fiascoes'
(p. 28). This tormented and lacerated personality, torn between a rigorous
desire and the gravity of action, has deep elective affinities with the most
orthodox Romanticism.

Yet Baudelaire went beyond Romanticism and assumed a critical attitude towards its 'cultural revolution', uncovering the traps lining the paths
of feeling and subjectivity, or, rather, of their stereotyped degenerations.
If Baudelaire called Musset a bad poet, it was because he rejected the
latter's introspective smugness, his pure lyrical effusion, and, above all, his
indulgence in all sorts of artistic facileness and licence. This last point in
particular is decisive for understanding Baudelaire's interest from 1845 on
in the small groups and movements that wished to return to the formal
rigour and seriousness of the poetic 'craft'.

Baudelaire was a good friend of Théophile Gautier, who, after having
been one of the pioneers of militant Romanticism, launched the theory of
'art for art'. The author of *Les fleurs du mal* was also seduced for a time by
the 'formalist' theories which gave birth, in the forties, to various schools
such as l'École Plastique or l'École Païenne. The very names of these

schools reveal the significance of their enterprise, especially the desire to put an end to the excesses of Romantic spirituality, to restore the cult of a pure, 'lay' beauty, and to privilege formal perfection over emotional 'authenticity'. From this poetic impeccability and virtuosity of verse, Baudelaire acquired the technical, linguistic tools and the awareness of the importance of the formal structures of poetry that were to leave their mark on the architecture of *Les fleurs du mal* as a whole and on the composition of each individual poem.

Some aspects of the 1845 formalism soon appeared, however, to be incompatible with Baudelaire's nature. A certain 'pagan materialism' in the professions of faith of the fashionable schools went against his spirituality and mysticism. Likewise, the naturalistic aspect of the movement was contrary to Baudelaire's diffidence toward the deep perturbations of human nature. Thus, beginning in 1848, Baudelaire distanced himself from Gautier and his friends. As a result, in the same period in which Gautier was broaching a formalism on the verge of sclerotization, Baudelaire realized that there can be no perfection without emotion, no craft without temperament. This also meant that art and criticism in their specific endeavours cannot be separated, to use the words of a surrealist poet, Louis Aragon, from a 'pedagogy of enthusiasm'. Gautier slipped, unawares, into one of the final traps of Classicism, while Baudelaire inaugurated, with complete awareness, the age of modernity.

In his critical activity, Baudelaire granted to painting not only a quantitative importance, but a qualitative one as well. This preference did not necessarily coincide with an aprioristic disdain of other forms of expression. It is true that sculpture often upset him, bored him and led him into misunderstandings, but music – that of Liszt, Beethoven and Wagner – often generated in him surprising states of enchantment and spiritual flight. Nevertheless, his intellect and sensitivity are consistently attracted by painters, to the point that his critical judgments in other fields often receive pictorial metaphors, as when he affirms that Hugo has become a 'painter in poetry' or that Wagner excels in 'painting space and depth'.

Why does painting have this preeminence for Baudelaire? The answer lies in the fact that the gift of the author of *Les fleurs du mal* is essentially visual, or even, in the strong sense of the term, visionary. When Baudelaire hears, listens and reads, he sees, picturing to himself things and emotions. Everything – the gamut of sounds, the dictionary lexicon, the essences of the perfumer's boutique – is the beneficiary in Baudelaire of a single system of representation which tends to 'display' images, to sketch 'pictures'. Painting, in his eyes, is the most explicit and immediate proof of representation, the one in which the presence or absence of the sensory quality is most clearly perceptible in the play of colours and lines. Painting, moreover, the privileged space, through its very surface, of the possible happy coincidence of two gazes, that of the artist and that of the viewer, and hence of two subjectivities invited to an unlimited correspondence in the finite place of the canvas. In both the old masters and the new, Baudelaire finds painters whose work is not only the occasion for controversial judgments, but is also the expression of desires, sensations and the luminous penetration into the night of the nonsensical and the invisible. The first of these 'beacons' of yesteryear that illuminate modernity on the march is Breughel the Elder and his oneiric chaos. And then there are, among others, Rubens, Rembrandt, Watteau, who dissolved the natural dimension in the carnival of his own artifices, Goya, who created the 'monstrous verisimilitude', and finally the Romantic Delacroix, for whom Baudelaire felt unbounded admiration. In Delacroix, Baudelaire recognized the modernity born from Romanticism that a lengthy comparison with Victor Hugo in the 'Salon du 1846' clarifies quite well:

In the works of [Hugo], there is nothing to guess; for he takes so much pleasure in showing his skill that he doesn't omit a blade of grass or a reflection from the streetlight. [Delacroix] in his works opens up deep avenues to the most adventurous imagination. The first possesses a certain serenity, let us say rather a certain disinterested egoism which envelops all his poetry with an indefinable coldness and placidity – qualities which the stubborn and splenetic passion of the second, in conflict with the patience necessary to his craft, does not always permit him to retain. The one begins with detail, the other with an intimate understanding of his subject, with the result that one goes only skin deep, while the other tears out the entrails. Too materialistic, too concerned with the exterior aspects of nature, M Victor Hugo has become a painter in poetry; Delacroix, always respectful of his ideal, is often unconsciously a poet in painting.   (p. 42)

If Delacroix was a 'poet in painting', it was because, first of all, he was able to make the real speak, to extract its secret word, of which the artist, and the viewer, retain a memory. Baudelaire sees Delacroix's art as a 'mnemotechnics of the Beautiful'; his paintings have their origin in memory and speak to memory. Baudelaire returns often to modern art's essential quality as an expression grounded in affective memory that touches affective memory (see D. Rincé *Baudelaire et la modernité poétique*). He speaks of a 'mnemonic art' in Constantin Guys, and he writes that almost all of Corot's works 'have the special gift of unity, which is one of the necessities of memory' (Baudelaire, *Œuvres complètes*, II: 482). Of Boudin, he writes instead, that if certain artists had seen 'several hundred pastel studies improvised before sea and sky, they would understand that which they seem not to understand, that is to say, the difference that separates a study from a painting. Nonetheless, M Boudin, who could take much pride in his devotion to his art, displays his collection in a most modest fashion. He knows full well that all of this becomes a picture via the poetic impression remembered at will' (p. 665). Writing of Wagner's

Tannhäuser, he observes that 'from the very first measures our nerves vibrate in unison with the melody; every creature of flesh endowed with memories begins to tremble' (*Selected essays*, p. 210). Finally, to cite once more one of the most beautiful metaphors in Baudelaire's comparison of Delacroix with Hugo, memory, in Delacroix and in the other painters of modern life, 'opens up deep avenues to the most adventurous imagination' (p. 42).

The imagination becomes the epicentre of aesthetic modernity, the faculty most friendly to seeing, speaking and showing the totality of the world. In emphasizing this quality in Delacroix, Baudelaire adhered to the theoretical concerns of Delacroix himself. In a part of his journal in which he proposed some definitions for a *Dictionnaire des beaux-arts*, Delacroix wrote:

Imagination. It is the primary quality among the artist's needs. It is no less necessary for the art lover. I cannot conceive the buying of pictures by a man devoid of imagination: in his case, vanity replaces imagination, and does so to the extent that the latter quality is lacking. Strange as it may seem, the majority of men do lack the quality. Not only do they fail to possess the ardent or penetrating imagination which would cause them to see objects in a vivid manner – which would introduce them to the very cause of things – but they also lack any clear comprehension of works wherein such imagination is dominant . . . although all men have sensation and memory, very few possess the imagination which, it is claimed, is composed of these two elements. In the artist, imagination does more than picture certain objects to itself: it combines them for the purpose which he seeks to achieve; imagination gives him images with which he composes at will. Where, then, is the acquired experience which can give that faculty of composition? (Delacroix, *Journal*, pp. 560–1)

Vis-à-vis Delacroix and his contemporaries, Baudelaire never ceased on his part to take up this last question. For him the imagination cannot simply be the putting into images or the putting into memory of the real. This is why he does not appreciate and poorly understands copies in sculpture that he judges to be too servile: 'Brutal and concrete like nature, it is at the same time vague and intangible, for it shows too many faces at once' (Baudelaire, *Œuvres*, p. 487). And this is why he mistrusts photography, despite a certain fascination and his friendship with Nadar. In the *Salon de 1859* he writes that photography runs the risk of lowering art to the level of a simple industrial practice of recording. Thanks to photography, 'art loses respect for itself daily; it prostrates itself before external reality, and the painter becomes evermore inclined to paint not what he dreams, but what he sees' (p. 619). Instead of trying to copy or imitate nature, Delacroix leafs through and consults his vast dictionary with a sure and penetrating eye. To imagine a composition, for him, means to combine known elements that have been seen with others present in the artist's interiority. From this point of view, modernity acquires, so to speak, a revolutionary character. And it acquires it, as certain critics have indicated, in the sense of a transference in the name of imagination from the primacy of the truth of the real to the truths of the Ego which seeks out the real by showing it and naming it. Once again the entire edifice of classical representation as the mimesis of an *a priori* given role is abandoned in favour of an aesthetics of intuition and suggestion (see Rincé *Beaudelaire*).

The overall supremacy that, in the theory of modernity, is conferred on the imagination, together with the new and scrupulous foregrounding of the poetic and critical imaginary, generate in Baudelaire a demanding way of life, with its constraints, pleasures and sufferings. Baudelaire evokes all of this in his pictorial and literary criticism through the expression 'the heroism of modern life'. In the last part of his 'Salon de 1846', entitled 'De l'héroisme de la vie moderne', Baudelaire sought to understand the 'essence' of this modernity, how to live it, how to imagine it, how to be its protagonist and messenger. In the process there emerged the awareness, at times implicit and other times explicit, and which will appear later in both symbolism and surrealism, that the 'modern hero' – whether he be an artist, critic or spectator – is he who is able to translate, i.e., to secularize, the transcendental sacredness of the absolute into the profane temporality of existence. He does this by immersing himself, as a creator with his creations, into the contemporaneously banal and terrible, obvious and sublime 'particularities' and 'differences' of the everyday. He is the generator, at least from Romanticism on, of all the 'greatnesses' and 'wretchednesses' of modern man.

3

The French Revolution

DAVID SIMPSON

Literary and cultural history is a hard task to pursue under the tutelage of postmodernity. Grand or master narratives are now discouraged, so that no one can any longer confidently propose Hegelian sequences describing the organic unfolding of events through time, or the immanent relation between phenomena within time, in the manner of the traditional *Geistesgeschichte*. The prevailing admonitions commonly appear as moral exhortations, telling us that to proliferate grand narratives is repressive and reprehensible. But the difficulties are also and even more exigently epistemological: how do we know how one thing is connected with another within a history or a culture? What does it mean to speak, as Hazlitt and many others did, of the 'spirit of the age'? How can one prevent even the simplest of little narratives from escalating into something grander, whether by tacit assumption or empirical accretion? Perhaps the safest literary history is once again the most traditional: that showing the influence of one writer or writing upon another, with citations in place and cases closed. But it is hard to restrict ourselves to this kind of literary history because we still inherit an Enlightenment disposition to do so much more, to explore and explain the inherence of literature and literary criticism to culture and history on the grandest scale.

What we call the French Revolution has functioned from the first both as an instance of and an apparent solution to this problem of cause and effect in culture and history. Unlike many other 'revolutions' whose presence marks the narratives of historians and critics – agricultural, industrial, demographic, consumer and so on – the French Revolution seems to have had a clear beginning in 1789 and an end by 1815 if not before. But there was arguably no single French revolution, and those who applauded the fall of the Bastille in 1789 often found themselves deploring some later development, whether it was the execution of the king, the Terror, the French invasion of Switzerland (actually more important than either of the above in changing European public opinion), or the appearance of first a consul and then an emperor. Nonetheless, there was from the very first an attempt to create a single revolution by rhetorical fiat. As early as January 1790, the Parisian press was referring to *the* revolution, and the habit has never disappeared.[1] And *the* revolution has, as if by virtue of its very nomination, figured as an obligatory reference point in all French and many other European reconstructions of eighteenth-century and subsequent histories. In the bicentennial year of 1989 François Furet was widely noticed for pronouncing that, at long last, the revolution was finished: only after a tortured process beginning with the Third Republic and ending during the Fifth Republic had France finally freed itself from the compulsion to repeat the gestures and the practical reinterpretations of 1789. These repetitions had appeared in practice in 1830, 1848 and 1871, and in theory throughout the nineteenth century.[2]

Other European and especially British observers would have been quite content to pronounce the revolution over by 1815 at the latest, and perhaps well before that. And on the question of its effect on literature and on literary criticism, most of them were either ambiguous or negative. The French Revolution was judged to have had very powerful consequences for European politics and political theory, and for social history. Governments and commentators took positions for and against liberty, and various kinds of liberty, in the light of their various interpretations of the French experience, as did the different radical movements contesting the legitimacy of those same governments. The rights and wrongs of man were employed to describe a whole range of national liberation movements (for instance in Germany and Italy) and democratic movements, so that the rhetoric of revolution came into inevitable conjunction with the literatures of the national cultures thus affected. One can find, among the literary critics and historians, judgments like that of Taine, who would write (much later, in the 1860s) that on the 'eve' of the nineteenth century 'the great modern revolution began in Europe. The thinking public and the human mind changed, and whilst these changes took place a new literature sprang up.'[3] But to read on in Taine's history is to discover that the revolution began not with 1789 but (at least for England) with the aesthetic and stylistic initiatives of Burns and Cowper, both of whom published their most significant work before the French Revolution broke out. His 'whilst these changes took place' is thus as much a historical dislocator as a locator; changes were already afoot, and in obedience to some longer chronology

---

[1] See Mona Ozouf, 'Revolution', in eds. François Furet and Mona Ozouf, *A Critical dictionary of the French Revolution*, Arthur Goldhammer (trans.), Cambridge, MA and London: Belknap Press, 1989, p. 810.
[2] See, for example, François Furet, *Interpreting the French Revolution*, Elborg Forster (trans.), Cambridge University Press, 1981. For an excellent survey of the historiography surrounding Furet's work, see Bernadette Fort, 'The French Revolution and the making of fictions', in Bernadette Fort (ed.), *Fictions of the French Revolution*, Evanston, IL: Northwestern University Press, 1991, pp. 3–32.
[3] Hippolyte Taine, *History of English literature*, H. van Laun (trans.), 4 vols., Philadelphia, PA: Altemus, 1908, III: 381.

than that of 1789. Literature and political history are evolving in some sort of conjunction, but not as cause and effect. Thus it is at least imaginable that even without 1789 the 'revolution' of which Taine writes could have still happened.

The same questions occur with Friedrich Schlegel's famous declaration in number 216 of the *Athenaeum* fragments: 'The French Revolution, Fichte's philosophy, and Goethe's *Meister* are the greatest tendencies of the age.'[4] The word 'tendencies' (*Tendenzen*) suggests but does not specify a causal energy; it leaves these three phenomena suspended somewhere between cause, effect, symptom and analogue. Later on, in fragment 424, Schlegel identifies the revolution as the 'center and apex of the French national character' (p. 233) – a symptom of what came before it rather than the origin of a new national order. And on another occasion it becomes 'a marvelous allegory about the system of transcendental idealism' (p. 263). There is no settled specification of any simple effect of which 1789 might have been the cause. The Revolution is significant, indeed, but how and of what it is significant is left in the language of allusion and suggestion. It cannot be ignored, but neither can it be pinned down as a single privileged cause or component of cultural and historical change.

Between them, Taine and Schlegel more or less set the terms of the predominant literary-critical evaluation of the relation of the French Revolution to literature and its reception. Few if any of the critics who set about the task of relating literature to history and society were willing to propose a definitive effect brought about by the revolution, and only the revolution. To some extent this can be explained by the degree to which the events of 1789 were themselves readily open to being explained as a consequence of the Enlightenment philosophical culture that came before them. Blaming everything on Rousseau and/or on the *philosophes* was a favourite tactic of the British conservative press throughout the 1790s, and the same connection also appealed to the radicals who sought to validate thereby the powerful consequences of books and ideas like their own. Such explanations made political change a consequence rather than a cause of mental and spiritual revolutions. They put at risk the intellectuals and men (and women) of letters who published ideas that could be retroactively or prophetically related to radical social changes, but they also enhanced the importance of a subculture of writers and philosophers existing, for the most part, outside the security of universities and thus highly dependent upon public opinion.

There were, then, many commentators who regarded the events of 1789 and thereafter as the summation of a historical tendency already fully

---

[4] *Friedrich Schlegel's 'Lucinde' and the Fragments*, Peter Firchow (trans.), Minneapolis, MN: University of Minnesota Press, 1971, p. 190.

developed in philosophical and aesthetic theory, and only awaiting the
right moment to solidify into political form: an explanation much assisted
by the habit of the revolutionaries themselves in invoking the authority of
Rousseau and others, and by the active involvement of intellectuals like
Condorcet in the reordering of French political life. Late twentieth-century
historians, with their emphasis on *mentalités*, and their renewed faith in
the power of cultural and symbolic formations in the creation of historical
events, have recovered much the same emphasis as a corrective to the
excesses of strictly political and economic models of revolutionary change.
Ideologies and aesthetics as systems of social significations (now no longer
attributed to individual writers but to representational syndromes) are
firmly back at the forefront of our contemporary historical explanations.[5]

The argument for the priority of ideas over events was not, however, the
principal one used to position literature and literary criticism in relation to
the Revolution. That argument worked better for the *philosophes* than for
those we now recognize as writers of literature, though the boundaries
were obviously crossed by Voltaire, Diderot and Rousseau among others.
Perhaps more important in both the immediate and subsequent literary-
critical tradition has been the invocation of chronologies that displace or
outflank 1789 as the key date in the formation of what was called Romanticism. In France, for example, the consensus has been that Romanticism
began as a traditionalist movement antithetical to the secular spirit of the
revolutionary decade. The appearance of Chateaubriand's *Génie du christianisme* in 1802, or of Staël's early writings, are often cited as the key textual events. The delayed influence of these writings and others like them on
other countries has pushed forward other European Romanticisms into
the 1820s and 1830s, if not beyond. This has brought about a historical
distancing of European Romanticism from the most important events
of the French Revolution. Even British Romanticism, deemed one of the
earliest, shows in its commonly accepted founding date of 1798 (the publication of *Lyrical ballads*) an important remove from the critical French
events of 1789–95. And the Friedrich Schlegel who had the greatest influence across Europe was the Catholic traditionalist of the 1800s rather than
the radical aesthetician of the 1790s.[6]

---

[5] A good example of the trend is Lynn Hunt, *Politics, culture and class in the French Revolution*, Berkeley, CA, Los Angeles, CA, London: University of California Press, 1984.

[6] Any detailed account of European Romanticisms is well beyond both the scope of this
essay and the abilities of its author. Historians of Spanish Romanticism are still constructing definitional categories that extend into the late 1830s, and have to take account of
conservative and liberal appropriations of the term, as well as of established regional predispositions: see, for example, E. Allison Peers, *A history of the Romantic movement in
Spain*, 2 vols., 1940; rpt New York and London: Hafner, 1964; and, most recently, Derek
Flitter, *Spanish Romantic literary theory and criticism*, Cambridge University Press, 1992.
For an introduction to Italian Romantic criticism see René Wellek, *A history of modern*

An even greater chronological realignment affected the relation of the French Revolution to a long-durational literary history, one that most commonly placed the significant events in the evolution of the 'modern' well before 1789, and located literature itself as responsive to quite different historical cycles than those inaugurated by mere political changes. Within this model, the French Revolution might remain an important moment in the evolution of modernity, but its claim to independent significance is diminished along with its significance for an ongoing literary culture. The paradigms were in place before the French Revolution. But the appetite for long-durational models of modernity in literary history was increased after 1789, as part of the effort to distinguish the profound effects manifest in art and literature from the superficial disturbances wrought by merely political shifts.

Hegel, for example, located the beginning of the 'romantic' spirit in the Christian Middle Ages, with the emergence of 'the absolute inner life as inherently infinite spiritual activity', and thus as a principle increasingly 'indifferent to the objective world'.[7] Schelling specified the origins of this compulsive inwardness – which of course reappears in many formulations of the romantic ego – in the Reformation. The supersession of Catholicism by Protestantism in much of Europe brought with it all the terrors and privileges of isolation from both public sphere and communicative God, and it is this isolation that the literature of modernity depends upon and explores.[8] The Reformation of course divided Protestant from Catholic states in a radical way, so that its primacy as an explanation of the history of literature invites also the discrimination of national literatures, all the more so because of the Reformation's own role in the processes of state formation and consolidation in the fifteenth and sixteenth centuries. Thomas Warton's *History of English poetry* (1774–81) was only the most extended of various eighteenth-century efforts at providing a pedigree for English literature that would prove too firmly established to tremble at

criticism, 1750–1950, vol. II: *The Romantic age*, New Haven, CT: Yale University Press, 1955, pp. 259–78. See also Wellek's important essay 'The concept of Romanticism in literary history' reprinted in his *Concepts of criticism*, New Haven, CT and London: Yale University Press, 1963, pp. 128–98. A very useful anthology of the German responses to the French Revolution specifically is *Die französische Revolution im Spiegel der deutschen Literatur*, Claus Träger (ed.), Frankfurt am Main: Röderberg, 1979. For an interpretive summary of the same materials, see Ernst Behler, 'Die Auffassung der Revolution in der deutschen Frühromantik', in *Essays in European literature in honor of Liselotte Dieckmann*, Peter Uwe Hohendahl, Herbert Lindenberger and Egon Schwarz (eds.), St Louis, WA: Washington University Press, 1972, pp. 191–215.

[7] G. W. F. Hegel, *Aesthetics: lectures on fine art*, T. M. Knox (trans.), 2 vols. (continuously paginated), Oxford: Clarendon Press, 1974, pp. 518, 609.

[8] See, for example, the selections from *The philosophy of art* and the essay 'On Dante in relation to philosophy', translated in David Simpson (ed.), *The origins of modern critical thought: German aesthetic and literary criticism from Lessing to Hegel*, Cambridge University Press, 1988, pp. 232–47.

the effects of someone else's revolution. Thomas Campbell, coming a little later, was able to repeat as a truism the idea that the 'literary character of England' was in place by 'the end of the sixteenth century'.[9] It was, in other words comfortably in place by the time that England had its own revolutions (in 1649 and 1688), and could thus function to preserve a crucial national continuity during politically strenuous times.

The French literary character was usually seen as having evolved in the period of Descartes and Racine, a compound of rationalism and classicism to which the eighteenth century added in the component of libertinism. German literary culture was however still short of national status, and could be thought of as still coming into being during the period of the French Revolution. But even here there was common recourse to ancestral Gothic models in defining its directions. A. W. Schlegel ended his influential *Lectures on dramatic art and literature* with a plea for a German literature employing German events, events 'thoroughly national' even before there was a nation, and working to publicize the 'indestructible unity' of all Germans.[10] His brother Friedrich predicted a special role for the Germans in the 'great internal awakening' taking place across Europe, by way of a love of 'old traditions and romantic poetry' that would operate as an alternative to 'bloody revolutions'.[11] Fichte defined a special role for the German language both in overcoming the political distinctions between the German-speaking states and principalities and in disseminating a uniquely appropriate and close connection between words and things. The calamities in France during the 1790s showed Germans, by omission, the proper way forward. Education must precede political change, and language is key to education. German, as long as it banishes any propensity for Latinate borrowings and abstractions, has for Fichte a primitive integrity, an 'immediate comprehensibility and definiteness', a liveliness akin to a 'force of nature'. Given this energy and authenticity, poetry above all can function to spread this 'spiritual culture' across a whole people, in a way that cannot happen in a Latinate speech culture like the French.[12]

The primitive energy of Gothic culture, native to northern Europe and approximately coincident with the Protestant nations, served as a common principle uniting, for example, English, German and Scandinavian literatures, and distinguishing them from the French, with their predilection

---

[9] Thomas Campbell, *Specimens of the British poets*, 7 vols., London: John Murray, 1819, I: 104.

[10] A. W. Schlegel, *Lectures on dramatic art and literature*, J. Black (trans.), rev. A. J. W. Morrison (ed.), London: Bohn, 1846, pp. 528–9.

[11] Friedrich Schlegel, *Lectures on the history of literature, ancient and modern*, John Frost (ed.), Philadelphia, PA: Moss & Co., 1863, p. 382. Like Schiller, Schlegel held out hope for an aesthetic revolution; see Behler, 'Die Auffassung der Revolution', p. 214.

[12] Johann Gottlieb Fichte, *Addresses to the German nation*, George Armstrong Kelly (ed.), New York and Evanston, IL: Harper & Row, 1968, pp. 57, 59, 68.

for reason, politeness, wit, abstraction and social distinction. This division of national literatures was certainly in place before 1789, and informed, for example, the popularity of such primitive paradigms as the Norse sagas and the (imagined) Ossian. But it certainly took on a renewed energy with the alliance of so many of these same nations and cultures against the French, and with the need to define or redefine either a general or a nationally specific incarnation of 'freedom' that was different from what was spoken of by that name in France. Even before 1789 France was losing its hold on cultural hegemony over the rest of Europe. When the northern, 'Gothic' alliance took arms against the republic, a military as well as cultural patriotism (the second conveniently embodied in Staël's influential *De l'Allemagne*) came into play. The final victory at Waterloo was thus also a victory for Gothic civilization. And well before Waterloo, the turn to a preclassical aesthetics had begun to appear in France itself. French Romanticism is indeed often described as having been inaugurated with the return to the primitive and to the past, and to Christianity, evident in the Gothic predilections of Chateaubriand, which began a century or more of struggles between the novelists for a definition of the revolutionary spirit. A similar turn in German culture came with the Schlegels' embrace of Catholicism and a new appetite for the Middle Ages, a movement that was analogous to French literary Romanticism even as it was part of a national political struggle against France itself. In Britain, William Blake declared that 'Gothic is Living Form', while that of the Greeks is merely 'Mathematic', and opposed to the prolific imagination he discovered in the Bible and in the primitive, native and Hebraic traditions.[13] British conservatives were highly sensitive to a perceived Jacobin element in German literature and philosophy in the first decade after 1789, but by 1815 they were able to accept some of the same writings as spiritual companions to the new Europe, though this acceptance was contested by those who tried to revive a new 'cult of the south' on behalf of the liberal programme.[14]

Two of the most profound literary-critical texts of the period contributed however to a weakening or sceptical unsettling of any simple relation between literature and national politics, of the sort that Staël was all too often reproducing, as they argued for a morally and psychologically regenerative function for aesthetic experience: Schiller's *On the aesthetic education of man* and Shelley's 'Defence of poetry'. It is reasonable to propose that the French Revolution exacerbated the gap between these two kinds of literary criticism, which we now recognize as the historical

[13] *The complete poetry and prose of William Blake*, revised edn David V. Erdman, Berkeley, CA and Los Angeles, CA: University of California Press, 1982, p. 270.
[14] See Marilyn Butler, *Romantics, rebels, and reactionaries: English literature and its background, 1760–1830*, New York: Oxford University Press, 1982, pp. 113–37.

and the aesthetic (with the 'formal' drawing variously upon both). Adapting the influential (though often misunderstood) account of the aesthetic judgment in Kant's *Critique of judgement*, Schiller seeks to displace attention from the political scene and toward the inner life of the individual mind: 'it is only through Beauty that man makes his way to Freedom'.[15] Without this inner freedom, no political establishment can survive in authentic form, and at least one interpretation of Schiller's treatise would suggest that all political establishments must by definition be inauthentic. The necessary division of labour in modern societies, the 'rigorous separation of ranks and occupations' (p. 33), produces only a 'mechanical kind of collective life' and an inevitable divorce of work from pleasure (p. 35), a situation with which Wordsworth and Carlyle are also preoccupied. The division of labour is good for society but bad for the individual social being, and the paradox will not go away. And as long as the 'split within man is not healed', no merely political solutions can be expected to work (p. 45).

Schiller suggests that the healing work of the aesthetic can best work for the individual, or for a small circle of like-minded individuals. Moreover, the experience of beauty is without 'result', and 'does not meddle in the business of either thinking or deciding' (p. 161). As such, its healthful effects are psychological, embodied in the process of play and imagination rather than in any empirical product, whether artifact or concept. The same priorities and paradigms explicitly inform the writings of I. A. Richards in the 1920s and 1930s, and they have remained implicit in a great deal of subsequent literary criticism. Literature functions properly only when it avoids or negates the didactic; it is most enlivening when it eschews morality. The most powerful expression in English of this same position comes from Shelley. 'Defence of poetry' is one of the masterpieces of British literary theory. For Shelley, 'poetry' is the radically creative energy in all of writing and culture, most apparent as itself in language, but not restricted to it. Its creativity depends upon its being free both from purposive moral or empirical intent as well as beyond the control of the conscious will of the poet. The poetic principle operates through the proliferation of pleasure and delight; it makes us transcend the 'dull vapours of the little world of self' and also the limitations of doctrine and political difference.[16] Poetry is to language and culture what love is in interpersonal relations; both depend upon the synthesizing energies of metaphor, bringing contraries together and 'turning all things to loveliness' (p. 505).

For Shelley, the power of this poetry can be traced throughout human history, subject to temporary eclipse but never completely destroyed. His

---

[15] Friedrich Schiller, *On the aesthetic education of man*, Elizabeth M. Wilkinson and L. A. Willoughby (ed. and trans.), Oxford: Clarendon Press, 1967, p. 9.

[16] *Shelley's poetry and prose*, Donald H. Reiman and Sharon B. Powers (eds.), New York and London: Norton, 1977, p. 497.

exposition can be read as a defence of the idea that poetry is progressive, against the more common view articulated by Peacock (whose 'Four ages of poetry' was the immediate occasion for Shelley's text) and already somewhat traditional, that poetry was, if anything, in a state of decline within the culture of modernization. But Shelley's model is not simply progressive, in the sense that some of the revolutionaries of the early 1790s imaged progress: a steady increase in sense and civilization coming from the circulation of truth in popularly available forms. Shelley does vindicate the poets of his own generation, in England, as full of 'electric life' and part of a 'great and free developement of the national will' (p. 508). But in the larger course of history, his case relies upon a justification that is necessarily tautological. When culture has blossomed, it has done so in tandem with great poetry; and when it has not, it has failed in its notice of the great poetry within it. Poetry (in Shelley's extended sense) is the rejuvenating element in culture, and therefore cannot be extinguished as long as we have life itself. But its legislation is 'unacknowledged' (p. 508), as it has to be to remain outside of the limitations of doctrines and institutions. Progress is by anarchistic contingency rather than (or as much as) by steadily incremental development. Poetry may lie dormant for centuries before being rediscovered and put to use. It contains 'within itself the seeds at once of its own and of social renovation' (p. 493), and each word is as 'a burning atom of inextinguishable thought' (p. 500). But we cannot know in advance when it will flame into blossom, nor how it will be revivified, so that the process of describing poetry's effects is always immediate or retrospective, never predictive. Shelley has saved the principle of progress, the credo of the early revolutionaries, but only by disconnecting it from empirical history and legislative fiat. Hegel too required a loosely and minimally detailed history in order to get away with the argument of *The phenomenology of spirit*, that *Geist* really was refining itself to perfection through the time of human history. But Shelley's model has no clear goal; it is the worship of the creative process itself. For all the things he says to the contrary, the logic of this paradigm is that of eternal recurrence rather than teleological fulfilment. And in this sense he remains, like Schiller, true to the spirit of the Kantian aesthetic judgment, whose power is in its empirical and historical neutrality.

Shelley's 'Defence' makes the strongest of all Romantic cases for the social and historical powers of poetry (or literature), even if it is marked, as I have suggested, by critical qualifications and retractions. And indeed Shelley was the inheritor of a literary culture for which the *disconnection* of good literature from the ordinary constraints of time and place was already a sort of given. Because the appreciation of literature functioned as a socially solidifying gesture carried on outside political life and largely among or on behalf of those excluded from significant political life (the 'bourgeoisie', as we sometimes say), such disconnection was its very reason for being.[17] On the one hand, then, Shelley had to make a case against the majority view that the best art and literature was created, as Hazlitt put it, 'soon after the birth of these arts', by those who 'lived in a state of society which was, in other respects, comparatively barbarous'.[18] This is the distinction between the arts and the sciences; that the one reaches perfection almost at once, the other never. On the other hand, he had to work against the notion that the best art and literature is defined as such by being detached from use value or from the power to change history. Many critics thus concluded that the violence of the French Revolution was antithetical to the health of French and European literature. Madame de Staël, who regarded the Revolution as progressive in the long term, saw its immediate effects as 'detrimental to manners, to literature, and philosophy'.[19] Her successors in the academy were often even more outspoken. Sainte-Beuve, writing in 1849 one year after another revolution, presented the decade of 1789–99 as 'totally revolutionary, without any rest, constantly shattered by catastrophes'.[20] Literary culture was suspended as all attention came to be fastened on purely immediate outcomes. Apart from a brief interval in 1795, there was no security for serious writers and no leisure for artistic production. At the end of the century, Gustave Lanson's pathbreaking *History of French literature* (1894) was even more emphatic. For literature, the revolutionary decade was a 'period of transition' producing 'useless writing' that 'only adds a dead weight to our literature'.[21] William Hazlitt made some analogous observations about the negative effects of the French Revolution on British literature and culture. He found that the revolutionary rhetoric's extreme polarizations of 'high and low' had disastrously reductive effects, threatening to destroy the Englishman's traditional appreciation of 'wit and humour' and of the 'glancing shades of life' (the stuff of good literature), as well as encouraging a habit of national self-regard in response to the threats from abroad.[22] Hazlitt does not attribute the changes in English literature directly to the Revolution but, like Schlegel and Taine, to the same 'sentiments and opinions which

---

[17] On this subject, see Terry Eagleton, *The function of criticism: from 'The Spectator' to post-structuralism*, London: Verso, 1984; and *The ideology of the aesthetic*, Oxford: Blackwell, 1990.

[18] *The complete works of William Hazlitt*, P. P. Howe (ed.), 21 vols., New York: AMS Press, 1967, XVIII: 6.

[19] Madame de Staël, *The influence of literature upon society*, Daniel Boileau (trans.), 2nd edn, 2 vols., London: Henry Colburn, 1812, II: 95.

[20] C.-A. Sainte-Beuve, *Chateaubriand et son groupe littéraire sous l'empire*, Maurice Allem (ed.), 2 vols., Paris: Garnier, 1948, I: 38.

[21] G. Lanson, *Histoire de la littérature française, remaniée et complétée pour la période 1850–1950*, Paul Tuffrau (ed.), Paris: Hachette, 1952, pp. 853–4.

[22] *Complete Works*, P. P. Howe (ed.), 21 vols., New York: AMS Press, 1967, vol. XVIII: pp. 400–1.

produced that revolution'. At the same time, the 'principles and events' of 1789 did act as a lightning rod, a clear 'impulse' speeding up the transmission of the historical energies that went into them. Thus British literature, in the hands of the Lake poets, went straight from 'the most servile imitation and tamest common-place, to the utmost pitch of singularity and paradox', in a process wherein 'nothing established was to be tolerated'.[23]

Hazlitt and other commentators typically recognized at least three specific functions to this 'impulse' coming from the French Revolution, an impulse that was already latent in the spirit of the age but which was hurried along by the Revolution at what most felt was far too reckless a pace: the fashion for commonplace subjects (in the spirit of democracy); the compulsion to self-reflection and thence to egotism; and the habit of theory.

The first of these, the inclination to populate literature with ordinary people in ordinary situations, in the spirit of the popular 'democracy', was enormously controversial, most famously in the responses to Wordsworth's Preface to the second edition of *Lyrical ballads* (1800). It was the perceived offence against decorum in the very appearance of these 'Botany Bay convicts, female vagrants, gipsies, meek daughters in the family of Christ, of ideot boys and mad mothers' (to cite Hazlitt again), rather than any avowed political or oppositional content to the poems, that caused the outcry.[24] Burns's protagonists had not been so different, but they were prerevolutionary, and insulated by the picturesque and localizing functions of the Scots dialect. But Wordsworth made extended and carefully theorized claims for the value of a diction drawn from 'the real language of men in a state of vivid sensation', and embedded those claims in a recognizable if often implicit political economy that was critical of the metropolitan culture upon which most writers had to rely for their living.[25] The representation of 'vivid sensation' conjured up the spectre of Rousseau with all its radical associations, and, along with the validation of 'ordinary language', seemed to threaten the control of an educated elite over the distribution of standards of taste. In adverting to the 'primary laws of our nature' Wordsworth took the risk of sounding like a philosopher; and in seeking to balance the claims of 'thought' and 'feeling' he was adapting into English the two elements of the French national character whose violent oscillation was seen to have marked the worst excesses of the 1790s.[26]

[23] *Ibid.*, vol. v: pp. 161–2.   [24] *Ibid.*, p. 163.
[25] *The prose works of William Wordsworth*, W. J. B. Owen and Jane Worthington Smyser (eds.), 3 vols., Oxford: Clarendon Press, 1974, vol. I: p. 118. For full accounts of this political economy and its coherence, see my *Wordsworth and the figurings of the real*, London: Macmillan, 1982, pp. 122–69; and *Wordsworth's historical imagination: the poetry of displacement*, London and New York: Methuen, 1987, pp. 56–78.
[26] *Prose Works*, vol. I: pp. 122, 126.

Wordsworth himself was no friend to mass culture or to the burgeoning reading public. He was making a case for a purified version of popular culture whose intentions later critics have as often judged reactionary as radical, and his appeal was not to ordinary people but on behalf of ordinary language to a specialized and educated readership. He set out to produce an alternative to the 'gross and violent stimulants' he saw in the popular literary culture, which he linked to the imprudent speed of political and social change and the 'craving for extraordinary incident which the rapid communication of intelligence hourly gratifies'.[27] Nonetheless his acceptance of some perceived democratic tendencies, however carefully disciplined, was enough to cause offence to those who were completely panicked at the increasingly rapid circulation of print itself. The radicals of the 1790s, like Godwin, Paine and Thelwall and some of their French precursors, believed that print would be the agent of world revolution. Innocent of any complex notion of ideology, they believed that as the reading public expanded, the truths of political liberty would take root (preferably by peaceful conviction rather than revolutionary violence). Hazlitt, writing a little later, described the French Revolution as 'a remote but inevitable result of the invention of the art of printing'. Books formed public opinion, and public opinion made the Revolution.[28] With this kind of faith in the power of the printed word, the Romantic generations were not surprisingly very anxious about what was published. Staël noted that one effect of the English passion for business was an uncritical use of leisure: 'continual labour, whether mental or corporeal, disposes the mind to be contented with every kind of diversion', as long as it is extravagant enough to puncture our habitual ennui and 'dejection'.[29] Wordsworth had exactly the same concerns. Under the pressures of modernization, the national imagination had become melodramatic, insensitive to the subtle nuances of language and feeling, and responsive only to 'gaudy and inane phraseology' and 'gross and violent stimulants'.[30] Melodrama, of course, had already been coded as central to the French revolutionary aesthetic. Whether in the great public spectacles organized by the state, or in the theatres or in private reading-rooms, the times were felt to require clear and loud messages and trenchant distinctions between good and bad, right and wrong. The rapid distribution of important information called for clarity and simplicity, whether by propositional abstraction or by representational melodrama.[31] The well-known Romantic 'anti-theatricality'

[27] *Ibid.*, p. 128.   [28] *Complete Works*, vol. XIII: p. 38.
[29] *Influence of literature*, vol. I: pp. 307–8.   [30] *Prose works*, vol. I: pp. 116, 128.
[31] The classic study of the place of melodrama is Peter Brooks, *The melodramatic imagination: Balzac, Henry James, melodrama, and the mode of excess*, New Haven, CT and London: Yale University Press, 1976. See also Mona Ozouf, *Festivals and the French Revolution*, Alan Sheridan (trans.), Cambridge, MA: Harvard University Press, 1988; and Ronald Paulson, *Representations of revolution (1789–1820)*, New Haven, CT and London: Yale University Press, 1983.

has much to do with the refusal of an aesthetic of public visibility and instant response, though it was tied in also with a polemic against popular culture and against the public display of female passion.[32] Furthermore, the spread of printed information about the European war was itself governed by the melodramatic mode, as one 'decisive' event succeeded another in the patriotic narrative favoured by the newspapers. Lanson, following Sainte-Beuve, described the 1790s as the decade of political oratory and journalism, arousing in the public a constant desire for novelty and excitement.[33] Coleridge noted, in 1814, something that Wordsworth had sensed in 1800: that 'these troublesome times occasioned thousands to acquire a habit, and almost a necessity, of reading', which the writer in peacetime must make it 'his object to retain by the gradual substitution of a milder stimulant, which though less intense is more permanent'.[34]

The gulf between 'good' literature and the satisfaction of a developing mass readership had been widening throughout the eighteenth century. Women writers and readers, frivolous plays, novels in general and Gothic novels in particular, had all been positioned as improper and even socially dangerous bearers of the printed word. The French Revolution did not initiate this controversy, but it did add a further element of urgency to those addressing it. In particular, it gave a push to those who were looking for something in the reading experience that might work to help head off revolution, whether by positive reform or by an alternative energizing of an aesthetic experience that would have no practical consequences whatsoever. In this way the Revolution assisted in the coming into being of an educational apparatus with an important place for 'good' literature, and for a literary criticism to tell us the difference between good and bad literature. Francis Jeffrey, one of the most influential of the reviewers of the Romantics, admitted that good poetry would not 'often turn out to be very popular poetry'. But he argued – and it is a very Wordsworthian argument, despite his notorious criticisms of Wordsworth – for a sliding scale of response connecting qualified and unqualified readers, rather than for an unbridgeable gulf between them. As long as 'the qualities in a poem that give most pleasure to the refined and fastidious critic, are in substance, ... the very same that delight the most injudicious of its admirers', then there is a potential for an educational process, a broadening of the class of

---

[32] See Marc Baer, *Theatre and disorder in late Georgian London*, Oxford: Clarendon Press, 1992, which offers a detailed account of the 'Old Prices' riots at Covent Garden in 1809 and concludes that the politics of the theatres was to say the least ambiguous and not entirely radical; and Julie A. Carlson, *In the theatre of Romanticism: Coleridge, nationalism, women*, Cambridge University Press, 1994, which argues for an antifeminist component to the case against the theatres.

[33] Lanson, *Histoire de la littérature française*, p. 856.

[34] 'On the principles of genial criticism', in *Biographia literaria, edited with his aesthetical essays*, J. Shawcross (ed.), 2 vols., Oxford University Press, 1962, vol. II: p. 220.

adequately responsive readers.[35] The focus on slow or close reading that would become the hallmark of literary criticism in the writings of I. A. Richards and the American New Critics takes a good deal of its cultural and historical energy from this same realization of the power of literature to educate us into careful response. If the French in the 1790s read bad literature too quickly and came to disastrously hasty and superficial conclusions, then the British in the 1800s and thereafter would be taught to read good literature very slowly, and on the understanding that few if any conclusions were to be drawn.[36] Twentieth-century critics deplore the 'stock response' in much the same terms as their Romantic precursors criticized unrestrained passion and hasty judgments. Wordsworth wanted to encourage this same slowness of reading and response, and in order to encourage it he pared down his poetry to the point where it risked seeming beneath any serious attention at all. Readers have always had to work hard at Wordsworth's poetry, seeking a significance in what can at first sight look merely trivial. In 1815, Wordsworth explained how all young readers and many uneducated older readers would remain under the influence of extravagant passions were it not for the sobering discipline of good poetry; while that same poetry rekindles the passions that in serious older readers have all too often been forgotten thanks to the deadening functions of doctrine or predisposition.[37]

Good poetry, in other words, is an anti-revolutionary tonic. It requires for its elucidation the same act of imagination that Coleridge defined as consisting in 'the balance or reconciliation of opposite or discordant qualities'.[38] As he grew older Coleridge looked more and more to religion and the Bible as the sources of social–literary education for the masses who, he implies, can never be rendered self-active enough to appreciate good literature. He was reluctant to broaden the constituency of those entitled to form judgments for themselves beyond that made up of a small, highly educated clerisy. But of course, within the secular, liberal–democratic culture of which Coleridge was so fearful, the literary education has functioned precisely to offer a wider access to the experience of self-formation and the creation of 'standards' than had been previously available. The special place of poetry in this process has depended not insignificantly upon its status as the slowest of all reading experiences; and its pedagogic career has been at least enhanced by the perceived lessons to be drawn

---

[35] Francis Jeffrey, reviewing Scott's *The lady of the lake* in 1810, in Francis Jeffrey, *Contributions to the 'Edinburgh review'*, 4 volumes in 1, Boston, MA: Phillips, Sampson and Co., 1854, pp. 368–9.

[36] See Chris Baldick, *The social mission of English criticism, 1848–1932*, Oxford: Clarendon Press, 1987.

[37] *Prose Works*, III: 62–5. Compare the remarks on metre in the 1800 preface, I: 148–9.

[38] *Biographia literaria*, James Engell and Walter Jackson Bate (eds.), 2 vols., London and Princeton, NJ: Routledge and Kegan Paul and Princeton University Press, 1983, II: 16.

from the French Revolution. Coleridge made this clear in *Biographia literaria*, when he spoke of the 'beneficial after-effects of verbal precision in the preclusion of fanaticism' (II: 143), and pointed to Wordsworth (properly purged of his deficiencies, of course) as an instance.

A second component of the 'impulse' provided by that Revolution was the turn to self-consciousness and thus, it was often said, to self-centredness. The long-durational genealogies of 'modern' literature located this syndrome as a result of the Protestant Reformation, which placed the individual in a more stressful and self-determining position than had been the case within Catholic culture. Once again, the preoccupation with selfhood did not originate in 1789. But the revolutionary years were regarded by many critics as radically intensifying this inherited tendency, partly because of the presence of Rousseau, the ultimate self-analyst in literary history thus far, and partly because of the apparent inclination to self-worship evident among the Jacobins and then again in the figure of Napoleon. Tocqueville has memorably theorized an inevitable profile for literature in a democratic culture: it will be 'vehement and bold' in style, rather than marked by order and regularity, and its authors, deprived of the traditional topics for poetry, are 'excited in reality only by a survey of themselves', as they seek to establish their place in the pantheon.[39] The claimants are many and the competition is fierce. Style will become an important signature as birth and breeding come to matter less and less. Schiller's treatise of 1795, *On naive and sentimental poetry*, identified the modern age as nostalgically drawn to an older world in which self-consciousness had not yet become obligatory, while remaining unable to reproduce that world except in forms governed by acute self-consciousness. De Quincey, citing Fichte, opined that revolutions only exacerbated the already dominant tendency of the creative mind to turn inward upon itself; and Hazlitt saw the 'spirit of Jacobinism' as a direct threat to a more liberal 'spirit of poetry' in that it converts 'the whole principle of admiration in the poet (which is the essence of poetry) into admiration of himself. The spirit of Jacobin poetry is rank egotism'.[40]

The great examples of this 'rank egotism' in British Romantic culture were, of course, Wordsworth and Byron. They provided the anti-types against which the more liberal ideal of poetry as many sided and cosmopolitan, requiring negative capability rather than the egotistical sublime, took shape. At the same time, as Schiller tells us, such alternative ideals are implicitly nostalgic, and look back to a time when the poet did not need to

[39] Alexis de Tocqueville, *Democracy in America*, 2 vols., New York: Random House, 1945, II: 62–3, 77.
[40] *The Collected writings of Thomas De Quincey*, new edition, David Masson (ed.), 14 vols., Edinburgh: Adam and Charles Black, 1889–90, X: 430; Hazlitt, *Complete works*, VII: 144.

appear, by historical compulsion, in his own creation (Homer and Shakespeare were the most commonly produced examples). The rediscovery of Classical culture from Shelley to Matthew Arnold had much to do with a desire to counteract the preoccupation with the self that was the legacy of Puritanism and Romantic poetry as it was also the perceived priority of an entrepreneurial, utilitarian economy.

Byron had little time for Wordsworth, whom he regarded as a political reactionary, but they both came under the same critical disapproval as literary egotists. Once again, we see at work what is to a modern reader a surprising disconnection between the 'content' of poetry and its critical evaluation. Romantic critics and reviewers were much less interested in the 'message' of a poem than in its diction, craftsmanship and general compliance with certain notions of decorum. Even the notoriously conservative *Anti-Jacobin review* gave a favourable notice of the first edition of *Lyrical ballads*; and Francis Jeffrey, comparing Crabbe and Goldsmith – a comparison that for us now would have to include discussion of antagonistic political ideologies – manages to occlude or fail to perceive these differences by reference to exclusively aesthetic categories.[41] In the same spirit, Byron is defined by Hazlitt as a 'liberal' only in his politics: 'his genius is haughty and aristocratic'. In its formal and aesthetic dimensions, his poetry is 'self-dependent', and 'governed by no law, but the impulses of its own will'.[42] Hazlitt's criticism of Byron is in this respect interchangeable with his criticisms of Wordsworth on the same grounds: both are egotists. And this judgment was the conventional judgment of Byron by the early reviewers. John Wilson linked him with Rousseau as creating only endless versions of himself, and Jeffrey expressed the familiar view that none of his plays have in them anything dramatic: all the characters are versions of himself.[43] Byron had of course an immense influence on European Romanticism, but even here what is registered is as often the power of individuality as the appeal of political doctrine. Mazzini, who perhaps found radical individualism a revolutionary thing by virtue of residence within a Catholic culture, made much of the 'principle of Individuality', though he also found it insufficient for the liberationist long run.[44]

The critics, then, were much more exercised by the possible consequences of the turn to the self than they were of the turn to nature that constituted the other familiar aspect of what we have come to know as Romanticism. The two came together in such analyses as Schiller's *On naive and sentimental poetry*, where the turn to nature is a symptom of the refusal of complex (and inorganic) human community and a further

---

[41] *Contributions*, pp. 380–1.
[42] *Byron: the critical heritage*, Andrew Rutherford (ed.), New York: Barnes & Noble, 1970, p. 270.
[43] *Ibid.*, p. 147; Jeffrey, *Contributions*, p. 319.   [44] *Byron: the critical heritage*, p. 330.

stimulus to reflective self-absorption. But Wordsworth could be made acceptable to the literary–pedagogical tradition, albeit at the expense of everything most interesting in his poetry, by being packaged as the poet of nature rather than the poet of the egotistical sublime, as he was by Matthew Arnold. John Morley, in 1870, brilliantly understands Byron as the poet of 'melodramatic individualism', and thus as doubly threatening to the emerging culture of literary criticism and its pedagogically normalizing ambitions. Temperament and intellect gave Byron 'the amazing copiousness and force that makes him the dazzling master of revolutionary emotion, because it fills his work with such variety of figures, such free change of incident, such diversity of passion, such a constant movement and agitation', and thus makes him the 'effective interpreter of the moral tumult of the epoch'.[45] Byron, in other words, represents the threatened return of what Wordsworth and the anti-melodramatic writers had tried to repress: that which militates, in its invitations to passionate response, against the emerging discipline of trained and restrained close reading. Byron's avowed beliefs and notorious personal habits were not the only reasons for his being marginalized by a literary pedagogy that has preferred Shakespeare to Milton, and has accepted Wordsworth largely by ignoring what so many of his contemporaries found most objectionable: the revolutionary personality and its portrayal in poetry.

The case of Byron demonstrates just how complex a task it is to draw firm conclusions about the effect of the French Revolution on literary culture. Here we have an aristocrat with liberal sympathies but exclusionary instincts, and a 'Romantic' with polemical preferences for the poetry of the eighteenth century. The third element of the revolutionary 'impulse' shows some of the same complexities. No sooner was there a turn to theory than there was a reaction against it, and the dialectic then consolidated (for it was, once again, not a completely original moment) has bedevilled and inspired literary criticism ever since. Looking back at Romanticism with the hindsight of the 1860s, Taine described how 'philosophy entered into literature, in order to widen and modify it', so that 'every poet, becoming theoretic, defined before producing the beautiful, laid down principles in his preface, and originated only after a preconceived system'. Taine did not approve, seeing here a 'doing violence to literature', and a 'rendering it rigid', an initiative for which he principally blamed the Germans.[46] Thirty years earlier, Heine had noted the influence of the Schlegels in establishing a 'critical examination of the art works of the past' along with 'a recipe for the art works of the future', though he wickedly

---

[45] *Ibid.*, p. 395. Morley also notes Byron's revolt 'on behalf of unconditioned individual rights, and against the family' (p. 404).

[46] *History of English literature*, vol. III: 442–4.

refused to allow them the authority of a 'fixed theory'.[47] But Friedrich Schlegel had indeed set the agenda for theorization in claiming that the history of modern poetry embodied the injunction that 'all art should become science and all science art; poetry and philosophy should be made one'.[48]

To say this, of course, was to threaten one of the traditional boundaries whose maintenance had always been thought necessary for the very existence of 'literature' and literary criticism, which defined themselves against the respective limitations of history and philosophy (for instance in Shelley's 'Defence of poetry'). The synthesis which Schlegel here proposes is indeed still being fought over and fought out in the debate about the postmodern.[49] And it was fiercely resisted at the time. Wordsworth, as is well known, drew much more fire for the preface to *Lyrical ballads* than had been occasioned by the poems themselves when they were published without the 'theory'. And Coleridge, who tried throughout his career to introduce the habit of systematic or philosophic thinking into aesthetics, often suffered dismissal as a crazy metaphysician. *Biographia literaria* may be read as an effort, however ungainly, to make literary theory friendly by weaving it into the narrative of a life.

Once again, the image of the French Revolution, frequently cast as the result of the delusions of theorists and metaphysicians, seems to have functioned to strengthen prejudices and predispositions that were already in place.[50] There was already, at least in Britain, a well-developed commitment to maintaining literature and its criticism as independent of systems, theories and doctrines, as well as of specialized terminologies. Edward Gibbon wrote against the 'fondness for systems' at the expense of the 'attention to particulars' which should be the business of literature and criticism in its commitment to 'the human heart and the representations of nature'. Criticism cannot be learned 'by rote or practice', nor does it consist in 'speculative truths' that remain 'purely theoretical'. The good critic is 'attached to beauties more than rules'.[51] Gibbon here speaks for a

[47] Heinrich Heine, *The Romantic school and other essays*, Jost Hermand and Robert C. Holub (eds.), New York: Continuum, 1985, pp. 16–17.

[48] Schlegel, *'Lucinde' and the fragments*, p. 157. The case for this aspect of the Jena circle's work as originating the modern notion of literature has been made by Philippe Lacoue-Labarthe and Jean-Luc Nancy, *The literary absolute: the theory of literature in German Romanticism*, Philip Barnard and Cheryl Lester (trans.), Albany, NY: State University of New York Press, 1988.

[49] See my *The academic postmodern and the rule of literature: a report on half-knowledge*, Chicago, IL and London: University of Chicago Press, 1995.

[50] See, among others, Seamus Deane, *The French Revolution and Enlightenment in England, 1789–1832*, Cambridge, MA and London: Harvard University Press, 1988; Margery Sabin, *English Romanticism and the French Revolution*, Cambridge, MA and London: Harvard University Press, 1976; David Simpson, *Romanticism, nationalism, and the revolt against theory*, Chicago, IL and London: University of Chicago Press, 1993.

[51] Edward Gibbon, *An essay on the study of literature*, London: Becket & De Hondt, 1764, pp. 3, 28, 62, 65.

consensus in place at least since *The spectator*, and very much enforced by the cultural functions of literature and literary reading as a release from the rigours of professional and occupational discipline and from political disputes. As literary criticism moved into the universities in the late nineteenth century, the same priorities tended to be preserved as a means of marking off the discipline (as it had now to be called) against other disciplines. At the same time the proximity of other disciplines has required some compromises with more exact methodologies, in order that literary criticism stay abreast and appear at least minimally professional. Hence we have the ongoing fights over 'literary theory'.

The contest of literature with theory really did become exceptionally acute in the revolutionary years; and, given the already in-place British disposition 'against theory' as a traditionally French preoccupation, theory never had much of a chance. Erasmus Darwin's efforts at putting biology (and sexology) into poetry were fiercely resisted both because they broke with disciplinary decorum and because they threatened to introduce the readers of literature (especially women readers) to indelicate information. Despite the widespread European interest in German *Naturphilosophie*, with its explicitly synthesizing ambitions, the long-term effect of the French Revolution, especially on Anglophone culture, appears to have worked to further separate literature from science and from all other exact languages, a tendency already perhaps inevitable with the remarkable and specialized advances in science and mathematics themselves. Blake, in no uncertain terms, wrote that 'SCIENCE is the Tree of DEATH', while 'ART is the Tree of LIFE'.[52] Hazlitt, as so often, is eloquent about the dangers of the 'contractedness and egotism of philosophical pursuits' of all kinds: 'because wherever an intense activity is given to any one faculty, it necessarily prevents the due and natural exercise of others'. Too much of this

> must check the genial expansion of the moral sentiments and social affections; must lead to a cold and dry abstraction, as they are found to suspend the animal functions, and relax the bodily frame. Hence the complaint of the want of natural sensibility and constitutional warmth of attachment in those persons who have been devoted to the pursuit of any art or science.[53]

Hazlitt is of course rehearsing the by then already familiar argument about the consequences of the division of labour, but he is applying it with particular energy in defence of the liberalizing effects of reading and writing good literature. We can see here the prefigurings of Matthew Arnold's Hellenism and of F. R. Leavis's ferocious attack on C. P. Snow and on the

---

[52] *Complete poetry and prose of William Blake*, rev. edn, David V. Erdman and Harold Bloom (eds.), Berkeley, CA: University of California Press, 1982, p. 274.
[53] Hazlitt, *Complete works*, IV: 117.

claims of scientific knowledge; we can see, in fact, the founding principles of literary pedagogy (including a rehabilitation of 'serious' theatre) for much of the following two centuries.

The less literature and criticism were seen to have to do with theories and systems, the more they had to do with particulars and localized forms of knowledge. The defining characteristic of the aesthetic as independent of empirical content and didactic effect placed an emphasis on the health of individual minds rather than of general groups; this too was a form of particularization. But the content of literature and the purpose of literary criticism were also reaffirmed after 1789 as more than ever local and particular rather than general and systematic. Blake's statements are again exemplary. In his annotation to the works of Sir Joshua Reynolds, he wrote that 'To Particularize is the Alone Distinction of Merit'; and in his own *Vision of the Last Judgment* he opined that 'he who enters into & discriminates most minutely the Manners & Intentions the Characters in all their branches is the alone Wise or Sensible Man & on this discrimination All Art is founded'. He deplored the move toward general standards which, like Burke, he blamed on France: 'since the French Revolution Englishmen are all Intermeasurable One by Another Certainly a happy state of Agreement to which I for One do not Agree'.[54] In a similar spirit, Taine's interpretation of the French Revolution involved attributing political disaster to an inherited French antipathy to localized rather than generalized representations.[55] Coleridge had already published an account of the limitations of 'Reason . . . taken singly and exclusively', and of 'the science of cosmopolitism without country, of philanthropy without neighbourliness or consanguinity, in short, of all the impostures of that philosophy of the French revolution, which would sacrifice each to the shadowy idol of ALL'.[56] Literature, then, would henceforth concentrate upon 'each' even more doggedly than it had done previously, and thence began the cult of exceptionalism and irreducibility, of the concrete example and the lived experience, that would characterize so much of later literary criticism in Britain especially.

For Hazlitt, literature in general and 'dramatic poetry' in particular offered the best means for tempting the public away from its preoccupation with the French Revolution and its consequences. These events had made us focus on 'the general progress of intellect, and the large vicissitudes of human affairs', with all the negative effects previously specified. Dramatic poetry brings us back to the contemplation of 'single suffering' and 'private sorrow' in 'the most trying and singular circumstances', and

[54] *Poetry and prose of Blake*, pp. 641, 560, 783.
[55] See Furet and Ozouf, *Critical dictionary*, p. 1015.
[56] Samuel Taylor Coleridge, *Lay sermons*, R. J. White (ed.), London and Princeton, NJ: Routledge and Kegan Paul and Princeton University Press, 1972, p. 63.

limits attention to 'personal and local attachments and antipathies'.[57] The egotism of Wordsworth and Byron prevents this particularization, as does the theoretical obsession of Godwin and of the short-lived 'Jacobin' novel of the 1790s. For a theorist like Hegel, with his grand narrative of the emergence of *Geist* and philosophic (generalized) prose out of the disappearance of art, literature's commitment to the local is an impediment, so that Goethe, for example, is praised exactly to the degree that he transcends his 'quite restricted material' and infuses his works with the energies of a larger history.[58] But for the British tradition, the localizing incentive would remain dominant, whether in the desire for a regional literature (Burns, Wordsworth, Clare, Hardy) or for a portrayal of ordinary people living reasonably ordinary lives (Austen, Lawrence and in at least one sense the Joyce of *Ulysses*).

One important aspect of this localization or domestication of literature and literary criticism, with all its associations of rural contentment, home and hearth, and patriotic self-sufficiency (especially powerful, of course, in an age of imperial expansion), was its redefinition of the role of women writers and readers. Throughout the eighteenth century the identity of literature as a feminine and feminized occupation was becoming more and more forceful.[59] More and more women wrote literature and, since it was by definition produced in English and announced as requiring no very systematic thought, more and more women (and ordinary men) who had not had the benefit of higher education read it, and were imagined as reading it. The incursion (as it was perceived) of women into the literary public sphere was already controversial before 1789, and after the Revolution it became more so, notwithstanding the evidence that the revolution itself was not especially kind to women after its first flush of democratic enthusiasm.[60] But Burke's accounts of mobs of violent women, together with the sexually liberating messages of the German dramas that were so popular (in translation) in the 1790s, were enough to ensure that the position of women became one of the dominant talking points of the revolutionary period. Educated male writers, who had a professional investment in upholding the integrity of an 'educated' literature and readership, were able to use the newly emphasized imperative toward particularization as a way of at once privileging literature as a whole (and hence themselves) while limiting the sphere of women within it. Francis Jeffrey, reviewing Felicia Hemans in 1829, points out that woman's 'proper and natural business is the regulation of private life, in all its bearings, affections, and concerns'. Thus they develop 'the finest perception of character

[57] Hazlitt, *Complete works*, XVIII: 305–06.   [58] Hegel, *Aesthetics*, pp. 191, 262, 1110.
[59] See, among others, Nancy Armstrong, *Desire and domestic fiction: a political history of the novel*, New York and Oxford: Oxford University Press, 1987.
[60] See Staël, *Influence of Literature*, II: 156–74.

and manners' – the perfect knowledge for writing literature. It will not of course be the whole of literature, and Hemans's own work does not show 'the very highest or most commanding genius'. But in the bourgeois sphere addressed by the domestic novel and by lyric poetry it will, presumably, do. Hemans's translations are praised for having made over into English the extravagant and 'revolting' prototypes of foreign literatures, and thus for performing the useful task of cultural domestication. Her weakness here is her strength. Her capacity for what is merely 'sweet, elegant, and tender' prevents her passing on whatever is 'vehement and overpowering'.[61]

This is the schematic profile of the Victorian woman of letters, resisted so strenuously by so many Victorian women writers. Women, whose political and personal enfranchisement, as much imagined as actual, had caused so much fear and trembling in the early Revolutionary period, are now offered as an alternative energy to the masculine sublime, the 'vehement and overpowering' mode that had seemed (remember Byron) the natural emanation of the revolutionary spirit. If unlicensed women could occasion the sublime spectacle, as they did for Burke, then women like Hemans could assist in the task of keeping it at bay for future generations. And because this gendered determination was very much in line with the general function of literary culture for a bourgeois society, it worked to reinforce the generically feminized role of that culture in relation to the developing scientific, utilitarian and professional vocations. This too may be related to, though it was in no sense exclusively caused by, the events of the French Revolution.

How, then, to sum up the impact of the French Revolution on Romantic literary criticism? We have seen various responses in various national or nationalizing cultures. In general, the Revolution confirmed even as it challenged the existing paradigms and stereotypes, except perhaps in France, where it was received by many as a radical break with the past. By strengthening the case of those who thought that great literature should be not so much of its time as for all times, it challenged (though it did not defeat) the cultural–historical criticism of the Enlightenment, which had sought to understand literature in its relation to other, contextual tendencies. It exacerbated the already anxious relation between popular and elite culture, and further emphasized the ambivalent potential of literary pedagogy as a mediator between the two. It certainly had the effect of further displacing French culture and literature from any claim to general European or world significance. It would be hard to argue that the French Revolution brought into being a single new literary genre, except perhaps the 'Jacobin' novel of the 1790s, which did not last. But it did consolidate the British predilection to applaud the free play of thought and feeling and left

---

[61] Jeffrey, *Contributions to the Edinburgh Review*, pp. 473–4.

British culture with an even more profound disdain for 'theory' than it had had before. It confirmed that the dominantly approved paradigm for British literature would be anti-metropolitan, rural and local (for the Revolution was imaged as a Parisian event), and it probably worked to reify the place of women in a literary culture that would hold nothing more sacred than the holiness of the heart's affections and the ultimate integrity of personal relations. For these reasons among others, it would be hard to argue that the French Revolution has even now finished its work with literary criticism.

4

Transcendental philosophy and Romantic criticism

DAVID SIMPSON

Most students of Romanticism will at some point find themselves confronting the challenge of theory and philosophy. This was not always so. The Romantics themselves certainly felt this challenge, perhaps most visibly in the career of Coleridge, but later commentators found ways to avoid it. John Stuart Mill's *Autobiography* presented a case for the therapeutic value of reading Wordsworth as a poet of the feelings rather than of ideas, and Matthew Arnold followed up with a recommendation that we ignore altogether the same poet's efforts at systematic thought and concentrate instead on his closeness to nature.[1] Wordsworth was seen by both men as a great poet but a poor philosopher, and as such he was taken to instance the generic divide between poetry and philosophy that had preoccupied so many critics from Sir Philip Sidney on. The general notion of the 'literary' has indeed for the last four or five hundred years involved the assumption that literature is *not* philosophical, that it offers access to different sorts of truth and different imaginative experiences from those associated with abstract thought and logical argument. This same general notion has also supposed that literature is to be distinguished from history, from the accumulation and arrangement of facts and records and from the grand narratives of world-historical change.

Criticism, however, has not always kept itself so pure. In the 1970s, especially in the United States, Romanticism was visibly associated with the development of literary theory, and with a philosophic foundation. Since then, the most notable ambition in Romantic studies has been a historical one, an effort to situate the major writers within the life and thought of their times, and to fill in our knowledge of the literary tradition by recovering and discussing other writers (including many women) whom we have ignored or dismissed as of no interest. The effort at holding on to a model of the literary that is neither philosophical nor historical has always been under pressure from one or other of these alternatives, and sometimes both at once.

---

[1] John Stuart Mill, *Autobiography*, John M. Robson (ed.), London: Penguin, 1989, pp. 120–2; Matthew Arnold, preface to *The poems of Wordsworth*, London: Macmillan, 1879.

Notwithstanding the recent turn to history, Romanticism has for a long time been implicated in and identified with philosophy, and particularly with German philosophy. Some critics have resented this, and some continue to resent it. The great nineteenth-century French literary historian Hippolyte Taine complained that the 'philosophical spirit . . . dragged literature through an agony of struggles and sufferings' thanks to the Romantic preoccupation with 'aesthetics' and the 'theoretic' and the compulsion to write 'after a preconceived system'.[2] Other readers then and since have concluded that Coleridge lost his poetic gifts as he became interested in philosophy, or that Wordsworth's poems are best appreciated by ignoring the 1800 Preface to *Lyrical ballads*, or that Keats showed admirable tact in never offering any systematic critical statements beyond the luminous informalities of his letters.

The resistance of literary criticism to the philosophical moment in Romanticism has also been by association a resistance to the political and even the revolutionary. Many British commentators of the 1790s and 1800s believed or chose to claim that philosophy and theory had been responsible for the French Revolution, so that any contamination of literature by philosophy looked like a threat not only to the autonomy of the imagination but also to the integrity of throne and altar.[3] Belief in the power or usefulness of systematic thought or theory was seen as a Jacobin trait, and welcomed or dismissed as such according to the political preferences of the reader or hearer. The dominant figures here were French: rationalists like Voltaire, materialists like Helvétius and La Mettrie, and above all the disturbingly complex man of feeling, Jean-Jacques Rousseau, who represented (especially after the publication of the second volume of his *Confessions*) a threat that was both sexual and political, erotic and rationalist. British political theorists like Paine, Priestley and Godwin were squarely placed in this French tradition by the defenders of the establishment, and treated accordingly.[4] Poets and novelists who read or referred to these figures, or who themselves dabbled in philosophy, risked the same treatment.

So insular was the British tradition, and so impulsive in its prejudices, that all foreign philosophy tended to appear threatening. German writers were particularly obscure, since almost no one spoke or read German, and

---

[2] H. A. Taine, *History of English literature*, H. van Laun (trans.), 4 vols., Philadelphia, PA: Altemus, 1908, I: 442–3.

[3] For a longer discussion, see David Simpson, *Romanticism, nationalism and the revolt against theory*, Chicago, IL and London: University of Chicago Press, 1993.

[4] See, among others, Margery Sabin, *English Romanticism and the French tradition*, Cambridge, MA and London: Harvard University Press, 1976; Seamus Deane, *The French Revolution and Enlightenment in England, 1789–1832*, Cambridge, MA and London: Harvard University Press, 1988; Marilyn Butler (ed.), *Burke, Paine, Godwin and the Revolution controversy*, Cambridge University Press, 1984.

opportunities for travel and the easy exchange of information were nar-
rowed during the wars with France that dominated the period we have
come to call (in Britain) Romantic. The arguments that dominated German philosophy in the late eighteenth century were also extraordinarily
difficult and technically challenging, and indeed they have remained so. In
Kant there is a transcendental philosophy but not a fully developed idealism. That is, while he is writing in declared opposition to the materialists
he resists the grand synthesis of mind and nature, subject and object, that
preoccupied some of his successors, Schelling and Hegel chief among
them. It is for these successors, at once influenced by Kant but critical of
his sceptical and negative efforts at limiting what philosophy could properly describe to what the mind thinks about its own operations, that the
term *transcendental idealism* is best reserved. These distinctions are hard
enough to adduce now, with the assistance of hindsight and competent
translation. They were more or less unavailable to most of the Romantics.
Early English translators of and commentators on Kant, to take the major
example, achieved only the most minimal understandings of his work,
even to the point of radical falsification.[5] Even the cosmopolitan Madame
de Staël, in her important book *De l' Allemagne*, translated into English in
1813 and a key text in introducing the second generation of Romantics to
German thought, managed only the vaguest summary of Kant's philosophical priorities: 'Kant wished to re-establish primitive truths and spontaneous activity in the soul, conscience in morals, and *the ideal* in the
arts.'[6] Staël is concerned to assimilate Kant to the model of Gothic spirituality that was by this time being invoked as a north-European intellectual
alternative, generally conservative, to the Franco–Mediterranean empire
of light and reason.[7] Consequently she finds in him an affirmative rather
than a critical intelligence, a healing commitment to the idea that 'we must
have a philosophy of belief, of enthusiasm, a philosophy which confirms
by reason, what sentiment reveals to us' (p. 94). The highly complicated
arguments of the *Critique of judgement*, the third of Kant's great critiques
and the one centrally concerned with aesthetics, are reduced to near-parody.
Where Kant writes about the assumption of consensus in judgments of
taste, Staël admires him for presenting the beautiful as an 'image which is
constantly present to the soul' (p. 89), and as a quality eliciting 'sentiments
of celestial origin' (p. 91). Philosophy here becomes a kind of sublimity-
machine: it 'inspires us with the necessity of rising to thoughts and sentiments without bounds' (p. 136).

[5] For an account, see René Wellek, *Immanuel Kant in England, 1793–1838*, Princeton, NJ:
Princeton University Press, 1931.
[6] Baroness de Staël, *Germany*, 3 vols., London: John Murray, 1813, III: 73.
[7] See Marilyn Butler, *Romantics, rebels and reactionaries: English literature and its background, 1760–1830*, Oxford and New York: Oxford University Press, 1982, pp. 129–37.

One can see here an instance of the way in which the unintelligible Kant could become the advocate of the ineffable experience. He has suffered the fate of some other major thinkers – Marx, Freud and Hegel come to mind – in being vaguely identified as responsible for all sorts of influences on the spirit of his age and invoked as such while seldom being closely read. What then are the main features of the argument of the *Critique of judgement*? What was their legacy in Romanticism and in subsequent aesthetic philosophy? What did Kant and those who came after him contribute to the formation of a specifically *literary* criticism? These are the questions I shall try to address in what remains of this essay.

The literary student will not find much that looks familiar on a first reading of the *Critique of judgement*, which hardly mentions works of art and almost completely ignores literature. This is a consequence of Kant's determination to avoid the sort of floundering in the empirical – this painting, that book, that statue – that in his view prevented the articulation of a systematic philosophy of the aesthetic. In his effort to produce a philosophical aesthetics, moreover, he is working against the familiar eighteenth-century British tradition from which he otherwise took over so much. Lord Kames, for example, whose *Elements of criticism* (first published in 1762) was among the most popular eighteenth-century works on aesthetics, promised his reader the 'gay and agreeable form of criticism' rather than a 'regular and laboured disquisition' of the sort that Kant would soon attempt.[8] Kames pronounced himself 'extremely sensible of the disgust men generally have to abstract speculation' (1: 26). Hugh Blair, whose *Lectures on rhetoric and belles lettres* (1783) became a familiar university textbook in the nineteenth century, regarded criticism as a 'liberal and humane art' whose demands are less 'severe' than those of logic and ethics.[9] Indeed, he is explicit about the value of good taste in profitably filling up the leisure hours of 'men of serious professions', who 'cannot always be on the stretch of serious thought': the 'pleasures of taste refresh the mind after the toils of the intellect, and the labours of abstract study' (p. 14). Addison had made much the same point in *The spectator*. With some exceptions (Hutcheson among them) eighteenth-century British aesthetics was in general conceived within the culture of politeness rather than of philosophical analysis.

Kant took over a good deal of the material for the *Critique of judgement* from his British precursors. Kames too was interested (though much less systematically than Kant) in beauty as a subjective quality that seems objective, as a category established apart from personal inclination or desire, and as a principle of communicability with analogies to moral

[8] Henry Home, Lord Kames, *Elements of criticism*, 6th edn, 2 vols., Edinburgh, 1785, I: 13.
[9] Hugh Blair, *Lectures on rhetoric and belles lettres*, 1783, rpt Philadelphia, PA: Troutman & Hayes, 1853, p. 13.

experience. But Kant is emphatically not interested in adjudicating good and bad taste: his concern is exclusively with the faculty of mind that makes judgments of taste possible. For him, the aesthetic judgment promised to fill in the space between the concepts of the understanding (*Verstand*) governing epistemology, which he had made the subject of the *Critique of pure reason*, and the judgments of reason (*Vernunft*) implicit in moral judgments and analysed in the *Critique of practical reason*. Moral judgments (properly defined) have no reference whatsoever to the empirical world, and do not depend upon their communicability. Though they are dependent upon the concepts of pure reason, they are final in themselves and do not depend upon contingent confirmation. I do not (in Kant's view) do the right thing because I expect to be understood or to be praised for my behaviour. Epistemological functions on the other hand orient us in the world, although it takes a metaphysical inquiry into the *a priori* categories of the mind to see what legitimates them. In the *Critique of judgement* Kant was exploring the middle ground. What interested him about judgments of taste – for instance my assertion that something is beautiful – was that these judgments feel as authoritative to us when we make them *as if* they were functions of the understanding or moral judgments. In other words, I am as sure that an object is beautiful as I am that this other object is a table. But while most normally functioning human beings do not spend much time arguing about what is and is not a table, consensus about what is and is not beautiful is very rare. This does not stop me assuming, when I make the statement, that all right-minded persons should or will agree. The judgment of taste is subjective, but presents itself as objective. When I call something beautiful I expect everyone to agree though I can never command that agreement by reference to concepts of the understanding.

This conundrum is for Kant important evidence that the judgment of taste has something to do with the transcendental component of the human mind – that which is revealed to us by the object world but is not itself of that world. This is what he wants to get at, and it explains his decision not to muddy the waters with sustained remarks about the respective qualities of particular works of art. He is not really interested in works of art or literature, so much as in what our responses to them tell us about transcendental subjectivity. Indeed the account of aesthetic judgment takes up only half of the *Critique*. The first part of the first half of the book, the 'Analytic of the Beautiful', makes the case for the beautiful as dependent upon disinterest, upon form and not content, and thus as inclining us to an assumption of consensus. After all, if we screen out what divides us from each other (particular likes and dislikes, 'interested' perspectives, the need or desire for empirical satisfaction) then what remains must be assumed to be common to all observers. The most appropriate kind of art for stimulating this reflection is visual, not literary. For with statues, shapes and paintings we have instant access to an intuition of form and to the disjunction between formal and empirical identity that is so important to aesthetic judgment as Kant defines it. In the 'Analytic of the sublime', which concludes the first part of the *Critique of judgement*, Kant moves from the discussion of limits to that of limitlessness. The experience of the sublime has more in common with the concepts of reason than with those of the understanding which appear to condition judgments about the beautiful. Hence we call things 'beautiful' even though we are finally to understand that beauty is not empirical, but we are much less tempted to call things (rather than our feelings about them) 'sublime' because we are responding to what is dynamic or limitless. The sublime, for this reason, has more in common with the moral than with the empirical judgment, and more readily persuades us of its purely subjective location.

The arguments Kant makes to accommodate the aesthetic to the moral are made by way of both the sublime and the beautiful. They are difficult and somewhat tentative arguments, scattered throughout the first part of the *Critique*. Beauty is a 'symbol' of morality: that is, it is analogous to the morally good in the feelings it gives rise to, although the perception ('intuition') of something as beautiful is not subsumable under the concepts of morality, nor indeed under any other concepts. This symbolic relation is the source of our pleasure in the beautiful. As with moral experience, so beauty 'gives us pleasure with an attendant claim to the agreement of every one else, whereupon the mind becomes conscious of a certain ennoblement and elevation above mere sensibility to pleasure from impressions of sense'.[10] The beautiful in nature is superior to this end to the beautiful in art, which has a more remote affinity with the moral because, insofar as it is a made thing, it has an end (imitation or delight) the awareness of which must interfere with the immediacy of our judgment (§ 42). The beauty of nature is closer to the sublime, which is also revealed in and through natural phenomena. It has nothing to do with ends, it is not purposive. With the sublime, in particular, we do not move from the aesthetic to the moral but rather the other way round. Kant says that without a moral education, the sublime will look merely terrifying (p. 115). In the last paragraph of the first part of the *Critique* Kant reiterates the priority of the moral as the 'true propaedeutic for laying the foundations of taste' (p. 225). Morality precedes beauty in the education of the human being, not the other way around. But this did not stop many who came after Kant from seeking his permission for all sorts of claims about the primary moral potential of both the sublime and the beautiful, including the beauty of art.

---

[10] *The critique of judgement*, James Creed Meredith (trans.), 1928; rpt Oxford: Clarendon Press, 1980, I: 224.

Strikingly Kant is not at all interested in the sublimity potential of art
or language. This had been the inherited emphasis of the British tradition
as evident in the writings of Burke, Kames, Blair and others. Following
Longinus, their account of the sublime was principally rhetorical, and
devoted to the presentation of exemplary passages from Homer, Virgil,
Shakespeare and Milton and their kind.[11] Kant's two modes of the sublime, the mathematical and the dynamic, use nature as their examples of
the stimuli through which the mind comes to awareness of its own sublimity. The second half of the *Critique*, the 'Critique of teleological judgement', is about our ideas of finality in relation to the perceived operations
of the physical world, of 'nature'. It has nothing to say about art. Nonetheless Kant's remarks about the subsumption of parts within wholes,
means within ends and causes within effects provided some later critics
(Coleridge for example) and philosophers (like Schelling) with paradigms
for the description of ideal works of art conceived within the parameters
of organic form.

If we take Kant as the prime representative of the philosophical moment
in Romanticism, then we would have to conclude that criticism took far
more from philosophy than philosophy was prepared to part with. One
view of Kant would specify his task as the stringent setting of limits, as
making sure that statements were limited to the spheres of experience to
which they properly applied. From this point of view we would have to
conclude that his successors and interpreters got him wrong, as they set
about taking down the fences he had so doggedly put up. Nor were the literary critics alone in this response: those we would describe as philosophers did much the same thing. But another view of Kant, the dominant
one in the recent commentaries, regards the coherence of his arguments
as merely tentative in the first place, and sometimes downright self-
contradictory. This construction of Kant makes everything fair game, and
regards his interpreters as no more or less unfaithful to the master than
the master was to himself. Some commentators see the Kantian system as
intrinsically open in its very efforts at closure; others locate the fissures in
the historical conditions of Kant's intellectual production, both in relation
to other philosophers (Herder, the Spinozists, Hume, Hutcheson) and to
the general pressures of theorizing a sphere of freedom in a culture of constraint.[12] It is clear that Kant's effort at the articulation of a transcendental

---

[11] For a good introduction to and selection from the major British treatments of the sublime
see Andrew Ashfield and Peter de Bolla (eds.), *The sublime: a reader in British eighteenth-
century aesthetic theory*, Cambridge University Press, 1996. The editors' introduction
stresses the continuity of the rhetorical sublime in the British tradition.
[12] Examples of the first include Jean-François Lyotard, *Lessons on the analytic of the sublime*, Elizabeth Rottenberg (trans.), Stanford, CA: Stanford University Press, 1994; and
Paul de Man, *Aesthetic ideology*, Andrzej Warminski (ed.), Minneapolis, MN: University
of Minnesota Press, 1996. Important historical studies include John H. Zammito, *The*

subjectivity was itself already reacting to a world in which empirical judgments and historicist explanations were becoming more and more important. As such it touched a sensitive nerve in the developing body of middle-class culture in relation to literature and the fine arts. That culture put a good deal of effort into imagining that the greatest creations of the human imagination might somehow be beyond the reach of time, change and history, and thus also beyond the sorts of disputes and frustrations that marked ordinary life in the everyday world. In his 'Essay on criticism' Pope identified Homer with an enduring nature and a common truth that took on surplus value with the passage of time, in contrast to the many other human endeavours (including those of other poets) that must always be subject to corruption and mutability. Samuel Johnson thought that the same status might be accorded to Shakespeare, if we should ever get far enough away from him to ignore the quibbles and the bombast that corrupt his plays. Transcendental subjectivity, whatever it might mean as a philosophical paradigm, must have appeared to many to be a very desirable thing for art and for the artist. Time and space are its tools and not its masters. That is one element of the message that Keats made his Grecian urn speak back to us out of its immunity to generational wasting.

But the notorious ventriloquism that ends Keats's most famous poem – 'Beauty is Truth, Truth Beauty' – has always been contested, not so much or not only because of the variable punctuations in the different texts but because this is a piece of poeticized (literary) criticism that was already mired in controversy and has remained so ever since. The traditional nexus of truth and beauty had been refigured (differently) by Boileau and Shaftesbury and interrogated by Kant,[13] for whom these terms came to represent not things in the world but attributes of transcendental subjectivity. That part of Kant's argument which can be read as contributing to critical formalism (see, for example, §§ 14–17 of the *Critique of judgement*) does not relate beauty to truth; it is the communicability of judgments of taste that most interests him (§§ 8–9), and in this way he displaces the rhetoric of subject and object almost entirely into the subjective sphere. Many of Kant's readers were not happy with this limitation on the usefulness of statements about the objective world, and with the condition of implicit isolation that it prescribed for the human mind and heart.

genesis of Kant's 'Critique of judgment', Chicago, IL and London: University of Chicago Press, 1992; and Howard Caygill, *Art of judgement*, Oxford: Blackwell, 1989. Zammito gives a thorough account of Kant's efforts at stemming the tide of *Sturm und Drang*. Frederick C. Beiser, *The fate of reason: German philosophy from Kant to Fichte*, Cambridge, MA and London: Harvard University Press, 1987, pp. 153–8, sees the attention to teleology in the *Critique of judgement* as a direct (and late) response to Herder and Forster.

13 See Ernst Cassirer, *The philosophy of the Enlightenment*, Fritz C. A. Koelln & James P. Pettegrove (trans.), Princeton, NJ: Princeton University Press, 1951, pp. 286–7, 313–14.

Chief among them was Schiller, whose response to Kant was at once philosophically opportunistic and very influential on a range of later critics including the likes of Matthew Arnold and Herbert Marcuse.[14] Schiller's critical writings resituate what is taken from Kant within a rhetoric that is simultaneously idealist and historicist, and thereby one that is exemplary of the effort at applying the arguments of the *Critique of judgement* to any specific literary or cultural phenomena in place and time. In a number of his critical essays Schiller worries about the incompatibility of the rational and the sensible as described by Kant. This was an exemplary concern among Kant's readers (including Coleridge): that human nature is divided instead of unified by the critical philosophy, with reason subsisting in its proper form only at the expense of the senses and the empirical life. In such writings as 'The moral utility of aesthetic manners' and 'On grace and dignity' Schiller argued for a common ground between the moral and sensuous instincts, proposing in the first that taste can compensate or prepare the way for moral virtue when it might otherwise be unattainable, and in the second that beauty happily unifies sense and intellect and that the properly moral person can trust his or her sensuous inclinations and spontaneous responses by virtue of possessing the 'beautiful soul' (*schöne Seele*).

While Schiller is fairly faithful to Kant in his writings on the sublime, his most extended critical statements are quite unlike the *Critique of judgement* in that they are explicitly historicised.[15] In *On naive and sentimental poetry* Schiller analyses the culture and literature of modernity, which he sees as obligated to a self-conscious meditation upon its own findings and procedures: a dialogue of the mind with itself. Only the Greeks managed the complete incorporation of object and feeling, self and other, real and ideal. The historical schema, which anticipates those of Schelling and Hegel and follows that of Herder (one of Kant's great rivals), inevitably puts pressure on the model of normative human subjectivity that underwrites transcendental idealism. Kant recognized this, and it explains his scrupulous effort at describing what remains to subjectivity after all contingent determinations have been thought away. But Schiller wanted to address precisely the contingencies. His major treatise *On the aesthetic education of man*, first published in 1795, once again turns to the Greeks as the embodiment of all the harmonies we have lost, and fully situates the debate about aesthetics within the debate about the division of labour that had preoccupied the eighteenth-century political economists (Smith, Ferguson, Kames and others). Not only was that debate historical and

---

[14] See Dieter Heinrich, 'Beauty and freedom: Schiller's struggle with Kant's aesthetics', in *Essays in Kant's aesthetics*, Ted Cohen and Paul Guyer (eds.), pp. 237–57.

[15] Some (but not all) of Schiller's writings on aesthetics are translated in *Friedrich Schiller: essays*, Walter Hinderer and Daniel O. Dahlstrom (eds.), New York: Continuum, 1995.

historicized, but it also threatened to explain aesthetic response and good taste as themselves the property of an exclusive subgroup of society, those with the wealth and leisure necessary to allow disinterest to develop, rather than as the radical common ground of humanity as a whole which was, it will be recalled, the qualification for entrance into the sphere of transcendental idealism. Although Kant had admitted along with almost everyone else (*Critique of judgement*, p. 160) that good taste would never be empirically common, he is interested in minimizing the familiar dissensus and in playing up the assumption of universal agreement that we make when we deliver a judgment of taste.

In his *Aesthetic education* Schiller indeed deploys a number of arguments derived or developed from Kant. But he offers a much more fully developed psychological model of the play drive as the core of the aesthetic experience which, he argues, cannot be had in its pure form (since it is impossible to be free from all determinations whatsoever) but can be understood and sustained in its maximally available forms through the encounter with genuine works of art. Kant had made a place for the free play of the mind in the aesthetic sphere, and for the role of *Geist* (mind-spirit) and 'genius', in sections 49 and 54 of the *Critique*. But he was relatively guarded in his rhetoric and emphasis, lest he be seen as approving the 'Storm and Stress' (*Sturm und Drang*) cult of feeling, with its belief in mere spontaneity and in the uselessness of all 'restraint' (p. 164).[16] Schiller makes much more of this component than had Kant, and adds a sustained analysis of the 'drives' (*Triebe*) that govern human behaviour. His psychological dynamism is very much in tune with the temporal–historical emphasis signified also in Herder and Fichte's *Kraft* (force, energy), Hegel's *Geist*, and Schopenhauer's *Wille*, all of which further disturbed the atemporal ambitions of Kant's critical philosophy. Later critics who pick up on the metaphor of the 'free play of the mind' (Arnold and Leavis for example) take their cue principally from Schiller, even though Kant is lurking behind him, *sotto voce*.

Schiller is not at all interested in Kant's emphasis on communicability and on the pivotal role of judgment in general (of which the aesthetic is just one form). He is, unlike Kant, very interested in the empirical existence of the aesthetic personality, which he embodies notably in the heroes and heroines of his blank-verse tragedies. And it is here that he proposes, much more vigorously than Kant, that there are limits on its potential universality. (Again, he is not concerned with Kant's careful explanation that his interest is in the assumption of universality, not the thing itself.) First, the

---

[16] Despite the restraint, Zammito, *Genesis*, p. 305, has argued that the 'metaphysical potential of the Idealist concept of *Geist* is already fully latent in the repressed speculations of Immanuel Kant', and especially in the third *Critique*.

aesthetic experience is always primarily a gift of nature: some people will just never have it (letters 22, 26). All humans are born with the capacity to appreciate 'semblance' (*Schein*) for its own sake by possession of eyes and ears, the non-tactile senses (an insight Schiller could have found in Kames). But only the optimal cultural and historical conditions (such as in Greece) can bring that potential to fruition for any but a small minority.

Schiller's historical sense also includes the admission that he is interested in the aesthetic as an explicit response to the failures of rational state-planning (the French Revolution) in bringing about any important improvement in the human condition. Paradoxically, then, the integrity of the aesthetic is measured by the degree to which it is neither political nor embodied in any formal state-sponsored pedagogy. Or, one might say that the message for such pedagogy is that a certain space must be encouraged within which the aesthetic can do its work (where it can work) without having to meet common standards of accountability and productivity. The aesthetic, in other words, is most useful when it is least subject to utilitarian demands.[17]

Perhaps its major use is that it preserves an image or experience of wholeness in an age of division: the divisions within the self as well as those of labour according to which the self takes on, Schiller suggests in letter 6, its own contemporary identity. This implicitly compensatory function is one that Kant preferred to leave undiscussed, since it threatens to position the aesthetic in relation to larger historical forces that compromise its incipient universality. It might also portend a historicizing of the aesthetic itself – a concept for which the Greeks, Schiller implies, would have had no need, but which we can only keep alive *as* a concept, by way of self-conscious, critical resuscitation. This compensatory dimension of the cultivation of taste had been evident enough in Addison and Steele (*The spectator*), but it was obviously hostile to the articulation of a purely philosophical aesthetics. Today it is easy to see how much of the discussion of the enduring greatness (or not) of Chaucer, Shakespeare, Spenser and Milton had to do with the culture of nationalism, and with the space opened for a literary-critical franchise that was broader than those offered by wealth, property or voting rights. Participation in the discussion of literary value was available to many men and all women who had no say in electing their representatives, and emphasizing the importance and sufficiency of semblance (Schiller's *Schein*) and disinterest was clearly a

[17] Some of Kant's thoughts about pedagogy can be found in *Critique of judgement* § 60. Because Kant is interested in communicability he is arguably less individualistic than Schiller in his sense of the uses of cultivating taste. See also Schiller's writings on the theatre, particularly 'Die Schaubühne als eine moralische Anstalt betrachtet' (1784) and the preface to *Die Braut von Messina*, entitled 'Über den Gebrauch des Chors in der Tragödie' (1803).

disciplinary tactic at a time when various sorts of interests and real possessions were to remain limited to a few.

The aesthetic, then, performed an ambivalent function. On the one hand it was compensatory, allowing a property in the response to the fine arts that might not have been available in real life; on the other hand it held forth a model of commonality and democracy of taste in which rank and wealth were deemed irrelevant.[18] Philosophical aesthetics, explicitly or implicitly, emphasized the second, whatever it may have carried with it of the first. It thus does not have a simple or single 'politics' or a predictable historical effect. To hold out the ideal of classical Greece, as Schiller and others did, is indeed to invite a mood of nostalgia within an unsatisfying present, but it is also to hold out a utopian image for possible future restorations, partial but nonetheless better than what we have. The history and historical consciousness that Kant tried in all three of the *Critiques* to displace could not be kept at a distance. It returns not only in Schiller and in Fichte's efforts at translating transcendental idealism into the language of the common reader,[19] but also in Schelling and Hegel.

With Schelling's philosophical aesthetics we have moved fully from the transcendental philosophy into transcendental *idealism*. There are many implications to this transition. For the purposes of the present account, we can say that Schelling is prepared to go much further than Schiller in spreading the spirit of wholeness, and a metaphysics supportive of it, into those areas where Kant's philosophy was either tentative (the relation of beauty to morality) or propaedeutically negative (the distinction between works of art, and objects in general, and our responses to them; the disaggregations of reason from sensibility, phenomena from noumena, religion from philosophy, man from nature). Spinoza and pantheism appear again on the philosophical menu, and the second half of Kant's third *Critique*, the 'Critique of teleological judgement', is adapted (and distorted) into the *Naturphilosophie* that Kant deliberately tried to pre-empt. Schelling alone among the great philosophers makes, at least at one stage of his career, the aesthetic into the *summum* of his system, in the spirit of the mandate aphoristically set forth by Friedrich Schlegel in number 115 of his 'Critical fragments': 'all art should become science and all science art; poetry and philosophy should be made one'.[20] This occurs in the *System of transcendental idealism* of 1800, where fine art is preferred to philosophy itself

---

[18] See Terry Eagleton, *The function of criticism*, London: Verso, 1984; and *The ideology of the aesthetic*, Oxford: Blackwell, 1990.

[19] See Simpson (ed.), *German aesthetic and literary criticism*, pp. 71–113.

[20] *Friedrich Schlegel's 'Lucinde' and the fragments*, Peter Firchow (trans.), Minneapolis, MN: University of Minnesota Press, 1971, p. 157. The importance of this conflation has been extensively argued by Philippe Lacoue-Labarthe and Jean-Luc Nancy, *The literary absolute: the theory of literature in German Romanticism*, Philip Barnard and Cheryl Lester (trans.), Albany, NY: State University of New York Press, 1988.

because of its capacity to embody and demonstrate the unity of mind and nature.[21] In 1802–3 Schelling delivered a course of lectures (published only in 1859) on the philosophy of art that fully explores the tension between the historical and the ideal or normative (which in Schelling is called the 'absolute') that Kant had sidestepped and Schiller reintroduced.[22] The rhetoric is affirmative in almost every place where Kant had been sceptical or tentative. The ideal of beauty is objective and exists in the world as art-object; beauty and truth are identical. Unlike Hegel, whose 1818 lectures on aesthetics (first published in 1835) were to be much more influential than Schelling's, Schelling does not subject the best art to an evolutionary historical model. What is true and real in art is so for all times and places (Ezra Pound would propose just this as part of the Imagist manifesto); it has a consistent metaphysical identity. It is this that makes it possible for us to receive Greek art (for Schelling as for Schiller the high point of the aesthetic) as it really is, was and ever will be. Insofar as art is great art, it is beyond the (essential) influence of place and time, even when the same art cannot be newly produced in a different place and time (as it cannot within a Christian culture whose premise is the division between temporal and eternal). Schelling operates not just with a *Zeitgeist*, a spirit of the age, but with a *Weltgeist*, a transhistorical reference point in the absolute. And because of the fundamental equivalence of all great art in relation to the absolute, he is under no pressure to prefer some cultures or historical periods to others. Some cultures enable things that others do not – hence the superiority of Calderón (and Catholicism) to Shakespeare (and Protestantism). But history is not progressive in the Hegelian (and nationalist) sense, leaving behind most of the past as it moves to a future end, because the absolute has already appeared in the great work of art, and can never become more absolute than it is already.

In later life Schelling moved away from the aesthetic and into religion and what he called 'mythology' as the organizing energies of his philosophical system. But he had made a major contribution to philosophical aesthetics in his attempt to combine historicism and idealism. Historicism

---

[21] See Simpson, *German aesthetic*, pp. 119–32. The entire text is translated by Peter Heath, *System of transcendental idealism (1800)*, Charlottesville, VA: University of Virginia Press, 1981. Also worthy of note is a short fragment of uncertain authorship (Hölderlin, Hegel or Schelling) from the mid-1790s published under the title 'Das älteste Systemprogramm des deutschen Idealismus'. This fragment is much discussed in the German scholarship as the earliest outline of transcendental idealism. For the text, see 'The oldest system-program of German idealism', in *Friedrich Hölderlin: essays and letters on theory*, Thomas Pfau (trans. and ed.), Albany, NY: State University of New York Press, 1987, pp. 154–6. See also Rüdiger Bubner (ed.), *Das älteste Systemprogramm: Studien zur Frühgeschichte des deutschen Idealismus* (*Hegel-Studien*, suppl. no. 9), Bonn: Bouvier, 1973.

[22] *The philosophy of art*, Douglas W. Stott (ed. and trans.), Minneapolis, MN: University of Minnesota Press, 1989. My foreword and the translator's introduction may be consulted for a more extended account of Schelling's lectures.

itself and the historical consciousness were not new. Herder in particular had described at great length the rootedness of works of art in time and place and called for a value-free historical criticism without a historical system (progressive or regressive), making him an awkward precursor for those committed to some or other form of idealism.[23] Schelling wants it both ways. He is able to propose, for example, that Dante is determined by the life conditions of the Christian Middle Ages, and Shakespeare by those of Early Modern northern (Protestant) Europe, so that the cultural profiles of each period and place can be read back through their writings, but at the same time he wants to maintain a transhistorical component to great art in its embodiment of the absolute. Herder's nonevaluative and more thoroughgoing historical criticism is arguably more in tune with our contemporary understanding of how we should go about reading the past, notwithstanding the degree to which the ambition to tell it 'as it was' has come under considerable pressure. But the hierarchy of value that is implicit in Schelling's system, whereby some works are exemplary while others are not, regardless of place and time, has generally proved more appealing to literary critics.

The dominant figure in the idealist tradition was not however Schelling but Hegel. There is no point in Hegel's career at which art takes pride of place, the way it does in Schelling's *System of transcendental idealism*. For Hegel, the mind–spirit (*Geist*) that is at work through human history will only come to its fullest development after having passed through the aesthetic into the spheres of religion and rational philosophy whose proper expression is prose. He does not mean to say that humans will simply stop creating works of art: the art instinct is and will remain a foundational impulse. And these works of art will always register the characteristics of their historical moment, so that in studying art we are also studying history. Hegel shares this emphasis with Schelling, and with much subsequent literary criticism. But Hegel differs from Schelling in proposing that the moment at which art most completely represents *Geist* has already long passed: that moment was classical Greece. Only here, before the Christian culture of inward spirituality and necessary self-consciousness had come into being, could the work of art, with its objective sufficiency (sculpture here being the dominant form), exist as an adequate representation of mind–spirit.[24] The evolution of *Geist* since that time has been

[23] See, for example, *Reflections on the philosophy of the history of mankind (1784–91)*, Frank E. Manuel (abridged and trans.), Chicago, IL: University of Chicago Press, 1968. Herder's relativism is not always absolute; his focus is dominantly European, and there are some arguments for progress through history. Nonetheless, he is remarkably affirmative about the integrity of other times and places.

[24] The fullest exposition is in Hegel's *Aesthetics: lectures on fine art*, T. M. Knox (trans.), 2 vols., Oxford: Clarendon Press, 1975.

marked by a passage out of materialization (of which architecture in pre-classical times had been an even more primitive form) and toward the immaterial. Literature, by virtue of its existence in writing, is the privileged art form of the modern period, which requires the priority of the inner life of consciousness. This remains the case even as art itself is no longer as important to modernity, as historically saturated with significance, as it had been for the Greeks. And within modern literature, poetry is the primary form, being the most self-conscious and spiritual expression open to the user of words. Unlike music, it remains committed to external form, and it can therefore dramatize the encounter of form and spirit that was so important to Hegel's notion of progressive self-consciousness. Indeed, the lyric poetry of Hegel's own times is at the opposite end of the sequence from architecture. Architecture is so thoroughly dependent upon material form that it can hardly manage to express any spiritual content whatsoever. Lyric poetry, on the other hand, risks leaving behind the material component completely, and almost passes wholly over into the spiritual. Since the essence of art is the synthesis of matter and spirit, lyric poetry signals the immanent transition of *Geist* out of art and beyond the aesthetic.

Hegel is well known and commonly critiqued for his adaptation of philosophical argument to German nationalist models of the state (most clearly in the *Philosophy of right*). The aesthetic manifestation of this is indeed partly a celebration of German poetry, and of an aesthetic that is in general (and more so than Schelling's) visibly Eurocentric. Hegel accords Christianity the critical role in world history, for it is the Christian moment that brings to life the all-important principle of self-consciousness that will be consummated in absolute mind–spirit. There is thus in Hegel little of the serious attention to and interest in non-European art and culture that had preoccupied Schelling, in his *Philosophy of art*, and Friedrich Schlegel, in his *On the language and wisdom of the Indians* (published in 1808), among others. Places like China and India are consigned to primitive history. One expression of this dismissal is the primacy accorded to the alphabet, which is central to Hegel's version of history as the Protestant world view writ large. For progress (real history) to occur there has to be self-consciousness and the privacy of experience required to nurture it. Alphabetic writing contributes to this because its analytical simplicity and minimalist basis allow the mind to pass quickly beyond the difficulties of sheer representation (in which the ideogram is forever mired) into reflection upon acts of the mind as well as into a progressive science. Writing as imitation (the ideogram) cultivates only servility: hence the notion of eastern countries as the natural home of despotism.[25] It follows then

[25] See *Lectures on the philosophy of history*, J. Sibree (trans.), New York: Dover, 1956, Part I, 'The Oriental World'.

that as the west is superior to the east in its invention of the alphabet so within the west it is writing that is superior to the other expressive forms as the vehicle of spiritual self-consciousness (as it is writing that allows for and encourages the experience of privacy). Oddly, it appears that poetry is in one way the highest form of artistic expression exactly to the degree that it is not the highest form of art.[26] We may envy the Greeks their happy ignorance of the inner life and their oneness with natural form (as Schiller did), but we can console ourselves with our greater proximity to absolute spirit imaged in the vanishing art-form that is poetry. Hegel is not the only one to see the centrality of poetry to what he himself would call (late) Romanticism – Shelley comes to mind among those writing in English – but he is surely the most exhaustive and systematic in his demonstration of why this is so. The idea of the Romantic period as an era of poetry rather than prose subsisted throughout the nineteenth century and well into the twentieth. It could be said to subsist even today.

Like Schelling and Schiller, Hegel was unhappy with the dualism in Kant's system, which he regarded as authentically prototypic but sadly limiting: he gives to Schiller the credit for healing the division of mind and for correcting the emphatically subjectivist Kantian priority (*Aesthetics*, pp. 60–1). But there is one crucial component of Kantian aesthetics that remains constant among the idealists who came after him and who differed from him in so many other ways: the insistence on the judgment of taste and the beautiful as being definitively independent of interest and desire. This congruity surely indicates just how threatening the powers of interest and desire were felt to be by those seeking to articulate a place for the aesthetic at the turn of the nineteenth century. Among the political economists interest had been related to the increasing division of labour apparent in the modernizing (and demographically expanding) economies. Specialization in the workplace was felt to produce specialization in the mind, so that one schooled only in a limited set of tasks or ways of thinking could no longer remain open to a full range of pleasures and responses. Open-mindedness itself was threatened. Schiller saw around him a culture composed only of fragments of human nature, and Wordsworth theorized the implications for readers of literature in his 1800 Preface to *Lyrical ballads*, where the 'uniformity of their occupations' renders city dwellers incapable of any pleasure not founded in 'gross and violent stimulants' resorted to as mere relief from monotony and alienation.[27] Samuel Johnson had worried about the English language in comparable terms, fearing that the proliferation of special dictions that came with the international-commercial economy and the increasing development of technically

---

[26] Compare § 53 of the *Critique of judgement*.
[27] *The prose works of William Wordsworth*, W. J. B. Owen and Jane Worthington Smyser (ed.), 3 vols., Oxford: Clarendon Press, 1974, I: 128.

differentiated job tasks would produce a vocabulary further and further away from commonality and more and more the register of limited, professional interests.

Kant thus had a powerful cultural–historical imperative operating in his definition of the beautiful as that which pleases apart from any interest. With so much in contemporary life working to divide persons from one another (including the sexual division of labour critically analysed by Mary Wollstonecraft), the aesthetic experience came under pressure as one of the few places (if not the only place) where consensus might be sought or (as for Kant himself) assumed or imagined. This same emphasis remained central in Schiller's writings, and in Hegel's. It is not just *interest*, the psychological manifestation of the divided labour economy, that is suspended in the aesthetic experience, but also *desire*, the psychosomatic impulse to possess, to grasp, to appropriate for oneself that is, even before the division of labour, fundamental to human nature and to the sexual and social contract. Art, when authentically experienced, then becomes a relief not just from occupational constraints but also from an exigent component of being human, of one's own empirical life in the world. This is its place in the writings of Schopenhauer, who was bitterly opposed to Hegel but who shared with him, and with Kant, this one primary belief in the availability of art (along with asceticism) as a way out of being subjected to the determinations of a world otherwise governed by an amoral and uncontrollable will.[28] Schopenhauerian pessimism and Hegelian progressivism meet at this one point in the emphasis on the freedom from desire in the experience of the aesthetic.

The emergence of a similar consensus in British Romantic literary criticism is however hard to imagine. Among the most prominent writers, only Coleridge attempted any full scale engagement with German philosophy. The effects of this have been much debated both by the early reviewers who attributed all of Coleridge's obscurities and infelicities to German metaphysics and by the latter-day critics and editors who have tried to establish what Coleridge borrowed, plagiarized or amended from his German sources.[29] Much of what has caused Anglophone readers most trouble in the central chapters of *Biographia literaria* comes from Schelling, although the borrowings are not straightforward enough for us to trace a

---

[28] See *The world as will and representation*, E. F. J. Payne (trans.), 2 vols., New York: Dover, 1969, vol. I, §§ 36ff.

[29] There is a voluminous secondary literature on this question. A start can be made with Gian N. G. Orsini, *Coleridge and German idealism: a study in the history of philosophy*, Carbondale, IL and Edwardsville, IL: University of Southern Illinois Press, 1969; Norman Fruman, *Coleridge, the damaged archangel*, New York: Braziller, 1971; and Thomas McFarland, *Coleridge and the pantheist tradition*, Oxford: Clarendon Press, 1969. Appropriate volumes of the *Collected works of Samuel Taylor Coleridge*, Kathleen Coburn *et al.* (eds.), in progress, should be consulted for further bibliography.

Schellingian system in Coleridge's writing.[30] There is no doubt that Coleridge's thoughts on the wholeness of the work of art, on organicism, and on various other aesthetic topics are significantly influenced by German idealism, though it is implausible to limit the influences to those sources. So many traditions and individual writers and philosophers contributed to the making of Coleridge's mind that it is very hard to be sure of the source of any single idea or emphasis. Coleridge does not, for example, reproduce the historical component of Schelling's aesthetics, of which he almost certainly did not know (see *Biographia*, I: cxx–cxxi), but neither does he reproduce the philosophical primacy of art *vis-à-vis* the Absolute that figures in Schelling's *System*, which he did know. The commitment to organic form that marks Coleridge's criticism of Wordsworth in the *Biographia* does seem to draw heavily on the spirit of idealist philosophy, but this same notion has a troubled career between Kant and Schelling. (See the chapter by Joel Black in this volume.) Nonetheless, the notion of poetry as bringing 'the whole soul of man into activity' (II: 15–16) that would continue to figure (and be refigured) in the writings of such later critics as Arnold, Richards and Leavis does seem to have come to Coleridge from Schiller and Schelling.

He would not, in other words, have found it in the writings of many of his recent British predecessors. Here the dominant spirit was still empiricist. When Hume writes about the difficulties of defining a standard of taste, he emphasizes the problems governing a standardization of experimental conditions; though the same experimental nexus allows taste to be taught and tested over time.[31] Hume discusses taste in relation to the 'forms and qualities' of objects (p. 233), taking over the vocabulary of Locke and Boyle. The same language figures in Archibald Alison's *Essays on the nature and principles of taste* (Edinburgh, 1790), where an argument for the predominant power of associations in governing judgments of taste sits awkwardly alongside a case for the relation between proper judgments and the 'simple emotions' that Alison derives from Locke's primary qualities, and therefore from things in themselves. Hume and Blair, like Pope and Johnson before them, take some comfort in the usefulness of repeated experiments for showing what really is the case: hence the survival of some works through extended histories – Homer and Virgil, chiefly – are a measure of the standard of taste. They are less interested in bringing 'the whole soul of man into activity', or in the connection of the

---

[30] The attempt to be specific commits one to the editorial sublime. See, for example, the editors' gloss to the famous distinction between primary and secondary imaginations, *Biographia literaria*, James Engell and W. Jackson Bate (eds.), 2 vols., Princeton University Press, 1983, I: 304–5.

[31] David Hume, 'Of the standard of taste', in *Essays moral, political and literary*, Eugene F. Miller (ed.), Indianapolis, IN: Liberty, 1985, pp. 226–49.

great works to any metaphysical identity that is revealed through them. The incorporation of the study of literature into the universities and into education generally was pushed through largely by those trained in rhetoric and *belles lettres*; the philosophical potential of aesthetics was very much a minority interest. Adam Smith, whose Glasgow lectures have been proposed as foundational for the development of academic literary criticism, was more rhetorician than metaphysician, and arguably implicated in the immediate project of making Scotsmen into Englishmen rather than in any ambition to rewrite philosophy or aesthetics.[32]

What many of these British writers do stress or suggest is the social–historical situatedness of judgments of taste. For Hume (as for Schiller), good taste must remain the property of an elite. Few can overcome the forces of personal and cultural preference to the point that their judgments can be relied upon ('Of the Standard of Taste', p. 243). So the inquiry into aesthetics is always an inquiry into social and historical conditions. Synchronically, good taste is an attribute of polite culture, and a force in the dissemination of civility and social discipline (as it is for Kames); diachronically art and literature are an index of the state of culture itself in different times and places. Kant, as we have seen, was not interested in the second analysis and modified the first toward a universalist application. He was also uninterested in the analysis of literature or art as itself the expression of ideological preferences, which sets him quite apart from the greatest British literary critic of the period, William Hazlitt, who indeed pronounced Kant's system to be 'the most wilful and monstrous absurdity that ever was invented'.[33]

Transcendentalism's post-Kantian formation of the aesthetic as a world-transcending or world-embodying category thus proved a divisive legacy for literary criticism. It inclines us toward seeing the experience of literature as non-instrumental or, as some of the radical utilitarians would suggest, useless. At the same time it proposes this exact sort of uselessness as itself useful for a culture all too preoccupied with getting and spending. In this way it reinscribes its own historical energy in the form of an anti-historical imperative. This paradox is worked through by Schiller, by Shelley in his 'Defence of poetry', and by Wordsworth in his project of breaking down the distinctions between work and leisure by way of an energized and productive reinvention of pleasure. The aesthetic project thus conceived cannot solve the question of art's general or exclusive availability, though literary criticism has wrestled with that question throughout its post-romantic history. It is almost a matter of definition that the aesthetic

[32] See Robert Crawford, *Devolving English literature*, Oxford: Clarendon Press, 1992.
[33] *The complete works of William Hazlitt*, P. P. Howe (ed.), 21 vols, 1930–4; rpt New York: AMS Press, 1967, XVI: 123.

cannot be generally experienced in a culture whose commitment to a proliferating division of labour seems to be irreversible. But that is also what makes it more and more precious and necessary that some people continue to experience it at all: that they make themselves specialists in keeping alive the doctrine of non-specialized response. The role of the aesthetic is in this way inevitably utopian and messianic. It is bound to be misunderstood and to remain a minority interest, as it is also compelled to publicize a better way of life and a different future. It is also bound to involve those invested in it (writers and critics) in difficult and conflicting acts of self-consciousness, wherein they face the alarming prospect that art and criticism are themselves nothing more than forms of divided labour, licensed oppositional leisure-time activities compensating for (and even cooperating with) the increasingly inhuman and unaesthetic progress of modern culture. An understanding of the evolution of Kantian and transcendental idealist aesthetics does much to suggest that modern questions about the end and purpose of art are designed not to be solved but to recur almost by definition. At the same time, the compulsion to self-consciousness and (after Kant) to a historical as well as an immanent critical analysis suggests that this antinomy itself must have a history that can be called up for inspection, even as that history can never leave behind the subject that lives it through and lays it out.

5
Nature
HELMUT J. SCHNEIDER

I

Of all ideas commonly associated with Romanticism in the arts, the idea of nature is perhaps the most inclusive and the most evocative. The only rival for this role would be the concept of creativity of the human mind and the power of the poetic imagination. Both ideas are closely interrelated. Romantic 'nature' is essentially a space of the imagination, which in turn draws from her most of its imagery. Romantic literature and painting abound in representations of pristine landscapes and scenes of blissful simplicity, of genuinely perceived particular phenomena of the natural world and bold visions of its overall harmony with the world of man. To be sure, there are also the experience of solitude and the adventure or despair of the wilderness, awesome and frightful sceneries symbolizing the abandonment of a soul adrift from the moorings of the familiar world. During the Romantic period, nature in its physical appearance emerged as the privileged material for expressing a human subject emancipated from the traditional restrictions of religion and society and experiencing the unfathomable depth of the soul. Confronted with a self-imposed freedom and the loss of sense of a 'natural' belonging, this subject developed, together with a rich and infinitely differentiated emotionality, an equally infinite longing for a lost unity and harmony resonantly evoked as 'nature'.

Indeed, one way of defining the Romantic movement in Europe between 1770 and 1830 and accounting for its unity and specificity across the varieties and differences of individuals, media, genres, chronologies and, last but not least, national traditions, is to regard it as an aesthetic reaction to, and compensation for, the thrust of an onrushing modernity. Romantic nostalgia developed in a period which saw a rapidly accelerating modernization in all domains of society and life – cultural, political, technological, economic, etc. The French Revolution represented the one momentous event which brought this all-pervasive process to consciousness. This is especially true of Germany and England, the two 'bystander' countries, where an intellectual debate ensued on the character and consequences of the shocking historical rupture. For all contemporaries regardless of political partisanship – and many early Romantics including

Wordsworth, Coleridge and Friedrich Schlegel began as fervent admirers of the revolutionary ideals, before they turned against their perceived betrayal and bloody perversion – the French Revolution represented an irreversible break with the old order and the advent of a yet unshaped, unpredictable future, bristling with promise and at the same time deeply frightening. Within the chasm between the new and the old, 'nature' became the suggestive shibboleth for the lost past and everything it seemed to embody; it conjured up a world of sheltered security and benevolent authority, a kind of symbolic cultural childhood.

Around the turn of the century, the Enlightenment alliance of 'reason' and 'nature' in the name of 'progress' broke apart. Instead of providing the unquestioned ontological foundation for infinite development, nature was now seen as threated in its very substance by human reason. Yet the profound shift in perspective did not represent a radical turn from the universalist and progressivist values of Enlightenment naturalism. Rather, it initiated a thorough reevaluation of both reason and nature. 'Nature' became the ambiguous, paradoxical object of nostalgic longing, but she also held the resources necessary to bring reason back under her fold; she represented to reason an absolute *a priori* agency which gave her the status of an all-powerful, all-inclusive subject. However, we shall see how the traditional dichotomy of 'subject' and 'object' was itself undercut in the new concept.

For this ambiguous role, the conceptual origin of the idea in the intellectual aftermath of the Revolution seems important. To begin with, contemporaries recognized that 'nature' was a retrospective ideal, and their theoretical reflection laid the groundwork for Romantic aesthetics. The Romantic espousal of nature was linked to the awareness of an emerging modernity in art and poetry, a modernity half regretted half welcomed and promoted. In two seminal treatises of the mid-nineties, at the height of Weimar classicism in Germany, Friedrich Schiller and the young Friedrich Schlegel attempted a philosophical definition of contemporary art against the background of the epochal transformation which in their view had made the classical model of aesthetics obsolete, although by no means less valuable. The two texts – *On naive and sentimental poetry* (*Über naive und sentimentalische Dichtung*, 1795) and *On the study of Greek poetry* (*Über das Studium der griechischen Poesie*, 1795–97) – can be regarded as the last and, arguably, the conclusive contributions to the secular European debate on the preference of the ancients over the moderns, the *querelle des anciens et des modernes*. Both authors accord the Greek and Roman artists the higher aesthetic rank because their works remained within the borders of the sensible, 'natural' world, the living beauty of which they had only needed to enhance. In contrast, the 'moderns' traded – and had to trade – the plastic objectivity of this self-evident cosmos for the mediated abstraction of a rationalized universe and the problematic self-reflexivity of a mind bent on its inner life. Yet the loss in aesthetic perfection was seen as a gain in spiritual content. It was a consoling theory, according to which modern art articulates the unlimited striving of the human intellect towards the realization of its potential. In a further and decisive dialectical twist, Schiller and Schlegel even made the modern condition the necessary prerequisite for the recognition of the past stage of classical art. The 'nature' of antiquity comes into full sight only in the perspective of loss and as an object of longing, or, as Schiller says, as 'ideal'. This insight did not remain limited to the frame of reference of the *querelle*, but it was extended into the principal philosophical issue of an imaginative construction of the past. 'Nature' as an aesthetic objectivation – be it of classical antiquity, be it of an external landscape, be it of childhood, etc. – always presupposes its loss and absence; it is marked by an unerasable difference for a rational subject who seeks in her precisely non-difference: the self-identity, self-manifestation, clarity of pure being.

Schiller named this differential perspective on the non-differential 'sentimental', to which he opposed the 'naive' object constituted by it. The two dialectically opposing categories were pivotal in shaping the modernist self-conception of the early German Romantics and in developing the discourse of historico–philosophical aesthetics. Furthermore, they illuminate the central import of the concept of nature in Romantic aesthetics and literary theory. For they define art and poetry principally in terms of their relation to nature: 'They [the Ancients] felt naturally; we [the Moderns] feel the natural [das Natürliche]'.[1] A fundamental lack in the Modern subject begets the sentimental ideal of nature and thereby characterizes the status and function of Modern art in general. The artist must always be, according to Schiller, the 'preserver of nature' ('Bewahrer der Natur'); for the Modern artist this means that he or she will 'seek for nature lost'.[2] Modern – sentimental or, for that matter, Romantic – art is nothing but an incessant and unremitting search for the lost encompassing whole. In the historico–philosophical scheme, this endeavour is oriented towards the utopian goal to recover nature through a fully developed reason; a civilization is envisioned which would, in its state of ultimate perfection, liberate nature from her status as object of domination and raise her to the rank of partner and friend. The utopian liberation of a nature presently subjugated and vilified signifies the final overcoming of alienation on all levels of human life.

If we turn from Schiller and Schlegel in Germany to Wordsworth in England, we find in the Preface to *Lyrical ballads* of 1800 a text of

---

[1] Friedrich Schiller, 'Über naive und sentimentalische Dichtung' (1795). *Sämtliche Werke*, Herbert G. Göpfert (ed.), Munich: Carl Hanser, 1960, V: 711.
[2] *Ibid.*, p. 712.

comparable importance for British Romanticism with a similar definition of the poet as 'the rock of defence of human nature; an upholder and preserver, carrying every where with him relationship and love'.[3] To be sure, Wordsworth offers not so much a critique of modern civilization's estrangement from nature as a positive assessment of the poet's ability to give 'human nature' its full expression. His direct critique is levelled against the rhetorical diction of the neoclassicist tradition, the artifice of which needed to be pushed aside in favour of 'the real language of nature'. This is reminiscent of the revolt against formal Enlightenment poetry in the German *Sturm-und-Drang* movement of the 1770s, which pitted the unrefined ingenuity of natural expression against the 'false embellishments' of art and rhetoric. Twenty years later, however, Schiller attacked the ideal of expressive immediacy and chastised Rousseau and nature poets in his vein for choosing an easy escape and shunning the labours of reason. For the Weimar idealist, legitimate nature poetry must not yield to regressive desire but must aspire to the highest 'ideal' of reason, for which elevated diction and symbolic representation are indispensable.[4] On this account, had Schiller been acquainted with it, he would have had to condemn Wordsworth's advocacy (and his practice) of a humble poetic language as blatant naturalism. (The same can be said of the Weimar Goethe, who had distanced himself long since from his earlier *Werther* period.)

German 'Classicism' appears historically displaced in comparison to England and France. It could join Classical form and Modern content only through a sharp turn against the dominant 'prosaic' tendencies of the age. The impossibility of fusing the old and the new gave the classicist project a constructivist character. The early German 'Romantics' around the Schlegel brothers were participants in this debate and owed to it their high degree of self-awareness as 'moderns'; in fact, this is one of the reasons for the distinct theoretical vein of the movement in Germany. Yet national differences should not blind us to fundamental congruities. For while Wordsworth was certainly not historico–philosophical idealist, his poetic 'defence of human nature' remains modernist. The poet is called upon to join the 'man of science' and bring the results of abstract knowledge to life. Poetical sympathy with nature does not shy away from scientific analysis, but acknowledges it and anchors it in the heart and the soul. In the humble language of the poet, the results of science are 'transfigured' into a universal bond of human society. On an emotional and individual, yet by no means

---

[3] William Wordsworth, Preface to *Lyrical ballads, with pastoral and other poems* (1802), in Stephen C. Gill (ed.), *The Oxford authors: William Wordsworth*, Oxford and New York: Oxford University Press, p. 606.

[4] Particularly illuminating on this sublimation of the landscape is the review essay on the nature poetry of a popular poet of the time: Friedrich Schiller, 'Über Matthisons Gedichte' (1794), in *Sämtliche Werke*, vol. v.

'regressive', level poetry thus takes on a reconciliatory quality not unlike that in the utopian conception of the German theorists.[5]

Romantic writers all wanted to reduce man's alienation from nature. Independently, in the late 1790s, German and English authors protested the one-sided rationalism which had sundered humans from their inner life, from the outer world and from one another. René Wellek was right, decades ago, to ground the unity and inner coherence of German, English and French Romanticisms in the 'endeavour to overcome the split between subject and object, the self and the world, the conscious and the unconscious'.[6] In this light, Romanticism appears to correct the course that European intellectual history had followed since the relentless secularization and rationalization in the Renaissance, in which the individual self gained autonomy from God and His worldly delegates through the subjection of nature. The young intellectuals around 1800, who had been educated in the well-established spirit of the rationalist Enlightenment, felt that the price paid for this freedom was too high. Man, who according to the Cartesian promise was to become 'the master and owner of nature', was confronted with a world which had been degraded to a soulless mechanism and left him only the role of instrumental manipulator. Thus 'nature' for Kant, one and a half centuries after Descartes and in consequential philosophical pursuit of the latter's separation of mind and matter, meant nothing but the 'existence of things as determined by general laws'.[7] When the young Goethe and his friends in the seventies read Holbach's *Système de la nature*, they felt depressed by its 'deadly and ghastly' materialist outlook. Instead of learning, as they had hoped, 'about suns and stars, planets and moons, about mountains, valleys, rivers and seas and everything which lives and thrives [*lebt und webt*] in them', they saw themselves in a 'dismal atheist half-darkness, in which the earth with all her shapes, the heaven with all its celestial bodies disappeared'.[8] The same frustration reverberates one generation later in countless remarks about a nature and human life turned into mechanical routine and threatened by imminent death if not *resurrected* by a new spirit of harmony with the soul.

The Romantic generation – the term taken as a psycho–sociological category proper may apply here for the first time in intellectual history – was confronted with what they saw as the desolate outcome of the modern

---

[5] Wordsworth, Preface, pp. 606ff.

[6] René Wellek, 'Romanticism re-examined', in *Romanticism reconsidered: selected papers from the English Institute*, Northrop Frye (ed.), New York & London: Columbia University Press, 1963, p. 133.

[7] Immanuel Kant, *Prolegomena zu einer jeden künftigen Metaphysik, die als Wissenschaft wird auftreten können*, § 14, in *Werkausgabe*, Wilhelm Weischedel (ed.), Frankfurt am Main: Suhrkamp Verlag, 1977, p. 159.

[8] Johann Wolfgang Goethe, *Aus meinem Leben: Dichtung und Wahrheit*, Klaus-Detlef Müller (ed.), Frankfurt am Main: Deutscher Klassiker Verlag, 1986, p. 535 (Part III, Book XI).

spirit of scientific analysis, secular critique and utilitarianism. At the same time, a return into the premodern world was at no time a debated alternative. Instead, the Romantic answer to the pervasive 'disenchantment' of the Modern world (as Max Weber was later to call it) was its poetic reenchantment. The dispelled myth and magic were to be recuperated, the severed bond between man and nature to be restored by aesthetic means. The basis was the newly established autonomy of art, conceived not as a modest self-restriction of the aesthetic but as an absolute claim to a 'higher' truth in all spheres of culture and society, including the scientific and political. For this mode of thinking, art's appeal to 'nature' had the overall function of an ontological, even metaphysical affirmation. The poetic reenchantment, or, as the German writers said, the 'Romanticization' of the world was not to lead into the land of illusory fairy tales, but to uncover the buried ground of the divine creation.

Or to start the creation anew. For Romantic thinking with respect to nature, inventing and discovering amounted principally to the same thing. We touch here on the basic paradox of the romantic project. It considered nature in its present state to be reified and enslaved, turned away from it to create a new world out of the subjective mind's boundless and quasi-divine power, yet looked for its ultimate reassurance in the transcendence of a 'true' nature. Depending on emphasis and perspective, the project appears either more progressivist or more conservative. But on the whole, despite the conservative overtones – which grew stronger as the movement wore on, especially in Germany, both on an individual and a generational level – it was not reactionary, and it started out with a revolutionary ambition. The early German Romantics in particular remained the sons and daughters of the philosophical Enlightenment and its luminary Kant, who combined an intensive feeling of the deficiencies of reason with an equally strong exertion to overcome them on the basis of the mind's hard-won autonomy and the individual's right to self-realization. In the 1790s a most significant philosophical fragment of uncertain authorship connected with the Tübingen student friends Schelling, Hölderlin and Hegel announced an imminent new 'mythology of reason'.[9] The disembodied intellect was to be reincarnated poetically, mechanized nature to be repoeticized, and a poetic community to be founded, not through a supernatural or superhuman revelation, but as a self-conscious production of the mind. The brief yet foundational text calls for liberating reason from the threatening powers of mythical fear and physical necessity – the concern of the Enlightenment – as well as from the soul-deadening compulsion to master and exploit nature, in order to commune with nature as an equal partner.

[9] *Mythologie der Vernunft: Hegels 'ältestes Systemprogramm' des deutschen Idealismus*, Christoph Jamme and Helmut Schneider (eds.), Frankfurt am Main: Suhrkamp Verlag, 1984. Today, there is serious contemplation of Schelling as the author of the fragment.

A century and a half later, Theodor W. Adorno formulated this utopian, even mystical project in an early Romantic spirit, while reducing the role of the autonomous subject. True enlightenment would transcend Baconian, rational instrumentality in order to realize a freedom not from but rather 'for the Other' of reason ('Freiheit fürs Andere').[10] Fulfilled enlightenment, Adorno postulates, would be 'nature perceptible through her alienation' ('Natur, die in ihrer Entfremdung vernehmbar wird').[11]

II

The reconciliation of 'reason' – as the agent of human autonomy – with 'nature' from which it had torn itself away, or the recovery of nature through a fully developed culture: this utopian vision on the one hand ties Romanticism back to the Enlightenment idea of historical progress, yet replaces straight linearity with the circular, more precisely spiral, figure of a return to origin.[12] But if reason was the decisive force behind this process, was nature then relegated to a merely passive role? How could nature, the independent 'Other' to the human mind, be engaged to disclose herself spontaneously to it? How could her voice, through her alienated state, be brought to bear?

Still more poignantly: Was the 'poetic', creative mind not just another way, more subtle and more thorough, of exerting human mastery over nature? This leads us to the crucial function of poetry for mediation and reconciliation. German philosophical idealism acknowledged modern alienation as the necessary dialectical step towards a 'higher' appreciation of nature, while Wordsworth and his circle proclaimed a refined susceptibility to nature's beauty and its transcendent value as the 'natural' equipment of the modern poet; in either case poetry – and, by implication, the arts in general – was assigned the privileged role of nature's substitute and advocate, speaking for her and on her behalf. At the same time, however, its function went beyond that of a mere substitutive representation. Art as 'poesy' in the emphatic Romantic sense became an ally of nature within the human mind itself. Through this 'natural force', the subject was intimately intertwined with the outer world even before any conscious activity. A preestablished consonance existed between mind and nature which then had to be articulated and refined by the mind so as to

[10] Theodor W. Adorno, *Ästhetische Theorie*, Frankfurt am Main: Suhrkamp Verlag, 1970, p. 98.
[11] Max Horkheimer and Theodor W. Adorno, *Dialektik der Aufklärung: philosophische Fragmente*, Frankfurt am Main: Suhrkamp Verlag, 1997, p. 57.
[12] The classical study of this circular figure of restoration through and after alienation and division in European Romanticism is M. H. Abrams, *Natural supernaturalism: tradition and revolution in Romantic literature*, New York & London: Norton, 1973.

develop its inherent potential. Speaking of the child in his depiction of the 'growth of a poet's mind', Wordsworth in *The prelude* formulates the programme: 'For feeling has to him [the child] imparted power / That through the growing faculties of sense / Doth like an agent of the one great Mind / Create, creator and receiver both, / Working but in alliance with the works / Which it beholds'.[13] The 'one great Mind' represents of course the divine mind, which is not the mind separated from the whole and opposing itself to it, but the encompassing and all-uniting creativity of which the child's and, by implication, the artist's active sensitivity is the 'agent' or reflection.

In the view of the Romantic writers, poetry was to redeem this originary synthesizing mind – *Geist*, in the German idealist terminology, or the 'primary imagination' which Coleridge characterized as the 'prime agent of all human perception, and as a repetition in the finite mind of the eternal act of creation in the infinite I Am'[14] – and to set free (again) the process of endless becoming blocked by one-sided instrumental rationality. While science cut like a 'sharp knife', killing 'friendly Nature' and leaving behind 'only dead, twitching relics', poetry brings her to life and speech 'as through spirited [*geistvollen*] wine'.[15] 'Poetry' was now no longer the 'art' classically opposed to nature, i.e. a structure of order imposed on a chaotic material. Aristotelian aesthetic theory, dominant in Europe since the Renaissance, had advocated imitating the formal order inherent in nature or imparted to her by the Creator. The artist followed the preexisting normative structure of the given world or of earlier 'classical' works imitating that same structure. The 'nature' touted by classicist poetics as the model of art had been the supreme artwork of the divine cosmos, and human art remained necessarily derivative. This hierarchy had remained fundamentally unchanged in the eighteenth century. Pope's famous lines, 'First follow *Nature*, and your judgment frame / By her just standard, which is still the same,'[16] still formulated an ontological as well as an aesthetic norm, albeit in a rationalized, 'enlightened' version. The descriptive nature poetry of the Enlightenment period, so popular both in England and Germany and an important precursor for the Romantics, laboured to reconcile the constructive empiricism of modern science with the inherited idea of a prior

---

[13] William Wordsworth, *The prelude* (1850), II: 255ff. *The prelude 1799, 1805, 1850: authoritative texts, contexts and reception. Recent critical essays*, J. Wordsworth, M. H. Abrams and S. Gill (eds.), New York & London: Norton, 1979, pp. 79ff.

[14] Samuel Taylor Coleridge, *Biographia literaria* in *The Oxford Authors: Samuel Taylor Coleridge*, H. J. Jackson (ed.), Oxford & New York: Oxford University Press, 1985, p. 313.

[15] Friedrich von Hardenberg (Novalis), *Die Lehrlinge zu Saïs* in *Schriften*, Paul Kluckhohn and Richard Samuel (eds.), Stuttgart: Kohlhammer Verlag, 1960, I: 84.

[16] Alexander Pope, 'An essay on criticism', lines 68ff. *Poetical works*, ed. Herbert Davis, London: Oxford University Press, p. 66 (emphasis original).

metaphysical entity, again in Pope's verses: 'Unerring Nature, still divinely bright, / One clear, unchang'd, and universal light . . . / At once the source, and end, and test of Art'. Only Romanticism left this metaphysical ground, simultaneously drawing the radical consequences from the modern scientific approach to the world and attempting to find a replacement for the dissolved cosmic order and its system of analogies between the physical and the moral world. It found it in the new principle of a human creativity which was grounded in the transsubjective and dynamic agency represented equally by the mind or *Geist* and by 'nature'.

Romantic philosophy distinguished between an 'absolute' subject and a relative one that splits off for the sake of self-recognition, creating the objective world of the non-ego. The priority of the absolute unity of the transcendental ego over the derived subject–object split is the crucial assumption of philosophical idealism, shared by all major German representatives of *Frühromantik*, including Hölderlin, Novalis, Friedrich and August Wilhelm Schlegel. 'Imagination' (or *Einbildungskraft*, to use the more active German term that Coleridge also invoked) was the poetic equivalent – a primordial unifying principle of spiritual creativity, which objectified itself (unconsciously) in separating nature from the individual mind and returned to its original unity by the conscious recognition of the unity of that duality. In the medium of the imagination the mind confronts the world as its own production, 'creator and receiver both'. Friedrich Schlegel called it the 'universally objective power in the human spirit'.[17] Nature is then not a mere projection or construct of the mind, nor is it an incomprehensible and foreign 'beyond'; both these ideas would correspond to a nature conceived as mind's opposite and opponent, which is *Verstand* or *Vernunft* and not *Geist*. Instead, she is a loving and responding partner to whom we are bound in an unthinkable depth of affinity and who still keeps her essential independence from us as limited, empirical beings. Thus, imaginative nature remains an intermediary between subject and object, the interior and the exterior, activity and passivity; a realm where this difference is itself kept in abeyance. The 'absolute', by definition inaccessible to consciousness, was made accessible through the 'image'. Romantic nature poetry symbolized this achievement of *Einbildungskraft* with imagery suggesting the indistinct fusion between the inner and outer worlds: the 'breeze' or wind, denoting the animated nature as well as the inspiration of the poet, may well be the most significant,[18] others are the aeolian harp, echo, twilight, veil, 'hovering' (*Schweben*).

[17] *Kritische Friedrich-Schlegel-Ausgabe*, Ernst Behler (ed.), XII: 421 (from *Kölner Vorlesungen*, 1804).
[18] Cf. M. H. Abrams, 'The correspondent breeze: a Romantic metaphor', in M. H. Abrams (ed.), *English Romantic poets: modern essays in criticism*, New York, London and Oxford: Oxford University Press, 1960.

Yet as these images also show, the imagination provided no firm ground for the subject to stand on. Far from being vanquished by the infinite enhancement of the mind's creative force, the spectre of solipsism haunting the self-empowered modern ego since Descartes was ever more forcefully conjured up. Until our period, both the thinking mind and the material world owed their existence to an authorizer such as the numinous world of Kantian 'things-in-themselves' beyond the transcendental reach of human knowledge. It remained to the Romantic philosophers and poets, heirs to an unprecedented explosion of scientific and technological productiveness and exposed to the seemingly boundless potential of the mind's creativity, to develop the corresponding anguish that a world owed solely to their making would collapse into nothing. The German novelist Jean Paul (Jean Paul Friedrich Richter), author of an insightful aesthetic theory containing a sharp (self-) critique of the Romantic movement (*Vorschule der Ästhetik*, 1804), coined the phrase 'poetic nihilism' in reference to this tendency.[19] Hence the remarkable vacillation between the extremes of creative euphoria and nihilist depression expressed in so many works of the period: in the first letters of Goethe's *Werther* of 1774, whose hero extols the universal life-giving power in his bosom only to fall into a void the instant it leaves him; in Coleridge's lament in the ode 'Dejection', 'we receive but what we give / And in our life alone does nature live';[20] in Jean Paul's nightmarish poetic visions of universal annihilation, Mary Shelley's *Frankenstein*, and Keats's and Hazlitt's criticism of the exploitively aestheticised 'egotism' with which Wordsworth contemplated nature.[21]

Again we encounter the essential Romantic paradox of an 'invention' and a 'discovery' of nature. Romantics who protested the costs of the modern world's immense heightening of power might relapse into religious faith from a yearning for a lost metaphysical certainty, but the more characteristic direction was forward to an enhancement and redirecting of the modern principle of unfettered human productivity. True, the world of objective phenomena needed to be rescued from the uniformity of an instrumentalizing reason, but it received its utopian self-sustaining status by grace of the autonomous power of the imagination. This is not to say, of course, that for the Romantic imagination nature served as a merely delusory or phantasmagoric screen (as it indeed sometimes did), nor that the search for the individual natural phenomenon was not genuine. In particular the poetic practice of the English authors demonstrated a keen adherence to an independent objective world. But as the debate on

---

[19] Jean Paul, *Vorschule der Ästhetik*, §2 in *Werke*, Norbert Miller (ed.), Munich: Carl Hanser, 1963, V: 31ff.

[20] 'Dejection: an ode' in *The Oxford authors: Coleridge*, 1985, p. 114.

[21] Cf. his essays on Wordsworth and 'The character of Rousseau', in *Selected writings*, Jon Cook (eds.), Oxford & New York: Oxford University Press, 1991.

Wordsworth's poetry illustrates, the question of the 'objectivity' of the nature representation remained a controversial issue. The yearning for absorption by the objective world compensated for an inverse fear of the void. We might say that the postulate of a spontaneous devotion to the object was itself a 'sentimental' ideal; as late as 1831 Thomas Carlyle pitted a poetic mood of 'being wholly possessed by the object' against 'the diseased self-conscious state of Literature' in works such as *Werther*.[22] Countless remarks such as Coleridge's early assertion – before his acquaintance with German philosophy – of the 'sweet and indissoluble union between the intellectual and the material world'[23] assume the character of a pious hope. Again and again poetic activity seeks to actualize this union, testifying to an ontological anxiety that the very creativity meant to (re-)animate nature – in Schlegel's formula 'the universally objective power in the human spirit' – was but another version of the modern tendency to hollow out the world's substance.

There was no logical escape out of the circle that transferred the transcendence of a divine creator to the inner transcendence of the human mind. More than half a century ago Arthur Lovejoy initiated a controversy among English-oriented scholars of Romanticism around the distinction between a 'primitivist' and a 'constructivist' tendency in the literature of the second half of the eighteenth century. Lovejoy contended that both had been indiscriminately and illegitimately attributed to Romanticism; in his view Romanticism (notably in Germany) was driven by an emphatically modernist constructivism while the aesthetic 'primitivism' or 'naturalism' belonged to the earlier sentimentalist, 'Rousseauistic' stage of literary history.[24] But in fact both tendencies worked closely together. If the word itself is any indication, then Schiller's modernist definition of 'sentimentalist' or *sentimentalisch*, which provided our starting point, would confirm the inner connection between the constructive and the retrospective aspects. In criticizing the popular 'sentimental' literature of his age for remaining stuck halfway between a nostalgic ('primitivist') nature illusion and a driving spiritual ideal, Schiller presupposes that the one builds on the other. Romanticism or 'true' sentimental poetry in the Schillerian sense is a sentimentalism grown self-reflexive about its modern condition; it acknowledges and bears out its inherent utopian impulse. It restores nature's sensible solidity and objectivity in a constructive aesthetic endeavour entrusted with an overriding philosophico–historical mission. (At the

---

[22] Thomas Carlyle, 'Characteristics' (1831) in *Romantic criticism*, R. A. Foakes ed. (The English Library), Columbia, SC: University of South Carolina Press, 1968, pp. 148ff.

[23] Introduction to *Pamphlet anthology of sonnets*, 1796.

[24] Arthur Lovejoy, 'On the discrimination of Romanticisms' in M. H. Abrams (ed.), *English Romantic poets: modern essays in criticism*, New York: Oxford University Press, 1960 (first 1924, then in Arthur Lovejoy, *Essays in the history of ideas*, 1949).

same time, it is precisely this mission, which by and large remained constitutive for Romanticism, which also places it on the far side of Modernist constructivism proper.)

The landscape, defined as the aesthetic perception and representation of outer nature in the form of an image, provided the outstanding symbol for the transformative power of the imagination. The very term 'Romantic' in its modern sense appears to have first been developed with respect to the landscape.[25] Even at its most abstract, the Romantic idea of nature always carried with it the suggestion of the sensually concrete – the visionary as visual – without which its allure would have been unthinkable. As the philosopher Joachim Ritter argued in an important essay little known in the English-speaking world, the modern experience of landscape supplants the Classical and Medieval tradition of 'theoria', the philosophical contemplation of a closed cosmos that was made obsolete by the post-Copernican scientific and technological approach to nature.[26] In place of the ('natural') 'given-ness' of the divine creation, there is the landscape as the aesthetic creation of a 'whole'. No longer content to receive the world out of the hand of the creator, the self needed reassurance of its sensual (primarily visible) perceptibility, its 'outness', in the term Coleridge adopted from Berkeley. If we follow Ritter's thesis, the Romantic 'landscape of the mind' was much more than the symbolic expression of an inner state of feeling; it fulfilled the function of an ontological guarantee.

The project of German idealism was to reconcile the autonomy of the human intellect and the world's independence. As is well known, Kant's successors attacked his infamous 'thing-in-itself', which presented them not only with a logical impasse, but an intolerable restriction of the mind's world-structuring activity. Yet while Fichte's principle of the 'absolute ego' (creating the empirical duality of 'ego' and 'non-ego') inspired the early Romantic credo of an unlimited creative capacity, it was rapidly attacked as a violent and tyrannical assault on the empirical world and nature. The Romantic motif of the 'rescue of nature' won out over the idealist motif of an absolute intellectual progressivism. In his tale, *The apprentices at Sais*, Novalis parodies the Fichtean preference of *a priori* 'absolute' knowledge over empirical nature: 'we are sitting at the wellspring of freedom and look out; it is the great magic mirror in which the whole of creation discloses itself in purity and clearness, in it the tender spirits and icons of all natural entities bathe themselves, and we see all chambers opened to us here. What need we wander labouriously through

[25] Cf. Lilian R. Furst, *Romanticism in perspective: a comparative study of aspects of the Romantic movements in England, France and Germany*, London: Macmillan, 1969.

[26] Cf. Joachim Ritter, 'Landschaft: zur Funktion des Ästhetischen in der modernen Gesellschaft' in *Subjektivität: sechs Aufsätze*, Frankfurt am Main: Suhrkamp Verlag, 1974.

the muddy world of the visible things? The purer world rests in ourselves, in this wellspring.'[27] As we shall see shortly, there is indeed a partial truth contained in this overbearing statement – but only a partial one.

The decisive step out of the quandary was made by the young Schelling. In his years as a teacher at the University of Jena, 1798–1800, close to Weimar and in intimate contact with the young Romantic poets, Schelling developed a philosophy of nature which became highly influential for German and – through mostly indirect ways – English Romanticism.[28] Even where no demonstrable historical influence existed, his (early) philosophy is undoubtedly the most significant theoretical contribution to the Romantic aesthetics of nature. Schelling is therefore an excellent point of reference to probe yet somewhat deeper into the paradoxes of the Romantic nature imagination.

III

When Pope exhorted man to look at the exterior world as an inscrutable work of divine art – 'All nature is but Art, unknown to thee'[29] – he had in mind God as the creator whose design had to be trusted in its totality even though the human intellect could only grasp it in small fragments. For Schelling, nature is likewise the product of a grand design, but the human mind is now the unconscious producer, 'before' (in a temporal as well as logical sense) confronting it on the basis of a dualist relationship. In its cognitive and instrumental function, the human intellect remains split from a nature reified as its foreign Other, unless reason attains to that higher stage of knowing which is the recognition that the objective world is its own work – that is, a product of spirit. Schelling calls this final stage of a reconciliation between the external and the internal, to which all knowledge and experience of the spirit aspires, 'intellectual intuition', *intellektuale Anschauung*. The concept was a provocation to Kantian philosophy, which had limited human knowledge to the realm of the senses. Human knowledge, Kant had insisted, always followed, belatedly and imperfectly, the act of production, and only a divine 'intellectus archetypus'

---

[27] Novalis, *Die Lehrlinge zu Saïs*, *Schriften*, 1: 89.
[28] Coleridge is, of course, the most important mediator. In chapters 12 and 13 of his *Biographia literaria*, he quotes extensively from Schelling's work, whom he calls 'my German predecessor'. He also attacks Fichte for his 'boastful and hyperstoic hostility to Nature' (p. 234). Cf. ch. 6 of René Wellek, *A history of modern criticism*, vol. 1, New Haven, CT: Yale University Press, 1955. For the special role played by Henry Crabb Robinson in transmitting Schelling's ideas to English and French circles, cf. Ernst Behler, 'Schellings Philosophie der Kunst in der Überlieferung Henry Crabb Robinsons' in *Studien zur Frühromantik und zur idealistischen Philosophie*, Paderborn: Schöningh, 1988. Besides Coleridge, Schelling's influence is especially marked in Emerson (see below).
[29] Pope, 'An essay on man', 1, line 289 in *Poetical works*, p. 249.

or an 'intuiting reason' (*anschauende Vernunft*) could know and produce the world in one identical act, recognizing itself completely in the object and the object in itself. Schelling proceeded to install such an intellect in the human mind.

In breaking the barrier between finite and infinite reason Schelling took the work of art as his model. In this respect, the Kant of the *Critique of judgement* of 1790 had been his precursor, as he had laid the groundwork for German idealist aesthetics in general. But for Kant the artwork, the 'work of genius' as he called it, stood under the explicit caveat of an 'as if'. A mere 'symbol' of the problematic, forever transcendental – not intuitable, not cognizable, not even positively assertable – unity of nature and freedom, it presented itself to the mind *as if* it was nature spontaneously agreeing with our cognitive outfit, *as if* nature through it would signal to reason her free consent with its rule, or, in Romantic vocabulary: *as if* through it nature would turn her smiling face to man and commune with him. For Schelling, this symbolic 'as if' of art took the place of a firm metaphysical truth. In its material presence the aesthetic artifact realizes the preexisting and unthinkable symbiosis of the mind with nature's unlimited productivity and hence manifests the essence of the world that the philosopher is to reconstruct and 'remember'. Art, Schelling therefore contends, is intellectual intuition become objective.

For Schelling, the task of philosophy after the demise of all substantialist versions of metaphysical knowledge lies in the demonstration of this absolute identity between the world and the spirit. Philosophy traces in reverse direction the road which the spirit, *Geist*, has travelled since its severance from nature. 'All philosophizing consists in a remembering of the stage in which we were one with nature.'[30] At the same time, this process of remembrance is propelled towards future restoration: 'Nature shall be the visible spirit, the spirit shall be invisible nature.'[31] But art contains already and in one finite intuition what speculative thinking can attain to only in the problematic form of its eschatological completion. Since reflexive thinking (thinking in the mode of the subject–object-dualism) always necessarily means 'splitting', the identical ground of the world and the mind necessarily eludes conscious thought; 'speculative' thinking, however, attempts to surmount the dualistic dilemma and to restore the 'unconscious' unity with nature from which the (finite) mind has broken away. On its infinite and tortuous journey towards self-recognition as the originating creative principle in and as nature, then, the

[30] F. W. J. Schelling, Allgemeine Deduktion . . . der Physik', in *Sämmtliche Werke*, K. F. A. Schelling (ed.), Stuttgart: Cotta, 1856–61, IV: 77.
[31] Friedrich Wilhelm Joseph von Schelling, *Einleitung zu: Ideen zu einer Philosophie der Natur*, in *Ausgewählte Schriften*, Manfred Frank (ed.), Frankfurt am Main: Suhrkamp Verlag, 1985, I: 294.

mind is presented with art's reassuring sensual plenitude. 'Art therefore represents to the philosopher the highest possible good, since it opens to him as it were the holy of holies wherein eternal and primordial union burns, as it were in one single flame, what in nature and history is separated.' The quote is taken from the concluding passage of the *System of transcendental idealism* of 1800, the work in which the leading function of art for speculative philosophy is stressed the most emphatically. Schelling continues in the same poetical diction invoking 'nature' as the mysterious space of the 'odyssey of the spirit':

The view of nature which the philosopher shapes to himself artificially [*künstlich*], for art is the most primordial and the most natural. What we call nature, is a poem residing sealed in secret writing. Yet if the enigma could disclose itself, we would see in it the odyssey of the spirit, which, wondrously deceived, in search of itself, flees from itself; for meaning glances through the sensual world only as though through [as many] words, only as through half-transparent fog [gleams] the land of the imagination for which we strive.[32]

This is the philosophical arche-story of the Romantic quest, which is the quest for a nature revealing herself to the mind as plenitude of its own meaning. Nature is a poem unaware of its own poetry (or rather poesy) since the spirit does not (yet) recognize itself fully as its author. (Notice how the conceptual language of philosophy here transcends itself in poetic imagery, so as to perform what it asserts.) Conversely, poetry in the finite, mundane sense of the production of poetic works partakes of this universal productivity; writing poetry is an – always partial and fragmentary – attempt at reading nature as poem, at deciphering a forgotten language. As 'universal trope of the spirit' ('*Universaltropus des Geistes*', Novalis[33]), nature invites, even demands a creative reading, and this reading in turn is but a response to the mind's own creativity unconsciously at work in her and recreated in aesthetic production.

But despite all its dialectical subtleties, this relationship between nature and mind cannot deny its essentially specular character. Idealist thinking in general evinces a 'narcissistic relation to itself',[34] and 'higher philosophy' betrays an incestuous tendency as it 'contemplates the marriage between nature and spirit'.[35] Novalis turns it on the positive side when he invokes an 'act of self-embracement' as the primordial source of our erotic relationship to the world, but he hastens to add that this autoeroticism remains a secret. 'The first kiss in this understanding is the principle of philosophy – the origin of a new world – the beginning of the absolute order of time

---

[32] Schelling, *System des transcendentalen Idealismus* in *Ausgewählte Schriften*, I: 696.
[33] Novalis, *Schriften*, II: 600.
[34] Ernst Behler, 'Die Kunst der Reflexion: Das frühromantische Denken im Hinblick auf Nietzsche' in *Studien zur Romantik*, p. 116.
[35] *Ibid.* (III: 375).

– the realisation of an infinitely growing self-union.'[36] The first kiss is, we might generously translate, the incipient recognition that it is only the mother we crave for. Yet the mind's speculations never achieve a final consummation. 'Idealism contemplates the world as a work of art, a poem', Friedrich Schlegel says, 'only it does not know it right away'.[37] The 'speculative' reading of the world remains the unreachable ideal of a universal understanding of nature, in Novalis's terms a 'system of mutual representation of the universe' (*Wechselrepräsentationslehre des Universums*).[38] By (re-)creating the text of nature, the Romantic text opens up an infinite play of significations that simultaneously offer themselves to and withdraw from the hero and reader. Operating across the distance between the strange and the familiar, the new and the old, the unconscious and the conscious, the dream and the world, or the internal and the external, the recognition of nature by art replaces the former reiteration according to the *imitatio naturae* principle. The 'sweet and indissoluble union between the intellectual and the material world' (Coleridge) must prove and perform itself again and again through a permanent process of poetic estrangement; the visible things of Novalis's muddy world are made visible in the first place by their removal from the ordinary course of life, through their 'reflection in the wellspring' of the inner being of the human mind. The routine of the everyday and the reduction of nature to a mechanical surface lend a false familiarity of standardized perception and practice that oppose the mind's deeply felt 'presentiment' (*Ahndung*) of a past and future harmony. The truth of nature can therefore paradoxically be regained only by veiling her in a mystery that entices the mind to seek in its depths something at once more wondrous and deeply familiar.

In a short prose fragment, *Die Lehrlinge zu Saïs* (*The apprentices at Saïs*, written 1798–9 and posthumously published in 1801), Novalis chooses the famous Egyptian sanctuary as the symbolic, hieroglyphic locale of a philosophical discussion on the truth of nature. His young narrator does not find it in any one of the diverse opinions he hears around him (although in their ensemble they may approach it, for nature is 'infinite communication') nor in the 'strange piles and figures' amassed in the chambers and reminiscent of contemporary nature cabinets, but in the telling of a simple fairy tale. It is a tale about a youth like the narrator himself, who leaves his home and his love, headed for the unknown truth, 'where the mother of things lives, the veiled virgin'. In a further *mise en abîme*, the wandering hero is put to sleep and receives a dream, 'since only dream was allowed to lead him to the innermost sanctuary'. Truth, then, is ultimately not achieved by penetrating into the physical secrets of nature

---

[36] Novalis, *Schriften*, II: 541 (no. 74).   [37] *Kritische Friedrich-Schlegel-Ausgabe*, XII: 105.
[38] Novalis, *Schriften*, III: 266.

(something, it should be mentioned, Novalis like many of his fellow Romantics in practice did not at all neglect) but revealed to the feeling soul. Alienated from his customary world and dissatisfied with the familiarity of normalcy, the youth is rewarded with the supernatural gift of his past: 'Everything appeared to him so well-known and yet in a glory never seen before, even the last worldly trace disappeared there as if consumed by air, there he lifted the light, splendorous veil, and Rosenblütchen sank into his arms.'[39] The spirit's odyssey has returned home to the origin: to the childhood landscape, to mother and to first love, all now prodigiously transfigured in poetic image.

If we abstract the nearly ubiquitous Romantic topos of estrangement and return from its philosophical and historico–philosophical background, we can describe it as a poetic device. In discovering the mind in nature and in exploring the mind through nature, the imagination creates a novel familiarity with the world. This poetic 'circuitous journey'[40] from nature to mind and back to nature never achieves closure in the circle of a perfect self-transparency. Fichte thought the mind could reach back to the ground of the preexisting unity to which it owes its existence, but his Romantic followers were more hesitant, arguing that the mind presupposes its ground but cannot 'grasp' it conceptually,[41] and their poetic nature imagery provides the only half-transparent medium – the veil, the mist, the twilight – for the self-recognition of the spirit. Each closing of the circle, such as the just quoted ending of Novalis's short tale, remains provisional, merely another promise for the ultimate utopia where 'the world becomes dream, the dream becomes world'.[42] The Romantic postulate of reciprocity between mind and nature, spirit and matter, called on the poet to transform everything external into the internal world, but also to transcend, constantly and permanently, the interiority of the soul by reaching into the otherness of the material world and in this manner to reveal progressively the transcendent world within. Again Novalis puts it succinctly: we understand 'everything foreign only through making ourselves foreign [*Selbstfremdmachung*] – self-changing – self-observation'.[43]

The transcendence of nature as the all-encompassing unity ever escaping the conscious mind is finally reflected in the ontological status of the work of art itself. Art, we remind ourselves, for Schelling and his followers is the only place for the mind's encounter with the 'absolute' – an absolute, however, in the paradoxical form of a finite and objective intuition. The

---

[39] *Ibid.* (I: 93 ff.).
[40] Cf. Abrams, *Natural supernaturalism*, esp. chs. 3 to 5.
[41] Manfred Frank has stressed this point of the priority of being in early romantic thinking in numerous studies, cf. in particular: 'Die philosophischen Grundlagen der Frühromantik', *Athenäum* 4 (1994).
[42] Novalis, *Schriften*, I: 319.   [43] *Ibid.* (III: 429) (no. 820).

artwork confronts the mind with the (limited) image of its unlimited creativity; through art as an autonomous object of the external world, 'nature' surprises the mind with its own autonomy. With respect to the creative activity of the artist, Schelling accentuates the 'unexpected harmony' between the subjective and the objective sides, which allows 'free' human creativity to coincide with the necessity of natural process. 'Through this union, it [the conscious creative activity] will feel taken by surprise and blessed, i.e. it will regard it [the union] as it were as a voluntary favour of a higher nature, having made possible through it the impossible.'[44]

The patently religious language here suggests the heritage of the divine gift of grace now embodied in the 'gift' of art. The experience of aesthetic recognition is characterized by a blissful gratuitousness beyond human control. Notwithstanding the speculative affirmation of their preexisting union, then, the actual coming together of the mind and the world constitutes a 'finding' in the emphatic sense of an incalculable event. As such, the work of art becomes a symbol of the non-disposable 'absolute', representing its unrepresentability.[45] Art stands in for the elusive, inconceivable and unpresentable absolute harmony of mind and nature precisely because it does not owe its existence to mere subjective achievement but to the 'supervening' of the objective or nature.[46]

Romantic poetry abounds with moments of such contingent bliss when images of nature flash on the human mind in sudden recognition, assuring the subject of its sympathetic bond with the external world. The function of nature imagery in the circular movement of externalization and internalization, splitting and uniting, lies in affirming the transcendence of the outer as that of the (as yet) unknown inner world and, since the circle will never completely close on itself, the transcendence of their synthesis. Thus, when Coleridge confesses that 'in looking at objects of Nature I seem rather to be seeking, as it were *asking* for, a symbolical language for something within me that already and forever exists, than observing anything new',[47] he does not advocate subjectivist psychological projection against scientific discovery; rather, his concern is with an external nature leading to the discovery and the poetic articulation of a foreign and hitherto impenetrable dimension within the self. The natural object challenges the beholder to turn within himself and 'reflect' it in the mirror of his soul by translating it into a language that reactivates the forgotten primeval bond between the subjective and the objective. Conversely, when Blake laments

[44] Schelling, *System des transcendentalen Idealismus*, I: 683.
[45] 'Representation of the unrepresentable' as a definition of the artwork is a recurring formula in Novalis, *Schriften*, III: 685 (no. 671), and p. 376 (no. 612).
[46] Schelling, *System des transcendentalen Idealismus*, I: 683ff.
[47] Quoted in Frye, 'Drunken Boat', in *Romanticism Reconsidered*, pp. 10ff.

the 'natural objects' which 'weaken, deaden and obliterate Imagination in Me',[48] he takes aim at the objects as perceived by the 'Corporeal or Vegetative Eye', which is the eye of the neutral observer who uses it for seeing 'through it and not with it'.[49] This desirable 'seeing with' is no less than the revelation of the human imagination as the ground of the external world: 'To the Eyes of the Man of Imagination, Nature is Imagination itself.'[50]

The symbolic mode for such 'seeing' of the imagination is the dream. Ultimately, Romantic nature is nature dreamt. In dreaming, the poetic mind does not withdraw from the exterior world into a realm of arbitrary inwardness but hallucinates the world in its 'true objectivity' which engulfs and transcends human subjectivity. In the dream landscape, the mind at once loses and finds itself – loses the limited, rational, quotidian identity 'as' individual subject and finds the true identity 'with' nature. In Novalis's unfinished novel *Heinrich von Ofterdingen* the artist hero was to find his initial dream – the famous dream about the 'blue flower' – fulfilled at the end of his quest journey; but this fulfilment was not to be understood as the realization of an individual motivating wish. Rather, within the dream structure of the poetic text itself the interiority of the soul and the externality of the world were to interfuse and ultimately become indistinguishable. The poetic (not the psychological) dream becomes identical with the artwork, which in turn becomes the visible symbol of what Schelling called the 'point of indifference' between the subjective and the objective, or mind and nature, which is the 'absolute'.

IV

In the light of the ambiguity of imagined nature as a space of absence from the real and of its recovery, it would seem a rather fruitless endeavour to classify individual poets as to their position within the mind–nature constellation, such as 'egotists' imposing their will on the natural appearances on the one side and 'sympathetic minds' submitting themselves to their autonomy on the other.[51] Of course, there are distinguishable dispositions and talents for the observation of individual phenomena, for which on the whole poets are more convincing advocates than philosophers. But the basic dilemma that the world's infinite multiplicity had to be rescued

---

[48] William Blake, Marginalia to Wordsworth, quoted in Geoffrey H. Hartman *Wordsworth's poetry, 1787–1815*, New Haven, CT: Yale University Press, 1962, p. 218.

[49] William Blake, *Poetry and prose*, Geoffrey Keynes (ed.), Oxford University Press, 1946, p. 617 ('Vision of the Last Judgment').

[50] Letter to Trusler, 23 August 1799, in *Romantic Criticism 1800–50*, R. A. Foakes (ed.), Columbia, SC: University of South Carolina Press, 1968, p. 19.

[51] Cf. Frederick Garber, 'Nature and the Romantic mind: egotism, empathy, irony', *Comparative literature* 29 (1977), pp. 193–212.

through an autonomous act of the human imagination – regardless of the regrounding of this faculty of the mind in a prior agency – remained the same. Emerson summed up in euphoric language the transcendentalist premise that 'the Universe is the externalisation of the soul'[52] and that the poet was the one able to repossess its spiritual content by reading its symbolic language and thus effectuating 'the passage of the world into the soul of man, to suffer there a change and reappear a new and higher fact'[53]; his monstrous incorporation of the world's otherness (especially in the last chapter of the famous 'Nature' essay), when he extols man's power over a nature who yields to his spiritual superiority, makes him sound like a true contemporary of Marx. But Emerson insists on the higher rank of the imaginative intellect over a purely instrumental and technological reason which, to be sure, it integrates; and his model is the poet who discloses the inner essence of natural appearances in a language which is 'not art, but a second nature, grown out of the first, as a leaf out of a tree' – just as if it were, Emerson says, a self-baptizing of nature.[54]

At the other end of the spectrum, late Romanticism in Germany increasingly stressed the objective against what was seen as the danger of excessive subjectivity. For the most popular German Romantic poet in the nineteenth century, Joseph von Eichendorff, nature represented God's creation, communicating with man through a 'hieroglyphic' language. To translate this message was the primary task of the artist, whose work then was more passive and receptive than that of his early Romantic predecessor. Subjective creativity now confronted its limits not in a pre- or supra-subjectivist 'absolute' of the mind (the inner transcendence), but in the 'objective' transcendence of the work of God. The substance of 'nature poetry' was placed firmly beyond the human disposition. Yet it still needed to be decoded; nature did not speak unless made to by a responsive subject. The primacy of the natural over the human, then, was not due to its mere objective reality but its character as emblem, or signature, of the divine.[55] The same translating function of (poetic) subjectivity distinguishes Eichendorff's conception of poetry from late Romanticism concepts of *Volkspoesie*, as expounded by Achim von Arnim and the Grimm brothers, who posited an anonymous collective subject as surrogate of the idealist 'absolute'; in their writings the 'self-revelation of nature' through the *Volk* eliminates every element of the rational subjectivity.[56]

---

[52] Ralph Waldo Emerson, 'The poet', *Selections from Ralph Waldo Emerson: an organic anthology*, Stephen E. Whicher (ed.), 1960, Boston, MA: Houghton Mifflin Company (Riverside Editions), p. 227.
[53] *Ibid.*, p. 230.   [54] *Ibid.*, p. 231.
[55] Alexander von Bormann, *Natura loquitur: Naturpoesie und emblematische Formel bei Joseph von Eichendorff*, Tübingen: Niemeyer, 1968, p. 105.
[56] Cf. for instance Jakob Grimm, *Kleinere Schriften*, Berlin: Duemmler, 1869, IV: 35.

The most prominent aesthetic concept for the transcendence of nature *vis-à-vis* the mind's creative power was the concept of the sublime. The sublime phenomena of external nature – such as rugged mountains, steep precipices, violent thunderstorms, vast oceans, the immensity of the open horizon or the starry sky – overwhelm the human capacity of sensory perception and imaginative comprehension; in instantaneously crushing the human apparatus of object reception, they assert painfully the priority and dominance of the objective world. But this is only the one half of the sublime experience. Already Enlightenment aesthetics, which discovered the natural sublime, had focussed on the fact that the mind found a strange 'delight' in these threatening objects and sought them for the calculated arousal of the mixed feelings of 'delightful horror' or 'tranquillity tinged with terror',[57] which shrank and extended the ego at the same time, extended it by shrinking it. Again it was Kant's transcendental explication of the experience (building on Burke's superb phenomenological description) in the *Critique of judgement* which put the matter most succinctly.[58] Kant attributed the elevating feeling inspired by the sublime not to the object, which served but as catalyst, but to the subject itself. In the midst of its sensory and bodily breakdown, the mind discovered the resistance of a superior faculty within itself, through which it rose above the sensual realm and found a firm halt in the cognitive and moral order of reason, *Vernunft*. Even more, the terrifying grandeur exuded by the 'sublime' object was ultimately owed to an unacknowledged projection by the mind itself, as Kant says: to a 'subreption of the imagination'. Only the mind possesses the power to extend the finite objects of the external world into infinity, and it does so by the work of the imagination which stretches itself beyond the limits of the conditioned under reason's imperative to seek an unconditional totality. Through the collapse of the overstretched imaginative power the mind 'incurs' the power of the unconditioned. The external object sets the process in motion and thereby becomes the negative representation of the absolute.

The fascination of the sublime was largely due to the fact that in it nature assumed the quality of the 'aweful' transcendence of God; the sublime natural object provided an apt substitute for waning religious belief. At the same time, however, it illustrates the way in which that otherworldly transcendence was conferred on the human subject. In the aesthetics of the sublime, the subject triumphed over the object, as did immanence over transcendence, imagination over reality and reason over the imagination. Eventually, it was the self-aggrandizement of the ego which prevailed over the incomprehensible non-ego, the positive over the

---

[57] Edmund Burke, *A philosophical inquiry into the origins of our ideas of the sublime and beautiful*, James T. Boulton (ed.), London 1958, p. 136.
[58] Cf. the paragraphs on the 'Analytic of the Sublime', *Critique of judgement*, §§ 23–9.

negative, the representation over the unrepresentable. When, in a famous section of the *Prelude* describing the crossing of the Simplon Pass in the Alps, Wordsworth celebrates the imagination as the power transcending reality – here, the reality of the sublime mountain scenery as well as the recollected initial enthusiasm of the French Revolution and its abrupt disappointment – he lets the sublime moment of sense extinction be followed by the conscious 'usurpation' of the greater power of the inner realm:

> That awful Power rose from the mind's abyss
> Like an unfathered vapour that enwraps,
> At once, some lonely traveller. I was lost;
> Halted without an effort to break through;
> But to my conscious soul I now can say –
> 'I recognise thy glory': in such strength
> Of usurpation, when the light of sense
> Goes out, but with a flash that has revealed
> The invisible world . . .[59]

Paul de Man and Geoffrey Hartman, among others, have stressed this pivotal moment of blindness that sets Romantic nature off from the tradition by denying the *imitatio naturae* principle and Enlightenment visualism, turning from the outward to the inward and establishing of the imaginative autonomy.[60] On the other hand, blindness is also insight – the 'flash upon that inward eye'[61] revealing the truth of nature, which, however, in its turn needs to be represented and 'visualized' – in metaphors, symbols, hieroglyphs, emblems. De Man specifically has stressed the Romantic 'nostalgia for the object' which attempts to ground the originating act of language in the ontological priority of the sensory world (and which, incidentally, he sees forsaken in the Wordsworth passage in question).[62] In the sublime object, the overbearing flagrancy of the sensual as it were extinguishes itself, becoming the inverted representation of 'the mind's abyss'. But this self-transcendence of nature into the 'nothingness' of the creative moment could all too easily be converted into the self-empowerment of a subject seeking – and staging – moments of weakness as tokens of its strength, testing as it were 'to what point, and how, / The mind is lord and master – outward sense / The obedient servant of her will'.[63] Otherness

---

[59] Wordsworth, *The prelude* (1850), VI, lines 594ff.

[60] Cf. Paul de Man, 'Wordsworth and Hölderlin', in *The rhetoric of Romanticism*, New York: Columbia University Press, 1984, esp. pp. 55ff. and 'The Intentional Structure of the Romantic image', in *Rhetoric*, pp. 11ff. Geoffrey H. Hartman, 'A poet's progress: Wordsworth and the "via naturaliter negativa"', *Modern philology* 59 (1961/62), esp. pp. 220ff.

[61] Cf. Wordsworth's poem 'I wandered lonely as a cloud'.

[62] De Man, 'Intentional structure', *Rhetoric*, pp. 15ff.

[63] Wordsworth, *Prelude* (1850), XII, lines 221ff.

is then subsumed by the ego, as appears symbolized in the final image of Mount Snowdon, 'the emblem of a mind / That feeds upon infinity, that broods / Over the dark abyss' – supreme fiction of a self not threatened, but as it were presiding 'over', even creating the limitless.[64]

---

[64] *Ibid.*, XIV, lines 70ff. Cf. Thomas Weiskel, *The Romantic sublime: studies in the structure and psychology of transcendence*, Baltimore, MD and London: The Johns Hopkins University Press, 1976, pp. 48ff.

6

Scientific models

JOEL BLACK

Poetic metaphors and scientific models

The century and a half preceding the Romantic period was marked not
only by an unprecedented succession of major scientific discoveries, but
also by the rise of entirely new domains of scientific knowledge. From
Newtonian mechanics to chemistry, from biology to psychology, each
new field disclosed natural phenomena that were increasingly inaccessible
to ordinary human observation. Such phenomena had to be apprehended
through technological innovations (telescopes, microscopes), and were
often only comprehended through the use of mathematical formulas and
conceptual models.

Amidst this growing scientific abstraction, Romantic writers have been
seen as conducting a valiant but ultimately futile crusade to save the
appearances. Goethe insisted that natural objects should not merely be
studied objectively – 'in themselves and in their relation to each other'[1] –
but viewed in relation to the observers themselves. Blake bitterly denounced
Newton's mechanistic world-view, and even Coleridge, while professing
admiration for Newton's scientific discoveries, deplored the passivity of
corporeal bodies in Newton's scheme of nature and, what for him was
worse, the passivity of Newton's concept of the mind itself. '[T]he Souls of
500 Sir Isaac Newtons would go to the making up of a Shakespeare or a
Milton', he wrote, adding that 'Newton was a mere materialist – Mind in
his system is always passive – a lazy looker-on on an external World.'[2] The
Romantics' suspicion of a scientific approach to nature is best expressed
in Wordsworth's line, 'we murder to dissect'.

Yet such criticism of Newtonian abstraction and materialism does not
mean that the Romantics were hostile to science itself. As shown by
the period's two great English literary manifestos – Wordsworth's 1802
Preface to *Lyrical ballads* and Shelley's 1821 'Defence of poetry' – most
Romantic writers viewed poetry and science as complementary human

[1] Walter D. Wetzels, 'Art and science: organicism and Goethe's Classical aesthetics', in
Approaches to organic form, Frederick Burwick (ed.), Dordrecht: Reidel, 1987, p. 75.
[2] *Collected letters of Samuel Taylor Coleridge*, E. L. Griggs (ed.), Oxford University Press,
1956–71, vol. II, p. 709.

endeavours. Wordsworth described poetry as 'the impassioned expression which is in the countenance of all Science', and as 'the first and last of all knowledge'; not only would the poet 'be ready to follow the steps of the Man of science . . . but he will be at his side, carrying sensation into the midst of the objects of the science itself'.[3] For Shelley, poetry was 'at once the centre and circumference of knowledge; it is that which comprehends all science and that to which all science must be referred'.[4] Such statements suggest the Romantics' acceptance of the sciences – as long as their poetic origins were acknowledged. This openness toward scientific inquiry contrasts sharply with the staunch opposition to modernity and scientific progress of later artistic movements such as the pre-Raphaelites and other groups associated with late nineteenth-century aestheticism.

Writers of the Romantic period were not necessarily averse to philosophical thinking or to the use of conceptual models as a means of grasping and representing deep truths about the natural world; their metaphorical language relies on a stock of metaphysical models – on 'older less precise but more comprehensive concepts of comprehending reality than modern scientific theories about the structure of and order among things'.[5] In 'The Eolian harp' (1795), the young Coleridge employed such a poetic image of nature:

> And what if all of animated nature
> Be but organic Harps diversely framed,
> That tremble into thought, as o'er them sweeps
> Plastic and vast, one intellectual breeze,
> At once the Soul of each, and God of all?[6]

This passage is the culmination of a succession of analogies in the poem, moving from simile to metaphor, in which the poet pushes his central image to the limit, using the physical motif of the harps for metaphysical purposes. In themselves, the harps are a mechanistic image (separate, individual, artificial instruments each made up of separate parts) which Coleridge recasts as an organic image (natural organisms, composed of interdependent parts, that are themselves interdependent parts in a larger ensemble). Yet this organic metaphor functions less as a model of external, created nature (*natura naturata*) than of the poetic, creative process itself (*natura naturans*) in which God, that all pervasive 'intellectual breeze', directly participates. It is impossible to stand outside this model,

---

[3] *The prose works of William Wordsworth*, W. J. B. Owen and Jane Worthington Smyser, Oxford: Clarendon Press, 1974, vol. I, p. 141.
[4] *Shelley's prose*, David Lee Clark (ed.), New York: New Amsterdam Books, 1988, p. 293.
[5] Wetzels, 'Art and science', pp. 72–3.
[6] Ian Wylie discusses an early draft of this passage with respect to Coleridge's early scientific studies in *Young Coleridge and the philosophers of nature*, Oxford: Clarendon Press, 1989, pp. 3–4.

to invoke God or to employ thought as a means of considering nature objectively, because God and thought are already included and involved in the model. It is unclear, in short, whether Coleridge's image of the 'organic harps' – in which thought is already implicated in nature, and in which the subject is already implicated in the object – is merely a poetic metaphor or a metaphysical (if not a scientific) model. Like Novalis's statement that 'language is a musical idea instrument',[7] Coleridge's image suggests the inseparable relation between mind and the physical world.

When Romantics writers employed involuted poetic metaphors like this, they were not indulging in the witty conceits of the metaphysical poets, nor were they attempting to give an objective, loco-descriptive account of nature. They were elaborating metaphysical models *of* nature – models that, on the one hand, presented nature as an intellectual, creative process, and on the other hand, presented themselves as products, instances, or demonstrations of this very process. When pushed to the limit, such models were bound to become strained and had to be appropriately qualified. Thus, when Shelley uses the image of the 'Æolean lyre' near the beginning of 'Defence of poetry' to describe man (rather than Coleridge's 'animated nature'), he acknowledges the inadequacy of this image:

But there is a principle within the human being, and perhaps within all sentient beings, which acts otherwise than in a lyre and produces not melody alone but harmony, by an internal adjustment of the sounds and motions thus excited to the impressions which excite them. It is as if the lyre could accommodate its chords to the motions of that which strikes them in a determined proportion of sound, even as the musician can accommodate his voice to the sound of the lyre.

(277)

If the lyre is of limited use as an image of human creativity, it is even more difficult to find a poetic metaphor that will make poetry itself intelligible. Of the various images of poetry Shelley experiments with in the 'Defence', perhaps the most successful is the 'scientific' model of light, which 'transmutes all that it touches, and every form moving within the radiance of its presence is changed by wondrous sympathy to an incarnation of the spirit which it breathes . . .' (295). Yet while this view of poetry is modelled on the contemporary scientific notion of sunlight's power to enliven the visual world,[8] such uses of scientific models must ultimately be

---

[7] Novalis, *Schriften*, Paul Kluckhohn and Richard Samuel (eds.), 2nd edn, Stuttgart: Kohlhammer, 1960–75, vol. III, p. 360.

[8] See Ted Underwood, 'The science in Shelley's theory of poetry', *Modern language quarterly* 58 (1997), pp. 298–321. Underwood cautions, however, that to 'say that this theory of poetry was "modeled" on science would understate the connection . . . Shelley could quite consistently argue that the scientific ideas he borrowed were already informed by the poetic imagination.'

reconciled with Shelley's dictum that poetry 'is that which comprehends all science and that to which all science must be referred'.

'What we know, we know only through analogy',[9] Herder declared, and what Novalis called '*den Zauberstab der Analogie*'[10] ['the magic wand of analogy'] could be counted on when logic and experimental observation were unable to yield positive, empirical knowledge. Implicitly repudiating the Royal Society's project in the mid-seventeenth century to develop a scientific discourse that would 'reject all the amplifications, digressions and swellings of style', and 'return [language] back' to a condition of 'primitive purity' and 'Mathematical plainness',[11] Romantics like Novalis and Friedrich Schlegel devised a poetic–philosophical discourse in which knowledge was neither immediate nor inaccessible, but thoroughly mediated by metaphors, models, and other symbolic figures, if not flagrantly distorted through the rhetorical techniques of irony, hyperbole and digression. Yet while cooler heads like Herder and Goethe remained aware 'that the models and metaphors of scientific discourse were not identical with nature',[12] and were therefore limited in their usefulness, Romantic writers tended, intentionally or not, to ignore any distinction between artificial models and nature. Like today's more radical scientific proponents of 'artificial life', they invested their metaphors with new significance as generative organons in their own right. Coleridge, for example, ascribed supreme creative power to the divine Logos and immense generative potential to human language, while Novalis and Gotthilf Heinrich Schubert treated nature itself as discourse.

Organic form

Given their penchant for ascribing creative and procreative powers to language, Romantic critics tended to exploit the analogy between the poetic artifact and the physical organism. Behind this analogy lay the concept of organic unity dating back to Plato in which a work's parts agreed with each other and with the whole;[13] in the guise of organic form, this concept assumed unprecedented significance in Romantic criticism. Coleridge contrasts form that is 'mechanic when on any given material we impress a predetermined form', with organic form that 'is innate, it shapes as it develops

[9] Johann Gottfried Herder, 'Vom Erkennen und Empfinden der menschlichen Seele', in *Sämmtliche Werke*, B. Suphan (ed.), Hildesheim: Georg Olm, 1967, vol. VIII, p. 170.
[10] Novalis, *Schriften*, vol. III, p. 518.
[11] Thomas Sprat, *The history of the Royal Society of London*, London, 1667, p. 112.
[12] Karl J. Fink, *Goethe's history of science*, Cambridge University Press, 1991, p. 90.
[13] See G. N. Giordano Orsini, *Organic unity in ancient and later poetics*, Carbondale, IL: Southern Illinois University Press, 1975, p. 21.

itself from within, and the fullness of its development is one and the same with the perfection of its outward Form'.[14] Natural organisms (especially plants) served as a model for artworks (especially poems); poetic creation consequently entailed, in M. H. Abrams's words, 'the metaphorical translation into the categories and norms of intellection of the attributes of a growing thing, which unfolds its inner form and assimilates to itself alien elements, until it reaches the fullness of its complex, organic unity'.[15] But, as W. K. Wimsatt observed, since a poem 'does not in fact look very much like a plant', even when it contains 'vegetable imagery', Coleridge emphasized the analogy's genetic aspect (what Wimsatt called 'the psychological doctrine, concerning the author's consciousness or unconsciousness'), rather than the structural or 'objective doctrine concerning poetic form'.[16]

By stressing the subjective aspect of organic form that pertained to issues of growth, Coleridge downplayed the concept's other aspects of wholeness, assimilation, internality, and interdependence.[17] Noting that the 'Romantic analogy between vegetable and poetic creation tended to assimilate the poetic to the vegetable by making the poetic as radically spontaneous as possible – that is, indeliberate, unconscious' (22), Wimsatt warned the

aesthetic organicist . . . in his dealing with poems . . . to appeal but cautiously to that analogy with the all too ragged physical organism. He may well be content to confine his appeal to a very purified post-Kantian version of the aesthetic properties: the individuality and uniqueness of each aesthetic whole, the priority of the whole to the parts, the congruence and interdependence of parts with parts and of parts with the whole, the uniqueness and irreplaceability of parts and their nonexistence prior to the aesthetic whole or outside it. (26)

While admitting that 'we should today be under the necessity of inventing' the concept of organic form if the Romantics hadn't already done so, Wimsatt cautioned that the concept has now become so 'very well-established' in contemporary criticism 'that both the metaphor and the

---

[14] Lecture 8 of the 1812–13 series (delivered Dec. 1812), in *The collected works of Samuel Taylor Coleridge*, Kathleen Coburn (ed.), Princeton, NJ: Princeton University Press, 1969–, vol. v, part 1, p. 495. See also lecture 9 of the 1811–12 series, delivered the previous year.

[15] M. H. Abrams, *Natural supernaturalism*, New York: Norton, 1971, p. 432.

[16] W. K. Wimsatt, 'Organic form: some questions about a metaphor', in *Romanticism: vistas, instances, continuities*, David Thorburn and Geoffrey Hartman (eds.), Ithaca: Cornell University Press, 1973, pp. 20–1.

[17] Goethe is not as constrained as Coleridge in this regard. For him, 'to apply the organic model in art means, in effect, to make reality transparent so that the unique interdependence of the part and the whole, the particular and the general, actually appears and can be perceived' (Wetzels, 'Art and science', p. 83).

literal idealist doctrine invite some not unreasonable questions' (26–7). It remained for poststructuralist critics like Paul de Man to deconstruct not only the metaphor of organic form, but the very concept of metaphor itself as the cornerstone of Coleridge's formalist criticism.[18]

Coleridge was not alone in exploiting the organic model as a genetic if not a formal analogue of poetry. Complaining of the 'lifeless mechanism' of eighteenth-century prose, Thomas De Quincey found fault with Dr Johnson's writing because it never 'GROWS a truth before your eyes whilst in the act of delivering it. His prose offers no process, no evolution, no movement of self-conflict or preparation.'[19] And besides the quasi-scientific description of poetry as transforming light in 'Defence of poetry', Shelley's culminating image is an unabashedly organic metaphor in which poetry is described as being 'at the same time the root and blossom of all other systems of thought; it is that from which all spring and that which adorns all; and that which, if blighted, denies the fruit and the seed, and withholds from the barren world the nourishment and the succession of the scions of the tree of life' (293).

For better or for worse, we are heirs not only to the Romantics' concept of organic form,[20] but to their symbolic and analogical habits of thinking. To see that this is so, we need only survey the history of attempts to describe the phenomenon of Romanticism itself: romanticists are often tempted to borrow metaphors from the writers whose work they are analysing. Critical discussions of Romanticism frequently demonstrate how one model of mind, nature, the self or the poetic text is replaced by another: the metaphor of the machine by the organism, the image of the mirror by the lamp, the shape of the circle by that of the ellipse.[21] How widely and how literally we apply these models plays a large part in determining our understanding of Romanticism.

[18] See Paul de Man, 'The rhetoric of temporality', in *Blindness and insight*, rev. edn, Minneapolis, MN: University of Minnesota Press, 1983, pp. 187–228, and *The rhetoric of Romanticism*, New York: Columbia University Press, 1984.

[19] *The collected writings of Thomas De Quincey*, David Masson (ed.), Edinburgh: Adam and Charles Black, 1890, vol. X, pp. 270–2. Cited by D. D. Devlin, *De Quincey, Wordsworth and the art of prose*, London: Macmillan, 1983, pp. 105–6, who comments that the 'capitalized "GROWS" suggests that De Quincey will need to create a prose that is (he uses the word) organic and exploratory' (p. 106).

[20] Cf. Fink: 'Even though we usually do not think of our technical culture as grounded in organic form, most scientific instrumentation is in some way based on perceptions of a natural model' ('Ontogeny recapitulates phylogeny', in *Approaches to organic form*, Burwick, p. 90). Fink gives the example of the computer as 'a crude representation of the brain'.

[21] Cf. Morse Peckham's observation that 'the new metaphor is not a machine; it is an organism' ('Toward a theory of Romanticism', *PMLA* [March 1951], pp. 5–23); regarding the circle and the ellipse, see Marshall Brown, *The shape of German Romanticism*, Ithaca, NY: Cornell University Press, 1979; and M. H. Abrams, *The mirror and the lamp*, New York: Oxford University Press, 1953.

Naturphilosophie: Metaphysical models of nature

The Romantics' extensive use of metaphysical models in their artistic and scientific endeavours followed Kant's claim – so much at odds with the positivist–empiricist inheritance of modern scientific thinking – that the natural sciences rested on metaphysical foundations.[22] Yet Kant's thesis that knowable, physical phenomena were grounded in a realm of unknowable, supersensible noumena was developed by Romantic thinkers in ways that enabled this metaphysical realm to become accessible and intelligible. The post-Kantian move inaugurated by Fichte, who held that the material world is posited by an unconscious act of the 'productive imagination' (*produktive Einbildungskraft*), was extended by Schelling in the characteristically Romantic brand of science known as *Naturphilosophie*. Schelling treated the natural phenomena studied by conventional science as products of prior generative powers that informed both mind and nature. In *Von der Weltseele* (1798), he reduced Kant's primal polarity of attraction and repulsion to that of weight (*Schwere*) and Light (*Licht*). From these, all the other polar forces found in nature were derived: magnetism, electricity, chemical reactions, organic and even psychical activities.

Naturphilosophie offered useful metaphysical models for Romantic writers who were inclined towards the sciences. Jean Paul regarded Schelling's entire system as an extended 'magnetic metaphor',[23] and Coleridge – who acknowledged attending Humphry Davy's lectures on chemistry for the purpose of adding to his supply of metaphors – found a rich poetic vocabulary in *Naturphilosophie*. After 1818, however, he became increasingly critical of this approach for being too abstract and pantheistic, and for its atheistic tendency to absolutize nature, which he instead envisioned as a structured hierarchy mediated by a system of symbolic representations.[24] Goethe also insisted upon a carefully differentiated system of symbolic representations of nature, distinguishing four linguistic modes of expressing nature: 'physically real' descriptions based on natural phenomena, 'aesthetically ideal' descriptions using figures of speech, 'mnemonic' references based on arbitrary relations, and finally,

---

[22] Immanuel Kant, *Metaphysische Anfangsgründe der Naturwissenschaft* (Riga: Hartknoch, 1786). Compare Coleridge's statement that 'A system of Science *presupposes* – a system of Philosophy' (autograph notebook no. 28 f21v; cited by Trevor H. Levere, *Poetry realized in nature*, Cambridge University Press, 1981, p. 4). Elsewhere, Coleridge echoed Schelling's objections to Kant's philosophy; see Raimonda Modiano, *Coleridge and the concept of nature*, Tallahassee, FL: Florida State University Press, 1985, pp. 153–60.
[23] *Jean Pauls Sämmtliche Werke*, E. Berend (ed.), Weimar, 1960, vol. IV: p. 166.
[24] Modiano notes 'Coleridge's insistence that a concept of mediation . . . be part of a viable system of nature' (*Coleridge*, p. 182), and his belief that 'if nature is to approximate at all the inner life of the Absolute, its grammar must include a system of symbolic expression' (p. 186).

mathematical descriptions based on intuitions that are 'in the highest sense identical with appearances'.[25]

Although Goethe's early awareness of the role of metaphors in scientific study has been hailed as a brilliant anticipation of the views of twentieth-century philosophers of science,[26] other, more identifiably Romantic writers also recognized the essential role of models as theoretical tools in science. Novalis envisioned nature as a system of cipher-writing (*Chiffernschrift*)[27] whose secrets could be detected by geologists and others trained in the sciences. His fragment *Die Lehrlinge zu Saïs* (1802) was intended to be 'ein ächtsinnbildlicher, Naturroman' ['a truly symbolic novel of nature'].[28] And the protagonist of his fragmentary novel *Heinrich von Ofterdingen* (1802), as Ralph Freedman has shown, is a passive, symbolic hero who 'enacts in fictional terms the main procedures of the early romantic dialectic' whereby 'self and non-self ultimately obliterate one another and, as the outcome of an infinite process, are transformed into the absolute self'.[29] The fact that Novalis's poetic and philosophical discourse is more symbolic and abstract than most of his fellow Romantics is understandable, considering that he followed Leibniz and Kant in their conviction that scientific knowledge was based on the model of mathematics: 'If one could only explain to people that language behaves like mathematical formulas – they form a world of their own, they play only with themselves, express nothing but their own wonderful nature, and for this very reason they are expressive, just because of this they mirror the strange interplay of objects.'[30] Instead of following the *Naturphilosophen* in reducing scientific thought, and even the forces of nature themselves, to a primal polarity, Novalis proposed that Schelling's dualist *binome* be replaced with an irreducible *infinitome*.[31] Such a plan is evident in Novalis's major imaginative works which consist of a multiplicity of voices and perspectives that all seem to be interrelated.

Besides organic, mineralogical and mathematical models, Romantic writers also found a crucial textual model in the Bible. Indeed, Friedrich

---

[25] Johann Wolfgang von Goethe, *Die Schriften zur Naturwissenschaft* (Leopoldina-Ausgabe), K. Lothar Wolf *et al.* (eds.), Weimar: Hermann Böhlaus Nachfolger, 1947–, Abt. I, XI: 56–7.

[26] Thus Fink (*Goethe's history of science*, pp. 46, 86–7) notes that present-day critics of scientific discourse like Max Black and Thomas Kuhn 'seem to have come to the same point to which Goethe arrived after a lifetime of observing and doing science, to that point, when we realize that the language of science and the "acts" of nature are not identical', and 'that science and poetry share tropological properties of language'.

[27] Novalis, *Schriften*, I: 79.

[28] 23 February 1800 letter to Tieck (Novalis, *Schriften*, IV: 323).

[29] Ralph Freedman, *The lyrical novel*, Princeton, NJ: Princeton University Press, 1963, p. 19.

[30] Novalis, *Schriften*, II: 672. Lorenz Oken also stressed the primacy of mathematics in the major fields of knowledge; see Brown, *German Romanticism*, pp. 19–20.

[31] Novalis, *Schriften*, III: 432; see John Neubauer, *Novalis*, Boston, MA: Twayne, 1980, p. 36.

Schlegel's tautological definition of the novel as 'a romantic book' ('Ein Roman ist ein romantisches Buch'[32]) could be revised for many of his fellow Romantics for whom the Bible was *the* Romantic book. Moreover, while Scripture was seen by writers like Schlegel and Blake as the basis for a new Romantic or revolutionary religion, it provided Novalis and Coleridge with a model for scientific inquiry. Coleridge based his philosophical cosmogony on Genesis by relating the various stages of creation to the hierarchy of powers proposed by the *Naturphilosophen*. Novalis envisioned his encyclopedic project – the *'Allgemeines brouillon'*, based on his mining studies at Freiberg – as 'a scientific bible, a real and ideal model [*Muster*], and the seed of all books'.[33] Such Romantic uses of the Bible for 'scientific' purposes – recently revived in the fad of seeking out hidden scriptural messages with computers[34] – stand in sharp contrast to Goethe's more sober interest in biblical history and criticism, and his attempts to distinguish historic fact from poetic symbolism in the case of specific episodes in Scripture.[35]

Scientific ideologies

While the *Naturphilosophen* provided a philosophical rationale for key Romantic concepts like organic form and dynamic polarities, they are frequently ridiculed for their metaphysical speculations and their unrestrained use of language.[36] Instead of disclosing new factual knowledge supported by experiment, they proposed fanciful analogies based on their assumptions that a single developmental tendency informs nature (the genetic view that was easily extended to poetry and the other arts as organic creations), and that all animals are based on a single plan (the structural view that proved less adaptable to the arts). Their most striking analogies involved biogenetic parallels such as Schubert's and J. F. Blumenbach's sense of a correspondence between the course of human history and the history of the earth,[37] or Lorenz Oken's, J. F. Meckel's and, later, Ernst Haeckel's attempts to relate the stages of embryonic

[32] Friedrich Schlegel, *Kritische Friedrich-Schlegel-Ausgabe*, ed. Ernst Behler, Paderborn: Schöningh, 1958–79, II: 335.
[33] Novalis, *Schriften*, III: 363.
[34] See Michael Drosnin, *The Bible code*, New York: Simon & Schuster, 1997.
[35] Thus his 'exegetic experiment', as Fink calls it, to determine the precise length of time that the Israelites wandered in the desert after the exodus from Egypt (*Goethe's history of science*, p. 62).
[36] See H. A. M. Snelders, 'Romanticism and Naturphilosophie and the inorganic natural sciences 1797–1840', *Studies in Romanticism* 9, no. 3 (Summer 1970), pp. 193–215.
[37] See Nicholas A. Rupke, 'Caves, fossils, and the history of the earth', in Andrew Cunningham and Nicholas Jardine, *Romanticism and the sciences*, Cambridge University Press, 1990, pp. 241–59.

development of higher animals to the series of adult forms of lower animals which appeared to be their evolutionary ancestors.[38] Today these
views are generally considered scientifically untenable if not bizarre. Yet
critics of *Naturphilosophie* who would deny its scientific importance under-
estimate the compelling power of its speculations. The notion that ontogeny
recapitulates phylogeny – that the organism's embryological development
parallels the species' evolutionary history – became an accepted doctrine
in nineteenth-century thought.[39] Perceptions of a developmental parallel
between individual and species are evident in Romantic 'culture theories'
and *Bildungsromane*.[40] Biologists are still intrigued by the idea of neoteny,
a corollary of recapitulation theory that suggests that species evolve by
retaining the juvenile features of their ancestors. Wordsworth's poetic
conceit that 'The Child is father of the Man' may prove to be scientifically
valid in a way he couldn't have foreseen.[41]

   While historians of science continue to debate whether the few major
discoveries made by investigators associated with the Romantic movement – electromagnetism by the Danish physicist Hans Christian Oersted,
electrochemistry by Davy (and, some have claimed, Johann Wilhelm
Ritter, who in any case discovered ultra-violet rays) – were inspired by,
or made in spite of, the speculative philosophy of Kant and Schelling,
literary scholars can be expected to pursue their inquiries into the impact
of scientific developments on individual Romantic writers.[42] As illuminating as such discussions are, they often overlook a fundamental distinction
between the natural and the human sciences – a distinction that the
romantics inadvertently announced in their writings, even as they
sought to affirm their premonition of an underlying unity between nature
and mind. Typically, the natural sciences are assumed to be exact and
predictable, while the human sciences are inexact and nonpredictable,
if, indeed, they are sciences at all.[43] As that precursor of Romanticism,

[38] Stephen Jay Gould gives a useful survey of theories of development proposed by the
    'Naturphilosophen' in *Ontogeny and phylogeny*, Cambridge, MA: Harvard University
    Press, 1977, pp. 38–47.
[39] Not only did the idea of recapitulation withstand an early attack by Carl Ernst von Baer in
    1828, but it went on to flourish in the wake of Darwin's evolutionary theory; under the
    sponsorship of Louis Agassiz it gained acceptance in the United States, and continued to
    be taught in science textbooks until the end of the century.
[40] See Fink, 'Ontogeny recapitulates phylogeny', pp. 91ff.
[41] See Stephen Jay Gould, 'The child as man's real father', in *Ever since Darwin*, New York:
    Norton, 1977, pp. 63–9.
[42] See studies by Ault, de Almeida, Grabo, Nisbet, Stephenson and Wyatt. Wylie addresses
    the question of whether Coleridge's early scientific interests contributed to or detracted
    from his poetic writing, and takes a somewhat different view of Coleridge's anti-
    Newtonianism than Levere.
[43] Cf. Michel Foucault's explanation in *The order of things* (New York: Random House,
    1970) that the human sciences 'are not sciences at all; the configuration that defines their
    positivity and gives them their roots in the modern *episteme* at the same time makes it

Giambattista Vico, maintained in the *New science*, the only objects that human beings can hope to know with any certainty and completeness are the artifacts and institutions that they themselves have made. As a divine creation, the natural world is beyond our ken and should be approached, not by 'rational metaphysics' which 'teaches that man becomes all things by understanding them', but by 'imaginative metaphysics' which 'shows that man becomes all things by *not* understanding them'.[44] Imaginative metaphysics is a primitive, mythic science, an interim form of knowledge based on poetic tropes and psychic defences that, in the absence of demonstrable, causal explanations of natural phenomena, provide provisional meaning. In our own time, Harold Bloom has concisely expressed this Vichian insight in his observation that 'poetry is born of our ignorance of causes',[45] while Georges Canguilhem has updated Vico's imaginative metaphysics with the concept of 'scientific ideology'. This refers to 'explanatory systems', speculative insights that fill the inevitable gaps in scientific knowledge. Scientific ideologies both precede 'the institution of science' in a given domain, and are 'preceded by a science in an adjunct domain that falls obliquely within the ideology's field of view'.[46]

The concept of scientific ideology helps us to recognize Romanticism as a transitional stage between periods of institutionalized science. Romanticism's transitional status is most apparent with respect to biology, evolutionary theory and psychology. In the absence of a developed science of biology founded on cell theory (which only became possible after 1829 with the invention of a more powerful microscope),[47] of a Darwinian account of evolution based on natural selection (which could only be formulated after Cuvier demonstrated the reality of extinction, and after his own teleological view of organic development was discredited[48]) and of a dynamic view of the unconscious as a realm of repressed desires (which could only receive serious consideration after psychiatry gained medical credibility at the end of the nineteenth century), Romanticism can be said to have sponsored such scientific ideologies as organicism, developmentalism,

impossible for them to be sciences; and if it is then asked why they assumed that title, it is sufficient to recall that it pertains' to the archaeological definition of their roots that they summon and receive the transference of models borrowed from the sciences (p. 366).
44 *The new science of Giambattista Vico*, Thomas Goddard Bergin and Max Harold Fisch (eds.), 1948; rev. edn, Ithaca, NY: Cornell University Press, 1984, p. 130.
45 Harold Bloom, *Poetry and repression*, New Haven, CT: Yale University Press, 1976, p. 5.
46 Georges Canguilhem, *Ideology and rationality in the history of the life sciences*, Arthur Goldhammer (trans.), Cambridge, MA: The MIT Press, 1988, p. 38.
47 See L. S. Jacyna, 'Romantic thought and the origins of cell theory', in *Romanticism and the sciences*, Cunningham and Jardine, pp. 161–8.
48 See Joel Black, 'The hermeneutics of extinction: denial and discovery in scientific literature', *Comparative criticism* 13, E. S. Shaffer (ed.), Cambridge University Press, 1991, pp. 147–69.

vital materialism and dipsychism.[49] The ultimate aspiration for many Romantics (as it continues to be for some of today's scientists) was to unify organic and psychic processes in a single conceptual system. The relation between Romantic criticism and the sciences can be clarified by briefly reviewing the situation of biology and psychology at the beginning of the nineteenth century, since the models employed in these new disciplines also informed Romantic criticism and poetics.

The biological model

When Michel Foucault declared that 'up to the end of the eighteenth century, . . . life does not exist: only living beings',[50] he meant that the concept of life was unthinkable in the classifying systems that prevailed in the Classical age. In contrast to eighteenth-century natural histories that classified every species of flora and fauna on the basis of fairly arbitrary criteria, and that supposed that living beings were simply the products of preformed germs, the beginning of the nineteenth century saw the appearance of the new term 'biology', coined by Lamarck in 1802 and described by Gottfried Treviranus in the same year as 'the Science of Life'. Rather than enumerate the fully developed features of organisms, this Romantic science[51] sought to uncover the immanent principles or underlying laws that determined their development in the first place; this was Coleridge's purpose in his *Theory of life*. Consequently, Foucault associates Romanticism with 'the reign of the biological model (man, his psyche, his group, his society, the language he speaks – all these exist in the Romantic period as living beings and in so far as they were, in fact, alive; their mode of being is organic and is analysed in terms of function)'.[52]

Romantic naturalists scoured nature in search of quintessential biological models.[53] Goethe's concepts in the 1780s of the *Urpflanze* and the *Urtier* were attempts to formulate a single ideal plan for the vast diversity of flowering plants and vertebrate animals. Yet even as he sought an ideal type in nature – somewhat like the antiquated concept of the ideal model

---

[49] Regarding 'vital materialism,' see Timothy Lenoir, 'Kant, Blumenbach, and vital materialism in German biology', *Isis* 71 (1980), pp. 77–108. Not only did Romanticism sponsor these scientific ideologies, but it has itself been identified as an ideology with its own poetic and political agenda; see Jerome J. McGann, *The Romantic ideology*, Chicago, IL: University of Chicago Press, 1983.

[50] Foucault, *Order*, p. 160.

[51] Cf. Hermione de Almeida's reference to biology as 'a discipline that could have arisen and flourished only in Romantic thought' (*Romantic medicine and John Keats*, New York: Oxford University Press, 1991, p. 63).

[52] Foucault, *Order*, p. 359.

[53] See Timothy Lenoir, 'Morphotypes and the historical–genetic method in romantic Biology', in *Romanticism and the sciences*, Cunningham and Jardine, pp. 119–29; p. 122.

in the arts[54] – Goethe resisted the inevitable associations with Plato's transcendent ideas. In his literary writing he always tried to achieve a certain degree of individualization, as in the characters depicted in *Wilhelm Meisters Lehrjahre*. Nevertheless, Novalis insisted that this novel had been constructed according to a 'variational principle' whereby all the characters were variations of a single type – a principle he planned to demonstrate in *Heinrich von Ofterdingen*, his own 'anti-*Meister*'.[55]

As a primal form or image, the *Urbild* is a strange combination of what Clifford Geertz has called models *for* and models *of* reality. Somewhat like a genetic programme, it achieves the 'communication of pattern' in living beings by incorporating a fundamental, reproducible code or plan. But while a code is not reducible to, and does not resemble, the recognizable pattern it generates, the *Urbild* is a purely symbolic representation whose function is 'not to provide sources of information in terms of which other processes can be patterned, but to represent those patterned processes as such, to express their structure in an alternative medium'.[56] Goethe struggled with the problem, especially after Schiller told him in 1794 that his sketch of a 'symbolic plant' was not an actual experience but an idea ('das ist keine Erfahrung, das ist eine Idee')[57] – a troubling compliment for Goethe who wanted to dissociate himself from all abstract theorizing. His eventual solution was to introduce the concept of the *Urphänomen* in the *Farbenlehre* (1810). Unlike ideal models and archetypal organisms, primal phenomena *were* observable; like Coleridge's 'central phenomenon',[58] they enabled the scientist to seek the idea in experience,[59] and to

---

[54] Goethe left unspecified just 'how closely' the 'scientific aspiration . . . to master the whole . . . is tied to the creative and imitative urges' (*Die Schriften*, Abt. 1, IX: 7). Although Fink believes that it was Goethe's 'generalized approach to a definition of "type" ' in his writings on morphology in the mid-1790s 'which marks [his] transition from romantic to classical science' (*Goethe's history of science*, p. 24), one wonders whether 'Romantic science' precedes a Classical phase, or whether, like Romantic art, it follows such a phase.

[55] For a detailed discussion of the Romantics' (chiefly Friedrich Schlegel's and Novalis's) ambivalent reception of Goethe's novel, see Ernst Behler, '*Wilhelm Meisters Lehrjahre* and the poetic unity of the novel in early German romanticism', in *Goethe's narrative fiction: the Irvine Goethe symposium*, William J. Lillyman (ed.), Berlin: de Gruyter, 1983, pp. 110–27.

[56] *The interpretation of cultures: selected essays by Clifford Geertz*, New York: Basic Books, 1973, p. 94. Henri Ellenberger inadvertently uses Geertz's terminology when he notes that Goethe 'believed in the *Urpflanze* (a primordial plant) as a model for all plants, of which each botanic species would partake to some degree' (*The discovery of the unconscious*, New York: Basic Books, 1970, p. 203).

[57] Goethe, *Die Schriften zur Naturwissenschaft*, Abt. 1, IX: 81.

[58] Levere finds Coleridge's concept to be 'perhaps even closer than the *Urphänomen* to the Platonic tradition' since it 'was at once phenomenon and symbol of an idea, embodying a law', rather than a mere representation (*Poetry*, pp. 93–4).

[59] Goethe, *Die Schriften zur Naturwissenschaft*, Abt. 1, X: 277. See Nisbet, *Goethe and the scientific tradition*, pp. 39–43.

perceive the general in the particular, 'not as dream and shadow, but as the living, instantaneous revelation of the impenetrable'.[60]

Despite the superficial resemblance between Goethe's *Urphänomen* and the archetypes of the *Naturphilosophen* (e.g., Richard Owen's 'typical vertebra' as the basis of animal structure[61] and Oken's crystal as a geological archetype), Goethe remained critical of speculative, static forms that purported to explain complex natural processes. His morphology relied instead on the organic concept of formation or *Bildung* to accomplish the more modest task of describing observable phenomena. Ultimately, Goethe came to regard the scientific conundrums of his time as discursive problems of symbolization and communication. In 1830, he characterized the Cuvier–Geoffroy debate in French zoology as a crisis resulting from a conflict of metaphors,[62] and sought

> to show how word usage in French discourse, indeed, in the polemics of admirable men, leads to significant misunderstandings. We think we are speaking in pure prose and are already speaking tropologically [*Man glaubt in reiner Prosa zu reden und man spricht schon tropisch*], the tropes are applied differently, are used in a related sense, and in this way the quarrel becomes endless and the riddle insoluble.[63]

To be sure, Goethe had himself made ample use of metaphors as a way of making analogies between the human and natural realms, referring to a magnet as a hermaphrodite, and to colours as the 'deeds and sufferings' (*Taten und Leiden*) of light, while in his 1809 novel *Die Wahlverwandschaften* he modelled human relations on chemical reactions.[64] Yet his sensitivity to language enabled him to understand what escaped most of his scientific colleagues – that the great crises in the history of science were to some degree an effect of discursive limitations and inadequacies. In short, Goethe may be said to have combined a topological with a tropological insight – a recognition of the need in science for figural (visual and experiential as opposed to abstract, metric) models, and figurative (verbal and metaphorical as opposed to exact, mathematical) language.

---

[60] Goethe (*Maximen und Reflexionen*, no. 314), *Sämtliche Werke*, XVII: 775.

[61] See Philip F. Rehbock, 'Transcendental anatomy', in *Romanticism and the sciences*, Cunningham and Jardine, pp. 144–60, and Ronald H. Brady, 'Form and cause in Goethe's morphology', in *Goethe and the sciences*, Frederick Amrine, Francis J. Zucker and Harvey Wheeler (eds.), Dordrecht: Reidel, 1987, pp. 257–300; esp. pp. 262–7.

[62] See Fink, *Goethe's history of science*, p. 89. After 1810, Fink notes, Goethe 'reduced most observations on science to questions about language' (p. 44).

[63] Goethe, *Die Schriften zur Naturwissenschaft*, Abt. 1, x: 398; cited by Fink (*Goethe's history of science*, p. 44), who remarks that 'Goethe's perception of the linguistic basis' of 'paradigm changes in the history of science . . . seems to be unique' (p. 87).

[64] See Nisbet, *Goethe and the scientific tradition*, p. 16.

Models of the mind: the Romantic unconscious

As a 'Science of Life', biology lasted only for the thirty years or so that investigators considered the organism the basic unit of life. When biology came into its own as a modern scientific discipline – when the organism was superseded by the cell, the whole by the part, as an object of study – it ceased to be a Romantic science. Romantic medicine has been viewed as 'a period of transition between the birth of the clinic and the discovery of the cell', a transition that is itself embedded in the larger 'change in the prevailing paradigm from theoretical physics to practical biology that occurred at the turn of the century'.[65] More broadly still, the Romantics were poised midway between Newton and Freud, and the discovery of the life sciences was a pivotal point of transition between the established physical sciences and the emerging human sciences.

Beyond their interest in the new science of biology which treated life as an *object* of study, the Romantics introduced a self-reflective approach to knowledge in which human beings (or human consciousness) were themselves the *subject* of various biohistories. Lacking a determinate object that conformed to universal laws as in the physical sciences, the human sciences were concerned with individual subjects, each of whom was different and unique. These emerging areas of research relied on a new kind of model, on 'historical hypotheses',[66] as a way of defining themselves as academic disciplines. The groundwork for the human sciences was laid during the Romantic period: by Kant, Blumenbach and Alexander von Humboldt in anthropology; by Christian Gottlieb Heyne, Friedrich Schlegel and Friedrich Creuzer in comparative mythology; by Herder, the Grimm brothers and Wilhelm von Humboldt in philology and linguistics; by the Schlegel brothers in comparative literature; by Friedrich Schleiermacher in hermeneutics. But the most significant human science inaugurated by Romantic writers may well have been psychology.

Besides celebrating such titanic male figures in classical mythology as Prometheus and Hyperion, Romantic poets rehabilitated the more modest figure of Psyche whom they reinvested with a new significance. No longer a symbol of the ancient philosophical and religious concept of the soul, Psyche was associated with the new biological concept of life and with emerging psychological theories of the mind. Keats's reference to this 'latest born' deity in his 'Ode to Psyche' (1819) suggests this figure's paradoxical nature as a personification of the human spirit of sceptical

[65] De Almeida, *Romantic medicine*, p. 3.
[66] See Paul Dumouchel, 'The role of fiction in evolutionary biology', *SubStance* 71/2 (1993), pp. 321–33; p. 323.

inquiry that brought about the gods' decline. Yet even this view of Psyche still accords with an Enlightenment view of the mind as a conscious activity. The Romantics' great critical achievement – as part of their effort to overcome the Enlightenment dialectic that set myth and reason in opposition to one another – was their investigation a century before Freud into the mind's vast unconscious processes.

The Romantics did not discover the unconscious; the mind's dark side had been known in a variety of forms since antiquity, and was conceptualized in the eighteenth century as the magnetic fluids and animal electricity which the mesmerists supposedly manipulated in an early form of hypnotism. But it was during the Romantic period that the role and range of unconscious operations in human life and artistic creation became widely recognized.[67] Schelling is generally credited with reformulating the neoplatonic concept of a universal soul in the post-Cartesian proposition that nature and human beings are informed by a single organizing principle which only attains consciousness *in* human beings.[68] In Albert Béguin's words, 'the unconscious of the Romantics is neither a sum of the old forgotten or repressed contents of the conscious (Freud), nor a larval conscious (Leibniz), nor even an obscure and dangerous region (Herder). It is the very root of the human being, its point of entry into the vast process of nature.'[69] In this expanded sense, the unconscious became what Foucault has called 'the most fundamental object' of the human sciences; it 'is not simply a problem within the human sciences which they can be thought of as encountering by chance in their steps; it is a problem that is ultimately coextensive with their very existence'.[70]

Beyond discerning the profound effect of the unconscious on human existence, the Romantics discovered that the unconscious had a structure – a discovery that not only informed their imaginative and critical writings, but was essential for establishing psychology and psychiatry as genuine sciences. As the Romantics had not been deterred by Kant's insistence on the unknowability of the noumenal world, so they were not put off by his denial that psychology, or a science of 'internal sensibility', was possible.[71] The most complete Romantic theory of the unconscious was Carl Gustav Carus's 1846 study *Psyche, zur Entwicklungsgeschichte der Seele*, which describes the soul's development from unconsciousness to

---

[67] Lancelot Law Whyte, *The unconscious before Freud*, 1960; rpt. London: Friedmann, 1978, p. 125; Albert Béguin, *L'âme romantique et le rêve*, 1939; rpt. Paris: Corti, 1946, p. 70.

[68] Claiming that Romantic writers did not discover the unconscious *per se*, but rather called attention to the diverse, unconscious functions of an embodied mind, Alan Richardson has recently argued that the Romantics were less the forerunners of psychoanalysis than of modern brain science. ('Romanticism and the unconscious: building a mind', paper presented 23 January 1998 at the American Conference on Romanticism in Athens, Georgia.)

[69] Béguin, *L'âme*, p. 76.   [70] Foucault, *Order*, pp. 372, 364.

[71] Kant, *Metaphysische Anfangsgründe*, p. x.

consciousness as a biological rather than a mental or spiritual process. (Carus was a physician as well as a painter and theorist.) Like Keats's 'latest born' Psyche, Carus's consciousness only evolved late in the individual's development, after the vital unconscious phase of embryonic existence (when the 'formative consciousness' emerged that regulated organic growth), and well after an even longer and earlier pre-embryonic period (during which the individual existed as a cell inside the mother's body). Clearly, Carus went much further than Freud – who read him – was to do in tracing unconscious impulses to very early stages of human development.

As unscientific as such early psychological speculations may be, they refute the popular notion that the discovery of the structure of the unconscious 'only began in the twentieth century'.[72] Such a view neglects what Henri Ellenberger calls 'the first dynamic psychiatry' of the period 1775 to 1900, during which 'a new model of the human mind was evolved . . . based on the duality of conscious and unconscious psychism'.[73] In Harold Bloom's view, the conflictual model of the mind developed by Blake not only anticipated Freud by a century, but surpassed him in subtlety: 'Blake allows . . . for two very different ideas of conflict in an individual consciousness, one between id and restraining ego against superego, the other between active and passive aspects of the true self.'[74] Another example of the dynamic model was G. H. Schubert's description of the individual as a 'double star' with two centres – the ego or individual soul, and a consciousness of Self (*Selbstbewusstsein*) or World Soul to which the individual gains access in certain 'cosmic moments'.[75] The phenomenon of 'dipsychism' not only informs the novels of Jean Paul (*Flegeljahre*) and E. T. A. Hoffmann (*Kater Murr*), but has been used to explain the Romantics' own creative processes. One early twentieth-century critic theorized that Novalis had two personalities – a normal, mundane self and a poetic, visionary self – that had developed alongside each other since he was a child.[76]

Today scholars are less likely to find a contradiction between Novalis's supposedly 'normal', professional life and his poetic vocation,[77] especially

---

[72] Whyte, *The unconscious*, p. 63. Cf. Jean Baudrillard's claim that 'the unconscious was created at the same time as psychoanalysis' (*Seduction*, Brian Singer (trans.), New York: St Martin's Press, 1990, p. 80), and n. 68 above.

[73] Ellenberger, *Discovery*, p. 111.

[74] Harold Bloom, *Blake's apocalypse*, 2nd edn, New York: Anchor, 1965, pp. 263–4.

[75] Ellenberger, *Discovery*, pp. 205, 729.

[76] Jean-Edouard Spenlé, *Essais sur l'idéalisme romantique en Allemagne*, Paris: Hachette, 1904. The related concept in Romantic psychology of cryptonesia was used to explain cases of literary plagiarism (see Ellenberger, *Discovery*, p. 170).

[77] While Hans Mayer viewed Novalis's professional and poetic activities as contradictory, later critics like Gerhard Schulz did not (Neubauer, *Novalis*, p. 173 n. 1). Behler (pp. 125–6) notes that in *Heinrich von Ofterdingen* the 'alternating between the worlds of the miraculous and common life, the inner self and the exterior world, is Novalis' literary technique of symbolizing the cohesion of those two spheres'.

since his profession as mining engineer and administrator was avidly studied by many other young writers between 1790 and 1820 in pre-industrial Germany.[78] Novalis's advanced training under Abraham Gottlob Werner at the famous Freiberg *Bergakademie* did not keep him from referring in his literary works to the archaic notion that metals are quasi-organic materials that actually 'grow' inside the earth's womb – a belief that 'continued to function powerfully as a governing metaphor' in the literature of the time.[79] This view was explicitly formulated by Schubert, Novalis's fellow student at Freiberg, who located the 'kingdom of metals . . . at the boundaries of the two worlds' of the inorganic and the organic, and ultimately of the unconscious and the conscious.[80] As a literal 'deep structure', the mine provided the Romantics with a key metaphor for the unconscious that superseded the classical metaphor of the underworld inhabited by the shades of the dead. From the Romantics' mining motifs to Freud's archaeological metaphor, the unconscious has been routinely conceptualized in subterranean images. And since Freud, the purely metaphorical nature of the unconscious has been increasingly acknowledged.[81]

Some of the most striking insights into the unconscious that were later developed in psychoanalytic theory can be found in the Romantics' imaginative writings. One thinks of Coleridge, whom Kathleen Coburn credits with inventing the word 'subconsciousness';[82] Blake, to whom Harold Bloom attributes 'a profundity of schematized psychological insight comparable to Freud's';[83] Goethe, whom Jung declared to be preoccupied with the unconscious in the second part of *Faust*; E. T. A. Hoffmann, whose tale 'Die Bergwerke zu Falun' was based on an incident in Schubert's *Ansichten*; Schelling, whose definition of the 'uncanny' as 'the name for everything that ought to have remained . . . secret and hidden but has come to light'[84] was – along with Hoffmann's story 'Der Sandmann' – a key source for Freud's 1919 essay 'The "Uncanny" '; and Edgar Allan Poe,

[78] Novalis's contemporaries who studied mining included Clemens Brentano, Eichendorff, Heinrich Steffens, Theodor Körner, Alexander von Humboldt, Franz von Baader and Gotthilf Heinrich Schubert. While not trained in mining, Goethe participated in efforts in 1776 to reopen copper and silver mines in the Ilmenau valley.

[79] Theodore Ziolkowski, *German Romanticism and its institutions*, Princeton, NJ: Princeton University Press, 1990, p. 31.

[80] Gotthilf Heinrich Schubert, *Ansichten von der Nachtseite der Naturwissenschaft* (Dresden: Arnold, 1808), p. 201; cited by Ziolkowski, who calls Schubert's work 'the standard textbook of Romantic *Naturphilosophie*' (*German Romanticism*, p. 31).

[81] Thus Donald P. Spence has argued that Freud's unconscious is a 'free-floating metaphor' with 'a life and will of its own' (*The Freudian metaphor* (New York: Norton, 1987), p. 39).

[82] *The notebooks of Samuel Taylor Coleridge*, Kathleen Coburn (ed.), Princeton, NJ: Princeton University Press, 1957–), notes to II: 2915 and IV: 4540.

[83] Harold Bloom and Lionel Trilling, *Romantic poetry and prose*, New York: Oxford University Press, 1973, p. 10.

[84] *The standard edition of the complete psychological works of Sigmund Freud*, James Strachey (trans.), London: The Hogarth Press, 1958, XVII: 224.

whose tale 'The Purloined Letter' provided Jacques Lacan with an exemplary case for his thesis that the unconscious is structured like a language.

Besides their speculations regarding the structure of the unconscious, the Romantics anticipated psychoanalysis and the other human sciences through the genetic approach they brought to scientific study. We have seen that as the ideal organic types behind Goethe's idea of metamorphosis, the *Urpflanze* and *Urtier* themselves underwent a transformation in his thinking, eventually becoming the *Urphänomen* in his work on colour theory. Goethe used this term to refer to certain primal phenomena observable in nature such as magnetism and colour, but he also traced his own scientific interest in colour back to a 'primal phenomenon': instead of examining what happened to light passing through a prism as Newton had described, Goethe looked through the prism and was struck by the bright colours that appeared along the borders of objects.[85] In effect, Goethe traced his own scientific knowledge back to a primal scene, much as Freud would do in the case of sexual knowledge. 'What are the Oedipus complex, the murder of the primordial father', asks Ellenberger, 'if not *Urphänomene*, which are postulated for mankind as a whole and described in individuals under their various metamorphoses? To Freud, it did not matter whether the murder of the primordial father had actually been perpetrated or not, no more than it did concern Goethe whether the *Urpflanze* actually existed as a botanical species. Important only were the relationships that could be deduced from it in regard to human culture, religion, the social order, and the psychology of the individual'.[86] The *Urphantasie* of Freud – who is said to have been inspired to become a medical student after reading Goethe's writings on nature – is the modern, psychoanalytic equivalent of Goethe's concept of the *Urphänomen* in the natural sciences, which Ellenberger calls the 'basic concept of Romantic philosophy'.[87] In describing primal fantasies as a phylogenetic inheritance that transcends the individual's own experience, Freud represents the culmination of the Romantic tradition of German science that aimed at 'the unfolding of a generative history of nature through an "original intuition"'.[88] It is not

[85] See Fink, *Goethe's history of science*, pp. 32, 35.
[86] Ellenberger, *Discovery*, p. 204.   [87] *Ibid.*, p. 203.
[88] Cunningham and Jardine, 'Introduction', *Romanticism and the sciences*, p. 5. Many intellectual historians see Freud continuing the romantic project. While Ellenberger declares that 'hardly a single concept of Freud or Jung [has] not been anticipated by the philosophy of nature and Romantic medicine' (p. 205), Michel de Certeau finds Freud resuming the Romantic critique of the Enlightenment concept of the individual. Whereas Enlightenment philosophy and positivism had relegated the study of the passions in the nineteenth century to a 'literary specialization', Freudianism 'returns relevancy to passions, to rhetoric, and to literature' by reincorporating them into a scientific discourse from which they had been excluded (*Heterologies*, Brian Massumi (trans.), Minneapolis, MN: University of Minnesota Press, 1986, pp. 25–6). Yet some Romantic writers were interested in the sciences, and investigated the passions in a scientific as well as a literary mode.

surprising that psychoanalysis's numerous critics in the late twentieth century have recycled the same arguments that were earlier used to repudiate Romantic *Naturphilosophie* as a pseudo-science.

Models of sexuality

If modern science has a primal scene, it is undoubtedly the legend of Newton's discovery of gravitation after witnessing an apple fall in an English garden. In a profound joke, Byron links the tale about the falling fruit that inaugurated the scientific revolution to the story of the fatal fruit that attracted Eve's notice in another garden and that precipitated humanity's fall from grace. The line 'Man fell with apples, and with apples rose' (*Don Juan*, x.ii.1) suggests that Newton's discovery and modern science may provide humanity with the means to overcome the first fall in Eden.[89] Yet Byron's notorious irony, the anti-Newtonianism of contemporaries like Goethe and Blake, and the intellectual hubris of figures like Faust and Frankenstein suggest a Romantic anticipation of the sceptical modern view that 'advances' in scientific knowledge may be plunging humanity into a far more calamitous 'Second Fall'.[90]

In Genesis and Milton's *Paradise lost*, the primal scene in Eden was concerned less with scientific knowledge in any developed sense than with a primitive act of sexual awareness. The title of Byron's poem makes it clear he had the rake's sexual progress in mind as well as the scientist's cognitive advancement. (So does the quip that the celibate Newton was 'the sole mortal who could grapple, / Since Adam – with a fall – or with an apple' (x.i.7–8) – or, it is implied, with a woman since Eve was typically blamed for the fall.) Sexual knowledge is more than a metaphor for scientific knowledge; as scripture, literature, and science (Genesis, Milton and Freud) all attest, it is, quite simply, the earliest form of knowledge.

Given orthodox religion's traditional subordination of the knowledge and pleasure associated with sexuality to the divine purpose of procreation, the act of becoming 'one flesh' could only be justified in a non-erotic sense as a necessary means of fulfilling the commandment to be fruitful and multiply. In Romantic *Naturphilosophie* too, sexuality was often regarded as natural because it was productive, and cosmogony itself was described as a metaphysical act of procreation. Oken declared that

---

[89] Cf. the end of Kleist's *Über das Marionettentheater*: 'Then we would have to eat again of the tree of knowledge, in order to fall back again into the state of innocence?' 'To be sure . . . That is the last chapter in the history of the world' (*Heinrich von Kleists Werke*, Wilhelm Waetzoldt (ed.), Berlin, n.d., v: 79).
[90] Stephen Spender, *The struggle of the modern*, London: Hamish Hamilton, 1963, p. 26.

'creation itself is nothing else than a fecundating act', that 'sex was foreseen from the beginning as a sacred bond that preserves all of nature', and
that 'whoever denies sex does not grasp the mystery of the universe'.[91] The
disastrous consequences of denying the affinity between human sexual
procreation and divine creation are depicted in Mary Shelley's *Frankenstein* (1818); in the creature produced in the laboratory 'we are confronted
immediately by the displacement of God and woman from the acts of conception and birth'.[92]

Procreation and productivity, however, do not explain the importance
that the Romantics attached to sexuality. More than a metaphor, sexual
love enabled men and women to recover a lost wholeness that preceded
the division of the sexes. Jakob Böhme's theosophy was influential in this
regard, revealing the 'original' sin in Eden as a second fall following the
more significant lapse brought about when an originally androgynous
Adam sought to 'know' his female half, the divine virgin Sophia. As a
result of Adam's lust, God separated the sexes and gave them 'bestial
members [*thierische Glieder*] for propagation'.[93] In his Romantic adaptation of Böhme's schema, Franz von Baader valorized human sexual union
as the only means of recovering androgynous totality. Novalis and the
young Friedrich Schlegel depicted the androgyne as *Urphänomen*, a symbol of the ideal of wholeness and perfection that could only be experienced momentarily in erotic union, and that could only be expressed in
fragmentary forms. Coleridge envisioned a golden age when the sexes
had been nearly the same, having 'just variety enough to permit and call
forth the gentle restlessness and final union of chaste love and individual
attachment, each seeking the beloved *one* by the natural affinity of their
Beings . . .'[94] Far from regarding sexuality as lust which, through the
agency of a woman, had caused the fall of man, many Romantics envisioned an erotics of creation whereby men and women could achieve
reunion and redemption. And once sexuality was no longer stigmatized as
the earliest instance of humanity's sinful desire for (scientific) knowledge,
it could become a field of scientific investigation in its own right.

The emergence of a science of sexuality began in the seventeenth century with the discovery of egg and sperm cells, a discovery that 'marked
the beginning of a long research program to find sexual reproduction

[91] Cited in Béguin, *L'âme*, p. 67.
[92] George Levine, 'The ambiguous heritage of Frankenstein,' in *The endurance of Frankenstein*, George Levine and U. C. Knoepflmacher (eds.), Berkeley, CA: University of California Press, 1979, p. 8.
[93] Jakob Böhme, *Sämmtliche Werke*, K. W. Schiebler (ed.), Leipzig: Barth, 1922, V: 95. See
Sara Friedrichsmeyer, *The androgyne in early German Romanticism*, Bern: Peter Lang,
1983, pp. 30–1.
[94] *The collected works of Samuel Taylor Coleridge*, IV: *The friend*, I: 7.

everywhere'.[95] By the end of the century the sexual nature of plants was known, inspiring Linnaeus to refer to blossoms as 'the nuptials of the flowers' and providing him with the principle for his system of classification. Coleridge praised this system, but found that the Swedish naturalist had reduced sexuality to 'a scheme of classific and distinctive marks' and had failed to grasp the 'inner necessity of sex itself'.[96] In *The loves of the plants*, Erasmus Darwin attempted the Lucretian feat of writing a scientific treatise in poetic form, while Goethe found theories of plant sexuality vulgar.[97]

The real 'revolution in scientific views of sexuality'[98] coincided with Romanticism. Along with a sense of the pervasiveness of sexuality in nature went an awareness of the distinctiveness of the two sexes themselves. The new 'two-sex model' was readily adopted by the Romantic *Naturphilosophen* who considered 'sexual difference as one of the fundamental dichotomies of nature, an unbridgeable chasm born not of the Pythagorean opposites but of the reproductive germs themselves and the organs that produced them'.[99] While reinforcing gender stereotypes,[100] increased awareness of the fundamentally different nature of the sexes made it possible to reexamine the relation between procreation and sexual pleasure – specifically, in women – and, by the 1820s, to reject the traditional views 'that rape was incompatible with pregnancy' and that 'a woman can not conceive unless she doth consent'.[101] We can thus appreciate Kleist's perspicacity in his account of the rape of the unconscious heroine in his 1808 tale 'Die Marquise von O–'. Based on conventional medical–legal wisdom, the story's original readers would have had to conclude that the pregnant Marquise had willingly 'surrendered' herself to the Count!

While the Church's strictly functional view of intercourse as a means of propagating the species was revised by writers like Schlegel and Novalis who presented sexual relations in an erotic or mystical guise, it was not

---

[95] Thomas Laqueur, *Making sex*, Cambridge, MA: Harvard University Press, 1990, p. 172.
[96] Coleridge, *The Friend*, I: 466–7.
[97] See Adolf Portman, 'Goethe and the concept of metamorphosis', in *Goethe and the sciences*, Amrine *et al.* (eds.), pp. 133–45.
[98] Londa Schiebinger, *The mind has no sex?*, Cambridge, MA: Harvard University Press, 1989, p. 189.
[99] Laqueur, *Making sex*, p. 172.
[100] See Schiebinger's criticism of Laqueur's account of 'the reevaluation of women's reproductive organs' which is 'simply one element in a much broader revolution . . . By the 1790s, European anatomists presented the male and female body as each having a distinct telos – physical and intellectual strength for the man, motherhood for the woman' (*The mind*, pp. 190–1).
[101] Laqueur, *Making sex*, p. 162. Cf. the best-selling novel *Le médecin de Pecq* (1839) by Léon Gozlan in which a man impregnates a woman while *he* is in a somnambulic state and subsequently has no recollection of the event. A somewhat similar occurrence is found in Wilkie Collins's *The moonstone*.

religious zealots who were most opposed to Romantic views of love, or who were most obsessed with procreation. The anti-Romantic reaction was most forcefully represented, on the one hand, by Sade with his programmatic fantasies about circumventing nature's generative processes in every conceivable way, and, on the other hand, by Schopenhauer with his profound suspicion of the sexual impulse as humanity's supreme illusion, a ruse of the Will that ensured procreation and perpetuated life. These pornographic and paranoiac extremes lie at the margins of conventional Romantic views of sexuality as a creative and redemptive activity. In their radical, quasi-scientific scepticism, Sade and Schopenhauer posed a greater philosophical challenge to the Romantics' sanguine views of sexuality than any repressive religious or cultural regime.

We have seen that an array of quasi-scientific concepts – organic form, polar contraries, primal phenomena, the dynamic unconscious and the androgyne – inform the poetic and critical discourse of Romanticism. Not only do these concepts function as metaphysical models of the physical world, but they are imaginative, poetic creations in their own right. A critical reading of the Romantics needs to attend to these models which generate many of the key images found in literary texts of the period. A problem for present-day readers of Romantic texts is that we have inherited some of these same models which have influenced our ways of seeing and feeling the world, and of reading literature. What the editors of a recent collection of critical essays on the concept of 'nature' have noted is even more true for us today than it was for the Romantics: 'increasingly, scientific theories and models have been taken up precisely as cultural metaphors which have material effects in transforming "ways of seeing" and "structures of feeling" '.[102] We need to bear in mind that these scientific models, which the Romantics borrowed from the physical sciences, have become the foundation of the relatively new disciplinary fields called the human sciences. And we should not forget that one of these new fields of study was the institutionalization of literary study as an academic discipline[103] – namely, literary criticism – itself.

---

[102] *Future natural*, George Robertson *et al.* (eds.), London: Routledge, 1996, p. 4.
[103] See Philippe Lacoue-Labarthe and Jean-Luc Nancy, *The literary absolute*, New York: State University of New York Press, 1988: 'it remains to be understood why romanticism should have been the first literary movement to demand entry into the University – into universality – in order to complete itself and lose itself there at the same time and in the same movement, thereby inaugurating the entire modern history of literature in the University (or of the University in literature)' (p. 82).

7

Religion and literature

E. S. SHAFFER

The close relations between religion and literature in most societies testify to the vital role of imagination in the sphere of human values. The secular terms in which this statement is cast are characteristic of the period from the late Enlightenment critiques of religion to the various forms of nineteenth-century apologetics, although the latter may appear draped in traditional language. The secular agenda and terms still dominate current thinking. This period, then, marks a major shift in the relations between religion and literature. It can be expressed by saying that literature becomes the dominant partner; if 'religion and literature' would have expressed a clear hierarchy at the beginning of the period, it is of 'literature and religion' that we have come to speak. Criticism finds its vocation in negotiating this shift.

The critiques of the Enlightenment went to the roots of religious claims to supernatural authority, rational validity, divine inspiration of the sacred books, and historical evidence. They often employed a mocking tone, in which literary modes of satire and irony were effective persuasive tools. One of the major works scrutinizing these claims was David Hume's *Dialogues concerning natural religion* (1776), and especially the essay 'Of miracles' (1752), which demonstrated the radical incoherence of claims to miraculous supernatural events including 'prophecy' (inasmuch as natural law could not be abrogated); this represents one of the first major victories for the scientific world-view over the religious.[1] Spinoza's *Tractatus theologico-politicus* (1670), questioning the infallibility of the Scriptures and regretting 'that human commentaries are accepted as divine records'[2] (while counselling external conformity to authority), had an underground circulation throughout the eighteenth century despite condemnation of Spinoza as an 'atheist', and his arguments were absorbed into the Deist works of John Toland and Conyers Middleton. In another vein, Spinoza's *Ethics* suggested a highly abstract divine substance that to some

---

[1] David Hume, *Of Miracles*. In: *Enquiries concerning human understanding*, ed. A. Selby-Bigge. A number of eighteenth-century attempts to refute Hume's argument are reprinted in *Hume on miracles*, Stanley Tweyman (ed. with an introduction), Bristol: Thoemmes Press, 1996 [Reviews].

[2] Spinoza, *Tractatus theologico-politicus*, S. Shirley (trans.), Leiden: E. J. Brill, 1991, p. 8.

was 'atheist pantheism' (because it denied personality to the deity), but for many Romantics was to prove a permanent attraction.[3] The higher critical movement stemming from Spinoza (and gathering strength from J. S. Semler and J. G. Eichhorn to D. F. Strauss's *Life of Jesus* (1835)) asserted the appropriateness of applying secular historical scholarship to the sacred books, and sifted the biblical texts, their authorship and dating, the process of canon-making, the relationship of the canon to the apocrypha and the roots of both in the myths, legends, and literary traditions of the societies in which they were first produced. Science again entered the arena, with the hypothesis that the earth must be far older than biblical chronology allowed; geology was to be one of the major challengers to the veracity of the Bible for more than a hundred years. A geological observer commented on 'how fatal the suspicion of the high antiquity of the globe has been to the credit of the Mosaic history, and consequently to religion and morality'.[4] Kant's *Critique of pure reason* (1781) attacked the rational basis of religious concepts, challenging all the major proofs of the existence of God (the ontological, the cosmological and the physico-theological or 'Argument from Design'), the claim to a substantial 'soul' and the claim to immortality. By the use of the 'antinomies' he showed that arguments could be constructed out of theological concepts that led to contrary conclusions, between which there could be no adjudication; such theological concepts were therefore futile and nugatory, and not part of the proper use of reason.

Against these devastating critiques there was a counter-movement which took several forms. Already by the mid-eighteenth century value began to be placed on the irrational, which was set in opposition to the exclusive claims to the superiority of reason. The value attached to irrationality, to feeling as a source of knowledge, especially in religion, was stressed by Pietist Protestant sects like the Herrnhüter or the Moravian Brothers, and by John Wesley's newly formed 'enthusiastic' group of Methodists, and was carried into literary realms by J. G. Hamann in *Socratic memorabilia* (1760). The argument from the 'need' for religion (regardless of its capacity for rational justification) gained ground, sometimes by reassertion of the traditional 'original sin', or in Kantian terms, of 'radical evil', or, increasingly, human 'psychological need'.

A characteristic countering technique was to found an apologetics on the basis of the newly won Enlightenment ground, that is, to employ its means with an opposite valuation. Perhaps the most successful such

---

[3] The word 'pantheist' was given currency in a positive sense by John Toland's *Pantheisticon*, 1718.
[4] Kirwan, *Geological essays*, 1799; quoted in C. C. Gillispie, *Genesis and geology: a study in the relations of scientific thought, natural theology, and social opinion in Great Britain, 1790–1850*, Cambridge, MA: Harvard University Press, 1951, p. 55.

counter-movement turned on the positive valuation placed on the mythology that had been dismissed with mockery as mere superstition by the
Enlightenment. Robert Lowth's *Lectures on the sacred poetry of the
Hebrews* (1749) suggested that religious belief was grounded in the folk
poetry and myth of a particular people, and treated the Old Testament
as literature, Oriental literature; moreover, his influential commentary on
the Book of Isaiah (1778) as the type of prophetic utterance, the irrational,
ecstatic, disordered language of Biblical prophecy, offered a new stylistic
model. The major German figure, J. G. Herder, standing at the turning-
point between Enlightenment and Romanticism, took up this theme in
The spirit of Hebrew poetry (1782), describing the emergence of the Old
Testament at the originary point where language itself was expressive and
poetic. The Gospels of the New Testament were themselves a form of
oral poetry, written down considerably later than the events supposedly
witnessed. The notion of the 'bard' as the voice of the community's innermost beliefs was to become an important theme of Romanticism. The
negative connotations of 'primitive' began to be overturned. From within
the higher critical camp a form of apologetics arose in which the myths
and legends which Voltaire, Bayle and Hume had mockingly identified in
Christianity as on all fours with myths and legends in other religions – in
short, those superstitions which all religions embraced and from which
reason only could deliver the human race – began to acquire a positive
value. These, as Herder showed in his *Ideas towards a philosophy of the
history of mankind*, could be seen to be intimately bound up with the
cultural achievements of different societies, all of which were valuable
permanent acquisitions by the human race, not just progressive steps up
from primitivism to civilization.

   Again it is Kant who constructs the most effective and subtle arguments
from within his own critiques of the nature and capacities of reason. In the
Critique of practical reason (1788) he showed that morality depended
on the practical employment of some ideas which could find no proof in
the philosophical or scientific sphere, in particular that of 'freedom' (as
against the actual material determination of all objects in the physical
sphere). In the *Critique of judgement* (1790), his treatise on aesthetics, he
offered the most plausible and productive set of ideas by which literature
and the other arts could assert their significance. Whereas ideas had no
embodiment in objects, art alone could fashion objects in the world which
were reminders of the mind's power to shape significance through 'regulat-
ive ideas' (of freedom, the soul and immortality) which otherwise had
no corresponding objects. At the same time, because the objects they
described were not objects in physical nature, they provided 'free play' to
human faculties. The post-Kantian idealists and the Romantic movement
would construct their position out of these pregnant suggestions. The

imaginative functions would serve as apologetic grounds for religious experience, shifting from dogmatic and institutional authority to aesthetic validation of the reflective ideas essential to religion. By these means the relative importance of religion and literature would be reversed. For literature provided the most persuasive example of the power of the imagination to fulfil human capacities in bringing about an unforced harmony of the faculties. 'Art' thus came into possession of much of the ground hitherto occupied by religion. Kant's ideas were mediated during the 1790s for the wider literary community by Friedrich Schiller's important essays on the function of art, especially *On the aesthetic education of man*. The more popular Romantic stereotypes began forming: the *Herzensergieß-ungen eines kunstliebenden Klosterbruders* (1797) [Heart-outpourings of an art-loving monk] by Wackenroder and Tieck, cast the creative artist in a fictional guise as a tragic young musician, the vehicle of the language of the art that were the bearer of pure, non-conceptual significance.

Kant's delicately balanced solution took time to find recognition. The work of William Paley, both *A view of the evidences of Christianity* (1792) and *Natural theology* (1794), had a considerable vogue even after the Kantian critiques had removed the foundations of his argument for 'evidence' of the existence of God in the forms of created nature; indeed, Paley's texts were still set for students in Cambridge into the twentieth century. This may be attributed to the fact that Newton's laws had in England been turned into a natural–theological 'proof' of God's design, and His power and beauty celebrated in sermon and poetry throughout the century.[5] A minor classic of natural history like the Reverend Gilbert White's attentive observations of the migration of birds while making his parish rounds shows that regularities in nature were construed as confirming God's law.[6] At the time of Paley's publications, moreover, there was an urgent need for affirmation of divine and rational order in Church and State in the face of the French Revolution, and Paley quickly received preferment.

In England the first to master the arguments of Kant and to deploy these thoroughly modern strategies was Samuel Taylor Coleridge (1772–1834). As a student at Cambridge, and afterwards in Bristol, in the early 1790s, he moved in radical dissenting, especially Unitarian, circles, at Jesus College

---

[5] See James Jacob, *Robert Boyle and the English Revolution: a study in social and intellectual change*, New York: B Franklin, 1977, for an account of how the religious interest annexed Newton to its own purposes; J. E. McGuire and P. M. Rattansi, 'Newton and the pipes of Pan', *Notes and records of the Royal Society of London* 21 (1966), pp. 108–43, outlines the interpretation of Newton in the light of traditional natural theology; Marjorie Nicolson, *Newton demands the muse: Newton and the eighteenth-century poets*, Princeton, NJ: Princeton University Press, 1946, shows the deployment of these ideas and images in eighteenth-century poetry.

[6] Gilbert White, *The natural history of Selborne* (1789), Paul Foster (ed.), Oxford University Press, 1993.

coming into contact with William Frend, and in Bristol belonging to the circle of Thomas Beddoes. Coleridge's Bristol Lectures in 1795 were politically and theologically radical, and he became aware of the new higher criticism of the Bible, which challenged the 'historical evidences of Christianity' by questioning the dating and authorship both of the Old Testament and the New. His decision to write a Life of Lessing ('the most formidable Infidel'), and to go to Germany to gather materials, reflected his awareness of the crucial importance of Lessing's view that the historical evidences of Christianity would not stand up to scrutiny. The historical religions, whose claim rested on supposed miraculous interventions by a deity in the order of nature (Christianity, Islam), were suspect by virtue of such claims; and the Scriptures themselves, once subjected to the same tests as secular documents, were unsound bases for such claims. As Lessing put it, 'Contingent historical truths can never serve as proof for necessary truths of reason.'[7] 'Contingent historical truths' included revelation, miracles and prophecy, as well as the events of the life of Jesus, for which there was no reliable testimony. Religion must be refounded on a spiritual basis that could animate the truths of reason. This set Coleridge's lifelong agenda. Paley's 'evidences' he held in contempt. In Germany, at the University of Göttingen in 1797–8, he heard the lectures of J. G. Eichhorn, whose *Introduction to the Old Testament* (1770) had already challenged the text, and who now proceeded onto the more dangerous ground of the New Testament. Coleridge was aware of the argument that the Gospels were not written by the Apostles, and that they were written long after the events described. Together with the Enlightenment challenges to miraculous claims, these challenges to the text undermined the notion of 'plenary inspiration' of the Bible; rather than the dictation of the Holy Ghost, the sacred book was to be treated to the same scrutiny of sources, language, editorial practice and later revisions as any secular historical text. During the 1790s, Eichhorn had extended his treatment of Genesis as oriental myth to certain parts of the New Testament. The full results were published in the *Introduction to the New Testament* (1804–18); thus Coleridge's acquaintance with his ideas was in advance of publication.[8] By the time of Johann Friedrich Strauss's *Life of Jesus* (1835), the New Testament was seen to be shaped by the mythic expectations set up in the Old Testament. It was from Eichhorn that Coleridge derived the significant revisionary notion of the biblical canon: the writings to be included in the Bible were not laid down by the Holy Spirit, nor by the

---

[7] G. E. Lessing, 'On the proof of the spirit and of power', *Theological writings: selections in translation*, Henry Chadwick (ed.), London: Adam and Charles Black, 1956, p. 53. This was Lessing's most influential essay.

[8] E. S. Shaffer, *'Kubla Khan' and 'The Fall of Jerusalem': the mythological school in Biblical criticism and secular literature, 1770–1880*, Cambridge University Press, 1975, pp. 21–3.

authority simply of the Church, but by 'tradition', interpreted as the continuing assent of the Christian community. That is, the canonicity of Scripture had to be renewed in every generation; and the Christian community had to be maintained and reformed so that such a renewal could take place. Maintaining the communal assent to the canonicity of the Scriptures required the reconstruction of past experience within the historical belief system of the community, as well as reconstruction in terms that would command current assent.[9] These notions were to be essential for Coleridge's later work: for the *Confessions of an inquiring spirit*, which in denying 'plenary inspiration' proposed the reading of the Bible as an aesthetic work of human imagination; *Aids to reflection*, which suggested an aesthetic solution to the problems of faith in a rationalist age; and *On the constitution of the church and state*, in which he proposed the notion of a 'clerisy' or intelligentsia composed partly of churchmen, partly of secular members. Coleridge concerned himself with the formation of groupings within society that could extend education and maintain culture against the inroads of commercialism; ideal notions such as 'the republic of letters' and the cultural 'Museum',[10] the 'Commonwealth' and the 'Constitution',[11] and the 'National Church' or the 'Clerisy' had powerful practical manifestations, for example, in the foundation of London University in the late 1820s. In these reconstructions of the communal experience the imagination played a key role.

Coleridge's exposition of the power of the imagination appears in *Biographia literaria* (1817). He adapts Schelling's account in the *System of transcendental philosophy* (1800), while giving practical critical examples of the creation of corresponding art objects from his own experience. In the *Biographia* the type of the genius embodying poetic imagination is Shakespeare; the example Coleridge gives, deriving from the sublime of Burke and Kant and supplying in turn the germ of Matthew Arnold's notion of the 'touchstone' of poetry, is the lines from *Venus and Adonis*:

> Look! how a bright star shooteth from the sky,
> So glides he in the night from Venus' eye.[12]

In Coleridge's work as a whole Milton and Wordsworth take their places with Shakespeare as the leading avatars of the Imagination. Chapter 13 of *Biographia literaria*, 'On the imagination', is introduced by an epigraph from Milton, ending with the lines of the archangel to Adam

---

[9] *Ibid.*, pp. 84–6.
[10] Coleridge discussed these in the *Biographia literaria*, J. Shawcross (ed.), Oxford University Press, 1907, ch. 3.
[11] For the radical interest the 'Commonwealth' remained a political ideal not fully realized in Cromwell's short-lived Commonwealth. The 'Constitution', by contrast, acquired in the hands of Burke the value of unwritten, time-honoured community allegiances.
[12] Coleridge, *Biographia literaria*, ch. 15, p. 18.

suggesting the analogy between 'organic form' in nature and in the faculties of mind.[13] One of the hallmarks of imagination is its ability to make new worlds, and thus to provide reminiscences of the mind's power to create through reflective ideas what can never be rationally proven. The ideas that Kant had singled out were those of supreme importance to the human race despite their unprovability – teleology, or the 'end' or destination of organic life; freedom, by which moral action is made possible; the soul, an idea of the self beyond what is sufficient simply to hold together the manifold of sense perceptions. These ideas are indispensable to humanity, as Kant and, following his lead, Schiller had argued. A poetry that carries out these high tasks will *ipso facto* have high seriousness; but it need not have an overtly solemn religious theme like Milton's *Paradise lost* or Wordsworth's *Ode: intimations of immortality*. The existential, hermeneutic and phenomenological traditions that have developed these lines of thought have stressed in Kant's *Critique of judgement* (1790) the idea of Life (generalized from the crucial part 3 on the teleological judgement, which provided the germ of Romantic philosophy), and have interpreted Coleridge's *Theory of life* in this sense.[14] The aesthetic and teleological portions of the *Critique of judgement* are united by the theme of creation. Thus, imagination projects a quickening, a moment of life, awareness, or consciousness. For Coleridge, the protean or 'myriad-minded' Shakespeare still holds the field as the type of creative genius. The lines from Shakespeare's *Venus and Adonis* quoted above are drawn from a genre (the Ovidian epyllion) that is the reverse of religious in character; yet genre is not the determining factor for Romanticism. Rather, a proof of original genius is that the poet 'darts his own life' into his images, whatever their ostensible genre or subject matter. This 'consciousness' that wakes us to the human capacity for reflective ideas is also the basis of religious experience. Shakespeare's lines have the qualities attributed to the sublime moment by eighteenth-century aesthetics: overwhelming speed, intensity and totality; and these in turn depend upon a religious original, namely God's creative word: '*Fiat lux*', 'Let there be light.' If Shakespeare kept

---

[13] . . . So from the root
Springs lighter the green stalk: from thence the leaves
More aerie: last, the bright consummat floure
Spirits odorous breathes. Floures and thir fruit,
Mans nourishment, by gradual scale sublim'd,
To *vital* spirits aspire: to *animal*:
To *intellectual*! – give both life and sense,
Fansie and understanding: whence the Soule
Reason receives. And reason is her *being*,
Discursive or Intuitive.   (*Paradise lost*, v.479–88; Coleridge's italics)

[14] Rudolf Makkreel, *Imagination and interpretation in Kant. The hermeneutical import of the 'Critique of judgment'*, Chicago, IL: University of Chicago Press, 1990, pp. 88–9 gives a good account of this train of thought in Continental theology.

to 'the highroad of life', as Dr Johnson had put it, in Coleridge's late manuscript 'Opus maximum', an attempt at a systematic formulation of his views, his Shakespeare criticism took another philosophic turn up the steep hill of meaning, and his searching account of Iago's nihilism is closely linked with his examination of radical evil in *Aids*.[15] The theory of the sublime forms the main line of continuity between eighteenth-century and Romantic aesthetics, as the Longinian rhetorical sublime is transformed into a process culminating in the activation of the powers of mind.

After the explication of the imagination, and of Shakespeare as the model of original genius, Coleridge moves in chapter 14 of the *Biographia* to his evaluation of Wordsworth in the context of their collaboration in *Lyrical ballads* (1798). Here the discussion of their aim to project supernatural effects bears centrally on religion. Their approach is what we would today call a psychological one, and it is generally agreed that some of the finest achievements of Romanticism lie in this realm. The subject of *Lyrical ballads* was the supernatural: '. . . the incidents and agents were to be, in part at least, supernatural . . .' This is no casual choice of subject; the very possibility of encounter with the supernatural was at issue. How far the claims had already shifted onto psychological ground is immediately made evident: 'And real in *this* sense they have been to every human being who, from whatever source of delusion, has at any time believed himself under supernatural agency.'[16] Coleridge's province was to project the supernatural; Wordsworth's to show its presence in common life:

In this idea originated the plan of the 'Lyrical Ballads'; in which it was agreed, that my endeavours should be directed to persons and characters supernatural, or at least romantic; yet so as to transfer from our inward nature a human interest and a semblance of truth sufficient to procure for these shadows of imagination that willing suspension of disbelief for the moment, which constitutes poetic faith.

Wordsworth's task was 'to excite a feeling analogous to the supernatural':

Mr Wordsworth, on the other hand, was to propose to himself as his object, to give the charm of novelty to things of every day, and to excite a feeling analogous to the supernatural, by awakening the mind's attention from the lethargy of custom and directing it to the loveliness and the wonders of the world before us; an inexhaustible treasure, but for which, in consequence of the film of familiarity and selfish solicitude we have eyes, yet see not, ears that hear not, and hearts that neither feel nor understand.

Coleridge's formulation shows that much in Wordsworth that is not overtly religious may be deemed ancillary to religion. This awareness of

---

[15] E. S. Shaffer, 'Iago's malignity motivated: Coleridge's unpublished "Opus magnum"', *Shakespeare quarterly* 19 (1968), pp. 195–203.
[16] Coleridge, *Biographia literaria*, ch. 14.

the possibility of the supernatural diffused through ordinary experience may prepare for an awakening of religious life. In writing of the effect of Wordsworth's poetry he says of the admiration that 'young men of strong sensibility and meditative minds' felt that it 'was distinguished by its intensity, I might almost say, by its *religious* fervour' (my italics). Yet as Wordsworth's poems of common life excited a 'feeling analogous to the supernatural', so the reader's response to it is analogous to 'religious fervour'. The affirmation of the everyday marks a decisive shift towards the importance of inwardness, what Charles Taylor has called 'resonance in a subject'. The meaning of natural phenomena as they resonate within us reflects a meaning really expressed in them. But access to this meaning requires that we turn within.[17]

The only partial equation 'supernatural, or at least romantic' exhibits the centrality of the supernatural to Romanticism, though it again implies that the subject is not the supernatural itself but the psychological groundwork for it, that is, rational explanation for the human capacity for supernatural experience seen in a positive rather than a debunking light. Coleridge was especially interested in effects that gave a powerful impression of the supernatural, yet were scientifically explicable, for example, the Brocken Spectre, or projection of the observer's own shadow before him in gigantic form when the sun is low.[18] This was the effect James Hogg also exploited in the novel *The private memoirs and confessions of a justified sinner* (1808), presaging the appearance of the devil, who is, appropriately, a projection of 'the indulgence we accord to our own selves'.[19] The scientifically based sublime, including modified forms of the Brocken Spectre, is still a presence in current literature.

The passages on the project of the *Lyrical ballads* from the *Biographia* are among the most telling in Romantic criticism. But Coleridge pursued the question of the supernatural throughout his writings. He saw that it was essential to separate the true supernatural reference from the false and meretricious effects that were rife in the whole period. The latter threatened to degrade the authentic experience altogether. He tirelessly and with all his critical acumen attacked the merely sensational, the undergrowth of Burke's notion that terror was the essential ingredient in the experience of the sublime. He revised *The ancient mariner*, excising the false 'gothick'

---

[17] Charles Taylor, *Sources of the self: the making of the modern identity*, Cambridge, MA: Harvard University Press, 1989, p. 301.

[18] This effect was reported in scientific journals: M. Jordan in J. F. Gmelin's *Göttingisches Journal der Wissenschaften* I, part 3 (1798), pp. 110–14. Coleridge translates the report in *Notebooks* I, entry 430 (May 1799).

[19] André Gide, Introduction to James Hogg, *The private memoirs and confessions of a justified sinner*, London: Cresset, 1947, p. xv. Gide perceived that Henry James's *The turn of the screw*, like Hogg's story, presented supernatural apparitions that were the product of 'mental derangement' vividly experienced by the narrator.

from his early versions. He wrote reviews critical of the bestseller *The monk*, by M. G. 'Monk' Lewis, and all its 'gothick' cousins; he bitterly attacked the meretricious dramatic works that littered the stage, especially the popular Kotzebue (author of, for example, *Lovers' vows*, used by Jane Austen in *Mansfield Park* as a litmus paper of false sensibility), and his English imitators, such as Charles Maturin's play *Bertram*.[20] He delicately but decisively separated Shakespeare's and Schiller's authentic power to suggest the supernatural from the merely sensational and titillating effects of Kotzebue (who was often confused with Schiller and throughout the 1790s was translated by the same hands). His whole œuvre is characterized by this vigilance; high Romanticism disowned what Mario Praz called 'the soft underbelly of romanticism'. Only by so doing could a serious religious reference be maintained. Mary Shelley in her Gothic novel *Frankenstein: or, The modern Prometheus* (1818) may be said to have benefited from these discussions, and to have drawn upon the strength of the religious ban against vying with God's creative power to achieve effects of genuine terror, incrimination and monstrosity in the overreaching Dr Frankenstein and his grotesque creature. She also explored the psychology of guilt which, as in Godwin's novel *Caleb Williams* (1798), replaced the theological analyses of sin. Even in Romantic theology proper, Schleiermacher categorized the religions of the world according to the nature and quality of the individual experience of their adherents. Although on these criteria he was still able to claim the superiority of the inward, subjective Christian experience, just as Hegel saw world religions as 'essential though subordinate moments' in Christianity,[21] this comparative and psychological approach would eventually lead to William James's pragmatic and non-sectarian explorations of *The varieties of religious experience* (1895).

In the early 1820s, turning his attention more fully to religious questions, Coleridge wrote the *Confessions of an inquiring spirit*, intended to preface his *Aids to reflection*: it is one of the most persuasive and attractive statements of the case for abandoning all notion of 'plenary inspiration' (the authorship of the entire biblical text by the Holy Spirit) in favour of a reading of the Bible in the way we read literature. We now speak of the 'Bible as literature' without any sense of the enormity of this step. Whether for practical reasons, or more probably for fear it would appear too radical, he published *Aids* without it; when it was posthumously published in 1840 it did indeed incur the obloquy of conservative members of the Church. Yet *Aids* itself was in effect a reading of the Bible as literature,

[20] Coleridge, 'Review of M. G. Lewis, *The monk*', in *Shorter works and fragments*; and 'Critique of *Bertram*', *Biographia literaria*, II, ch. 23.
[21] Hegel, *Lectures on the philosophy of religion*, E. B. Spiers and J. Burdon Sanderson (trans.), London: Kegan Paul, 1895, I, pp. 76–7, 262–3.

through the medium of previous religious writings like the seventeenth-century aphorisms of Robert Leighton which he used as a framework for the book. Coleridge's rereadings of the seventeenth century, both of poetry and religious writings, constitute an imaginative reconstruction of the past without which, as Schleiermacher argued, there can be no continuity of the religious or the literary community.

In general, Coleridge's aesthetic grounding of the 'spiritual religion' was the solution that appealed most to the ever-growing group of believers who saw that the 'evidences of Christianity' would no longer hold, whether on historical, philosophical or scientific grounds. His brilliant apologetics held its ground throughout the nineteenth century, taking root also in the young New England transcendentalists, through the introductory essay to the American edition of *Aids* (1828) by the influential James Marsh, who perceived its Kantian basis.[22] Coleridge's solution did much to give an adequate programme to the 'clerisy' that he advocated in *On the constitution of the church and state* (1829), that is, the intellectual class, partly within, partly outside the Church, who would carry out the task of cultural education of the nation. Coleridge's 'national church' is not to be confused with the Anglican or Established Church of England, nor even with a Christian church; it is an idea to be served and forwarded by the clerisy whose task it is to ground civilization in *'cultivation*, in the harmonious development of those qualities and faculties that characterize our *humanity'*.[23] If this obligation to educate and to cultivate is not fulfilled, the people are released from their reciprocal obligations to the state, for they have lost the moral freedom (in Kant's sense) which would fit them to discharge these duties.

It is important for the whole period that the 'religion' that is related in a variety of ways to poetry is rarely that of a specific institution, but rather constitutes or calls upon an ideal entity, whether it be Kant's 'church of Reason', with its *Klerisei* (the source of Coleridge's coinage 'clerisy'), the angelic correspondences of the Swedenborgian New Jerusalem Church, the idea of a National Church or of the 'historical' community (in which that history is variously construed or fictionalized). The Idea (no longer dogmatically provable) becomes the bearer of value in the world, whether

---

[22] On the Transcendentalists see René Wellek, *Confrontations: studies in the intellectual and literary relations between Germany, England, and the United States during the nineteenth century*, Princeton, NJ: Princeton University Press, 1965, pp. 155–7; and Marjorie Nicolson, 'James Marsh and the Vermont transcendentalists', *Philosophical review* 34 (1925), pp. 28–50. On the hermeneutic programme of reanimation of the past, see E. S. Shaffer, 'Coleridge and Schleiermacher: the hermeneutic community', in *The Coleridge connection: Essays for Thomas McFarland*, Richard Gravil and Molly Lefebure (eds.), Basingstoke: Macmillan, 1990, pp. 200–32.

[23] Coleridge, *On the constitution of the church and state according to the idea of each*, John Barrell (ed.), London: Dent & Sons, 1972, pp. 33–4.

through dialectically evolving historical process, as in Hegel's *Phenomenology of mind* (1807), or through art that encapsulates the significant moment of spirit (as in all aesthetic systems following in Kant's wake).[24]

The Romantic period was characterized by its suspicion of institutions (both of the *ancien régime* – 'all institutes for ever blotted out / That legalized exclusion'[25] – and afterwards of its unsatisfactory revolutionary and counter-revolutionary successors), and by its imaginative recreation of them in literature. Wordsworth described the Wanderer in *The excursion* as 'Rapt into still communion that transcends / The imperfect offices of prayer and praise.'[26] Poetic reinventions of ceremonies of initiation, passage and communion, often placed within imagined temples, domes or fanes (one of Shelley's was hung with 'spell-inwoven clouds', and its aisles were 'more bright / With their own radiance than the Heaven of Day' *Revolt of Islam*, lines 589, 597–8), are one of the features of the literature of the period, as they were of the secularized calendar of the French Revolution. These reinvented institutions anticipate Ludwig's Feuerbach's regrounding of religious ritual in everyday experience in *The essence of Christianity* (1830).

A partial exception may be found in the Catholic revival on the Continent, especially in post-Napoleonic France in the 1820s, where state power and religious dogma, or 'Crown and Altar', were again allied by Joseph de Maistre, Louis Bonald and Pierre-Simon Ballanche; the latter also wrote the prose epic *La ville des expiations* [*The city of expiations*] (1827), restoring the operation of divine retribution and the expiation of nations through individual suffering in history. Victor Hugo later gave this religious theme a sharply ironic secular twist, in his poem *L'expiation*, in which Napoleon's 'expiation' takes place not through his defeat or his lonely death, but through the rise of the upstart Napoleon III. The ultramontanist priest, Felicité-Robert de Lamennais, who invested in the institutional power of the Church, and tried to set it against a corrupt state, suffered an almost tragic rejection by the papal authority, which placed his books on the Index, in particular the *Paroles d'un croyant* [*Words of a believer*] (1834), written in a sweeping biblical style and advocating the democracy of the early Church.[27] The Catholic revival had an aesthetic as well as a political aspect, perhaps best expressed by Chateaubriand's *Le Génie du christianisme* [*The genius of Christianity*] (1802), which evokes

---

[24] Hegel's tendency in his later writings to identify the Prussian State with the moment of spirit has been widely viewed as a betrayal of his own philosophical insight.

[25] Wordsworth, *The prelude (1805)*, in *The prelude 1799, 1805, 1850*, Jonathan Wordsworth, M. H. Abrams and Stephen Gill (eds.), New York: Norton, 1979, IX.527–8.

[26] Wordsworth, *The excursion*, I. 215–16.

[27] Lamennais's influence on the Oxford Movement was considerable; see W. G. Roe, *Lamennais and England: the reception of Lamennais's religious ideas in England in the nineteenth century*, Oxford University Press, 1966, pp. 93–114.

in fine prose style the moral, poetic and artistic contributions of Christianity to the development of mankind. In Germany too the second generation of Romantics, for example Clemens Brentano, responded to the aesthetic ceremonial of the Roman Church, which claimed a number of converts, most notably the innovative critic Friedrich Schlegel. But this revival came late to England, in the form of Newman's conversion to Rome in 1845. Despite notable works of apologetics from Newman, the Catholic revival finds an authentic poetic voice only later in Gerard Manley Hopkins (1844–89).

Coleridge's own poetry includes poems on overtly religious topics, ranging from poetry on public themes to intimate treatments of personal dread, guilt and despair. For the most direct accounts of the experience that lay behind the latter one must go to his private notebooks and to some of his letters and marginalia. These private experiences (often exacerbated by the not wholly comprehended effects of opium addiction) throw light also on his philosophic concerns: his conviction that the unaided will may be inadequate to lift us into Kant's 'kingdom of ends' where our actions are guided by the categorical imperative (a maxim fit to be a universal rule). In the intensity of his private dread, and its impact on his religious thought, as well as in his minting of a poetic–philosophic prose style, Coleridge may be compared with the Danish writer Søren Kierkegaard, whose existential exploration of *angst* through his diaries and more formally in *The concept of dread*, his vivid reinterpretation of biblical stories (*Fear and trembling*), and his fictionalized presentation of life alternatives (for example, the 'Diary of a seducer' in *Either/or*) have their roots in a similar range of German philosophical thought. This anxiety, itself a mark of the spirit ('the less spirit, the less dread', as Kierkegaard put it),[28] is the dread of nothingness traced in the later existential tradition by Heidegger and Sartre, as well as in psychoanalysis.[29] The opposition of contraries becomes itself an aspect of the dialectic of the sublime.

Coleridge's poem 'Religious musings' (1795) shows the use of biblical imagery in the service of political ideas, especially the imagery of the apocalypse from the Book of Revelation, one of the most widely quoted texts during the revolutionary period. The later poetry often speaks of 'last things' in a profound way bordering on allegory. But it is the poetry that embeds these concerns in a vivified mental inscape that speaks most powerfully: the speaker's sympathy at a distance with his friend's experience, in 'the one life within us and abroad' from 'This lime-tree bower my prison'; or the craving to transform the inner as well as the outer world in

---

[28] S. Kierkegaard, *The concept of dread*, Walter Lowrie (trans.), Princeton, NJ: Princeton University Press, 1957, p. 41.

[29] Thomas McFarland, 'Coleridge's anxiety', in *Coleridge's variety: bicentenary studies*, John Beer (ed.), Pittsburgh, PA: University of Pittsburgh Press, 1974, pp. 160–163, suggests this approach; there is no full study.

'Dejection: an ode': 'O Lady, we receive but what we give'. In 'The ancient mariner' recognizably religious themes of guilt, retribution and grace are played out in an impressive natural setting, shot through with supernatural traces that may be supplied by the narrator's credulous temperament. The mariner (like the fishermen of the Gospels) bears witness to a searing experience that can never be forgotten nor explained away.

Yet the symbolism of the poem is a subtle blend of Christianity and the mythology of nature:

> Nor dim nor red, like God's own head,
> The glorious Sun uprist:
> Then all averred, I had killed the bird
> That brought the fog and mist. (97–100)

The negative invocation of God, the intensification of the contrast between God and the Sun, the uncertainty of the colour reference, the awe-inspiring speed of the sun's rise in the strange pseudo-archaic verb form, is followed by the shock of the accusation, as if the godhead rose only to terrify and judge. The intermingling of pagan and Christian imagery restores a primitive terror and an unpredictability to the train of events; the reference system of the mariner, the crew and the reader is disoriented. The poem conveys an archetypal religious experience, not tied to sect or dogma.[30]

Coleridge, although criticized at the time for what Southey called 'a Dutch attempt at German sublimity', attained his aim, at least in this case, of representing supernatural characters; it is no longer the allegorical figures of Sin and Death familiar from Milton and from a century of pictorial renderings, but the symbolic natural setting for all the creatures invoked that suggests the supernatural. In his critique of Wordsworth's poetry in *Biographia* Coleridge did not enter into discussion of Wordsworth's analogues to the supernatural, but rather to what in his poetry might operate to baulk the effect – simplistic diction, bathos, inadequate metrics. Since then, 'Tintern Abbey' has been the most commented on poem of *Lyrical ballads*; the lyric persona, revisiting his feelings on again seeing Tintern Abbey from the Wye, speaks of 'a sense sublime / Of something far more deeply interfused / Whose dwelling is the light of setting suns / And the round ocean and the living air, / And the blue sky, and in the mind of man . . .' (lines 96–100).

A more overtly religious poem, such as Wordsworth's 'Ode: intimations of immortality' (1802–4), has sometimes been taken as marking a transition

30 Among the many commentaries on this poem see Robert Penn Warren, in James D. Boulger (ed.), *Twentieth-century interpretations of 'The rime of the ancient mariner': a collection of critical essays*, Englewood Cliffs, NJ: Prentice Hall, 1969; and J. B. Beer, *Coleridge the visionary*, London: Chatto & Windus, 1959.

from the pantheist affirmation of divine power in nature to a more conventional Christian (Anglican) position. This shift is also associated with
his sense of the 'failure' of the French Revolution (he was then writing the
books of *The prelude* that deal with his French sojourns), as well as with a
new personal maturity, in which the 'visionary gleam' is exchanged for 'the
philosophic mind'. A lively debate has centred on whether this turning-
point marks the beginning of a decline, which would relegate his later
poetry, not least his religious poetry, to the second rank. Lionel Trilling
argued persuasively (from a secular point of view) that the poetry of maturity – 'the still, sad music of humanity' (already heard in 'Tintern Abbey') –
was no less powerfully imaginative than that of youthful joy.[31] Subsequent
debate has focussed on the various versions of the *Prelude*.

In Wordsworth's reworking of his autobiographical epic, the *Prelude*,
finished in thirteen books in 1805 but several times revised, and published
only after his death (1850), he altered many phrases and lines to bring
them more nearly into line with institutional orthodoxy:

> 1805   in the place
>   The holiest that I knew of my own soul (X.379–80).
> 1850
>   In the last place of refuge – my own soul (X.415).

> 1805
>   The feeling of life endless, the great thought
>   By which we live, infinity and God (XIII.183–4).
> 1850
>   Faith in life endless, the sustaining thought
>   Of human Being, Eternity, and God (XIV.204–5).

The stress on the infinite feeling of life – a hallmark of Romantic sensibility
– becomes the theistic avowal of faith in immortality. The 1805 *Prelude* –
the first version Wordsworth read aloud to Coleridge – was not published
until the twentieth century, and since the two were published side by side,
a variety of different revisions of the poem over Wordsworth's lifetime
have been published. A recent critic has argued that the 1850 *Prelude* convincingly reworks the poem's major theme of travel via the visit to the
monastery of the Grande Chartreuse (which figured in Wordsworth's
early *Descriptive sketches* (1793), as well as in the earlier versions of *The
prelude*, and indeed in much contemporary poetry and prose), so that
'travel becomes a fully religious process':[32]

---

[31] Lionel Trilling, 'The Immortality ode', *The Liberal imagination: essays on literature and
society*, Garden City, NY: Doubleday, 1950, pp. 123–51.
[32] Howard Erskine-Hill, *Poetry of opposition and revolution, Dryden to Wordsworth*,
Oxford University Press, 1996, p. 218.

In different quarters of the bending sky,
The cross of Jesus stand[s] erect, as if
Hands of angelic powers had fixed it there,
Memorial reverenced by a thousand storms;

(1850 *Prelude* VI.483–6)

But the differing aims and conventions of pilgrimage, Grand Tourism, and aesthetic meditation on 'spots of time' need to be carefully observed.[33] The 'as if' formulation of this passage was widely employed in the period, together with similitudes of varying degrees of difference ('like', aided by such phrases as 'methought' and 'seemed', and various phrases employing 'as'), to present religious images and views to which the writer can no longer literally subscribe.[34] 'As if' is of special importance, for it draws on Kant's '*als ob*', the fulcrum of moral action: to be a moral being one must behave 'as if' one had freedom of the will, although all objects in the world are in fact materially determined. In Coleridge's late manuscripts, where he attempted a final formulation of his system, the argument is based on a counterfactual conditional: if ~p then p.

Few modern readers turn to those more overtly religious or sectarian of Wordsworth's poems – 'Seathwaite Chapel', or 'Devotional incitements' or the 'Ecclesiastical sonnets' – those which led Leslie Stephen to claim that 'his ethical system is as distinctive and as capable of exposition as Bishop Butler's'; indeed, a remarkable recent reading of 'Tintern Abbey' has chosen to dwell upon the absence of mention of the vagrants within the ruined church.[35] Yet the gap between 'the Wordsworthians', who looked to him for theologized wisdom, and those who valued him as a poet, was pointed out by Matthew Arnold; Wordsworth himself, although like many Romantics he sometimes borrowed religious terms to describe the 'calling' of the poet ('dedicated spirit'),[36] had subscribed to the distinction between 'religion in poetry' and 'versified religion', and declined to handle 'the Mysteries of Religion'.[37] Arnold, defending him as a poet, indeed as a great European poet, chose to praise him for his depiction of 'moral ideas', that is, the ideas 'on man, on nature, and on human life' (in Wordsworth's words), the subjects of Wordsworth's and Coleridge's early

[33] Geoffrey H. Hartman, 'The halted traveller', in *Wordsworth's Poetry 1787–1814*, New Haven, CT: Yale University Press, 1964, pp. 3–30.
[34] Susan J. Wolfson, 'The formings of simile', *Formal charges: the shaping of poetry in British Romanticism*, Stanford, CA: Stanford University Press, 1997, pp. 63–99.
[35] Marjorie Levinson, *Wordsworth's great period poems: four essays*, Cambridge University Press, 1986, pp. 14–57.
[36] Wordsworth, *Prelude* (1850) IV.337.
[37] Wordsworth, *Essay supplementary to the preface of 1815*, in *Prose works*, W. J. B. Owen and Jane Worthington Smyser (eds.), 3 vols., Oxford: Clarendon Press, 1974; and letter to Henry Alford, 20 February 1840, *The letters of William and Dorothy Wordsworth: The later years*, part IV, Alan G. Hill (ed.), Oxford: Clarendon Press, 1988, p. 23.

proposal to write a 'grand philosophical poem' on 'Man, Nature, and Society'. We recognize here the Kantian shift towards the oblique salvage of the religious sphere through the aesthetically rendered 'moral idea'. Arnold, indeed, picking up the thread from Coleridge, stresses in particular the 'idea of Life': 'A poetry of revolt against moral ideas is a poetry of revolt against *life*; a poetry of indifference towards moral ideas is a poetry of indifference towards *life*.'[38]

Wordsworth's handling of the 'moral idea' of life in the late poetry may be characterized by 'After-thought', one of the 'River Duddon' sonnet sequence (1828), whose last five lines are

> Enough, if something from our hands have power
> To live, and act, and serve the future hour;
> And if, as tow'rd the silent tomb we go,
> Through love, through hope, and faith's transcendent dower,
> We feel that we are greater than we know.[39]

'Faith's transcendent dower' is present here, yet it is subordinate to the sublime reflective idea of human greatness, which is 'felt', in aesthetic form, not 'known'.

If Coleridge was by far the most intelligent and subtle English apologist for religion, who had modernized it in accordance with the most radical critiques, almost without the full recognition of that fact by his contemporaries, the younger generation of English Romantics were more impatient. The radical tradition that Coleridge had been part of as a young man was carried forward in the circle of William Godwin (author of *Political justice* (1794)) and Mary Wollstonecraft (author of the *Rights of woman*) into the next generation, when Wollstonecraft's daughter Mary joined forces with Percy Bysshe Shelley (1792–1821), the self-proclaimed atheist, political radical and poet. The attack on the older Wordsworth, Coleridge and Southey, whom they viewed as turncoats – a band of 'sworn brothers in the same cause of righteous apostasy', as Hazlitt put it[40] – became especially strong after the fall of Napoleon, when the forces of reform in Britain emerged from the period of enforced consensus during the war against France. At this juncture the radical sources of transcendentalism in Enlight-enment critique were forgotten, as the state in both Germany and England veered to the right and 'organic theory' was deployed to defend conservatism. The use of religious language for political satire evident in Hazlitt's phrase characterizes the attack. Byron is his ally in this, and no attack on the older generation of 'apostate' poets is sharper or more hilarious than his satirical passage on Southey's reception by St Peter at the

---

[38] Matthew Arnold, Preface to *Poems of Wordsworth*, p. xvi. The Preface was reprinted as 'Wordsworth' in *Essays in criticism*, Second Series, 1888, but should be read in the context of his illuminating selection of Wordsworth's short poems.
[39] *Poems of Wordsworth*, p. 220.   [40] William Hazlitt, in *The examiner*, 5 April 1817.

pearly gates in the *Vision of judgement*. Yet despite Byron's mockery there is a trace of the Calvinism in which he was brought up, in particular in the 'Byronic hero', fated, doomed by some hidden sin or fault, or ill-doing (sometimes only the thought of an evil or criminal act, or a deed into which he has been led by others).

The contrast between the two generations is most sharply focussed in the poems on 'Mont Blanc' by Coleridge and Shelley. Both poems refer to one of the main themes of the sublime (an aesthetic term that largely came to displace beauty as the measure of aesthetic value), the grandeur of mountain landscape. The sublime moment had been much elaborated in the course of the eighteenth century, incorporating Longinus's Greek view of 'great nature' as inspiring human emulation into a complex Christian response which included awe and humility in the face of divine power as well as affirmation of God's beneficent workings in the natural order. Burke's *Inquiry* stressed the importance of the instinct for self-preservation that led to the suspension of action in a moment of terror in which all perceptions were heightened, before giving way to practical action (fight or flight). In Kant's critical account the literalness of the physico-theological proof of God's existence (or the 'Argument from Design') was denied, and the operation of the sublime took place through the power of the human imagination to create unity out of its perceptions, and by this to be reminded of other reflective ideas. The invocation of sublime nature thus lent itself to affirmations of divine power, on the one hand, and of human power on the other. Coleridge reworked the Dano–German poet Friederike Brun's ode 'Chamouni beym Sonnenaufgange' for his 'Hymn before sun-rise, in the Vale of Chamouni'. Brun's poem is couched as a series of Blakean questions as to what power has wrought this scene, and in the final verse nature itself replies: 'Jehovah'. Coleridge's version stresses the voice of God whose sublime fiat may be symbolized in the frozen moment of the glaciated abyss, whereas Shelley's poem, deliberately play-ing off Coleridge, reinterprets the voice in a political and atheist sense:

> Thou hast a voice, great Mountain, to repeal
> Large codes of fraud and woe; not understood
> By all, but which the wise, and great, and good
> Interpret, or make felt, or deeply feel.[41]

> ('Mont Blanc. Lines written in the Vale of Chamouni,
> lines 80–3)

'Large codes of fraud and woe' refer to the familiar radical linkage of political oppression and its religious colluders ('priestcraft'). The role of

---

[41] Geoffrey Matthews and Kelvin Everest (eds.), *The poems of Shelley*, vol. I, 'Mont Blanc. Lines written in the Vale of Chamouni', pp. 532–41. See headnote for further references to Shelley's atheism at Mont Blanc.

human intermediaries is made explicit. In the final stanza (5) the mountain becomes 'voiceless' – and silence is grander than all the babble of religion.

Coleridge in turn may well have been alluding to Wordsworth's handling of the Alpine sublime, both in the early poem from *Descriptive sketches* (1793), which Coleridge cites in *Biographia literaria*, and in the now more famous passage from *The prelude* on 'crossing the Alps'. Wordsworth turned his experience of failure to be aware of the long-awaited moment of crossing the summit into an invocation of imagination, and its powers of creating significance: the transcendental indirectness of the reference of the sublime to divine power is here fully registered. The contrasting extremities of the alpine landscape

> Were all like working of one mind, the features
> Of the same face, blossoms upon one tree,
> Characters of the great Apocalypse,
> The types and symbols of Eternity,
> Of first, and last, and midst and without end.

> (*Prelude* (1805) VI.568–72)

Despite conflict between the generations Coleridge, Wordsworth and Shelley can be seen to be using the same underlying poetics of imagination, and shifting the expression of religious experience more or less openly into a secular mode. Shelley adopted the language of Platonism, which had the advantage of being pagan, to express the high calling of poetic imagination (in 'A defence of poetry') and as a vehicle for aesthetic and political idealism. Yet Plato had long been absorbed into Christian thought. The traditional co-opting of platonic tropes in religious thought in the West, and the renewed confluence of Platonism, especially in its neoplatonic forms, with German idealism ensure a close kinship between Coleridge's and Shelley's handling of the sublime as a technique for projecting ideas of value. Wordsworth (who rejected the use of the Greek and Roman pantheon as an 'outworn creed') felt able in the Immortality ode to employ a platonic myth to express a Christian thought, just as Shelley used platonic myths to project revolutionary and anti-religious aspirations.

There is no doubt, however, that for a readership still more familiar with Paley than with Kant, or than with Coleridge's *Aids*, poetry in the sublime style could have the effect of underpinning faith, suggesting consolation in nature, and creating a bond of sympathy between God's creation and mankind, as well as promoting a community of believers. 'The pleasing sense of merit, which religious feelings used to bring to you in former times, still present themselves to you, but you feel that they can no longer find a footing within your bosom', George Grote wrote with a certain sarcasm to his sister in 1823; poetry could supply it. (Grote recommended instead Bentham's principle of utility as the only rule to be relied on! Presumably he agreed with Bentham that pushpin was as good as poetry.) The experience of many readers throughout the nineteenth century confirms that Wordsworth in particular continued to have these effects; the best-known is J. S. Mill's testimonial in his *Autobiography* to the healing power of Wordsworth's poetry after the death of his father. In the longer run, the success of the aesthetic strategy contributed to the notion that poetry could fill the place of religion ('poetry is spilt religion'), and perpetuated the religiose tone of criticism to the time of T. S. Eliot.

Coleridge represents the fullest and most adequate British response through Romantic aesthetics and poetry to the intellectual crisis in religious thought and institutions, corresponding to Schleiermacher and Hegel on the Continent, while Wordsworth's poetry represents the most successful body of poetic work in which a harmony between the inner life and the world of nature is postulated and maintained. Their collaborative work and significance had a powerful echo down the century in Britain. The Godwin and Shelley circles represent the radical opposition over two generations, developing a range of characteristic vehicles, from the grand ode and shorter lyric (shared with Wordsworth and Coleridge) to the political satire and cosmic drama, political poetry in which the role of priest and church was an aspect of oppression, and the Gothic novel. Both generations produced a literary criticism and a cultural critique saturated with political concerns. It was in this period that 'criticism' as we now know it came into being.

The construction of a new literary history and genealogy belongs to every movement, and the Romantics were especially active in reformulating the past. They presented themselves (this was more marked and explicit in Continental theory, in Schiller, Friedrich Schlegel, Chateaubriand) as anti-classical, that is, as Christian European, subjective and spiritual; for Schiller this is often attached to a nostalgia for a more robust classical paganism that responded directly to nature; for Schlegel, especially after his conversion to Catholicism, Dante was the religious poet par excellence who with the retrieval of the medieval period came to the fore again. The translations, especially Henry Francis Cary's Dante, favourably reviewed by Coleridge in 1814, became the Romantic Dante (although Shelley, Byron and Coleridge read the original). The development parallels that in the German Romantics, especially Friedrich Schlegel, for whom Shakespeare was the great poet of the imagination, but Dante of the transcendent. If the rediscovery of Dante began with the Ugolino episode, it was followed by the rest of the *Inferno*, and further episodes, especially that of Paolo and Francesca, the illicit young lovers (canto 5), became a favourite reference point. Coleridge ended his last book, *On the constitution of the church and state* (1830), with a quotation from Dante's *Paradiso*, avowing that the white light of reason could have been seen, had it not been obscured by false imaginings ('falso immaginar').[42] Shelley's last poem, 'The triumph of life' (1822), is in Dante's *terza rima*.[43] The two Romantic generations, opposed in so many ways, agreed in according Dante their ultimate homage.

If Coleridge and Wordsworth represent the main stream of modern literary accommodations to the critique of religion, and Shelley and Byron continue the attack on the new apologetics while adopting the language of the imagination, the most original poet and thinker who attempted a synthesis between religion and literature was William Blake (1743–1827). He has in recent years been assimilated to the Romantic movement, on the basis of his series of mythological poems which use biblical styles to convey a personal and idiosyncratic reconstruction of the myths of the fall and redemption of man, from *Vala* (1798) and *The Four Zoas* (1800), which sets out his mythic narrative most fully, to *Milton* (1804) and *Jerusalem* (begun 1804, engraved 1820). His earlier *Songs of innocence and experience* (1789–91) were then incorporated, which makes the onset of the Romantic movement conveniently coincide with the French Revolution. Some have even tried to incorporate *Poetical sketches* (1764).[44] But he has always been a unique figure. Belonging to an earlier generation than Wordsworth and Coleridge, he had his roots deep in the eighteenth century; and as an engraver by trade he belonged to the artisan class rather than, like Wordsworth and Coleridge, the middle class, or like Byron and Shelley, the upper class. He was little known as a poet in his day, and was dubbed an 'unfortunate lunatic' by the press at the time of his failed exhibition (1808), although Coleridge wrote of him appreciatively in 1815. Only when D. G. Rossetti, another poet–painter, took him up in mid-century, did his poetry begin to be known.

He was in touch with radical religious movements, especially Swedenborgianism and the heirs of the Protestant sects of the Civil Wars (their role in the eighteenth century is still a matter of dispute), and he moved in the radical political circles of the Corresponding Societies in the 1790s. His early *Prophecies*, in the years just following the Revolution, encode the developments in current politics, first in hope, then in increasing frustration. The mythological poems then recast his hopes for a redemption of man in a less immediate, more fully imagined form – the double fall and redemption, at once Biblical and Miltonic.

Religion and revolution are closely interwined in his visionary hope, as it was for the figures of the Civil War whose heir he is sometimes seen to

---

[42] Coleridge, *On the constitution of the church and state*, pp. 162–3.

[43] Shelley is credited with reviving Dante's verse form for English poetry, matched only by Eliot in *Little Gidding*. See Timothy Webb, *The violet and the crucible: Shelley and translation*, Oxford: Clarendon Press, 1976, pp. 326–9.

[44] Northrop Frye argued that the *Poetical sketches* give 'the main outlines of Blake's archetypal myth': *Fearful symmetry: a study of William Blake*, Princeton, NJ: Princeton University Press, 1947, p. 182.

be; his direct and personal relation to the text of the Bible is also reminiscent of the Puritan imagination. He is the poet most nearly a 'visionary' of the kind described with a certain wistfulness by Coleridge in *Biographia literaria* as having a direct form of intuition which was closed to his own age, citing Jakob Boehme, the sixteenth-century German shoemaker and mystic as his main example. Only Blake among the self-consciously 'belated' Romantics dared to make the direct visionary claim: 'The Prophets Isaiah and Ezekiel dined with me last night' ('Marriage of Heaven and Hell', plate 12). He was certain that he saw visions, and he drew and described what he saw.

Much controversy has arisen over attempts by historians to establish the continuity of the revolutionary sects of the Civil War, the Diggers and Levellers, and especially the Muggletonians, into Blake's time.[45] There is at any rate no doubt that Blake was an 'antinomian', that is, a believer in the doctrine that faith in Christ abrogated the law of the Old Testament.[46] In its extreme form, the doctrine of justification by faith not works could absolve the Elect from blame for any of their actions; but Blake was not a predestinarian, a calvinist believer in an Elect chosen by God regardless of deserts. He did, however, deploy the antinomian position against the oppressive laws of God, nature and man. This became a major theme in his poetry, fuelling protest against the patriarchal law of God ('Nobodaddy', or a Jehovah-like figure known as Urizen in his personal mythology), the state, the church and the family.

In the *Songs of innocence and experience* he drew on the hymns of Isaac Watts and John and Charles Wesley for his deceptively simple form, and on the literature of moral and religious admonition to children, which he transformed into a plea for the oppressed – for children, the poor, the exploited and the repressed. The Church and its priests played a repressive role, not only as hypocritical agents of the State power, but as the inhibitors of joy, including all the pleasures of the senses. As he wrote in 'The garden of love':

> And I saw it was filled with graves,
> And tombstones where flowers should be:
> And Priests in black gowns, were walking their rounds,
> And binding with briars, my joys & desires.   (lines 9–12)

His best-known poem 'Tyger, Tyger, burning bright / In the forests of the Night' is a strong statement of God's ambivalent power, both creative and destructive; the benevolent God of eighteenth-century theodicies is here abandoned.

---

[45] F. G. A. Pocock, Christopher Hill, and E. P. Thompson have all argued for this link, in varying degrees.

[46] E. P. Thompson, *Witness against the beast: William Blake and the moral law*, Cambridge University Press, 1993.

His antinomian position finds powerful expression in the aphorisms of
The marriage of Heaven and Hell (1790–3), which challenge and reverse
common moral assumptions in order to release energy for change: 'Without contraries is no progression.' He speaks in the voice of the Devil and
delivers the Proverbs of Hell: 'Prisons are built with stones of the Law,
Brothels with bricks of Religion.' 'The Tygers of wrath are wiser than the
Horses of instruction' (plate 9). Jesus appears as a liberator, and the
Gospel of Christ is brought into direct antagonism to the moral law: 'I tell
you no virtue can exist without breaking these ten commandments . . .
Jesus was all virtue, and acted from impulse, not from rules' (plate 23).
This line of thought recurs in Blake, culminating in 'The everlasting
Gospel' (1818), the name given to the Gospel construed as in opposition to
the law (Thompson, *Witness*, p. 19).

In the mythological poems the revolutionary moment is absorbed into a
more fully evolved process of a double fall and redemption, which is both
personal and historical. A moment of cleansing violence takes place at the
bottom of the second fall. The redemption is conceived in Biblical terms, in
two phases, first as 'Beulah', then as the New Jerusalem that follows the
Apocalypse in the Book of Revelation – a Book whose canonicity was long
in doubt and which retained its popularity with millenarians of all kinds.
Blake's extended mythological poems have been read only in the twentieth
century, and they have been found difficult, private, like the language of
other Romantic mythological worlds, for example, Friedrich Hölderlin's
late odes. It has been argued that as the Jacobin current went underground
towards the end of the 1790s, and Blake became more and more isolated,
he had no 'answerable language'; against this it is argued that Blake was
using 'the well-known idiom of millenarianism' (*ibid.*) (not a private language). There is no doubt that there was an idiom of millenarianism, but it
is misleading to derive it from the sectaries of the seventeenth century;
Blake was thoroughly up to date, and his Jesus is not that of the 'Saints' but
of the society that required liberating at the end of the eighteenth century.
He was well aware of current political terms, and of the new biblical criticism. While there are some overlaps with millenarians like Richard Brothers
(imprisoned in 1797) and Joanna Southcott (whose movement survived
the failure of the Second Coming into the 1830s), mainly through the use
of apocalyptic biblical imagery and the heightened tone of 'prophecy',
Blake's language is a complex literary product, in which the language and
form of Milton and the eighteenth-century imitators of the Miltonic sublime mingle with ballad, hymn and the 'wiry outlines' of a unique visual
imagination.[47]

---

[47] E. S. Shaffer, 'Secular apocalypse: prophets and apocalyptics at the end of the eighteenth
century', in *Apocalypse theory and the ends of the world*, M. Bull (ed.), Oxford: Blackwell, 1995, pp. 137–58.

Finally, Blake too is a proponent of the Romantic imagination. His activist and politically engaged poetics does not, from a theoretical point of view, stand in opposition to a 'Kantian ideal of disinterested art' represented by Coleridge and Wordsworth.[48] The Blakean use of imagination transposes the Shaftesbury–Akenside premise of the intuitive capacity for aesthetic response onto all perceptual judgments, and so represents a parallel rather than a contrasting development to the imaginative construction of the desired objects of the ideas of reason.[49] The doctrine of 'Eternal Forms' may be primarily platonic in origin, but Kantian and post-Kantian transcendentalism was itself a neoplatonic movement. Both display a complex debt to Burkean aesthetics. By attending to the realm of religion, however, it becomes clear that for all parties religious emotion was still a force to be summoned up through the newly fashioned imagination and to be put to many, often contestatory and increasingly secular uses.

[48] This view, expressed by Jerome McGann in *The Romantic ideology: a critical investigation*, Chicago, IL: University of Chicago Press, 1985, is representative of a whole series of books debunking the 'aesthetic ideology' in apparent ignorance of its sources in the philosophical recognition of the illusory nature of theological concepts.

[49] Jonathan Mee, 'Is there an antinomian in the house?', in *Historicizing Blake*, S. Clarke and D. Worrall (eds.), New York: St Martin's Press, 1994, p. 16.

8

Language theory and the art of understanding

KURT MUELLER-VOLLMER

> For not even the desire to communicate could be communicated if, before any agreed upon understanding takes place, humans did not already understand each other.
>
> August Wilhelm Schlegel

> Nobody understands himself only by being himself and not also somebody else at the same time.
>
> Friedrich Schlegel

I Poetics, language, hermeneutics

I.I

A persistent concern for problems of language that was shared by most Romantic writers did not come to them as an afterthought. Rather, their novel poetics, which posited the primacy of the creative imagination over an inherited system of rules and conventions, would make them focus on the poetic medium, language itself, and put them on a collision course not only with eighteenth-century neoclassical aesthetics, but also with the linguistic opinions that had been handed down to them by Enlightenment philosophers and theoreticians. Kantian and idealist philosophy on the other hand, whose basic beliefs they shared, though it stressed the creative nature of the human mind and ascribed a formative function to the imagination, did not engender any new philosophy of language. In fact, the rise and flowering of linguistic thought during the seventeenth and eighteenth centuries was so much part of the empiricist and rationalist traditions that in the eyes of the idealists the entire linguistic enterprise had become flawed. Thus the Romantics felt obligated to raise for themselves the fundamental issues of language, that is, its relation to thought, the nature of reality and human creativity, and to articulate linguistic theories that would be relevant to their own endeavours. This was their way of breaking with the rationalist and empiricist traditions and the deeply ingrained representational notion of language upon which neoclassicism had erected its mimetic ideals of literature. It is not surprising, therefore, that Romantic literature not only reveals a new and different conception of language that we can refer to broadly as Romantic,[1] but that the major writers such as the Schlegel brothers, Novalis, Schleiermacher in Germany, Madame de Staël and Benjamin Constant in France and Samuel Taylor Coleridge in England have articulated a coherent conception of language that takes issue with and replaces the traditional seventeenth- and eighteenth-century views associated with the names of Hobbes, Descartes, Locke and Condillac. Inspiration is drawn instead from a different set of thinkers, from Leibniz, Michaelis, Rousseau, Herder and above all from Kant and Fichte and their new philosophy of the mind.

I.2

If the Romantics' preoccupation with language was a direct outgrowth of their new poetics, the same holds true for their interest in hermeneutics or, in the words of Schleiermacher, 'the art of interpretation'. We must, however, distinguish between this art and its theory on the one hand, and the new attitude of the Romantics toward poetry, literature, philosophy and culture that accompanied them. What mattered to them was first of all a sympathetic understanding of the individuality and the creative spirit manifest in products of the mind rather than any judicious attempt to judge these by the preconceived standards of neoclassicist aesthetics. The poetic spirit for the Romantics had many incarnations – in different individuals and national literatures ancient and modern. Yet accepting the multiplicity of individual spirits also entailed a confirmation of their own distinct being. They thought that by recognizing the creative spirit in other cultures and other geniuses one would become aware of one's own indelible individuality. For the Romantics that meant crossing the borders of their national literatures and exploring what lay outside and had been previously taken merely as foreign and, frequently, inferior. The new attitude, first articulated by Herder, found its most effective embodiment in Madame de Staël's book *On Germany* (1810, 1813), which was not only the first portrayal of another national culture, but a testimony also to the new Romantic internationalism when, after having been rendered into English, it enjoyed an expeditious success with an influential readership in England and America.

---

[1] See Helmut Gipper, 'Sprachphilosophie in der Romantik' in Marcelo Dascal (ed.), *Sprachphilosophie, Philosophy of language, La philosophie du langage, Ein internationales Handbuch zeitgenössischer Forschung*, Berlin, New York: de Gruyter, 1992, I: 197–233 and my earlier 'From aesthetics to linguistics: Wilhelm von Humboldt and the Romantic idea of language', in *Le Groupe de Coppet: actes et documents du deuxième Colloque de Coppet 10–13 juillet 1974*, Geneva: Slatkine; Paris: Champion, 1977, pp. 195–215.

The openness toward and appropriation of works from other national literatures that is characteristic of the Romantic writers of Europe makes us aware of the linguistic dimension that is a necessary part of the new attitude. Looking at the Schlegels and Tieck in Germany, Madame de Staël in France or Coleridge and Carlyle in England, we find that these writers did not only study other modern languages in order to read the literature written in them, but were actively engaged in the business of translation, and frequently reflected upon this activity of cultural mediation. It is against this background that the various approaches to hermeneutics and hermeneutic thought must be viewed. As far as translation is concerned, there was an ongoing reciprocity between the practice of translation and hermeneutic theory proper.[2] Schleiermacher's and Humboldt's exemplary statements on the nature and function of literary translation grew from this environment and highlight once more the linguistic dimension that is so peculiar to Romantic hermeneutics. For what makes it distinct from its historicist academic successors, such as Ast, Droysen, Boeckh and Dilthey, is more than anything else its linguistic orientation. A notion of the linguisticality of all understanding lies at the core of both Schleiermacher's and Humboldt's hermeneutic thought. Hence the rise of hermeneutics goes hand in hand with a new approach to language; in fact the latter must be seen as its indispensable prerequisite.

2   A new conception of language

2.1

Romantic notions about language manifest themselves in a variety of ways and in different genres of texts. Linguistic ideas are frequently found integrated into literary and poetic texts, as in Coleridge's 'The ancient mariner' or more conspicuously in Novalis's *The apprentices at Saïs* where use is made of Augustinian semiology to bring across the idea of correspondence between mind and nature. Often linguistic reflections are a part of longer or shorter theoretical texts, as with F. Schlegel and Madame de Staël. Yet most important are the outright theoretical statements that the writers associated with the early Romantic movement have produced. They represent but different versions of the non-representational view of language that is characteristic of the early Romantic movement, from about 1795 to 1816. The break that occurred between the radical Romanticism of the Jena group and the later writers is reflected in the marked

---

[2] Antoine Berman, *The experience of the foreign: culture and translation in Romantic Germany*. Tr. S. Heyvaert, Albany, NY: State University of New York Press, 1992.

disappearance of its urgent concern for linguistic problems. We no longer find this same concern among the Arnims, Eichendorff and Brentano.

A disparity of equal magnitude exists between the early Romantics' pre-occupation with linguistic philosophy, and the views espoused afterwards by the representatives of the new academic discipline of historical linguistics. The latter has often misleadingly been called Romantic or described as an outgrowth of the Romantic movement. Indeed, literary and cultural historians, when they discuss Romantic ideas of language, do not usually refer to the poets, critics and theorists of the Romantic movement, but to linguists like Rask, Grimm or Bopp.[3] So powerful has been the identification of historical Indo-European philology with Romanticism, that it led Foucault to choose Bopp rather than Humboldt as the prototype of the new linguistic paradigm that replaced the classical representational model of language for him.[4] Yet Bopp's taxonomic reconstructions of the historical parentage of the Indo-European languages and its underlying reductionist conception of the nature of language are as far removed as can be from the linguistic ideas of the Romantics. Neither Rask, Grimm nor Bopp shared their philosophical conception of language and what these linguists had to say in these matters seems utterly naive and unsophisticated compared to the complex theoretical statements of the Schlegels, Novalis, Schleiermacher or Humboldt. Among these it was Humboldt who, in order 'to measure out the human capacity for language', translated his philosophical concerns into a programme of empirical investigation and created a linguistics that in its universalist and comparatist dimensions represented a true counterpart to the Schlegels' encyclopedic treatment of the history of European literature. But like the Schlegels' conception of a comparative literary history, Humboldt's linguistics did not enter the academic mainstream, and after his death it was ignored by the official representatives of the discipline. From its very start the triumphant Indo-European linguistics had abandoned any interest in the philosophical questions of language.[5] On the other hand, Humboldt, A. W. Schlegel and Novalis had revolutionized language philosophy and had developed positions far beyond the reach and interest of succeeding generations of academic linguists for whom language had become an isolated object of scientific inquiry.[6] The linguistic turn that was inaugurated by Saussure's

[3] Helmut Gipper and Peter Schmitter, *Sprachwissenschaft und Sprachphilosophie im Zeitalter der Romantik*, Tübingen: Günter Narr Verlag, 1979.
[4] Michel Foucault, *The order of things. An archeology of the human sciences*, New York: Vintage Books, 1973, pp. 280–94.
[5] On this issue see my 'Mutter Sanskrit und die Nacktheit der Südseesprachen. Das Begräbnis von Humboldts Sprachwissenschaft', *Athenäum: Jahrbuch für Romantik* 1 (1991), pp. 109–33.
[6] This was already noticed by Eva Fiesel in her ground-breaking and long-ignored work, *Die Sprachphilosophie der deutschen Romantik*, Tübingen: Mohr, 1927, p. 215.

Cours de linguistique early in this century has brought back with a ven-
geance many of the problems that the nineteenth century linguists had tried
to forget.

2.2

Among the Romantic writers and theorists, August Wilhelm Schlegel
(1767–1845), the older of the brothers, was the first for whom language
became a critical issue. 'With impatience I am waiting for your *Poetic letters*', his brother Friedrich wrote to him in the autumn of 1795. 'What
good and beautiful things will they bring? . . . undoubtedly there will be
much that is entirely new and foreign to me . . . We start from very different intuitions and concepts.'[7] The 'very different intuitions and concepts'
referred to the linguistic problems that the two brothers' new approach to
literary theory had raised. It was precisely in the area of language philosophy that August Wilhelm would undertake something akin to the transcendental approach to literary theory attempted by his brother Friedrich,
namely to provide a linguistic basis for the new poetics. That his role within
Romanticism has often wrongly been confined to that of the ubiquitous
critic–translator whose main contribution was to help his brother's novel
ideas achieve international success, is due to a long-standing neglect of the
linguistic dimension of Romanticism in general and of the linguistic work
of August Wilhelm in particular.[8]

His *Poetic letters* appeared in the same year in Schiller's journal *Die
Horen* as 'Letters on poetry, prosody and language'. The essay offers a
brilliant investigation into the character of poetic discourse and raises
issues that traditional normative poetics had failed to address. At stake
was the question whether rhythm and poetic metre inherently belonged to
poetic discourse rather than being mere conventional features and ornaments of speech. Schlegel believed the former to be the case. Since to prove
his point a close analysis of the relation between poetry and its linguistic
medium was called for, Schlegel devoted a major portion of the piece to
linguistic criticism. It is apparent that he had prepared himself well for
his task, because his argumentation reveals a state-of-the-art knowledge
of eighteenth-century English, French and German language philosophy.

---

[7] *Friedrich Schlegel's Briefe an seinen Bruder August Wilhelm*, Oskar Walzel (ed.), Berlin:
Speyer and Peters, 1890, p. 242.
[8] Philippe Lacoue-Labarthe and Jean-Luc Nancy in their popular *The literary absolute*,
Philip Barnard and Cheryl Lester (trans.), Albany, NY: State University Press of New York,
1988, fail to discuss the linguistic dimension of Romantic literary theory altogether, and
while calling the *Kunstlehre* one of its principal texts, along with the *Dialogue on poetry*,
they do not consider it. The late Ernst Behler had begun a new critical edition of August
Wilhelm Schlegel's lectures – including the hitherto unpublished ones. *Kritische Ausgabe
der Vorlesungen*, Paderborn, Schöningh, 1989, vol. 1.

Schlegel's initial position is in close agreement with the views of Herder and Rousseau, even though their names are not mentioned. Taking up the controversy over the origin of language, he rejects both the theory of the divine origin of language and the opposing conventionalist account advanced by the empiricist philosophers. For whether God is taken to have taught humans language, or whether they are believed to have themselves given names to objects 'in the same way you baptize your children', the proponents of either opinion presuppose human language ability, the ability namely 'to fix and to recall our ideas through signs', which means that 'people understood each other before possessing the means of understanding'.[9] When Schlegel discusses the origin of language, he does not mean the tracing back of existing natural languages to a common 'Ursprache', which he considered an impossible task, requiring 'a deadly leap of faith', but rather a 'philosophical theory' of how language must have originated, a theoretical model in other words, that would explain how language operates at all times. For Schlegel only three such theoretical accounts were possible. Either language is derived from the emotions, from the imitation of objects or from a combination of both. Since human speech contains both emotive and imitative elements, only the third alternative seems acceptable. But the problem Schlegel faces is how he could arrive at a unified conception of language that would overcome the difficulties inherent in the representational or, to use Charles Taylor's term, designative view of language that is shared equally by the rationalist and the empiricist tradition, and is represented by such diverse thinkers as Descartes, Hobbes and Locke[10] and how at the same time he could account for its relationship to other human expressions such as gestures, music, song and dance.

If, according to adherents of the designative view, language imitates objects, this means that verbal signs stand for objects as their semiotic representations, and that the objects and meanings exist independently of and prior to their being represented by signs. Here language is perceived merely as a tool for the communication of fixed meanings – a far cry from Schlegel's invocation of the poetic powers of language at the beginning of the essay. It was thus not possible to arrive at a unified conception of language as Schlegel desired, by combining the two origin-theories to form a third position. Instead an entirely new approach was called for. Although

---

[9] 'Briefe über Poesie, Silbenmass und Sprache', August Wilhelm Schlegel, *Kritische Schriften und Briefe*, Edgar Lohner (ed.), Stuttgart: Kohlhammer, 1962, vol. 1, *Sprache und Poetik*, p. 150. This statement echoes Herder's *The origin of language* in its critique of Condillac's account of the origin of language which implied for him that 'words must have arisen before there were words'. Johann Gottfried Herder *Sämmtliche Werke*, Bernard Suphan (ed.), Berlin: Weidmannsche Buchhandlung, 1891, v: 20.

[10] Charles Taylor, 'Language and human nature' in *Human agency and language, philosophical papers*, Cambridge University Press, 1985, 1: 215–47.

the *Horen* essay falls short in this respect, Schlegel gives his readers an indication how such an approach would have to combine Herder's linguistic insights with Fichtean idealism, that is, Herder's notion of reflection (*Besonnenheit*) had to be fused with Fichte's idea of the spontaneous activity of the human mind.

2.3   To understand Fichte better than himself

Johann Gottlieb Fichte's (1762–1814) transcendental idealism has been a starting point and catalyser for the creation not only of Romantic poetics and literary theory, but of language philosophy as well. But whereas the appropriation of Fichtean modes of thinking into Romantic literary theory has been well studied and documented, the same cannot be said about their impact on Romantic language philosophy. There is probably no better illustration for the Romantics' often quoted maxim that one ought 'to understand an author better than the author himself', than the way the Jena group (and Coleridge for that matter[11]) would understand Fichte's philosophy better than its originator.

Novalis wrote in his 'Logological fragments', that one should think of Fichte as the discoverer of an entirely new way of thinking for which our language had no name yet. Even if the discoverer himself were not the most apt and ingenious artist to master his new instrument, he asserted, 'there probably are or will be individuals much better at "Fichtecizing" (*Fichtisieren*), than Fichte himself. Incredible works of art could come into being – once we begin "Fichtecizing" as artists.'[12]

Language theory would prove to be a most fertile ground for such Fichtecizing. Paradoxically though, Fichte's impact on language philosophy seems to be rather negative on first glance. German idealism, having completed the Copernican Revolution of thought begun by Kant and having replaced the preceding empiricist and rationalist epistemologies, was not interested in producing a new language philosophy. Already Kant in his critical philosophy when he distinguished strictly between ideal and empirical components of the subject, had implied that mental representations are produced by the mechanism of the mind independent from experience and linguistic usage.[13]

---

[11] On Coleridge's occupation with language and the relation of his linguistic theories to those of Leibniz, Herder, Rousseau, Fichte and Humboldt, see James C. McKusick, *Coleridge's philosophy of language*, New Haven, CT: Yale University Press, 1986.

[12] Novalis, *Schriften*, Richard Samuel, Hans-Joachim Mähl and G. Schulz (eds), vol. II, Darmstadt: Wissenschaftliche Buchgesellschaft, 1965, 'Logologische Fragmente', no. 11, p. 524.

[13] Lia Formigari, *Signs, science and politics: philosophies of language in Europe, 1700–1830*, Amsterdam Benjamins, 1993, 169–71.

Things seem similar with Fichte at first. While attempting in his *Organon of science* (*Wissenschaftslehre*) to delineate the operations of the mind as they obey an unconscious system of rules and to deduce the system of these rules, Fichte treated the production of knowledge and the self-constitution of the subject, the 'I', as a purely cognitive and language-independent activity. However, the Romantic language theorists thought that the cognitive processes described by Fichte could only be understood as mediated by language. Thus their approach is governed by an intent to redefine the Fichtean model of mental production in linguistic terms, something that they thought Fichte himself had failed to do. Yet it was Fichte who, in 1795 with his essay 'On human language ability and the origin of language', had provided the occasion for the advent of what might rightfully be called the Romantic linguistic turn. His was the first (and the last) attempt by an idealist philosopher to revive language philosophy under the banner of transcendental idealism. Because the author did not carry his transcendental approach far enough, his attempt was only partially successful: his arguments still betray an adherence to the representational notion of language that was characteristic of the rationalist and empiricist thinkers. Both Descartes and Locke had assumed that thoughts and ideas existed prior to and independently of their expression through linguistic signs. In holding with this view Fichte defined language as 'the expression of our thoughts through arbitrary signs'[14] thereby making language into the handmaiden of thought rather than conceiving of it as an organ of thought itself.

This may be the reason for the Schlegel brothers' harsh criticism of Fichte's piece. The only thing positive that Friedrich found in it he summarized as follows: 'He who does not show how language had to originate, may stay at home. Everybody can dream how it could have arisen.' Schlegel's dictum (echoing Fichte's own formulation at the beginning of the essay) expresses a fundamental notion of Romantic language theories. From now on the question of the origin of language is no longer seen from the vantage point of Condillac's, Rousseau's and Herder's historicizing a-temporal constructions or Locke's and Berkeley's epistemological models, but instead the attempt is made, in Fichte's words, 'to derive the necessity of the invention of language from the nature of human reason itself' (p. 97). Seen from this vantage point, the problem of the origin of language becomes a question of the human capacity for language that calls for a transcendental analysis, a task that Fichte did not live up to in this essay. Yet the text contains one very important insight which Friedrich Schlegel had missed completely in his critique, but which his brother, Novalis and

---

[14] 'Von der Sprachfähigkeit und dem Ursprung der Sprache' (1795), Johann Gottlieb Fichte, *Gesamtausgabe*, R. Lauth and H. Jacob (eds.), Stuttgart-Bad Cannstatt: Frommann, 1966, III: 97.

Humboldt – each in their own way – would make their own: the derivation of language from human interaction. According to Fichte humans possess a drive that leads them to search for manifestations of rationality (*Vernunftmäßigkeit*) outside themselves, 'to enter into a contact with their own kind', and to search for mutual recognition through communication of their thoughts and ideas. Whenever humans enter into a relationship of this kind with each other the idea is 'aroused' in them 'to indicate their thoughts through arbitrary signs, in a word: the idea of language. Hence, the drive to find signs of rationality outside themselves harbors the particular drive to create a language' (p. 103).

Interaction and thus a human existence for Fichte is only possible through a process of sharing one's thoughts and ideas with others. The 'I', or subject, of *The Organon of science* (*Wissenschaftslehre*) is revealed ultimately then as an interactive concept, and the conditions for the possibility of mutual sharing are rooted in man's language ability. Language thus assumes a decisive function for the constitution of the human world. Without language there can be no intersubjectivity which institutes man as an intellectual and spiritual being. In Hegel's *Phenomenology of the spirit* (1807) self-consciousness and mutual recognition will result from the Hobbesian life–death struggle in which the master prevails over the slave. Fichte stands at the opposite end of this issue, language for him is the vehicle of communicative interaction through which alone mutual recognition can be achieved.

3 Language theories: issues and directions

3.1

It was Fichte's student August Ferdinand Bernhardi (1770–1820), brother-in-law of the poet Ludwig Tieck in Berlin and himself a noted literary critic, who elaborated and unfolded his teacher's ideas into a comprehensive philosophy of language. In his *Linguistic organon* (*Sprachlehre*) of 1801[15] the initial question (as for August Wilhelm Schlegel before and for Coleridge in his *Biographia literaria* later[16]) concerned the nature and function of poetic discourse. As it turns out, language as 'the organ of poetry' is shown by Bernhardi to be itself poetic, and the power of poetic speech is that of language itself in constituting the human world.

Bernhardi's work demonstrates convincingly the interdependency of poetic, linguistic and hermeneutic thought that is the mark of Romantic

---

[15] August F. Bernhardi, *Sprachlehre*, 2 vols, Berlin: H. Fröhlich, 1801.
[16] Coleridge writes (*Biographia literaria*, J. Shawcross (ed.), London: Oxford University Press, 1965, 1907), I: 1) that he intended 'to effect, as far as possible, a settlement of the long continued controversy concerning the true nature of poetic diction'.

critical discourse. But this interdependency is also indicative of the Romantic writers' rejection of the traditional Kantian concept of a language-independent human subject that formed the basis of the critique of reason. In fact their philosophy of language can be viewed as an attempt to recast the notion of the human subject in linguistic terms. In his work Bernhardi shows (as did Novalis in his semiotics and Humboldt in his linguistic writings) that human reason (*Vernunft*) in order to unite rationality with the imagination must articulate itself and bring something to 'presentation'. But this requires a subject that 'presents' and another that receives the 'presentation' (*Darstellung*)[17] from the first. In actual life this means that one person is addressing another, with whom he or she communicates, and whenever this happens, Bernhardi argues, language turns into speech. The essence of speech then for Bernhardi – as for Humboldt, the Schlegels, Schleiermacher and Novalis – consists of dialogue (*Gespräch*). But he believed language itself provides human speech with its dialogical structure. Therefore, in the first volume of his *Linguistic organon* he attempts to uncover within the grammatical structures of language 'the traces' of its dialogical origin,[18] whereas in the second he develops a theory of scientific and poetic discourse.

3.2

When August Wilhelm Schlegel praised Bernhardi's work in his brother's journal *Europa* in 1803, he had already overcome the short-comings of his earlier attempts. He wholly shared Bernhardi's views regarding language, its dialogical structure and the importance of language philosophy for an understanding of poetry, of literature and of culture in general. He expressed his own ideas on these matters in a series of lectures between 1798 and 1804, held at Jena and in Berlin,[19] in which he divulged the new

---

[17] The concept of *Darstellung* (presentation) lies at the centre of the anti-mimetic idea of language held by the Romantics. It can therefore not be rendered as 'representation'. Apparently it was Schelling who first used the term in this sense to describe the nature art in his *System of transcendental idealism* of 1800, a work widely read and discussed by the Romantics.

[18] This is Bernhardi's way of redefining the Cartesian notion of universal grammar in terms of transcendental idealism. The strongest evidence for the dialogical origin he believed to have found in the system of personal pronouns. Humboldt, who studied Bernhardi's work was to embark on large-scale empirical investigations into the pronominal systems of a large number of languages. On this, see his Academy Addresses 'On the dual' (1827) and 'On the affinity of the adverbs of place with the personal pronoun in some languages' (1829) which provided some of the linguistic underpinnings for J. Habermas's theory of communicative action.

[19] These are the Lectures *Über philosophische Kunstlehre* or *Aesthetic organon* of 1798–9 (the neologism parallels Fichte's term *Wissenschaftslehre*), a more elaborate version of the same from 1801–2, and the *Lectures on the encyclopaedia of the sciences* of 1803.

Romantic philosophy in a systematic fashion before a public forum – thus setting the stage for its dissemination in Germany and abroad. It is in these lectures that the Romantic position on language is stated authoritatively and consistently.[20]

We can single out some major components in Schlegel's argument that help us summarize his position, and measure out the circumference of the Romantic conception of language found in most other writers. The first is the attempt to overcome the dichotomy of eighteenth-century language theories to explain the origin of language from either animal communication or as a result of arbitrary convention. To simply combine the two, a solution he had still favoured in his 1795 essay, would not do, for there is no way for instinct-triggered animal communication to evolve into a language system based on convention. Conventionalists on the other hand had overlooked that 'not even the desire to communicate could be communicated if, before any agreed-upon understanding takes place, humans did not already understand each other'.

Schlegel's solution to the problem is to reinterpret Herder's position from a modified Fichtean standpoint. The beginnings of language for him are simultaneous with the 'first stirrings of a human kind of existence', indeed, the two coincide. But it is through language that man 'tears himself away from nature' and 'constitutes himself'. The constitution of the subject which had been defined as a self-positing process by Fichte in his *Organon of science* is thus given its linguistic turn. Fichtean 'self-activity' is made responsible for both, human speech and the constitution of the subject, but it is through speech that the subject truly comes into being. For without the ability to act spontaneously rather than simply react to what is imposed upon them by the environment, humans would lack any sense of continuity and self-identity. Only by comparing impressions with another could there be a sense of continuity. Presupposed in this mental activity, however, is a capability to fix impressions through symbols and to recall them at will; and this is precisely how Schlegel defines speech.[21]

Secondly, although language ability is a universal human trait, natural languages are 'communal products' (*Vereinwerk*), vehicles as well as products of sociability (*Geselligkeit*) of a particular society or nation. Like Fichte and his other Romantic followers, Schlegel believed that language arises from the desire to establish a communal bond among rational beings, and that speech is the medium of mutual recognition among them.

Thirdly, language is neither a passive response mechanism to external stimuli and sensations nor is it the product of arbitrary invention with the

[20] I am grateful to the late Ernst Behler who has provided me with the proofs of his transcript of A. W. Schlegel's *Lectures on the encyclopaedia of the sciences* from 1803 to be published in volume 2 of the *Kritische Ausgabe*.
[21] August Wilhelm Schlegel, *Kritische Ausgabe der Vorlesungen*, 1: 6.

purpose of representing an independent realm of objects, meanings or ideas. Instead – and here Schlegel anticipates Humboldt's classical formulation, language is the 'formative presentation' (*bildende Darstellung*), of all of these, and thus is 'poetic' in its essence.[22]

Finally, the formative (or poetic) power of language lies in its symbolizing ability. Hence the concept of symbolization is the centrepiece of Schlegel's *Aesthetic organon*. It is the one place where his aesthetics and language theory intersect. To accomplish this, he had to transform Schelling's definition of the beautiful from 'the infinite finitely presented' to 'symbolic presentation of the infinite'. If all art is understood as symbolic, poetry must be its prototype, because it arises from and builds upon the symbolization process that is language. World according to Schlegel exists for us only through language's work of symbolization. Languages therefore cannot be judged as to whether or not their metaphors and images correspond to some imputed reality,[23] but instead reality for us exists through them. Like Vico, Herder and Rousseau before him, Schlegel believes in the primacy of metaphors over abstract discourse. Language is always poetic at first, but as metaphors and tropes come to designate intellectual phenomena, it turns conventional. A language can never become totally unpoetic, and will always preserve some poetic elements. Languages live and expand by producing a continuous chain of comparisons, new metaphors come into being, signs become signs of other signs, so that we have what Humboldt called 'the web of language' that encompasses all its speakers. A word is more than a sign, because it possesses an individuality of its own, on account of the particular aspect through which it presents an object to us, and in regard to what Novalis calls its 'aura', the fact that a word transcends its semiotic function by reflecting its historical position within the language. These are not only Schlegel's views, they are those of Novalis, Humboldt and Schleiermacher as well.

3.3.1

Because eighteenth-century language philosophy was anchored in semiotic concepts, its notion of the sign, a veritable citadel of the representational ideal of language, became the principal target for attack and criticism by the Romantics. Prominently among them was August Wilhelm Schlegel, as we saw, but also Coleridge, Germaine de Staël (as early as 1800), and F. Schlegel with his impressive (though inconclusive) forays into the

---

[22] Humboldt called language 'the formative organ of thought', *Gesammelte Schriften*, A. Leitzmann (ed.), Berlin: Behr, 1903–36, VII: 152.

[23] For example Nietzsche, in his much quoted essay 'On truth and lies in an extra-moral sense' measures language from an extraneous concept of 'reality' and reiterates the traditional designative–representational view of language first introduced by Aristotle in his work *On interpretation*.

unchartered territories of linguistic thought.[24] The most consequential attack and subsequent transformation of the concept of the sign we owe to Novalis and Wilhelm von Humboldt. What they were attempting might be called a transcendental semiotics, in the sense that they were concerned with the conditions for the possibility of communication through verbal signs. In the case of Humboldt this semiotics would form the basis not only of a new conception of language, but for a novel kind of linguistics as well. Novalis, because of his early death, was not able to bring to completion his ambitious project of a comprehensive semiotic theory. What he (and Humboldt for that matter) did write on this subject was not published until the twentieth century. If their writings had been published earlier, much of de Saussure's and his followers' work would have been robbed of its originality.

3.3.2

Friedrich von Hardenberg, or Novalis (1772–1801), is perceived by many as one of the founders of aesthetic Modernism who prepared the way for the poetry and poetics of symbolist writers like Mallarmé or Rimbaud. This was mostly on the strength of some brilliant aphorisms, the longest and most explicit a forty-line piece, 'Monologue', which depicts language as a self-sustained system, 'concerned only with itself – regardless of what its speakers intended', 'constituting a world for itself' like the 'formulas of mathematics that play only with themselves' (*Schriften*, II: 672). Whatever significance one may attribute to this text, the centre of Novalis's language philosophy lies in his semiotics and its 'Theory of the Sign' (*ibid*. pp. 108–10). It is his most concentrated and innovative contribution to Romantic language philosophy.[25]

In raising the fundamental issue of how truth can be obtained through 'the medium of language' Novalis questions the very autonomy and independence of thought from language that Fichte had upheld. Like Fichte before him, he defines the problem of language in semiotic terms, but then parts company with him. To grasp Novalis's argument, it is necessary first to clarify his understanding of the verbal sign that marks a radical break with the eighteenth-century semiotic tradition by which the sign is moved from its previous position of detachment and placed into a communicative context. Novalis distinguishes first between the signifying medium (sound

---

[24] On F. Schlegel's linguistic views see Heinrich Nüsse, *Die Sprachtheorie Friedrich Schlegels*, Heidelberg: Winter, 1962 where he also examines the importance Schlegel's *Language and wisdom of the Hindus* (1808) has had for nineteenth-century language studies.

[25] On Novalis's semiotics and its importance for his philosophy and his other writings see Wm. Arctander O'Brien, *Novalis: signs of revolution*, Durham, NC: Duke University Press, 1995, Part III, pp. 77–118.

or letter) which he calls the sign, and the signified. Because a sign is always intended for someone, it is termed a 'hypothetical intuition' by him. This is a crucial definition, because it introduces Kantian/idealist philosophy into semiotics. For, if concepts without intuitions are blind, as Kant had maintained, a sign, in order to denote a concept had to rely on intuition in order to be understood as a sign. But how can signs express our thinking? Novalis views thinking as a mental, non-spatial, activity, a 'freely enacted process of successive isolation' of ideas. Speaking and writing on the other hand as sign-producing activities are spatial processes of 'successive isolation' of elements; they are 'definite spatial presentation(s) of thinking'. But because the activities of speaking and writing involve succession also, the two join together what according to Kant, are the two basic forms of our sensory intuition, namely time and space. In short, verbal and written signs combine spatial and temporal elements,[26] a feat that thinking alone would not accomplish, Novalis thought.

In contradistinction to Saussure, and many structuralist and poststructuralist theorists today, who consider the sign as the linkage of signifier and signified, Novalis, in translating the Fichtean notion of interactive mutual recognition into a semiotic model of communication, discerned the nature of the sign in a four-part relationship. It consists of a 'first signifier', that is someone who signifies; secondly, the sign itself, and thirdly, what is signified by it; and fourth, a sign being always directed at someone, a 'second signifier' who, like the first signifier, must perform an act of signifying (or semiosis) in order to actualize the 'hypothetical intuition' intended by the sign. In other words, the sign is defined by Novalis by its function within a model of communication.

Characteristically, in this model communication is conceived not as in many contemporary theories as a kind of data-transfer from a 'sender' to a 'receiver', but one that calls for two equal agents. Communication between them rests on their mutual acts of signification. In order that there can be a convergence of meaning between the two agents, Novalis assumed the existence of a sphere of 'homogeneity' that they had in common. He tried to elaborate the precise nature of this 'homogeneity' in a highly technical analysis that utilized Kant's theory of mental schemata. It breaks off unfinished, but suggests that Novalis's semiotic model of communication should be seen as part of the larger system of language.

If Novalis had redefined the notion of the sign and placed it into the context of intersubjective communication, it was Wilhelm von Humboldt (1767–1835) who in a short and tersely written piece, 'Thinking and speaking' (1795–6) analysed the structure of the linguistic sign in its

---

[26] Saussure is usually credited with the discovery of the 'linearity of the linguistic sign'. Yet it was Novalis and Humboldt who expressed this idea long before him.

relationship to thought.[27] Eighteenth-century language philosophy had taken signs to be like a class of objects to which meanings could somehow be attached. By focussing attention on the act of speaking, rather than its product, Humboldt discovered that the linguistic sign was not like an ordinary sensory object, but instead possessed a complex conformation that resulted from the structuring process of the human mind. He showed that speaking consisted of a joining together of two strings of articulation, a series of sounds, the signifiers, and of the thoughts signified. What Humboldt discovered linguists today refer to as the principle of double articulation and is regarded a cornerstone of modern structural linguistics. But there is also a philosophical side to Humboldt's analysis. If thinking consists of 'reflecting', as Humboldt maintains, that is 'the act by which the thinking subject differentiates itself from its thought', it can do so only with the help of speech. In order to separate from the stream of consciousness individual ideas, compare and distinguish them from each other, and to be aware of oneself as distinct from these acts, we need language. For Humboldt thus, as for August Wilhelm Schlegel, the act of speaking is constitutive for the consciousness of self, and we can see how Humboldt's semiotic reflections can provide a linguistic model for the transcendental foundation of philosophy that the idealist thinkers did not furnish. In his later linguistic writings he developed his ideas into a full-fledged communicative model of speech and pointed the way toward those branches of hermeneutic philosophy and critical theory in this century that attempt to locate the foundations of the sciences of man and of society in 'the Apriori of the Speech Community'.[28]

4   Hermeneutics: philology and the concept of understanding

4.1

Although it has been widely accepted that twentieth-century hermeneutic philosophy and interpretation theories have their roots in early Romanticism, our knowledge of its complex hermeneutic theories and practices is still rather insular. Much more needs to be learned about the actual contributions made by individual authors, their relationship to the hermeneutic tradition and the intense exchange of ideas that occurred among them, before a full assessment of their important body of thought can be under-

---

[27] Wilhelm von Humboldt, 'Denken und Sprechen' (1795–6), *Gesammelte Schriften*, VII: 581–3.
[28] K.-O. Apel, 'The apriori of communication and the foundation of the humanities' *Man and world: an international philosophical review* 5 (1972), pp. 3–37; On Jürgen Habermas's indebtedness to Humboldt see his 'Reply', in *The theory of communicative action*, A. Honneth and H. Joas (eds.), Cambridge, MA: The MIT Press, 1991, pp. 214–50.

taken. Until recently critical attention was concentrated on nineteenth-century academic hermeneutics and its major representatives, the later Schleiermacher, his student, the classicist Boeckh, the historian Droysen and the philosopher Dilthey.[29] Yet most of their ideas had originated in the philosophical and literary climate of Jena Romanticism and its Berlin extension during the years from 1795 to 1805. As it turns out, the Schlegel brothers, Humboldt, Novalis and, last but not least, Schleiermacher were the true pioneers. To understand the new hermeneutics and properly assess its achievements we must distinguish between its two major components. The first concerns the transformation of classical philology into a cultural science, whose task was defined as the critical authentication of the extant bodies of texts from Greek and Roman civilization through a process of reconstitution, classification and interpretation, with the aim of reconstructing in their entirety the cultures that had produced them. This transformation led to the encyclopedic systems of the philologists and historians of the nineteenth century and has shaped the history of the human sciences until today.[30] The second component is 'general hermeneutics', or hermeneutic theory proper as an independent field of inquiry. It is centred around the notion of understanding. Wilhelm von Humboldt, and above all Friedrich Schlegel, are largely responsible for the transformation of philology, whereas Schleiermacher must be credited for having created a unified theory of hermeneutics that is grounded in a philosophical and linguistic conception of understanding.

4.2

Friedrich Schlegel's (1772–1829) most explicit statement of his hermeneutic views can be found in a section of his literary notebooks called *On the philosophy of philology*, from 1795–6. Although only published in the twentieth century,[31] many of its ideas had been discussed widely among the Jena group, as we find often similar statements on the same issues in the writings of other members of the group and in those of the early Humboldt. Schlegel's text is exceedingly rich, complex, suggestive and often paradoxical in its formulations as it explores the relationship between

[29] As for example in H.-G. Gadamer's influential work, *Truth and method*. Ironically, academic hermeneutics was largely the product of an oral tradition. Its major texts were only published toward the end of the century. Droysen's *Historik* only appeared in this century.
[30] The best known representative of the genre is August Boeckh's *Encyclopedia and methodology of the philological sciences*, 1877.
[31] 'Friedrich Schlegel's *Philosophie der Philologie*. Mit einer Einleitung herausgegeben von Josef Körner', in *Logos: Internationale Zeitschrift für Philosophie und Kultur* XVIII (1928) no. 1, pp. 1–72. Friedrich Schlegel, *Kritische Friedrich-Schlegel-Ausgabe*, Ernst Behler et al. (eds.), Paderborn Schöningh, XVI: *Zur Philologie*, Hans Eichner (ed.), pp. 33–81. All references are to this edition.

philosophy and philology. It must be read as the attempt to transform traditional, formal philology into a historical discipline by supplying it with new theoretical foundations and enriching it with the 'material study' of ancient civilization in order to make it part of the 'humane study of the history of mankind'.[32] In reconstructing Schlegel's concept of philology, it would be a mistake to rely on his use of the term hermeneutics and read a modern meaning into it. This holds as well for Humboldt who did not use this term in his theory of understanding. In the academic tradition – both Humboldt and Schlegel had studied classics at the University of Göttingen with the same teacher, Christian Gottlob Heyne – hermeneutics was one of the components of classical scholarship, together with textual criticism and grammar, and referred to the textual explanation of obscure or difficult passages. Hence, in Schlegel's (in our sense of the term) 'hermeneutic' conception of philology as a historical, cultural science, hermeneutics as textual interpretation remains a distinct part of philological scholarship, even though he insisted on its 'absolute' interdependence with criticism.

In fact, Schlegel sees the relationship among the different activities of classical scholarship as an hermeneutic one (in our sense), because interpretation is involved in all of them: 'Interpretation can only start where and with whom one is in the clear about language. Obviously, grammar is also required for hermeneutics; but the same holds true for poetics' (*Kritische Friedrich-Schlegel-Ausgabe*, XVI: 48). But the question whether criticism or hermeneutics should be accorded primary importance he finds a 'true antinomy'. Yet he also reasons that a 'philosophy of hermeneutics' should precede the creation of a philological encyclopedia, that is, the systematic treatment of the contents, sources and procedures of philology. But he does not explain what this 'philosophy of hermeneutics' should look like. It is apparent, however, that for him criticism is the quintessence of philology: it must become 'a science of its own' (pp. 50, 48, 55, 69). But it is a criticism that has been thoroughly imbued with the historical and aesthetic sensibility of the philologist, in fact to be a philologist meant 'to cultivate one's historical sense'. Although Schlegel's conception of philology combined the idea of a comprehensive historical and cultural discipline with the call for a new criticism, this criticism was to be applied only to the classical texts of antiquity of an 'aesthetic' or 'historical' nature. To be excluded were 'political' and 'moral' works, and, not being a classical book, the Bible as well (p. 74). We find left out of the philologist's domain not only many genres of culturally important texts, but entire periods in

---

[32] This wording from the *Athenaeum* fragment 404 echoes Humboldt's formulation from his essay 'On the study of Classical antiquity' from 1793, *Gesammelte Schriften*, II: 255–81), the manuscript of which Schlegel probably knew. Parts of Humboldt's text were incorporated later by F. A. Wolf in his *Darstellung der Alterumswissenschaft* published in 1807.

cultural and literary history. There is a reason for this exclusive definition of philology. For Schlegel philology depends on the art of interpretation, and this art can only show itself in full light when it deals with those works of a 'semiotic nature' (p. 46) that represent as he states in one of his fragments, 'the classical and the purely eternal' (*Athenaeum* fragment 404). Only in dealing with such enduring texts the critic finds 'everything is joined together . . . poetic, grammatical, philological, historical, and philosophical criticism' (Fragment 47).

But have not political, moral and religious works come down to us, we should note, because of their semiotic nature? And are they any less important for the cultural history of nations than their aesthetic productions? In one instance Schlegel does speculate about philology to provide a blueprint for the treatment of modern national literatures (Fragment 48). Yet it was the older Schlegel in his Berlin lectures of 1803–4 on *The encyclopaedia of sciences* who overcame the limitations built into his brother's approach by conceiving of philology as a comprehensive interpretive science that would include the languages and literatures of the modern European nations.[33] As pertains to the theory of hermeneutics, it was up to Schleiermacher to do away with the ambiguities in Friedrich Schlegel's *Philosophy of philology* by focussing his attention on the operation of understanding itself rather than on specific classes of texts. It was he who redefined the task of hermeneutics, completed its transcendental reorientation and joined together many of Schlegel's ideas in a systematic fashion.

4.3

Friedrich Schleiermacher (1768–1834) has characterized succinctly the momentous difference that separates traditional rationalist from the new hermeneutics: 'Two definitions of understanding: Everything is understood when nothing nonsensical remains. Nothing is understood that is not construed.'[34] Rationalist hermeneutics had assumed that all utterances, as long as they were 'reasonable', that is, as long as they embodied the rules of their particular genre, can be understood. Problems could arise only when there were difficult or obscure passages that the interpreter had to explain. However, with the historization of the traditional literary genres

[33] August Wilhelm Schlegel, *Vorlesungen zur Encyklopaedie der Wissenschaften*, Dritter Teil, 'Philologie', see footnotes 8 and 22.
[34] *Hermeneutics: the handwritten manuscripts* by Friedrich Schleiermacher, Heinz Kimmerle (ed.), James Duke and Jack Forstman (trans.), Atlanta, GA: Scholars Press, 1977, pp. 41, 68. For a complete text of Schleiermacher's lectures together with his notes and manuscripts see, *Schleiermacher: Hermeneutik und Kritik, mit einem Anhang sprachphilosophischer Texte*, Manfred Frank (ed.), Frankfurt: Suhrkamp, 1977.

by the Romantics, textual understanding itself became problematic. A conviction that understanding could not be taken for granted and an acute awareness of its limitations pervades the new hermeneutics. This conviction was articulated most eloquently by Friedrich Schlegel in his essay 'On the incomprehensible'. Humboldt too believed that 'all understanding is at the same time a non-understanding'. All understanding being problematic – and this is the starting point for Schleiermacher's theory of hermeneutics – it follows that everything we believe we understand must be subject to a controlled process of construal and reconstruction. In other words, textual understanding must rely on a procedure of falsification, to use a modern term, that is governed by language. In fact, for Schleiermacher 'language is the only presupposition in hermeneutics; and everything that is to be discovered, including all remaining objective and subjective presuppositions, must be discovered in language' (p. 50). This is how Schleiermacher himself proceeded in elaborating his hermeneutic system. With its profound philosophical insights and critical acumen, its technical intricacies, its typology of readings and misreadings, it has remained the most complex and sophisticated theory of textual interpretation that has come down to us. Among its distinctive features is the grounding of the concept of understanding in language. That is Schleiermacher locates the prototype of human understanding in the everyday use of language, and its dialogical structures. Speaking and understanding are seen as correlative. Speaker and addressee must rely on their linguistic competence when they communicate with each other, or, as Humboldt, who shared Schleiermacher's views, put it: 'I understand someone else's speech because I could have uttered it myself.' Understanding must thus be defined, in Schleiermacher's terms, as a 'speech act' in reverse (p. 97).

In textual understanding another set of conditions comes into play. A text forms part of the linguistic system of the language in which it is written, while it is at the same time the utterance of an individual in a particular historical situation. Hermeneutic reconstruction therefore must treat the text as a point of intersection of these two aspects. Thus we can identify two distinct types of interpretation, one that considers the work strictly in its linguistic context, as part of a larger historical discourse, and another that concentrates on its individual traits, its constitution, its style, its relation to the author and his or her psychology. Schleiermacher's point is that both types of interpretation are rooted in the linguistic nature of its object, for, 'even an act of speaking cannot be understood as a fact of the mind unless it is also understood in its relationship to language, because it is modified by the linguistic heritage [of the speaker]' (pp. 98–9).

Schleiermacher supplied a linguistic explanation for two Romantic topoi, namely the idea of the hermeneutic circle, and the notion that one ought to understand an author better than himself. The first refers to the apparent paradox that our understanding of a particular is always conditioned by an understanding of the whole of a work, and vice versa. There are different ways in which this circle will manifest itself. As Schleiermacher points out, understanding a work requires first of all a knowledge of the language in which it is written, but this knowledge, as the case of so-called dead languages shows, is to be derived frequently from the very same texts we want to understand. Furthermore, understanding a period in the history of a language presupposes a knowledge of its history which is impossible without a knowledge of the whole language (p. 48). In dealing with a literary text, we encounter still other variations of the circle. For example when it comes to the relationship between different features of a work and the dominant aesthetic and stylistic order that constitutes its individuality, its style, understanding the former requires a grasp of the latter, and vice versa. Schleiermacher explains how this apparent circle is overcome by the interpreter and describes the operations he performs. They encompass different procedures like contextualizing, hypothesizing (divination), construction and reconstruction. Schleiermacher thought that in the human sciences 'all knowledge must be constructed in this manner' (p. 113).

The celebrated maxim that one ought to understand an author better than himself has seen many conflicting interpretations. Yet it is employed and explained by Schleiermacher in a rather unambiguous fashion. For example, when Kant used the words 'your most humble servant' he was, in Schleiermacher's eyes, not aware of the fact that he was merely expressing cliches, 'pseudo- words'. Here his interpreter must step forth and bring to conscious awareness the linguistic state of affairs of which Kant had remained unperceiving. More basic is the example with respect to what Schleiermacher calls the 'First Canon of Grammatical Interpretation' which states that specific problems of textual interpretation should be decided only on the basis of the linguistic sphere common to the author and his public. This sphere includes both grammatical and sociolinguistic factors of which the author was not consciously aware but that the interpreter must know so that he in fact will have to place himself in a position where he can understand the author better than himself (p. 112).

Schleiermacher's interest in hermeneutics dates from the time he lived in Berlin in close contact with Friedrich Schlegel, and it is not surprising that his ideas should have been written down as fragments in the vein of the other Romantic theorists. He drew on them later to prepare his influential lecture course on 'Hermeneutics and criticism' at the newly founded University of Berlin, and it was in this form that his ideas were to enter the nineteenth-century academic tradition. But Schleiermacher had already made his views known earlier in 1800, albeit in unacademic, rudimentary form, in his defence of Friedrich Schlegel's controversial novel *Lucinde*.

Here he had addressed from the basis of the new Romantic poetics the problems of interpreting contemporary works of literature.[35]

4.4

Main-stream historians of the German hermeneutic tradition and the representatives of twentieth-century hermeneutic philosophy, notably Heidegger and Gadamer, have accorded Wilhelm von Humboldt something like an honorary place within that tradition. Indeed, his Academy address 'On the task of the historian' (1821), much written about by generations of historians can be seen as the birth-place of the notion of 'effective history', and the constructivist nature of historical narratives. This being said, we should recognize that the core and the bulk of Humboldt's contributions to hermeneutic theory and thought clearly lie in his linguistics and language philosophy. Whereas his linguistics, which encompassed so many of the major and many minor languages of the world and combined structural, comparative, pragmatic, functionalist, generative and typological interests,[36] evince an outspoken anthropological intent, Humboldt's procedures betray a basic hermeneutic orientation. As early as 1801 he had stated that different languages are not just as many designations of the same matter, but rather different views of it, and that once we leave the realm of sensory perception, they present us with just as many differently constituted objects (*Gesammelte Schriften*, VII: 602). Human beings, in other words, live with the objects of their thought as their particular language presents these objects to them, because languages as organized systems do not mirror the world, but rather present different views of it. In some sense Humboldt's entire linguistics and language philosophy can be construed as a theoretical and empirical unfolding of this thesis. Madame de Staël's dictum in her book *On Germany* that 'acquiring another language means acquiring another world for one's mind' can be cited as evidence that it is shared by other Romantic writers.[37]

It would however be erroneous to characterize Humboldt's, Schleiermacher's or the Schlegels' position as linguistic relativism. In fact, its powerful universalist ingredient separates Romantic language philosophy and hermeneutics from postmodern and poststructuralist theories. Languages are not like windowless monads for the Romantics, their diversity is rather a condition for the cultural diversification of mankind and thus mutual

---

[35] *Vertraute Briefe über Friedrich Schlegels 'Lucinde'*, Lübeck, Leipzig: Bohn, 1800.
[36] For the languages that Humboldt knew or studied see my *Wilhelm von Humboldts Sprachwissenschaft: ein Verzeichnis des sprachwissenschaftlichen Nachlasses*, Paderborn, Vienna, Zürich: F. Schöningh, 1993, 454–60.
[37] *De l'Allemagne*, nouvelle édition, Jean de Pange and Simone de Balayé (eds.), 5 vols., Paris: Hachette, 1958, II: 179.

sharing among cultures. For despite their separateness languages share essential qualities. Specifically, humans understand each other through speech, Humboldt reasoned, on account of some fundamental commonalities, among them sameness of human nature, and, as Kant and Fichte had taught him, common mental structures and dispositions, and springing from these, a system of linguistic universals forming a 'linguistic prototype' underlying all natural languages, and lastly the grammatical and semantic structures of particular languages that make communication through speech possible.

If languages are like spheres or circles enclosing nations, as Humboldt argued, may humans ever escape their 'prison-house of language' (Jean Paul)? The answer is both yes and no, because we may always enter the world of another language, whereas an escape from language itself is unthinkable unless we first shed our human condition (*Gesammelte Schriften*, VII: 602). Language while separating cultures from each other is the condition not only for their separate individuality, Humboldt insisted, but also provides the means to bridge the gap between them. It is apparent then that the problem of translation is central to the new hermeneutics. In his *Philosophy of philology* Friedrich Schlegel had already disclosed some of its complexities, and there are pertinent utterances by the older Schlegel and Madame de Staël, yet it is to Humboldt and Schleiermacher that we owe the most insightful statements on translation theory. They have become classical texts since. Although produced for different occasions, an 'Introduction' to his translation of Aeschylus' *Agamemnon* (1816) in the case of Humboldt, and an address to the Royal Academy of Berlin (1813) in the case of Schleiermacher, there is extensive agreement between them as regards the relevant philosophical and linguistic problems and the significance they assign to translation activity.[38] Its problematics did not lie for them in the rendering of everyday and strictly business communications, but in the task of translating works of original scholarship, philosophy, literature and poetry, from one language to another, because these works, in contrast to the former, rely on the creative use of the structures and powers of symbolization peculiar to their respective language. In comparing languages with each other Schleiermacher noted that 'the system of concepts and their signs' are not synchronically identical in the source and target languages, but cut across each other. This means that in a given language concepts connect with and complement each other forming a tightly woven system whose individual parts do not correspond to any of those in another language.

---

[38] Wilhelm von Humboldt, *Gesammelte Schriften*, VIII: 119–46; F. Schleiermacher, 'Methoden des Übersetzens', *Sämmtliche Werke*, dritte Abteilung, Berlin: Reimer, 1938, II: 207–45. Partial English translations in *Theories of translation: an anthology of essays from Dryden to Derrida*, Rainer Schulte and John Biguenet (eds.), Chicago, IL: University of Chicago Press, 1992, pp. 36–59.

The outlook then for translation appears bleak if not to say hopeless, if this view of language holds. But it is precisely against this seemingly forbidding state of affairs that Humboldt and Schleiermacher attempted to define the task of the translator and delineate the space within which he is able to exercise his craft. What is required is first of all familiarity with the source language, and an understanding of the work embedded in it. To these prerequisites the mastery of the target language must be added and the ability to recreate in this medium the work and its meaning as the translator has understood it. Hence the competency required for translation far exceeds what is demanded of the ordinary critic and interpreter who is operating within a monolingual environment. Schleiermacher thought that there were just two kinds of translation possible, one where the translator attempts to 'move the author toward the reader', that is, makes it appear as if the author had written in the language of the reader, and the other where he tries to move the reader in the opposite direction 'toward the author'. Only the second alternative is acceptable to Schleiermacher and Humboldt, because it does not tend to obliterate the difference between the two languages and to neutralize the 'foreign' (Humboldt) or, in today's parlance, the 'otherness' of the work when it is brought into our own culture. However he fails in his task, if the work appears merely strange and becomes inaccessible to its readers. He is successful only if he brings the 'foreign' into the target language. Translation thus by expanding the limits of one's language, enlarges the horizon of one's own culture. We only have to think of the Schlegels' rendering of the plays of Shakespeare, of Constant's, Coleridge's and Carlyle's translations of works by Schiller, Goethe and Jean Paul, and of the awe-inspiring translations from the Greek undertaken by Hölderlin and Humboldt to discern that the Romantic theory of translation is accompanied by an equally imposing practice. Both together reflect what we identified earlier as the Romantics' desire to find self-affirmation in the discovery of different creative manifestations of the human spirit.

If however, all interpretation is an infinite task, as Schleiermacher claims, the same is true for translation, as both he and Humboldt see the matter. As the translator can never sever the meaning of the original work from its language, he is equally bound by the conditions imposed upon him by his own language, its synchronic and diachronic structures. Translations are thus transitory and not lasting. They are, as Humboldt put it, more like labours undertaken to probe the state of the target language than permanent works, and must therefore be undertaken again and again. Stated in modern terminology then, translations have their own historicity, they are an integral part of a nation's history and culture, and this is yet another momentous insight that we owe to Romantic theory.

9

The transformation of rhetoric

DAVID E. WELLBERY

The difficulty of our topic emerges into view when we consider Words-worth's claim in the Preface to *Lyrical ballads* (1800), certainly one of the key programmatic statements of European Romanticism, that the poet has 'taken as much pains to avoid . . . as others ordinarily take to produce' what he calls 'poetic diction'.[1] The term refers to exactly that sort of linguistic stylization that traditional rhetorical doctrine, from antiquity to the eighteenth century, had prescribed as the ornamental technique appro-priate to poetic speech. Wordsworth's insistence throughout the Preface on the 'very language of men' or even the 'real language of nature' as the proper stylistic paradigm of poetry amounts, then, to a radical dis-sociation of poetic writing from the prescriptions of rhetorical doctrine.[2] Coleridge, of course, did not share Wordsworth's adherence to common parlance, but his contention that 'whatever lines can be translated into other words of the same language, without diminution of their signific-ance, either in sense, or association, or in any worthy feeling, are so far vicious in their diction' nevertheless implies a cognate renunciation of rhetoric insofar as the principle of the substitutability of expressions is the foundation of traditional rhetorical *elocutio*.[3] Nor are these dispar-agements of rhetorical doctrine unique to their authors; they exemplify a widespread attitude formulated as early as the 1770s and characteristic of Romanticism generally. In this sense, one can agree with the historical diagnosis of Ernst Robert Curtius that Romanticism represents a decisive rupture in the European literary tradition precisely to the extent that it

---

[1] William Wordsworth, *Prose works*, J. B. O. Warwick and J. W. Smyser (eds.), Oxford: Clarendon Press, 1974, I: 130.

[2] Wordsworth, *ibid.*, pp. 131, 142. Of course, it is possible to see this turn to the common language of men as itself a rhetorical option, a preference for the 'humble style' as con-ceived in the traditional rhetorical hierarchy of styles. For an interpretation of Wordsworth along these lines see Klaus Dockhorn, *Macht und Wirkung der Rhetorik*, Bad Homburg, Berlin and Zurich: Gehlen, 1968, pp. 68–91; Derek Attridge, *Peculiar language*, London, 1988, pp. 46–89.

[3] Samuel Taylor Coleridge, *Biographia literaria*, J. Shawcross (ed.), Oxford University Press, 1907, I: 167. On the doctrine of *elocutio*, see Heinrich Lausberg, *Handbuch der liter-arischen Rhetorik: eine Grundlegung der Literaturwissenschaft*, Munich: Hueber, 1960; Roland Barthes, 'The old rhetoric: an aide-memoire', in *The semiotic challenge*, New York: Hill and Wang, 1988, pp. 11–94.

evacuates rhetorical doctrine, which had linked that tradition to its roots in antiquity, of theoretical and pedagogical significance.[4]

The peculiar difficulty of our subject matter, then, would seem to reside in the fact that the Romantic theory of poetry and, more generally, of literature is not, at least in the traditional sense of the term, a rhetorical theory at all. But this difficulty is compounded to the point of paradox when one considers that the recent revival of rhetorical terminology in deconstructive criticism has, from its beginnings, demonstrated its cogency principally with reference to Romantic texts.[5] Deconstructive or rhetorical criticism is concerned with the relations between literal and figural meanings and the ways in which these relations engender uncertainties regarding the epistemological status of texts and the ontological status of the major thematic units (e.g., 'self' or 'nature') those texts apparently refer to. This is not the agenda we shall follow here. Nevertheless, we take the fact that the deconstructive strain of rhetorical criticism has drawn support from both Romantic literary production and theory as an indication that the demise of traditional rhetorical doctrine at the end of the eighteenth century is accompanied by a rethinking of key rhetorical concepts. The relationship of Romanticism to rhetoric should be conceived less as the abandonment of a tradition than as its transformation.

The historical developments contributing to the withering of rhetorical doctrine as a codification of rules for literary production, evaluation and education intertwine in a complex cultural web. A major factor, certainly, is the reorientation of the literary system from retrospection to innovation. Until well into the eighteenth century the standards of literary achievement were held to be timeless and the task of the writer was to conform to those standards. The first loosening of the hold of past greatness over the present can be registered in the *querelle des anciens et des modernes* that broke out in the seventeenth century and remained, especially with regard to the arts,

---

[4] Ernst Robert Curtius, *European literature and the Latin Middle Ages*, Princeton, NJ: Princeton University Press, 1990.
[5] This revival begins with Paul de Man's masterful essay 'The rhetoric of temporality', reprinted in *Blindness and insight*, expanded edition, Minneapolis, MN: University of Minnesota Press, 1983, pp. 187–228. See by the same author *Allegories of reading*, New Haven, CT: Yale University Press, 1979 and *The rhetoric of Romanticism*, New York: Columbia University Press, 1984. An important collection of work in the deconstructive or rhetorical tradition of Romanticism studies initiated by de Man is Arden Reed (ed.), *Romanticism and language*, Ithaca, NY: Cornell University Press, 1984. Also in this tradition is Cynthia Chase, *Decomposing figures: rhetorical readings in the Romantic tradition*, Baltimore, MD: The Johns Hopkins University Press, 1986. For critical discussions of this work see Tilottama Rajan, 'Displacing post-structuralism: Romantic studies after Paul de Man', *Studies in Romanticism* 24 (1985), pp. 451–74; Thomas Pfau, 'Rhetoric and the existential: Romantic studies and the question of the subject', *Studies in Romanticism* 26 (1987), pp. 487–512.

an issue of debate well into the 1790s.[6] With the advent of innovation as a primary literary value, rhetorical doctrine lost its position as a master code of literary production, for not only was rhetoric organized around examples of greatness held to be timelessly normative, its efficacy rested on the presupposition of standardized situations. One need only think of the doctrine of commonplaces and *topoi*, which was nothing other than a compendium that preserved and made available for readaptation what had already been thought and said. Late redactions of rhetorical doctrine such as Adam Smith's lectures at the University of Glasgow in 1762–3 dispensed with this component altogether.[7] Gradually the rhetorical term *inventio*, which designated the finding of what is stored in cultural memory, ceded place to the concept of originality.[8] The entire field of art and literature was caught up in the 'temporalization of complexity' that, by the end of the eighteenth century, yielded the Romantic concept of history as a 'collective singular'.[9] Historical consciousness, the awareness that time ceaselessly alters the framework of human life, rendered classical rhetoric defunct.

A second major trend of the eighteenth century that undermined the authority of rhetoric was the privatization of literary experience. Rhetoric was an emphatically social art. Its field of application was the immediacy of face-to-face communication and interaction, a field stratified, of course, according to social rank. That is why classical rhetorical doctrine included, in addition to the sub-components *inventio*, *dispositio* and *elocutio*, those of *memoria* and *actio*. The orator had to be skilled in memory so that he could reproduce, with appropriate situational adjustments, his speech; and he had to master the rules of delivery, know the appropriate gestures and intonational patterns, in order to be able to persuade his audience. Interestingly, just these two sub-components of rhetorical doctrine were the first to fall into desuetude as the participants in literary communication

---

[6] See Hans Robert Jauss, 'Schlegels und Schillers Replik auf die "Querelle des Anciens et des Modernes"', *Literaturgeschichte als Provokation*, Frankfurt am Main: Suhrkamp, 1970, pp. 72–95. On the prehistory of the 'querelle' in the Renaissance see Robert Black, 'Ancients and moderns in the Renaissance: rhetoric and history in Accolti's *Dialogue on the preeminence of men of his own time*', *Journal of the history of ideas* 43 (1982), pp. 3–32.

[7] Adam Smith, *Lectures on rhetoric and belles lettres*, J. C. Bryce (ed.), Indianapolis, IN: Liberty Fund, 1985.

[8] A decisive text in this connection is Edward Young, 'Conjectures on original composition' (1759), *The complete works*, Hildesheim: Georg Olms, 1968, reprint of the 1854 London edition, pp. 547–86.

[9] See Niklas Luhmann, 'Temporalisierung von Komplexität: zur Semantik neuzeitlicher Zeitbegriffe', *Gesellschaftsstruktur und Semantik*, Frankfurt am Main: Suhrkamp, 1980, I: 235–300; Reinhart Koselleck, 'Die Herausbildung des modernen Geschichtsbegriffs', in Otto Bruner, Werner Conze and Reinhart Koselleck (eds.), *Geschichtliche Grundbegriffe*, vol. II: *E–G*, Stuttgart: Klett-Cotta, 1975, pp. 647–717.

extricated themselves from the constraints of oratorical interaction. The privatization of literary experience, in other words, occurred within a cultural situation organized around the medium of print, a literary culture of writers and readers. Needless to say, the invention of print in the fifteenth century preceded the demise of rhetoric; indeed the first two centuries of print culture coincided with the neohumanist reinvigoration of rhetorical doctrine. But this is because the printed word remained embedded in a social context the principal structures of which were still oral and interactional and in which reading had yet to gain its concentrated inward quality. Such internalization of the act of reading was an achievement of the latter half of the eighteenth century as the visual representations of readers produced during that time unmistakably demonstrate.[10] Like the ideal beholder of a painting in the theory of Diderot, the reader sensed him- or herself no longer as the member of an audience to a theatrical or oratorical performance, but, rather, as one absorbed into the world of the work.[11] And the opportunities for such absorptive reading were available to a degree previously unheard of. Indeed, the later eighteenth century has been identified as a major turning point in the history of reading, the shift from repeated readings in a few, mostly religious texts, to one-time readings of indefinitely many texts.[12] Romanticism is perhaps the first major epoch in cultural history to have shaped itself within the medium of print. 'Books', the Romantic poet Novalis noted, 'are a modern species of historical being – but a most significant one. Perhaps they have replaced traditions.'[13] Certainly this observation holds for the tradition of classical rhetoric.

The claim that these large-scale cultural trends – the emergence of historical consciousness, the privatization of reading within a broadly accessible print culture – eroded the authority of rhetorical doctrine is confirmed when one attends to specific theoretical and pedagogical developments. Thus, where late eighteenth-century theoreticians continued to employ rhetorical terminology, they tended to restrict themselves to the doctrine of tropes and figures, as if rhetoric were little more than a theory of metaphor. And, whereas traditional rhetorical doctrine had conceived of the tropes as deviations from normal linguistic usage that call attention to their artfulness while producing an affective response in the audience,

[10] See Erich Schön, *Der Verlust der Sinnlichkeit oder die Verwandlungen des Lesers: Mentalitätswandel um 1800*, Stuttgart: Klett-Cotta, 1987.

[11] See Michael Fried, *Absorption and theatricality: painting and beholder in the age of Diderot*, Berkeley, CA: University of California Press, 1980.

[12] Rolf Engelsing, *Analphabetentum und Lektüre: zur Sozialgeschichte des Lesens in Deutschland zwischen feudaler und industrieller Gesellschaft*, Stuttgart: Metzler, 1973.

[13] Novalis, *Schriften. Die Werke Friedrich von Hardenbergs*, Paul Kluckhohn and Richard Samuel in collaboration with Hans-Joachim Mähl and Gerhard Schulz (eds.), Stuttgart: Kohlhammer, 1960–8, III: 586.

eighteenth-century theories traced them to the cognitive faculties (attention, imagination, emotion, wit) that produced them.[14] Rhetoric, in short, was naturalized and psychologized, transformed from a highly coded art into a human representational capacity. In the secondary schools, a parallel development took place. Rhetorical training, which had culminated in a Latin *imitatio* of an exemplary classical text, was gradually replaced by readings in the best vernacular writers.[15] The language into which pupils were initiated was no longer a restricted code that could only be replicated, but a flexible instrument of individual expression. In the context of the present investigation, however, the most significant innovation of the eighteenth century was certainly the development of the theory of autonomous art.

Two aspects of this theory were incompatible with a grounding of literature in rhetorical doctrine: the notion that art is necessarily independent of external purposes and the related notion that artworks derive their unity and significance from the interdependence of their parts. The idea that art, including literary art, serves no other aim than its own self-presentation is inimical to rhetoric because rhetoric is an instrumental technique of language, its entire design is determined by the perlocutionary effects, most notably 'persuasion', it seeks to bring about. As long as literature derived its functions from other social spheres such as politics, religion and morality, rhetorical doctrine provided it with a mechanism of effective intervention. With the establishment of a self-regulating (autonomous) social system of art in the second half of the eighteenth century, however, rhetorical instrumentality was perceived as an extraneously imposed restriction of imaginative freedom.[16] Precisely this motivated Kant, in a passage to which we shall return, sharply to distinguish rhetoric from true poetry. The notion of the self-sufficient unity of the work, the 'parts of which', according to Coleridge, 'support and mutually explain each other' (*Biographia*, 1: 318), brought about the obsolescence of rhetoric by reformulating the very conception of the literary text. Never in its history had rhetorical doctrine produced an emphatic notion of the literary work as an instanding unity. On the contrary, the rhetorical attitude toward texts was pulverizing, isolating particular *loci*, which were viewed not in terms of their cohesion with others and their place in the whole, but in terms of their individual defects or perfections and with a view to their substitutability. The notion of the work as its own

---

[14] See Rüdiger Campe, 'Die Zwei Perioden des Stils', *Comparatio* 2:3 (1991), pp. 73–99.
[15] See the amply documented study by Heinrich Bosse, ' "Dichter kann man nicht bilden": zur Veränderung der Schulrhetorik nach 1770', *Jahrbuch für internationale Germanistik* 2 (1976), pp. 80–125.
[16] See Niklas Luhmann, 'The work of art and the self-reproduction of art', *Thesis eleven* 12 (1985), pp. 4–27.

self-description required an altogether different attitude toward texts, a reflective stance that considers each part with respect to the whole and the whole with respect to the parts in a kind of circular movement. Precisely this attitude found its codification in philosophical hermeneutics, which can be considered the Romantic successor to rhetoric as the foundational discipline for dealing with texts.[17]

The final factor to be considered here returns us to our starting point with Wordsworth and his valorization of the 'real language of nature'. By the 1770s the values of nature (artlessness) and the primordial, which Edward Young had promulgated so effectively, were in such ascendance, especially in the German-speaking lands, as to revamp the classical literary canon. Certainly the central figure in this connection was Herder, who, in a discussion of what he calls 'Oriental poetry', makes the following claim: 'Not poetry, but rather nature, the entire world of passion and action that lies within the poet and that he strives to bring out of himself – that is what has an effect. Language is merely a channel, the true poet merely a translator, or, more literally, the bringer of nature into the soul and heart of his brothers.'[18] It is clear that such a conception of original poetry leaves no room for the tactically calculated selections and elaborate ornamentations of the rhetorically trained poet. For this reason, according to Herder, his own culture, schooled in the artificiality of what Wordsworth would later call 'poetic diction', has such difficulty in reproducing the poetry of nature. With regard to his own translation of the 'Song of songs', he notes: 'An additional factor is that nothing is so different as Oriental poetry, language and love from ours' (Sämmtliche Werke, VIII: 534). And he glosses this difference with the remark: 'I would sooner claim to render the lalling of my child and the cooing of the turtle dove in the oratorical language of Cicero such that both would remain what they are' (ibid.). The task of the poet, then, is to draw on the inner resources of his own lived experience and to shape these as naturally, as spontaneously and immediately, as possible. The non-rhetorical language of nature, of the child, and of the unschooled folk poets becomes the privileged stylistic paradigm; poetry is no longer considered a learnable art, but an inborn gift (genius).

A more thoroughgoing rejection of the tenets of classical rhetorical doctrine could hardly be imagined. And yet this fascination with the origin, which establishes one of the cornerstones of Romanticism generally, discloses the possibility of a new rhetoric: 'The words of childhood – these our early playmates in the dawn of life! with which our entire soul formed itself – how could we fail to recognize them, how could we ever forget

---

[17] See Glenn W. Most, 'Rhetorik und Hermeneutik: zur Konstitution der Neuzeitlichkeit', *Antike und Abendland* 30 (1984), pp. 62–79.
[18] Johann Gottfried Herder, *Sämmtliche Werke*, Bernhard Suphan (ed.), Berlin: Weidmann, 1877–1913, VIII: 340.

them? Our mother language was simultaneously the first world we saw, the first sensations we felt, the first activity and happiness we enjoyed."[19] Precisely the process of self- and world-formation posited in this remarkable passage by Herder becomes the proper domain of Romantic rhetoric. The aim of Romantic rhetorical theory is no longer to establish rules governing the attainment of communicative influence, but to expose the operations that, prior to artfulness and yet exemplified in all art, are constitutive of human experience.

A crucial text for an evaluation of the Romantic transformation of rhetoric is certainly Kant's *Critique of judgement* (1790), not only one of the important source texts for all Romantic theories of art, but also, as mentioned above, a text that explicitly repudiates rhetoric in the traditional sense of oratorical art. Thus, the *Critique of judgement* enables us to observe quite clearly both the historical collapse of rhetorical doctrine and the emergence of a revised sense of the rhetorical. The reason for Kant's repudiation of rhetoric is, simply put, that the rhetorician uses the techniques of poetry for the purpose of persuading the listener to his – the rhetorician's – cause. A component of this argument, then, is the acknowledgment of an affinity between the poet and the rhetorician insofar as both employ the same (let us say) ideational technique, the enlivening of the recipient's spirit through the production of a 'beautiful semblance'. But the poet produces this semblance for its own sake, not as a means toward an extraneous purpose. Moreover, this 'honest and sincere' presentation of semblance has the additional advantage of being attuned to the understanding such that what is presented as a 'merely entertaining play of the imagination' nonetheless promotes the work of the higher faculties. The rhetorician, however, uses the beautiful semblance as an instrument of deception insofar as he seeks to secure adherence to a particular practical viewpoint on the part of his listener. And even if this viewpoint (say, commitment to a particular course of action) happens to be in itself good, its rhetorical solicitation is still 'condemnable' insofar as the listener adopts it not because it is good, but on account of the charm of semblance. The deficiency of the rhetorician's art (his technique) derives not merely from its potential for such abuses as the confusion of minds and the promotion of nefarious ends, as Enlightenment critiques of rhetoric from Bacon on had maintained. Even if all rhetoricians endeavoured to convey true opinions and to convince their listeners to do what is right, even if their *ethos* were impeccable, their enterprise would nevertheless be objectionable because they endeavour to achieve something – anything – rhetorically. Serious, goal-oriented human discourse is a matter of right

---

[19] Johann Gottfried Herder, *Abhandlung über den Ursprung der Sprache: Text, Materialien, Kommentar*, Wolfgang Proß (ed.), Munich: Hanser, 1978, p. 89.

reasoning and to introduce the appeal of semblance in the place of reasons is to denigrate the moral freedom of the interlocutors. The abuse Kant assails is not contingent, but categorical, a perniciousness in principle, and in this sense his argument marks an historical caesura. Since Aristotle, the presupposition that the rhetorician's art is essential to deliberation in practical affairs, where limited knowledge and the pressure of decisions do not allow for a genuinely philosophical consideration of the issues, had served as the primary legitimation of rhetoric. Kant removes the very ground of this legitimation by claiming that, just because it is employed practically, rhetoric is morally deleterious.[20]

And yet, even as the *Critique of judgement* repudiates rhetorical persuasion, it also discloses the possibility of a new rhetoric, a rhetoric of what I shall call ideational presentation. The term designates the process through which concepts are rendered in an intuitive (perceptual or imaginary) configuration. This can occur in two ways. In the case of empirical concepts, the imagination shapes sensate material according to a rule, or set of rules, specified by the concept. Kant calls this rule cluster for the intuitive actualization of empirical concepts a schema. Schemata mediate between the non-intuitive concept and the manifold of intuited sense impressions by moulding the latter according to the parameters set down in the former, producing in the process an intuitive presentation of the concept. There are, however, concepts which are not susceptible to such schematic actualization because they have no instances in the domain of empirical experience. Such are the 'ideas of reason'. Although these ideas (e.g., 'moral freedom') have no congruence with empirical objects, they are nonetheless indirectly presentable via what Kant calls 'symbols'. A symbol provides an indirect presentation in that its internal arrangement solicits a form of reflection that bears structural similarity to the form of reflection required to think the idea. To take one of Kant's examples, a monarchical state can be represented as a soul-animated body when it is governed according to laws formulated by the people, or as a merely mechanical device, say a coffee mill, when it is ruled by an absolute and sovereign will. In both cases, the state is represented through a schematic representation (the body or the mill), but this schematic representation is not taken as a direct representation. Rather, the inner relations of the schematic components are projected onto the idea actually represented. The schema of the coffee mill presents us with just the coffee mill; the coffee mill as symbol presents us with the idea of the absolutist state as something that is set into motion by the will of its sovereign operator.

---

[20] All citations in this paragraph are from Immanuel Kant, *Kritik der Urteilskraft*, *Werkausgabe*, Wilhelm Weischedel (ed.), Frankfurt am Main: Suhrkamp, 1974, X: 265–7 (para. 53).

To designate the class that subsumes both schematic or direct presentations and symbolic or indirect presentations, Kant introduces a term from traditional rhetorical theory: hypotyposis. The term refers to the supreme elocutionary achievement of the rhetorician, the crafting of a representation capable of bringing its object to the reader's or listener's mind with such force that it is experienced as if before one's eyes. This use of a highly charged rhetorical term is rather surprising in view of Kant's rejection of oratorical art discussed previously, for it amounts to a massive expansion of the domain of rhetoric. Kant effectively conceives even our normal perception and designation of the world as a rhetorical (in the sense of 'presentational') operation. Experience itself, even in its most direct or schematic variant, is a rhetorical–imaginative product; there are no neutral or merely literal presentations. What distinguishes the schematic from the symbolic is not that the latter is rhetorical and the former not, but, rather, the operation of judgment involved in each. In the schematic hypotyposis, what is meant is both the formal and contentual properties of the presentation, whereas in the symbolic hypotyposis the faculty of judgment abstracts certain formal properties and projects these onto an intuitively unavailable object. Kant further notes that our language is replete with symbolic presentations, including such philosophically significant terms as 'ground', 'depend', 'follow from' and 'substance'. The danger such terms as well as many key religious concepts harbour is that they are all too easily taken for schematic concepts, for direct rather than indirect presentations. Such confusion of the types of hypotyposis reduces the ideas of reason, and thus the free rational subject, to the status of an empirical object. But Kant's point in introducing the notion of symbolic presentation is not to criticize such false objectifications; rather, his major concern bears on the status of the beautiful as the correlate of judgments of taste. For Kant's claim is that the beautiful is a symbol, in the sense here specified, of the morally good. Kant's theory of art in the *Critique of judgement*, then, is a rhetorical theory, not in the sense of the traditional rhetoric of persuasion, but in the sense of a rhetoric of presentation, of hypotyposis. In the beautiful our moral freedom, otherwise only dimly thinkable, is rendered as if intuitively present because the form of reflection elicited by the beautiful object corresponds to the form of reflection required to think the morally good.[21]

Kant's cautionary observation that several crucial philosophical terms are symbolic terms often confused with schematic representations is promoted by the Romantics to the status of a fundamental problem. This

---

[21] The doctrine of schematic and symbolic hypotyposis discussed in this and the previous paragraph is set forth in Kant, *Kritik der Urteilskraft*, pp. 294–9 (para. 53). For a detailed discussion of Kant's views on rhetoric see Rodolphe Gasché, 'Überlegungen zum Begriff der Hypotypose bei Kant', Christiaan L. Hart Nibbrig (ed.), *Was heißt 'Darstellen'?*, Frankfurt am Main: Suhrkamp, 1994, pp. 152–74.

occurs due to the centring of theoretical attention on the structure of self-consciousness, which, following Fichte, is held to be the originary ground of all experience. When Coleridge writes: 'The primary imagination I hold to be the living power and prime agent of all human perception, and as a repetition in the finite mind of the eternal act of creation in the infinite I Am' (*Biographia*, I: 167),[22] he is alluding to the Fichtean thesis that the primordial act that brings forth the world is the self-positing of the absolute ego. To see the rhetorical relevance of this thesis, however, we must turn to the work of Friedrich von Hardenberg (Novalis). In his *Foundation of the entire doctrine of science*, Fichte had attempted to show that even the principle of identity (a=a) upon which all rational inquiry rests presupposes the prior identity of the ego with itself, which can be expressed in the formula: 'ego=ego' or 'I am I'.[23] This formulation of the underlying identity of the ego to itself is exactly what Novalis latches onto in his notes on Fichte:

In the proposition *a* is *a* there lies nothing but a positing, distinguishing and binding. It is a philosophical parallelism. To make *a* more distinct, A is divided. *Is* is set up as the universal content, *a* as the determinate form. The essence of identity can only be set up in a *semblance-proposition*. We leave the *identical* in order to present it. (*Schriften*, II: 104)

The philosophical point of Novalis's remark is that every endeavour to present the pure self-identity of the ego to itself dissimulates that identity. But the more remarkable claim, from the point of view of the present inquiry, is that the propositional form of such distorting presentations is a parallelism, that is, a poetic–rhetorical schema structured as a doubling of terms or of larger syntactic units.[24] This means that an unconscious and ineluctable rhetorical operation distances self-consciousness from itself in the very act through which it attempts to grasp itself. Kant had already argued, of course, that the imagination is the faculty through which all presentations, be they schematic or symbolic, are produced as hypotyposes, but he nevertheless considered it possible to hold these two forms of presentation apart and to avoid the pitfalls they pose for cognition. Novalis's argument accepts this generalization of the rhetorical to include all forms of imaginary presentation, but at the same time lends it a critical accent.

---

[22] For Fichte's influence on Coleridge, see Kurt Müller-Vollmer, 'Fichte und die romantische Sprachtheorie', in Klaus Hammacher (ed.), *Der transzendentale Gedanke: die gegenwärtige Darstellung der Philosophie Fichtes*, Hamburg: Felix Meiner, 1981, pp. 442–61.

[23] Johann Gottlieb Fichte, *Grundlage der gesamten Wissenschaftslehre*, ed. Wilhelm G. Jacobs, Hamburg: Felix Meiner, p. 14.

[24] On the prevalence of the notion of parallelism and of related figures of doubling in Romantic literary theory, see Winfried Menninghaus, *Unendliche Verdopplung: die frühromantische Grundlegung der Kunsttheorie im Begriff absoluter Selbstreflexion*, Frankfurt am Main: Suhrkamp, 1987.

The irreducible rhetoricity of the imagination imports an element of deception into all its products: 'In this field, delusion of the imagination or of
reflection is unavoidable – in presentation' (*Schriften*, II: 122).

The line of theoretical development illustrated here with respect to Kant
and Novalis takes us to one of the epicentres of the transformed rhetoric
produced in Romanticism. If it is the task of poetic art to provide access to
the 'eternal act of creation in the infinite I Am', as Coleridge maintained,
if the purpose of poetic art, in other words, is to present the freedom of
absolute subjectivity, then this project is inevitably condemned to failure
insofar as all such presentations are accomplished through rhetorical
operations that betray or distort that very freedom. The absolute ego
has no alternative but to objectify itself rhetorically and yet it can never
coincide with any of its rhetorical objectifications. The solution to this
dilemma is the invention of a concept that lends Romantic literary theory
its individual signature, a concept that emerges, as in the case of Kant's
use of the term 'hypotyposis', through the expansion and deepening of an
inherited rhetorical notion. In traditional rhetorical doctrine, the term
'irony' refers to a characteristic of individual utterances through which
one thing is said and its opposite is meant. In this sense, irony bespeaks a
double consciousness on the part of speaker and recipient: an awareness of
the straightforward or apparent meaning of the ironic utterance on the one
hand and of its inverted, ironic meaning on the other. The step taken by
the Romantics is to generalize this split consciousness, to conceive of it not
as a characteristic of local statements, but as a structure that suffuses the
entire text. Friedrich Schlegel, the preeminent theoretician of *Romantic
irony*, sees this generalized ironic consciousness as the feature that distinguishes a truly philosophical irony – a characteristic of every genuine poetic
achievement – from the irony exercised in traditional rhetorical oration:
'Only poetry can also reach the heights of philosophy in this way, and only
poetry does not restrict itself to isolated ironical passages, as rhetoric
does.'[25] The crucial matter in the Romantic reformulation of the concept of irony, however, is the aspect of reflexivity which enables the concept to function as a solution to the dilemma of rhetorical objectification.
Romantic irony is a meta-rhetorical awareness inscribed in the very structure of poetic texts, an awareness that outstrips the first-order rhetorical
formulations of the text through a critical negation of their rhetoricity.
In what Schlegel calls a 'constant alternation of self-creation and self-
annihilation' (p. 151) the poetic subject at once objectifies itself rhetorically
and transcends this objectification. Romantic irony is the presentation of
subjectivity as that which eludes presentation.

[25] *Kritische Friedrich-Schlegel-Ausgabe*, ed. Ernst Behler with the collaboration of Jean-
Jacques Anstett, Hans Eichner, *et al.*, Paderborn: Schöningh, 1958–, II: 152.

The idea that ironic subjectivity detaches itself from its first-order
rhetorical objectifications in order critically to mark their rhetoricity is
captured in an early formulation of Friedrich Schlegel's: 'Irony is a permanent *parabasis*' (XVIII: 85). The term is drawn from the tradition of classical
comedy and designates the disruption of the dramatic illusion through
an address to the audience. This theatrical practice embodies the double
character of ironic consciousness insofar as it is structured as a commentary on the play made from within the dramatic world. But one should not
assume on the basis of this definition that irony is only present where such
explicit addresses to the audience or reader are employed. The key element
in Schlegel's definition, rather, is the claim that in irony the *parabasis* is
permanent; that is, it permeates the entire text, even those portions where
no explicit authorial gloss is proffered. This is evidenced, for example, by
Schlegel's claim in his *Conversation on poetry* that the works of Cervantes
and Shakespeare are characterized by an 'artfully ordered confusion, this
charming symmetry of contradictions, this wonderfully perennial alternation of enthusiasm and irony which lives even in the smallest parts of
the whole' (*Kritische Friedrich-Schlegel-Ausgabe*, II: 318–19). Here the
Romantic transformation of rhetoric we have been tracing achieves its
most extreme formulation: irony, as meta-rhetorical consciousness, is
reconceived as the very structure of literature (or poetry). The historical
consequence of this reconceptualization is to detach poetry from the tradition of rhetorical doctrine, which had provided the instruments of literary
theory since antiquity, and to ally it with philosophy. Indeed, it can be
argued that the overall thrust of Schlegel's – and more broadly the Romantics' – theorizing is to demonstrate the internal and systematic relation
between philosophy and literature. Thus, in a famous formulation, Schlegel
imports the transcendental turn in philosophy initiated by Kant into the
very notion of the poetic work: 'There is a kind of poetry whose essence
lies in the relation between the ideal and the real, and which therefore, by
analogy with philosophical terminology, should be called transcendental
poetry' (p. 204). In Kant the term 'transcendental' designates a mode of
inquiry that is directed not at external objects but at the conditions of
possibility for the cognition of such objects. Transcendental poetry, therefore, is one that presents 'the producer along with the product', that is
'simultaneously poetry and the poetry of poetry' (*ibid.*). Exactly this
reflective turn characterizes Schlegel's notion of Romantic irony. With
Romanticism, the poetic work is reconceived as a transcendental rhetoric,
as a mode of language use that simultaneously produces rhetorical objectifications of self and world and critically reflects on, and thus transcends,
those objectifications.

As noted at the outset, one of the cultural factors contributing to the
demise of traditional rhetoric is the emergence, at the end of the eighteenth

century, of historical consciousness. In the theory of Romantic irony this connection between historical consciousness and the Romantic transformation of rhetoric becomes forcefully evident. The notion that literary works as such are ironic implies that they are essentially historical. Literary texts are not historical merely because they are located in time; historicity is internal to their structure. The irony of the work, in other words, marks its imperfection and thereby situates the work within the historical dimension of what Schlegel, following Condorcet, called 'infinite perfectibility'.[26] This is true even of 'classical' works, whose status as timeless standards is conceived by Schlegel as a relative achievement, as it were a preliminary perfection. Hence Schlegel's notion of criticism, the task of which is not to measure the work with respect to a universally valid standard, but to complete the work by marking the discrepancy between its own unique ideal and its actualization. Criticism is the mobilization, in discursive, reflective language, of the ironic potential of the work itself, an outstripping of the work that historicizes it by reintegrating it within the historical context of infinite perfectibility. Criticism, then, transforms its objects of investigation into Romantic works: 'The romantic kind of poetry is still in the state of becoming: that, in fact, is its real essence: that it should forever be becoming and never perfected. It can be exhausted by no theory and only a divinatory criticism would dare try to characterize its ideal' (*Kritische Friedrich-Schlegel-Ausgabe*, II: 183).

The notion that the rhetorical constitution of the poetic text involves an internal conflict and that it is through this conflict that the infinite is set free finds a unique and intellectually powerful formulation in Hölderlin's theory of poetic tones.[27] Hölderlin distinguishes three poetic tones, the naive, the heroic and the ideal, and it seems plausible that this distinction involves a transformation of the traditional rhetorical distinction between levels of style. The decisive matter, however, is not that traditional doctrine is reformulated here in the terms of post-Kantian aesthetics (although the term 'naive' at least, and probably 'ideal' as well, is derived from Schiller), but that the distinction no longer functions to discriminate genres. All three tones are at work in the poetic text, sequenced and combined in various ways according to the overall intention of the poem. Moreover, they operate on two levels: the level of presentation or language (also designated the 'artistic character') of the text and the level of subjective attitude, the 'intellectual treatment' or 'basic tone or mood', that underlies the manifest character of the text. The elaborate technical apparatus

---

[26] See Ernst Behler, *German Romantic literary theory*, Cambridge University Press, 1993, pp. 65–71.

[27] The theory of tones is discussed most thoroughly in Hölderlin's essay 'Über die Verfahrensweise des poetischen Geistes', in Friedrich Hölderlin, *Sämtliche Werke. Große Stuttgarter Ausgabe*, Friedrich Beißner (ed.), Stuttgart: Kohlhammer, 1843–85, N-I: 241–65.

Hölderlin develops – and his is the most technical, the most calculated, and in this sense the closest to traditional rhetoric of any of its contemporary theoretical endeavours – hinges on the fact that the two levels are in a state of irreducible conflict. No poem is entirely pure in the sense that its language and mood coincide. Rather, the two dimensions are in constant tension with one another and it is this tension that drives the poem forward until it reaches its conflictual apex, a turn or reversal (a sort of peripeteia), at which the oppositional structure is suspended in harmony. At this point of 'harmonious opposition' the 'Spirit in its infinity can be felt' (pp. 249–50). It is clear that this conception is kindred to the Schlegelian notion of irony, but it differs from the latter in that it conceives of the release of the spirit as occurring not through an act of semantic negation, but rather as a result of the dynamics of rhythm and form unfolded in the poem. The ironic solution to the problem of form is playful and reflective; Hölderlin's notion, by comparison, is austere and, finally, tragic. His transformed rhetoric, although certainly rooted, like Schlegel's, in Fichte's idealism, is a rhetoric of finitude that measures the distance between the human word and the divine.

The transcendental and historical transformation of rhetoric which we have reviewed here with respect to the concept of Romantic irony is perhaps the best known component of Romantic literary theory. But rhetoric, in its traditional form, was also a theory of the relation between language and emotion, passion and affect, and an account of the Romantic transformation of rhetoric requires that we consider this dimension of Romantic rhetorical theory as well. Traditionally, the task of the orator was conceived as arousing affect in his listeners, as 'moving' them, and this was achieved by simulating just those passions the speaker wished to awaken. The imitative capacity of the speaker, his ability to act out the emotions, is what enables him to bring forth those very emotions in his audience. This effective actualization of passion or affect is transformed by the Romantics into a more distanced relation to emotionality, as illustrated in Wordsworth's famous definition: 'I have said that Poetry is the spontaneous overflow of powerful feelings: it takes its origin from emotion recollected in tranquillity: the emotion is contemplated till by a species of reaction the tranquillity gradually disappears, and an emotion, similar to that which was before the subject of contemplation, is gradually produced, and does itself actually exist in the mind' (*Prose works*, I: 148). The emotion whose spontaneous overflow the poet calls forth within himself is not the actually lived affective movement, but one framed within the tranquillity of a contemplative attitude. It is an emotion neutralized by the temporal distance of recollection, an emotion gathered and condensed in the absence of the lived situation that actually produced it. Within this neutralizing frame, contemplation calls forth a mental experience of the emotion, which is to say: the emotion in its purified form. The task of the poet, then, is to provide access to emotion in such a way that it is felt through the filter of reflective distance. The result of this process is 'that the understanding of the being to whom we address ourselves . . . must necessarily be in some degree enlightened, his taste exalted, and his affections ameliorated' (p. 126). Amelioration of affect, not its instigation, is the rhetorical task.

Wordsworth's account of the affective dimension of poetic rhetoric conforms to the basic tendency of Romantic literary theory insofar as it valorizes reflective freedom. The theoretical interest of his claim, however, lies in the fact that it pursues this question within a domain that is located beneath the level of deliberate thought, a domain, one might say, that is inaccessible to ironic self-criticism. This is indicated by the fact that the production of the poetic emotion within the contemplating subject occurs through a process Wordsworth terms 'a species of reaction' and which he specifies in another passage as rooted in our 'organic sensibility', a sphere in which 'habits of mind' are 'obeyed blindly and mechanically' (*ibid.*). The language of blind and mechanical habit, of automatic reaction, would seem to be irreconcilable with the notion of reflective freedom and precisely this irreconcilability constitutes the theoretical provocation of Wordsworth's claim. The tension between the natural sphere of mechanical habit and reaction and the sphere of reflective freedom can only be resolved in a theoretical construct that embraces these two domains. What is required is an anthropological rhetoric of the passions that attends to what Wordsworth calls our 'organic sensibility'.

Just such an anthropological transformation of rhetoric is elaborated in the *Letters on poetry, metre and language* that August Wilhelm Schlegel published in 1795. Like Wordsworth, Schlegel attributes the difference between actually experienced affect and its poetic rendering and communication to the neutralizing, distancing effect of time. The sort of temporality that interests Schlegel, however, is not the gap between the lived emotion and its later contemplation, not the time of recollection. Rather, it is the sort of temporality internal to the poetic articulation of the emotion, which is to say: the temporal ordering, or rhythm, of the expression itself. Since such ordering relates one moment to another according to a law of repetition and variation, it involves a reflective component, an implicit comparison among various instants. Affect, in its immediate, lived actuality, exhausts itself in time; it is sheer expressivity obeying solely the inner impetus – typically a type of pain or desire – at its source. Rhythm, however, is temporal form; it binds the evanescent to a pattern. The question that Schlegel's anthropological rhetoric attempts to answer is: how is the intellectualization, the distancing and free organization evinced in the temporal binding of affect as rhythm, possible?

The answer to this question that Schlegel is keen to reject would have it that rhythm and metrical pattern are the products of convention. Conventional agreement is a function of the understanding, an artifact of a relatively late stage of cultivation, and cannot, therefore, be presupposed as operative during the earliest, most primitive stages of human development. There exists, however, no social group, regardless of its degree of primitiveness, which does not employ internally ordered, rhythmic expressions in song and dance. And if this is the case, as the records of travellers to such places as America and New Zealand indeed indicate, then the origin of rhythmical order must be located in a natural, or anthropological, factor, and not in arbitrarily imposed, conventional restrictions. Just such a natural origin of rhythm, hence of a reflective distance to the thrall of emotion, forms the centrepiece of Schlegel's argument. And the reason he can make this argument is that, in contrast to Wordsworth, he views our 'organic sensibility' as something other than a set of mechanical reactions and blind habits:

Our body is a living clockwork; without any conscious intervention on our part various movements occur continuously within it, for example the heartbeat and breathing, in equivalent intervals, such that any deviation from this regular course tends to indicate a disorder in the machine. In other movements that are dependent on our will, for example walking or speaking, we easily fall, especially when we perform them continuously, of ourselves and without knowing it into a certain temporal pattern. If we undertake several such actions simultaneously, for example walking and speaking, then the speed of the one usually conforms to the speed of the other, unless we deliberately disrupt the correspondence between them. And in just this way several individuals involved in joint endeavours assume a regular movement without intending to do so and without conventional agreement.[28]

The body naturally organizes its movements according to regular temporal patterns and, insofar as it does so (insofar as it is self-organizing), it is a natural anticipation of reflective freedom. In this sense, our organic sensibility provides the means of endowing affective expression, which in the human being is not merely keyed to needs and satisfactions, but exhibits an intrinsically excessive character, with a rhythmic ordering that neutralizes the lived actuality of the emotion and enables it to be experienced as a patterned sequence, as temporal form. Not the intellectual coordination achieved through the imposition of conventions, not the reflective distance of recollection, but rather the spontaneity of organic self-organization is the source of rhythmical song.

[28] August Wilhelm Schlegel, *Sämmtliche Werke*, Eduard Böcking (ed.), Leipzig: Weidmann'sche Buchhandlung, 1846, VII: 133.

By virtue of the 'law of organization' (Schlegel, *Sämmtliche Werke*, VII: 133) that characterizes the body, then, nature 'mediates between the senses and reason' (p. 145). Rhythm introduces into the fury of uncontrolled passion a law of regularity that, by harnessing the dissipative expenditure, at once enlivens and soothes. Such is the civilizing force of poetry that Wordsworth designates as 'amelioration'. But Schlegel's theory conceives of this civilizing effect in much broader terms. The internal coordination of passion and corporeal rhythm has as its external, pragmatic correlate the coordination of diverse individual experiences into a collective whole. 'It is therefore not surprising that song and dance was, and still is, the soul of all gatherings among less civilized peoples' (p. 150). This social coordination, accomplished 'without intention, almost without consciousness' (*ibid.*), then becomes the basis for further cultural development, including the formation of convention and the more elaborate exercises of reasoning. In contrast to traditional rhetoric, which was an instrumental theory of the instigation of affect within a social context, Schlegel's anthropological rhetoric views the harnessing of affect in temporal form as the condition of possibility of sociality as such.

The two strands of Romantic rhetoric reviewed here – Friedrich Schlegel's theory of Romantic irony and August Wilhelm Schlegel's theory of temporal measure – represent impressive contributions in themselves. If we are to attain a synthetic understanding of the Romantic transformation of rhetoric, however, we must ask what the conceptual unity of these contributions consists in. An answer to this question is suggested in a brief text by Novalis entitled *Monologue*, in which the poet sets forth, and ironically dramatizes, his concept of language. The traditional rhetorical dichotomy of *res* and *verba*, things and words, is abandoned altogether and language is reconceived as a system of self-defining terms: 'it is with language as with mathematical formulas – they constitute a world by themselves, they play only among themselves, express nothing but their own marvellous nature, and for that reason they are so expressive and mirror the singular interplay of things' (*Schriften*, II: 672). The implication of this statement, as the title of Novalis's text likewise indicates, is that reference, in the sense of connection with the external world, and communication, in the sense of the transfer of thoughts from one individual to another, are illusions. Language organizes itself into a system that is 'monological', not in the sense that it is spoken by one person, but in the sense that it only speaks of and to itself. A rhetoric that would investigate this monological domain, then, would of necessity be a rhetoric of reflexivity and self-reference. Its concepts would not be ontological, but autological, and its field of inquiry would include all the levels at which self-constitution is achieved. This is the case both for the transcendental rhetoric of irony as meta-rhetorical consciousness and for the anthropological rhetoric of temporal form as an effect of corporeal self-organization. Romantic rhetoric, in short, is a rhetoric of autopoetic systems, of systems that are formed by establishing recursive loops among the elements they produce. Such a rhetoric is bound to include itself, that is, to understand its own theoretical enterprise as a self-organizing system or, in Novalis's terms, as 'monological'.

10

Romantic irony

GARY HANDWERK

Introduction

More than any other element of Romantic aesthetics, Romantic irony contradicts the pervasive popular view of what Romanticism means. Irony is the other side of Romanticism, attuned to rationality rather than feeling, to calculation rather than sentiment, to self-reflection rather than self-expression. Conventional accounts of Romanticism have often been distorted by failing to take account of its central role for romantic aesthetics, not just in the theoretical sites where one might expect to find it (most notably the German romantic theories of Friedrich Schlegel and Karl Solger), but in innumerable literary texts where one might simply read past it (the poetry of Keats, for instance, or Mary Shelley's *Frankenstein*). Seen genetically, Romantic irony links Romanticism both to the immediate past (to such late Enlightenment figures as Immanuel Kant or William Godwin) and to subsequent revivals of romantic sensibility or epistemology (Friedrich Nietzsche's self-critical romanticism, Oscar Wilde's aestheticism, even postmodern theory and practice). Indeed, a scrupulous genealogy of Romantic irony might well confirm Friedrich Schlegel's claim that it is the incomprehensibilities of irony on which, 'the salvation of families and nations rests . . . and of states and systems' ('Ber die Unverständlichkeit', *Kritische Ausgabe*, II, p. 370). Or if not that much, a good deal nonetheless.

Although irony has long had its own secure niche within literary criticism, it was the New Criticism of the 1940s that gave it a particularly privileged position within Anglo–American critical discourse.[1] Cleanth Brooks articulated most forcefully the new role assigned to irony when he described it as 'the most general term we have for the kind of qualification which the various elements in a context receive from the context'. For Brooks, there can scarcely be any statement 'devoid of an ironic potential', a quality especially evident in poetry where 'any "statement" made in the

---

[1] Helpful overviews of the evolution of irony in Anglo–American criticism can be found in Douglas Muecke's *The compass of irony*, London: Methuen, 1969 and Lillian Furst's *Fictions of Romantic irony*, Cambridge, MA: Harvard University Press, 1984. A classic study of preromantic irony is Norman Knox, *The word 'irony' and its contexts: 1500–1755*, Durham, NC: Duke University Press, 1961.

poem bears the pressure of the context and has its meaning modified by the context'.[2] The presence of irony thus serves as an index of the specifically literary qualities of a given text; recognizing irony means seeing the density of internal connections formed when every statement or judgment in that text has its force inflected by the larger discourse within which it occurs. While all discourse may build up meaning in similar ways, irony brings to the surface the ambiguities that can result when multiple frames of reference bear simultaneously upon an individual statement.

New Critical attention to irony as a matter of literary structure was significantly redirected by three seminal works of the late 1960s and early 1970s: Douglas Muecke's *The compass of irony*, Paul de Man's 'The rhetoric of temporality', and Wayne Booth's *A rhetoric of irony*.[3] Different though they are in approach and emphasis, all three works share an interest in the rhetorical dimensions of irony that a formal analysis tends to leave aside. Rhetorical analysis of irony begins with the recognition that standard dictionary definitions of the term – saying one thing and meaning something else – fail to adequately explain the complex purposes that might motivate such ironic indirection. Why not just say what one means or, to adopt Brooks's language, why allow the context to 'warp' the sense of a given statement rather than having context and statement simply reinforce each other? Classical rhetoric had of course focussed on precisely such questions, but typically limited its concern to the persuasive strategies implicit in individual utterances. By contrast, Muecke, de Man and Booth saw the intent of an ironic stance reaching well beyond even the cumulative impact of pervasive local ironies. As an attitude toward the world, irony enacts within discourse fundamental questions about epistemology (how sure we can be of what we know) and ethics (how reliable our assessments of behaviour and motives can be).

Both Muecke and Booth strive to reduce irony to order by distinguishing its various species and subspecies. Muecke sets up a comprehensive classification of ironies, but supplements his abstract categories with a thorough historical account of what irony has meant within literary criticism and with an examination of the specifically philosophical purposes of Romantic and postromantic irony. He sees irony as an essentially aesthetic phenomenon; although it does alert us to 'the ambivalences of the human condition . . . irony is properly to be regarded as more an intellectual than

---

[2] These quotes come from *The well wrought urn*, New York: Harcourt Brace, 1947, p. 191, and 'Irony as a principle of literary structure', originally published in 1949 and reprinted in Hazard Adams (ed.), *Critical theory since Plato*, New York: Harcourt Brace Jovanovich, 1971, pp. 969 and 973.

[3] 'The rhetoric of temporality' originally appeared in 1969 and has been reprinted in *Blindness and insight: essays in the rhetoric of contemporary criticism*, Minneapolis, MN: University of Minnesota Press, 1983; Wayne Booth, *A rhetoric of irony*, Chicago, IL: University of Chicago Press, 1974.

a moral activity' (*Compass*, p. 247). Booth likewise classifies, and his categories overlap to some extent with Muecke's. But Booth is ultimately less concerned with what kinds of irony exist than with what occurs as we unpack the meanings within ironic discourse. This cognitive analysis is itself preliminary to his consideration of the ethical implications of the process. Booth contends that an ironist typically tries to establish a community of assent by leading the audience through an intricate process of decoding that validates their own sense of intellectual ingenuity. Showing that ingenuity as something they share with the ironist prompts them also to share the values that the ironist is promoting. From Booth's perspective, recuperable ironies, those that deal with relatively stable, determinate meanings, accomplish this convergence of attitudes most successfully and define the norm.

Unlike Muecke and Booth, de Man deals with only a single sort of irony, but a kind so pervasive that one can scarcely imagine areas of human discourse it would not affect. Irony begins for him with the recognition that 'the relationship between sign and meaning is discontinuous' ('Rhetoric', p. 209), hence inherently unstable. This situation arises because the relation of the human subject to itself, of its reflective or linguistic consciousness to its practical activity, is likewise discontinuous. 'The reflective disjunction not only occurs *by means of* language as a privileged category, but it transfers the self out of the empirical world into a world constituted out of, and in, language' (p. 213). Conceiving ourselves in language thus creates a gap that will never be fully recuperated. We can never reconcile the linguistic world of imaginative possibility with the actual world that we inhabit (p. 219); the subject 'can know this inauthenticity but can never overcome it' (p. 222). Irony thus 'engenders a temporal sequence of acts of consciousness [a pursuit of self-totalization] which is endless' (p. 220), an infinite deferral and pursuit of the self's own identity and meaning, with profoundly unsettling consequences for any discursive situation.

Although these three critics speak of irony in general, their expansive redefinitions of irony share a common point of historical reference. All of them take their bearings from the trajectory given to irony by Romantic thought, specifically by Friedrich Schlegel (even Brooks found his paradigmatic case of irony in one of Wordsworth's Lucy poems). Muecke and de Man make direct use of Schlegel in extending the philosophical scope of irony; Booth does so indirectly by dealing with *The concept of irony*, Søren Kierkegaard's sharply critical, Hegelian reading of Romantic irony. For Muecke and Booth, Romantic irony marks the far end of a continuum of ironies, signalling the most unstable form of this particular trope – precisely the features that make it the norm for de Man. In its renewed interest in this most radical kind of irony, Anglo–American criticism converges with a long-standing line of inquiry within the German literary and philosophical tradition, carried forward from Romanticism by such authors as Musil, Mann and Kafka, and explored by numerous twentieth-century critics.[4]

Irony came to seem of particular concern for modern criticism as its interests began to echo specifically Romantic concerns and as the dominance of a realist aesthetic began to wane. Like their Romantic predecessors, contemporary critics see irony putting into question the predominant modern understanding of self-identity (variously denominated Cartesian, humanist, bourgeois or liberal). How coherent is the subject's identity and where does the source of that coherence lie? How conscious of its own impulses and motives can the subject ever be? How fully in control of the meaning of its words or the consequences of its actions, i.e., how much of an agent in the philosophical sense, can it expect to be?

Besides serving as a nexus for specific philosophical questions, irony of the Romantic sort displays a second distinctive trait – its connection to strategies of aesthetic disruption. Romantic theorists saw irony as a device to foreground, within the aesthetic artifact itself, the processes of aesthetic production and reception. A specifically Romantic irony can therefore be said to be present when texts become self-reflective about their construction as texts and authors show genuine scepticism about their own aesthetic control of their products. Ironic texts confront their audiences, shattering the facade of aesthetic illusion and acknowledging the artificiality of aesthetic experience. Romantic irony thus represents a countermovement within European literary history to the increasing predominance, dating from the eighteenth century, of a realist aesthetic.

Despite its intrinsic affinity with central issues of Romantic aesthetics, the emergence of Romantic irony as a term for critical discourse provides a perfect case study for how literary history most often comes to be constructed – retrospectively and polemically. The phrase 'Romantic irony' was virtually never used during the Romantic period to characterise specifically Romantic texts, and debates persist even today about what

---

[4] Twentieth-century reconsideration of irony in the Germanic studies was sparked by Walter Benjamin's *Der Begriff der Kunstkritik in der deutschen Romantik*, in *Gesammelte Schriften*, Rolf Tiedemann and Hermann Schweppenhäuser (eds.), Frankfurt am Main: Suhrkamp Verlag, 1980, I: 1, pp. 7–122. Subsequent important treatments of irony include Beda Allemann, *Ironie und Dichtung*, Pfullingen: Verlag Neske, 1956; Erich Heller, *The ironic German*, Boston, MA: Little, Brown, 1958; Ingrid Strohschneider-Kohrs, *Die romantische Ironie in Theorie und Gestaltung*, Tübingen: Niemeyer, 1960; and Peter Szondi, *Schriften*, Frankfurt am Main: Suhrkamp Verlag, 1978; Szondi's Schlegel essays are included in *On textual understanding and other essays*, Minneapolis, MN: University of Minnesota Press, 1986. The most prominent French studies, Vladimir Jankélévitch, *L'ironie, ou la bonne conscience*, Paris: F. Alcan, 1936 and Philippe Lacoue-Labarthe and Jean-Luc Nancy, *L'absolu littéraire: théorie de la littérature du romantisme allemand*, Paris: Editions du Seuil, 1978, take this German tradition as their starting point.

texts best exhibit it. Yet the concept persistently reemerges in later discussions of Romantic aesthetics, centred upon an ongoing debate about how crucial a component of Romanticism irony should be taken to be. For Romantic irony has proven ideally suited to at least one purpose, serving as a marker for what different critics have taken to be the fundamental aesthetic, ethical and ideological implications of Romantic thought and practice.

As a technical device, Romantic irony has most typically been identified as the disruption within a text or performance of its aura of aesthetic illusion. This disruption can take the form of direct intrusion by the author or narrator in commenting upon the process by which the text has been produced (while authorial asides that simply comment in a direct way upon the characters or events, as in so many nineteenth-century novels, for instance, are not necessarily ironic). It can also manifest itself in the self-reflexivity that occurs when characters see or read the text in which they themselves appear. Or it can simply show up in abruptly disjunctive transitions from one mode of reality and one narrative thread to another. In all these cases, the disruption signals the fictional status of literary artifacts and the provisional nature of aesthetic experience. Sterne's *Tristram Shandy*, Diderot's *Jacques le fataliste*, the plays of Aristophanes and Tieck, Byron's *Don Juan* and Pushkin's *Eugene Onegin* provide signal instances of the first trait. Part two of Cervantes's *Don Quixote*, Brentano's *Godwi*, Goethe's *Wilhelm Meisters Wanderjahre*, and Novalis's *Heinrich von Ofterdingen* contain striking examples of the second. The tales of E. T. A. Hoffmann (*Kater Murr* and others), the plays of Shakespeare (with their plays within plays), and even the echoing between framing tale and main narrative set up in Romantic novels such as Shelley's *Frankenstein* neatly illustrate the third.

As nearly as any idea can be, Romantic irony was the progeny of a single person, Friedrich Schlegel, whose work has been a touchstone for almost every recent theoretical discussion of irony. Hence any exposition of Romantic irony needs to take its bearings from a detailed consideration of his work. Schlegel was the foremost theorist of that most theoretical of Romanticisms, the German variety, and at the centre of the early phase of Romantic activity based in Jena and Berlin. Although the lectures of his brother, August Wilhelm, on literary history and the later lectures of Friedrich Schleiermacher on hermeneutics were more directly and widely influential than Schlegel's own works in defining the public perception of a Romantic movement, Friedrich had the largest role in shaping Romantic thought into a self-conscious literary theory and programme. Surprisingly, though, there are only a handful of places in his works where Schlegel himself used the term 'Romantic irony', and irony as a general concept held a central place in his aesthetic and philosophical projects for only a very brief period.[5] His major texts dealing with this idea were all written within a four-year period, and even most broadly construed include only three essays, one on Lessing (1797, revised 1801), one on Goethe's *Wilhelm Meister* (1798), one called 'On incomprehensibility' (1800), and two sets of fragments, the Lyceum fragments of 1797 and the *Athenaeum* fragments of 1798, all of which were published in relatively small circulation literary journals of the period. There are supplementary references to irony in his philosophical and aesthetic notebooks, almost all of which date from the same years, but little of that material was available until publication of the *Kritische Ausgabe* of his works began in the 1950s.[6]

Yet Schlegel's concern with irony was less idiosyncratic than this pattern might suggest. He used 'irony' as a term to focus a set of general problems that were at the heart of Romantic aesthetics; it served as a conceptual catalyst for his reflections upon subjectivity, epistemology and aesthetic representation. The term does in fact capture a set of concerns that were widespread during and after the Romantic period, though other figures used different terms to survey quite similar ground. Both Novalis and Jean Paul, for instance, associate many of the traits that Schlegel would have described as ironic with 'humour'. As Novalis noted in a fragment of 1797, 'What Schlegel characterises so sharply as irony is in my opinion nothing other – than the consequence and the character of genuine self-possession – true presence of mind. . . . Schlegel's irony seems to me to be genuine humour.'[7]

---

[5]   The sole occurrences of 'romantische Ironie' can be found in Schlegel's literary notebooks of 1797, vol. XVI, p. 126 (Fragment 503), p. 145 (Fragments 709, 713), p. 146 (Fragment 716). References to Schlegel's works are taken from Ernst Behler, Jean-Jacques Anstett, Hans Eichner (eds.), *Kritische Friedrich-Schlegel-Ausgabe*, Paderborn: Verlag Ferdinand Schöningh, 1958–, cited by volume, page and, where appropriate, fragment number. All translations from these and other texts are mine, except where noted.

[6]   Schlegel's early works of literary criticism were not widely available during the nineteenth century, nor was any of his voluminous notebook material in print prior to Josef Körner's 1935 edition of Schlegel's *Neue philosophische Schriften* and Hans Eichner's 1957 edition of the *Literary notebooks*. They were not included in his collected works (Vienna: 1822–5), hence his later lectures on history, literary history and aesthetics provided the material for English translations by John Lockhart (1818), John Frost (1844) and E. J. Millington (1849), all of which were reprinted multiple times in the subsequent decades. Wider dissemination of Schlegel's theories was made possible by Jakob Minor's *Fr. Schlegel: seine prosaischen Jugendschriften* (1883) and Oskar Walzel's 1890 edition of Schlegel's letters to his brother. Multiple editions of the fragments appeared in the first two decades of the twentieth century, including an English version translated by Paul Bernard Thomas and Louis H. Gray in 1913. Schlegel's essays and fragments are in volume II of the *Kritische Ausgabe*; English translations of most of them are included either in Peter Firchow (trans.), *Friedrich Schlegel's 'Lucinde' and the fragments*, Minneapolis, MN: University of Minnesota Press, 1971, or Kathleen Wheeler (ed.), *German aesthetic and literary criticism: the Romantic ironists and Goethe*, Cambridge University Press, 1984. The notebook material is in volumes XVI and XVIII of the *Kritische Ausgabe*, which have yet to be translated in their entirety.

[7]   Novalis, *Schriften*, Richard Samuel, Hans-Joachim Mähl, Gerhard Schulz (eds.), Stuttgart: W. Kohlhammer Verlag, 1960, vol. II, p. 428. Jean Paul's comments can be found in his *Vorschule der Ästhetik* (*The horn of Oberon*), especially in the sections on Romantic and humorous poetry (I: v and I: vii).

Schlegel's idea of irony is closely connected as well with the literary hermeneutics that grew out of work by himself, Novalis and Schleiermacher, in particular the idea that works could be produced in collaborative 'Symphilosophie' or 'Sympoesie' and engaged by readers whom Novalis described as authors in the second degree. 'The true reader must be the extended author. He is the higher instance, who receives his subject-matter after it has already been worked over by a lower instance' (II, p. 470).

There is nonetheless an historical irony in the way that discussion of Romantic irony was actually extended more by its opponents than by its advocates. Although Schlegel's most immediate heirs in Germany, Adam Müller and Karl Solger, gave wider circulation to the idea through their own publications, they added relatively little to his philosophical formulation of the concept.[8] In contrast, the attacks upon Romantic irony by Hegel, Kierkegaard and others helped considerably in establishing why such irony should be considered central in assessing the implications of Romanticism. For Hegel, the Romantic subject's belief in its absolute power to create itself led it to conceive all the concrete forms in which it might realize itself as arbitrary forms that it had the power to abolish at its own discretion. He felt that the 'infinite absolute negativity' latent in irony represented a highly suspect refusal of philosophical and ethical seriousness, which erred by absolutizing the negative moment in the dialectical progression of consciousness.[9] Regardless of how fair Hegel was in identifying Romantic irony with an egocentric aestheticism, his critique did bring to the foreground questions about the ethical consequences of an ironic aesthetic. Recent criticism has renewed Hegel's focus on the ethical and, by extension, the political aspects of irony, although different critics have valorized irony's subversive potential in quite different ways.[10]

If the conceptual centre of irony seems hard to locate amid the claims and counterclaims of various theorists, its status as a literary category can seem equally elusive. Clear-cut literary manifestations of Romantic irony are at best scattered and sporadic. Such irony seems more characteristic of individual authors or works than pervasive as a trait within specific movements or periods. Even the greatest theoretical exertions can make the

[8] For consideration of their respective roles, see Ernst Behler's comprehensive historical essay on Romantic irony in Frederick Garber (ed.), *Romantic irony*, Budapest: Akadémiai Kiadó, 1988, pp. 65–75.

[9] Georg Wilhelm Friedrich Hegel, *Vorlesungen über die Ästhetik*, *Werke* (Frankfurt am Main: Suhrkamp Verlag, 1970), vol. XIII, pp. 93–100. See also Søren Kierkegaard's elaboration of Hegel's criticism in *The concept of irony*, Lee M. Capel (trans.), Bloomington, IN: Indiana University Press, 1965, pp. 289–335.

[10] An outstanding recent treatment of irony's ideological force is Linda Hutcheon's *Irony's edge: the theory and politics of irony*, New York: Routledge, 1994. Studies specifically on Romantic irony include David Simpson, *Irony and authority in Romantic poetry*, London: Macmillan, 1979 and Joseph Dane, *The critical mythology of irony*, Athens, GA: University of Georgia Press, 1991.

term fit at most a minority of Romantic writers, while at the same time it seems equally applicable to a number of writers not now taken to be Romantic (though Schlegel did use the term for Shakespeare or Cervantes, for instance). So Romantic irony can ultimately appear to be more a question of literary temperament or style than a stable or historically specific doctrine.

Romantic irony has in fact attained its greatest importance for literary criticism within the last few decades. The term has by now been extended well beyond the German tradition and well outside the Romantic period, without particular concern on the part of many critics for any direct lines of influence. Lilian Furst, for instance, emphatically insists that the 'archetypal' aspect of Romantic irony matters more than its historical one, so that the term itself is an 'unfortunate misnomer' (*Fictions*, p. 238).[11] Yet there is a certain aptness in this critical reincarnation of the term, since Romantic irony has once again begun to serve a role much like the one it had for Friedrich Schlegel – as a critical tool for reshaping the literary canon, for realigning generic classifications and for highlighting the philosophical, self-reflexive potential of literary discourse.

Between logical beauty and transcendental buffoonery

Tracking irony through Friedrich Schlegel's texts can be an extremely problematic endeavour, for it is not sufficient to trace any of his terms in an isolated way. Irony was too densely connected to his other ideas, too deeply embedded in his larger projects for this method to produce a comprehensive account of its role in his thinking. From the start, however, irony was a pivotal idea for Schlegel's effort to critically engage Friedrich Schiller's historicist mediation of the long-standing debate about the relative superiority of ancient or modern literatures.[12]

As highly contested as the definition, implications and application of Romantic irony may be, its ancestry remains relatively straightforward. Schlegel's irony was an amalgamation of two influences, one drawn from

---

[11] See also Anne Mellor, *English Romantic irony*, Cambridge, MA: Harvard University Press, 1980; Gary Handwerk, *Irony and ethics in narrative*, New Haven, CT: Yale University Press, 1984; Clyde de L. Ryals, *A world of possibilities: Romantic irony in Victorian literature*, Columbus, OH: Ohio State University Press, 1990; Candace Lang, *Irony/humour: critical paradigms*, Baltimore, MD: The Johns Hopkins University Press, 1988.

[12] Among the most useful efforts to sort out the Schiller–Schlegel debate are Richard Brinkmann, 'Romantische Dichtungstheorie in Friedrich Schlegels Frühschriften und Schillers Begriffe des Naiven und Sentimentalischen: Vorzeichen einer Emanzipation des Historischen', *Deutsche Vierteljahrsschrift für Literaturwissenschaft und Geistesgeschichte* 32 (1958), pp. 344–71; Peter Szondi, 'Das Naive ist das Sentimentalische', *Schriften*, pp. 59–106; and Ernst Behler's introduction to *Kritische Ausgabe*, vol. I, pp. clxi–clxxiv.

classical Greek philosophy and literature, the other from contemporary German philosophy. Although Romanticism is often credited with over-turning the assumed superiority of the ancients to the moderns, Schlegel himself advocated not a rejection of the Classical tradition, but its assimilation and revivification. Repudiating the codifying aesthetic of Aristotelian neoclassicism did not for him entail an absolute break with the literary past. Irony provides a good instance, in fact, of how he sought to recover elements of classical thought that had been domesticated by the intervening tradition of literary criticism. Quintilian, for example, attributed to irony a relatively narrow figural force. Although he does concede that the whole life of someone such as Socrates may be 'coloured' by irony, he restricts his analysis to its use in local contexts as a conscious, strategically motivated rhetorical ploy.[13] In contrast, Schlegel's version of classical irony is a much more ambitious composite of two distinct threads, the one Socratic and epistemological, the other Aristophanic and performative. By interweaving these threads, Romantic irony foregrounds both the pervasive presence of evaluation within discourse and the situational contingency of the evaluative act.

Generally speaking, the force of the terms '*eiron*' and '*eironia*' was considerably narrower in classical Greek than the force that we give to their modern equivalents. The Greek words often imply an active dissimulation, such as the feigned ignorance of which Socrates is accused in various Platonic dialogues (as at *Republic* 337a) or the lack of truthfulness that for Aristotle is characteristic of the ironist (*Nicomachean ethics*, 4.92–4.95). As Gregory Vlastos has noted, however, the terms had by the time of Quintilian shed their strictly negative connotations, becoming a mode of 'mockery innocent of deceit'.[14] Yet even when associated with someone's personality or rhetorical style, they were not seen to be related in any essential way to methodological or epistemological issues. For Friedrich Schlegel, the narrowness with which traditional rhetoric conceived irony came from not taking seriously enough Socrates' profession of his own ignorance.

Schlegel was the first interpreter of Socrates to work out the profound affinities between Socrates' ironic pose and his philosophical methods, and thus to recognize how essential irony was to Socrates' project of philosophical inquiry and social critique. This insight is evident in the longest of Schlegel's fragments dealing with Socratic irony, Lyceum fragment 108 (*Kritische Ausgabe*, II: 160). It begins by noting that 'Socratic irony is the only fully involuntary and yet fully deliberate dissimulation'. It is impossible either to feign such irony or to betray its presence, and yet it

---

[13] Quintilian, *Institutio oratoria*, Book IX, ii. 44–53.
[14] Gregory Vlastos, *Socrates, ironist and moral philosopher*, Ithaca, NY: Cornell University Press, 1991, p. 28.

is not meant to deceive anyone, except perhaps 'those who take it to be deceptive'. The function of this irony, then, is not rhetorical, but epistemological and ethical; it indicates not that the ironist is presuming to adopt a superior position for himself, but that he is in the same place as his ostensible victim, for he does not have final control over its presence or its meaning.

Socratic irony combines the most opposite attitudes, being at the same time completely playful and yet completely serious, completely sincere and open and yet deeply dissimulating. 'It springs from the union of an artistic feeling for life (*Lebenskunstsinn*) and a scientific spirit', thus foreshadowing what was for Schlegel the programmatic aim of modern poetry, that 'All art should become science, and all science become art; poetry and philosophy should be united' (II: 161, Fragment 115). It adopts a transcendental rather than a rhetorical view of language, because it 'contains and arouses a feeling for the insoluble conflict between the absolute and the conditioned, between the impossibility and the necessity of complete communication'. On the one hand 'the freest of all licences', it is on the other hand 'the most regulated', precisely because of its absolute necessity. It manifests itself as 'continual self-parody', where the subject never abides long in any particular form, but where the meaning of its movement is difficult to discern. Socratic irony thus enacts the fundamentally contradictory nature of human experience, both with respect to what we can know and what we can say.

Evocative as these formulations may be, they are less precise than we might wish in clarifying why Plato's Socrates intrigued Friedrich Schlegel or what the actual purposes of Socratic irony were. Providing an answer to these questions requires going a step further and sifting through other comments scattered throughout Schlegel's work, not only his fragments, but also the more systematic remarks about Socrates and Plato in his later lectures on philosophy (especially the unpublished Cologne lectures of 1804–5).

Schlegel's fundamental insight was that the ironic posture assumed by Socrates in his assertion of ignorance had specific consequences for his philosophical method, as Plato clearly understood in shaping his dialogues. 'Plato had only a philosophy and not a system . . . philosophy itself is more of a striving for knowledge than a completed science of knowledge . . . he is never finished with his thinking, so that the characteristic element of his philosophy must be sought . . . in this eternal becoming, developing, and shaping of his ideas which he sought to represent in aesthetic form in his dialogues' (XII: 209). As Lyceum fragment 42 adds, 'anywhere that someone is philosophising in oral or written dialogues and not just in a completely systematic way, he should both enact and insist upon irony' (II: 152). Furthermore, this process is necessarily interactive because an individual has at best partial access to the truth. Socrates' ignorance is what drives him to seek out conversation with others; it pushes him beyond any possible philosophical self-reliance. 'Plato's dialogues are representations of this communal thinking for oneself' (xii: 210), a method that Schlegel explicated further in his analyses of Lessing (besides the 1797–1801 essay, Schlegel published a piece on 'Lessing's thoughts and opinions' in 1804; *Kritische Ausgabe*, iii: 46–102).

Irony as a philosophical method proceeds by pushing definitions beyond their ordinary range of use, even to the point where they rupture. The procedure of many Socratic dialogues thus involves shifting a term from one context to another in order to determine the limits of its applications, the measure of its particular truth. This method aims as much at assessing the speaker as at weighing the truth content of any particular proposition, and can therefore be aptly described in Charles Altieri's terms as 'dramatistic analysis, in which an agent is judged by his awareness of conditions of relevance'.[15] This procedure raises questions about how much of the field of human experience a particular definition of courage, of piety, of justice, can be stretched to cover, and how aware we remain of those limits. In extending a term by assembling an array of relevant cases, the acknowledgment of any contradictions that emerge is crucial, for they signal how far we have got with our definitions. Thus *Athenaeum* fragment 121 defines an idea as 'a concept that has been perfected to the point of irony, an absolute synthesis of absolute antitheses, the continually self-generating interchange of conflicting thoughts' (ii: 184). Only when a concept has been tested by being balanced against its most absolute inversion does it begin to become an idea. This formal structure, the suspension of judgment between opposites, is what Lyceum fragment 42 has in mind when it asserts, 'Philosophy is the real home of irony, which one might like to define as logical beauty' (ii: 152). This is the aspect of Romantic irony taken up by Nietzsche, whose genealogical method aims to uncover the ambivalent motives behind our values. Nietzsche is very much the heir of Schlegel when he asserts, '*Everything* human deserves to be viewed ironically in regard to its *origin*: that is why there is such an *excess* of irony in the world' (*Human, all too human*, aphorism 252).

Yet for Schlegel, the force of such philosophical irony in uncovering contradictions and measuring the limits of our truths is expansive and connective, not simply disruptive and corrosive; this is where Hegel and Kierkegaard (among others) go wrong in reading him. As a notebook fragment succinctly states, 'irony is the idea, *universum*', for the practice of irony is motivated by an aspiration toward intellectual unity (xviii:

---

[15] Charles Altieri, *Act and quality*, Amherst, MA: University of Massachusetts Press, 1981, p. 79.

206, Fragment 114). Schlegel's irony has a specific cognitive force of the kind that critics such as Booth and Hutcheon have been instrumental in defining; the ironist aims to make us see things within a wider context. His interrogative mode goes well beyond any model that sees communication merely as the transmission of clearly conceived ideas. The ironic play with the concepts and categories of language that so deeply offended Hegel was – for Schlegel as for Plato – meant to be purposive and heuristic.

Its purposes, however, are as much pedagogical and ethical as cognitive; they are oriented toward the interactive dimensions of the dialogue situation as much as toward the discovery of truth. The Cologne lectures praise Socrates most highly as a teacher, for 'nobody worked so powerfully and variously upon the characters and ways of thinking of his auditors as he did, and his pre-eminence in this regard is so great that people have almost compared him to Christ' (XII: 198). Schlegel connected irony closely to *Bildung*, that expansive German term whose range of meanings includes education, cultivation, formation. '*Bildung* is antithetical synthesis and perfection to the point of irony' (XVIII: 82, Fragment 637), a decidedly unsentimental education. Despite what Hegel thought, Schlegel did recognize the provisional status of irony as a moment and the consequent responsibility of the ironist to help direct the sceptical impulses that he rouses. Yet Socratic–Schlegelian irony demands a great deal from its auditors as well. As Vlastos points out, such irony aims at enhancing the moral autonomy of others; its open-endedness is a provocation that seeks to move others toward specific sorts of self-reflection (*Socrates*, chapter 1).

Can the philosophical self-reflexiveness of this Socratic ironist really go beyond 'continual self-parody', though? Taking one's ignorance seriously means engaging in the sort of rigorous intellectual self-examination that Plato's Socrates puts at the heart of the dialectical method. This involves 'making the hypotheses not beginnings but really hypotheses – that is, steppingstones and springboards – in order to reach what is free from hypothesis at the beginning of the whole'.[16] Schlegel may have been less certain than Plato that philosophy can ever raise itself free from hypotheses, but he emphatically endorses the need to recall where one has stepped.

Thus, what Schlegel took most seriously in the Platonic dialogues was their literary form as the essential manifestation of their philosophical truths. 'This procedure in the Platonic dialogues is fully in accord with the spirit of philosophy; they go up to the gates of the highest things and satisfy themselves with merely hinting ambiguously at the infinite, the divine, which does not allow itself to be denoted and explained philosophically'

---

[16] Allan Bloom (trans.), *The Republic of Plato*, New York: Basic Books, 1968, p. 191. See besides this passage (511c–511d), also 533b–533c and 537d. Schlegel links dialectic and irony at *Kritische Ausgabe*, vol. XVIII, p. 392 (878).

(XII: 210). Schlegel's critique of a mimetic theory of truth clearly involves reading against certain elements of the Platonic texts, but it anticipates the linguistic turn that Wittgenstein gave to philosophy in this century, a turn as clearly signalled by the stylistic distance between the *Tractatus* and the *Philosophical investigations* as by the difference in their subject-matter. If all philosophy is allegorical, if 'all knowledge is symbolic', then truth lies as much in presentation as in ascertainable facts (XII: 9).

As important as the idea of logical beauty for Schlegel's Romantic irony, then, is the second component named in Lyceum fragment 42, the practice of transcendental buffoonery. If irony's interior consists of an earnest pursuit of reflective self-transcendence, its exterior is, Silenus-like, the mask of Italian buffo with all of the latter's vulgar wit. Schlegel saw this element in the classical tradition as well, most clearly in Aristophanic comedy. Schlegel's interest in Aristophanes goes back to his earliest philological work, which includes an essay on 'The aesthetic worth of Greek comedy' and extensive comments on comedy in his historical studies of Greek literature. In another emphatic revaluation of received wisdom (one that prefigures Nietzsche's *Birth of tragedy*), he took comedy to be an essential complement to tragedy. Indeed, Attic comedy could be seen as a philosophical counterpoise to the Parmenidean–Platonic stress upon unity, for it paid homage to those aspects of human experience represented by Dionysus, 'the god of immortal joy, of wondrous abundance and eternal liberation' (I: 20).

Aristophanes' plays have their share of deceptive *eirons*, to be sure, among them Socrates himself in *The clouds*. As with Socrates, however, Schlegel recognized a more far-reaching dimension of irony in elements of those texts to which the term 'irony' had not traditionally been applied. Irony was most evident for him in an aesthetic strategy peculiar to Greek comedy, the *parabasis*. This scene was a regular part of Aristophanic comedy; it consisted of a direct address by the chorus to the audience that interrupted the play's action with commentary on the play itself, often directly self-reflexive but sometimes highly indirect. The author frequently used this interlude to make a plea that the judges recognize the superiority of his play, as Aristophanes does so deftly in *The clouds* or *The wasps*. The parabasis thus called attention to the actual conditions of performance in Attic theatre. Greek drama was presented competitively, with three plays vying for first prize at the festival of Dionysus, and in an historically self-conscious way. The parabasis often sought to define the aesthetic criteria for a play's own superiority by referring to its predecessors as well as to its immediate rivals.

Schlegel saw this interruption of aesthetic illusion as an ironic acknowledgment by the dramatic text of its own nature as representation and of the limits of such representation. The parabasis calls attention to the

fundamental duality of the aesthetic object, at once mimetic and performative, and forces the audience to consider both dimensions at once. A performative aesthetic expands a mimetic aesthetic in two different respects.
First, an interruptive parabasis reminds the audience that a play, like any
aesthetic artifact, has been produced by an individual author and reflects
some particular perspective. It therefore calls upon us to evaluate the
author's views and purposes apart from the views and purposes of those
characters represented within the text. Second, by addressing the audience, the parabasis locates the play's purposes within publicly determined
conditions of performance that help determine its meaning.

By highlighting its own status as performance, comedy destabilizes the
autonomy of the artwork, a feature that has often been taken by critics as
an essential (and unselfconscious) determinant of Romantic aesthetics. At
the same time, an ironic reading of comedy moves beyond the covertly
strategic purposes that traditional rhetorical analysis can handle. Romantic
irony thus anticipates the increasingly crucial role played by the narrator
in modern fiction, especially the meta-fictional acknowledgment that a
tale is always constructed, told from a particular perspective and with an
eye toward engaging the audience in specific sorts of ways. The characteristic romantic turn on this strategy, however, is its insistence upon the
limits of even this acknowledgment, its recognition that we do not escape
the paradoxes of reciprocal intentionalities simply by portraying them.

The real force of aesthetic parabasis for Romanticism, though, stems
from Schlegel's ingenuity in forging a link between it and Socratic dialectic.
Just as seeing the comic parabasis in light of Socrates brings out its epistemological implications, so Schlegel's reflections on Aristophanes alerted
him to the performative features of the Platonic dialogue. In practical
terms, parabasis also provided the romantic tradition with an immensely
adaptable device for injecting irony into literary texts. Critics have most
often identified Romantic irony as literary practice with some form of
parabasis, 'the drastic violation of illusion by reference within a literary
work to its author and the process of its creation, to the transgression of
the boundary which separates our level of reality as readers of a book or
as audience in a theatre from the reality of the characters in that book or
play'.[17] Among the German Romantics, irony of this sort was most systematically employed by Ludwig Tieck in various plays, including *Puss
in boots*, *The world turned upside-down* and *Prince Zerbino*, the last of
which Schlegel described as the modern drama that came closest to the
Aristophanic spirit (XI: 94). Tieck's plays involve characters, author,
director, critics and audiences in hilariously inconclusive debates about

---

[17] Raymond Immerwahr, 'The practice of irony in early German Romanticism', in Garber,
   Romantic irony. The essays throughout this volume are a rich compilation of such
   instances.

the quality and direction of the performance. He trumps Aristophanes by incorporating even the reactions of his audience within his fictional world, and sets the stage for the anti-illusionist modern plays of Brecht, Genet, Beckett and others.

So even though the term 'Romantic irony' was not then current, it does fit many of the most characteristic features of the literary experimentalism that sprang from Romantic aesthetics. We can find parabasis indirectly at work in the structural juxtapositions and self-commentary that show up in Romantic and post-romantic literature. Schlegel himself had already argued that 'Parabasis in the novel must be concealed, not out in the open as in ancient comedy', and Romantic writers did in fact find multiple ways of deploying it (XVI: 118, Fragment 397). Schlegel's own 'novel', *Lucinde*, Novalis's *Heinrich von Ofterdingen*, Brentano's *Märchen*, E. T. A. Hoffmann's tales, Shelley's *Frankenstein*, Hogg's *Memoirs and confessions of a justified sinner*, and De Quincey's *Confessions of an English opium eater* and *Suspiria de profundis* all utilize an interruptive structure similar to parabasis in their abrupt shifts from one narrative level to another, from fairy tale or fantasy or dream to realism and back again. Even within a consistently sustained realism, juxtapositions of the kind employed by Stendhal or Flaubert raise the same sort of evaluative questions about the connectedness of events and the motives of characters (and authors) that a parabasis would raise explicitly. The interventionist narrators of Byron's *Don Juan*, Carlyle's *Sartor resartus*, or Pushkin's *Eugene Onegin*, and even the more sober I of Wordsworth's *Prelude*, comment extensively upon their difficulties in orchestrating their texts, blurring as they do so the generic lines between biography and fiction.

Our peculiar fate

Much of the originality in Schlegel's renewal of classical irony came from viewing it through the lens of contemporary German philosophy. Plato and Aristophanes provided Schlegel with rich models of irony, but it was Kant and Fichte who gave him the philosophical framework for explaining why such irony was necessary and for justifying how far it needed to be extended. Through his intensive study of German idealism as it emerged, Schlegel came to conceive of the paradoxical and perspectival nature of human knowledge as an inevitable consequence of the structure of human consciousness.

Kant's influence makes itself felt here, and indeed throughout Romantic literary theory, as the essential impetus. The philosophical spark for Romantic aesthetics was given by Kant's transcendental turn, with its rigorously argued demonstration of the self-reflexivity and self-limitation of reason. It was the *Critique of pure reason* rather than the *Critique of judgement*, with the latter's more explicit aesthetic concerns, that was most influential for Schlegel and the other Romantics; this took as its starting point the seemingly paradoxical nature of reason, its apparent and perplexing inability to fulfil the tasks that it sets for itself. The *Critique of pure reason* opens by saying, 'Human reason has this peculiar fate that in one species of its knowledge it is burdened by questions which, as prescribed by the very nature of reason itself, it is not able to ignore, but which, as transcending all its powers, it is also not able to answer.'[18]

There is already an ironic displacement of consciousness from itself in the main premise of the *Critique of pure reason*. Kant contends that although we cannot apprehend things-in-themselves directly and can therefore know things only as phenomena, only as they appear to us, we can come to understand the conditions of possibility for the knowledge (of phenomena) that we do have, that is, the objective (shared) grounds for our subjective (human) experience and knowledge. We can therefore also understand the necessity by which reason is confronted with apparent paradoxes and recognize the inevitability of certain limits. The *Critique of pure reason* endeavours to systematize the *a priori* concepts that we use to organize and thus even to apprehend our world. 'Understanding has rules which I must presuppose as being in me prior to objects being given to me, and therefore as being *a priori*. They find expression in *a priori* concepts to which all objects of experience necessarily conform' (p. 23).

Yet the fundamental ideas of reason, in contrast to the concepts of understanding, are not only required for the operation of understanding, but also unknowable by that understanding. 'I understand by idea a necessary concept of reason to which no corresponding object can be given in sense-experience. . . . [Transcendental ideas] are concepts of pure reason, in that they view all knowledge gained in experience as being determined through an absolute totality of conditions' (p. 319). Despite being unknowable, these ideas of reason – God, freedom, immortality – underlie the unity we project into (or find within) our experience and regulate our aspirations and our behaviour. We presume a unity in our experience, an autonomy in our identity, a purpose in our being that we can never adequately demonstrate, but do so by necessity in making any use whatsoever of our mental faculties; such unity is for Kant therefore not simply a matter of faith, but an intrinsic feature of everyday experience. Human existence can thus be said to be bipolar, empirical and ideal at the same time, with two non-convergent centres.[19]

---

[18] Immanuel Kant, *Critique of pure reason*, Norman Kemp Smith (trans.), New York: St Martin's Press, 1965, p. 7.

[19] On this tension, see in particular chapter 3 of Marshall Brown, *The shape of German Romanticism*, Ithaca, NY: Cornell University Press, 1979.

Schlegel clearly recognized the importance of the Kantian revolution in philosophy, while assessing its implications in this way. 'Kant introduced the concept of the negative into the world's wisdom. Might it not now be a useful endeavour to introduce the concept of the positive into philosophy as well?' (II: 166, Fragment 3). While Kant had demonstrated the existence of intrinsic limits upon human knowledge because of the inevitably partial status of our reason and understanding, he refused to acknowledge the generative and transformative power of the subject to transcend its own formulations. He remained fundamentally empirical and sceptical in his rationalism, his unifying ideas of reason poised precariously above an intellectual abyss.

For the positive possibility that Schlegel envisaged, he turned to Johann Gottlieb Fichte, the German philosopher who gave Kant's transcendentalism its distinctively idealist form. Kant's philosophy, because of its systematic aspirations and presentation, remained to Schlegel's mind essentially static. It ultimately took both the mind (in its categories and ideas) and phenomena (in their mode of apprehension) as stable and self-identical entities, thus failing to work through the consequences of its own ironic insight. Fichte's *Wissenschaftslehre* (1794), in contrast, began by taking thinking as active, dynamic, self-transcending. Fichte's foundational thesis is that the subject is that which posits itself or sets itself forth (*Das Ich setzt sich*). In thus positing itself, the subject creates the possibility of seeing itself as split between positing and posited, hence exceeding the very form in which it has just posited itself, which therefore becomes a limit rather than an adequate representation for itself – though also a necessary stage in that it provides an object for self-reflection. In Schlegel's rendering of Fichte, this becomes the idea that we are always only a part of ourselves. '*Human beings are omnipotent and omniscient and wholly good*; only humanity is *not wholly* present in the individual, but there only in part. The human being can never be present' (XVIII: pp. 506, 509; see also XII, pp. 337 and 343). We can take this partial presence of the subject to itself in various ways, in a psychological, a sociological or a political sense as well as a philosophical one, as the romantic solipsism that Hegel saw or as the sign of an intersubjectivity where the subject is recognized as a repository of ideas and affects whose availability for consciousness is intermittent at best.[20] It is crucial, however, to see that Schlegel's ironic subject hovers between its realizations and its potential, no more one than the other. Its essence is an unstable combination of these opposites; its dynamism results from its insufficiency to itself, but also from its dissatisfaction with that insufficiency.

---

[20] See Handwerk, *Irony and ethics*, especially chapters 1 and 2.

For Schlegel, the fundamental idealist premise was the priority of becoming over being, and here he might well have claimed that Kant simply failed to push his ironic ignorance far enough. Schlegel credited Fichte with discovering the laws of thought and thus with discovering how to move beyond the scepticism of classical Greek philosophy, with its intuition of experience as mere flux (XII: 291–2). So it is not surprising that Schlegel's own version of idealist dialectic (in the Jena lectures of 1801–2) is not all that different from Fichte's. He is perhaps more emphatic in his stress upon its destabilizing consequences, upon the necessity of going beyond the very laws of logic that Fichte took as constitutive of the subject – the laws of identity and non-contradiction in particular. And he does raise two specific objections against Fichte in the later Cologne lectures. First, he contends that Fichte did not follow out the implications of his own model for conceiving the subject in process. 'The sole difference between our philosophy and that of Fichte consists in this, that Fichte says: *the ego is at the same time subject and object*, whereas in our language he would have had to have said: the ego *becomes* itself an *object* for itself' (XII: 342). Second, he draws a further consequence from his view that the subject can only be present to itself in a partial way. 'In that we are inconceivable to ourselves, only appear to ourselves as a part of ourselves, we cannot possibly be a work of ourselves'; that is, the subject does not in any literal sense engender itself (XII: 343). Thus Schlegel carefully deflects Hegel's criticism that the romantic subject asserted a self-creative power as absolute as that claimed by Fichte's ego. Hegel denounced this as a purely abstract claim, allowing the subject to hypostasize the moment of negativity as uncontrolled subjective licence and to repudiate even its self-created reality as inessential. Instead, as his own later work confirms, Schlegel recognized that irony set the foundation for a model of subjectivity that was fundamentally temporal, indeed historical, in nature.[21]

Seeing the epistemological status of the subject as ironic has important methodological consequences for Schlegel's view of philosophy and literature. First, it explains his reiterated claim that 'if the object of philosophy is positive *knowledge* of infinite reality, it is easy to see that this task can never be completed' (XII: 166). Philosophy must instead (as Nietzsche also saw) become historical, focussing not upon formal, systematic modes of analysis, but genetic ones. 'Only the historical, constructive representation is *objective*, that which no longer requires any demonstrative form' (XVIII: 35, Fragment 174). These principles lay behind Schlegel's own choice to shape his personal notebooks as *Philosophische Lehrjahre*, records of his

---

[21] This line of thought has produced some of the finest recent work on Schlegel and on Romantic irony. Sparked by Benjamin's essay, it includes de Man's work, as well as Manfred Frank, *Das Problem 'Zeit' in der deutschen Romantik*, Munich: Winkler Verlag, 1972 and Jochen Hörisch, *Die fröhliche Wissenschaft der Poesie*, Frankfurt am Main: Suhrkamp Verlag, 1976.

years of philosophical apprenticeship. It is telling, however, that he did not discover any suitable mode of publication for such records and reverted in his own later work to the expository form of the lecture. Second, the representation of such partial knowledge obtained in the pursuit of knowledge must be performative, enacting that which it describes. This, as Werner Hamacher has noted, leads to a revolutionary aesthetic, in that, 'a radically new place is assigned to aesthetics; it is its own ground and no longer mimesis of the idea or *imitatio naturae*, it is the *form of action* of the human spirit and no longer the reproduction of an action, be it that of nature or of consciousness'.[22] It turns philosophy into aesthetics, into a science of representation and of self-reflexivity about representation. Fichte's philosophy thus allows Schlegel to give a much more precise philosophical force and structure to literary parabasis, defining it as a process of self-creation and self-destruction that aims to put the subject itself into question. At the same time, Romantic irony gives a literary impulse to Fichte's philosophical formulations, re-immersing that subject in the particularity characteristic of literary texts and moving it past the formalism of Fichte's method.

This idealist irony, then, accepts as its problem the issue that Kant's *Critique of pure reason* tried to bracket, by acknowledging the continually paradoxical nature of human thought. If the mind cannot fully grasp itself, even the conditions of possibility for or the ultimate limits of the acts that it itself performs, its aspiration to self-sufficiency will always be frustrated. Its knowledge will necessarily be an allegorical representation of its own suspension between intuitive insight and discursive incapacity. This consequence can be felt either as a liberation or as a loss. But to emphasize the incapacity over the aspiration, as does the melancholic irony of Karl Solger's *Erwin* (1815) or the blinded insight of de Man, is to take the part for the whole. For though the subject may always be less than it is, it is also more. 'But voluntarily to displace oneself from this sphere into that one . . . not simply with understanding and imagination, but with one's entire soul; freely to renounce now this, now that part of one's being and to limit oneself wholly to another one; to seek for and to find one's one and all now in this, now in that individual and intentionally to forget all others: that can be done only by a spirit who contains within himself a number of spirits and a whole system of persons, and in whose interior the universe, which as we say ought to sprout in every monad, has grown and ripened' (*Kritische Ausgabe*, II: 185, Fragment 121).

Schlegel's formulation here gives a recipe for one of the dominant narrative subgenres of the last two hundred years, the *Bildungsroman*. Such novels of education treat this pattern of internal revolution within a central character as a developmental process. Schlegel's early praise for

---

[22] Werner Hamacher, 'Der Satz der Gattung: Friedrich Schlegels poetologische Umsetzung von Fichtes unbedingtem Grundsatz', *MLN* 95 (1980), p. 1161.

Goethe's *Wilhelm Meister* and his own, less successful effort at the genre, *Lucinde*, provide theoretical models for the innumerable *Bildungsromane* that followed, from Stendhal's *The red and the black* and Dickens's *David Copperfield* through Flaubert's *Sentimental education* to Mann's *Dr Faustus* and Rushdie's *Midnight's children*.

Given its own transformative imperative, it seems inevitable that 'irony' itself, as a term, would be provisional as well. That it vanishes from Schlegel's writings is clear; what it becomes remains a matter of debate. With an eye to Schlegel's conversion to Catholicism, Strohschneider-Kohrs has suggested 'love' as its surrogate, and elsewhere 'conscience' seems to invoke a familiar network of related terms; Frank has argued that 'irony' becomes 'time', and Behler that it turns into Hegel's irony of history.[23] What we can perhaps more reliably measure are the immediate consequences of Romantic irony for literary theory and literary practice.

From literary theory to literary history

Since other essays in this volume deal with many specific problems in Romantic aesthetics, I want simply to signal a few general implications of Romantic irony for the practice of literary criticism during the Romantic period itself. Abstract though his formulations can seem, Schlegel's reflections on irony had a broadly historical as well as a theoretical basis. His concept of irony emerged deductively from his sustained meditation on a very specific group of philosophers and artists, but also inductively from his wide-ranging studies in numerous European literatures. It served him well as a concept because it was sufficiently capacious to hold together his eclectic collection of literary forebears and yet sufficiently precise to signal the coherence of his choices. The expansive sense that Schlegel gave to 'modernity' is evident in *Athenaeum* fragment 247, which lists Dante, Shakespeare and Goethe as the great triad of modern poetry, describing them as transcendental or Romantic writers who implicitly share the self-reflexive ambitions of Romantic irony. We can trace the continuity of Schlegel's theory of irony with his literary historical concerns by looking briefly at three specific areas, literary hermeneutics, the literary canon and genre theory.

Schlegel's hermeneutics are centred upon the active integration of all the different components of aesthetic experience, even those most often presumed to be quite distinct. Even the violation of aesthetic illusion was not meant to be an entirely negative and disruptive force. Schlegel saw it, in fact, as an opening into the mingling of poetry and philosophy, as a way to

---

[23] Strohschneider-Kohrs, *Die romantische Ironie*, pp. 80–8; Handwerk, *Irony and ethics*, pp. 40–3; Frank, *Das Problem 'Zeit'*, pp. 181–93; Behler, 'The theory of irony', in Garber, *Romantic irony*, pp. 62–7, 76–80.

demonstrate that imaginative fiction and analytical reflection could work as interdependent modes of knowledge. A parabatic interlude should not just interrupt the dramatic action, but connect to it and even advance it, just as the dramatic plot of a given text should consciously strive to extend the implications of its reflective digressions.

At the same time, by denying the immediate self-presence of a self-identical subject, irony complicates the issue of where literary meaning can be located. This point is articulated by two of the most perfectly (albeit briefly) sustained examples of Romantic irony, Novalis's 'Monologue' and Schlegel's 'On incomprehensibility'. The latter piece was Schlegel's parting address in the *Athenaeum* and opens by questioning the very foundation of hermeneutics. 'Of all that has to do with the communication of ideas, what could be more intriguing than the question of whether it is possible at all?' (II: 363).[24] It goes on to assert that language typically frustrates our communicative intentions, not, as we might expect, because of various insufficiencies in it, but because it actually says more than we intend. 'Words often understand themselves better than do those who are using them' (II: 364). Yet the fact that we are not fully in control of our language is, as Novalis emphasizes, as much an opportunity as a restriction. 'For if someone speaks merely for the sake of speaking, he utters the most splendid, most original truths. But if he wants to say something specific, whimsical language makes him say the most ridiculous and upside-down things' (II: 372). His monologue works its metaphoric way through comparisons of language to mathematics and to music, arguing that we speak the most truly when we allow our language the freest rein. Alert to its own paradoxical status, however, 'Monologue' finally turns around to question whether it can possibly have expressed this 'truth' about language adequately, precisely because it has been trying to do so – which of course leaves open the possibility that it may unwittingly have spoken a different truth.

A parallel openness with respect to meaning exists at the other end of the communicative chain as well, captured in Novalis's idea of the reader as an 'extended author'. One reason why a speaker or author cannot hope to control the significance of what he expresses is that the full meaning of his words lies not in him alone, but in the expansive force that they have as they move through other people. 'That one person understands another is philosophically inconceivable, but indeed magical. It is the secret of becoming divine; the blossoms of the one become the seed for the other' (XVIII: 253, Fragment 713). Schlegel's attempt in 'On incomprehensibility' to categorize the whole array of possible ironies breaks down into a

---

[24] For a careful study of the multiple turns of Schlegel's text, see Cathy Comstock, ' "Transcendental buffoonery": irony as process in Schlegel's "Über die Unverständlichkeit" ', *Studies in Romanticism* 26 (1987), pp. 445–64.

predictable chaos, but its conclusion is that there is a positive power in incomprehensibility. 'As anyone can readily discern, the most precious thing that human beings possess, their own inner satisfaction, finally depends upon some such point that must be left in the dark, yet which for that very reason bears and supports the whole, and which would lose its force at the very moment we wished to dissolve it into understanding' (II: 370). It is those texts and those statements that do not presume to control their own meanings and leave sufficient space for their readers that are for him the most intellectually fruitful.

Schlegel's ironic perspective logically tends, then, to privilege many works and genres that had been left aside or even deemed incomprehensible by the traditional literary canon. Shakespeare holds the most central place in Schlegel's romantic realignment, for his texts contain in abundance virtually every literary strategy that one might consider ironic – the mingling of comic and tragic elements, the play within a play that comments on the nature of dramatic representation, and the metaphoric interrogation of the relation between representation and reality in such images as the world as stage. Yet these surface features matter less for Schlegel than the underlying sensibility that transforms all these incongruities into wholeness. *Athenaeum* fragment 253 turns the neoclassical suspicion of Shakespeare on its head by insisting upon the 'correctness' of his plays. By correctness, Schlegel means the internal resonances that indicate an author's cognizance of the multiple relations among the various parts of a given text. '[Shakespeare] is also systematic as no one else is: now through those antitheses that allow individuals, masses, even worlds to contrast with one another in picturesque groupings; now through musical symmetry on the same great scale, through gigantic repetitions and refrains; often through parody of the letter and through irony directed at the spirit of romantic drama, and always through the highest and most complete individuality and the most many-sided representation of it, uniting all the stages of poetry' (II: 208, Fragment 253). As in his essay on Goethe, Schlegel sees irony here as a spirit hovering over the most variegated, internally manifold sort of work, suggesting a unity that need not be explicitly visible in any specific moment of synthesis within the text itself and cannot begin to exist apart from a reader's assistance in constructing it.

Yet it is prose fiction, especially in the modern form of the novel, that offers the greatest possibilities for irony. Not only does Schlegel advocate a realignment of traditional genre hierarchies to privilege this relatively new form, but he strives to find a place within his renovated canon for such 'frivolous' authors as Cervantes and Sterne. He ranks *Don Quixote* with the greatest works of Romantic art, *Hamlet* and *Wilhelm Meister*, in the 'Dialogue on poetry' (II: 282–3, Fragment 346). Like his more respectable counterparts, Cervantes underscores the ironic gap between ideals and reality, yet his sentimental tendencies keep the irony from degenerating into mere parody. Cervantes practises irony on a large structural scale as well, with part two of *Don Quixote* serving as commentary on all of part one, so that the first part becomes in a sense the hero of the second part. *Tristram Shandy* has very similar self-commentary on its surface as well, as the act of writing becomes itself the subject and even the main character in the text. As with Cervantes, it is essential for Schlegel that this reflective irony be balanced by the sentimental features so evident in Sterne's text; the irony requires the adventures of the Shandy family in order to balance its intellectual dimensions with ethical purposiveness.

Besides reconstituting the literary past, Romantic irony looks toward a literature of the future as well, most obviously in its implications for genre. An obvious device for disrupting aesthetic illusion is the mingling of distinctive, even discordant genres. In his 'Letter on the Novel', Schlegel recommends a literature that would recombine authors and texts from the past in a theory of the novel that would itself be a novel, as Goethe's *Wilhelm Meister* so brilliantly manages to do. Nor do the boundaries of literature stop at fiction, since 'true history is the foundation of all romantic poetry' (II: 337).

While reaching out toward a 'progressive universal poetry', Romantic irony also turns back toward the most minute aesthetic objects and most circumscribed aesthetic forms. Its acknowledgment of the perspectival nature of knowledge lays the foundation for a theory of the fragment as form. Fragments provided not only a setting for the sort of finely polished, provocatively formulated insight that Schlegel loved, but also an occasion for the active practice of *Symphilosophie*. The *Athenaeum*, Blütenstaub and Ideen collections of fragments were all to some degree communal, as Schlegel sowed contributions from his Romantic associates into the distillations he had drawn from his own notebook materials. The suggestiveness of the fragment form, which Schlegel often described as '*échappées de vue* into the infinite' or as 'critical wit', made it an ideal way to spark the interactive response that Schlegel thought essential in literary or philosophical practice.

The allure of Romantic irony as a concept derives in large part from the sense that it could be connected to almost any other Romantic idea, in a process itself reaching to infinity. Yet since Schlegel has over the course of literary history so rarely had the last word, even with respect to irony, it might not be out of place to let him have it here, with an ironic reminder from the essay on incomprehensibility. 'The highest truths of every kind are thoroughly trivial and for that very reason nothing is more necessary than expressing them in ever new and, where possible, in ever more paradoxical ways, so that it will not be forgotten that they still exist and that they can never really be fully expressed' (II: 366).

11

Theories of genre

TILOTTAMA RAJAN

I

To argue for a Romantic genre theory may seem surprising. This is the period when William Wordsworth writes that every author must '*creat[e] the taste by which he is to be enjoyed*', when Madame de Staël praises Germany as opposed to France because its authors 'form [their] public', and when Victor Hugo insists that writers be judged by the 'laws of their personal organisation' instead of 'rules and genres'.[1] But as Hugo indicates Romanticism may not so much reject genre as expand its provenance so that it is no longer a system of exclusion. Noting that a work's 'defects' are often the 'condition of [its] qualities' (p. 107), Hugo questions the equation of genre with achieved form. He also points to what is more systematically theorized in Germany as *hermeneutics*: the understanding of culturally or historically different texts through a reading that is 'psychological' as well as 'grammatical' and 'technical'.[2] Wilhelm Dilthey later links a specifically *Romantic* hermeneutics to a tradition leading from Leibniz through Goethe and Herder to the post-Kantians, one that sees 'the shaping structure of the soul behind the appearance' of natural and cultural phenomena.[3] Instituting a hermeneutics of genre, romanticism replaces earlier pragmatic or formalist approaches with a *phenomenological* approach to genres as expressing sometimes conflicted states of (cultural) consciousness. Genres are seen not in terms of effects or structural features, but as sites of negotiation between subject and object, inwardness and its externalization, or as (in)adequate embodiments of the 'Idea'.

[1] William Wordsworth, 'Essay supplementary to the preface', in *Literary criticism of William Wordsworth*, Paul M. Zall (ed.), Lincoln, NE: University of Nebraska Press, 1966, p. 182; Madame de Staël, *De l'Allemagne*, Paris, n.d., pp. 110–11 (translation mine); Victor Hugo, Preface to *Cromwell*, Paris: Garnier-Flammarion, 1968, p. 107 (hereafter cited in the text – translations mine).
[2] The terms are those of Friedrich Schleiermacher, whose work is best initially approached through 'The Hermeneutics: the Outline of the 1819 Lectures', J. Wojcik and R. Haas (trans.), *New literary history* 10 (1978), pp. 1–16. For further discussion of Romantic hermeneutics see Tilottama Rajan, *The supplement of reading: figures of understanding in Romantic theory and practice*, Ithaca, NY: Cornell University Press, 1990, pp. 15–99.
[3] Wilhelm Dilthey, 'The Schleiermacher biography', in *Dilthey: selected writings*, H. P. Rickman (ed.), Cambridge University Press, 1976, p. 53. See more generally pp. 50–67.

This essay traces the emergence of 'philosophical genre theory' up to its temporary consolidation by Hegel. But the influence of this theory continues beyond his *Aesthetics*, in theorists as different as Kierkegaard, Nietzsche, Benjamin, Lukács, Bakhtin and de Man, as well as in a metathematics of cultural forms that extends beyond literature or even the arts.

Two discussions of Romantic genre theory are relevant here. Peter Szondi views the transition from 'the Enlightenment to German idealism' as a shift 'from a pragmatic to a philosophical' theory of genres.[4] Szondi sees Friedrich Schlegel as initiating concerns teleologically completed by Hegel, who synthesizes a new awareness of historical change with the systematic claims of 'philosophy'. In contrast, I approach Hegel's *Aesthetics* not as the resolution of earlier tendencies but as a watershed text that opens new directions. Szondi makes aesthetics part of a philosophical imaginary that provides a metanarrative and not just a methodology for the study of art: aesthetics is the 'mirror' in which, as Schelling says, the philosopher views 'the inner essence of his own discipline' made concrete and real.[5] But despite the totalizing seductions of philosophy, its real contribution was methodological. Instead of taking philosophy as the master discipline of Romanticism and aesthetics as its exemplification, I therefore see the Romantics as *interdisciplinary* thinkers who approach genres in philosophical (and psychological) rather than mechanical ways. The role of 'philosophy' is not to confer a systematic order on history; rather (post-)Hegelian theory sees genres as attempts at philosophical problem-solving that are finally subject to historical and cultural difference.

Cyrus Hamlin, though laying less emphasis on the systematic, also locates the contribution of German romanticism in its 'philosophical' genre theory. He traces its debt to Goethe's theory of morphology: like plants, genres have a *Gestalt* which is not 'an abstract schema or norm' but the 'individual and characteristic *shape* of the work'. Hamlin also contextualizes Romantic genre theory in post-Kantian idealism's theory of 'consciousness (*Bewußtsein*) and its dialectical development, or education (*Bildung*)', so as to emphasize that the Romantics saw genres as expressing a 'state of mind'.[6] Hamlin, however, limits Romantic genre theory to what Alastair Fowler calls the 'central genres' as opposed to 'extended literature'. But while Goethe names epic, lyric and drama as the 'natural forms of poetry',[7] Friedrich Schlegel confines this division to classical literature,

---

[4] Peter Szondi, *On textual understanding and other essays*, Harvey Mendelsohn (trans.), Minneapolis, MN: University of Minnesota Press, 1986, p. 78.

[5] F. W. J. Schelling, *The philosophy of art*, Douglas W. Stott (ed. and trans.), Minneapolis, MN: University of Minnesota Press, 1989, p. 8.

[6] Cyrus Hamlin, 'The origins of a philosophical genre theory in German Romanticism', *European Romantic review* 5, no. 1 (1994), pp. 9–11.

[7] Alastair Fowler, *Kinds of literature: an introduction to the theory of genres and modes*, Cambridge, MA: Harvard University Press, 1982, p. 17; Hamlin, 'Origins', p. 13.

arguing that 'of the modern genres there exists only one or infinitely many'.[8] Thus, while the actual term *Gattung* (species) may have been used restrictively, in practice Romanticism greatly expands the reach of genre by theorizing semiotic genres such as irony and allegory along with genres or 'kinds' of sensibility such as the naive and the sentimental. The pheno-menological expansion of genre is the result of a tension between the theories of morphology and consciousness that Hamlin sees as complementary. On the one hand Goethe's notion of *Gestalt* leads to a definition of genre as a '*natural*, rather than . . . arbitrary phenomenon';[9] genres are under-stood as organic expressions of consciousness, and are grasped in terms of what Coleridge calls 'form as proceeding' rather than 'shape as super-induced'.[10] On the other hand, because this consciousness is involved in the process of *Bildung*, the 'natural' is historicized, allowing new genres to emerge.

This essay, then, locates Romanticism's contribution in the shift from a formalist to a phenomenological theory of genre, in the resulting expan-sion of generic analysis to other forms of cultural consciousness, and in the recognition of these forms as historical. I deal largely with German Romanticism because I focus on genre at the level of 'theory' – an epi-stemic form that is rarer in England, where 'criticism' predominates and where 'aesthetics' has not yet been constituted as a separate discipline. Whereas 'criticism' from Pope to Arnold is oriented to the public sphere, aesthetic 'theory' is constituted upon the sense of aesthetic judgment as autonomous. Klaus Berghahn has described the dominance in enlighten-ment Germany of just such a literary criticism committed through *taste* to the constitution of the bourgeois public, and carried on in the socially responsive media of reviews and periodicals.[11] The *Sturm-und-Drang* period, however, witnesses a growing emphasis on the artist himself and the ideal intention or inner spirit of artworks. The promotion of *genius* can take an anthropological form (as in Herder's advocacy of the *Volk*), or an individual form (as in the hermeneutic emphasis on understanding the author better than he understood himself). In both cases artworks and cultures are considered as being *sui generis*, and it is from this openness to their individuality that a rethinking of genre develops.

The emphasis on individuality lays the ground for the aesthetic to have its own discursive space, so that the paradigm shift in Germany between

---

[8] Friedrich Schlegel, *Literary notebooks 1797–1801*, Hans Eichner (ed.), Toronto: University of Toronto Press, 1957, p. 110. (When cited: translations mine.)

[9] Hamlin, 'Origins', p. 10.

[10] Samuel Taylor Coleridge, 'On poesy or art', in *Biographia literaria, with his aesthetical essays*, J. Shawcross (ed.), 2 vols., Oxford University Press, 1907/73, vol. II, p. 262.

[11] Klaus Berghahn, 'From Classicist to Classical literary criticism, 1730–1806', in *A history of German literary criticism*, Peter Uwe Hohendahl (ed.), Lincoln, NE: University of Nebraska Press, 1988, p. 21.

1730 and 1830 can also be traced through a subordination of the review and the amateur essay to the treatise, the academic lecture, and somewhat differently the fragment. This shift is considerably less marked in England. For only in Shelley and Coleridge do we find traces of the discursive genres characteristic of German Romanticism: of the system or treatise that constructs aesthetics as an autonomous discipline (as in Schelling or Hegel), or the theoretical aphorism that resists both systematization and empirical contextualization (as in Schlegel). More commonly English criticism consists of essays and reviews, or of literary histories written to accompany the early anthologies through which Thomas Campbell and Robert Southey constructed a national literature.[12] Indeed the mixed nature of Coleridge's *Biographia literaria* (1817) as a miscellany of post-Kantian theory and empirical criticism testifies to the anxiety attending any reconfiguration of the dominant (social) model of criticism. The power of the public sphere remains evident even in Shelley, even though he argues that a poet 'would do ill' to write according to contemporaneous 'conceptions of right and wrong'.[13] For despite resemblances to Jena Romanticism, 'Defence of poetry' (1821) places itself in an 'aesthetic public sphere'[14] defensively constituted in response to Peacock's attack on poetry in *The four ages of poetry* (1820). Shelley's theory of genres is thus judgmental rather than systematic or historicizing. Narrative is inferior to poetry because its particularity disfigures the idealist project (p. 485); and (in an account that recurs in conservative literary histories such as Campbell's), drama, unless it 'continues to express poetry', is a source of mimetic and affective contagion because of the way it 'sympathises' with 'the decay of social life' (p. 491).

To be sure, English Romanticism also experiments with 'decoupling' art from the public sphere, notably in the theory of Coleridge and Shelley, and earlier in Edward Young's *Conjectures on original composition* (1759). Concomitantly, the literature is rich in generic experimentation, and its 'unwritten poetics'[15] calls for precisely the innovative genre theory developed in Germany. Parallels to J. G. Herder's recognition (discussed in the next section) that different cultures write different 'kinds' of poetry can also be found in antiquarian attempts to recover the 'specimens' of

---

[12] I refer to Thomas Campbell, *Specimens of the British poets; with biographical and critical notices, and an essay on English poetry*, 7 vols., London: John Murray, 1819, and to Robert Southey, *Specimens of the later English poets*, 3 vols., London: Longman, Hurst, Rees and Orme, 1807, *Select works of the British poets from Chaucer to Jonson*, London: Longman, Rees, Orme, Brown and Green, 1831, and *The lives and works of the uneducated poets*, 1831; rpt. London: H. Milford, 1925.

[13] Percy Bysshe Shelley, 'Defence of poetry', in *Shelley's poetry and prose*, Donald H. Reiman and Sharon B. Powers (eds.), New York: Norton, 1977, p. 488.

[14] Berghahn, 'From Classicist', p. 97.

[15] See Claudio Guillen, *Literature as system: essays toward the theory of literary history*, Princeton, NJ: Princeton University Press, 1971, p. 127.

early English poetry, or to uncover a tradition of 'uneducated poets' as in Southey's *The lives and works of the uneducated poets* (1831). Nevertheless Southey stops short of dignifying the non-canonical as part of the *Volk*, preferring to define his poets by subtraction as 'uneducated'. In this he continues the treatment of generic otherness as a 'relique' or curiosity characteristic of Thomas Percy, who recovers the marginal genre of the ballad within a narrative of 'improvement' to which his own project is apologetically related. Interspersing older ballads with 'elegant' lyrics so as to appeal to contemporary 'taste', Percy fails to deal with the ballad as epistemically different both from narrative and from lyric (into which he assimilates it because of its 'sung' quality).[16] Despite concessions to cultural difference such criticism therefore remains firmly located in the contemporary public sphere.

English criticism, then, assumes that genre participates in constructing the appropriate public through 'taste' and 'judgment'. Thus Wordsworth dismisses 'frantic novels' and 'sickly . . . German tragedies' which apply 'gross and violent stimulants' to the mind, while Coleridge criticizes novels for 'painfully' affecting the 'feelings' and exciting 'curiosity and sensibility'.[17] There were, of course, different opinions of the various genres. William Godwin's 'Of choice in reading' opens by observing that 'daughters' are often 'prohibited from the reading of novels'.[18] Arguing that a text is constituted by its 'effect' and that effect cannot be regulated, Godwin makes both drama and the novel vehicles for rethinking the norms of gender and society. One could develop a more complex account of such revisability by dealing not only with the scattered critical comments on genre, but also with literary texts that reflect on genre, through subtitles or scenes of writing and reading. New *theoretical* approaches to genre, however, are to be found elsewhere.

II

The need for a 'philosophical' genre theory is first intimated by Herder, who complains that we have 'mechanical rules governing the *modes of poetry*', but lack a 'complete *aesthetics* of poetic art, and even less a whole metaphysics of the *fine arts*'. Herder thus continues Baumgarten's institution of aesthetics as an autonomous discipline that defines 'the essence of

---

[16] Thomas Percy, *Reliques of ancient English poetry*, J. V. Prichard (ed.), 2 vols., New York: Crowell, 1876, I: viii, x.

[17] William Wordsworth, Preface to *Lyrical ballads* (1800), *Literary criticism* p. 21; Samuel Taylor Coleridge, *The Friend* (1818), Barbara E. Rooke (ed.), 2 vols., Princeton, NJ: Princeton University Press, 1969, vol. I, pp. 179, 132, 20.

[18] William Godwin, *The enquirer; reflections on education, manners, and literature in a series of essays*, 1797; rpt. New York: Kelley, 1965, p. 129.

the *beautiful* in every . . . form of art'. Unlike Schelling and Hegel after him, he does not propose to 'begin this building . . . at the top', but to start 'from below' with the ode.[19] Though Herder falls short of a 'philosophical' account of even this one genre, his 'Fragments of a treatise on the ode' (1765) and his 'Essay on a history of lyrical poetry' (1766) enunciate certain seminal analytic principles. He links genre to *'sensibility'* or 'sensation' (*Early works*, pp. 35–6) – an idea developed further by Schiller. He also emphasizes the relativity of *'aesthetic sense'*: 'What a nation at one time holds as good' can later be seen as 'ugly, as useless, as displeasing, as false' (p. 67). He is critical of genre theory for drawing its standards from '*one* kind, manifested by *one* people' in relation to which other forms are 'deviations' (p. 71). The appeal to sensibility is thus connected, not simply with a shift to the subjective, but also with an emphasis on cultural and historical difference.

Herder institutes certain tensions that recur from Jena Romanticism to Hegel between the desire for unity and the recognition of difference: tensions evident in his use of a systematizing language alongside an organicism itself overdetermined by the competing discourses of history and biology. Thus the figure of a 'building' anticipates the German craving for system. But on another level it is the very amplitude of this 'building' (and later *Bildung*) that accommodates different kinds of art. The tension between essentialism and difference is continued in Herder's 'genetical' conception of genre on the analogy of a plant. A stemmatic approach traces genres back to their 'source' as the tree is 'derived from its root'. The ode is thus the root of elegy, lyric and pastoral (p. 50) – a suggestion that typifies a Romantic desire for a point of unification that Schlegel will re-project from the past to the future in making the novel the synthesis of all other genres. Here we see the desire for system: for taxonomies that reduce multiplicity to unity. On the other hand, Herder is as interested in the 'offshoots' as in the 'stem', thus disclosing another aspect of organicism: the notion that genres grow and change. As he observes of the ode, 'Since my subject is constantly changing, I do not know where I shall find oneness' (pp. 70–1). Organicism thus becomes cognate with history, understood disseminatively rather than as a teleological unity.

Herder's style is marked by his use of the fragment and of deliberately asystematic arguments. In choosing him as a point of emergence, I approach Romantic genre theory as similarly open-ended, despite its propensity for systems. Of particular importance is Herder's view that a 'philosophical elaboration' of genre requires a critic who is a 'poetic philologist', a philosopher and a 'poetological psychologist' (pp. 50–1, 252).

---

[19] Johann Gottfried Herder, *Selected early works, 1764–7*, Ernest A. Menze and Michael Palma (trans.), University Park, PA: Pennsylvania State University Press, 1992, pp. 50–1.

But it is Schiller who more specifically exemplifies the movement from 'poetics' to 'philosophy'. Schiller contrasts the naive poet, who is united with his world and art, to his sentimental counterpart, who is estranged from nature and seeks as *'idea* and *object'* what has 'disappear[ed] from human life as *experience'.*[20] His essay *'On naive and sentimental poetry'* (1795) thus distinguishes two forms of consciousness, which he analyses in psychological and historical terms that are loosely 'philosophical' rather than formalist. Thereby, Schiller shifts genre study from a technical to a phenomenological basis. On the face of it 'mode' is not a new concept: Aristotle uses it when he distinguishes genres in terms of the medium employed, the object and the mode of imitation. In Aristotle's *Poetics* modes are not alternatives to genres but tools for analysing them. Schiller shares this emphasis but analyses genres through their mode of sensibility (*Empfindungsweise*) rather than their 'form of presentation' ('Naive and sentimental poetry', 126n). In so doing he not only makes mode into an incipient alternative to genre, but also recognizes genre itself as a cultural category.

In empirical terms Schiller's contribution may seem unsatisfactory and minor. While conceding that the 'mode of perception' may not be uniform 'even in a single work' (p. 126n.), he names only two modes, thus identifying all post-classical literature with the sentimental. Nevertheless he introduces a *metacritical* tool that works in several registers, thus profoundly enriching the 'phenomenology' of genre. The naive and the sentimental are not simply moods, as is sometimes argued. They represent something closer to what Schlegel calls *Ton*: an adjectival form of genre that allows him to speak of the novel as 'color[ing] all of modern poetry'.[21] We can also read Schiller through Heinrich Wölfflin's extension of mood (as *Lebensgefühl*) to architectural forms such as Classical and Gothic.[22] As the parallel suggests, the sentimental is not only an affect but also a cultural category, arising from the disappearance of nature in a post-agrarian society. Analogous to what Pierre Bourdieu calls a *habitus*,[23] *Empfindungsweise* is a semiotic sensibility produced by the fact that what the writer seeks 'is outside of him, as an idea still to be realized' ('Naive and sentimental

---

[20] Friedrich von Schiller, *Naive and sentimental poetry and On the sublime*, Julius A. Elias (trans.), New York: Ungar, 1966, p. 105.

[21] Friedrich Schlegel, *Philosophical fragments*, Peter Firchow (trans.), Minneapolis, MN: University of Minnesota Press, 1991, p. 36. Hereafter cited as *Fragments*. The concept of *Ton* is also used by Hölderlin: see *Friedrich Hölderlin: essays and letters on theory*, Thomas Pfau (trans. and ed.), Albany, NY: State University of New York Press, 1988, pp. 83–8.

[22] Heinrich Wölfflin, 'Prolegomena to a psychology of architecture' (1886), in *Empathy, form, and space: problems in German aesthetics 1873–1893*, Harry Francis Mallgrave and Eleftherios Ikonomou (eds.), Santa Monica, CA: Getty Centre for the History of Art and Humanities, 1994, pp. 149–51, 159.

[23] Pierre Bourdieu, *The logic of practice*, Richard Nice (trans.), Stanford, CA: Stanford University Press, 1990, pp. 52–79.

poetry', p. 111). Thus for the naive poet 'language springs as by some inner necessity out of thought', while for the sentimental writer 'the sign ... [is] heterogeneous and alien to the thing signified' (p. 98).

The influence of Schiller can be seen in Victor Hugo's Preface to *Cromwell* (1827), which posits three periods (primitive, ancient and modern/ Romantic) corresponding to lyric, epic and drama. For in making epic a generic figure for Classicism, Hugo uses 'epic' modally to describe not only Homer but also the sensibility of Herodotus (p. 64). Where Aeschylus is thus 'epic', 'drama' paradoxically is 'modern', expressing the conflicted sensibility of 'Romanticism' in such modes as the grotesque, with its mixture of melancholy and irony (pp. 65, 69–71). However, it is easy to overlook the complexity of Schiller's concept if we read it through its appropriations. Reworked in A. W. Schlegel's distinction between classical and romantic, which was popularized in Staël's *De l'Allemagne* (1810), sensibility becomes an emotional category used to underwrite sweeping generalizations about entire cultures rather than to understand generic and formal difference.[24] Its most complex deployment remains within a post-romantic tradition of philosophical genre theory, as in Paul de Man's discussion of allegory (1969), which turns back Schiller's understanding of the tropological structure of sentimentality into an analysis of the sensibility implicit in tropes.[25]

The affiliation of genre with sensibility through the connective category of mode has far-reaching ramifications. A. W. Schlegel already recognizes that a 'general theory' of 'the beautiful' must be supplemented by an awareness that 'every art ... has its own special theory', which must be 'adapt[ed] ... to the peculiarities of other ages and nations'.[26] Yet he elides the difference between a normative account of 'what ought to be accomplished' in art and an empirico–historical account of what 'has been' done (*Lectures*, pp. 17–18). It is thus left to his brother to pursue the consequences for *genre* (*theory*) of distinguishing Romantic from Classical sensibility.

Schlegel's comments on genre are deliberately abstract and incomplete. It is thus misleading to systematize them through 'Hegel' (as Szondi does) and more appropriate to read them through his own view of the fragment as criticism and irony. For Schlegel fragments are 'tendencies, ruins, and raw materials': 'subjective embryo[s]' of a system and marks of its limitations

---

[24] The culmination of this trend can be seen in the ethnological criticism of Ernest Renan and to a lesser extent Matthew Arnold. The decoupling of sensibility from genre criticism, and thus from the understanding of culturally strange forms, leads to a crossing of the thin line dividing the hermeneutics of cultures from a racial (stereo)typology.

[25] Paul de Man, 'The Rhetoric of Temporality', *Blindness and insight: essays in the rhetoric of contemporary criticism*, Minneapolis, MN: University of Minnesota Press, 1983, pp. 187–208.

[26] August Wilhelm Schlegel, *A course of lectures on dramatic art and literature* (1808), John Black (trans.), London: Bohn, 1846, pp. 17–18.

(*Fragments*, pp. 1, 20). The fragmentary nature of Schlegel's comments is thus an integral part of his attempt to reinscribe *genre theory* in a Romantic/modern rather than Classical mode. For the Schlegel of the Jena period there is an 'absolute difference between ancient and modern' (p. 37), which are structural and epistemic, not simply thematic, terms. While A. W. Schlegel sees Romanticism thematically as a 'mental culture' (*Bildung*) distinguished from Classicism by its longing for spirit (*Lectures*, pp. 24–7), Friedrich contrasts the terms formally with respect to closure: 'In the ancients we see the perfected letter of all poetry; in the moderns we see its growing spirit' (*Fragments*, p. 11). Unlike his brother, Friedrich associates longing with excess rather than lack, and he often speaks in consequence of three and not two kinds of literature: the naive, the sentimental and the 'progressive' (*Notebooks*, p. 32), elaborated in the concept of 'a progressive universal poetry' (*Fragments*, p. 31). Romanticism is progressive rather than sentimental, characterized by expanding horizons and not melancholic longing.

Originally in his unfinished history of Greek literature, Schlegel had wanted to organize classical literature as a dialectic between subjective and objective worked out through the central genres. It is perhaps on this basis that Hamlin connects his genre theory with Goethe's notes to the *West-östlicher Divan* (1819), where epic, lyric and drama are described as the 'natural' forms of poetry.[27] Schlegel, however, does not confine himself to the *Naturformen der Dichtung*; rather, he proposes a hierarchical binary between 'natural' and 'artificial', or *Natur-* and *Kunstpoesie*, that is intended to keep *Kunstpoesie* at bay. At the same time he is neither able to articulate his dialectic consistently nor to preserve the alignment of *Natur-* and *Kunstpoesie* with ancient and modern. Schlegel is undecided on how to narrativize ancient literature. For while lyric is subjective, epic at one point is 'merely objective', while at another point it takes over from drama the synthesizing of subjective and objective (*Notebooks*, pp. 175, 204). Unsure of how to narrativize ancient literature so as to match theory to history, Schlegel often credits the Greeks with the same variety of genres as the moderns, and even finds the preeminently modern form of the 'novel' in such ancient forms as Socratic dialogue, symposia, biographies and annals (p. 164).[28] In the Jena period, 'Classical' and 'modern' thus

---

[27] Hamlin, 'Origins', pp. 10–13. Goethe distinguishes a wider range of *Dichtarten* from these *Naturformen der Dichtung*, but gives priority to the latter. On Goethe see also Guillen, *Literature as system*, pp. 115–6.

[28] This explains why, even after his supposed turn around 1796 from the valorizing of ancient to modern poetry, Schlegel continues to see the 'original body of Greek poetry' as 'poetry itself' ('Dialogue on poetry and literary aphorisms', Ernst Behler and Roman Struc (trans.), University Park, PA: Pennsylvania State University Press, 1968, p. 63). Greek poetry in the 'Dialogue' is conspicuously not narrativized in terms of the dialectic of epic, lyric and dramatic (cf. p. 102).

become critical approaches rather than historical categories, with the modern being at once the symptom, the cause and the corrective for Schlegel's failure to work out a 'classical' approach to ancient poetry. The 'classical poetical genres', he writes, 'have now become ridiculous in their rigid purity' (*Fragments*, p. 8). Raising the question of why we have 'no concept' of genre, despite the existence of 'so many theories' on the subject, Schlegel suggests that we would then 'have to make do with a single theory' of genre (p. 8). His interest in the 'modern' therefore arises from his reluctance to make do with a single (classical) theory which would restrict what counts as a genre, given that the 'romantic kind of poetry' is still 'becoming' and 'can be exhausted by no theory' (p. 32).

Kunstpoesie, according to Schlegel, is written by individuals and thus is not limited to the *Naturformen der Dichtung*. In his earliest work Schlegel had dismissed such literature as *interessant*, as impure in its 'mixing . . . of genres' and its 'inclusion of even the ugly and the monstrous'. But in the Jena period the 'minus signs . . . in front of the characterization of the moderns' are changed to 'plus signs'.[29] As the metagenre of the modern Schlegel picks the novel or *Roman*, which becomes an etymological metaphor for all 'romantische Poesie'. In the restrictively generic sense also used by Goethe or Schelling the novel (as Lukács later argued) is a 'prosaisches Epos' (*Notebooks*, p. 54), and is an umbrella term for prose forms including biographies, annals, travel writings, confessions and oriental tales, which can be modally 'epic, lyric, dramatic, idyllic, [or] satirical' (*Notebooks*, pp. 163–4, 33). But Schlegel generalizes the term to make it a principle of experience, claiming that 'every human being . . . contains a novel within himself' (*Fragments*, p. 10). On these grounds Schlegel even insists that he 'detest[s] the novel as far as it wants to be a separate genre' ('Dialogue', p. 101). The novel represents a principle of openness, or as Bakhtin argues, of dialogue.[30] It is the 'new' (*Fragments*, p. 11), and thus the progressive, which 'often negates itself, but also immediately creates itself again' (*Notebook*, p. 32). In this sense it becomes 'like the epic . . . an image of the age' (*Fragments*, pp. 31–2), in spirit though not in politics.

The novel is thus the metasignifier of a more inclusive and modern genre theory. This inclusiveness might appear to abandon 'genre', since if there are so many genres that 'every poem [is] a genre for itself' (*Notebook*, pp. 72, 116), the category seemingly becomes useless. We must nevertheless take Schlegel at his word when he argues that a genre theory 'is what we lack' and that it will provide 'the true aesthetics of literature' ('Dialogue', p. 76) by allowing us to name the new. When he asks if poetry should

---

[29] René Wellek, *A history of modern criticism 1750–1950*, 4 vols., New Haven, CT: Yale University Press, 1955, vol. II, pp. 11–12. My own view, however, is that this turn involves a rejection of Classical canons of criticism rather than of Classical literature.

[30] Schlegel himself says 'Novels are the Socratic dialogues of our time' (*Fragments*, p. 3).

'simply be divided up' or if it should 'remain one and indivisible', Schlegel is questioning the 'pedantry' of the 'usual classifications' rather than expressing a Romantic antipathy to 'division' *per se* (*Fragments*, p. 90; 'Dialogue', p. 76). 'Oneness' paradoxically protects difference by resisting classifications based on the 'limited vision' of current critics (*Fragments*, p. 90), so that the 'one' is not so much a synonym for 'the chaotic generalization of poetry' ('Dialogue', p. 76) as a differential and diacritical term.

   Schlegel, in short, sees a place for genre as a way of articulating how the imagination 'must limit and divide itself' (p. 76), but reconceives the system of genre as what Georges Bataille would call a 'general' or open rather than 'restricted' and closed economy.[31] Extending *Gattung* beyond the literary, and picking up his own notion of *interessante Poesie*, he writes that 'even if something is nothing in itself, still it must contribute something to the definition of some species. And in this sense one could say that nobody is uninteresting' (*Fragments*, p. 27). That Schlegel writes in fragments is fully appropriate, since the fragment allows him to be interested in everything. Its aphoristic thrust, moreover, produces a phenomenology of these 'subcategories' (p. 18) by bracketing all empirical interferences so as to grasp their invariant structure. It does so, however, asystematically. For in Schlegel's own unparaphraseable wit, 'a fragment, like a miniature work of art, has to be entirely isolated from the surrounding world and complete in itself like a porcupine [*Igel*]' (p. 45).

III

Schlegel's general economy recognizes individuality. Where some criticize Dutch painters as limited, he argues that 'they have created their own genres for themselves' (*Fragments*, p. 41), thus preparing the way for the philosophical understanding of Dutch still life by Schopenhauer (1818) and of cultural styles in general by Wilhelm Worringer (1909).[32] Following upon Herder's relativism, Schlegel's theory has radical consequences both for the social concept of taste and for its more 'disinterested' aesthetic reinscription as beauty. If different art-forms 'limit' themselves differently, the very term 'beauty' proves limited, as Herder suggests in his essay on 'The Transformation of Taste' (*Early works*, p. 67). The philosophical study of genre thus eventually jeopardizes the philosophical project of unity and identity attributed to aesthetics by Szondi. For if genres disclose

[31] Georges Bataille, *The accursed share: an essay on general economy*, Robert Hurley (trans.), New York: Zone, 1991, vol. I, pp. 19–26.
[32] Arthur Schopenhauer, *The world as will and representation*, E. F. J. Payne (trans.), 2 vols., New York: Dover, 1969, vol. I, p. 197; Wilhelm Worringer, *Abstraction and empathy: a contribution to the psychology of style*, Michael Bullock (trans.), Cleveland, OH: Meridian, 1967.

different forms of consciousness, then neither poetry nor philosophy itself – and its cognate disciplines from architecture to mathematics – are necessarily 'one and indivisible'. The Indeed Schelling complains that we now have a philosophy of agriculture, will soon have a philosophy of 'vehicles', and that eventually there will be 'as many philosophies as there are objects' such that their sheer quantity 'will make us lose philosophy itself entirely' (*Philosophy*, p. 14).

The German systems of the fine arts respond to this anxiety about difference. As a whole the *Geisteswissenschaften* attempted to control the permeability of ideal to empirical versions of 'reality' produced by new disciplines that according to Schopenhauer ranged from mathematics to horticulture (*World*, 1: 218, 222). Still, systems are not intellectual state apparatuses, since Romantic systems-philosophy is self-revising: within the same *habitus* of the system, Schopenhauer and Nietzsche create inverse dialectics that actually critique 'philosophy'. Structurally, moreover, systems differ from the grand narratives they often incorporate. Narratives such as Hugo's Preface and Peacock's *Four ages* match genres to periods in monotonal ways. But because systems try to account for everything, their argumentative line is overdetermined by the ramifications of their details. In this sense they resemble the Romantic project of the encyclopedia, which Ernst Behler describes as 'a system in fragments'.[33] Like the novel which is 'infinitely many' but 'only one', the encyclopedia is ideally a totality but is empirically without closure. Indeed its 'totality' is the condition of its openness, a form of insurance that allows it to explore multiplicity.

This synonymity of the ideal and the empirical likewise marks the paradoxically 'romantic' and 'modern' status of the great nineteenth-century systems. For it is no accident that Schlegel used both terms to describe his period. As the first such system, Friedrich Schelling's lectures on *The philosophy of art* (given between 1799 and 1805) is Romantic in its metaphysics of art, yet modern in a concern with methodology that institutes our own culture of professionalization. 'Method' is a key motif in Schelling, who argues that aesthetics must become a 'science'. The scientific ideal requires an investigation of the 'multifarious' genres of art (*Philosophy*, p. 11). Yet these 'divisions' threaten the very identity of art as the 'magic and symbolic mirror' of a unified 'philosophy' (pp. 14, 8). The result is a syncresis: a system disseminated into everything it contains, a radical empiricism recontained as idealizing metaphysics.

Schelling provides a systematic rationale for Jena Romanticism's notion of a literary absolute in which art is the culmination of transcendental philosophy. He posits three modes – the schematic, the allegorical and the symbolic – thus developing Goethe's distinction between symbol and

[33] Ernst Behler, *German Romantic literary theory*, Cambridge University Press, 1993, p. 283.

allegory dialectically. The schematic and allegorical reflect differing imbalances between the universal and the particular, and the symbolic provides the system's normative centre. While the former separate the Idea from its embodiment, in the symbolic the 'subject not only signifies . . . the idea, but *is itself the idea*' (p. 151). Schelling's own 'schema' tries to account for the real and the ideal in one unified system, by using the principles of 'duplicity' and 'triplicity' to organize individual artforms. There are two 'series': music, painting and plastic art make up the 'real' series in which matter is made a symbol of the Idea, while lyric, epic and drama form the 'ideal' series. In theory these central artforms are divided into subgenres according to the principle of triplicity, so as to introduce even more permutations. Reducing time to space, Schelling's system simulates the 'indifference' of the real and the ideal. Thus while art differentiates itself into various forms in finite situations, it remains 'one' in the absolute, as the paradoxical synchrony of what is diachronically different. Correspondingly, Schelling sees no incompatibility between aesthetic difference and philosophical identity, insisting that art is the highest objectification of philosophy (p. 13).

Schelling's view that the various genres are perspectives on an 'undivided whole' (p. 14) is echoed by others. We see traces of it in Shelley's comments on the relation of narrative and drama to a metageneric 'poetry' that in Schlegel's words is 'more than a kind' (*Fragments*, p. 32). Insofar as poetry is 'a mirror which makes beautiful that which is distorted' while narrative is a 'mirror which . . . distorts that which should be beautiful' ('Defence', p. 485), narrative is potential or lapsed poetry, while dramatic multiplicity is likewise recuperable as poetic unity. Indeed the 'duplicity' of unity and dissemination in a drama committed to 'poetry' is figured in Shelley's description of drama (repeated by Hugo *Cromwell*, p. 90) as a 'prismatic and many-sided mirror' that 'multiplies' yet also synthesises (*Defence*, p. 491). Constructing genres as emanations from 'the chaos of a cyclic poem', Shelley speaks of individual 'fragments' as 'episodes' in a progressive, universal poetry 'built up since the beginning of the world' (pp. 481, 493). Closer to Schelling's own circle, this 'generalized translatability' is the principle behind Novalis's *Encyclopaedia*, which is concerned not with the self-differentiation of art through its various forms but with that of spirit through its disciplines. Reversing difference by 'poeticizing' the sciences, Novalis posits a principle of 'versability' or of the *'translatability of everything into everything'*. He postulates a 'poetics of mathematics, a grammar of mathematics, a physics of mathematics' and 'a mathematics of nature'.[34]

---

[34] Antoine Berman, *The experience of the foreign: culture and translation in Romantic Germany*, S. Heyvaert (trans.), Albany, NY: State University of New York Press, 1992, pp. 82–4.

On one level, then, *The philosophy of art* is the culmination of 'philosophical genre theory' in Szondi's sense, idealizing what in Schlegel remains chaotically 'modern'. But on another level its form is deceptive, the system being an example of Schlegel's 'romantic genre' which 'can never be completed' (*Fragments*, p. 32). Schelling, like Hegel, developed his theory in unpublished lectures, and his synchronization of 'potences' and artforms is not sustained. For instance he uses the triple scheme of the allegorical, the schematic and the symbolic in discussing painting, but forgets it when he comes to literature. We can infer that drama, as the synthesis of the particular and the universal, of lyric subjectivity and epic objectivity, is 'symbolic'. But nowhere is it said that epic is 'schematic' – perhaps because such a description is not helpful. Indeed when Schelling gets to epic he abandons his approach of deducing the genres that ought to exist, and theorizes an array of actual genres under the nominal rubric of 'epic'. It is hard to see what procedure organizes this, the most fascinating section of the lectures. At times Schelling proceeds by logical deduction: he subdivides the epic into objective and subjective versions so as to produce, Polonius-like, a subjective–objective genre (the elegy), an objective–objective form (the idyll), an objective–subjective form (satire) and so on (p. 220). Common sense, however, leads him to recognize that the satire might also be thought of as an intersection between epic and dramatic modes (p. 226). And common sense also suggests that the inclusion of elegy under epic rather than lyric is an experimental reclassification designed to make us aware of '*historical*' elements in some elegies that complicate their identity as 'poem[s] of lament' dominated by a single mood (p. 221).

Moreover, Schelling also uses the stemmatic approach of Herder and Goethe, deriving elegy metamorphically from the 'root' of epic. If the logical shades insensibly into the genetic, the genetic in turn produces the historical, despite Schelling's determination not to be historical (p. 207). Thus he borrows from the Schlegels the notion that there are Classical and Romantic (or modern) genres, and introduces two modern forms of epic: the romance and the novel (pp. 229–32). Nor is the chaos of this section summed up by saying that it (con)fuses logical, genetic and historical approaches, since Schelling introduces forms not accounted for by any of these models. The 'sentimental biography in verse form' seems to be not even an 'offshoot' but a hybrid, which cannot be described 'if we are to preserve even a modicum of purity within this genre', and which Schelling does nevertheless describe as 'neither a true epic nor a genuine novel (which must be written in prose)' (p. 228). Some of the forms he describes are not even genres: for instance parables, dialogue and episodes (p. 217).

What we discover in Schelling's lectures is thus an overdetermination of theory by practice. Their formal layout invites a diagram that reduces

them to a closed combinatorial system in which differences are permutations of pre-established unities. But in practice they are a compendium of
existing criticism from Goethe, Schiller and the Schlegels, which Schelling
does not always work into his own system. Thus when he takes over
Schiller's distinction on a theoretical level, he makes the naive and the sentimental into 'two directions' within the same 'poesy', eliding their historical difference by representing them as exchangeable perspectives within a
synchronic space (pp. 91–2). But when he uses Schiller in more practical
ways, Schelling lays the groundwork for Lukács's historicizing of genre in
The theory of the novel (1920) by presenting the novel as the modern or
sentimental form of epic (Fragments, pp. 231–2).

As a system that is less unified than it seems, the lectures are the inverted
mirror image of Schlegel's 'Athenaeum fragments', which vaunt their
fragmentation but gesture towards the systematic as a 'project' (Schelling,
Fragments, p. 58). Moreover, as a medley of existing criticism, they replicate the tensions that traverse the Romantic corpus. Foremost among these
is the use of cognitive defences to explore precisely what they are meant to
resist. Thus the stemmatic approach should be used to reduce elegy to epic,
and to return the multiplicity of genres to a central trinity which is then
resolved into a poetry that is 'one and indivisible'. But in fact what interested Schelling are differences: the way the lyrical element in the novella
differentiates it from epic, and the way the epic strand in elegy distinguishes
it from lyric.

In a sense the lectures spell the failure of the philosophy of identity,
given that Schelling himself asks what it means that epic 'as the highest
identity' proves capable of 'real difference' (p. 220). But this failure can
also be read more positively if we see the systematic as a rhetoric that per-
mits Romantic thinkers to claim for aesthetics a disciplinary autonomy
which allows for the asystematic study of whatever kinds one chooses
in terms of their own phenomenology. Schelling himself defines schematism as a 'rough outline' produced according to an 'intuition', or a faculty
for grasping the particular through the universal, to be complemented
by the reverse move from the universal to the particular (pp. 46–7). In
other words systematizing schemas are no more than heuristic categories.
Schelling does sometimes use genre prescriptively, as when he claims that
there are only two novels or that no poem has achieved 'the true archetype'
of the didactic genre (pp. 234, 226). But he also uses it to recognize new
kinds, as when he argues that The divine comedy is 'a genre unto itself'
which 'requires its own theory' (pp. 240–1). Insofar as Dante's text is a
'completely unique, organic mixture' of all the genres (p. 240), Schelling's
analysis also indicates what Schlegel may have had in mind when he
described the novel as uniting all other genres. For the novel is a non-genre,
a signifier for the fact that cultural artifacts are finally sui generis: 'It

embraces everything that is purely poetic, from the greatest systems of art' to a 'sigh [or] kiss' (*Fragments*, p. 31).

Like the 'novel', the system provides a space for exploring difference. Already in Schelling's lectures we find the beginnings of a method more thoroughly developed by his successors, in which a *noetic* account of the (cultural) consciousness that produces a genre is integrated with a *noematic* account of the motifs and structures (or the 'world') that accompany this genre. These accounts combine what Fredric Jameson calls a 'semantic' treatment of genre as a *mode* of 'generalized existential experience' with a 'syntactic' analysis of 'mechanisms and structure[s]'[35] whose phenomenology Romanticism also seeks to discern. The phenomenological approach naturally adapts itself to the study not just of genres but a variety of cultural phenomena. This is already true even in Schelling's discussion of literature, which deals with 'episodes' – a structural component of epic that metamorphically produces the picaresque novel. But Schelling also deals with mythology (*Philosophy*, pp. 47–83) and hieroglyphics (p. 148), anticipating the spirit of Walter Benjamin's explorations of the phenomenology of cultural practices such as storytelling and collecting. While the term 'genre' remains viable, genre criticism is extended to cultural practices that are not genres, and even to dispositions (mental or emotional) that are not signifying practices.

In short, although generic study may be one of its outcomes, the metasemiotics of culture characteristic of Romantic aesthetic systems begins with pre-generic categories such as the naive – or Nietzsche's Dionysian and Apollonian – that describe a mode of perception in terms that are affective, philosophical and/or semiotic. These categories constitute a *langue*, or to adapt Karl Viëtor a series of *Grundhaltungen*, from which develop the particular artforms and genres that are the *parole* of the system.[36] But another way to approach our subject is to see genre theory itself in terms of 'metamorphosis'. In Goethe's model as Dilthey analyses it 'organisms display a disguised . . . repetition of the same parts . . . It is the same leaf which appears first as the shoot, then the stamen' and so on ('Schleiermacher biography', p. 61). This model can be used stemmatically in the service of a unifying organicism but can also function disseminatively in producing offshoots and transformations of the original root. In this sense the phenomenology of culture can be seen as a methodological organism composed by the repetition of the same analytic procedures

---

[35] Fredric Jameson, *The political unconscious: narrative as a socially symbolic act*, Ithaca, NY: Cornell University Press, 1981, pp. 107–8.

[36] For further discussion of this point, see Tilottama Rajan, 'Phenomenology and Romantic criticism: Hegel and the subversion of aesthetics', in *Questioning Romanticism*, John Beer (ed.), Baltimore, MD: The Johns Hopkins University Press, 1995, pp. 168–9. On Viëtor see Guillen, *Literature as System*, pp. 117–8.

with reference to different 'parts': the sensibility and the cognitive structures that produce genres, the genres themselves, their structural components and the cultural practices (ritual or other art forms) that are offshoots
of this same sensibility.

An interesting case is 'allegory', which occupies several positions in
the metamorphic network. As theorized by Dante in his 'Letter to Can
Grande' it is not a genre but an exegetical method. By Goethe's time it has
become a property of texts, though as figure rather than genre. Goethe's
philosophical treatment of the figure in terms of a thematics of the universal and the particular, infinity and limitation,[37] allows Schelling to see the
allegorical as a basic mental structure, alongside the 'schematic'. Unlike
others Schelling is sympathetic to allegory, and makes it into a way of
understanding the teleological unity that binds nature to spirit. Thus the
plant is an 'allegory' of the animal and the animal an allegory of the
human. And at an even more general level allegory describes the process
by which the unconscious is made conscious of the 'infinite concept'
embodied in finite beings ('Fragments', pp. 49, 148). Genre, cognitive
structure, figure and exegesis are all bound together in the metamorphic
migrations of the term 'allegory'.

Limiting Romantic genre theory to its discussions of literary kinds thus
ignores its theoretical legacy. Precisely because the phenomenological
method extends to other disciplines (epistemology, history, linguistics),
these disciplines reciprocally inflect the expansion of genre study beyond
formalism. As important, Romanticism is hesitant about limiting genres
to those that have already been socially encoded, preparing the way for
modern attempts to decouple genre study from existing theories of genre.
Thus Bakhtin extends the category of genre to 'speech genres' – a move
continued in feminist discussions of the genres of everyday life. Bakhtin
also invents an alternative terminology to that of genre in his notion of
'chronotope': a distinctive sense of space–time intended as part of a 'historical poetics' sensitive to 'generic heterogeneity'. Although he applies
the term to subgenres such as 'the adventure-novel of ordeal', he also
discusses topoi such as 'the road', thus aligning a variety of literary units
on one morphological stem. Moreover, for Bakhtin (as more briefly for
Schlegel) the 'novel' provides an excuse for exploring extra-literary
phenomena, including travel, letters, eschatology, parlours and salons.[38]
Bakhtin's metamorphic phenomenology of genre develops directly from

---

[37] J. W. von Goethe, 'Aphorisms on art and art history', in *German aesthetic and literary
criticism: the Romantic ironists and Goethe*, Kathleen Wheeler (ed.), Cambridge University Press, 1984, p. 229.

[38] Mikhail Bakhtin, 'Forms of time and chronotope in the novel', *The dialogic imagination*,
Caryl Emerson and Michael Holquist (trans.), Austin, TX: University of Texas Press, 1981,
pp. 84–6, 98, 103, 143, 148, 246.

his Romantic forefathers, but since they had no encompassing name for their practice, the Romantic contribution, though profoundly influential, has remained unrecognized.

Other alternative terminologies, which also reciprocally refigure genre, are 'mode' and 'mood'. Modes can of course be defined stemmatically and conservatively as adjectival derivatives of genres, such that the pastoral mode arises only after the eclogue (Fowler, *Kinds of literature*, p. 16). But in practice mode is a more disseminative concept. In allegory the mode generates the genre, and in the epistolary mode the literary form is actually generated by a practice from social life. As forms of collective consciousness, modes can include everything from cultures such as the Apollonian to artistic styles such as the grotesque or tropes that have been expanded into forms of experience, such as Kierkegaard's irony. Indeed this expanded use of the term is still evident when we speak of the 'mode' of print. As an alternative to genre, mode thus brings new material into culture. And while the concept predates Romanticism, it is the Romantics who first theorized mode, liberating it from its dependence on parental literary genres.

As for 'mood' or *Stimmung*, traces of it exist in earlier theory, but it is named and legitimized only in the Romantic period. It is not entirely true, as Stanley Corngold suggests, that mood in the Romantic–Idealist tradition is 'viewed as "inside"' and as possessing 'no correlative domain of objects'.[39] Though moods can be purely inward, they can also be forms of sensibility, like Schiller's 'sentimental', which calls for cultural as well as tonal analysis.[40] Unlike mode, however, 'mood' decisively shifts aesthetic judgment outside of the public sphere. Kant's *Critique of judgement* (1790) already subjectivizes judgment by legitimating the sublime and the beautiful as aesthetic phenomena alongside (or even in place of) romance and epic. Moreover, as Jean-François Lyotard points out, the analytic of the sublime is particularly radical in inviting us to think beyond existing concepts to pre-conceptual 'representations' that exceed what we can grasp in a 'form'.[41] Kant's analysis is the condition of possibility for our own interest in genres of affect such as melancholia, even if the moods that now preoccupy us were not the ones explicitly theorized by the Romantics. For our present purposes it is enough to say that by theorizing mood Kant adds it to the morphological network in which genre is inscribed, and allows affect to become part of the analysis of genre.

---

[39] Stanley Corngold, *The fate of the self: German writers and French theory*, New York: Columbia University Press, 1986, p. 206; 'Nietzsche's Moods', *Studies in Romanticism* 29 (1990), p. 72.

[40] For further discussion of this issue see Rajan, 'Phenomenology', pp. 166–7.

[41] Jean-François Lyotard, *Lessons on the analytic of the sublime*, Elizabeth Rottenberg (trans.), Stanford, CA: Stanford University Press, 1994, pp. 31–2, 53.

IV

If Schelling's lectures are conflictedly Romantic and modern, metaphysics also competes with methodology in Hegel's *Aesthetics* (1823–9). Hegel's idealist apotheosis of 'philosophy' appears to put disciplinary imperialism in the service of cultural hegemony. Indeed he is often criticized as a proto-structuralist who absorbs 'the temporal articulation of history' into 'spatial subdivisions interacting on a vast historical chessboard' that subordinates East to West.[42] Thus in his section on 'poetry', he deals only with 'the proper species of poetic art', and narrows epic, lyric and dramatic from modes to genres.[43] As with Schelling, however, the system is the cirumferential form of excess. Somewhere in the *Aesthetics* Hegel accommodates everything from pyramids to sacrifice and metamorphosis. In these byways and margins he also includes 'hybrid transitional stages' of literature such as fable and parable, and '[im]proper' forms such as the didactic, on the grounds that he needs to describe genres that 'will not fit' in order to define properly the boundaries of a 'symbolic' art which itself does not 'fit' the norms of art (pp. 382, 423).

The lectures are organized in two parts, consisting of supplementary and overlapping grids. In the first Hegel deals with the aesthetic sensibilities of the symbolic, the Classical and the Romantic. These 'art-forms' express various relationships between 'inwardness' and its 'externalization' or between the 'Idea' and its 'embodiment'. To each there corresponds a specific 'art': architecture in the case of the symbolic, sculpture in the case of Classicism, and poetry and music in the case of the Romantic. In the second part Hegel takes up these arts, dividing them in terms of the various artforms. Thus the phylogeny traced in the first part with reference to a world history of artforms is repeated in the second as an ontogeny of individual arts, such that architecture in the first part is symbolic, while in the second it has symbolic, Classical and Romantic subdivisions. Hegel 'explains' these overlaps so as to recontain an encyclopedic content in a systematic form. But the schemas are non-synchronous,[44] and the taxonomies merely heuristic, so that as principles of exclusion they must be readjusted by

---

[42] Henry Sussman, 'An American history lesson: Hegel and the historiography of superimposition', in Bainard Cowan and Joseph G. Kronick (eds.), *Theorizing American literature: Hegel, the sign and history*, Baton Rouge, LA: Louisiana State University Press, 1991, p. 33.

[43] G. W. F. Hegel, *Aesthetics: Lectures on Fine Art*, T. M. Knox (trans.), 2 vols., Oxford: Clarendon Press, 1975, p. 382. Hegel's lectures were edited from notes by H. G. Hotho in 1835.

[44] Interestingly the dominant figure of the section on poetry is 'synthesis': poetry is the synthesis of interiority and exteriority, music and painting, while within poetry itself drama plays its traditional role as a synthesis of epic and lyric. Yet in part I poetry is a Romantic mode and thus associated with the dissolution of synthesis.

other schemas of inclusion. Thus the identification of 'poetry' with versification (as distinct from a broader use of 'poesy' to mean literary 'making')
compels Hegel to exclude prose from part two. The novel is, however,
included in part one, although oddly and sketchily as a disappointment,
a prosaic negative of Romanticism in which 'romance' is displaced and
recontained in the bourgeois epic.

In what follows I approach Hegel methodologically, by focussing as
much on the form as on the content of his thought, so as to emphasize not
its cultural prejudices (particularly evident in his treatment of Indian art)
but the innovations it subsequently facilitates. For the *Aesthetics* inaug-
urates a structural phenomenology of culture, divided between a desire
to place and control on the one hand and to understand on the other.
Instituting what is later called 'genetic structuralism',[45] Hegel's lectures
operate in terms of multiple homologies, so that phenomena as disparate
as the epic and the house can be reduced to the same isomorphic form
of 'classicism'. Hegel thus works out 'scientifically' the morphological
network that develops more organically and unpredictably in previous
German thought. More specifically for our purposes he places genre in
this network, thus facilitating its analysis in terms of the *episteme* from
which it emerges. That the network can become rigid is undeniable, especially if we read the *Aesthetics* syntagmatically as a fearful symmetry of
parallel disciplinary narratives. It is possible, however, to emphasize its
interdisciplinarity and to inhabit its space more paradigmatically by using
other art forms as suggestive metonymies for literary genres.[46]

Like Schelling, Hegel posits three *Grundhaltungen* that involve differing (im)balances between spirit and matter, expressive of different stages in
consciousness's attempt to actualize the 'Idea'. Hegel's dialectic, however,
is diachronic rather than synchronic and transcendental. For Schelling's
purely formal triad he substitutes a progress from the symbolic, through
the Classical to the Romantic. The symbolic, associated with Oriental art,
fails because of a deficiency in self-consciousness that leaves the Idea still

---

[45] The term refers to the work of Lucien Goldmann and the early Roland Barthes, but also
describes Michel Foucault's *The order of things*.

[46] The striking analysis of the pyramids, for instance, could be translated into an account of
the relationship between death and inwardness in one form of the elegiac. The pyramids
are 'prodigious crystals which conceal . . . an inner meaning' but in a form that is 'mute
and motionless' because spirit has 'not really found its own inner life' (*Aesthetics*, pp. 356,
354). As a representation of death that differs from its Christian counterparts in concentrating on the 'preservation [of] corpses' rather than the 'immortality of the soul' (p. 355),
the pyramids might provide an analogue for an elegy that questions the economy of successful mourning by 'introjecting' rather than 'incorporating' the lost object. Eugenio
Donato explores the literary extensions of such mourning in *The script of decadence:
essays on the fictions of Flaubert and the poetics of Romanticism*, New York: Oxford University Press, 1993, pp. 202–7. Donato also discusses Hegel (pp. 131–8, 146–9) but does
not make a link between the pyramids and the elegiac.

'indeterminate'. The Classical phase temporarily resolves the tension, through 'the adequate embodiment of the Idea' (*Aesthetics*, p. 77). But it returns on a higher level in the final, Romantic phase, where matter rather than spirit proves deficient, external forms being unable to embody an Idea that is now fully developed.

As a phenomenology of culture that uses philosophy to deal with the material of other disciplines, Hegel's work also draws these disciplines into philosophy in a way that Kant's does not. His analysis of artforms in terms of matter and spirit is philosophical, but it is also proto-psychological in its emphasis on inwardness and externalization as well as on the history of art as a *Bildung* in which an (un)happy consciousness tries to understand and become identical with itself. The analysis is semiotic as well, since Hegel is more concerned than his precursors with the difficult relationship between 'meaning' and 'shape'. His analyses of the relation between form and content prefigure both the understanding of artforms in terms of discrepancies between signifier and signified later developed by Benjamin and de Man in their analyses of allegory, and the more general discussion by the early Derrida of the impossibility of a consciousness fully present to itself in the unification of 'concept and reality' (p. 341).

To the interdisciplinary analysis of art Hegel also adds a social dimension. He approaches Dutch still-life psychologically by relating its focus on 'the smallest and commonest things' to that 'satisfaction in present-day life' (p. 597) that Worringer later terms 'empathy'. This account continues Schopenhauer's discussion of Dutch painting as a pure representation free from the will (*World*, 1: 197). But Hegel also analyses the semiotics of Dutch realism as an expression of a bourgeois Protestantism that values the ordinary rather than the aristocratic, and the secular and plain over the religious and symbolic (*Aesthetics*, p. 598). Because he supplements a philosophical with a sociological approach, he is more tolerant of Dutch painting than Schopenhauer.[47] Social phenomenology can be the Achilles' heel of Hegel's prejudices, as in his assumption of a homology between the 'symbolic' and tyranny (pp. 436–7). Yet it is Hegel who allows subsequent aestheticians such as Alois Riegl and Worringer to argue that the generic 'peculiarities of past epochs' are not 'explained by lack of ability, but by a differently directed volition'.[48] Worringer, for instance, focusses on the flat schematism of Egyptian art as a 'failure' to be like Classical realism in representing the Concrete Universal, and traces this 'abstraction' from history to an outlook for which 'history' itself would be an ideological formation

---

[47] For example, since Schopenhauer approaches art only in philosophical and psychological terms, he can see no purpose to the Dutch inclusion of food in its still lives (*World*, 1: 208).

[48] Worringer, *Abstraction and empathy*, p. 9. See also Alois Riegl, *Questions of style: foundations for a history of ornament* (1893), Evelyn Kain (trans.), Princeton, NJ: Princeton University Press, 1992.

(*Abstraction and empathy*, pp. 14–16). Extracting Hegel's approach from its Eurocentric narrative, Worringer uses the form rather than the content of this approach. Methodology does in fact break out of ideology in Hegel's analysis of Dutch painting. For in general he sees the emphasis on the 'prosaic' (*Aesthetics*, 595) as unaesthetic, devaluing descriptive poetry for this reason. The account of Dutch painting, however, is an attempt to understand on its own terms 'the prose of life' as a form unaccounted for by an emphasis on Romanticism that is itself part of an idealist ideology (pp. 592–8).

Hegel's work consolidates much previous German theory. But he also moves beyond his precursors in historicizing artforms as incomplete expressions of a consciousness still in process. His attitude to such forms is deeply divided. The normative emphasis on 'beauty' envisions a 'free totality' in which 'content' and 'shape', the artist and his 'topic', are united (pp. 431, 602). Yet Hegel seems more interested in disfigured artforms that defer any synthesis. For when Classical 'Spirit' transcends the symbolic's inability to realize the Idea, it proves limiting and must be displaced by the Romantic, in which the Idea once again cannot be represented. Read syntagmatically Hegel's triad recovers the crisis in representation that mobilizes the *Aesthetics*, along a racial axis that protects West from East. The relationship of the Romantic to the symbolic is thus narrativized, so that the problems first disclosed in Oriental art are dialectically resolved in the 'non-correspondence' of matter and spirit in Christianity. But as a paradigmatic arrangement Hegel's system is organized by repetition rather than dialectic. For the Romantic is perpetually haunted by its affinity to the symbolic, so that we are never sure whether the Idea exists but cannot be represented, or whether it is always indeterminate. The system is the conflicted transcript of a process in which the very nature of art as 'classical' perfection (p. 441) is being reconfigured. Thus while Hegel accedes to taste in dismissing as 'symbolic' an art that fails to achieve self-identity, he also privileges such art through the 'romantic'. The opposition between the two keeps collapsing, as in the uncertainty as to whether the symbolic artist 'strives to imagine a . . . meaning for the shape' or 'a shape for the meaning' (pp. 438, 440), whether symbolism stems from a lack or an excess of inwardness, whether the Oriental is not in fact the abjected form of the Romantic.

Hegel's fascination with an art in which meaning and shape stand 'in a relation of mere affinity and allusiveness' (p. 427) is empirically confined to 'supplementary forms' (p. 422) which he treats only briefly. More important is the metasignifying possibility he constructs through the symbolic, in which this dissociation figures the 'restless fermentation' and 'labour' of a consciousness still involved in 'producing its content and making it clear to itself' (pp. 440, 438). Hegel's discussion of the symbolic is radically innovative in allowing us to think of these forms as 'art', and of art as a 'shape' that has meaning 'without being able to express it perfectly' (p. 372). The consequences for genre are significant. Genre, as Guillen suggests in a formulation that recalls Schiller's interest in the reconciliation of the *Stofftrieb* and the *Formtrieb*, is a 'problem-solving model' that matches 'matter and form' (*Literature as System*). A genre in this sense would be a 'free totality' that reconciles the material with its expression so as to leave nothing unsaid (*Aesthetics*, p. 431). But after Hegel art itself is not necessarily the unification of form and content, or 'ability' and 'volition'. Correspondingly genres are neither wholly 'free' nor wholly determined. Instead they are collective expressions of a disparity between 'form as proceeding' and 'shape as superinduced', or between inwardness and the socially constrained shapes in which it expresses itself.

By the late nineteenth century the psycho–philosophical study of cultural forms was well established. But although the systematic drive of German Romanticism has been continued by theorists such as Arnold Hauser, Ernst Bloch and Northrop Frye,[49] aesthetics after Hegel has also picked up on the Romantic privileging of singularity by concentrating atomistically on the individual genre. Later continuations of idealist genre theory thus recast 'Hegel' through the genre on which they focus. Lukács's precise debt to Hegel differs at different points in his career, but it is notable that when in *The meaning of contemporary realism* he develops the *Grundhaltungen* of allegory and realism within the normative framework of a search for 'totality', he is less receptive than Hegel to styles that separate meaning and shape. Yet this latter aspect of Hegel is precisely the stimulus for Kierkegaard, who generalizes the trope into the mode of irony as 'infinite absolute negativity'. While *The concept of irony* is a subversion of idealism that concentrates on the one mode Hegel could not accommodate in his teleology (*Aesthetics*, pp. 64–9), Hegel himself valorizes 'infinite negativity' through the Romantic (p. 521). In this sense Kierkegaard reads the *Aesthetics* against the grain so as to bring out its unconscious fascination with a hermeneutics of forms that do not cohere.

The subsequent diversity of philosophical genre theory testifies to the unresolved complexities of its Romantic matrix. Still untheorized, however, is the legacy of approaching art as incomplete. Such an approach also derives from Schopenhauer, on whom Wölfflin draws in positing an 'immanent will' that 'works its way out of matter . . . toward form' but that 'cannot always fulfil itself' ('Prologomena', pp. 159–62). But where

---

[49] Arnold Hauser, *The social history of art*, Stanley Godman (trans.), 4 vols., New York: Random House, 1951; Ernst Bloch, *The principle of hope*, Neville Plaice, Steven Plaice and Paul Knight (trans.), 3 vols., Oxford: Blackwell, 1986; Northrop Frye, *Anatomy of criticism: four essays*, Princeton, NJ: Princeton University Press, 1957.

Schopenhauer's framework is biological and psychological, Hegel's is historical. Conceiving art as a will that strives for representation, the Romantic (as distinct from the conservative) Hegel explains crises in representation through sociohistorical conditions that result in Spirit not being 'clear to itself' (*Aesthetics*, p. 433). He thus reads the 'insufficiently articulated' artwork (p. 162) as a meaning de-formed by existing shapes, so as to extricate from the conditions that determine it the possibility of future 'freedom'.

The terminology of 'Spirit' and 'freedom' will sound mystified to a contemporary ear. Nevertheless it also underwrites the dialectic of enlightenment pursued by both cultural and feminist criticism. For such criticism genres are not straightforwardly expressive, nor are they social 'contracts' for the regulation of artistic behaviour. Jameson, for instance, approaches texts as overdetermined structures in which form and content function as semi-autonomous parts. He locates the text in relation to its political unconscious, by analysing how the form says something different from the content, or how the content is de-formed by the shape it assumes. But it is Hegel who institutes this understanding of artistic kinds in terms of the 'form of content' and the 'content of form' (*Political unconscious*, p. 242). For even as he sees the Classical as synthesizing form and content, he also theorizes through the symbolic and the Romantic the structural possibility of their disparity.

One example of this disparity is the novel, considered as a transposition of romance into 'prosaic *objectivity*' (*Aesthetics*, p. 595). In effect 'Romantic fiction' is what Jameson calls a 'symbolic' or provisional resolution of underlying contradictions between a Romantic content and the prose of 'civil society' (*Aesthetics*, p. 592). Since a wide range of genres are symbolic or 'imaginary' resolutions of such disjunctions, Hegel initiates a rethinking of genre that has yet to be theorized fully. Both in structural terms and in its reconstitution of the relation between genre and the public sphere, this reconception is a culmination of 'Romanticism'. For the Classical artist as Hegel characterizes him, 'the content must already be there cut and dried', such that its nature as 'personal or national' belief is already 'settled', and the artist can concentrate on finding an appropriate 'shape'. Genres provide a 'special sort of assistance' in this process, since they name a 'fitting of matter to form [that] has *already* taken place' (Guillen, *Literature as system*, p. 111). Genre in Classicism is thus a component of a mimetic ideology in which the artist 'only [gives] a shape' to existing belief-systems (*Aesthetics*, p. 439). In symbolic and Romantic art, by contrast, 'representations . . . intended to be expositions of the content' remain 'problems', their very indeterminacy reflecting a 'fermentation' in which 'belief' cannot be settled (p. 438). Genre, as a way of recognizing the forms that such incompleteness assumes, is at the heart of this collective self-understanding.

12

Theory of the novel

MARSHALL BROWN

Like genre theory in general, Romantic novel theory in particular takes radically different guises in different countries. My chapter, like Tilottama Rajan's, highlights German contributions, which are systematic and abstract in ways that are rare in other countries. However, the theory of the novel is by nature more oriented toward practice, which makes the more empirical and pragmatic English and French expressions more worthy of extended notice than is the case for genre theory. A central question is whether it makes sense to speak of Romantic novel theory as a whole, given the radical national differences becoming manifest. I begin with a survey of the situation of the novel and of novel theory confronting the first generation of Romantic writers; a common tradition guaranteed a certain commonality of approach, while growing divergences foreground the question of unity. I proceed with a synopsis of leading themes of novel criticism, mostly linked to two famous, synthesizing utterances of Friedrich Schlegel. Having defined some common ground, I then present the four most distinctive Romantic contributions: Goethe's comments on the novel in *Wilhelm Meister*, Friedrich Schlegel's essay on *Wilhelm Meister*, the novelist Jean Paul Friedrich Richter's *Aesthetic primer*, and the writings of Walter Scott. Scott's work sums up the tendencies formalized in the German writers and forecasts leading concerns of subsequent novel theory; a brief closing consideration of Balzac's preface to the *Comédie humaine* characterizes the later destiny of Romantic thinking about the novel.

*

The novel reached its independence in the Romantic period. A great many books we now recognize as novels were, of course, written earlier. But there is little evidence that authors and readers considered the novel to be a distinctive form. While 'novel' starts appearing on English title pages by the 1660s, the early appearances are in translations from the French and, more tellingly, are conjoined with numerous other generic designations. Eighteenth-century fictions might be identified by a vast range of categories, including story, history, tale, adventures, memoirs, letters, life. The eighteenth-century authors considered canonical then and now wrote few

works of fiction and designated genres almost randomly: *Joseph Andrews*
is a history of the adventures, *Tom Jones* a history, *Jonathan Wild* a history of the life; Marivaux's *Paysan parvenu* is memoirs (but the Dutch
translation is a strange but true happening and one German translation is
remarkable incidents), his *Vie de Marianne* is adventures, and so it goes.
Meanwhile, more prolific authors often mixed short and long fictions,
or obscured the lines between fiction and non-fiction (Defoe), or essayed
narratives in verse as well as in prose (Wieland). Indeed, Spanish still
has a single word, 'novela', for long and short prose fictions. Only around
1800 do we start seeing title pages such as *Sense and sensibility: a novel.
In three volumes*, or the very spare *Lucinde: ein Roman*.[1] And only with
Jean Paul in Germany, Scott in Britain, and finally Balzac in France do
we find authors of high aesthetic ambitions who specialized – still not
exclusively – in the production of numerous novels. It is, then, not surprising, that something we could recognizably call a theory or a discourse
of the novel only begins to coalesce in the same decades.

A brief review of earlier writings will set the stage. The only influential
early book on the novel was Pierre Daniel Huet's *Traité de l'origine des
romans*, a ninety-nine-page essay published in 1670 (translated into English
in a rare publication of 1672 and into German in 1682). Huet's definition would serve – at least as a starting point – to this very day: 'What
are properly called novels [*Romans*] are fictions of amorous adventures,
written in Prose with art, for the pleasure and instruction of Readers'
(pp. 4–5). With considerable learning Huet tells the story of fiction in
antiquity, in the Orient, and in the Middle Ages, as 'good Novels' that
'serve . . . to fashion the spirit and make it proper for the world' (p. 96)
gradually emerged from their origins in fantastic tales and in histories.
Huet praises form and order – 'the Novel should resemble a perfect body,
& be composed of several different parts proportioned under a single
head' (p. 44) – and he distinguishes novels from 'romances' (i.e., Spanish
ballads). Still, Huet's canon is so limited and so dominated by the prose
romances of the sixteenth and seventeenth centuries that his book bears
little relevance to writing about the novel after 1800. He uses some of the
same words as later writers, but they mean different things when applied
to *Le grand Cyrus* and to *Emma*.

For the next century authors accepted Huet's positioning of the genre
even if they differed in evaluation. The notably brief, one-page article on
'roman' in the French *Encyclopédie* (by the philosopher Jaucourt) follows
Huet in deriving the novel from baroque prose romances, but condemns

[1] Pope's dedication to *The rape of the lock* says one of his sources 'both in its Title and Size
is so like a *Novel*, that many of the Fair Sex have read it for one by Mistake'. The book,
Le Comte de Gabalis, is eighty-eight pages. It is evident that Pope used the term for what
we would call a novella.

these in favour of more moral authors, Madame de La Fayette, Richardson, Fielding and Rousseau. A leading fiction writer (Marmontel) was called in for the three pages on 'fiction', but the article is almost entirely concerned with history painting. Richard Hurd's *Letters on chivalry and romance* (1762, much expanded in 1765 and 1788) was famous and influential in praising romance plotting, gothic form, and (in his concluding phrase) the 'world of fine fabling', but focusses on the tradition of Ariosto; John Dunlop's two-volume *History of prose fiction* (1805 – much the earliest book so titled) still concentrates on ancient works and chivalric romances, arriving at French and English novels only late in the second volume. Only with the novelist Clara Reeve's dialogue, *The progress of romance* (1785), was there finally an influential attempt to separate off the novel as a distinct kind. The passage merits quoting in full, since it sets the terms of much subsequent discussion. 'The Romance is an heroic fable, which treats of fabulous persons and things. – The Novel is a picture of real life and manners, and of the times in which it is written. The Romance in lofty and elevated language, describes what never happened nor is likely to happen. – The Novel gives a familiar relation of such things, as pass every day before our eyes, such as may happen to our friend, or to ourselves; and the perfection of it, is to represent every scene, in so easy and natural a manner, and to make them appear so probable, as to deceive us into a persuasion . . . that all is real, until we are affected by the joys or distresses, of the persons in the story, as if they were our own' (p. 111). Historical dictionaries catalogue only meanings, not systems of discourse, but this passage makes it clear that only toward the Romantic period did the novel acquire something like the systematic place and separate generic status it has today.[2] The relationships of the real to the romantic, prose to poetic language, the ordinary to the exotic, and the probable to the marvellous are issues that remain central for all Romantic (indeed all nineteenth-century) thinking about the novel.

Unquestionably the outstanding case for the novel before the Romantic period had been made by Fielding in the prefaces and the introductory chapters to the various parts of *Joseph Andrews* (1742) and *Tom Jones* (1749). While Fielding did not use the term 'novel' for serious purposes,

---

[2] Reeve's definitions are to some extent anticipated in Armand-Pierre Jacquin, *Entretiens sur les romans*, 1755; rpt Geneva: Slatkine, 1970. Jacquin distinguishes novel from history as being primarily fictional; from epic as being less elevated, more digressive and softer; and from fable as being verisimilar and about men or pagan divinities and not animals (pp. 18–23). Jacquin devotes three quarters of his 365-page text to the uselessness and the dangers of novels, of which Fénelon's *Télémaque* is 'the most perfect and the least dangerous' (p. 148); he finds Huet too indulgent (p. 117) and does not think that the modern sensations (Madame de Graffigny's *Peruvian letters*, Richardson's novels, *Tom Jones*) will last (pp. 100–1). While Jacquin also discusses *Gil Blas* and Prévost's *Cleveland*, his canon, with acknowledgement to Huet, consists overwhelmingly of prose and verse romances, including a recent Milton imitation, the *Christiade*.

his famous accounts of the 'comic epic-poem in prose' and of 'prosai-comi-epic writing' (Preface to *Joseph Andrews, Tom Jones* v.i) were repeatedly echoed by later writers who did: Anna Barbauld's 'Origin and progress of novel-writing' (1810) says, 'a good novel is an epic in prose, with more of character and less (indeed in modern novels nothing) of the supernatural machinery' (p. 3); Hegel, whose massive *Aesthetics* devotes only three scattered paragraphs to the novel (*Roman*, with unspecified generic range), calls it 'the modern bourgeois epic' of 'a reality that has become prosaic in its ordering' ('eine bereits zur *Prosa* geordnete Wirklichkeit', II: 452). Designed for a middle-class audience sophisticated enough to relish irony and clever allusion, Fielding's essays apply Aristotelian and Horatian norms to the contemporary, relatively realistic fictions he was writing. A number of the essays concern the craft of writing: management of the plot, stylistic resource, authorial learning and such details as chapter divisions and the naming of characters. On the moral side, Fielding asserts the didactic value of representing mixed characters in plausible situations, with foibles rather than passions as the focus. Playful in tone but serious in the effort to position prose fiction as the heir of Homer and of Cervantes, Fielding established the terms in which the dignity of the novel would henceforth be debated as a distinctively modern, stylistically intermediate, intellectually and artistically polished form of writing.

Still, it would be misleading to speak of a developing theory of the novel in the later eighteenth century. Rather, with Fielding hovering in the background, the more or less explicit topic often seems to be whether novels should be written at all. In *Rambler* no. 4 (1750) Samuel Johnson opposed the modern fashion that favours 'the comedy of romance', 'natural events [brought about] by easy means', and 'life in its true state, diversified only by accidents that daily happen in the world'; instead he recommends 'the most perfect idea of virtue; of virtue not angelical, nor above probability'. Silencing the name of his nemesis, Johnson clearly would like to stem a tide; indeed, his only extended work of fiction was not a novel but the allegorical Eastern tale, *Rasselas* (1759). Johnson prefers reality to mere realism: 'I cannot see . . . why it may not be as safe to turn the eye immediately upon mankind as upon a mirror which shows all that presents itself without discrimination.' The distance traversed in the Romantic period can be measured by noting that what Johnson hates is precisely what Stendhal's *The red and the black* (1830) famously propounds: 'Eh, monsieur, a novel is a mirror travelling on a highway. Now it reflects the azure skies, now the mud puddles in the road. And the man carrying the mirror in his basket will be accused by you of immorality!' (II. xix). Equally typical in resisting Fielding's modernity was Rousseau, whose *Julie, or the new Eloise* – one of a great many novels written against novels – includes in its prefaces and its main text diatribes against 'the makers of Novels and Comedies': 'Novels are perhaps the last instruction remaining to give to a people so corrupted that any other is useless' (II, letter 21; p. 277; repeated almost verbatim by Jaucourt in 'Roman'). Perhaps because of his very success in promoting the novel, Fielding drew attacks and left defenders of the novel on the defensive.

Therefore, in writing about literature generally, it remained easiest simply to ignore the novel, as Kant did, and as Herder, Schiller and Hegel almost did as well.[3] Treatises on general literary topics like the sublime were prone to confine themselves to verse and drama while giving prose fiction a wide berth. And in England, Hugh Blair's *Lectures on rhetoric and belles lettres*, first published in 1783, is similarly inclined. The last ten of the forty-seven lectures survey the various reputable poetic kinds: lyric and descriptive poetry, epic, drama. Just preceding them, lecture 37 concerns 'Philosophical Writing – Dialogue – Epistolary Writing [i.e., letters, not epistolary novels] – Fictitious History'. The three embarrassed pages devoted to fiction describe 'a very numerous, though, in general, a very insignificant class of writings, known by the name of romances and novels'. Blair, the great defender of Macpherson's pseudo-primitive prose romance *Ossian*, actually likes fictions; he summarizes Huet's history, adding Lesage, Marivaux, and Rousseau at the French end and *Robinson Crusoe, Tom Jones* and *Clarissa* to uphold the honour of England. He even calls the last two novels. But the conclusion is apologetic in the extreme: 'characteristical novels . . . might furnish an agreeable and useful entertainment to the mind; yet . . . they oftener tend to dissipation and idleness, than to any good purpose. Let us now, therefore, make our retreat from these regions of fiction.' Mary Wollstonecraft similarly denigrates 'women who are amused by the reveries of the stupid novelists' but allows that even reading novels is better than nothing (*A vindication of the rights of women*, 13 §2). And the Preface to *Lyrical ballads* contains a famous wisecrack about the 'degrading thirst after outrageous stimulation' that favours 'frantic novels' and other popular forms at the expense of Shakespeare and Milton; though Wordsworth blames the problem on current events, he is really reviving an established topos. So long as novels caused this much embarrassment they could not be the subject of much refined reflection.

---

[3] Herder's meagre comments, mostly about the novel's primitive roots, mostly postdate *Wilhelm Meister*, from the very end of his long and prolific career. Though Schiller had some notoriety as a prose fiction writer, a page in *Über naive und sentimentalische Dichtung* denies that novel writers, *Romanenschreiber*, compose poetry, *Dichtung*. Earlier, Sulzer's influential *Allgemeine Theorie der schönen Künste* (1771–4, revised 1792 with the novel theorist Blanckenburg as coeditor) has an entry for 'romanhaft' but not for 'Roman', 'Fiktion' or 'Novelle', and discusses verse narrative only in the entry for 'Erzählung'.

Indeed, only one general eighteenth-century book about the novel – Friedrich von Blanckenburg's 528-page *Versuch über den Roman* (1774) – has enjoyed any afterlife, having become a standard reference point in German scholarship since its reprinting in 1965.[4] An apologist for the German Enlightenment novelist Christoph Martin Wieland (whose licentious verse-novella *Musarion* figures almost as largely in the book as the Bildungsroman *Agathon*), Blanckenburg sets out to combat the usual association of the novel with passion. Opposing both perfect and 'romantic' characters (2 §15), he introduces the formula that the novel portrays 'possible men in the real world' (2 §2: 'mögliche Menschen der wirklichen Welt'). The epic, with its machines and its citizens (by which Blanckenburg evidently means its focus on societies), has yielded to stories of individual character. Hence the novel resembles the drama more than the epic; indeed, Shakespeare, Lessing and Diderot often serve Blanckenburg as models for character representation, and his penultimate chapter advocates approximating dramatic dialogue in novels. Also inspired by drama is Blanckenburg's concern with construction. He criticizes epistolary novels in general and Richardson's longueurs in particular; he wants every incident to be essential to the whole, with a necessary unfolding of cause and effect, 'nowhere a leap or a gap' (a formula found twice, with trivial variations, pp. 267 and 315). Terror generates sympathy and is thus subsumed under pity; humour (Sterne above all) likewise shows us real men, who are best illuminated by 'small traits' (1 §18); the aim is to educate readers in the progress toward virtue.

Blanckenburg's *Versuch* was not reprinted in its own day and was seldom referred to. Many of its themes seem to look forward to Romantic novel theories – reality, drama, totality and (albeit not very fully developed) formalism. On the other hand, his moralism and his generic prescriptivism seem rather old-fashioned. His book is of interest not as an original, let alone an influential, document, but as an intelligent encounter with the still rather shapeless debates about the validity of writing prose fictions at all. (To this day German has no settled word for 'novelist'; Blanckenburg uses 'Romanendichter' – roughly, narrative artist – rather than Schiller's condescending 'Romanenschreiber'.) If fiction was attacked for pandering to primitive passions, it was natural to defend it insofar as it could be represented as a serious, sober, up-to-date adaptation of time-honoured

---

[4] In 'Zur französischen Romantheorie des 18. Jahrhunderts', *Nachahmung und Illusion*, ed. Hans R. Jauss, Munich: Eidos, 1964, pp. 60–71, Werner Krauss lists two books on the novel by N.-A. Lenglet-Dufresnoy, one of which has been reprinted: *De l'usage des romans*, 1734, rpt. 2 vols. in 1, Geneva: Slatkine, 1970. Volume one defends a miscellaneous assemblage of narratives in prose and verse; volume two is a vast and capriciously organized bibliography. Krauss also lists the book by Jacquin discussed in note 2 above and a 1736 Latin oration by Charles Porée, *De libris qui vulgo dicuntur romances* (the OCLC database gives the last word as 'romanenses').

artistic principles. So much anyone might have thought in 1774; nor did it seem to anyone else interesting and profitable to say it at such length.

More than any other factor, then, what shapes romantic discussions of the novel was simply the existence of a corpus of works considered distinctive and important enough to be worth examining. A canon was generally recognized and largely shared by English, French and German authors: Madame de La Fayette, Lesage, Marivaux and Rousseau in France; Defoe, Richardson, Fielding, Smollett in England (with Sterne and Goldsmith added when humorists were cited, Behn and Burney when women writers were at issue); Wieland in Germany (*Werther* seems to have been little noticed among the theorists). These authors provided a range of models whose techniques and merits could be differentiated and thus facilitated inquiry into how novels did or might work, rather than merely global debates about whether they should be tolerated and recognized at all. They allowed for a differentiation between such serious writing and the sensation writers of gothic, or sentimental, or women's fiction. And, perhaps most significant of all, the recognition of a canon gave the novel a history. Instead of degraded epics or romances – or even retreaded picaresques and latter-day Quixotes – readers could now feel they were encountering a distinctive body of work, with its own aims and tendencies. Separated in kind, and not just in degree, from romance and other narrative genres, the novel appeared as the newest of poetic kinds, just emerging into prominence. Increasingly associated with the middle classes in subject matter (and of course in readership as well), and generally telling the story of young people just entering on adult life, the novel established itself as the signature poetic form of modernity.

*

But which modernity? While literary culture had been largely international – often in a one-directional way, of course – literature in the Romantic period was becoming far more national and monoglot. National traditions were growing apart just as a theory of the novel started coming together. The only truly international form of fiction in the Romantic period was the least theorized one, the gothic novel. The German novel in the Romantic period, when it wasn't gothic, was dominated by the ironically self-reflexive, generically mongrel, philosophically abstruse tradition following on *Wilhelm Meisters Lehrjahre*. These works have desultory plots set in ethereal versions of either the present or the romantic past (our Middle Ages and Renaissance being seen as a unit); they incorporate poems, letters, inserted tales and legends, essays, in one case (Eduard Mörike's *Maler Nolten*) a whole – if bizarre – play; they mix the natural with the supernatural, the social and political with the domestic and psychological, reality with dream. Distinctively English in this period were the novel of manners and the national and historical novels eventually popularized on the Continent through Scott and Cooper. In both countries, except in gothic fictions, third-person narrators became the norm: the 'Confessions of a Beautiful Soul' was a self-consciously archaizing insert in *Wilhelm Meister*, Rob Roy was a one-time experiment for Scott; epistolary fictions were old-fashioned or fitful (Hölderlin's *Hyperion*, the first parts of Brentano's *Godwi* and of Scott's *Redgauntlet*). In the much thinner production of France and Italy, however, the older first-person forms predominated, whether as memoir (Constant's erotic novel *Adolphe*, the primary narrative sequences in Chateaubriand's American novellas) or as epistolary narration (Senancour's *Obermann*, Foscolo's *Ultime lettere di Jacopo Ortis*). And in Russia, still struggling to establish itself as a nation of culture, literary production remained mired in sensibility, so that a theory of the novel began to emerge in advance of any fictional output that could satisfy it. International influences in the Romantic period were running only from England to Germany, with the very strong return influence of Goethe, Novalis and Hoffmann upon English and French letters still to come. Apart from Goethe, the only genuinely cosmopolitan writer was Madame de Staël, who was fated to become an exile in her own land. Among the various national discourses it is not easy to see commonalities.

What they do share, however, is the heritage I have already described and the attitudes accompanying it. A shared past and sense of the novel's historical position promote resemblances among apparently unrelated discourses; though discordant in tone and approach, they continue to sound allied themes. In this section of my chapter I will summarize these themes in relation to the twin utterances by Friedrich Schlegel that are the most important slogans of Romantic novel criticism: 'Die romantische Poesie ist eine progressive Universalpoesie' (Romantic poetry is a progressive universal poetry, *Athenaeum* Fragment 116, 1798), and 'Ein Roman ist ein romantisches Buch' (A novel is a romantic book, 'Letter on the novel' in *Conversation on poetry*, 1800). Neither slogan is meant to be univocal; thus, Schlegel regularly applies the term 'Roman' to Dante, Petrarch, Shakespeare and many others who were not 'novelists', and two sentences before defining the novel as romantic book he denies that the novel is 'a distinct kind'. Still, the slogans clearly embrace much of what critics in the following decades were to say about the novel. At least five motifs can be identified.

(1) Schlegel links the Romantic with modernity. Throughout his life, and even around 1800 at the high point of his 'Romantic' phase, Schlegel remained ambivalent about the value he attributed to Romanticism and to modernity. The novel was not to be constrained to representing the world as it is, but should be a transformation or even (as Schlegel wrote about Cervantes in his 1815 lectures on the history of literature) a 'transfiguration

of all things in a magic mirror' that 'reaches . . . into the future' ('Goethes Werke', p. 603). Hence the 'Letter on the novel' emphasizes that the Romantic is not identical with modernity. But, it argues, the Romantic – with the novel as its vehicle – expresses the tendency of modernity: 'everything excellent in modern poetry inclines in spirit and even in type towards it'. That is what is implied likewise by the word 'progressive' in the *Athenaeum* slogan. Or, as another famous fragment has it, 'the French Revolution, Fichte's *Doctrine of knowledge* and *Wilhelm Meister* are the three great tendencies of the age' (*Athenaeum* Fragment 216).[5] If not necessarily the form of the now, the novel is surely the form of the new.

(2) The novel is 'universal'. While modernity distinguishes novel from epic, totality distinguishes it from its nearer neighbour, the drama, which is 'an applied novel' ('Letter', p. 15). Totality is a motif whose application varies widely among different Romantic critics. For Schlegel it means, first, that the novel is comprehensive in its contents, 'a mirror of the entire surrounding world, a picture of the age' (*Athenaeum*). Second it is formally comprehensive. In a number of places Schlegel says the novel is not a genre; it knows no law but encompasses all forms. Every novel is unique and experimental, witty and virtuosic, or, in another specifically Schlegelian term, 'arabesque'. (See Rajan's chapter for an elaboration of the philosophical underpinnings linking totality with uniqueness.) Only German novels of the period are flamboyant in this way, and only Schlegel recommends such flamboyance, but a more general sense that the novel is a developing genre constantly building on prior achievements is widespread in both theory and practice: whereas eighteenth-century novels often originate in parody of a particular model, Romantic novelists adopt motifs from a range of dramatic and poetic as well as fictional predecessors, often signalling the borrowings in their texts, and several also wrote discursively about predecessors and contemporaries. Finally, in addition to its comprehensive content and form, the novel's universality also entails multiple levels of awareness. It must have a reflective and philosophical dimension, doubling its plot with philosophical sophistication, its objective content with subjective self-consciousness. To make the point, Schlegel rather wilfully concludes the 'Letter' by exalting Rousseau's *Confessions* and Gibbon's *Memoirs*. Again, while the more pointed claims only relate to the German situation, the concern for authorial self-awareness and compositional sophistication are widespread and – with the usual qualified exception of Fielding's jocular essays – new in the Romantic period. The Romantic novel becomes both a subject and a vehicle for speculation.

---

[5] In Schlegel's notebooks the sentence about 'the three greatest tendencies of the age' is completed by the phrase, 'but only tendencies, without thoroughgoing execution'. It is significant that Schlegel dropped the qualification in print.

(3) The novel also becomes 'poetry'. Poetry first of all means craft. The English reader may think here of a famous epistolary comment by Jane Austen, representing the author as careful maker rather than as casual finder-out: 'the little bit (two Inches wide) of Ivory on which I work with so fine a Brush, as produces little effect after much labour'.[6] Earlier, it was more characteristic for writings to defend the subject matter and the morality of the novel. Smollett's preface to *Roderick Random* (1748), to take one example, is entirely absorbed with the selection of the hero (also Fielding's starting point): 'I have attempted to represent modest merit . . . I have allowed him the advantages of birth and education . . . I have not deviated from nature', and so forth. In marked contrast, many hundreds of Schlegel's fragments seek quasi-scientific determinations of the system of poetic genres, with the novel frequently prominent among them. But in the Romantic context poetry means more than this – it means an alliance with the highest aims of art. For Blanckenburg, as for Wieland, *Bildung* meant moral instruction, which is typical of eighteenth-century defences of the novel; Smollett, for instance, offers the alternatives of 'wonder' and 'judgement', obviously preferring the latter. But Schlegel wants Romantic poetry to be so refined, fully organized, mystically perfect that it elevates and transforms the soul.

Again, the idealist exaltation is specifically German, but the impulse to accord the highest dignity to the novel is often felt in Romantic discussions elsewhere, and sometimes made explicit. An important case in point is Madame de Staël's early, forty-page 'Essai sur les fictions' (1795, translated the same year into German by Goethe). Her aim is 'to prove that novels painting life as it is, with finesse, eloquence, profundity and morality, would be the most useful of all the kinds of fiction' (p. 178). The essay is in three parts: (1) marvellous fictions, comprising childish fables (which are best if they stress character) and allegories which are abstract (Fénelon, 'Spencer') or else incomprehensible (Samuel Butler's *Hudibras*); (2) historical fictions, briefly scorned for watering down real history and for their dependence on love plots; and (3) natural or probable fictions, which are 'like a history . . . of the future' and give 'intimate knowledge of the human heart' by exercising reflection. Examples of the last class are *Tom Jones*, *Julie* and *Caleb Williams*, and they have virtues resembling the metaphysical *Bildung* denied to the novel by Schiller and accorded to it by Schlegel: 'He who distracts man from himself and from others, who suspends the working of the passions to substitute independent enjoyments, would be the dispenser of the only true happiness of which human nature is susceptible.' The breadth of Madame de Staël's literary culture is already

---

[6] Letter to James Edward Austen, 16 December 1816, in *Jane Austen's letters*, ed. Deirdre Le Faye, Oxford University Press, 1995, p. 322.

evident in this essay; also noteworthy is the tendency (with some exceptions) to winnow out other genres and focus in on the novel as the bearer of the purest aesthetic mission.

(4) Yet insofar as it is 'progressive', the novel is also quintessentially concerned with the unfolding of events in time and hence with reality. To be sure, 'real' is not a new term in criticism, but hitherto it generally implied merely subjective vividness; in this sense it is prominent in Diderot's criticism, including the influential 'Eloge de Richardson' of 1762. More widespread terms, however, had been truth and probability, which survive more sporadically in Romantic novel criticism; Sade's 'Idée sur les romans' (1800), for instance, wants plots that are probable (*vraisemblable*) rather than true (*vrai*), local descriptions that are real (*réelles*) or else probable, and conclusions that are natural and probable (though Sade says his own are extreme and legitimated only by 'the extreme truth of the characters'). Increasingly, however, it was becoming common to take reality as an intrinsic value in art: one thinks of Wordsworth's advocacy of 'the real language of real men', of the growing estimation of Dutch genre painting and of the gradual incorporation of historical and contemporary reality into opera and even concert music (such as Beethoven's *Eroica* symphony or the 'Jena symphony' formerly attributed to him). In a notable early use of the derived abstraction (which was decades away from becoming common in this sense), fragment 449 from Schlegel's *Literary notebooks* explicitly attributes 'Realismus' in the modern sense to novels ('The novel must necessarily relate to a particular point in time; this realism is grounded in its nature'). His published essays also occasionally use the abstract noun, and the last mention of novels in the 'Letter on the novel' criticizes Burney and Goldsmith for deficient realism: 'But how sparingly, drop by drop, does the small dose of the real get delivered in all these books! And which journey, which collection of letters, which history of oneself would not be a better novel, if read in a Romantic way, than the best of these?' Again, Schlegel's formulas encapsulate Romantic commonplaces, both in and out of Germany. They are preceded by Reeve's 'real life and manners' and Staël's 'life as it is' as well as by titles like Robert Bage's *Man as he is* (1792) and Godwin's *Things as they are; or, the adventures of Caleb Williams* (1794). For subsequent writing, Hazlitt's not very abundant essays on novels are symptomatic: 'real' is a leitmotif in the lecture 'On the English novelists' in the *Lectures on the English comic writers* (1819); the chapter on Scott in *The spirit of the age* (1825) calls him 'the amanuensis of truth and history'; 'Sir Walter Scott, Racine, and Shakespear' (from *The plain speaker*, 1826) condescends to Scott's 'matter-of-fact imagination', though a short unsigned 1829 piece, 'The Waverley notes', argues that the novels are not harmed if readers know how they are based in reality.

(5) Finally, for Schlegel, as for many writers of the period, *Roman* retained its associations with one of the more colloquial uses of 'romantic'. Romance as a genre is invoked mostly as a point of departure: Wilhelm Meister, for instance, gets his start in literature by adapting Tasso for the theatre, but the aim of the novel is, arguably, to wean him from romance entanglements. On the other hand, it remained commonplace to consider the novel to be a story of love. The romantic element was often associated with women writers and characters, and not always praised; it is noteworthy that the three women essayists I have cited (chronologically, Reeve, Staël and Barbauld) all polemicize against women writers for pandering to base emotions. Another interesting case is Mary Wollstonecraft, who repeatedly attacked love novels in the *Analytical review* in the 1780s, then eventually undertook an anguished novel *Maria*, left incomplete at her death, to undo the erotic subordination of women.[7] With the exception of some gothic writers (Staël mentions Godwin – whose later novels do, however, have love plots – and Brown and Poe are others), love is a nearly ubiquitous topic in Romantic novels, whereas it figures only incidentally or not at all in several leading eighteenth-century fictions, most obviously *Robinson Crusoe* and *Gulliver's travels*, but among others also *The vicar of Wakefield* (which subordinates the children's love entanglements to the father's financial woes) and even the first two instalments of *Tristram Shandy*. Schlegel himself wrote a small libertine novel (*Lucinde*) that is schematic to the point of abstraction, yet representative in imparting to romantic love the general aestheticizing tendency of the Romantic novel. The novel portrays emotions, rather than adventures, but the emotions should be both portrayed in real situations and purified through their representation in a work of art.

The importance of the 'Letter on the novel' – especially when supplemented as I have suggested by *Athenaeum* fragment 116 – lies in its synthesis of so many leading motifs of Romantic novel criticism. Modern, universal, poetic, realistic, erotic: as the novel comes into prominence as the latest literary form to gain an identity and a history, these are the characteristics that naturally accrue to it in all the major European traditions, however the criticism varies in genre and tone. Two other topics that do not figure in Schlegel, one old and one new, can round out the list. The old topic that continues in Romantic period writing about the novel is the problematic morality of novels, the subject for much mirth and some grief in the many fictional episodes describing books that characters read. For obvious reasons, comments on what is good or bad, and hence on

---

[7] On Wollstonecraft's troubles with the novel, in her *Vindication of the rights of women* and in *Maria*, see Daniel O'Quinn, 'Trembling: Wollstonecraft, Godwin, and the resistance to Literature', *ELH* 64 (1997), pp. 761–88.

vices and virtues, are more common in prefaces and reviews than in more general essays (of which Jean-François Marmontel's 1787 'Essai sur les romans, considérés du côté moral' is more notable than Hugh Murray's multiply condescending *Morality of fiction* of 1805).[8] The new topic is the novel as voice of the nation or of the region; though Schlegel says, 'It belongs to the very concept of a novel not to have a nationality' (*Literary notebooks* 465; two fragments later Schlegel assigns nationality to the drama), Louis-Sébastien Mercier sounds what would become a refrain, especially of Scott criticism, when he writes in *Mon bonnet de nuit* (1784), 'ROMANCES, which are esteemed as frivolous by some serious characters, but who are short sighted, are the most faithful history of the morals and customs of a nation.'[9] It can, of course, be someone else's nation, hence exotic regions beyond the reader's experience, as notably in Charles Nodier, who was known for his Scottish and Slovenian settings and whose reviews are a source for discussion of this topic. And it can be a nation of the future: in Russia the Romantic novelist Bestuzhev (publishing under the name Marlinsky after participating in the failed 1825 Decembrist uprising) and the critic Belinsky made *narodnost'*, or popularism, the watchword for the narratives of a nation not yet truly forged.

The themes I have itemized recur in countless variations in Romantic reviews and essays and eventually make their way into the histories of literature or of the novel.[10] The value of particular works is debated repeatedly, in terms that mostly continue from the eighteenth century. Most noteworthy perhaps were the enduring contest between the emotional Richardson's ideal characters (the Continental favourite) and the down-to-earth Fielding's mixed characters. There were, likewise, debates about Sterne, with whom the Germans often ranged Goldsmith: the English Romantics admired the sentiments but often remained intolerant of Sterne's bawdy comedy, the German discussions weighed pointed wit against the more ethereal humour. Rather than surveying in any detail such instances

---

[8] American criticism in the period does not seem to have risen above primitive attacks and occasional defences of the morality of novels; see the survey in Cathy N. Davidson, *Revolution and the word: the rise of the novel in America*, Oxford University Press, 1986, pp. 38–54.

[9] *Nightcap*, Philadelphia, PA: Spottswood, 1788, II: 227. 'Les romans, regardés comme frivoles par quelques personnes graves, mais qui ont la vue courte, sont la plus fidelle histoire des mœurs & des usages d'une nation.' *Mon bonnet de nuit*, Neuchatel: Société bibliographique, 1785, p. 276.

[10] Large-scale histories of the novel are, however, a very late arrival. The only one I am familiar with that can legitimately be attached to the Romantic period is *Der deutsche Roman des achtzehnten Jahrhunderts in seinem Verhältniß zum Christenthum* (1851), by the great Catholic poet and prose fiction writer Joseph von Eichendorff (1783–1857). Parochial and judgemental, but far more comprehensive than its title indicates, systematic in its elaboration, committed to understanding novelistic production in relation to social (specifically religious) forces, and written with remarkable ardour for so aged an author, the book deserves more sympathetic attention than it has hitherto received.

of the Romantic ordinary, I shall devote the remainder of this chapter to considering a few texts that stand out from the crowd.

*

I.

In Germany *Wilhelm Meister's Apprenticeship* (1795–6) was the break-through text, for both fiction and the theory of fiction. A radically innovative work from an author who had hitherto been given to imitation and adaptation, it fostered new ways of thinking about the novel and even articulated a few. In the middle books the novel's hero participates in a production of *Hamlet*. The influential discussions of Shakespeare scattered throughout this episode are reported by Jonathan Arac elsewhere in this volume; chapter seven of book five, however, contains as fine a single page of novel criticism as is to be found in the entire period. Presented as 'approximately' the result of discussions among the characters, the page distinguishes between novel and drama. While drama concerns 'characters and actions' subject to the workings of fate, the novel portrays 'sentiments and occurrences'. The dramatic hero 'must hasten to the conclusion and may only be delayed', whereas 'the novel must go slowly', to allow the sentiments to develop. In the drama, dominated by conflict, 'everything resists [the hero], and he clears and moves the obstacles out of his way, or succumbs to them'; the novel opts for chance, even if 'steered and led by the sentiments of the personages'. The novel's more gradual pace, without winners and losers, calls for more accommodating personalities; 'the novel hero must be passive, or at least not greatly active'. Above all, the novel takes time, and 'Grandison, Clarissa, Pamela, the Vicar of Wakefield, Tom Jones himself are, if not passive, yet retarding personages'.

This passage serves first of all to define terms for approaching the novel in which it appears. As such, it satisfies the criterion of reflexivity that was soon to become a centrepiece of Friedrich Schlegel's theory of Romanticism. Wilhelm's initiatives are repeatedly sidetracked and his progress delayed by interruptions and accidents. The frequent use of free indirect discourse focusses attention on the sentiments of Wilhelm and, occasionally, other characters. Fate plays a role only in the ironic form of the shadowy Society of the Tower that watches over Wilhelm's development without markedly intruding; their goal, it might well be said, is to help Wilhelm use his chance encounters to reflect and further his true nature, that is, to let contingency be guided by sentiment. Fortune is the novel's guiding spirit, with the word *Glück* prominent throughout and featured twice in the closing sentences. Wilhelm is impulsive in judgment and action, but neither combative nor stubborn; he does not allow himself to sink into tragic regrets either for his lost first love Mariane or for the mysterious and tragic Mignon, and he yields to greater wisdom when the bluntest member of the Tower, Jarno, tells him he has no talent for his chosen vocation of actor. 'Passive, or at least not greatly active' is the perfect description for the hero whose gradual entry into the unpredictable modern world – a poetic universe slightly marked by traces of developing capitalism and of the French Revolution – we are to witness. Whereas *Tom Jones* rushes to conclusion with the threads of its plot drawn ever tighter in the press of incidents and explanations, the retrospective narrations in *Wilhelm Meister* and the disposition of character and incident in the ending work to counteract haste and intention and, instead, celebrate serendipity. Goethe hardly ever mentioned Fielding and never discussed him; clearly a polemical rethinking is entailed by the surprising inclusion of 'Tom Jones himself' in Goethe's list of passive heroes. Whether or not novelists abroad read *Wilhelm Meister* (Carlyle's 1824 translation was the first in English, and those in most other languages came far later, but two French versions appeared in 1802), the terms Goethe proposes – the decisive importance and greater complexity of temporal unfolding in narratives, the breadth of the hero's entanglements, the dispersal of interest away from a commanding dramatic centre – are of enormous relevance to the slow, quiet, inward development of the characters of Austen, Scott and their fictional progeny. And perhaps equally noteworthy is the tone of the chapter: it provides a model for criticism of the novel that is thoughtful and deliberative rather than judgmental, prescriptive or (as in Fielding and Schlegel) witty.[11]

Wilhelm Meister aroused an immediate and strong response. Schiller's letters during and after the composition (published 1829) have remained a touchstone. His observation of 'a strange alternation between a prosaic and a poetic mood' (20 October 1797) characterizes the novel's manifold worlds in terms related to his own account of naive and sentimental poetry. 'The form of *Meister*, like the form of every novel whatsoever, is simply not poetic; it lies wholly in the realm of the understanding . . . [but] it is

[11] Two years after the publication of *Wilhelm Meister* Goethe and Schiller co-authored a brief essay, 'On epic and dramatic poetry' (1797, published 1827) that echoes the discussion in the novel while diverging in significant details. In chapter five of *Goethe and the novel* Eric Blackall scrupulously inventories the differences in order to argue that what we read in the novel reflects the characters' transient interests rather than Goethe's settled views. For purposes of this volume it is not necessary to decide whether the novel criticism (and likewise the *Hamlet* criticism) in *Wilhelm Meister* expresses Goethe's views or Wilhelm's; either way, they remain important documents of Romantic literary criticism. Still, without being able to argue the case in detail here, I would say that Blackall mistakes terminological discrepancies between the novel and the essay for real ones: rather than saying different things about a single concept of retardation, they actually use the same term to refer to different concepts. And he also overlooks the occasion of 'On epic and dramatic poetry', which was prompted by Goethe's epic poem *Hermann und Dorothea* and thus is not properly a theory of the novel at all.

a genuine poetic spirit that uses this form and in this form expresses the most poetic circumstances . . . There is clearly too much [of] the portentous, the incomprehensible, the subjectively marvellous, which comports well with poetic depth and darkness, but not with the clarity that must reign in a novel.' Another touchstone is the reaction of Schlegel's brilliant young friend Novalis (Friedrich von Hardenberg). After initially extolling Goethe (in 1798) for the 'rightness and strength' of his classical mastery and for his richly Romantic and ironic retarding style, Novalis later soured; a much-quoted fragment of 1800 (first published in 1901) turns to sarcasm:

> The whole thing is a nobilitated novel.
> Wilhelm Meisters Lehrjahre, or The Pilgrimage to a Patent of Nobility.
> WM is actually a Candide directed against poetry.

What is revealing about Novalis's abuse in the context of a general discussion is how close his terms are to Schiller's. '*Wilhelm Meisters Lehrjahre* is, so to speak, altogether *prosaic* – and modern . . . It is a poetized bourgeois and domestic story. The marvellous in it is explicitly treated as poetry and enthusiasm.' Though the balance of their judgements differs radically, the terms used by Schiller and Novalis are almost identical: both see in *Wilhelm Meister* a combination of the everyday real with the unusual and mysterious, and both find the combination falling short of actual fusion. Surely, their comments eventually became touchstones at least partly because they reflect widespread issues.[12] We will meet similar terms again in Scott's criticism.

2.

The response to *Wilhelm Meister* that clearly belongs to the history of criticism and not just to the history of Goethe's reputation is Schlegel's twenty-page essay of 1798, 'On Goethe's Meister', surely one of the greatest exercises in practical criticism of the entire century. While Schlegel resembles Novalis in his desire for an ideal aesthetic fusion, his taste, which in this one case never varied,[13] stays closer to Schiller's. Consequently,

[12] Novalis's other comments about novels – a few published in his lifetime, a few in 1846, most in 1901 – are scattered, vague, inconsistent, derivative and mostly cursory. For example, where Schlegel's notebooks insistently seek to place the novel within ever-shifting systems of genres, Novalis mostly relies on the traditional triad of lyric, epic and drama, occasionally either assimilating novel to epic or replacing epic by novel. Sometimes he blames novels for everydayness, sometimes praises them for being poetic. I noticed only one fragment among thousands linking 'Roman' with 'romantisch', but blandly and without development: 'Love has forever [von jeher] played novels, or the art of love has always been romantic' (*Schriften*, III: 692).

[13] Important subsequent discussions of *Wilhelm Meister* by Schlegel are found in the final section of the *Dialogue on poetry* (a 'spirit of antiquity . . . under a modern shell', 'wholly progressive'), and in a review of an 1806 collected edition of Goethe's works ('the novel,

the essay paints Goethe's novel in rich detail as the perfected form of Romantic narrative.

The essay takes the deceptively naive guise of a summary of Goethe's plot, with running commentary interspersed. Extended reviews in the period generally consist of summaries bloated with lengthy excerpts and supplemented by evaluative remarks. Scott's are typical (and shorn of much quotation in Ioan Williams's collected edition); Balzac's massive 1842 review of Stendhal's *Charterhouse of Parma* is an extreme, that virtually rewrites the desultory novel into the form of a dramatic Balzacian plot; Francis Jeffrey, when he reprinted his reviews of the Waverley Novels, felt it would be silly to include the summaries and excerpts, but still apologizes for the 'sad shrinking' and the 'naked and jejune appearance' to which his texts were thereby reduced. Schlegel, however, was a reviewer in the modern sense, and the summary in the *Meister* essay is mimetic rather than descriptive; there are no marked quotations but rather continual allusions to incidents, characters and even locutions presumed already to be familiar to the reader. (The embedded words and phrases are not always recognizable in translation.) Applying his view that the romantic novel is inseparable from its theoretical self-reflection, he has written an essay that has to be read alongside the book to be appreciated.

'On Goethe's Meister' is the supreme instance of Schlegel's interpretive method. Paralleling the novel rather than imposing a framework on it, Schlegel characterizes the different elements of the book (sections, incidents, styles, as well as major and minor personages). The interpretation is in part intuitive – 'divinatory' is Schlegel's word in *Athenaeum* fragment 116 – as it evokes the dominants in mood and pace, and in part structural as it defines roles and units separately and in their organic interrelations. In its procedures the essay is thus a document in the general history of hermeneutic practice; its importance for the generic theory of the novel lies in its principled application of the procedures to a novel. Schlegel treats the novel as *Dichtung* (literature in the highest sense), abolishing traditional hierarchies. Conventional markers of the novel are transmuted into poetic virtues: the 'comedy' of 'caricatures' and of 'foolishness' becomes 'ethereal merriment' ('Äther der Fröhlichkeit'); the Pedant's prosaic reality becomes a touchstone for the prevailing 'poetic mood'; 'even chance here is an educated [*gebildeter*] man' (Schlegel's allusion to the Abbé who guides the Tower Society), who then turns out not to be but to 'play fate'. Thinking

like the epic poem, is often . . . the common product of the poet and of the age'; 'A distinguishing characteristic of modern literature is its precise relationship to criticism and theory, and the determining influence of the latter'; 'In the modern novel . . . it is the whole complex modern world of the understanding, with all its petty details . . . on which the poet must demonstrate his poetic sense and proceed to victory in the face of such refractory material').

through the novel's seeming loose joints, Schlegel shows how each one is motivated, even necessary – the verb *müssen* should be tracked through the essay – so that the Romantic qualities become both the support and the refined adornments of the book's Classical architectonics. ('On Goethe's Meister' does not actually use the term 'Classical', but the Goethe segment of the *Conversation on poetry* speaks of *Wilhelm Meister*'s 'harmony of the Classical and the Romantic'.) At once unique and representative, particularizing and totalizing, immediate and reflective, serious and comic, *Wilhelm Meister* not only portrays *Bildung* but perfectly exemplifies it, long before the term *Bildungsroman* was ever thought of.[14] While Schlegel does not make the claim explicitly, the essay's title allows the character Wilhelm to fuse with the book and, implicitly, with author and reader as well, as all are simultaneously 'formed' or 'educated' into what the last sentence calls the terrain 'of the most holy, and we suddenly find ourselves on a height where everything is divine and self-possessed [*gelassen*] and pure'.

3.

Schlegel's 'Letter on the novel' of 1800 is couched as a defence of the novels of Jean Paul. The latter resumes the discussion, much in Schlegel's spirit though without appealing directly to him, in his *Vorschule der Ästhetik* of 1804 (*Aesthetic primer*, well translated into English under the title *The horn of Oberon*), perhaps the first general treatise on aesthetics to devote a substantial section specifically to the novel.[15] The *Vorschule* consists of fifteen parts (each called a *Programm* [course]), followed by three series of 'lectures'. The novel gets the twenty-three pages of the twelfth course, following 'The historical plot of drama and epic' and preceding a brief course on 'The lyric' – not a climactic position, in others words, but an advanced one nevertheless. The first chapter in the course on the novel is titled 'On its poetic value', directly posing the question implicit in the Romantic recognition of the novel as an independent genre. It is difficult,

[14] A little-read essay by Karl Morgenstern, 'Über das Wesen des Bildungsromans' (1820–1) seems to be the first coinage of the term; it only gained currency late in the century, in the wake of Wilhelm Dilthey's *Das Erlebnis und die Dichtung*.
[15] Friedrich Schelling's *Philosophy of art* devotes half a dozen pages to novels as the perfected mythology of the modern age, but acknowledges only *Don Quixote* and *Wilhelm Meister* as successful novels and points toward a call for a renewal of epic; the lectures, delivered in 1802–3, were not published until 1859. Karl Heinrich Ludwig Pölitz's 680-page *Aesthetik für gebildete Leute* (1807) allots only seven pages of text and bibliography to the novel (perfected form despite the absence of metre; idealized humanity; lyric, didactic and epic subgenres) as the fifth of six forms of epic. In Friedrich Bouterwek's vast, positivist *Geschichte der Poesie und Beredsamkeit* (11 vols., 1801–19) older novels are well represented, scattered throughout and without any clear genre definition; modern English novels get twenty-six pages of volume eight versus forty-eight pages for other prose; German novels since 1770 get only eight pages of volume eleven, and Goethe's novels are barely mentioned in the nine pages devoted to him.

Jean Paul says, to maintain unity over so much larger a space than the epic encompasses, and difficult to maintain the intensity of the lyric. Hence the novel must above all possess 'das Romantische'; that is, it must not be tied to reality (*Wirklichkeit*) or to doctrines. It must be general in import – humanity speaking to humanity, 'not this man to these men'. And though 'poetry teaches', what it teaches is 'how to read' the signs surrounding us in 'the whole world, the whole of time'.

The exemplary importance of Jean Paul's treatment lies in the specificity it gives to this Romantic impulse. Beginning with the most rarefied Schlegelian ambitions, he settles not into mythology and mysticism (as Schelling regularly does, Novalis frequently and Schlegel also at times) but into practical matters. There are epic novels and dramatic novels, with different strengths. There are three stylistic levels, which Jean Paul relates to national proclivities (though the examples are broadly international): the high, or Italian; middle, German; and low, Dutch. The bourgeois German middle is the most difficult form, but also the form of *Wilhelm Meister*; because it is refractory to poetizing, success with the middle world constitutes the true 'poetry of poetry'. Then, following an interpolation on the idyll, a bit under half the course is devoted to 'Rules and hints for novelists' – unity, episodes, plot and character, love and friendship, naming, counting chapters. When a Romantic novelist writes a Romantic theory of the novel, genius and technique jockey for attention, spirituality and worldliness, poetry and prose.

If the Romantic period poetized the novel, it may also be said to have novelized literature. A novel-based programme could have been an incitement to rampant idealizing, even of realistic modes. But the more far-reaching tendency was the reverse – that of tethering ideals back to the concreteness of plot, characters, setting and socially determined modes and levels of expression. In practical terms the double valence of the Romantic novel was most visibly displayed in the many gothic and German novels that mixed poetry with prose and most subtly conceived in the encounter of an 'imaginist' like Austen's Emma (the word is coined in volume 3, chapter 3) with everyday life. In theory, where bringing the novel up to snuff and bringing poetry down to earth proved to be complementary developments, the double valence implied by Jean Paul's treatment became the most important legacy of the Romantics to the theorists and practitioners in the rest of the century.

4.

The crucial figure in concretizing novel theory was Walter Scott. Until the reputation of Hegel's brief comments ballooned under the influence of Lukács, Scott was surely the most lastingly influential Romantic theorist of the novel. Some long surveys (not in the Ioan Williams collection), about two dozen reviews and introductions to the work of other novelists, together with a number of programmatic prefaces to his own novels, make up an unprepossessingly desultory corpus. Still, when collected the reviews and prefaces alone make up one of the fattest volumes discussing the novel by any author of the period, famous or not.

Because of the form Scott's criticism takes, René Wellek found it 'difficult to consider him an important critic'.[16] Yet while far from the grand flights of idealist criticism, Scott cares about novels and combines a seriousness unthinkable in the obsessively witty Schlegel and Jean Paul with a practical regard inaccessible to abstract philosophical criticism. He feels the need to defend novels, though he does so on the grounds of plea- sure and charm, nothing higher. About Fielding he writes, 'The professed moral of a piece is usually what the reader is least interested in' (p. 54). Hence Fielding's licentiousness leaves him unruffled, and he even concedes that Sterne's bawdy is 'harmless as to morals' (p. 72), however greatly it may 'sin against taste'. He admires well-contrived plots, but finds few of them – certainly not his own plots, which he criticizes harshly both at the start of the self-review he wrote of the anonymously published *Black dwarf* and *Old mortality* and also in the preface to *The fortunes of Nigel*. Instead, time and again he warms up to heart-warming, vivid characters, in Richardson, Goldsmith, Bage, Smith; even the disgusting Sterne is redeemed by his sentimental characters, even the dramatist Fielding creat- ed characters who outshine his plot. Fundamentally, then, Scott values fiction for its unique ability to capture and project feelings. He carves out for novels a terrain all the more aesthetic for being ordinary, unexalted and hence free from the German Romantic contamination of aesthetics by theology that Elinor Shaffer discusses elsewhere in this volume.

The novel for Scott conveys the feeling of real life. Like so many Romantic critics of the novel, Scott is an instinctive, unobtrusive propon- ent of realism. The topic is ubiquitous, but perhaps most pronounced in the opening of the self-review: 'These coincidences between fiction and reality are perhaps the very circumstances to which the success of these novels is in a great measure to be attributed' (p. 238). Of many other passing remarks that might be cited, I will mention only the praise of 'the unequalled dexterity with which [Defoe] has given an appearance of REALITY to the incidents which he narrates' (p. 172). This passage is revealing because Scott continues by praising Defoe's artlessness as the root of the effect: the appearance of reality is valued even above artifice, or above reality itself. Hence the frequency of Scott's thematized or incid- ental references to painting and painters, such as the well-known compar- ison of Austen to a Dutch painter (p. 235). Reality for Scott is primarily spatial, visual, external; literary portraiture is the vehicle of true feeling.

---

[16] René Wellek, *A history of modern criticism, 1750–1950*, vol. II: *The Romantic age*, New Haven, CT: Yale University Press, 1955, pp. 121–2.

Still, however much Scott may admire 'an air of reality' or 'an appearance of reality' (pp. 43, 151, Richardson and Swift respectively), 'Something more than a mere sign-post likeness is also demanded' (p. 231, Austen). The real must also be vivid, affecting, not just 'correct' but 'correct and striking' (p. 230), or, in a more common term, it must be 'interesting'. 'Between the concentric circles of probability and possibility' (p. 228) the novelist balances the ordinary and the exceptional. Schiller, Novalis and many others position the novel between such poles; Scott is the writer to do so most insistently. Plot is the realm of interest, curiosity, excitement. Hence reality must always be coloured and enriched by 'romance'. Romance is Scott's most general term for the artistry of novels.[17] He uses it for all the dimensions of 'das Romantische' except the most abstrusely philosophical or ironic: for love (p. 236, end of the Austen review), for exoticism (pp. 317–25, Hoffmann), incessantly for the supernatural, and for the contrivances of plot in general. The rise of the novel – not to existence, but to independence – entailed a double status, reconciling or at least juggling life and art, prose and poetry, the aesthetic or imaginative and the social or natural, the epic and the dramatic, character and plot. If the German critics imply such balances, it is Scott who makes them the cardinal presumption of his evaluations.

Balance can be difficult, however. 'It is not perhaps possible, at the same time, to preserve consistency and probability, and attain the interest of novelty' (p. 308, Galt). Consequently lesser but still worthy novelists are often found shuttling between the two poles, or favouring one at the expense of the other: now painting reality, truth, nature, now inventing plot, adventure, interest, romance. For his own work, as critics have long discussed, Scott preferred a semi-distant perspective from which events could appear true, yet hazed by the romance of uncertainty – a perspective perfectly embodied by the two generations' distance and moderately remote settings of his first novel, *Waverley; or, 'tis sixty years since*. However, as Scott often reiterates, novelty is abraded by repetition, so that Romantic elements quickly lose their force. As he worked into the vocation of a historical novelist, basing his stories increasingly on research rather than experience and accumulating documentation to validate his invention, he came increasingly to value the Romantic *within* the real rather than alongside it. As the young lawyer Hardie says in the discussion about novels from the first chapter of *The heart of Mid-Lothian*, 'the heroes of romance' grow predictable more rapidly than 'the real records of human vagaries', and 'The true thing will triumph over the brightest inventions of the most ardent imagination.' Through such realignments Scott, who began his writing career as a Romantic poet, became the

---

[17] Scott's accomplishment, however, did not satisfy Alessandro Manzoni, whose long essay 'Del romanzo storico' (begun in 1828, published in 1850) concludes that Scott was not 'truer than history' but rather 'less historical' than truth.

fountainhead of realism in fiction.[18] The historical logic from which the romantic novel benefited promoted its further transformation into the mid-nineteenth century epic of society and the late-century slice of life. And the polarity on which Scott's criticism rests sets the terms for most of the discussion of the form and function of the novel for the entire period. Virtually every novelist from Scott to Woolf sets as a more or less conscious task an adjudication of the competing claims of the true or the real and the interesting or the romantic. In particular, critics writing on the (to my mind spurious) topic of 'the American romance' would do well to realize the degree to which Hawthorne and his fellows were merely inflecting a debate within European literature that preceded and outlasted their writings.

*

Which is not to say, of course, that either the nineteenth-century novel or nineteenth-century novel criticism stops developing after the Romantic period. I will finish with a glance at the text that may be said to have put an end to my topic, Balzac's 1842 preface to the *Comédie humaine*. Balzac's career as a serious writer began in imitation of Scott and of the gothic novelists, and he shares the Romantic aim of creating a mythology of modern life by balancing external fact (such as occupation) with internal essence, the ordinary with the unique and (a topic he highlights in his theory more than any of the critics I have mentioned except Wollstonecraft) men with women. At once philosophical and practical, and drawing key inspirations from Romantic scientists, Balzac at a certain level seems to fuse the German and the English traditions of thinking about the novel. But reading Balzac's preface is nothing like reading either Schlegel or Scott. In a torrent of names and pointed polemics, Balzac's preface showcases his learning. If the German critic is a wise or clever thinker and the English one an experienced and informed practitioner, Balzac promotes a distinctly unromantic image of the novelist as scientist, man of vast knowledge. Romance means to him much what it meant to Romantic critics (though he emphasizes drama to a greater degree than any predecessor), but his reality is less the thing encountered, experienced or intuited than the world known. Neither Scott's 'air of reality' nor Schlegel's Platonic 'mysteries of realism' (*Conversation*, p. 506) approach the total system of worldly knowledge that Balzac makes his claim to fame. The novelist becomes not a craftsman but a specialist in fiction. And so the Romantic legacy is simultaneously perpetuated and overthrown.

[18] The long essay 'Romance' that Scott wrote for the *Encyclopedia Britannica* in 1823 sets up the framework differently from the writings included in the Williams collection. In the opening paragraph Scott contrasts novels as stories of everyday life to romances. However, he proceeds to acknowledge the prevalence of mixed examples, never again mentions novels, and concludes with a brief paragraph praising Defoe and Swift as preeminent romancers. Clearly the mixed form is the norm here too, even though the novel is nominally defined as a pure type.

13

The impact of Shakespeare

JONATHAN ARAC

The impact of Shakespeare on Romantic literary criticism may be measured in at least three ways. First, his place in the canon: starting in the later eighteenth century, a transformation in taste, led and articulated by critical writings, radically changed the value of Shakespeare. In the world of culture and learning, Shakespeare ceased to be primarily a source of pleasure and of interest almost exclusively in England; he became by the 1830s a universal genius known and admired, throughout the West, for his deep insight into the human condition. His newly exemplary pedagogical value made Shakespeare the basis for England's educational mission in India.[1] Shakespeare's cultural destiny was thus linked to Britain's rise to world power in the decades from the Seven Years' War through the Napoleonic struggles; Britain's wars against France counterpointed and reinforced the challenge Shakespeare offered to the literary values of the French neoclassicism that dominated European thought for more than a century. Second, the place of Romantic critics in the canon of Shakespeare studies: German works by August Wilhelm Schlegel and English works by Samuel Taylor Coleridge and William Hazlitt are landmarks that still serve as points of departure for fresh thinking nearly two centuries later. Third, Shakespeare was a crucial starting point for important Romantic writers as they made innovative contributions in poetry and fiction, as well as in literary criticism and theory: Johann Wolfgang von Goethe, Friedrich Schlegel, John Keats, Herman Melville.

In 1850 the American poet and essayist Ralph Waldo Emerson published *Representative men*, choosing Shakespeare to represent 'The Poet'. Looking back over the period covered by this chapter, Emerson defined the change: 'Now, literature, philosophy, and thought are Shakspearized.' Emerson asserts that only in the nineteenth century could 'the tragedy of Hamlet find such wondering readers', and the reason is because the 'speculative genius' of the century is itself 'a sort of living Hamlet'. Emerson

---

[1] The best brief, internationally focussed, summary of Shakespeare's rise to preeminence is Harry Levin, 'The primacy of Shakespeare', in *Shakespeare and the revolution of the times*, New York: Oxford University Press, 1976. On India, where Shakespeare began to occupy a central place in pedagogy in the 1830s, earlier than was regularly the case in England, see Gauri Viswanathan, *Masks of conquest*, New York: Columbia University Press, 1989.

compares the place Shakespeare had assumed to that which religion was relinquishing: 'there is in all cultivated minds a silent appreciation of his superlative power and beauty, which like Christianity, qualifies the period'.[2]

In the writings about Shakespeare by those who were in the first generation to feel his power as a tremendous, surprising discovery, rather than as part of an already known literary culture, there is indeed a feel of religious conversion. Through his interchange with Johann Gottfried Herder, the young Goethe came to a new awareness of Shakespeare. Goethe's first public text on Shakespeare, composed to be read among friends at the celebration of Shakespeare's name day in 1771, testifies, 'The first page I read of him made me his own for life, and when I had finished the first play I stood as a man born blind to whom a miraculous hand had returned sight in an instant.'[3]

Such enthusiasm had not characterized the language of Samuel Johnson, even when Johnson judged Shakespeare unmatched except by Homer in the powers of invention and innovation. Scarcely had Johnson consolidated one point of view in the preface to his edition of Shakespeare (1765, two centuries after Shakespeare's birth in 1564), than quite a different way of writing about Shakespeare began to emerge in Germany, led by Herder's 'Shakespeare' (1771). Herder at this time exercised an immense effect on Goethe, whose Götz von Berlichingen (1771) was a history play clearly inspired by Shakespeare, but Goethe's Shakespeare was most importantly enunciated in his novel Wilhelm Meister's apprenticeship (1796). This novel, and its use of Shakespeare, formed a major nucleus for the thoughts of the younger generation in Germany, especially the brothers Friedrich and August Wilhelm Schlegel, whose writings in their journal The Athenaeum (1798–1800) activated the term Romantic, which is now used for the whole movement leading up to them and extending well into the nineteenth century. A. W. Schlegel contributed to German culture the verse translation of Shakespeare (seventeen plays from 1797 to 1810) that made Shakespeare an accepted masterpiece of German literature. As a critic his 1808 Vienna lectures on dramatic art and literature, published the next year as a book, made the conception of organic unity widely known.[4]

The most dynamic critical intelligence in England from the 1790s was that of Samuel Taylor Coleridge, and in 1798 he travelled to Germany to

[2] Ralph Waldo Emerson, Essays and lectures, New York: Viking, 1983, p. 718.
[3] Johann Wolfgang von Goethe, 'Shakespeare: a tribute', in John Gearey (ed.), Goethe: essays on art and literature, Princeton, NJ: Princeton University Press, 1994, p. 163. I have altered the translation in the interest of literality.
[4] Augustus William Schlegel, A course of lectures on dramatic art and literature, tr. John Black, rev. A. J. W. Morrison, London: Bohn, 1846.

improve his knowledge of the tremendous intellectual work there being accomplished. In his literary lectures, starting in 1808 and continuing until 1819, and in his *Biographia literaria* (1817), Shakespeare formed the crux for Coleridge's thinking, which made possible – slowly in a process extending into the twentieth century – a new mode of critical writing in English. Shakespeare was not new in English culture, but even so, a manuscript document testifies to the impact of Shakespeare on Coleridge as he made the decision around 1800 to focus his energies on criticism rather than on poetry (at this date, Coleridge had published considerable political prose and several volumes of poetry, including *Lyrical ballads* with Wordsworth, but none of the critical writing by which he is known). Coleridge's 'Memoranda for a History of English Poetry' lays out a rather bland agenda (e.g., '3. Spenser – with connecting introduction') until item five which is briefer and by far more emphatic than any of the preceding: 'Shakespeare!!!' (*Collected works*, vol. XI, 1: 108).

Coleridge helped to inspire – to emulation and at times to controversy – the essayists Charles Lamb and William Hazlitt, as well as the Scottish historian and social prophet Thomas Carlyle. Carlyle began his career as a highly active and significant bridge between Britain and Germany through his many essays and translations – notably the first, and long-standard, English version of Goethe's *Wilhelm Meister* (1824). Besides essays and a selection, with commentary, of *Specimens of English dramatic poets who lived about the time of Shakespeare* (1808), Lamb wrote with his sister Mary *Tales from Shakespeare* ('designed for the use of young persons', 1807).[5] Criticism and retellings are two of the various ways by which Romantics lovingly turned Shakespeare's poetry and drama into prose and narrative. Hazlitt's writing is saturated with Shakespeare in quotation and allusion; his direct critical address to Shakespeare includes 'Shakespeare and Milton' in *Lectures on the English Poets* (1818) and a volume, also from lectures, *Characters of Shakespeare's Plays* (1817), which a knowledgeable judge has declared the founder of a genre, the 'one-volume critical introduction which surveys the full range of the plays'.[6] What now would be a university course was then open to the public by subscription. Carlyle's contemporary John Keats took his critical bearings to a large extent from Hazlitt, and Herman Melville, a novelist of America's belated Romanticism, echoes both Keats and Carlyle on Shakespeare just as he is asserting his own most idiosyncratic self-orientation.

[5] For the larger issue of how women responded to Shakespeare in the nineteenth century, see Nina Auerbach, *Woman and the demon*, Cambridge, MA: Harvard University Press, 1982, chapter 6; and Marianne Novy, *Engaging with Shakespeare: responses of George Eliot and other women novelists*, Athens, GA: University of Georgia Press, 1994, esp. chapters 1 and 2.

[6] Jonathan Bate, *Shakespearian constitutions: politics, theatre, criticism 1730–1830*, Oxford University Press, 1989, p. 144.

This is the cast of characters most important to this chapter, for the English- and German-speaking cultures felt Shakespeare's impact first and most powerfully. It soon spread more widely. As the question of Romanticism became an issue for European cultural polemics, Shakespeare was a touchstone by which the Romantics could distinguish themselves from their adversaries.[7] Before his career as a novelist, Stendhal began his pamphlet *Racine and Shakespeare* (1823, 1825) with a debate in dialogue between 'The Academician' and 'The Romantic' on the neo-Aristotelian unities of place and time that had dominated French critical thought and dramatic practice since the later seventeenth century. The upshot of Stendhal's argument was to value Shakespeare, and the Romantic, as what was most vital in the present cultural moment. In the manifesto serving to preface his never staged drama *Cromwell* (1827), Victor Hugo elaborated German metahistorical typologies to define the centrality of Shakespeare and launch a Romantic movement in France. Hugo schematizes the history of poetry as the interrelation of ode, epic and drama, identified with the Bible, Homer and Shakespeare. Drama, which Shakespeare embodies, 'combines in one breath the grotesque and the sublime, the terrible and the absurd, tragedy and comedy'. This comprehensive mixture is the defining characteristic of 'the third epoch of poetry, of the literature of to-day'.[8]

In Italy Alessandro Manzoni published a letter in French explicating and defending the practice of *Othello* against that of Voltaire's *Zaïre* with regard to the unity of time.[9] In Russia likewise, Aleksander Sergeyevich Pushkin demonstrated the key issue in the impact of Shakespeare: during the Romantic period the most consequential writers of the various Western national cultures found Shakespeare an indispensable means of defining their own innovations.[10] Romanticism has been seen as a 'revival' of earlier literary modes and as a 'revolution' that overturned existing modes and made literature new. Shakespeare's impact demonstrates the close connection of revival and revolution.

The impact of Shakespeare operated most importantly at a higher level than that of work-to-work influence. Romantics through their engagement with Shakespeare conceptualized a mode of writing that seemed quite different from the prevailing modes of the later eighteenth and earlier

---

[7] See Paul Van Tieghem, *Le romantisme dans la littérature européenne*, Paris: A. Michel, 1969, p. 287.

[8] Victor-Marie Hugo, Preface to *Cromwell*, I. G. Burnham (trans.), in Jonathan Bate (ed.), *The Romantics on Shakespeare*, London: Penguin, 1992, pp. 226, 225.

[9] Alessandro Manzoni, 'Letter to M Chauvet on the unities of time and place in tragedy', excerpted in Oswald LeWinter (ed.), *Shakespeare in Europe*, New York: Meridian, 1963, pp. 130–5.

[10] See LeWinter, *Shakespeare in Europe*, pp. 161–2, for an example of Pushkin's table-talk on characters from Shakespeare.

nineteenth centuries and that seemed to offer opportunities for originality, the creation of new forms. In Friedrich Schlegel's review-essay on Goethe's *Wilhelm Meister*, the most innovative critic of the age is discussing the major novel of the era's most influential writer. It is a crucial fact of this period that both these figures are German; but it is equally crucial that Goethe's Wilhelm breaks through toward his maturity by engaging with Shakespeare. This novel as the founding exemplar of what later came to be called the *Bildungsroman* offers a model of development, and Shakespeare is an essential part of that development. Schlegel argues that 'there is an immeasurably wide gulf between the first apprehensions and elements of poetry with which the first volume concerned Wilhelm and the reader' and the point later in the novel 'where man becomes capable of grasping both the highest and the most profound'.[11] The 'passage' across such a gulf, Schlegel thinks, always requires 'a leap', and this leap is made possible by 'the mediation of a great model'. This formulation of Schlegel's catches the crucial dimension of Shakespeare's impact. For many of the most important Romantic writers the model is Shakespeare, because of all poets, he is 'the one who deserves so eminently to be called unlimited'.

Because Shakespeare is unlimited, it is not possible simply to copy the externals of his practice. Rather, to make use of Shakespeare requires the modern writer to grasp the productive principles by which Shakespeare achieved his art. That is, an act of critical formulation necessarily precedes innovative creation. Such an argument is fundamental to the decades-long critical theorizations of Coleridge. As early as a notebook entry of 1804, he reflects on the structure of similarity and difference that makes possible linguistic symbolization and links it to 'the *imitation* instead of *copy* which is illustrated in very nature *shakespearianized*'.[12] And in the *Biographia literaria*, he contrasts Shakespeare's representation of madness in *King Lear* with a mad passage in Thomas Otway's *Venice preserved* (1682) in order to elucidate the dynamic at work in Shakespeare. He explains that such critical theorization is necessary for the future of great writing: 'To admire on principle is the only way to imitate without loss of originality.'[13] In the structure of the *Biographia*, Shakespeare is the hinge between German theory (chapters 5–13) and English poetry (specifically the discussion of Wordsworth that begins in chapter 4 and then occupies chapters 17–22). The contrast of Otway to Shakespeare opens the topic of the imagination, provoked by Wordsworth's poetry and pursued theoretically

[11] Friedrich Schlegel, 'On Goethe's *Meister*' (1798), in Kathleen Wheeler (ed.), *German aesthetic and literary criticism: the Romantic ironists and Goethe*, Cambridge University Press, 1984, p. 68. The quotations in the rest of this paragraph also come from this page.

[12] Kathleen Coburn, ed., *The notebooks of Samuel Taylor Coleridge*, vol. II, Princeton, NJ: Princeton University Press, 1961, [unpaginated] entry no. 2274.

[13] James Engell and W. Jackson Bate (eds.), *Biographia literaria*, vol. VII of *The collected works of Samuel Taylor Coleridge*, Princeton, NJ: Princeton University Press, 1983, I: 85.

by Coleridge. Then, after the definition of imagination (chapter 13) and the related characterization of 'the poet, described in *ideal* perfection' (chapter 14),[14] chapter 15 prepares for the later analysis of Wordsworth's strength and weaknesses by using Shakespeare's *Venus and Adonis* as the proof-text for the application of the theory. The term Coleridge introduces for his performance has had a great fortune in twentieth-century Anglophone literary criticism: 'practical criticism'.[15] Shelves of books have been written in this new form.

Schlegel in his discussion of Shakespeare in Goethe's *Meister* made a point similar to Coleridge's: to understand Shakespeare is to understand a force like that of nature which operates by the laws of its nature. It is not simply 'the greatness of [Shakespeare's] nature' that is the crux for Wilhelm and Goethe and Schlegel, but rather 'his profound artistry and purposefulness'.[16] In his notebooks from this period, Schlegel cited John Milton's characterization in 'L'Allegro' of Shakespeare's 'warbling his native woodnotes wild' as 'the earliest wrong view' of Shakespeare.[17] Shakespeare's great nature is manifested only through his great art. Therefore, Schlegel argues, Goethe's novel engages Wilhelm with a specific work of Shakespeare's, *Hamlet*, for 'no other play . . . offers the occasion for such varied and interesting debate on what the secret intention of the artist might be'.[18]

The impact of Shakespeare mediates the relations between criticism and new creative work. Some of this new creative work is by major poets who also wrote important criticism, such as Goethe and Coleridge. Some of the new creative work is itself criticism, as in essays by Lamb, Hazlitt and Thomas De Quincey, and in the writing of Friedrich Schlegel himself, whose 'fragments' helped to define a characteristic Romantic literary practice. These interrelations between critical thinking about Shakespeare and the new creative work of the era helped to open larger theoretical perspectives and arguments about the category of 'literature'. Coleridge's theory of the imagination may be understood as beginning from his intuition that what he felt to be the greatest work of his own time, the poetry of William Wordsworth, had some fundamental relation to what was valuable in Shakespeare, and in turn the combined work of Wordsworth and Coleridge allowed Thomas De Quincey to make his distinction between the 'literature of knowledge' and the 'literature of power', which codifies the understanding of imaginative *belles-lettres* that still guides much critical and pedagogical debate at the end of the twentieth century.[19]

[14] *Ibid.*, vol. II, p. 15.   [15] *Ibid.*, vol. II, p. 19.   [16] Schlegel, 'On Goethe's *Meister*', p. 68.
[17] Hans Eichner (ed.), Friedrich Schlegel, *Literary notebooks 1797–1801*, London: Athlone Press, 1957, entry no. 1150.
[18] F. Schlegel, 'On Goethe's *Meister*', p. 68.
[19] See John E. Jordan (ed.), *De Quincey as critic*, London: Routledge and Kegan Paul, 1973, pp. 268–72 (in the midst of an essay on Alexander Pope).

These new understandings of literature, in turn, helped writers to orient their own work – as for instance in the case of Keats's letters reflecting on Shakespeare in dialogue with Hazlitt's critical views – and they also provided means by which readers, including a posterity still active at the end of the twentieth century, can understand that work.

The impact of Shakespeare in Romantic criticism is a case study of the role of literary criticism in a larger literary history. This history proves to be international, and therefore its study must be comparative. There is a compelling story to be told that would work only with the British impact of Shakespeare, but an account is richer and more significant for including not only Germany and France, but also the United States.[20] The crucial role of Goethe's *Meister* – both as a powerful new understanding of Shakespeare and in its provocation to Schlegel's metacritical theorization – indicates that this larger literary history in which the impact of Shakespeare figures is inseparable from the greatly emergent form of the Western nineteenth century – the novel.

No less than in the case of the fictional Wilhelm Meister, the career of John Keats suggests the use a culturally ambitious young man of high powers could make of the 'mediation of a great model'. As with Friedrich Schlegel, for whom thinking about the great past figure of Shakespeare went together with thinking about the great contemporary figure of Goethe, so for Keats Shakespeare signalled the possibility of a path to poetic accomplishment that might be different from that of William Wordsworth.[21] Keats's reflections in his letters show that his process of thought was enriched by the critical writings, lectures and conversation of William Hazlitt.[22]

April 1817 was a crucial moment in Keats's career. Just after the publication of his first volume of poems, he determined to test his powers by writing the long narrative *Endymion* in six months. At the opening of this process, he bought himself a set of Shakespeare (preserved now in Harvard's Houghton Library) and also, by chance, came into possession of a picture of Shakespeare, which he set over his desk and kept with him

---

[20] On the British story, see Jonathan Bate, *Shakespeare and the English Romantic imagination*, Oxford: Clarendon Press, 1986 and *Shakespearean constitutions*. Bate extends the range to France and Germany in his edited anthology, *The Romantics on Shakespeare*.

[21] The argument developed here concerning the role of critical thought about Shakespeare in enabling important, innovative writing differs from, but owes much to, several lines of twentieth-century theorists of literary history, specifically on the process by which the practice of poetry is carried forward: T. S. Eliot, 'Tradition and the individual talent'; W. J. Bate, *The burden of the past and the English poet*, Cambridge, MA: Harvard University Press, 1970, and Harold Bloom, *The anxiety of influence: a theory of poetry*, New York: Oxford University Press, 1973.

[22] The analysis that follows is indebted to the classic discussion by Walter Jackson Bate, *John Keats*, Cambridge, MA: Harvard University Press, 1963, esp. ch. 10, 'Negative capability', pp. 233–63.

through various moves until the end of his life. In the letter (May 11) in which he told his friend, the painter Benjamin Robert Haydon, about the acquisition of this image, Keats refers to Haydon's belief that there was 'a good genius presiding over you' and applies the belief to himself: 'Is it too daring to fancy Shakespeare this presider?'[23] The same letter, near its opening, draws from *King Lear* a phrase to characterize Keats's state of mind, and near its end returns to link his state of mind to Shakespeare: 'I never quite despair and I read Shakespeare – indeed I shall I think never read any other book much . . . I am very near Agreeing with Hazlitt that Shakespeare is enough for us.'[24]

Hazlitt's 'depth of Taste' was for Keats one of the 'three things to rejoice at in this Age',[25] and Hazlitt's specific way of thinking seems to have helped Keats to a formulation concerning Shakespeare that not only is crucial in understanding Keats's own trajectory as a writer but also has been highly influential in the continuing conversations of criticism at large. In December 1817, after finishing his self-appointed task of *Endymion*, Keats reported suddenly being struck with an insight into 'what quality went to form a Man of Achievement especially in Literature and which Shakespeare possessed so enormously'. That quality Keats calls, somewhat mysteriously, '*Negative Capability*'. He explains it thus: 'when man is capable of being in uncertainties, Mysteries, doubts, without any irritable reaching after fact and reason',[26] and he contrasts this condition with Coleridge's quest for systematizing his thought.

The contrast of Keats with Coleridge, of 'negative capability' with the 'balance or reconciliation of opposite or discordant qualities' that is for Coleridge the mark of 'the poet, described in *ideal* perfection' in chapter 14 of the *Biographia literaria*,[27] became a crucial concern for the rejection of Coleridge-inspired New Criticism by postmodern criticism in the United States.[28] The key term in this postmodern discourse is the highly romantic *openness*, and this is what, it may be argued, Keats found in Hazlitt's critical response to Shakespeare.

Hazlitt's fundamental intellectual experience was his discovery of what has since been called the sympathetic imagination. His aim was to rebut the long tradition that explained morality by self-interest, and he did it by unbinding the self. He argued that my connection to my future self can only be made by an act of imagination not different in kind from the

[23] Hyder Edward Rollins (ed.), *The letters of John Keats: 1814–21*, 2 vols., Cambridge, MA: Harvard University Press, 1958, I: 142. In quotations from this edition, I have in a few cases regularized spelling.
[24] *Ibid.*, p. 143.   [25] *Ibid.*, p. 203.   [26] *Ibid.*, p. 193.
[27] Bate and Engell, eds., *Biographia literaria*, II: 15–16.
[28] See William V. Spanos, 'Charles Olson and negative capability: A de-structive interpretation', in *Repetitions: the postmodern occasion in literature and culture*, Baton Rouge, LA: Louisiana State University Press, 1987, pp. 107–48.

imaginative leap by which I link myself to other persons,[29] and he thereby erased in theory the difference between self and other, not by making everything me (as German idealism often seems to) but by opening the possibility of oneself as another. This was the theory. Shakespeare was the practice. Hazlitt asserted in his lectures on the English poets that Shakespeare 'was the least of an egotist that it was possible to be'. He was 'nothing in himself', but he 'had only to think of anything in order to become that thing'.[30]

Keats, in a letter of October 1818, just preceding his year of great accomplishment, returned to Shakespeare as model, and it is clearly a Shakespeare he shares with Hazlitt. Against the most powerful poet of his own time, William Wordsworth, who strongly asserted his selfhood, Keats posed Shakespeare. Wordsworth represented the 'egotistical sublime', but the true 'poetical Character', of which Keats considered himself 'a Member', can be defined as a substance only negatively: 'it is not itself – it has no self . . . It has no character . . . has no Identity'. Positively, it may be defined by feelings and actions: 'it enjoys light and shade; it lives in gusto'. But by allusion, it has a name, for 'It has as much delight in conceiving an Iago as an Imogen.'[31] Tragic villain or romantic heroine, it is all the same to Shakespeare. And many readers have felt that Keats's poetic accomplishment, though in lyric rather than drama, was similarly an outgoing that found its fullest self-realization through the particulars of other lives and ways of being.

By the middle of the nineteenth century, the response to Keats by Matthew Arnold, for all he owed to Coleridge, marks an ossifying of the Romantic Shakespeare. Arnold warned that Keats, and the Elizabethans, were not sufficiently 'mature' to achieve the 'very plain direct and severe' style required for 'modern poetry'. Their 'exuberance of expression' and 'richness of images' seemed to Arnold only 'ornamental work' that ignored the 'whole', while the crux for modern poetry must be 'its contents'.[32] Arnold's critique shows that he has lost the substance of the empathetic form that Keats achieved through his engagement with Hazlitt and Shakespeare.

In the Romantic period, the impact of Shakespeare played a large role in the newly emerging definition of 'literature', and in turn this new conception of literature led to a theoretical remaking of Shakespeare. Difficulties,

[29] Hazlitt himself presents this account in his 1819 polemical and autobiographical pamphlet, 'A letter to William Gifford, Esq.', in William Hazlitt, *The spirit of the age*, 4th edn, W. Carew Hazlitt (ed.), London: Bell and Sons, 1904, pp. 444–56.
[30] William Hazlitt, *Lectures on the English poets and the English comic writers*, William Carew Hazlitt (ed.), London: Bell and Sons, 1894, pp. 62–3.
[31] Rollins, ed., *Letters of John Keats*, vol. I, pp. 386–7.
[32] Cecil Y. Lang (ed.), *The letters of Matthew Arnold: volume I, 1829–1859*, Charlottesville, VA: University of Virginia Press, 1996, pp. 245–6.

challenges to understanding, that had once been condemned as obscurity were newly praised as deep meaning. Four emphases seem most important: the shift from stage to page; the shift from judgment to interpretation; the changed character of mimesis, by which the work becomes a resource for learning; and the tendency to understand what is learned as involving 'uniqueness', a particularity.

The shift from stage to page redefines Shakespeare as producing literature to be read rather than drama to be staged, watched and heard. The larger shift in which this is implicated is the long-ongoing definition of a canon of high culture in the vernacular languages. As Greek and Latin became standard for an ever-smaller percentage of the total reading public, a select group of honoured works in the modern literatures played an increasing role as alternatives to commercialized mass culture, what Wordsworth in his 1800 Preface to *Lyrical ballads* called 'gross and violent stimulants'.[33] This cultural struggle, in turn, was involved with what Lionel Trilling called in an important retrospective essay 'The Fate of Pleasure'.[34] Samuel Johnson had defined his high evaluation of Shakespeare in response to the question of what 'can please many, and please long'.[35] Shakespeare, it began to seem, offered a 'higher', 'deeper', overall more challenging and difficult experience than the term *pleasure* conveys. The discourse of the sublime was one influential way of conveying Shakespeare's value in a new affective idiom.

The best known text in English that links Shakespeare's sublimity to his status as difficult text rather than easy watching pleasure is Charles Lamb's 1811 essay, 'On the tragedies of Shakespeare, with reference to their fitness for stage representation'. Lamb finds actors inadequate to convey, and spectators inadequate to receive, Shakespeare's meaning. Instead, his model is individual and private, the reflective response of an elite, as against the vulgar theatre-goer who lacks 'the very idea of *what an author is*'.[36] The value of Shakespeare becomes a spiritual communion between readers' minds and the mind of the author. Lamb no longer finds the value of Shakespeare's works in the pleasure we gain from the representation of an action; instead the value comes from our process of understanding the meaning of the play's expression of mind. As readers of Shakespeare, we become interpreters, in quest for something not evident

---

[33] W. J. B. Owen and Jane Worthington Smyser (eds.), *Prose works of William Wordsworth*, 2 vols., Oxford: Clarendon Press, 1974, I: 129.

[34] Lionel Trilling, 'The fate of pleasure: Wordsworth to Dostoevsky', in Northrop Frye (ed.), *Romanticism reconsidered*, New York: Columbia University Press, 1963, pp. 73–106.

[35] Arthur Sherbo (ed.), *Johnson on Shakespeare*, New Haven, CT: Yale University Press, 1968. The Yale Edition of the Works of Samuel Johnson, VII: 61.

[36] Charles Lamb, 'On the tragedies of Shakespeare, with reference to their fitness for stage representation', in *Complete works and letters*, New York: Modern Library, 1935, p. 291.

on the stage, in the action. We become connoisseurs of a text, distinguished from, and elevated above, the masses who applaud the play.[37]

A comparable pattern prevails in Goethe's *Wilhelm Meister* (1796). Although Wilhelm's crucial engagement with *Hamlet* comes through his attempt to become an educator for Germany by bringing great works to popular performance, the overall effect of his encounter with Shakespeare is to turn him away from this public role and toward the self-development with which the German ideal of *Bildung* has become associated – and this use of Shakespeare occurs in a novel to be read.[38] A belated and parodic echo of *Wilhelm Meister* may be found in James Joyce's *Ulysses* (1922), in the ninth chapter ('Scylla and Charybdis'). Stephen Dedalus holds forth in the Dublin library his theory of how Shakespeare came to write *Hamlet*. Through Stephen, Joyce mocks the century of impassioned biographical speculation that had grown from Romantic ideas about Shakespeare, but in the instance of Stephen he also reflects critically on the relation of the innovative artist to culture and nation. At the end of *A portrait of the artist as a young man* (1914), Stephen had hoped 'to forge in the smithy of my soul the uncreated conscience of my race',[39] but no such public function may be found in the character of Stephen in *Ulysses*. Like Wilhelm, the intended path of national artistic education proves instead individual and solitary – and in the case of Stephen by no means successful.

In the generation before the Romantics, whether on the negative with Voltaire or more positively with Samuel Johnson, it had been understood as the critic's task to judge Shakespeare and his works. In *Wilhelm Meister*, it has become far more important to understand, to interpret, than to judge. One of the newspaper reports from a lecture of Coleridge's strikes the keynote for this Romantic tendency. It speaks of Coleridge's comments on the history plays as 'deciphering the character of Falstaff'.[40] Across the range of Romantic critical writing, and more widely yet, the notion of the 'hieroglyph', the riddle that needs unravelling recurs. The play's action only inscribes the mystery of the productive mind, which becomes the true object of critical attention.

---

[37] Jonathan Arac, 'The media of sublimity: Johnson and Lamb on *King Lear*', *Studies in Romanticism* 26 (1987), pp. 209–20; and more broadly, Jonas M. Barish, *The antitheatrical prejudice*, Berkeley and Los Angeles, CA: University of California Press, 1981.

[38] See Nicholas Boyle, *Goethe: the poet and the age*, vol. I: *The poetry of desire*, Oxford University Press, 1991, on 'the printed book' as the indispensable means for 'the literary transformation of Germany' in Goethe's lifetime, especially through 'the literary drama': 'In so far as it was a book like other books, [it] linked intellectuals from all over the German-speaking world in the study of feeling and in social, moral and historical reflection' (p. 365).

[39] James Joyce, *A portrait of the artist as a young man*, in Harry Levin (ed.), *The portable James Joyce*, rev. edn, New York: Vintage, 1966, p. 526.

[40] R. A. Foakes (ed.), *Lectures 1808–19 on literature*, 2 vols., vol. v of Kathleen Coburn (ed.), *Collected works of Samuel Taylor Coleridge*, I: 575.

As Wilhelm Meister begins to study the role of Hamlet, he finds himself lost in a 'strange labyrinth', where 'the further I progressed . . . the more difficult did it become for me to perceive the structure of the whole'.[41] Wilhelm defines his task as an actor in trying to make sense of the play as a whole and of its central character. It all seemed a mystery until he discovered a means of interpretation by which he 'really entered the mind of the author'.[42] Only in the Romantic period did Hamlet first become a mystery, and only then did it become necessary to solve the mystery through an act of psychological interpretation.

Wilhelm unravelled the mystery by searching for 'any clues to Hamlet's character previous to the death of his father. I observed what this . . . young man had been like without reference to that sad event . . . and considered what he might have become without them.'[43] In other words, Wilhelm treats Hamlet as a real person and performs a speculative psychological interpretation of his whole character and development. This form of 'character criticism' became almost universal in Germany and English-speaking countries for well over a century.[44] Its spread was closely linked to changes in the human science of psychology. In the letter in which Freud first proposed the Oedipus complex, he immediately went on to suggest its applicability to Hamlet.[45] By this interpretive path backwards into the character's past, Wilhelm finds a way to escape from the labyrinth in which he had wandered. Finally, he discovers 'the key to Hamlet's whole behaviour' in the exclamation,

> The time is out of joint: O cursed spite,
> That ever I was born to set it right!

This specific analysis of *Hamlet* became a point of reference for generations of subsequent criticism. Wilhelm argues that 'Shakespeare set out to portray . . . a heavy deed placed on a soul which is not adequate to cope with it'. This formulation explains how 'the whole play [is] constructed'. Wilhelm's interpretation is sealed by a metaphor: 'an oak-tree planted in a precious pot which should have only have held delicate flowers. The roots spread out, the vessel is shattered.'[46]

---

[41] Johann Wolfgang von Goethe, *Wilhelm Meister's apprenticeship*, Eric A. Blackall and Victor Lange (trans.), Princeton, NJ: Princeton University Press, 1995, p. 128. The relevant passages from the novel may also be found in Wheeler (ed.), *German aesthetic and literary criticism*, pp. 231–6.

[42] Goethe, *Wilhelm Meister*, p. 129.   [43] *Ibid.*, p. 128.

[44] See Jonathan Arac, 'Hamlet, *Little Dorrit*, and the history of character', *South Atlantic quarterly* 87 (1988), pp. 311–28.

[45] Sigmund Freud, *The origins of psychoanalysis: letters to Wilhelm Fliess, drafts and notes, 1887–1902*, Marie Bonaparte, Anna Freud and Ernst Kris (eds.), Eric Mosbacher and James Strachey (trans.), Garden City, NY: Doubleday, 1954, p. 224.

[46] Goethe, *Wilhelm Meister*, p. 146.

Wilhelm's criterion of the 'structure of the whole' is a crucial feature of the new Romantic understanding. As Friedrich Schlegel put it, 'there probably is no modern poet more correct than Shakespeare', when that term so dear to earlier generations of *correct* is understood 'in the nobler and more original sense of the word – meaning a conscious main and subordinate development of the inmost and most minute aspects of a work in line with the spirit of the whole'.[47] In the neo-Aristotelian discourse the key term had been *unity*. Coleridge stands as strongly as Schlegel for a new criterion: 'Instead of unity of action, I should great[ly] prefer the more appropriate, tho' scholastic and uncouth words – Homogeneity, proportionateness, and totality of interest.' This shift in terminology, for Coleridge, brought out the difference between the 'skill of mechanical Talent' and the 'creative Life-power of inspired Genius'.[48]

Shakespeare had been criticized in neoclassical criticism for his failure to observe the unities, but the question of the 'whole' is not at all the same as the question of 'unity'. As Herder put it in the primal text for the German Romantic response to Shakespeare, 'whereas in Sophocles's drama the unity of a single action is dominant, Shakespeare aims at the entirety of an event'. The distinction is that Sophocles 'makes a *single* tone predominate', but in contrast Shakespeare 'uses *all* the characters, estates, walks of life he needs to produce the concerted sound of his drama'.[49] The 'concerted sound' is what later critics will theorize as 'polyphony' versus the 'monologic' classical.

This criterion of wholeness was developed influentially by A. W. Schlegel and Coleridge in the metaphor of the organism. Coleridge contrasts 'mechanical regularity' to 'organic form':

The form is mechanic when on any given material we impress a pre-determined form, not necessarily arising out of the properties of the material – as when to a mass of wet clay we give whatever shape we wish it to retain when hardened – The organic form on the other hand is innate, it shapes, as it developes itself from within, and the fullness of its development is one & the same with the perfection of its outward Form. Such is the life, such is the form.[50]

[47] Friedrich Schlegel, *Philosophical fragments*, Peter Firchow (trans.), Minneapolis, MN: University of Minnesota Press, 1991, p. 53.
[48] Foakes, ed., *Lectures 1808–1819*, II: 362.
[49] Johann Gottfried Herder, 'Shakespeare', Joyce P. Crick (trans.), in J. Bate (ed.), *The Romantics on Shakespeare*, p. 41 (emphasis added). The German translated as 'concerted sound' is 'Hauptklang seines Konzerts', J. G. Herder, *Von der Urpoesie der Völker*, Konrad Nussbächer (ed.), Stuttgart: Reclam, 1969, p. 27.
[50] Foakes, ed., *Lectures 1808–1819*, I: 495. I have omitted from my quotation words crossed out by Coleridge in the manuscript from which Foakes transcribes.
    This passage is a close paraphrase by Coleridge from A. W. Schlegel's Vienna lectures: 'Form is mechanical when, through external force, it is imparted to any material merely as an accidental addition without reference to its quality; as, for example, when we give a particular shape to a soft mass that may retain the same after its induration. Organical

Such organic power is the power of 'Nature, the prime Genial Artist', and 'our own Shakespear' is 'himself a Nature humanized', whose 'genial Understanding' wields 'self-consciously a power and a[n] implicit wisdom deeper than Consciousness'. Shakespeare, then, as a power like that of nature has his own laws, which must be studied and learned even as are those of nature.[51] Contrary to the neoclassical critics who had condemned Shakespeare as wild and irregular, Coleridge asserted that 'Genius' must not and cannot be 'lawless', for every 'work of true Genius' achieves 'its appropriate Form'; the very definition of genius is 'the power of acting creatively under laws of its own origination'.[52] This power, which has often been called *autonomy*, was attributed by Romantic theorists in various contexts to the work, the author, the culture or 'spirit' of a nation and to every person as an individual.

By this logic, we cannot know in advance what we will find in Shakespeare's work, or in the works of any other genius. We must learn from the work. The very sense of the key term *nature* is shifted. For Samuel Johnson it was Shakespeare's greatness that he was 'above all writers, at least above all modern writers, the poet of nature', but this meant that Shakespeare better than any other 'holds up to his readers a faithful mirrour of manners and of life'.[53] Nature here is the way things already are, what we recognize in human passions and experience. For Coleridge, in contrast, nature is a shaping force actively in process:

Whence the Harmony that strikes us in the wildest natural landscapes? In the relative shapes of rocks, the harmony of colours in the Heath, Ferns, and Lichens, the Leaves of the Beech and Oak, the stems and rich choc[ol]ate-brown Branches of the Birch, and other mountain Trees, varying from . . . Autumn to returning spring? . . . [They] are effected by a single energy, modified ab intra [from within]

form, again, is innate; it unfolds itself from within, and acquires its determination contemporaneously with the perfect development of the germ.' A. W. Schlegel, *Course of lectures*, p. 340.

The passage from Coleridge, which was first published in his posthumous *Literary remains*, Henry Nelson Coleridge (ed.), 4 vols., London: W. Pickering, 1836–9, without the manuscript's acknowledgement to 'a Continental Critic', exemplifies the empirical basis for the double controversy over Coleridge's critical character and achievement: was he a plagiarist? was he original? Current landmarks in this controversy include the fair but devastating diminishment of Coleridge in René Wellek, *A history of modern criticism*, New Haven, CT: Yale University Press, 1955, vol. II, esp. pp. 151–57; the remarkable reconceptualization by Thomas McFarland in chapter 1 of *Coleridge and the pantheist tradition*, Oxford: Clarendon Press, 1969; the impassioned prosecutor's brief by Norman Fruman, *Coleridge, the damaged archangel*, New York: Braziller, 1971; and the rescue operation by the editors of the *Collected works* of Coleridge, especially Bate and Engell in the *Biographia* and Foakes in the *Lectures 1808–1819*, esp. I: lx–lxiv.

[51] For the larger resonances of this topic, see M. H. Abrams, *The mirror and the lamp: Romantic theory and the critical tradition*, Oxford University Press, 1953, on 'The poem as heterocosm', pp. 272–84.

[52] Foakes, ed., *Lectures 1808–1819*, I: 494–5.

[53] Sherbo, ed., *Johnson on Shakespeare*, p. 62.

in each component part. Now . . . this is the particular excellence of the Shakespearean Dramas.[54]

By long tradition, nature might be understood as the book in which God had written his teachings,[55] and in the same spirit by which Shakespeare's power as nature was assimilated to divine power, so was Shakespeare's text assimilated to that of God's other book, the Bible, as the expression of an incomparable inner power, requiring endless exegesis.[56]

Friedrich Schlegel defined a 'classical text' (not in this usage to be distinguished from Romantic) as one which 'must never be entirely comprehensible'. Such a text requires, solicits and rewards, an endless process of interpretation: 'those who are cultivated and who cultivate themselves must always want to learn more from it'.[57]

For Friedrich Schlegel, Goethe's choice of *Hamlet* for his definitive accomplishment in *Wilhelm Meister* demonstrated an affinity between Shakespearean drama and the novel. Both, in Schlegel's terms, were *Romantic*, a connection made easier in German because an adjectival form derived from the word for novel (*Roman*) is *romantisch*, which is identical with the term for *Romantic*.[58] One of Schlegel's fragments links drama and novel in ways that take us immediately to *Wilhelm Meister* on *Hamlet*:

Many of the very best novels are compendia, encyclopaedias of the whole spiritual life of a brilliant individual. Works which have this quality, even if they are cast in a completely different mould – like *Nathan* [referring to the play *Nathan the Wise* by Lessing] – thereby take on a novelistic hue. And every human being who is cultivated and cultivates himself contains a novel within himself.[59]

In *Wilhelm Meister*, consideration of *Hamlet* leads to larger debates over genre. Novels are contrasted to drama, insofar as in novels 'it is predominantly *sentiments* and *events* that are to be presented', but in the drama, 'it is *characters* and *deeds*'. As opposed to the active hero of drama, 'the hero of a novel must be passive', or at least function as a 'retarding' personage. From this insight, the application was made back to *Hamlet*: 'the hero . . . really only has sentiments, and it is only external events that work on him, so that this play has something of the breadth of a novel'.[60]

[54] Foakes, ed., *Lectures 1808–1819*, II: 362.
[55] See Ernst Robert Curtius, *European literature and the Latin Middle Ages*, Willard R. Trask (trans.), New York: Harper and Row, 1963, chapter 16, 'The book as symbol', esp. pp. 319–26 on 'The book of nature'.
[56] On Friedrich Schlegel's 'romantic polysemism' in relation to the traditions of biblical hermeneutics, see Abrams, *Mirror and lamp*, 239–41.
[57] Schlegel, *Philosophical fragments*, p. 2.
[58] For an authoritative treatment of the complex etymology and semantics of *Roman* and *romantisch*, which, however, I do not wholly follow, see Hans Eichner, *Friedrich Schlegel*, New York: Twayne, 1970, pp. 48–54.
[59] Schlegel, *Philosophical fragments*, p. 10.
[60] Goethe, *Wilhelm Meister's apprenticeship*, p. 186.

In studying and endlessly interpreting Shakespeare as we do the Bible, what we learn is not universal truth but rather a uniqueness, something highly particular. The contrast of Johnson in 1765 with Herder in 1771 again makes the point very starkly. Johnson finds that Shakespeare's characters are 'not modified by the customs of particular places'; rather, they are 'common humanity, such as the world will always supply'. This means that Shakespeare's 'persons act and speak by the influence of those general passions and principles by which all minds are agitated'. For most writers 'a character is too often an individual', but in the plays of Shakespeare a character is 'commonly a species'.[61] It is Shakespeare's praise that 'his story requires Romans or kings, but he thinks only on men'.[62]

For Herder, however, different circumstances of life not only mean that characters will be different, but that the whole aesthetic of one culture will differ from that of another culture. Sophocles is taken as representing not simply classical drama but a whole Greek way of life, and Shakespeare exemplifies the way of life of the 'North'. If, in contrast to the Greek world, the Northern world did not offer such 'simplicity in its history, traditions, domestic, political, and religious conditions', then correspondingly Northern drama will not display any such simplicity. A different 'world' will 'create its drama out of its own history, the spirit of its age, customs, views, language, national attitudes, traditions and pastimes, even if they are carnival farces or puppet-plays'.[63] Since Shakespeare 'found nothing like the simplicity of the Greek national character', his works build instead from 'a multiplicity of estates, ways of life, attitudes, nations, and styles of speech'.[64] Johnson found Shakespeare essentially human, but Herder understood him as quite local. The work itself builds out of these local details a 'splendid poetic whole' that is its own particularity.[65] In this register we again confront the prestige of the 'whole' – valued as rich – over the earlier criterion of 'unity' – devalued as simplistic.

The impact of Shakespeare on Romantic criticism was sometimes muffled. Romantic criticism was capable of finding in Shakespeare commonplace banalities. When Coleridge boasted that 'Hamlet was the play, or rather Hamlet himself was the Character, in the intuition and exposition of which I first made my turn for Philosophical criticism, and especially for insight into the genius of Shakespeare, *noticed*',[66] it is quite disappointing to learn from him that in *Hamlet*, Shakespeare seems to have 'wished to exemplify the moral necessity of a due Balance between our attention to outward objectives, and our meditation on inward Thoughts – a due Balance between the real and the imaginary World'.[67]

---

[61] Sherbo, ed., *Johnson on Shakespeare*, p. 62.   [62] *Ibid.*, p. 65.
[63] Herder, 'Shakespeare', p. 40.   [64] *Ibid.*, p. 41.   [65] *Ibid.*, p. 41.
[66] Foakes, ed., *Lectures 1808–1819*, II: 293.   [67] *Ibid.*, I: 539.

More characteristic was a crucial feature of much Romantic criticism, the need for criticism itself to be(come) poetic. Friedrich Schlegel was the figure who most theorized this view, as well as being one of the many brilliant critical performers in prose of the period. Here is one of his slogans for this perspective, 'Poetry can only be criticized by way of poetry. A critical judgment of an artistic production has no civil rights in the realm of art if it isn't itself a work of art.'[68]

Schlegel in this spirit praises Goethe's discussion of *Hamlet* in *Wilhelm Meister* because it is 'not so much criticism as high poetry'.[69] He asks, 'what else but a poem can come into being when a poet in full possession of his powers contemplates a work of art and represents it in his own?' This 'poetic criticism' does not arise simply because a critic 'makes suppositions and assertions which go beyond the visible work'; for Schlegel any criticism must do that much, 'because every great work . . . knows more than it says', which the critic therefore must explicate. The key to poetic criticism for Schlegel is rather in its own formal relation to the work being criticized. The analytic procedure of poetic criticism will only divide the whole of the work under discussion into its 'articulated parts and masses', but will 'not break it down into its original constituents', because these raw materials 'in respect of the work are dead things'. Coleridge made a similar point in his description of the secondary imagination, which 'dissolves, diffuses, dissipates, in order to re-create' and in doing so is *vital*, whereas 'all objects (*as* objects) are essentially fixed and dead'.[70] For Schlegel, the 'living unity' of a work of art has transformed the elements it has taken in from 'the universe', so that they should no longer be related back to that first source, but only to the newly organic role they play in the poetic composition. This is a theory of contextual rather than referential criticism, which has strong echoes in the arguments of American New Criticism in the middle twentieth century. But unlike the modest stance of New Critics as servants to the poem, Schlegel was willing to acknowledge the competitive artistic ambitions of the critic, even as the critic honours the work from which the critic's new work is formed.

Friedrich Schlegel was the great activator of the term *Romantic*, and Shakespeare was the great activator of Schlegel's thinking about the Romantic. The term signalled the contrast of modern, vernacular Germanic and romance languages to the ancient, classical languages of Greece and Rome; and of Northern and Christian cultures to Southern and pagan cultures, but an important further dimension of the romantic for Schlegel was also its element of the prosaic, the 'interesting', the 'characteristic', in opposition to the universal purity associated with the classical.

---

[68] Schlegel, *Philosophical fragments*, p. 14.
[69] All Schlegel quotations in this paragraph from 'On Goethe's *Meister*', p. 69.
[70] Bate and Engell, eds., *Biographia literaria*, I: 304.

As early as 1795 in the midst of his essay 'On the study of Greek poetry', the impact of Shakespeare erupts in a way that links it to Schlegel's understanding of the literature of his own time, as represented by Goethe.[71] The 'aesthetic tragedy' accomplished by the Greeks finds its 'complete antithesis' in the more recent 'philosophical tragedy', which is the highest form of 'characteristic' poetry. Although the outcome of philosophical tragedy is tragic, the work as a whole is not cast in this single mode; the 'purity' of aesthetic tragedy contrasts to the 'disharmony' which is the 'truth' of this modern mode. To illustrate this idea of philosophical tragedy, Schlegel cites 'one of the most important documents for the "characteristic" qualities of modern poetry': Hamlet. As against those who praise this work for particular passages, Schlegel asserts its 'coherence'; he emphasizes, however, that the 'basis of this coherence' is not readily evident but lies 'deeply hidden'. Schlegel locates the 'centre of the whole' in 'the character of the hero'. Hamlet's self-division exemplifies the 'most perfect representation of irresolvable discord, which is the true subject of philosophical tragedy'.

Schlegel names Shakespeare as the figure who 'most completely and most strikingly embodies the spirit of modern poetry' and who in crucial respects has 'anticipated the developments of our own age'. These are the features that Schlegel attributes to Shakespeare and to the most important writing of his own age: 'the inexhaustible supply of what is interesting'; the 'intensity of all passions'; the 'inimitable truth of the "characteristic"'; and finally, 'unique originality'. Then Schlegel brings into dialogue with Hamlet the fragment of Faust that Goethe had published in 1790; if it were completed Schlegel thinks it might even surpass Shakespeare. In the next year Goethe's new novel incorporated a discussion of Hamlet considerably in the spirit of Schlegel's own. Goethe's Hamlet interpretation had been in manuscript for at least a decade, showing the extent to which Shakespeare's impact was working across the culture in ways not simply calculable by measures of influence.

In this discussion of Shakespeare, Schlegel's crucial conceptualization is the notion of a whole composed by 'dissonance'. Leading twentieth-century theorists of the novel, schooled in the traditions of German philology and aesthetics that Schlegel did so much to form, include Mikhail Bakhtin and György Lukács, both of whom fundamentally characterize the novel as a form that must deal with, and build itself from, dissonance.[72]

[71] Quotations in this and the next paragraph are taken from Friedrich Schlegel, 'On Hamlet and Faust as philosophical tragedies', translated by Cyrus Hamlin from 'On the study of Greek poesy', in Hamlin's Norton Critical Edition of Johann Wolfgang von Goethe, Faust, New York: Norton, 1976, pp. 435–7.

[72] On Schlegel and Bakhtin, see Tzvetan Todorov, Mikhail Bakhtin: the dialogical principle, Wlad Godzich (trans.), Minneapolis, MN: University of Minnesota Press, 1984, pp. 86–87.

Schlegel, as we have seen, places Shakespeare at the defining centre of what for him was equally the 'modern' and the 'Romantic'. The 'great triple chord of modern poetry', the core of any 'critical anthology of the classics of modern poetry', for Schlegel, would be defined by Dante's 'transcendental poetry', the 'purely poetical poetry' of Goethe, and at the very 'centre of Romantic art', he places 'Shakespeare'.[73] In his *Dialogue on poetry*, Schlegel distinguishes between the work of his own time and that of 'the older moderns', such as Shakespeare and Cervantes. It is these older moderns who are above all Romantic, and it is Shakespeare who forms 'the actual centre, the core of the romantic imagination'.[74] This Romantic imagination includes both the goals of the highest synthesis and also the disruptions of deep irony – the technique corresponding to what Schlegel had earlier called 'dissonance'.

In his 1800 essay of self-reflection, 'On incomprehensibility', Schlegel comments on the modes of irony of his own essays and fragments of the last several years and warns of the self-annihilating spiral of 'the irony of irony'. He asks, 'what gods will rescue us from all these ironies?' but he abandons hope of finding 'an irony that might be able to swallow up all these big and little ironies' and thereby get rid of them. For irony, Schlegel argues, is too serious and complex to be evaded: 'irony is something one simply cannot play games with', and 'it can have incredibly long-lasting after effects'. Even 'hundreds of years after their deaths', the 'most conscious artists' continue to exercise ironical power over their 'followers and admirers'. The only writer mentioned in this discussion of irony is Shakespeare, because he 'has so infinitely many depths, subterfuges, and intentions' that the 'insidious traps in his works' snare the 'cleverest artists of posterity'.[75] Yet the dissonances of irony are themselves part of a project that Schlegel understands as one of totalization: 'The whole history of modern poetry is a running commentary on the following brief philosophical text: all art should become science and all science art; poetry and philosophy should be made one.'[76] It is important to recognize that in German the term translated as 'science' is *Wissenschaft*, which has the sense of 'an organized body of thought and learning' rather than exclusively its usual current English sense of an empirical and mathematical discipline.

On Schlegel and Lukács, see Peter Szondi, *On textual understanding and other essays*, Harvey Mendelson (trans.), Minneapolis, MN: University of Minnesota Press, 1986, pp. 63, 82.
[73] Schlegel, *Philosophical fragments*, p. 52.
[74] Friedrich Schlegel, 'Letter about the novel', in Wheeler (ed.), *German aesthetic and literary criticism*, p. 77.
[75] All quotations up to this point in the paragraph from Friedrich Schlegel, 'On incomprehensibility', in Wheeler, ed., *German Aesthetic and Literary Criticism*, p. 37.
[76] Friedrich Schlegel, *Philosophical fragments*, p. 14.

Schlegel's most quoted text, fragment 116 from the *Athenaeum*, takes as its subject 'Romantic poetry' in its largest sense.[77] The classical is 'perfected' and thus limited, but Romantic poetry is 'infinite' and therefore 'free'. It is the 'only kind of poetry that is more than a kind' – that is, it is the genre that transcends genre because it is both 'progressive' and 'universal', thus going beyond fixity and limitation. In this fragment Schlegel sums up his thoughts from an intensely creative period of theorization, and its terms resonate with those from his discussion of Shakespeare: 'to reunite all the separate species of poetry and put poetry in touch with philosophy and rhetoric', to 'mix and fuse poetry and prose, inspiration and criticism, the poetry of art and the poetry of nature'. This kind of work 'can so lose itself in what it describes that one might believe that it exists only to characterize poetical individuals of all sorts; and yet there is still no form so fit for expressing the entire spirit of an author'. 'Like the epic' it wields large mimetic power; it forms 'a mirror of the whole circumambient world, and image of the age', but its armament of mirrors is multiple. Therefore, Romantic poetry 'more than any other form' can 'hover at the midpoint between the portrayed and the portrayer . . . on the wings of poetic reflection'. This capacity to 'raise that reflection again and again to a higher power', to 'multiply it in an endless succession of mirrors' is, we have seen, the power of irony in which Shakespeare is preeminent.

Schlegel had in mind not only Shakespeare but also the crucial form of his own age, the novel. *Romantische poesie*, 'Romantic poetry', is also 'novelistic poesis'. And so in the midst of Schlegel's *Dialogue on Poetry*, there is interposed a 'Letter on the novel'.[78] This disruption of the play of voices in conversation by a written text mimics the generic crux of the novel. For Schlegel, 'A novel is a "romantic book"'. The self-conscious 'tautology' here ('Ein Roman ist ein romantisches Buch') allows the weight to fall on the material means and its implications. The 'manner of presentation' of a novel will differ from that of drama because it is 'for reading', not for viewing; and in thinking of a book, one thinks of 'a work, an existing whole'. Here Schlegel anticipates the 'rhetorical' basis of Northrop Frye's theory of genre, in which prose 'fiction' is the genre of the written word.[79]

This distinction – the special force of literature in its form as book – was crucial for Coleridge some decades later as he reflected on why so fine a

---

[77] For *Athenaeum* fragment 116, see Schlegel, *Philosophical fragments*, pp. 31–2.
[78] Friedrich Schlegel, 'Letter on the novel', in Wheeler (ed.), *German aesthetic and literary criticism*, quotations in this paragraph from p. 78. The sentence in German comes from Friedrich Schlegel, *Charakteristiken und Kritiken I (1796–1801)*, Hans Eichner (ed.), Munich: Schöningh, 1967, p. 335. This is vol. II of Ernst Behler (ed.), *Kritische Friedrich-Schlegel-Ausgabe*.
[79] Northrop Frye, *Anatomy of criticism: four essays*, Princeton, NJ: Princeton University Press, 1957, esp. pp. 246–8.

critical mind as Ben Jonson had been unable to recognize Shakespeare's greatness so fully as Coleridge thinks he should have. The answer is that Jonson had only the plays, one after another 'as acted', to respond to; only since 1623 have we had the book that allows us to think about the plays in relation to each other and thereby 'to form a just notion of the mighty mind that produced the whole'.[80]

Schlegel argues against those who derive the novel only from epic. Because of its distinctive 'mixture' of various forms, it is rather Shakespearean drama 'which is the true foundation of the novel'.[81] For Schlegel a true theory of the novel 'would have to be itself a novel', and in its pages 'Shakespeare would converse intimately with Cervantes'.[82]

No less than in Schlegel's exemplary case of *Wilhelm Meister*, the 'mediation of [the] great model' of Shakespeare fostered Herman Melville's radically innovative *Moby-Dick*.[83] In the midst of writing *Moby-Dick*, Melville registered a double encounter with literary greatness which, scholars have argued, caused him to reconceive his work in progress at a higher level of ambition and complexity. He had been passionately reading in a recently acquired edition of Shakespeare (now in Harvard's Houghton Library) that had print large enough for his bad eyes.[84] The fruits of this reading mark his letters and found their first printed form in 'Hawthorne and his Mosses' (1850), a review-essay on Nathaniel Hawthorne, to whom *Moby-Dick* was dedicated when it appeared in 1851. Melville's praise of Hawthorne at its highest point is caught up in the web of Romantic writing on Shakespeare. His essay pursues the contrast of stage and page, the need for appreciative interpretation, the sense that Shakespeare does not so much confirm our understanding of life as give us new, particular knowledge. Melville draws especially from his reading of 'The hero as poet' in Thomas Carlyle's *On heroes, hero-worship, and the heroic in history* (1840),[85] a work that culminates some twenty years in which Carlyle had been translating and discussing German works in the hope of transforming his Anglophone audiences.

In the key passage, Melville begins by singling out for praise and attention a feature of Hawthorne now familiar but far less recognized by his

[80] H. J. Jackson and George Whalley (eds.), *Marginalia*, Princeton, NJ: Princeton University Press, 1992, III: 187; volume XII in Kathleen Coburn (ed.), *Collected works of Samuel Taylor Coleridge*.

[81] Wheeler, ed., *German aesthetic and literary criticism*, p. 78.   [82] *Ibid.*, p. 79.

[83] The classic discussion of *Moby-Dick* and Shakespeare is F. O. Matthiessen, *American Renaissance: art and expression in the age of Emerson and Whitman*, Oxford University Press, 1941, pp. 405–67.

[84] His notes are reproduced, with commentary, in *Moby-Dick or the whale*, Harrison Hayford, Hershel Parker and G. Thomas Tanselle (eds.), *Writings of Herman Melville*, Evanston: Northwestern University Press, 1968–, VI: 955–70.

[85] On this connection between Melville and Carlyle, see Jonathan Arac, *Commissioned spirits*, New York: Columbia University Press, 1989, pp. 148–56.

early readers, 'that blackness in Hawthorne'.[86] This 'infinite obscure' in Hawthorne recalls to Melville the example of Shakespeare, who, Melville believes, is admired by theatrical crowds for 'Richard-the-Third humps and Macbeth daggers' but who is valued by 'philosophers' as the 'profoundest of thinkers': 'It is those deep, far-away things in him; those occasional flashings-forth of the intuitive Truth in him; those short, quick probings at the very axis of reality: – these are the things that make Shakespeare, Shakespeare.' Melville invokes the theme of interpretation: 'few of his endless commentators and critics seem to have remembered, or even perceived, that the immediate products of a great mind are not so great, as that undeveloped (and sometimes undevelopable) yet dimly discernible greatness, to which these immediate products are but the infallible indices. In Shakespeare's tomb lies more than Shakespeare ever wrote.'

Melville here closely resumes Carlyle's rhetoric in 'The Hero as Poet'. Because Shakespeare is a force like that of nature, Carlyle writes, his works 'grow up withal *un*consciously from the unknown deeps in him; – as the oak-tree grows from the Earth's bosom'. This comparison allows Carlyle to emphasize 'How much in Shakespeare lies hid; his sorrows, his silent struggles known to himself; much that was not known at all, not speakable at all: like *roots*, like sap and forces working underground!' Carlyle concludes this passage with a sentence that became a commonplace, circulating far more widely than in the criticism of Shakespeare: 'Speech is great; but Silence is greater.'[87]

Through Shakespeare, Melville feels his own powers. To be original, and thus like Shakespeare, is for Melville to be fully human, and thereby also to be not abstractly universal but rather peculiarly national. For 'to write like a man' means that a writer 'will be sure to write like an American'.[88] For Carlyle, too, in 'The hero as poet', an original writer plays a national role: 'it is a great thing for a Nation that it get an articulate voice'.[89]

This topic of Shakespeare and national identity had been part of the Romantic Shakespeare, from Herder on. For the Germans in the later eighteenth century, Shakespeare was a compelling alternative to the previously dominant canons of French neoclassicism (in the aftermath of the English triumph over France in the Seven Years' War), and then in the age of the French Revolutionary wars for both Germany and for Britain Shakespeare played an even larger polemical role as an antithesis to French

---

[86] Herman Melville, 'Hawthorne and his Mosses', in Harrison Hayford and Hershel Parker (eds.), *Moby-Dick*, New York: Norton, 1967. Quotations in this paragraph come from pp. 541–2.

[87] Thomas Carlyle, 'The hero as poet', in D. Nichol Smith (ed.), *Shakespeare criticism: a selection*, Oxford University Press, 1935, p. 409.

[88] Melville, 'Hawthorne and his mosses', p. 546.   [89] Carlyle, 'The hero as poet', p. 416.

culture, as one may see at various moments in Coleridge that are now rather embarrassing. He ended a lecture in 1813 by noting that 'England, justly proud as she had a right to be, of a Shakespear, a Milton, a Bacon, and a Newton, could also boast of a Nelson and a Wellington.'[90] The same valence operated in Russia in the decades after the Napoleonic Wars in which German cultural values – including Shakespeare – prevailed among many of the intelligentsia over the longstanding prestige of French as the culture and language of international politesse. In the United States, Melville made his use of Shakespeare part of his democratic commitment to bring 'republican progressiveness into Literature'.[91]

Shakespeare as a political issue is not at all absent from Romantic criticism, but also not generally integrated within it. Hazlitt was provoked by the open politics of *Coriolanus* to argue that 'the language of poetry naturally falls in with the language of power', because the imagination is a 'monopolising faculty' and therefore 'aristocratic'.[92] This is the 'original sin in poetry'.[93] But he does not carry this extraordinarily challenging claim into relation with his analysis of Shakespeare's selflessly outgoing imagination.

Carlyle, in contrast, is explicitly concerned in *Heroes and hero-worship* with the varying modes in which power may be exercised (heroes have appeared 'as' poet, prophet, priest or king). The modes are not at all fully exchangeable. Carlyle concludes 'The Hero as Poet' with questions of how poetry relates to global politics, of nations in the world. He contrasts Italy to Russia: Italy is politically fragmented but nationally 'bound together' through Dante, while Russia is a vast empire 'which cannot yet speak'.[94] (Carlyle, like most Western intellectuals of his time, was evidently unaware of the work of Pushkin, who had recently died.) Shakespeare, in Carlyle's model, does even more than Dante, for Shakespeare has represented England not simply to itself but to the whole world. Carlyle asks his contemporaries a question that sets cultural power against political power: 'will you give up your Indian Empire, or your Shakespeare?' He argues that the empire in any case 'will go . . . some day', but that Shakespeare 'lasts forever'. (At least, Shakespeare is still very widely taught in Indian schools.[95]) Even after the loss of British political sovereignty over 'America', Shakespeare is unparalleled for his continuing '*in*destructible'

---

[90] Foakes (ed.), *Lectures 1808–19*, I: 546.
[91] Melville, 'Hawthorne and his mosses', p. 543.
[92] William Hazlitt, *Characters of Shakespeare's plays*, London: Bell and Sons, 1909, p. 50.
[93] Hazlitt, 'Letter to William Gifford', p. 423.   [94] Carlyle, 'The hero as poet', p. 416.
[95] See Ania Loomba, *Gender, race, Renaissance drama*, Delhi: Oxford University Press, 1992, p. 10: 'More students probably read *Othello* in the University of Delhi every year than in all British universities combined.'

power as the 'noblest, gentlest, yet strongest of rallying-signs' that gives him cultural 'sovereignty' as 'King Shakespeare'.[96]

The impact of Shakespeare moved Carlyle to imagine culture as a category that may have more power than politics does to organize the way people live with one another. This insight illuminates the Shakespearean inspiration for much of the work done in and since the nineteenth century by novelists, in the 'romantic' genre beyond genre.

---

[96] Carlyle, 'The hero as poet,' pp. 414–15.

14

The vocation of criticism and the crisis of the republic of letters

JON KLANCHER

To whom did the critic speak, and who could occupy the office of 'critic'? This chapter explores the roles of men and women of 'letters' in the Romantic age as a framework for understanding the vocation of Romantic criticism. Until the beginning of the nineteenth century, critics and reviewers of poetry, drama or the novel worked within the wider context of two closely related early modern categories: 'polite literature' and the 'republic of letters'. The crisis of both categories, between 1780 and 1830, produced changes in culture and criticism that would profoundly alter the status of literature itself in the nineteenth and twentieth centuries. 'Polite letters' embraced the genres of historiography, natural philosophy, moral philosophy and political discourse as well as poetry, drama and criticism itself, while significantly excluding the new genre of the novel. Resting on this basis, the early modern idea of a 'republic of letters' defined a territory that existed on no European map – an 'elusive, often deliberately mysterious domain', as Elizabeth Eisenstein remarks – yet shaped the self-understanding of European criticism until the last decade of the eighteenth century.[1]

At that point, the historian's road map to the republic of letters becomes more obscure. By 1800 its authority over the organization of reading and writing seems to have diminished as quickly as Edmund Burke's 'political Men of Letters' were discredited in the French Revolution controversy of the 1790s. Instead of an idealized unity of critical reasoners embedded in modern print culture, the republic of letters became in the Romantic age a confusing clash of those 'sects and systems' that, according to David Hume, the early modern republic had triumphantly suppressed. Instead of the sociability or politeness known to the mid-eighteenth-century republic, ideological dispute and personal attack pervaded literary life. Instead

---

[1] Elizabeth Eisenstein, *The printing revolution in Early Modern Europe*, Cambridge University Press, 1983, p. 99; in this chapter I draw on extensive research into the history of the republic of letters begun by Eisenstein; Dena Goodman, *The republic of letters: a cultural history of the French Enlightenment*, Ithaca, NY: Cornell University Press; Anne Goldgar, *Impolite learning: conduct and community in the republic of letters, 1680–1750*, New Haven, CT: Yale University Press, 1995; Lorraine Daston, 'The ideal and reality of the republic of letters' *Science in context* 4 (1991), pp. 367–91.

of a cosmopolitan discourse, nationalism suffused the languages of criticism. One critical function, 'literature as a calling' or vocation, began to be distinguished from another, 'literature as a trade', and the formerly authoritative 'man of letters' began to be seen as a slavish creature of the market. Theoretical criticism turned away from criticism oriented to a public, while at the same time a newly authoritative 'public opinion' divided the audiences that had formerly seemed to be a single reading public.

Yet even the apparent end of the older bourgeois republic of letters at the turn of the nineteenth century was not the end of those powerful configurations of intellectual or critical identity and practice it generated – as a network or class of scholars; a marketplace of ideas situated in civil society; or a formation of political intellectuals pressing reform or revolution. In the Romantic period these divergent institutionalizations of criticism became unavoidably confrontational as the relation of criticism to its public had to be redefined under new historical and cultural conditions. In this chapter, I first sketch a brief history of the literary republic as early moderns understood it, keeping in mind its peculiar quality as an *illusio* that focussed real practices and relationships. I then look more closely at the Romantic rethinking of critic and public in British and German writings of the turn of the nineteenth century.

I 'Thinking for Ourselves': forms of the republic of letters until 1800

When Samuel Coleridge remarked in 1817 that 'Bacon, Harrington, Machiavel and Spinoza are not read, because Hume, Condillac and Voltaire *are*', he was observing an old, but not well-remembered distinction between the *érudit* and *mondain* epochs of the early modern republic of letters (*Biographia literaria*, in *Works*, VII: 54). As recent historians have reconstructed the distinction, it developed in the seventeenth century as an international network of scholars who corresponded in Latin across the diplomatic channels of Western Europe. These scholars were individually based in academies, learned societies, churches or civil office and contributed vigorously to building the enlightened absolutist states of Louis XIV and Charles II. Encyclopedia frontispieces would depict them in Greek and Roman settings as they invented an ancient history for themselves and joined a classicist 'tradition' to the power of the early modern authoritarian state. Meanwhile they formed a public among themselves, exchanging letters within a circle of the learned.[2]

[2] Paul Dibon, 'Communication in the respublica literaria of the seventeenth century' *Res publica litterarum* 1 (1978), pp. 43–9; Martin Ultee, 'The republic of letters: learned correspondence, 1680–1720', *Seventeenth century* 2 (January 1987), pp. 78–98.

Between 1683 and 1720, the Quarrel of Ancients and Moderns marked the opening of the communicational network to new markets for print.[3] According to Pierre Bayle's influential definition, the modernized republic emerging in the 1680s and 90s distinguished itself as a state-within-a-state whose members were free from attachment to any existing institutions of power, building an 'empire of truth and reason' through publication. Intellectual war was to be waged by anybody against anybody, while 'everyone is both ruler and subject of everyone else'.[4] Locally Hobbesian but globally Cartesian – fighting one another at home, we reason together abroad – Bayle's literary republic would proclaim its autonomy from Europe's post-Reformation institutions of state or academy by forging a new power network among the publishing houses, periodicals, coffee-houses, and salons of early eighteenth-century Britain and France and late eighteenth-century Berlin.[5] The republic of letters would now address a far wider reading public than the circle of scholars who earlier corresponded by letter.

The most provocative new idea was that nearly anyone could be a critic. Jean Baptiste Dubos spoke for many others in *Reflexions critiques sur la poésie et sur la peinture* (1719) when he insisted, 'one can read the work for oneself, just as thousands of others have done'.[6] In England the Third Earl of Shaftesbury celebrated 'that reigning liberty and high spirit of a people, which arises from the habit of judging in the highest matters for themselves'.[7] The principle of 'thinking for ourselves' seemed to make it unnecessary to depend upon formal institutions or literary rules. 'Rules and formulas', Kant reminded German literary republicans sixty-five years later, are the 'shackles of a permanent immaturity'.[8] Long before Kant defined philosophical critique as the courage to free oneself from the

---

[3] Joan DeJean *Ancients against moderns: culture wars and the making of a fin de siècle*, Chicago, IL: Chicago University Press, 1997; Joseph M. Levine, *The battle of the books: history and literature in the Augustan age*, Princeton, NJ: Princeton University Press, 1991.

[4] Goldgar, *Impolite learning*, p. 161; Goodman, *Republic of letters*, p. 10; Pierre Bourdieu, *The field of cultural production*, Richard Nice (trans.), Stanford, CA: Stanford University Press, 1993, p. 163.

[5] Michael Mann, *The sources of social power*, Cambridge University Press, 1986, II: 35–41; see also, on the modern and ancient men of letters, Jerome Christensen, *Practicing Enlightenment: Hume and the formation of a literary career* (Madison, WI: University of Wisconsin Press), pp. 125–7; Goodman, *Republic of letters*, ch. 1.

[6] Quoted in Klaus Berghahn, 'From Classicist to Classical literary criticism, 1730–1806', John R. Blazer (trans.) in *A history of German literary criticism*, Peter Uwe Hohendahl (ed.), Lincoln, NE: University of Nebraska Press, 1988, p. 42.

[7] Barrell cites Shaftesbury's notion of 'judging in the highest matters for themselves' the cornerstone of the 'discourse of civic humanism', but it seems to have been common to French critics like Bayle and Du Bos who had not adopted this Florentine language of civic virtue, and it persisted through all later liberal or 'commercial' forms of the literary republic as well; John Barrell, *Political theory of painting from Reynolds to Hazlitt: 'the body of the public'*, New Haven, CT: Yale University Press, 1986, p. 34.

[8] I. Kant, 'What is enlightenment?' 1784, in Ted Humphrey (trans.), *Perpetual peace and other essays*, Indianapolis, IN: Hackett, 1983, p. 41.

tutelage of tradition, advocates of literary modernity were urging writers and readers to 'think for themselves' even as they jostled for position and distinction within the literary republic. Connected across distant locales and conditions, the republic encompassed the emergent institutions of civil society – from the publishing houses to the salons and philosophical societies – without being fully contained by any of them. In 1775 Chrétien Malesherbes marked the key distinction for France: 'What the orators of Rome and Athens were, in the midst of a people *assembled*, men of letters are in the midst of a *dispersed* people.'[9] The *Gelehrtenrepublik* gathered the far-flung German-speaking territories into a virtual nation, according to Friedrich Nicolai, a leader of the German Enlightenment and longtime editor of the *Allgemeine deutsche Bibliothek* (1765–1806).[10] In London, as William Hazlitt would later remark, 'we have a sort of abstract existence; and a community of ideas and knowledge (rather than local proximity) is the bond of society and good fellowship' ('On Londoners and country people', *Writings*, XII: 77).

Unlike the phrase 'polite literature' – whose very terms signified the educational level and social privilege that restricted access to literary culture – the language of the 'republic of letters' claimed inclusiveness. In 1699 Bonaventure d'Argonne claimed that it was 'composed of all nationalities, all social classes, all ages, and both sexes'.[11] Actually, it was stationed mostly in France, Holland, Britain and Germany, and except for artisans who worked the printing presses, its social composition was confined to aristocratic and middle-class writers and readers. In his later world of commercialized letters, political dissent and female authorship, Coleridge would memorialize the seventeenth-century republicans of letters as 'masculine intellects, formed under the robust discipline of an age memorable for keenness of research, and iron industry!' (*Statesman's Manual*, 1816, *Works*, VI: 107–8). Yet however, the *querelle des anciens et des modernes* seems itself to have been stimulated, at least in part, by the growth of prose fiction and its audience of women in the 1670s and 80s, who provoked ancients like Nicolas Boileau to defend 'masculine intellects' against the *précieuses* (DeJean, *Ancients against moderns*, pp. 24–36). Recent cultural historians of print have also shown a significant participation of women in the salons and discussion circles of Louis XIV in the mid-seventeenth century, and by the mid-eighteenth century a female-defined politeness and 'politics of sociability' suffused the literary republic of the

---

[9] Quoted in Eisenstein, *Printing revolution*, p. 94.
[10] Hans Erich Bodeker, 'Journals and public opinion: the politicization of the German Enlightenment in the second half of the eighteenth century', in Eckhart Hellmuth (ed.), *The transformation of political culture: England and Germany in the late eighteenth century*, Oxford University Press, 1990, p. 424.
[11] Writing as M. de Vigneul-Marville, *Mélanges d'histoire et de littérature*, cited in Dibon, 'Communication in the respublica literaria', p. 43.

Paris salons.[12] Still, despite governing the salons with a mixed-gender conversation between female *salonnières* and male literary talkers, women rarely had the chance to voice their critical opinions in print and found 'going public' fraught with obstacles.[13]

The imagined commonwealth called the 'republic of letters' thus fashioned a rhetoric of community that increasingly played against its actual contradictions and exclusions. Cosmopolitan ethics forestalled ethnic and religious particularisms across Europe. Friedrich Gottlieb Klopstock suggested without irony in *Die deutsche Gelehrtenrepublik* (1774) that the republic's own commitment to reason was a 'true religion', unifying Jews, Moslems, Protestants, Catholics and pagans.[14] 'Our connection with each other, as men of letters', David Hume commented similarly, 'is greater than our difference as adhering to different sects or systems'.[15] The militant language of Bayle's *Dictionary* soon became Hume's politely phrased account of how the natural and moral philosophers of the literary republic achieved ends no one had foreseen as 'the united judgments of men correct and confirm each other by communication'. Likewise, the network of personal connection seemed to supersede the division of labour and the inflections of social class. To be a man of letters was to take a local or particular problem as a universal one, and thereby to write as a generalist beyond the local idiolects of occupation – in Samuel Johnson's version, against limitations of 'the sailor, the academick, the lawyer, the mechanick, and the courtier', who 'have all a cast of talk peculiar to their own fraternity'.[16]

Generalizing across boundaries of social class and profession, the man of letters learned to forge a broad, 'common' vocabulary, often by resisting the coterie or professional languages emerging among the new knowledges and vocations of the eighteenth century (Christensen, *Practicing Enlightenment*, pp. 6, 178). In the new London literary reviews of mid-century, the *Monthly review* (started 1749) and *Critical review* (started 1756), Johnson, Hume and other generalists competed with unknown

---

[12] Goodman, *Republic of letters*, pp. 5–7; a broader picture of women's participation in the seventeenth- and eighteenth-century versions of the literary republic appears in Elizabeth Goldsmith and Dena Goodman (eds.), *Going public: women and publishing in Early Modern France*, Ithaca, NY: Cornell University Press, 1995, pp. 1–12.

[13] Timothy J. Reiss, *The meaning of literature*, Ithaca, NY: Cornell University Press, 1992, pp. 192–225; Goldsmith and Goodman, *Going public*, p. 6; see also Folger Collective, *Women critics 1660–1820*.

[14] Max Kirchstein, *Klopstocks deutsche Gelehrtenrepublik*, Berlin: Walter de Gruyter, 1928.

[15] *The letters of David Hume*, J. Y. T. Greig (ed.), Oxford, 1932, I: 172–3.

[16] Johnson, *The idler*, no. 70, in W. J. Bate *et al.* (eds.), *The Yale edition of the works of Samuel Johnson*, New Haven, CT: Yale University Press, 1958–, II: 217–20; *The rambler*, no. 99, in *Works*, IV: 166–9.

but prolific scholars who reported the newest researches of natural philosophy, historiography, moral philosophy and philology. Such reviewing journals also stimulated a fourfold increase in British book publication by the end of the century.[17] Meanwhile, the older Battle of the Books became a 'battle of the booksellers' as the new literary productivity crystallized a long-unresolved question of intellectual property rights: in 1774 the *Donaldson v. Beckett* decision cancelled the publishers' copyright-in-perpetuity in favour of a fourteen-year term. Many writers lauded the decision as a stimulus to the literary republic's principle of the 'encouragement of learning' and dissemination of ideas, since it seemed to diminish a publisher's monopoly over their work.[18] Yet the decision soon opened the publishers' coffers to the lucrative cheap-reprint market that flourished over the next half-century, while inducing among men of letters a new anxiety about authorship and status in the culture of print.[19] Notions of 'originality' and 'genius' would increasingly become rationales for authors' demands to extend copyright protection to the writer's lifetime and beyond.

In this and other ways, the commercialization of authorship and intensified competition among the specializing knowledge-producers seemed increasingly to erode the stability of Bayle's urbane literary republic. 'Instead of being stiled a republic of letters', Oliver Goldsmith's Citizen of the World complained in 1760, it should be called 'an anarchy of literature' where 'every member of this fancied republic is desirous of governing, and none willing to obey'. In *An enquiry into polite learning*, Goldsmith cited a crisis in the ancient republic of learning that began when Roman writers, 'destitute of experiment, had recourse to theory, and gave up what was useful for refinement'. As in the ancient world, the new expertise being transmitted by the *Monthly* or *Critical* reviewers now seemed likely to undermine 'civil society' and even political authority in London: 'the authors I refer to, are not only for disuniting society, but kingdoms also'.[20]

---

[17] For the controversy over paid authorship, see Linda Zionkowski, 'Territorial disputes in the republic of letters: canon formation and the literary profession', *The eighteenth century: theory and interpretation* 31 (1990), pp. 3–22.

[18] As Johnson put it, 'whatever valuable work has once been created by an author, and issued out by him, should be understood as no longer in his power, but as belonging to the publick'. Cited in Mark Rose, *Authors and owners: the invention of copyright*, Cambridge, MA: Harvard University Press, 1993, p. 85; see also John Feather, *Publishing, piracy, and politics: an historical study of copyright in Britain*, London: Mansell, 1994, p. 122.

[19] On the opportunity for new kinds of canon-formation as formerly copyrighted works were now opened to anthologies like John Bell's *The poets of Great Britain*, see also Thomas Bonnell, 'Bookselling and canon-making: the trade rivalry over the English poets, 1776–83', *Studies in eighteenth-century culture* 19 (1989), pp. 53–69.

[20] Goldsmith, *Citizen of the world* (1760) in *Works*, II: 86; *Enquiry into polite learning* (1759) in *Works*, I: 265–7.

The difference between the polite, generalizing men of letters Goldsmith longed to join in England and the new specialists of the periodicals became more pronounced among the descendants of the *Encyclopédie* in France. Instead of Bayle's war-of-anyone-against-anyone, Louis-Sébastien Mercier would speak of waging 'the liveliest war between the *gens de lettres* and *les grands*' and observed that literary republicans were becoming, by 1778, 'a substitute for the magistracy, forming the national spirit and directing national ideas'.[21] 'National ideas' would translate most precisely as the new meaning of 'public opinion' that cultural historians now attribute to the more aggressive republic of letters emerging after 1770 in France and after 1780 in England and Germany. The term *republic* itself began to admit political self-definitions reaching far beyond the boundaries of the polite literary sphere and its origins in the city-state. The cosmopolitan rhetoric of the literary world would harbour emergent and eventually explosive nationalisms across the metropoles of Paris, London, Berlin and elsewhere by the end of the eighteenth century, as European maps were redrawn to represent transformed republics, entrenched monarchies, new-born nations and timeless 'peoples'.

II   Critical 'sects and systems' in Britain, 1790–1800

The 'political Men of Letters' attacked by Edmund Burke in 1790 thus belonged to a third incarnation of the literary republic – if we periodize this history somewhat schematically – following the *respublica*'s closed network of scholars and the urbane commercial republic's polite 'market-place of ideas'. Where David Hume had enjoyed the intricate connections among men of letters across vast distances, Edmund Burke was seeing himself marooned among the 'sects and systems' that had, in fact, always been a distinct possibility in the literary republic as defined by the moderns around 1700. No longer marketing ideas or fighting *corpo a corpo*, the new political men (and in Britain, women) of letters were acting together 'as a body', according to Burke, as theorists and agents of a new kind of movement spreading 'a kind of electrick communication everywhere'.[22] Against them, Burke defended the polite mid-eighteenth-century literary republic he had shared with Johnson, Hume and Adam Smith. But he replaced its cosmopolitanism with a frankly nativist and familial discourse

---

[21] Quoted in Goodman, *Republic of letters*, p. 239.
[22] Edmund Burke, *Reflections on the Revolution in France*, Conor Cruise O'Brien (ed.), Baltimore, MD: Penguin Books 1969, p. 213; see also Tom Furniss, *Edmund Burke's aesthetic ideology: language, gender, and political economy in revolution*, Cambridge University Press, 1993, pp. 251–260.

on inheritance and transmission. The 'nation is a moral essence', he insisted, detailing its slow, insensible, unplanned formation through the history of its prejudices and habits.[23]

The literary reformers of the 1780s and 90s forged a historicizing relation to the early modern republic as they attempted to recharter its most fundamental claim. Thomas Christie cast his contributors to the *Analytical review* (1788) as retrospective 'HISTORIANS of the republic of letters', a phrase which partly meant returning to the first principles of the modernizing Republic as Jean le Clerc (publisher of *Bibliothèque universelle et historique*) and Michel de la Roche (publisher of *Mémoires de littérature*) had once represented it. 'While they gave their own opinions of books', Christie reminded readers, they 'did not lose sight of the necessity of enabling their readers to judge for themselves'. The Rational Dissenters writing for the *Analytical* fused the original mission of the republic of letters with a new sense of 'public opinion' defined as a normative, not capricious, popular judgment of broad political questions. 'A People Are Free', ran the motto to Samuel Coleridge's radical newspaper *The watchman* (1796), 'in Proportion as They Form Their Own Opinion'. In the early 1790s all four leading literary reviews in Britain were being edited by Dissenters, making any appeal to some earlier institutionalisation of the Republic a political gesture in its own right.[24]

Yet the claim to 'think for ourselves' could also mask the failures of the literary republic. On the one hand, Thomas Paine in *The rights of man* (1791–2) based the reformers' political arguments for natural rights and 'wise laws' on the republic of letters' guarantee of 'giving to genius a fair and universal chance'.[25] 'An hereditary governer is as inconsistent as an hereditary author', he reminded readers of Burke. According to Mary Wollstonecraft's *Vindication of the rights of woman* (1792) or Mary Hays's *Letters and essays* (1793), however, there was no such thing as a 'fair and universal chance' for women writers in the republic of letters, since women had been, with rare exceptions, tacitly or overtly excluded from access to its means of critical production. Wollstonecraft named the category of 'polite literature' as the discourse to which women must be extended access by means of reforming the system of British education.[26]

The widening reach of the British novel also underscored the exclusiveness of a 'republic of letters' whose constituency was still being trumpeted

[23] Cited in David Simpson, *Romanticism, nationalism, and the revolt against theory*, Chicago, IL: University of Chicago Press, 1993, p. 178.

[24] Coleridge, *The watchman*, 1795, in *Works*, I: 4; for a far more detailed study of the tensions in the literary republic in the 1790s, see Paul Keen, 'Whispers in the state: Romanticism and the public sphere', diss. University of York, 1996.

[25] Thomas Paine, *The rights of man*, Harmondsworth: Penguin, 1982, pp. 198, 171.

[26] Wollstonecraft, *Vindication*, chaps. 4, 12; Mary Hays, *Letters and essays, moral and miscellaneous*, London: T. Knott, 1793, p. 26.

by Isaac D'Israeli in 1791 as composed of all social classes and both sexes.[27] William Godwin made the republic of letters a necessary yet insufficient condition to a fair and universal state in *An enquiry concerning political justice* (1793). He argued that even if 'truth' is 'struck out by the collision of mind against mind' in the Baylesian literary republic, its central category of 'literature', founded on the truth-claims of Locke and Newton, nevertheless 'exists only as the portion of the few'.[28] The legitimacy of public opinion as a vast tribunal of truth and justice put in question the public's access to the kind of educated cultural capital previously defined as the many discursive genres of 'literature'. Godwin's novel *Things as they are; or the adventures of Caleb Williams* (1794) advanced arguments for political justice to popular audiences well beyond the republic of letters, within which the novel still had no literary status.

In 1810, Anna Barbauld extended the critique of 'polite letters' to a new form of literary history in her 'Origin and progress of novel-writing', an introduction to a 50-volume edition of *British novelists*. Barbauld showed that fictional narratives had appeared everywhere in the history of 'polite literature' – in epics, romances, satires and moral fables – until the modern age of novels. Thereby she challenged the criteria for judging genres within 'polite literature', not by suggesting the novel was more poetic than usually supposed, but by tracing its complex kinship to historiographic and encyclopaedist discourses of knowledge. Eighteen of the forty novelists she anthologized in this edition were women.[29]

From 1790 to 1830, as questions of right, law and justice made 'public opinion' the currency of all sides in fractious cultural debates,[30] the ambiguities of the crucial category of 'republic' became unavoidable. Its anti-absolutist meaning – power 'lodged in more than one', according to the *Monthly magazine* for July 1796 – no longer answered the immediate questions: how many more than 'one'? Few? Some? All? 'Aristocratical, representative, or democratical'?[31] An 'opinion' that had formerly belonged to the literary-critical republic now confronted a 'public opinion' recognized as authoritative by Parliament, king, tailor and plebeian reformer. A division emerged between the established market of 'taste-criticism' promoted by the reviewing organs and the newly defined market of what

---

[27] D'Israeli, *Curiosities of literature*, London: Murray, 1791, pp. 3–6.
[28] William Godwin, *An enquiry concerning political justice*, London: Robinson, 1793, I: 22.
[29] Anna Letitia Barbauld, 'On the origin and progress of novel-writing', in *The British novelists*, I: 1–8.
[30] For a detailed picture of the rise of 'public opinion' after 1800, see Drohr Wahrman, 'Public opinion, violence and the limits of constitutional politics', in *Re-reading the constitution: new narratives in the political history of England's long nineteenth century*, James Vernon (ed.), Cambridge University Press, 1996, pp. 83–122.
[31] J[ohn] A[ikin], 'On the words republic and commonwealth', *Monthly magazine* 1 (April 1796), pp. 179–81.

might be called 'criticism for critics', a theoretical criticism that takes criticism itself as its object. It would be here that 'literature' in the new, restricted sense of the imaginative genres was to be formulated long before it would be recognized by the leading reviews and magazines, in Britain, by the 1820s.[32]

At the same time, the older claim of the literary republic to independence from established power (as 'state within-a-state') became severely strained. We can measure this strain by a simple test – after 1800 it is extremely difficult to find any positive defences of a 'republic of letters' by Britain's men and women of letters, and certainly none of the kind often printed or republished throughout the eighteenth century. Instead of such defences, we find emerging after 1798 those striking Romantic formulations of a community of writers and readers, emphasizing new kinds of intensive intellectual, literary and political exchange. Though literary history has generally understood Romantic reformulations of reading and writing as opposing the established eighteenth-century sphere of polite and professional letters, the most famous versions suggest rather an attempt to reinvent the original face-to-face character of a 'literary republic'.[33] Imagine England 'divided into forty republics', Shelley proposed, each the size of a city-state like Athens: 'each would produce philosophers and poets equal to those who (if we except Shakespeare) have never been surpassed . . . the companions and forerunners of some unimagined change in our social condition or the opinions which cement it'.[34] Wordsworth's ideal of a 'man speaking to men' in Preface to *Lyrical ballads* refashioned the poet–audience relation according to the norms of modern prose, the *lingua franca* of the republic of letters, rather than by bardic or other standards proper to a more insular history of poetry. Even Keats's slogan of a 'negative capability', meant as a criticism of Wordsworth's own authorial egoism, resisted the new authority vested in professional authorship by dispersing that subject-position into multiplicity and echo. In another form, the republic of letters persisted in microcosm as what Raymond Williams called a 'cultural formation' – a 'Shelley circle', a 'Wordsworth circle', or in Germany (as the next section will show) a Jena circle (Williams, *Marxism*, pp. 117–20). Such circles – close-knit groupings of writers who practised and crossed many genres while struggling to redefine the relation of politics and literariness – would accentuate the intimacy of the old

---

[32] On the transformation of 'polite letters' into the more restricted category of imaginative 'literature', see Reiss, *Meaning of literature*, pp. 182–85, 227–33, 338–47; John Guillory, *Cultural capital: the problem of literary canon formation*, Chicago, IL: University of Chicago Press, 1993, pp. 121–3; Raymond Williams, *Marxism and literature*, Oxford University Press, 1977, pp. 46–7.

[33] The classic example is Abrams, *The mirror and the lamp*.

[34] Shelley, 'Preface to *Prometheus unbound*' in E. B. Murray (ed.), *The prose works of Percy Bysshe Shelley*, Oxford: Clarendon, 1993, p. 328.

literary republic while defining Romanticism itself as resisting the divisive, differentiating forces of modernity.

III The 'vocation' of criticism in early German Romanticism, 1797–1806

The German literary republic Coleridge found in 1798 was more weakly commercialized than Britain's and more stiffly institutional. The *Popular-philosophen* of the belated Berlin Enlightenment had launched public reviewing journals in the 1760s to expand the scope of Germany's vanishingly small *Gelehrtenrepublik*, which Friedrich Nicolai estimated at only 20,000 among a population of twenty million. The new journals, led by Nicolai's *Allgemeine deutsche Bibliothek* (1765–1806), generated an increase in annual German book production from 755 titles in 1740 to 2,569 in 1800 – about a quarter of Britain's output in both years.[35] In the enlightened absolutist state of Frederick II, the *Gelehrtenrepublik's* frankly paternalist reviewers were determined to tell readers what to think and campaigned to bind scientific and literary instruction to good citizenship (Berghahn, 'From Classicist to Classical', pp. 23, 64–8). Their pedantic criticism favoured a rule-governed poetics and Wolffian aesthetic philosophy, to which Nicolai devoted fully a quarter of his articles.

Responding to its authoritarian character, Kant's essay 'What is enlightenment?' (1784) provocatively introduced Horace's motto 'Have the courage to think for yourselves!' [*Sapere aude*!] as the first principle of modernity's international republic of letters. Perhaps Kant's most far-reaching claim was that reasoned debate on public matters is grounded within, but also necessarily surpasses, the boundaries of the *Gelehrtenrepublik*: all those who emerged from private life and addressed the public '*in the role* of the scholar' and before 'the entire literate world' were using their reason and thereby learning to think for themselves. The civil servant could adopt the 'role of the scholar' to speak publicly about the most universal matters

---

[35] Rolf Engelsing, *Analphabetentum und Lektüre: Zur Sozialgeschichte des Lesens in Deutschland zwischen feudaler und industrieller Gesellschaft*, Stuttgart: Metzler, 1973, pp. 53–89; W. H. Bruford, 'The profession of letters' in *Germany in the eighteenth century: the social background of the literary revival*, Cambridge University Press, 1959; Bodecker pp. 427–29; Herbert Rowland and Karl J. Fink, *The eighteenth century German book review*, Heidelberg: C. Winter, 1995. For British book production in the same years, see James Raven, *Judging new wealth: popular publishing and responses to commerce in England, 1750–1800*, Oxford University Press, 1992. The Berlin reviews included Christoph Martin Wieland's *Der teutsche Merkur* (1773–1810), A. L. von Schlozer's *Briefwechsel* (1776–82), Johann Erich Biester's *Berlinische Monatsschrift*, (1783–1811), Christian Gottlob Heyne's *Göttinger gelehrte Anzeigen* and others that achieved circulations of 1,200 to 2,000 per month (compared to the *Monthly review*'s circulation of 6,500–8,000).

even while he could not dare to speak freely in his private capacity as employee. Though far from democratic, Kant's 'public sphere' nonetheless opened the 'age of criticism' to a potentially volatile dialogue.[36] Johann Gottlieb Fichte adopted and radicalized Kant's conception of a critical public in his popularizing lectures on the vocation of the scholar at the University of Jena. As the reforming *Analytical* reviewers had attempted to do for a commercial public in England, Fichte used his 1794 'Lectures on the Vocation of the Scholar' to challenge the norms of the *Gelehrtenrepublik*, redefining the scholar–critic as 'educator of the human race' who could show a public how to learn for itself.[37] The meaning of *Gelehrter* shifted in these lectures in two directions at once: toward its broadest meanings of 'educated person', yet also toward a highly specialized 'scholar', leaving Berlin *Aufklärer* like Friedrich Nicolai in the excluded middle (Fichte, *Early philosophical writings*, p. 141).

Following his political expulsion from Jena in 1799, Fichte's 1805 lectures at Erlangen on the scholar's vocation, *Über das Wesen des Gelehrten*, pointedly contrasted the commercial reviewing market and the redefined 'vocation' of the critical scholar. His defence of a 'literary calling' against a 'literary trade' responded most immediately to the intensifying commercialization of the literary marketplace that reviews like Nicolai's *Bibliothek* had long been catering.[38] But another, apparently unrelated Fichtean distinction between the 'productive' critical scholar and the merely 'reproductive' traditional scholar in the university also depended on the notion of a commodifying of writing. So Fichte's lectures contrasted scholars of genuine innovative intellectual production to scholars merely engaged in cultural transmission. The critical scholar 'must not conceive of scientific knowledge in a merely historical fashion, only as it is received from others; he must have worked through it ideally and for himself . . . and produce in it a self-creative, new and hitherto unknown form' (p. 216).[39] Fichte's lectures effectively identified the traditional routines of the German university to the consumption habits of the commercial *Gelehrtenrepublik* outside

---

[36] Kant, 'What is enlightenment?' in *Perpetual peace*, p. 42; see also Jürgen Habermas, *The structural transformation of the public sphere: an inquiry into a category of bourgeois society*, Thomas Burger (trans.), Cambridge MA: The MIT Press, 1989, p. 105. On Kant's critique of the Berlin Enlightenment's authoritarianism, see John Christian Laursen, 'The subversive Kant: the vocabulary of "public" and "publicity" ', in James Schmidt (ed.), *What is enlightenment? Eighteenth-century answers and twentieth-century questions*, Berkeley, CA: University of California Press, 1996, pp. 253–69.

[37] Johann Gottlieb Fichte, 'Some lectures concerning the scholar's vocation' (1794) in Daniel Breazeale (ed.), *Fichte: early philosophical writings*, Ithaca, NY: Cornell University Press, p. 146; See also Frederick Beiser, *The fate of reason: German philosophy from Kant to Fichte*, Cambridge, MA: Harvard University Press, 1987, pp. 63, 75–76.

[38] Fichte, 'On the nature of the scholar' (1805) in David Simpson, *Origins of modern critical thought*, Cambridge University Press, 1988, p. 216.

[39] On the Kantian origin of this distinction between 'productive' and 'reproductive' knowledge, see Engell, *Creative imagination*, pp. 130–6.

it – the received canon of learning as a commodification of knowledge. The price of this insight, it would now seem, was that Fichte's 1805 lectures also seem to have diminished the range of the scholar's vocation by absolutizing its productive character. The critical scholar does not meet any particular audience of students, but must produce his audience from whole cloth: 'He has no specific reader in view; he forms his reader, and lays down to him the law which he must obey.' In effect, Fichte was replacing the critical principle of 'thinking for ourselves' with the newly defined disciplinary 'vocation' of the scholar, a 'calling' rather than the 'trade' he associated with the popularizing Berlin *Aufklärung*, a mode of scholarly 'production' rather than the academic transmission practised by the traditionalists at Jena.[40]

Such concepts of 'vocation' and 'production' led Fichte toward proposals for the restructuring of the academic *Gelehrtenrepublik* into modern disciplines. But central to his thinking was the reformation of public reading. In his popular lectures *Characteristics of the present age* (1806), he dramatically announces that 'the scientific effort of the Age' – to equip everyone to think for himself – 'has destroyed itself' by means of the very power of print culture that had promoted it. He describes the spiral of authority by which writers first rose to power over readers in the early, classicist republic of Johann Gottsched and then the 'critic species' came to command authority over writers in the republic of Friedrich Nicolai. With this decisive step, the capacity to 'think for oneself' has disappeared into the print-driven 'reading mania' of the present German literary republic. Fichte's answer was to reserve the reader's power to think for himself for the reading of Science, while surrendering himself to the aesthetic pleasure of the Literary work without recourse to the 'common theories' of literary and art criticism. Fichte eliminated poetics, genre theory, ethical analysis or any other mode of a recognizable literary theory in a strike against the poetics-dominated agenda of Nicolai's print enlightenment ('The scientific condition of the third age', *Characteristics*, p. 146). A year after these lectures, Napoleon invaded Jena, and Fichte turned the impasse of the *Gelehrtenrepublik* into the programme of German education, and the most influentially programmatic outline of modern nationalism, in *Addresses to the German nation* in 1808.

From Kant to Fichte, Friedrich Schiller and the early German Romantics, the various critiques of the Berlin Enlightenment all moved toward one or another version of distinguishing imaginative literature and criticism (as well as science) as 'autonomous'. Schiller clashed repeatedly with

---

[40] On Fichte's role in educational reform more broadly, see also Elinor S. Shaffer, 'Romantic philosophy and the organization of the disciplines: the founding of the Humboldt University of Berlin', in *Romanticism and the sciences*, Andrew Cunningham and Nicholas Jardine (eds.), Cambridge University Press, 1990, pp. 45–7.

Nicolai and other *Aufklärer* as effectively denying sensuous and communicative freedom. His *Letters on the aesthetic education of man* (1794) elaborately aligned the enlightened–despotic critics with the law-decreeing 'formal drive' which prevented the coming-to-consciousness of human sensuality in the aesthetic 'play' of spirit and matter. Schiller wanted his journal *Die Horen* (1795–7), whose contributors included Goethe, Fichte, Friedrich Schlegel and Wilhelm von Humboldt, to replace Nicolai's widely dispersed public with a focussed intellectual model of intensive critical exchange; Nicolai himself attacked the journal as too scholastic and self-absorbed to impress its style of critical inquiry on the general audience (Berghahn, 'From Classicist to Classical', pp. 91, 69). Meanwhile, Friedrich and August Schlegel, who were early colleagues and admirers of Fichte, began rethinking the function of criticism as a more reflexive, open-ended kind of discourse. They mounted a new journal at Jena, the *Athenaeum* (1798–1800), developing a collective, 'sympoetic' community of scholars and poets: Friedrich Schelling, Dorothea Veit-Schlegel and Caroline Schlegel-Schelling, Friedrich Schleiermacher, Ludwig Tieck, Wilhelm von Humboldt and Novalis, that would powerfully redefine the cultural meanings of a literary 'republic'.[41]

To the Berlin *Aufklärung*'s authoritarian idea of the function of criticism – 'to educate one's readers' – Friedrich Schlegel curtly answered, 'Whoever wants to be educated, let him educate himself' (*Philosophical fragments*, p. 10). This fragment, as dismissive as it sounds, essentially restated the premise of the British and French republics of letters against the top–down programmes of Germany's paternalist criticism. Earlier than Fichte, Schlegel criticized the quantifying and commodifying of the 'public' in the programmes of the Berlin reviewers, who 'speak of the public as if it were someone with whom they have had dinner at the Leipzig Fair in the Hotel de Saxe'. Schlegel responded, with considerable ambiguity, 'The public is not a thing [*res*] but rather an idea, a postulate, like the Church.' Instead of measurable empirical figures, Schlegel argued, the notions of 'Author and Public' could well be redefined as 'literary concepts', or positions constructed through texts within a field of literary and political relations.[42] Nothing more clearly expressed this aim than Lyceum fragment 112:

the analytic writer observes the reader as he is; and accordingly he makes his calculations and sets up his machines in order to make the proper impression on him. [But] the synthetic writer constructs and creates a reader as he should be;

---

[41] Schlegel, 'The concept of republicanism' in F. Beiser (ed.), *Early political writings of the German Romantics*, Cambridge University Press, 1996, pp. 95–112.

[42] Schlegel, Philological fragment 155, in Jochen Schulte-Sasse *et al.* (ed.), *Theory as practice: a critical anthology of early German Romantic writings*, Minneapolis, MN: University of Minnesota Press, 1997, p. 353.

he doesn't imagine him calm and dead, but alive and critical. He allows whatever he has created to take shape gradually before the reader's eyes, or else he tempts him to discover it for himself. He doesn't try to make any particular impression on him, but enters with him into the sacred relationship of deepest symphilosophy or sympoetry.   (*Philosophical fragments*, p. 14)

Thus did Schlegel define a 'sympoetic' or 'symphilosophic' ideal of a community of critical readers and writers. The hybridized poetic–philosophical discourse of the *Athenaeum* group might be understood as a short-lived but in the long run a powerfully suggestive effort to reinvent the early, cellular form of the republic of letters where 'everyone is a critic' and thinks for himself or herself. Next to this mixed-gender enclave, where Dorothea and Caroline Schlegel participated in the salon at Jena, the 'old-hat Berlin Enlightenment' appeared masculinist.[43] The 'vocation' of criticism was to merge criticism with poetical production – 'to penetrate the essence of poiesy', in Lacoue-Labarthe's words – by dissociating criticism from summary evaluation and stimulating 'active and critical' readers again to 'think for themselves'. All across Schlegel's 1797 and 1798 critical fragments is the idea that literature is theory and theory a kind of literature: in a famous phrase, 'the theory of the novel must itself be a novel'. The resulting critical procedure was not transcendent – speaking from above the texts under commentary – but immanent, arising from within the object of criticism. For author and public alike, 'Reading is freeing the bound spirit, in other words, a magic action.' This mode of reading made the true critic reflexive, 'an author to the second power'.[44]

Where Fichte's response to the existing academic and commercial *Aufklärung* pointed toward the departments and disciplines of a new university, accentuating the sciences, Schlegel's thinking bisected the original republic of letters. One part was the broad field of 'taste criticism' where the general critic or 'man of letters' continued to be preoccupied with tastes, 'standards', effects and markets as he mediated works to publics; the other part was a restricted field of theoretical authorship 'to the second power'. It was as if the form of the earlier, public or 'naive' criticism had now become, as it were, the content of the new second-order, reflexive vocation of Romantic critical theory. Hence, while establishing a barrier between the broader world of literary producers who write to the 'public'

---

[43] On Caroline and Dorothea Schlegel's roles in the *Athenaeum* group, see Sara Friedrichsmeyer, 'Caroline Schlegel-Schelling: "a good woman, and no heroine" ', in Katherine R. Goodman and Edith Waldstein (eds.), *In the shadow of Olympus: German women writers around 1800*, Albany, NY: State University of New York Press, 1992, pp. 115–36.

[44] Quoted in Azade Seyhan, *Representation and its discontents: the critical legacy of German Romanticism*, Berkeley, CA: University of California Press, 1992, p. 85, and Philippe Lacoue-Labarthe and Jean-Luc Nancy, *The literary absolute: the theory of literature in German Romanticism*, Philip Barnard and Cherel Lester (trans.), Albany, NY: State University of New York Press, 1988, p. xviii.

and that self-limiting critical enclave who write first of all for themselves, the early German Romantics also put in question the divisions between categories formerly defining the literary republic. They crossed boundaries between philosophy, religion, science, art, criticism, politics, poetry, novels and history, and seemed to undermine the distinctions between such discursive genres of classical knowledge. No longer poor relations to the *Gelehrtenrepublik*, novels emerged among the vast range of modern prose forms as the most characteristically and challengingly mixed of genres, seeming therefore to be an encyclopedic project crossed by philosophical dialogues, conversations and histories.

By reinventing the ethos of the original Republic in the midst of their polemic against the existing literary republic of the Berliner *Aufklärer*, the Jena Romantics effectively divided the literary republic into distinct markets for critical production. Members of the *Athenaeum* group formed their own market as critical producers writing for other producers, in polemical opposition to the large-scale, taste-forming criticism of the Berliners meant to influence buyers at the Leipzig book fairs. This gesture of 'literary theory' meant to break altogether with the language and aims of the general literariness of the *Gelehrtenrepublik* by radicalizing its norms – the *Frühromantiker* would truly, as writers and readers, 'think for themselves'. Or, to adopt the terms favoured by Percy Shelley, Schlegel aimed to replace traditional prescriptive criticism with a spirit of questioning and analysis that would act as the 'unacknowledged legislator' of the republic of letters. Between Schlegel's world, a restricted, theory-producing enclave, and Nicolai's, a taste-shaping majority of critics and publicists, criticism appeared for the first time in turn-of-the-century Germany, in Pierre Bourdieu's sense, as a complex field of modern cultural production. The philosophical–critical essay thus became a major specialty of the German Romantics, paying refined attention to the formal properties of the work as well as its immediate cultural context. Friedrich Schlegel's essays on Boccaccio, Georg Forster, Lessing, Goethe and others showed him to be perhaps the most brilliant practitioner of this critical mode.

Both the claim for critical autonomy and its ambiguous political implications can be measured in Schlegel's Lyceum fragment 65: 'Poetry is republican speech: a speech which is its own law and end unto itself, and in which all the parts are free citizens and have the right to vote.' To call poetry 'republican speech' was to invoke a political ideal – republican independence – and to thereby assert poetry's (and theoretical criticism's) autonomy from the wider and still authoritarian republic of scholars. But the term also asserted criticism's new authority over that republic. In this fragment, critical theory re-enacts the original founding of the modern republic of letters, asserting autonomy against wider powers by transforming the charter of Pierre Bayle. There is no mistaking Schlegel's ambition in a fragment of 1800: '*State within a state*, an idea that should be raised to the power of the infinite. Intellectuals will be artists, artists will be intellectuals, and agriculture will be an art.'[45]

Thus the early German Romantics evolved a political conception of criticism and critical theory, making Romanticism, in Frederick Beiser's phrase, 'the aesthetics of republicanism'.[46] The republican politics of the *Athenaeum* group were defined more by the literary field they restructured, however, than by any recognizable political programme beyond the frame of the *Gelehrtenrepublik*. As the politics internal to a modern, differentiating field of cultural production, the romantic aesthetics of republicanism proved unstable enough to be constantly redefined over the next six years, revealing an increasingly hierarchical tendency toward a spiritual governing board within the sympathy-based aesthetic community of the *Athenaeum* project of 1798. 'There is no republic without an ephorat', Schlegel would write in 1800, 'and only the spiritual class can execute this'. Moreover, 'a perfect republic would have to be not just democratic, but aristocratic and monarchic at the same time; to legislate justly and freely, the educated would have to outweigh and guide the uneducated'.[47] Over time, the romantic politics of republicanism lost its utopian accents and reproduced, now in an explicitly nationalist register, the educative criticism that it set out to oppose. With Schlegel's conversion to Catholicism and an arch-conservative nationalism by 1808, the experiment in remaking the *Gelehrtenrepublik* by learning anew how to 'think (read) for oneself' was over.

IV   Critical vocation in Britain, 1802–30

Civic yet commercial, exclusive yet claiming the universal, the literary republic formed an increasingly unstable referent for new critical programmes in Britain through the 1820s. After 1800, the critical 'men of letters' were gradually displaced from command of the whole field of modern educated discourse formerly designated by the category of 'literature'; by 1830 they were being clearly distinguished from 'men of science' and from 'scholars' (T. W. Heyck, *The transformation of Intellectual Life in Victorian England*, pp. 24–46).[48] 'Literature' as polite letters was becoming

[45] Fragment 203, Epoch VII, 'Philosophical fragments from the "Philosophical apprenticeship"', in Beiser, *Early political writings*, p. 168.

[46] F. C. Beiser, *Enlightenment, Revolution, and Romanticism: the genesis of modern German political thought, 1790–1820*, Cambridge, MA: Harvard University Press, 1992, p. 260.

[47] Schlegel, Fragment 998, Second Epoch II, of 'Philosophical fragments' in Beiser, *Early political writings*, p. 167; *Athenaeum* fragment 214, 'Philosophical fragments', p. 46.

[48] London: Croom Helm, 1982.

the more restricted category of literature as imaginative writing, a distinction clearly marked by Thomas De Quincey's distinction between books of 'knowledge' and of imaginative 'power' in the *London magazine* for 1823 ('Letters to a young man whose education has been neglected', *Writings*, X: 46–52). The Romantic vocation of criticism, for Samuel Coleridge as for the Schlegels, was to be defined in terms of this emerging reformulation of 'literature' and no longer in terms of its expansive and polite early modern scope. Critical vocation would also be defined as effectively distant or autonomous from the marketing of opinion by the major literary reviews.

The apparent exception to this pattern descended from the world of Hume and Adam Smith. Founding the *Edinburgh review* in 1802, Francis Jeffrey and his cohort tried to restore to criticism the ideal of a 'civil society' and its polite commercial literary republic as 'knit together in all its parts by a thousand means of communication and ties of mutual interest and sympathy'. Yet this new version of polite letters carried with it a distinctly aggressive and snobbish tone, as Marilyn Butler remarks, toward other conceivable recharterings of the enlightened republic of letters.[49] Unlike Hume, Jeffrey understood the new literary republic more as a field of rivalrous 'sects and systems' than as network of personal connections, and what kept these fractions from open war was a carefully mobilized 'public opinion' that operates, according to Henry Brougham, 'by its preventive influence, and renders it unnecessary to employ force' (*Edinburgh review*, 27 September 1816, p. 250). The appeal to politeness now had to be more explicitly couched in the language of class and cultural status. Typically, the *Edinburgh* qualified its claim that 'the actual power of the State resides in the great body of the people' by adding 'especially among the more wealthy and intelligent' (Jeffrey, *Contributions*, p. 571). Its advocacy of Scottish political economy gave polite literary criticism the task of discriminating polite opinion, which would be consistent with the aims and expansion of commercial society, from illegitimate or plebeian opinion at odds with that growth. Likewise, Germaine de Staël's *De la littérature considérée dans ses rapports avec les institutions sociales* (1800), translated into English by 1803, urged 'politeness' as the ethos of a literary world proper to the form of commercial republic born in post-revolutionary France, and far safer than the alternative republican conception of a 'revolution in literature' that would level the 'laws of taste', a notion widely bandied about in France as well as in England's Preface to *Lyrical ballads*.

[49] Francis Jeffrey, *Contributions to the 'Edinburgh review'*, London: Longman, Brown, Green & Longmans, 1854, p. 574; Marilyn Butler, 'Culture's medium: the role of the review', in Stuart Curran (ed.), *The Cambridge companion to British Romanticism*, Cambridge University Press, 1993, pp. 131–33.

314   Jon Klancher

Yet few British critics of the early nineteenth century followed Staël's or Jeffrey's counsel of politeness, adopting more often the language of *Kulturkampf*, vivid polemical combat, or the glare of the 'jealous leer malign' (M. Aske, 'Critical disfigurings: the "jealous leer malign" in Romantic criticism').[50] Attacking persons as much as principles, the reviewers and critics of Romantic Britain positioned one another as often according to their social habitus as to their critical postures. Class and gender associations became means of crediting or discrediting a bewilderingly various array of critical positions. In a dispute about the politics of Shakespeare's plays, William Gifford, editor of the Tory *Quarterly review*, maligned Hazlitt as a vulgar Cockney 'slang-whanger'; Hazlitt replied by assuming the mantle of legitimate man-of-letters while questioning Gifford's credentials for the office of critic. Conservative and radical critics alike vied to keep the republic of letters masculine, although they defined the feminizing of literature according to different social classes. To Hazlitt, female writers flourished in an 'aristocracy of letters' where bluestockings and successful novelists like Frances Burney earned their undeserved status with the aristocratic capital of the leisured classes. To John Wilson at *Blackwood's*, critics from lower-middle-class origins became feminine when they affected to speak of reason and art in the journals of criticism. Leigh Hunt's urbane pose for *The examiner* (1808–1821) earned the remark from *Blackwood's magazine* that he wrote like a 'mincing boarding-school mistress'.[51]

What Coleridge called the 'sting of personal malignity' in contemporary criticism could also be grasped as a test of modern authorship and intellectual property: 'Has the poet no property in his works?' he demanded in chapter 3 of the *Biographia literaria*; 'Is the character and property of the individual, who labours for our intellectual pleasures, less entitled to a share of our fellow feeling than that of the wine merchant or milliner?' A complicated set of issues about poetic genius, the professionalizing of authorship, and the 'public good' defined by the eighteenth-century republic of letters thus emerged in renewed challenges to British copyright law. 'With what justice, or under what pretext of public good', asked Robert Southey in 1819, 'are men of letters deprived of a perpetual property in the produce of their own labours, when all other persons enjoy it as their indefeasible right?'[52] To invoke him as appellant to the *Becket v. Donaldson*

Pp. 49–61 in John Beer (ed.), *Questioning Romanticism*, Baltimore, MD: The Johns Hopkins University Press, 1995.
[51] John Wilson, quoted in John Gross, *The rise and fall of the man of letters: aspects of English literary life since 1800*, London: Weidenfeld & Nicholson, 1969, p. 14.
[52] Coleridge, *Biographia literaria* in *Works*, VII: 43; Robert Southey, 'Inquiry into the Copyright Act', *Quarterly review* 21 (1819), p. 212; see also Rose, *Authors and owners*, pp. 110–12.

copyright decision was also to reveal how far the 'man of letters' had been absorbed into the new category of Romantic authorship, more distant now from the networks of intellectual exchange prized by the older literary republic.

Was there a literary 'theory' in Britain comparable to anything produced at Jena in the late 1790s? That question has often focussed on the career of Samuel Coleridge, whose advice in *Biographia literaria* to be 'not merely a man of letters' was founded on the difficult attempt to forge a German-inspired philosophical criticism in the midst of Europe's most powerful commercial literary establishment. The vocation of criticism Coleridge evolved out of his Shakespeare lectures, *The friend* (1818), and the *Biographia literaria* asserted autonomy against the economics of literary authorship and reviewing. As Jerome Christensen's portrait of his career suggests, Coleridge could easily fall back into the order of commercial print he struggled to surpass (*Coleridge's blessed machine of language*, pp. 118–85).[53] But unlike earlier plaintiffs against the republic of letters' 'anarchy' or commercialization, Coleridge was its most provocative and perhaps illuminating Romantic historian. He grasped its evolution as a complex process of differentiating spheres, citing 'three silent revolutions in England, (1) When the Professions fell off from the Church; (2) when Literature fell off from the Professions; (3) when the Press fell off from Literature' (Table talk (April 1832), *Works*, XIV: 285). As in Germany, understanding modernity as a process of differentiation entailed forging an idea of 'vocation' distinct from the market-based 'man of letters' who was fast losing whatever philosophical credentials he had acquired in the mid-eighteenth century. Significantly subtitled '*My* literary life and opinions', Coleridge's *Biographia literaria* in 1817 repudiated the devolution of the polite, vernacular republic of letters into its current, review-centred commercial form, its title alluding to the *respublica literaria* even as his subtitle reasserted the modernizing claim to 'think for myself'. In the Romantic age Samuel Coleridge would call for restoring the 'ex-dignitaries of the *Book-republic* from their forgotten origins in the *respublica literaria* ('Statesman's manual', *Works*, VI: 107).

As rough drafts for what Coleridge would theorize as the 'clerisy' in *On the constitution of church and state*, his literary lectures used August Schlegel's untranslated formulations from the *Athenaeum* era. No longer rule-structured from without, the poetic text was now said to be 'organized' from within: 'It must embody order to reveal itself; but a living body is of necessity an organized one' ('Lectures on literature, 1808–19', *Works*, V: 494). And yet the substitution of 'organization' for 'rules' was a displacement, not a rejection, of the early *respublica literaria*'s analogy

---

[53] Ithaca, NY: Cornell University Press, 1981.

between rules of state and rules of literary production. The category of 'organization' reflected the profound influence of the new sciences, especially John Hunter's physiology in England and Schelling's *Naturphilosophie* in Germany, where the 'organizing' of bodies became the focus of debates about divine or material sources of life's origin. (See Joel Black's chapter in this volume.) Moreover, unlike 'rules', 'organization' referred socially to the 'organizing' of the emerging institutional order, as it were, from 'within' – guided by a 'clerisy', a learned class of those who thought, read and wrote for themselves but no longer directly for the public. In 1828, a new literary journal, *The athenaeum*, was begun in Britain by a group calling themselves the Apostles, the readers most convinced by Coleridge of the need to reinvent the oldest literary republic.

But print was not the only medium for extending or reinventing some version of the early modern republic of letters. In an extraordinary gesture, Coleridge insisted that his most important 'publicity' was occurring beyond the print-based literary republic altogether. 'Are books the only channel through which the stream of intellectual usefulness can flow?', he asked readers of chapter 10 in the *Biographia*. 'Is the diffusion of truth to be estimated by publications; or publications by the truth, which they diffuse or at least contain?' The place and power of 'my opinions' were affirmed, not in print, but rather among the 'numerous and respectable audiences, which at different times and in different places honoured my lecture rooms with their attendance' (p. 220). To avoid being a 'mere man of letters', Coleridge became, as Byron quipped, 'the man of lectures', establishing a career as literary critic and theorist in the newest cultural institutions on the London scene, the scientific and literary lecturing institutions modelled by the Royal Institution on Albemarle Street since 1800. This venue proved unexpectedly productive for both memorializing and restructuring the legacy of the early modern republic of letters. For nineteenth-century literary and scientific historians alike, Coleridge's lecturing career and association with Humphry Davy were to become the symbol of symmetrical literary and scientific fields emergent from the older republic of letters. Both the mutual fascination and the growing antagonism between 'literature' and 'science', as elaborated in these Romantic-age institutions, was clearly a condition of the way the literary and scientific fields were co-producing each other, before the same audiences and under the same roof. Multi-disciplinary lecturing programmes featured Coleridge on poetry, Sidney Smith on moral philosophy, and Humphry Davy on chemistry (among many others). These lecturing agendas would prove, over thirty years' time, a powerful way to distinguish the distinctive claims of what would be recognized by the 1830s and beyond as the increasingly autonomous domains of science, social science, and the humanities. The interdisciplinary dialogues held in the old republic of letters were becoming the nineteenth-century's order of modern disciplines of knowledge.[54]

As Coleridge evolved a vocation of philosophical criticism, often by transmitting Shakespeare as a 'philosophical aristocrat' among poets, critics like Hazlitt took note of the way Coleridge avoided locating himself among the 'sects and systems' of contemporary political debate. 'Would any one catch *him* in the trammels of a sect? Would any one make *him* swear to the dogmas of a party?' Hazlitt asked in the *Yellow dwarf*. 'You can no more know where to have him than an otter. You might as well hedge the cuckoo' ('Mr Coleridge's lectures' (1818), *Works*, xix: 210). Hazlitt, by contrast, always professed a political position within the republic of letters: 'Any one knows where to have *me*', he boasted in his memoirs; 'what I have once made up my mind to, I abide by to the end of the chapter'.[55] Others have thought Hazlitt was far less consistent beyond the scope of an individual chapter or essay, but the point remains revealing for what it says about the composition of the British literary field at 1818. Professing to be 'careless of public opinion', Coleridge defined 'vocation' as the opposite of what Fichte had called, in *Characteristics of the present age*, 'wandering recklessly about in the empty domain of unsettled opinion'. Coleridge evaded being positioned in the broad field of taste-criticism for a wide reading public, eluding political identifications so that criticism might speak only through the texts and authors that it interpreted. This was criticism as political allegory instead of political affiliation, using what Coleridge elsewhere called a '*disguised* system of politics and morals'.[56]

Meanwhile Hazlitt, a frequent contributor to Hunt's *Examiner* as well as Jeffrey's *Edinburgh review*, arrived at a clearer sense of the difference between a 'republic of letters' (or of 'taste') and a public sphere of contested opinion. His apparently contradictory commentaries on public opinion – extolling its legitimacy in one essay, its insidiousness in another – seem to depend on whether Hazlitt frames the question as one of '*popular feeling* and public opinion' expressed by 'the people', or rather of 'the fortress of public opinion' manned by leading reviewers in the publishing industry. In 'On public opinion', Hazlitt portrayed a self-confirming circle of editors, critics, and readers who never say publicly what they really think: 'thus everyone joins in asserting, propagating, and in outwardly approving what everyone, in his private and unbiased judgment, believes and knows to be scandalous and untrue' (*Works*, xvii: 305). Like Fichte

---

[54] On Coleridge in the lecturing world, see also my 'Transmission failure: from the London lecturing empire to the *Collected Coleridge*' in *Harvard literary studies*, Cambridge, MA, 1991, pp. 77–95.

[55] Quoted in W. Carew Hazlitt, *Memoirs of William Hazlitt*, London, 1867, II, p. 227.

[56] *The collected letters of Samuel Taylor Coleridge*, Earl Leslie Griggs (ed.), 6 vols., Oxford: Clarendon Press, 1956–71, I: 632.

describing the 'reading mania' in turn-of-century Germany, Hazlitt scoffs to see 'a dozen or a score of my countrymen, with their faces fixed, and their eyes glued to a newspaper, a magazine, a review – reading, swallowing, profoundly ruminating on the lie, the cant, the sophism of the day!' Elsewhere Hazlitt described public opinion as invasively corporeal, 'always pressing upon the mind, and, like the air we breathe, [it] acts unseen, unfelt ... supplies the living current of our thoughts and infects without our knowledge. It taints the blood and is taken into the smallest pores' ('On the consistency of opinion' (1821), p. 27).

These powerful notices of a mediatic invasion of everyday life belong to the 1820s, when 'criticism' itself had seemed to become a 'system' or fortress in Britain bearing down on the smallest acts of personal knowledge and mocking the old promise of the literary republic to teach us to 'think for ourselves'. Nonetheless, Hazlitt as late as 1828 could mount the counter-argument to cynicism about the public sphere, recalling how in its overall rise to strength in the last two centuries, 'the press opens the eyes of the community beyond the *actual* sphere in which each moves' so that 'a public sense is thus formed, free from slavish awe or the traditional assumption of insolent superiority' ('Life of Napoleon' (1828), XIII: 41). In the more optimistic year 1817, amid a groundswell of popular dissent and public meetings, Hazlitt appealed to the combined power of 'popular feeling and public opinion' in essays like 'What is the people?' Wherever he opted for the long view, spanning the past two centuries as a critical measure of the 'actual' opinionating powers of the 1820s, Hazlitt strenuously held open, against recurring doubts, the normative perspective of the 'long revolution' of a democratizing modernity empowered by print-based public reason.

As a 'man of letters', however, Hazlitt drew defensive, increasingly nationalist pictures of a gentrifying literary republic overrun by bluestocking women, aristocratic fashion and Frenchifying taste in the age of Bourbon restoration. Female authors, aristocrats and the jumbled, miscellaneous format of newspapers struck Hazlitt as equally symptomatic of a decaying literary republic. In the newspapers we find 'odd combinations' of text and promiscuous 'cross-readings' among genres and categories, according to Hazlitt in 'On the conversation of lords' (1826). This melange of print makes the painter Rubens equivalent to the poet Quarles, and what thereby disappears are the distinctively separate histories of the various arts. The pseudo-aristocrats of letters differ from the classical republicans of letters in the way they so easily convert social connections into literary capital; Hazlitt contrasts them to the Grub Street authors who hack away without pedigree or without 'protection for [one's] person'. With the criteria of authentic literary distinction now confused, Hazlitt resorts to the focussed, unified and completed entity of the 'book' over the newspaper, the disciplined and intensive reader over the genre-crossing 'lord'. Yet this dispirited essay often suggests Hazlitt would rather have shared the pleasures and promiscuities of the literary lords than doggedly making a case for the 'forlorn hope' of genius in books (XVII: 168–73).

Hazlitt's essays of the 1820s mingled class, sexual and national identifications in describing this market-driven republic of commercial-aristocratic letters. Frenchifying and feminizing, the undeserving celebrities of letters in the 1820s seem to have reinvented the mid-eighteenth century cosmopolitan world of salon-letters, only now in the transformed context of Europe's Holy Alliance. This is why Hazlitt's lonely, unsung and underpaid 'authors' have an especially home-grown flavour and why later commentators, like Crane Brinton, would not be entirely wrong to note that Hazlitt shifted his advocacy for the French revolutionary republic, his referent for the power of 'public opinion', to a late-career promotion of all things English.[57]

Through the 1820s, the 'republic of letters' was passing into cultural myth; Hazlitt's disillusioned essays on the literary republic in the mid-1820s belong to the last detailed pictures of this early modern imagined community. The phrase began to name a vague, floating ideal that was no longer attached to any actual structure of learning, politics or literature. In one important form, the republic of letters was transmuted into the ideal of a European Romantic criticism reaching beyond the literary worlds of individual nations. Introducing 'The state of German literature' to British readers in the *Edinburgh review* for 1827, Thomas Carlyle measured the uneven pace of advanced national cultures and found at least two nation's cultural histories keeping the same time:

The past and present aspect of German literature illustrates the literature of England in more than one way. Its history keeps pace with that of ours; for so closely are all European communities connected, that the phases of mind in any one country, so far as these represent its general circumstances and intellectual position, are but modified repetitions of its phases in every other . . .[58]

Carlyle's picture no longer measured Europe as a whole against the 'primitive' cultures of the North American natives or the Scottish Highlanders, as in the heyday of the enlightened republic of letters. Instead he assessed the progress or backwardness of particular European literary cultures, with

[57] Crane Brinton, *The political ideas of the English Romantics*, Ann Arbor, MI: University of Michigan Press, 1966, p. 130; see also Gerald Newman, *The rise of English nationalism: a cultural history 1720–1830*, New York: St. Martin's, 1987, pp. 233–44; Marlon B. Ross, 'Romancing the nation-state: the poetics of Romantic nationalism' in Jonathan Arac and Harriet Ritvo (eds.), *Macropolitics of nineteenth-century literature: nationalism, exoticism, imperialism*, Durham, NC: Duke University Press, 1995, pp. 56–85.
[58] Thomas Carlyle, 'The state of German literature' [1827] in Henry Duff Trail (ed.), *Critical and miscellaneous essays*, London: Chapman & Hall, 1899, pp. 67–8.

an eye especially to the fate of the Enlightenment following the French Revolution. What mediated the national poetries was the category of criticism: 'Far from being behind other nations in the practice or science of Criticism . . . they are distinctly and even considerably in advance' (p. 51).

Late Romantic essays like this shaped the public's reception of Romanticism as a synchronized European phenomenon and helped erase the memory of the older 'republic of letters' itself. In a portrait of the 'hero as man of letters' in 1841, Carlyle featured representative men of letters (the unlikely company of Samuel Johnson, Jean-Jacques Rousseau, Robert Burns) while professing an inability to imagine any 'organization' to which the modern man of letters might belong. In a century of academic discipline-formation and professionalization, Trollope's backhanded compliment to the man of letters – an office that requires 'no capital, no special education, no training . . . an art no one teaches' – found him at the margins of organized modern discourse by 1879.[59] Yet the critical vocations, disciplines of knowledge and transformed place of the humanities that contributed to the decline of the 'man of letters' had important debts to the early modern republic of letters that was transformed in the Romantic age. While the details of this debate lie beyond the scope of the present volume, its signal importance for grasping the outcomes of Romantic criticism suggest the ongoing character of the restructured critical field that Romantic-age writers made out of the crisis of the early modern republic of letters.

[59] Cited in Heyck, *Transformation of intellectual life*, 28–9.

15

Women, gender and literary criticism

Theresa M. Kelley

The failure of the French Revolution to extend the rights of citizens to women marks a critical turning point in the European and British debate about women and gender.[1] In literary criticism of the period, this failure and its cultural aftermath inflect consideration of these topics: sex in souls, the passions, sensibility, the ideal, beautiful or twin female soul, the sublime, creativity, androgyny, love, dissent or revolution and slavery. Even in Britain, where an extensive tradition of published writing by women included criticism, antipathy toward women who wrote or aspired to a public role as intellects and cultural critics intensified after the Revolution.[2] We cannot assess literary criticism about and by women during the Romantic period without taking these cultural and historical pressures into account. Because women who wrote as critics often did so under the literary cover of poetry, fiction, letters, translations, even conversations of the kind practised in European salons, the range of critical discussion necessarily extends well beyond critical essays and reviews. This essay and its bibliographies offer a preliminary survey of this diverse body of material.

In France, literary discussions of women and gender which begin with Rousseau tend to emphasize the problematic status of his fictional women and the role of passion in a civil society. In Germany, such discussions emphasize or critique the idealist identification of woman as the beautiful or ideal soul, particularly when this soul can be made to sponsor an androgynous model of imaginative creativity in male authors. In Britain, Wollstonecraft's 1792 call for 'a revolution in female manners' in *Vindication of the rights of woman* defends reason over the passions and sensibility. Without such a revolution under the banner of French philosophic reason, she warns, women who are not educated, like slaves and standing armies, may revolt in less auspicious ways. After she had lived in revolutionary Paris and moderated her earlier enthusiasm for the Revolution,

---

[1] Dena Goodman, *Republic* 8–10. I am grateful to these scholars for assistance with research for this essay: Daniel Reiss, Thomas Baylis, Anne Mellor, Lori Marso, Ann Gardiner, Jeffrey Cox, Julie Carlson, Jane Brown and Marshall Brown.
[2] Lonsdale, ed., *Eighteenth-Century women poets*, Oxford University Press, 1990, pp. xxxix–xl; Anne K. Mellor and Richard E. Matlak, eds., *British literature 1780–1830*, Fort Worth, TX: Harcourt Brace, 1996, p. 33.

Wollstonecraft also moderated her earlier rejection of the imagination and the passions by identifying them as components of rational thought. This familiar Romantic alliance, together with Wollstonecraft's earlier dismissal of sensibility as injurious to women, register both sides of a sustained debate among writers of the period, particularly women writers, about the appropriate role of sensibility and the passions in poetic creativity, fiction, drama and the lives of women.

Germaine de Staël's criticism and fiction witness the radical side of the Enlightenment and Romantic debate about the 'woman question'. Although she refuses the model of female privacy and subordination which Rousseau had assigned to Sophie in *Emile* and to Julie in *La nouvelle Héloïse*, Staël defends Julie's passionate fidelity as the (discarded) moral and aesthetic basis for post-revolutionary republican society.[3] Whereas men tend to resort to calculations to simplify human reality and thereby err in their ideological excess – what Staël calls philosophical fanaticism – women remain available to 'humanity, generosity, delicacy' to the degree that they retain the capacity for strong feelings for individuals and thereby for the sufferings of others. This aesthetic informs her brief for realism and the novel and her rejection of idealism, traditional allegory, and rigidly circumscribed classical forms. In *De la littérature* (1800), she suggests that women writers in modern republics should devote themselves to literature and men to philosophy. Although this programme appears to defer to contemporary arguments that women who wrote for the public ought to confine themselves to writing novels (which Staël had not thus far written), it masks a more radical project – her defence of the passions and spontaneity as a strong moral basis for a liberal republic.

In *De la littérature*, political and philosophical convictions work in tandem with literary principles. Staël prefers modern writers, especially English poets. Some of the grounds for this preference convey an idealized vision of the Britain she visited in 1789, not the political reality of the 1790s. Her view of France is, in contrast, sharply attentive to points where politics and literary activity intersect. She aligns theatrical convention with aristocratic rank to argue that post-revolutionary French theatre lacks, and desperately needs, 'real heroes with weaknesses instead of ideal ones'.[4] She observes the implicit political function of the literary salon in the *ancien régime*: the freedom of salon conversation put a good, because superficial, face on absolute authority.

In *De l'influence des passions*, *De la littérature* and the novels, Staël insists that those who have strong passions need 'philosophy' to steady

---

[3] Lori Marso, *(Un)manly citizens: the subversive feminine presence in J. J. Rousseau and Germaine de Staël*, Baltimore, MD: The Johns Hopkins University Press, 1998, ch. 1.

[4] Madame de Staël, *De la littérature considerée dans ses rapports avec les institutions sociales*, Pans: Charpentier, 1887, p. 190.

their enthusiasm, to guide its moral ends (Staël rarely uses the term 'reason' in this context, perhaps because she had observed that the fanaticism of the Reign of Terror began with the Jacobin cult of reason). For similar reasons, in De la littérature she defends poetic rhyme and verse drama because they help to contain and make bearable the passion and sorrow that are 'inexhaustible sources of reflections for genius' (p. 330). In the chapter on women writers, she forecasts the ambivalence that will mark her presentation of her fictional heroines, who have passions and sorrows enough for several novels. An earlier distinction in this essay between 'tragedy' and 'drama' suggests one version of this ambivalence: whereas genuine tragedy deals with public subjects, drama occurs wholly in the domestic, private sphere. It is the achievement and the curse of Staël's heroines that they tend to be highly public characters who also demonstrate the passionate capacity for love and domestic intimacy that she identifies with modern women and the excellence of modern literature.

Staël's protagonists embody the strong passions whose moral and imaginative power she had first presented in De l'influence des passions sur le bonheur des individus et des nations (begun 1792, published 1796), Essai sur les fictions (1795), and De la littérature. The heroines of Delphine (1802) and Corinne (1807) do not thrive long in the rigidly traditional cultures to which their male lovers believe themselves to be honour bound. Yet both are tragic exemplars of traits and moral strengths that helped to define Romanticism in Britain and on the Continent. The Italian Corinne and the English Delphine display a sensibility and disinterested love of country and others which make them larger than life heroines, or at least larger in spirit and strength of character than the men to whom they lose their hearts but not their principles. Corinne in particular warned women of the period of the price they would likely pay for being Romantic enthusiasts in the public view.

Until she encounters English (and Scottish) deference to tradition and the law of the father in the person of her beloved Oswald, Corinne escapes ridicule and hatred because she resides in Italy, where her public life and talents have made her a celebrated public poet who seeks to communicate her interior spirit in ways that encourage enlightened progress in society. As Staël's readers immediately recognized, Corinne's improvisational brilliance, her predilection for sublimity in landscape and in virtue, and her swift intuition are as much the hallmark of her creator's genius as her own. At Coppet in Switzerland, a post-revolutionary network of visitors and correspondents that extended the intellectual range and influence of the pre-revolutionary salon,[5] Staël would draft a section of De la littérature in the morning, then present its argument to visitors in the afternoon. One

[5] See Ann Gardiner's forthcoming social history of the Coppet Circle.

of her listeners later asserted that these informal presentations were more brilliant than the written text, or so Sainte-Beuve took pleasure to repeat.[6] Although Coleridge would by 1817 make an allied claim for the dream that inspired 'Kubla Khan', the link between women and improvisation in the form of brilliant conversation is reiterated throughout the period. For more conservative French writers like Stéphanie-Félicité de Genlis, Staël's *Corinne* (and by extension its author) violates the code of domestic retreat that Genlis uses to defend women writers of fiction like herself. As a 'sedentary' activity, writing would keep women at home, away from theatrical spectacles. By becoming one such spectacle, Corinne exceeds the limits Genlis applied to women writers in her *De l'influence des femmes sur la littérature française* (1811) and other essays.

Staël's *De l'Allemagne*, confiscated in 1810 by the Parisian police and finally published in London in 1813, has been credited with introducing the tenets of German Romanticism to French and British readers. In fact, it reflects her appreciation for the pre-Romantic *Sturm-und-Drang* period, the early Goethe, and the early Romantic community at Jena.[7] Yet Staël's view of Germany predicts many of the preoccupations of Romanticism: poetic genius, passionate sensibility and the visionary idealism which she later admired in A. W. von Schlegel. Within Germany, idealist arguments about women, creativity and the sexes continually took different literary forms, from the ideal (and submissive) feminine or 'beautiful soul' of the sister in one of Goethe's early autobiographical dramas, *Sister and brother* (*Die Geschwister*), Mignon and Natalie in *Wilhelm Meister's apprenticeship*, Margarete in *Faust*, Part 1, Iphigenie in *Iphigenie in Tauris*, to the female protagonist of Friedrich Schlegel's *Lucinde*.

From within or at the edges of the Romantic circles in Jena, Berlin, or around Goethe in Weimar, women who challenged the role assigned them in idealist Romantic aesthetics tended to do so obliquely, often by fictional means, much as Charlotte von Stein, Goethe's model for the heroine of the 1779 tragedy *Iphigenie*, replied years later by writing *Dido*, which she circulated in manuscript. Based on sources that predate Virgil's, Stein's tragedy presents Dido's death as the choice she makes to save herself from an unwanted marriage to a barbarian king. Unlike Goethe's Iphigenie, who submits to being sacrificed but is saved in the end by the power of her speech to her captor, the barbarian Thoas, Stein's Dido submits to no one, choosing instead to die, unaided by her brother Pygmalion. Unlike the protective brother Orest in *Iphigenie*, whom Goethe modelled on himself and whose part he acted when the play was first performed, Stein's Pygmalion, who had murdered his sister's husband, is her first predator.

[6] Gretchen Besser, *Germaine de Staël revisited*, New York: Twayne, 1994, p. 63.
[7] Lilian Furst, *The contours of European Romanticism*, London: Macmillan, 1979, pp. 56–73.

Replying to Goethe's idealist drama in which the violent conflict of Orest and Thoas is in the end transformed by Iphigenie's submission and passionate call for peace, Stein imagines a female heroine who is not luminously submissive, who chooses death because it preserves her identity in and from a world controlled by a brother and a tyrant who are not receptive to transformation. Studded with allusions to court intrigues at Weimar and Goethe's earlier conversations and letters, *Dido* puts a more satiric, more realist spin on Goethe's character to refuse an ideal of womanly submission for which Stein had been the model.[8]

In the early years of German Romanticism, such idealizations of women support a vision of poetic unity and androgynous genius. In Friedrich Schlegel's *Dialogue on poetry* (1800), Petrarch's Laura conveys the poetic value of the beautiful, female soul: '[Petrarch's] songs are the essence of his life and a spirit animates and forms them into one indivisible work: eternal Rome on earth and the Madonna in heaven as reflection of the only Laura of his heart symbolize and capture in beautiful freedom the spiritual unity of his entire poetry.'[9] Novalis's 1798 fragments 'On Goethe' rehearse a similar view of Goethe's early heroines. In 'Studies in the visual arts' (1799), Novalis reads landscape as the visible counterpart to the inner dynamic of Romantic androgyne: 'Fluid Firm – *Masculine* – *Feminine*. Geognostic [geologic] Landscapes. Nature Variations.'[10] Men have the bones, women the body.

Schlegel's *Dialogue* identifies women characters as participants in intellectual and literary dialogue insofar as their questions to male characters get the dialogues going. The men are the interlocutors who dominate the ensuing metaphysical and aesthetic exchange (p. 57). When Amalia comments on genre and classification, 'I always shudder when I open a book where the imagination and its works are classified under headings', Marcus replies dismissively, 'no one expects you to read such despicable books. Yet a theory of genres is just what we lack.' He then directs his remarks to Ludovico, presumably because this interlocutor is more like to recognize the lack that Amalia neither recognizes nor supplies. To her fictional credit, Amalia continues to defend the ethical and aesthetic indivisibility and harmony of the imagination and its works (pp. 75–7), a critical argument in keeping with her near-emblematic status as the embodiment, like

---

[8] Katherine Goodman, 'The sign speaks', *In the shadow of Olympus: German women writers around 1800*, Katherine R. and Edith Waldstein (eds.), Albany, NY, State University of New York Press, pp. 71–94.

[9] Friedrich Schlegel, *Dialogue on poetry and literary aphorisms*, University Park, PA: Pennsylvania State University Press, 1968, p. 68; *Gespräch über die Poesie*, in *Kritische Friedrich-Schlegel-Ausgabe*, vol. II: *Charakteristiken und Kritiken I (1796–1801)*, Hans Eichner (ed.), Munich: Schöningh, 1967, pp. 284–351.

[10] *German aesthetic and literary criticism* p. 109.

Petrarch's Laura, of poetry's spiritual unity. Antonio suggests in a letter to Amalia that literary theory is 'too learned a pleasure for you' because she had dismissed his definition of the novel (a definition she had asked for) as 'a romantic book', calling it a 'meaningless tautology' (pp. 98–101). Antonio had forged on with further definitions that deal with the differences between the novel, drama and epic. According to her interlocutor, Amalia remains unconvinced, possibly bored: 'Afterwards you forgot your thesis or gave it up, and decided to claim that all those divisions lead to nothing; that there is *one* poetry, and what counts is whether something is beautiful, and only a pedant would bother with titles and headings' (p. 102).

In one sense, Amalia sustains one important tenet in Schlegel's over-arching thesis about poetry, whereas Antonio and other male interlocutors uphold another – the analysis of genres. Together the two define the oscillations that constitute Romantic irony, which here as elsewhere holds in productive suspension two apparently opposed, but mutually sustaining hermeneutic and philosophical claims. Yet the condescension with which fictional male speakers address their female counterparts echoes Friedrich Schlegel's comment in 'Über die Philosophie: An Dorothea' that 'it is not the destiny of women which is domestic, it is their *nature* and *situation*' and Schiller's earlier identification of women and children with naive poetic genius.[11] As Rousseau's imaginary reconstruction of a state of nature had also implied, because natural or naive genius requires the sentimental poet to be brought into modern (i.e., Romantic) consciousness, the latter gains a critical power over the former – men have the bones, women the body. For if it is the case that women are poetry, that their unwillingness to make critical or theoretical distinctions is in some sense an allegorical statement of this fact, women cannot be self-conscious sentimental poets anymore than they can be effective critics.

This polarization looks very little like the programme asserted by and about the early Romantic circle at Jena. In 1799 the brothers Schlegel settled there with A. W. Schlegel's wife Caroline (who later married Schelling) and Friedrich Schlegel's lover Dorothea Veit (who later married him). These four were soon joined by the poet Ludwig Tieck, then Fichte and Schelling, the poet Novalis, and Clemens Brentano, the brother of Bettine von Arnim, who afterward established an important salon in Berlin. Living in one house and others nearby, members of this group identified their collective enterprise of philosophical and poetic conversation and writing as *Lebenskunst*. The women of the Jena commune, Caroline Schlegel and Dorothea Veit, contributed to or co-authored articles for Friedrich Schlegel's *Athenaeum*; Caroline and A. W. Schlegel worked on a

---

[11] Schlegel's remark is quoted by Goodman and Waldstein, "Introduction," *In the shadow of Olympus*, pp. 22–3; Friedrich von Schiller, *Naïve and sentimental poetry, On the sublime*, Julius A. Elias (trans.), New York: Ungar, 1966, pp. 97–8.

translation of Shakespeare and Dorothea Veit wrote the novel *Florentin*.[12] Although the group soon dispersed, the literary record of this brief experiment suggests that key differences about gender and creativity existed in the group. Caroline Schlegel-Schelling's life and career offer a telling, if circumspect, case in point.

At Jena, Caroline's letters document her expanding confidence about her literary judgments. In reviews she wrote for the *Athenaeum* during the Jena period, she preferred works that linked public concerns with private feeling. Indeed, her 1801 parody of her then brother-in-law's Friedrich's dissertation insists that 'philosophical morality is to be ranked lower than the political'. Although she was the domestic mainstay of the group and preferred to have her work as well as work written jointly with Schlegel published under only his name to avoid criticism of women writers, once she left Jena and Schlegel for Schelling and households in other cities, her literary taste and ambition turned still more sharply away from the idealism and subjective focus of early Romanticism. A brilliant conversationalist and letter writer, she preferred the critical exchange these forms sponsored over diaries, autobiographies and the wildly fantastic, sentimental plots of contemporary novels. Although she began an autobiographical novel, she soon abandoned it. Her letters suggest why. During an era when to be a heroine like Goethe's Margarete and Iphigenie required self-sacrifice, Caroline Schlegel-Schelling described herself as 'a good woman, and no heroine' and flatly asserted, 'I do not believe in sacrifice.'[13]

Dorothea Veit's novel *Florentin* (1801), long dismissed as an insipid *Frauenroman*, may reply parodically to Schlegel's *Lucinde* (1799) by offering female characters whose flat submissiveness registers the status of women writers in early German Romanticism. The career of the novel's eponymous hero recalls the plot of Goethe's *Wilhelm Meister's apprenticeship*, the work which Schlegel believed to be essentially Romantic, on which he based *Lucinde* and to which Veit herself responded with marked distaste. By engaging in a series of relationships with women, the male hero of Goethe's fiction seeks to 'define himself aesthetically through the "eternal feminine" '.[14] Recognizing the masculinist emphasis of this plot in *Lucinde*, Schlegel called it 'Part One' and promised an analysis of the feminine in a later instalment which never materialized. For if the hero Lucinde is a woman, she functions principally as the passive agent of her lover Julius's androgynous identity. In *Florentin*, ironic inversions of *Lucinde* invite scrutiny of its assumptions about gender, women and Romantic subjecthood. Veit makes her hero a man (Florentin), gives him a

[12] Goodman and Waldstein, *ibid.*, pp. 19–21.
[13] Sara Friedrichsmeyer, 'Caroline Schlegel-Schelling', in *ibid.*, pp. 125–6; 124.
[14] Martha B. Helfer, 'Dorothea Veit-Schlegel's *Florentin*: constructing a feminist Romantic aesthetic', *German quarterly* 69 (1996), p. 151.

half-feminized name and a female lover named Juliane, and chronicles his
thwarted effort to father a child in his own image as a vehicle for giving birth
to his own identity. Considered together, these echoes recreate the sexual
–aesthetic dynamic of the androgynous Romantic soul in a fictional form
that exposes its literary cost to women thus idealized and thus put aside.

*

These impulses in early German Romanticism extend well into the period,
particularly in Berlin, where von Arnim and Rahel von Varnhagen von
Ense established salons where the critical practice of Romantic conversation between women and men continued. Like Frederike Helene Unger, the
wife of Goethe's publisher for *Wilhelm Meister's apprenticeship*, whose
letters to Goethe and subsequent fiction revisit his idealist view of the
beautiful female soul,[15] Arnim and Varnhagen imagined 'conversations'
with Goethe marked by rivalry as well as adulation. Arnim's first novel,
Goethe's correspondence with a child, uses the form of epistolary fiction to describe a reciprocal creativity whose Romantic traits are passion, spontaneity and intuition. The last third of the work, which shifts
from the epistolary form, registers Arnim's disappointment with Goethe's
lack of reciprocity in their real exchange of letters. Her second novel *Die
Günderode* memorializes another, more satisfying exchange of letters and
mutual passion between Arnim and Karoline von Günderode.[16] As such, it
records an aspiration that is more often honoured in the breach in the history of the European salon, where conversation in which women were full
partners prompted as much anxiety as pleasure.

In England as on the Continent, questions about gender and women
writers dominate the cult of sensibility. The most persistent criticism
argues that women, including women writers, display or exploit weak
sensibility – a susceptibility to emotion and moral failure which lacks the
ballast of reason. With this risk in mind, Wollstonecraft and Austen argue
that women who curb their sensibility are more likely to become rational,
moral beings. After 1793, Wollstonecraft, Staël and some later Romantic
women writers who did not witness the repressive political climate of
revolutionary France praised reason less and feeling more, perhaps because
the cult of reason invoked by Robespierre and the Committee for Public
Safety made reason less salubrious, but also because the passions and sensibility are prominent in the criticism of the period, particularly when
women, gender and genius are at issue.

The complex Romantic brief for passion, including the rhetorical passions, helps to explain the sustained popularity of Staël's writing, especially

---

[15] Susanne Zantop, 'The beautiful soul writes herself', in *In the shadow of Olympus*, Goodman and Waldstein (eds.), pp. 30–51.
[16] Waldstein, 'Goethe and beyond', in *ibid.*, pp. 98–113.

her fiction, throughout the period. Maria Jane Jewsbury's *History of an enthusiast*, whose story of a young woman's thirst for fame echoes the plot of *Corinne*, suggests that what attracted English and especially women writers to the novel was not simply its paeans to sensibility, but the possibility of a heroine whose passions and capacities warranted a public literary existence. Polwhele's 1798 verse diatribe against such ambitions offers one instance of the post-Revolutionary backlash against women who had some measure of visibility and therefore a role in the public sphere as writers of fiction, poetry and criticism. Mellor and others identify two responses to this antagonism among women poets – that of the 'poetess' – Hemans, Landon and others who wrote but counselled the domestic probity of such activity, as had Genlis at the beginning of the century – and women critics and poets like Barbauld, Smith, More, Williams and Opie, who appropriated the stance of dissenting women preachers to authorize their public voices as writers and critics.[17]

Whether they regarded themselves as essentially private beings who wrote for the public out of necessity or from within the domestic sphere or writers in the public arena of literary culture, women in or from England, Scotland, Ireland and Wales produced a significant volume of published as well as privately circulated literary criticism during this period. Romantic poems and novels offer more oblique because figurative discussions of women and gender. Dramatists like Baillie and Inchbald produced substantial published criticism. Baillie's concerns dramatic theory, Inchbald's the history of dramatic criticism and theatrical production. Poets like Robinson, Seward and especially Barbauld were significant literary critics. In Barbauld's case, the range of criticism extends from the eighteenth-century essay, from the history of the British novel, to politics and poetics. For writers like Smith and More, distinct pedagogical, ethical and poetic perspectives share the same critical and literary space. More women than presently recognized published in magazines and reviews.

A number of published women writers of the period, including Edgeworth and Burney, as well as some who preferred not to publish their work, such as Dorothy Wordsworth, convey literary judgments in forms that appear to be incidental, or social (letters to friends) or improvised. In published works, improvisation serves the persona of the Romantic 'poetess' who claims to write less threatening because less premeditated verbal art.[18] Yet this persona may have been more subversive than submissive in English heroines who recall Staël's Corinne, among them Jewsbury's female 'enthusiast', and the protagonist of Landon's *The improvisatrice*.

---

[17] Anne K. Mellor, 'The female poet and the poetess: two traditions of British women's poetry, 1780–1830', *Studies in Romanticism* 36 (1997), pp. 261–76.
[18] Richard C. Sha, *The visual and verbal sketch in British Romanticism*, Philadelphia, PA: University of Pennsylvania Press, 1998, p. 125.

The last of Lucy Aikin's *Epistles on women* makes female improvisation one feature of a poetics grounded in conversation, social intercourse and public debate.[19] Once a virtual set piece in poetic attacks on women (remember Pope), female improvisation and conversation are now forms of literary criticism.

This view of women and criticism was hardly unanimous. Wolfson's investigation of how Romantic writers defined 'sex in souls' suggests why. Wollstonecraft believed souls had no sex, a position that allowed her to do an end run around earlier claims that souls have sex and the better soul is male. Put in context, Coleridge's remark that 'a great mind must be androgynous' argues for the presence of feminine attributes in great male minds. Similarly, his conviction that there is sex in souls imagines that a feminine soul reflects the attributes of a feminine body and, further, that female souls provide quasi-bodily assistance for God's divine (and male) inspiration. Jewsbury's *History of an enthusiast* appropriates the language of Percy Shelley's Asia in *Prometheus unbound* to celebrate the intellectual power of her heroine's female soul and thereby rewrites Shelley's early poetic alliances of women with nature and matter. Ambivalence about gender and sex differently complicate the poetic personas of Keats and Byron, making them strange bedfellows indeed. The edgy, misogynist and heterosexual poetic voice Keats employs is complicated by his awareness of critical jibes at his Cockney effeminacy. The figurative language Byron uses to present heroes like the Corsair, Sardanapalus and Don Juan is subject to telling confusions about gender and putatively masculine agency as Romantic heroes grow introspective and inactive, and female characters act, often to the distress of their male creators. Like Beatrice in *The Cenci*, such female characters disturb existing structures of masculine power (critical and dramatic) by acting them out.[20]

The antitheatrical complaint that, as Carlson puts it, 'theatre, with its plays on identity and the body, threatens culture like a woman',[21] finds more ample ground in Romantic drama and criticism. By this time women had assumed female roles which had before been acted by men; those women who were dramatists and critics took careful measure of female characters and the role of women in the theatre. The anxiety that permeates Coleridge's dramatic representations of female characters and his ambivalence towards actresses on whom his theatrical success depended together suggest the underlying suspicion and antagonism that persisted even after

---

[19] Mellor, 'The female poet and the poetess', p. 276.

[20] Susan J. Wolfson, 'Gendering the soul', in *Romantic women writers: voices and countervoices*, Paula R. Feldman and Theresa M. Kelley (eds.), Hanover, NY: University Press of New England, 1995, pp. 33–62.

[21] Julie A. Carlson, *In the theatre of Romanticism: Coleridge, nationalism, women*, Cambridge University Press, 1994, p. 7.

the actress Mrs Siddons had become the 'tragic muse' of Joshua Reynolds's painting, not simply its model. The figural and real violence that is one consequence of Hazlitt's erotic and critical confusion of women with actresses, and both with self *dis*-possession, more overtly convey that antagonism.[22] Romantic women critics differently recognize this and other critical tensions in which gender is part of the subplot.

In the 'Introductory discourse' to her *A series of plays*, each of which presents characters who dramatize a passion or the conflict of passions, Joanna Baillie reorients discussion of the rhetorical and dramatic passions and female sensibility by situating both in an aesthetic that is realist rather than allegorical. She argues accordingly for the dramatic interest of characters whose passions and motives are mixed. Such characters matter to us, she asserts, because we recognize them. Turning the tables on tragic and epic norms of heroism and, more subtly, on then-current efforts to exclude women from public arenas like the theatre, she argues that dramatic protagonists are more likely to engage our ethical and sympathetic interest if their travails are 'more familiar and domestick': 'A King driven from his throne, will not move our sympathy so strongly, as a private man torn from the bosom of his family.' Or as a private woman like Jane de Montfort in *De Montfort*, whose status as the presumptive non-titular heroine of this play may well have been secured in production because Mrs Siddons took the part. Baillie grants the extension of her argument to women in a note: 'With some degree of softening and refinement, each class of the tragick heroes I have mentioned has its corresponding one amongst the heroines' including the 'great and magnanimous', the 'passionate and impetuous' as well as the 'tender and pathetick'.[23] Baillie suggests that the dramatic category most easily assimilated to canonical understanding of female sensibility – the tender and pathetic – offers too narrow a frame for female passion. At the same time, Baillie recuperates the domestic sphere to which critics like Polwhele so wished to confine women by reimagining it as the arena of tragic action and feeling which is likely to matter to a reading and viewing public that tacitly includes women and men.

In the multi-volume *The British theatre*, which grew from twelve to twenty-five volumes in editions printed between 1806 and 1823, Elizabeth Inchbald's 'Remarks' provide brief critical commentaries and stage histories for each play. Inchbald's practical criticism is grounded in realist and ethicist principles and an informed regard for Shakespeare's dramatic achievement. She observes that Thomas Southern's *Oroonoko* is never staged in Liverpool, where it should be performed inasmuch as 'merchants

[22] *Ibid.*, pp. 117–32 and 147.
[23] Joanna Baillie, 'Introductory discourse', in *A series of plays*, 1798, rpt. London: Routledge, 1996, vol. I, pp. 35–6.

of that great city acquired their riches by the slave trade'.[24] To objections that the villains in her play *Lovers' vows* are never punished, she replies by offering a more interior moral scheme in which conscience is itself the punishment (II: 7). She has nothing good to say about productions of *Romeo and Juliet* and *Lear* which tacked on happy endings.

Inchbald's brief for women in the theatre is judiciously nuanced. Her partial defence of Susannah Centlivre's *A bold stroke for a woman* admits that it pleases 'the degraded taste of the public', but then takes aim at male playwrights who are as willing to do likewise, though their 'fortunes were not wholly dependent on their mental exertions' (IX: 3–4). Inchbald dryly observes that Shakespeare's Leontes in *The winter's tale* looks better for the female company he keeps (XII: 5). Reviewing a production of Southern's *Isabella* in which the mature Mrs Siddons took the female lead, and was 'enthusiastically worshipped' as she had not been when she performed on the London stage 'in the prime of youth and of beauty', Inchbald urges, against claims to the contrary, 'Who will allege, that mental powers have no charm in the female sex?' (IX: 3). She admires Baillie as 'a woman of genius' but critiques the hero of *De Monfort* on the grounds that his unspecified motivation for his all-consuming hatred suggests less a tragic hero than the 'mind of the lunatic generally tyrannized by one obstinate idea' (X: 3–4).

Anna Jameson's *Characteristics of women, moral, poetical, and historical* offers more sustained critical reflections on women as dramatic characters. Although she sounds decorous to a fault as she assigns Ophelia traits of modesty, grace and tenderness without which 'a woman is no woman',[25] the critical distance from this assessment to her essay on Lady Macbeth is immense. Jameson notes that except for acknowledging her one of Shakespeare's 'most sublime creations', critics have had little else to say about this character. The length and heft of what Jameson has to say redresses this imbalance. She begins with Mrs Siddons's reflection on the role: 'I have heard her say, that after playing the part for thirty years, she never read it over without discovering something in it new' (p. 322). Reviewing the 'sagacity of critics and the reflections of commentators', Jameson lists Dr Johnson (who says the character is detestable), Schlegel (who dismisses her as a 'species of female Fury') and other critics who mention Lady Macbeth in passing. Although she grants that Hazlitt had recognized the power of this character, Jameson diplomatically conveys a key reservation: the limited space he was able to give to this topic led him to 'stop . . . short of the *whole* truth – it is a little superficial, and a little too harsh' (p. 323).

---

[24] Inchbald, 'Remarks', in *The British theatre*, 25 vols., London: Longman, 1808, vol. v, p. 4.
[25] Anna Jameson, *Characteristics of women, moral, poetical, and historical*, 2nd edn, New York: Wiley and Putnam, 1847, p. 134.

Jameson's commentary begins where we might imagine she would have ended had moral censure been her project. She readily grants that Lady Macbeth is so dominated by ambition that she sacrifices 'every just and generous principle, and every feminine feeling'; that she 'is doubly, trebly, dyed in guilt and blood' (p. 323). Nonetheless, Jameson continues, 'Lady Macbeth's amazing power of intellect, her inexorable determination of purpose, her superhuman strength of nerve, render her as fearful in herself as her deeds are hateful; yet she is not a mere monster of depravity, with whom we have nothing in common . . . she is a terrible impersonation of evil passions and mighty powers, never so far removed from our own nature as to be cast beyond the pale of our sympathies; for the woman herself remains a woman to the last, – still linked with her sex and with humanity' (pp. 324–5). Among all the other women characters in dramatic literature, only the Medea of Euripides comes close. Jameson measures how close by alluding, as we might now say, to her subject-position: 'as far as a woman may judge of a woman . . . although the passions of Medea are more feminine [than those of Lady Macbeth], the character is less so' (p. 340). Together, these two characters illustrate Schlegel's distinction between ancient (Medea) and modern or romantic drama (Lady Macbeth). With this sleight of (critical) hand, Jameson reverses Schlegel's dismissive treatment of Lady Macbeth such that she now becomes the Shakespearean character who exemplifies the 'gothic grandeur, the rich chiaroscuro' of Romantic drama.

In *The British novelists* (1820), a fifty-volume edition for which Anna Letitia Barbauld as editor provided extensive introductions, her essay 'On the origin and progress of novel-writing' rehearses the widely held critical preference for realist fiction among Romantic women writers. If romance belongs, according to Barbauld, to a medieval culture nurtured by a curious mix of amorous chivalry, metaphysics, and battle, the achievement of the novel beginning with Defoe's *Robinson Crusoe* is, within the limits available to fiction, to convey 'some knowledge of the world'.[26] Her assessment of the extent to which individual novels do or can provide such knowledge is rigorous and pragmatic about the difference between art and life, as in 'real life is a kind of chance-medley, consisting of many unconnected scenes. The great author of the drama of life has not finished his piece; but the author [of a novel] must finish his.' The evident religiosity of Barbauld's critical temperament should not be misconstrued. She can be censorious, as when she notes the excessive attention to love in novels. Yet unlike Clare Reeve, who asserts in *The progress of romance* (1785) that it is the 'gentleman in a Novel' not the 'Hero in Romance'

---

[26] Anna Letitia Barbauld, 'On the origin and progress of novel-writing', in *The British novelists*, 50 vols., London: Rivington, 1810, vol. I, pp. 1–59.

who is likely to mislead a young female reader,[27] Barbauld suggests that the evils widely attributed to novel reading are exaggerated. Her assessment of Sterne's *Tristram Shandy* is unconstrained by the moral censure with which she begins: 'The indelicacies of these volumes are very reprehensible, indeed in a clergyman scandalous, particularly in the first publication, which however has the richest vein of humour.' Her moral scrutiny of Rousseau's *Julie* challenges the driving moral of its plot – that Julie becomes the good, the holy 'nouvelle Héloïse' by separating herself from St Preux and consenting to marry Wolmar. Instead of chastizing the sexual relationship between the unmarried lovers, Julie and St Preux, she makes it the moral basis that Julie (with a hefty assist from parental authority) abandons: 'Rousseau has not reflected that Julie ought to have considered herself as indissolubly united to St Preux; her marriage with another was the infidelity.'

Edgeworth's praise for Inchbald's *A simple story* is likewise attentive to its mimetic claims: 'I never read any novel that affected me so strongly, or that so completely possessed me with the belief in the real existence of all the people it represents.'[28] The unspecified critical premise of this remark shows how far from the language of sensibility such discussions of the realist novel are. This particular reader's affective response to Inchbald's novel is the subjective guarantor of its mimetic claims, not a generalized grammar of sensibility in which key plot turns, landscapes and character types constitute the norm.

Such readjustments may illustrate how some Romantic writers dislodged the gender mapping held in place by eighteenth-century sensibility and aesthetic theory. So long as the carefully crafted alignment of women with softness, beauty and a sensibility that made them quintessentially vulnerable or malleable was secure, in fiction as in life, Wollstonecraft and Hannah More, among others, could hardly defend the alliance of women and sensibility. Austen and Mary Shelley offer different novelistic assessments of this dilemma. Austen's mockery of sensibility indicts characters who rush to judgment without knowing particulars about a person or situation. In a literary register wholly unlike Staël's, novelistic particularity and realism jointly sponsor affective passions that cannot be made to serve abstractions, be they aesthetic or political. The communicative arena in which Austen's characters often work their way toward this recognition suggests further that isolated, self-absorbed reflection is likely to be sealed off from the world of persons and particulars to which such judgments must refer. Shelley's *Frankenstein* orchestrates a hauntingly

---

[27] Clara Reeve, *The progress of romance through times, countries, and manners*, 1785, rpt. New York: Garland, 1970, p. vi.

[28] Maria Edgeworth, 14 January 1810, quoted in *Women critics 1660–1820: an anthology*, Folger Collective on Early Women Critics (ed.), Bloomington, IN: Indiana University Press, 1995, p. 376.

negative assessment of what happens to fictional women who are identified with sensibility and the beautiful (the novel is not much kinder to male characters caught in a similar alignment).[29] Female characters and interlocutors are either off the map of the story (Walton's sister Margaret), dead (Victor's mother), aborted (the monster's would-be mate), or they don't live long (Justine and Elizabeth). As such, they are good Romantic candidates for the sex which is not one. The metaphorical and fictive shape of Shelley's critical reply to cultural rehearsals of the ties that bind gender, aesthetic theory and literary sensibility registers a covert critique of the aesthetic location of women in the scheme of the sublime, Romantic hero/villain.

Throughout the nineteenth century critics assented to Francis Jeffrey's 1829 presentation of Felicia Hemans as a poet whose career illustrated the strengths (which also turn out to be the limitations) of 'Female Poetry': a 'disabling delicacy' and 'inexperience of the realities they might wish to describe' confirmed the propriety of their sequestration in 'the practical regulation of private life'.[30] Hemans's rueful account of being pursued by 'household troops' so relentless that she begins to think of moving her workplace to the cellar suggests an ambivalence about the domestic sphere that her poems also record.[31] Some mark and thereby question the social determinants that make it the woman's task to suffer (a theme which Landon and Smith play in related keys), others present female characters whose heroic intensity or actions disturb the prescriptive alignment of women with domestic, private life. The poetic history of this ambivalence in Hemans's *Records of Woman* includes a self-reflexive eulogy to Mary Tighe in 'The Grave of a Poetess' which implies that her eternal rest requires bifurcating the poet from the woman. In 'Woman and Fame', Hemans contrasts the public fame of Staël's Corinne with the greater happiness of 'she that makes the humblest heath / lovely but to one on earth'.[32]

Charlotte Smith's poetic resistance to this gendered domestic economy works in counterpoint to the prefaces she composed for successive editions of *Elegiac sonnets*. In the first edition, she claims that the poems are sonnets only in the sense that they are fourteen lines long. But in later prefaces she avers that some were attempted 'on the Petrarchan model',

---

[29] Anne K. Mellor, *Mary Shelley: her life, her fiction, her monsters*, New York: Routledge, 1988, p. 126; Fredericks, 'On the sublime and the beautiful in Mary Shelley's *Frankenstein*', *Essays in literature* 23 (1996), pp. 178–89.

[30] Francis Jeffrey, ' "Records of women" and "The Forest Sanctuary" by Felicia Hemans', *Edinburgh review* 50 (1829), p. 32; Susan Wolfson, 'Domestic affections', in *Re-visioning Romanticism*, C. S. Wilson and J. Haefner (eds.), Philadelphia, PA: University of Pennsylvania Press, 1994, pp. 129–30.

[31] Wolfson, *ibid.*, p. 133.

[32] *Ibid.*, pp. 140–60; Kevin Eubanks, 'Minerva's veil: Hemans, critics, and the construction of gender', *European Romantic review* 8 (1997), pp. 341–59.

including a few that are translations from Petrarch. Curran points out that the sonnets so identified are not translations.[33] Mary Robinson's account of the 'legitimate' or Petrarchan sonnet, which defends Smith's sonnets against the claim that they were not legitimate, recognizes what Smith assumes: that poetic legitimacy requires some demonstration, even if feigned, of a tradition.[34] The real poetic story of Smith's *Sonnets* and later poetry may have less to do with their purported legitimacy than with their crafted departures from gendered as well as poetic norms, departures all the more surprising when read against the self-pity that is also evident in the prefaces, which steadily remind readers of the link between feeling or sensibility, economic powerlessness and woman.

In part because they emerge from a dissenting tradition that had produced dynamic female preachers, Hannah More, Helen Maria Williams and Barbauld openly respecify the location of women and gender on the poetic landscape. In 'Slavery', More deploys the traditional identification of the muses and personified virtues as female, here named Liberty and Mercy, to array the full moral force of the aesthetics of sensibility against slavery. In *Peru*, Williams opposes the rapaciousness of the Spanish conquest to the domestic, familial affections of the Peruvian chiefs, and the mildness of their priests. Thus 'feminized' insofar as they are situated within the aesthetic arena created in part to set women and female virtue in a separate space, Williams's Peruvians are morally superior. The itinerary of Barbauld's poetic interest in women and gender is openly declared in 'Eighteen hundred and eleven', an anti-progress poem that chronicles the moral path of England's decline. As Mellor observes, here Famine, Disease and Rapine are the work of 'Man', whereas a female 'Glad Nature' finds her bounty destroyed by 'frantic man at strike'.[35] Coming from a poet–critic like Barbauld, who anatomized the perplexities of figurative agency in Collins's poems long before modern critics would, this gendered conflict of personifications in 'Eighteen hundred and eleven' looks neither accidental nor incidental to its argument. Other critics have suggested more oblique evidence of the role of gender in Barbauld's poetry. McCarthy finds evidence of Barbauld's resistance to the patriarchal ethos of the dissenting culture in which she wrote and lived.[36] Armstrong suggests that Barbauld and other Romantic women poets work out poetic relations to sense, nature and culture that have little to do with the sex of sensibility. They have more to do with the rub of nature against culture, contemporary dis-

---

[33] Stuart Curran, ed., *Poems of Charlotte Smith*, p. 4.
[34] Mary Robinson, *Sappho and Phaon*, 1796, rpt. Delmar, NY: Scholars' Facsimiles & Reprints, 1995, pp. 3–4.
[35] Mellor, 'Female poet and the poetess', pp. 262–71.
[36] William McCarthy, 'We hoped the *woman* was going to appear', in *Romantic women writers*, Feldman and Kelley (eds.), pp. 113–25.

courses about economics and philosophy, and a sensuous poetic texture quite unlike that identified with the 'effeminate' Keats, so regarded by Romantic critics in part because of his poetic (over)fondness for sensuous imagery.[37] By such inversions, women and gender refigure the landscape of Romantic literature and its criticism.

[37] Isobel Armstrong, 'The gush of the feminine', in *ibid.*, pp. 13–19; Susan J. Wolfson, 'Feminizing Keats', in *Critical essays on John Keats*, Hermione de Almeida (ed.), Boston, MA: Hall, 1990, pp. 317–56.

16
Literary history and historicism

DAVID PERKINS

I

Literary history was created in the Romantic age. René Wellek traces its origins to English and Scottish intellectuals of the eighteenth century – Robert Lowth, Thomas Percy, John Brown, Thomas Warton and many another. They thought their way to the basic concepts of literary history (*The rise of English literary history*, pp. 200–1).[1] If their contributions are now less remembered, a reason is that in Germany Herder collected their ideas, along with those of Leibniz, Kant, Hamann and Winckelmann, and voiced them more assertively. He is perhaps the father of literary history – at least of its programme, though he was unready to chew as much straw as is necessary to write it. There were important essays by French writers, such as Madame de Staël's *On literature considered in its relations with social institutions* (1800) and Chateaubriand's *Genius of Christianity* (1802), but after the 1780s, the development of literary history proceeded mainly in Germany.

Which was the first literary history? We are speaking, of course, of the first in a modern kind. The older kind was a history of learning, *historia litterarum*, a project Francis Bacon had recommended: 'the general state of learning to be described and represented from age to age . . . without which the history of the world seemeth to me to be as the statua of Polyphemus with his eye out; that part being wanting which doth most show the spirit and life of the person'.[2] As time passed, the histories of learning became more sophisticated, but as late as 1839, in Henry Hallam's impressive volumes,[3] they were still essentially compendia. They rehearsed what was known about authors in the various fields of *belles lettres*, history, philosophy, classical philology, theology and so forth, and if the authors were arranged in chronological series, this was what Hallam understood by 'history'. Thomas Warton's great *History of English poetry*

---

[1] Chapel Hill, NC: The University of North Carolina Press, 1941.
[2] Francis Bacon, *Works*, ed. James Spedding, *et al.*, 14 vols., London: Longman, 1857–74, III: 329–30.
[3] Henry Hallam, *Introduction to the literature of Europe in the fifteenth, sixteenth, and seventeenth centuries*, 4 vols., Paris: Baudry's European Library, 1837–9.

(1774–81) did not quite dissolve this form. Much of it is a chronicle with bibliographies. The first modern literary history – developmental, sociological, organic – was Friedrich Schlegel's unfinished *History of the poetry of the Greeks and Romans* (1798), a dazzling performance. Other notable literary histories of the Romantic age were A. W. Schlegel's *Lectures on dramatic art and literature* (1809–11); J. C. L. Sismondi's *On the literature of the south of Europe* (1813); and Friedrich Schlegel's *History of ancient and modern literature* (1815). The first complete history of English literature – for Warton's book dealt only with poetry and only down to the Elizabethans – was by Robert Chambers in 1837. Chambers, a Scott, wrote this as a hopefully profitable venture in popular education. The first history of German literature, by Georg Gottfried Gervinus, appeared from 1835 to 1842. Romantic literary history foregrounded origins, continuous development and teleology. It gave prominence to the primitive, folk, medieval and early modern, and found in these the national. Thus literary history was part of the stream of becoming that dissolved the world vision of the Enlightenment.

But in the years we now bracket as the Romantic age, discourse about literature was not usually historical. This statement will, I suppose, seem doubtful or simply wrong to many readers, even to those who most know the critical writing of the time. Certainly the Romantics frequently viewed and evaluated the literature of their own time in comparison with that of the past. I explore this topic later, in connection with the widespread fear of decline in the arts and the distinction between the modern or romantic and the classical. Whether hopeful or pessimistic, comparison of the present with the past indicates a concern for the situation and rank of the present moment in history. In such comparison, a certain view or interpretation of the past, or of a selected portion of it, shapes one's view of the present. The hunger to understand the present through history motivated brilliant analyses of present-day culture. One thinks of passages in Friedrich Schlegel's 'On the study of Greek poetry' (1795), Schiller's 'On Naive and Sentimental Poetry' (1795–96), Wordsworth's Preface to the second edition (1800) of *Lyrical ballads*, Francis Jeffrey's 1810 review of Sir Walter Scott's *The lady of the lake* and 1815 review of the *Works* of Jonathan Swift, Shelley's 'Defence of poetry' (1821), and Hazlitt's *Spirit of the age* (1825). In these analyses, the traits of the present were accounted for by citing contextual factors, whether the French Revolution, industrialism, methodism or the influence of speculative philosophy. 'The spirit of the age' was an omnipresent phrase in German discourse and common also in England after Madame de Staël's *On Germany* was translated in 1813. The phrase testified to a feeling that the present was a demarcation within the stream of becoming, a cultural unity, a chapter in the narrative of history. As a movement, Romanticism trumpeted its own newness. Like the Pre-Raphaelites, the Futurists, and the Modernists, the Romantics defined themselves and seized their place in cultural history with full self-consciousness, though less so in England than in Germany and France. In order to break with the recent past, they required a description of that past. Always the avant-garde reconstructs the past in order to reject it. They also required a description of remote pasts that might now be revived. The Romantic enthusiasm for the Middle Ages and the Renaissance expresses a pervasive historical consciousness.

Moreover, even those critics, from Samuel Johnson to Coleridge and Shelley, who usually approached authors without a strong sense of historical context and difference, could espouse historicist principles on occasion. Goethe had no sense of history, according to Gervinus, but in speaking of his own career, Goethe historicized. 'The man', says Coleridge, 'who reads a work meant for immediate effect on one age with the notions and feelings of another, may be a refined gentleman, but must be a sorry critic' (*Complete works*, IV: 306).[4] Fine words! But Coleridge was often this man, at least until he read the Schlegel brothers. No one has put the concept of a literary period better than Shelley:

> there must be a resemblance which does not depend upon their own will, between all the writers of any particular age. They cannot escape from subjection to a common influence which arises out of an infinite combination of circumstances belonging to the times in which they live, though each is in a degree the author of the very influence by which his being is thus pervaded.[5]
>
>   (Preface to 'Laon and Cythna')

Nevertheless, when in 'A defence of poetry' Shelley sketched the history of his art, his concept of poetry was universal and normative, and hence the main difference between periods was that in some the footsteps of poetry departed from the world and in others they returned (*Complete works*, VII: 118–31).

All critics invoked history as an exculpation, when the seeming faults of loved authors could not be ignored. 'Every man's performances', said Johnson, 'to be rightly estimated, must be compared with the state of the age in which he lived' (Preface to 'Shakespeare').[6] 'The times' were enlisted to explain Homer's attitude to women, Milton's asperities in controversy, and Shakespeare's conceits and puns – for when accompanied by strong emotion, conceits and puns seemed unnatural and insincere. Romantic encounters with Shakespeare's sonnets are a comedy. By the assumptions

---

[4] W. G. T. Shedd (ed.), 7 vols., New York: Harper & Brothers, 1853.

[5] *Complete works*, Roger Ingpen and Walter E. Peck (eds.), 10 vols., New York: Gordian Press, 1965, I: 244.

[6] *Johnson on Shakespeare*, Arthur Sherbo (ed.), New Haven, CT: Yale University Press, 1968, p. 81.

of the age, the sonnets were personal self-expression, yet the object of their passion was male, an unthinkable circumstance. History saved this situation by showing that in Shakespeare's days friends used the language of lovers without erotic implications.

If all this is true, how can it be said that Romantic literary criticism, on the whole, was not historical? I can only appeal to each reader's sense of this discourse. Certainly a lot of literary history was produced. Certainly a historical consciousness was often implied even though genesis and context were not discussed. And yet for the most part Romantic critics did not situate books and authors within history or read them contextually. Certain aesthetic conceptions of the age inhibited them from doing so. Moreover, they had more interesting and more pressing critical concerns. They characterized and appreciated; they analysed the creative processes and traits of genius; they theorized about the sublime and the ironical; they sought to define art, poetry and beauty; they speculated on the relation of these to nature or truth, and on their formative impact on the individual and on society. In the great volume of Romantic literary criticism, historical thinking is present but not dominant. One can think of many similar instances, in which one generation created a discourse without widely adopting it, and the next generations made it an orthodoxy. In the present, the future is always marginal.

Among the assumptions of Romantic aesthetics, the idea of genius made difficulties for historical thinking. For a typically Romantic rhetoric on this point we can cite William Gray's *Historical sketch of the origin of English prose literature and of its progress till the reign of James I* (1835). Gray believed that literature is progressive, but wondered how, in this case, to explain Homer, Chaucer, Shakespeare – the great writer in a rude and barbarous age. 'These wonder-working ancients stand "themselves alone," ' ... as privileged and unaccountable spirits who are allowed to "o'erleap the bounds of space and time" ' (pp. 92–3).[7] Genius has no derivations. Coleridge comments tartly on 'Ritson and other Dullards', who trace 'the growth of poetic Genius by ancestry: as if Dante or Milton were *creatures* of *wandering* Bards'.[8] If genius transcends the age, literary history becomes impossible except as chronicle. As A. W. Schlegel put it, a genius is 'something on which one cannot reckon, a mere gift of nature'. But literary history exhibits works as determined in a chain; it strives to 'discover a lawful process in the chaos of phenomena'. With this contradiction, we 'stand on the limits of knowledge', unable to see further.[9]

---

[7] Oxford: D. A. Talboys, 1835.
[8] Samuel Taylor Coleridge, *Coleridge on the seventeenth century*, Roberta Florence Brinkley (ed.), Durham, NC: Duke University Press, 1955, pp. 586–7.
[9] August Wilhelm Schlegel, *Vorlesungen über schöne Literatur und Kunst*, in *Vorlesungen über Ästhetik I*, Ernst Behler (ed.), Paderborn: Schöningh, 1989, p. 192.

For a literary historian, the factors that shape literature are general, influence most authors in a certain time and place, explaining the observable similarities between their works. But a lyric, by Romantic assumptions, is an individual expression, a cry of a personal occasion. A lyric might still be historically typical or representative, for history formed the poet and his passions. Yet as compared with novels and plays, the historical, social context was less apparent in a lyric and was possibly less determining. And even novels and plays were, after all, fictions, which meant, within Romantic premises, that each depicted its own world, 'a little closed world', explained Friedrich Schlegel, proceeding on its 'own conditions and laws of inner possibility' ('Über das Studium der griechischen Poesie' (1795)).[10] In his essay on 'The artificial comedy of the last century' Charles Lamb took for granted that Restoration comedies did not reliably picture upper-class life at the end of the seventeenth century. He did not speak of literary stylization and convention, as we might now do, but viewed the plays as heterocosms. This concept makes the fictional reflection of history indirect and hard to extrapolate. Finally, there were the multiple difficulties for literary history created by the concept of art as beauty. The question, as Peter Szondi puts it, was how can there be 'different types of the beautiful', or how can the beautiful itself be 'susceptible of change'.[11] Moreover, if we think art expresses beauty or the ideal, we cannot also find that it directly reflects social reality.

The situation most reveals itself in critics who were also historians, such as Thomas Carlyle, Thomas Babington Macaulay and Georg Gottfried Gervinus. Macaulay's *History of England from the accession of James II* (1849–55) reconstructs a past society, but his essays in literary criticism largely elide historical information and context as causal factors. Gervinus was trained as a historian in the school of Wilhelm von Humboldt and F. C. Schlosser, and applied his considerable talents to literary history. He stoutly maintained the irrelevance of critical evaluation to his project. Whoever 'is inclined to make aesthetic judgments thereby loses the point of view of a writer of history. The literary historian has nothing to do with aesthetic criticism.'[12] As for Carlyle, the future historian of the *French revolution* (1837) and of *Frederick II of Prussia* (1858–65) had himself tried to write, around 1830, a history of German literature. He spent maybe a

[10] In Ernst Behler *et al.* (eds.), *Kritische Ausgabe*, 35 vols., Paderborn: Schöningh, 1979, I: 314–15.
[11] Peter Szondi, *Poetik und Geschichtsphilosophie I. Studienausgabe der Vorlesungen*, vol. II, in *Antike und Moderne in der Ästhetik der Goethezeit*, ed. Senta Metz and Hans-Hagen Hildebrandt, Frankfurt am Main: Suhrkamp, 1974, p. 17.
[12] Georg Gottfried Gervinus, 'Prinzipien einer deutschen Literaturgeschichtsschreibung', *Heidelbergisches Jahrbuch der Literatur* (1833), reprinted in Thomas Cramer and Horst Wenzel (eds.), *Literaturwissenschaft und Literaturgeschichte*, Munich: Fink, 1975, p. 20.

year on it, working so earnestly that 'it sickens me and inflames my nerves, as if it were a *Poem!*'[13] Yet Carlyle also harboured the deepest reservations about this project. In its highest ideal, literature embodies, as Carlyle believed, a transcendent, spiritual essence – Beauty – that is continuous with morality and religion. Hence Carlyle could not conceivably accept a sociological or material history of literature. To deduce 'the inward and spiritual exclusively from the outward and material' is a fallacy. 'Poetry above all . . . is one of those mysterious things whose origin and development never can be what we call explained'.[14] This does not mean that poetry lacks a history, for 'each age . . . demands a different representation of the Divine Idea' (*Critical essays*, 1: 57). But historical inquiries about poetry are of secondary importance. In fact, a literary history is 'a trivial insignificant book' (*Two notebooks*, p. 156). The 'grand question' concerns 'the essence and peculiar life of poetry itself' – what it is and to what end (*Critical essays*, 1: 49).

Eventually a time of dominance arrived for literary history. Works were studied within its perspective more often than not. This period, which lasted with peaks and valleys roughly from 1840 to 1940, may be thought an aberration in the 2,400 years of western criticism. It is neither natural nor obviously desirable, and certainly it is not necessary, to read, interpret or evaluate literary works within historical contexts. Every work has a double aspect, that in which it relates to its own time and that in which it transcends it by speaking to us. Readers and critics are free to emphasize the former or the latter. To imagine that a work addresses us the more, the more we conceptualize it in its own time, is a present-day ingenuity that could occur only to literary historians on the defensive.

One might seek the historical causes of this brief ascendancy. But this topic is for a different essay, and I merely remark here that literary history satisfied the criteria of a university discipline. Neither criticism nor poetics could be modelled as a progressive body of knowledge. If by philology we mean linguistic research and the editing of texts, this was useful for classical and medieval writings but less so for modern literature. But study of the biographical, sociological, intellectual, literary *contexts* of works was a different case. It could be taught and – essential criterion for an academic discipline – persons of ordinary abilities could make contributions. The piling up of information could be presented as an increase in knowledge. Disputes over methods and theories of literary history might be taken as signs of healthy life in a discipline.

[13] Thomas Carlyle, *Two notebooks*, Charles Eliot Norton (ed.), New York: The Grolier Club, 1898, p. 156.
[14] Thomas Carlyle, 'Early German literature' (1831), in *Critical and miscellaneous essays*, 3 vols., Boston: Dana Estes and Charles E. Lauriat, 1884, II: 254–5.

II

To this point my argument has been that though literary history was indeed a product of the Romantic age, as is generally supposed, it was not yet then the dominant critical discourse. Historicism could not easily be integrated with other premises and interests to which critics and readers were strongly committed. Nevertheless, much narrative literary history was written, much historical conceptualizing, explanation, and interpretation of texts, and much research into the literary past. To this I now turn as my subject for the rest of this chapter. In discussing Romantic literary history, moreover, I try to see it in relation to other modes or models of literary history, especially those of the present day. On the one hand, Romantic literary historians necessarily followed procedures and adopted assumptions that are intrinsic to the genre. On the other hand, their work had features that are not characteristic of the naturalist, positivist, modernist or post-modernist literary histories that came later. It is certainly not correct, as one sometimes hears, that literary history is inherently or always a Romantic genre. Instead, there is a distinctively Romantic type of literary history.

Already the Romantics had enough information to make historical reconstructions that were detailed and plausible. The great work of reacquiring medieval and Renaissance literature, of discovering manuscripts, learning languages, preparing bibliographies, editions and commentaries, continued in full spate from the eighteenth century. The close knowledge of medieval literature possessed by Gray and Warton as early as the 1760s is astonishing, the more so since most of this literature was still only in manuscript. The manners and material life of the past became a subject of research, as histories ceased to focus only on political events. The old histories of learning gradually transformed themselves into histories of culture. Thanks to this collective effort of scholarship, a minor literatus such as Nathan Drake could produce *Shakespeare and his times* (1817).[15] This book pretends to offer nothing more than background for reading the plays. It describes the schools of Shakespeare's time, the spread of literacy, the knowledge of foreign literatures, the price of books, religious beliefs, folklore and the material culture and ways of life of the Elizabethan upper, middle and lower classes, all in rich detail. It is a fat, useful, impressive work, and makes my point that historical information was richly available.

Certain concepts or cultural attitudes must be diffused before literature will be viewed historically, and the attainment and diffusion of these was

---

[15] Paris: Baudry's European Library, 1843.

the work of the later eighteenth century. When in 1717 Samuel Garth prefaced a recent translation of the *Metamorphoses*, he did not discuss the historical context in which Ovid's poem was created.[16] Garth took for granted, of course, that Ovid's pagan, slave-holding Rome was unlike contemporary England. But apparently the differences did not seem important to him. At any rate, they did not erect a barrier between himself and Ovid, whom he discussed as though he were a contemporary, criticizing his versification. The recognition of an alien mentality emerged strongly, however, as attention turned to the literature of the Middle Ages. A similar feeling of historical distance developed gradually throughout the eighteenth century in discussions of ancient literature and of the Renaissance. Literary history presupposes that the past is different and attempts to overcome this distance. It compiles information, explains the past, makes it intelligible. But more effectively and deeply the historical approach intensifies the sense of difference by positing it, by taking it as a fundamental assumption. In the modern world, to place a work in the past is automatically to view it as expressing an alien mentality.

George Frederick Nott, an admirable but conservative scholar, produced in 1815 an edition of Surrey and Wyatt. Surrey, he said, established 'the laws of English versification, such as they . . . have been adopted by our standard writers . . . ever since'. 'Improvements' in literature, Nott believed, are not the work of collective processes but of single individuals.[17] Romantic literary history assumes the opposite. Something supraindividual – the age, milieu, generational experience, in short, context – forms the work because it forms the author. Reading Cicero, Madame de Staël encountered 'the nation in the man'.[18] 'As a language belongs to an entire nation', said Herder, 'so also do certain favourite processes of imagination, turns and objects of thought, in short, a genius that expresses itself in the dearest works of its spirit and heart without regard to individual differences' (*Sämmtliche Werke*, XVIII: 58). An author, Herder wrote elsewhere, 'stands rooted in his century like a tree, and draws his sap from it'. He bears the 'birthmarks of his age'. It is true that these 'birthmarks' are also 'wounds', 'fetters' – in short, they are limitations (II: 265). But they limit only as individuality does, and Herder believed that every human achievement grounds itself in a nation and an age as well as a personal identity.

[16] Sir Samuel Garth (ed.), *Ovid's metamorphosis*, trans. by John Dryden, *et al.*, 5th edn, London: Tonson & Draper, 1751.

[17] George Frederick Nott, 'Dissertation on the state of English poetry before the sixteenth century', in *The works of Henry Howard Earl of Surrey and of Sir Thomas Wyatt the Elder*, 2 vols. (London: Longman, Hurst, Rees, Orme, and Brown, 1815), pp. clxxxii, cxxxviii.

[18] Madame de Staël-Holstein, *De la littérature considérée dans ses rapports avec les institutions sociales*, Paul van Tieghem (ed.), 2 vols., Paris: M. J. Minaird, 1959, I: 111.

Because of the role they assign to context, literary histories have a split focus. They dwell both on literary works and on the causal factors at work in shaping them. Romantic literary history invokes as contexts geography, race, politics, manners, social institutions, folklore, religious faith, philosophical beliefs, other arts and previous literature, and usually combines these different contexts in its explanations. Why did drama and oratory flourish in ancient Athens? Paper was expensive, says De Quincey, invoking a material factor, and the voice was the most efficient mode of publication.[19] Why did English poetry decline after Chaucer? Or German poetry after the Hohenstaufen dynasty? We need only consider the political anarchy of those times, according to Thomas Campbell in his 1819 'Essay on English poetry' and Thomas Carlyle in his 1831 'Early German literature'.[20] In his *History of prose fiction* (1814) John Colin Dunlop explains why Italians did not write chivalric prose romances: their low opinion of the military profession; their mercantile spirit; their closeness to classical culture. For these causes he cites other sociological or historical causes.[21] Comparing English with French tragedy, Shakespeare with Racine, Francis Jeffrey finds 'more than an analogy' between the form of tragedy and the form of government. 'Our drama has all along partaken of the mixed nature of our government – persons of all degrees take a share in both . . . In England, too, the stage has in general been dependent on the nation at large, and not on the favour of the Court.'[22]

With few exceptions, Romantic literary history assumes that literature's reflection of the age is very direct. 'We should really be at a loss', Hazlitt wrote, 'where to find, in any authentic document of the same period, so satisfactory an account of the general state of society, and of moral, political, and religious feeling, in the reign of George II as we meet in the Adventures of Joseph Andrews'.[23] Dunlop believed that romances of chivalry were 'the offspring of existing manners . . . merely an exaggerated picture of the actual state of society'. (Dragons and enchanters were 'ornaments'; Dunlop, *History*, I: 128, 126.) Only slowly and reluctantly did readers accept the argument of Sismondi, that 'the system of chivalry is an invention almost entirely poetical': the documents of the supposedly chivalric ages 'give us a clear, detailed, and complete account of the vices

[19] Thomas De Quincey, 'Style', in David Masson (ed.), *Collected writings*, 14 vols., Edinburgh: Adam and Charles Black, 1889–90, X: 237.
[20] Thomas Campbell, 'An essay on English poetry', in *Specimens of the British poets*, 2nd edn, London: John Murray, 1841, p. xlv; Carlyle, *Critical essays*, II: 253.
[21] John Colin Dunlop, *History of prose fiction: a new edition revised with notes, appendices and index*, Henry Wilson (ed.), 2 vols., 1906: reprinted New York: AMS Press, 1969, II: 2–3.
[22] Francis Jeffrey, *Contributions to the 'Edinburgh review'*, 3 vols., London: Longman, Brown, Green & Longmans, 1846, I: 356–7.
[23] William Hazlitt, *Complete works*, P. P. Howe (ed.), 21 vols., London: Dent & Sons, 1933, XVI: 5.

of court and the great, of the ferocity or corruption of the nobles, and of the servility of the people'. One 'is astonished to find the poets, after a long lapse of time, adorning the very same ages with the most splendid fictions of grace, virtue, and loyalty'.[24]

In a circular method, Romantic critics frequently derived their information about an 'age' from its literature and used this information to explain the literature. For lectures of 1818 Coleridge planned 'to exemplify the positions of my last lecture concerning the morals, manners, and specific genius of the Middle Ages from the old Tales, Songs, and Metrical Romances . . . For in these we possess not only the most amusing illustrations, but actually the fairest and least objectionable proofs, of the true character of the Times, in which they were written.'[25] Herder and Madame de Staël have especially been charged with this circular fallacy.[26] It is a fallacy because literary representations may be stylized, traditional, conventional and ideological and, in such cases, do not directly reflect the social world in which they are produced. This now seems obvious, but such considerations were largely ignored in Romantic literary history.

Literary history aspired at this time to become an 'inner history' in which events were seen as causally interrelated and therefore necessary. Rightly or wrongly, this form of historiography was thought a great advance over the older compilations and chronicles. Such a history is more selective in what it includes and more tightly organized than, for example, the Wartonian catchall or the Gibbonian panorama, and it is shaped teleologically. Its purpose is not merely to describe the past but to explain some phenomenon, such as 'Shakespearean tragedy', by tracing its derivations. Or it may seek to make the present or some aspect of it intelligible or to predict the future. Its form is thus linear – it traces a chain of events to a chosen terminal point – and it is developmental. The latter term implies a succession of changes in which, as Dilthey put it, 'each is possible only on the basis of the previous one'.[27] Goethe's supposed classicism motivated German critics also to notice that influence can take long leaps. 'Only after centuries', said A. W. Schlegel, 'does a great spirit speak to a related one, who is able to form works corresponding to his own' (*Vorlesungen über schöne Literatur*, p. 194). Nevertheless, Schlegel was fully committed to a developmental literary history. Alternative models

[24] J. C. L. Simonde de Sismondi, *Historical view of the literature of the south of Europe*, Thomas Roscoe (trans.), 3rd. edn, 2 vols., London: Henry G. Bohn, 1850, I: 79.
[25] Samuel Taylor Coleridge, *Notebooks: 1808–19*, ed. Kathleen Coburn, 2 vols., Princeton, NJ: Princeton University Press, 1973, vol. I, entry 4384.
[26] René Wellek, *A history of modern criticism: 1750–1950*, 8 vols., New Haven, CT: Yale University Press, 1955–, vol. I: *The later eighteenth century*, p. 197; Paul van Tieghem Introduction to Staël, *De la littérature*.
[27] Wilhelm Dilthey, *Der Aufbau der geschichtlichen Welt in den Geisteswissenschaften*, Frankfurt am Main: Suhrkamp, 1970, p. 201.

of change, corresponding to different perceptions of reality, are more in favour at present. We observe randomness, contingency or discontinuity where Romantic historians saw continuous transition and constructed their narratives accordingly.

German thinkers often described historical development as organic. Every event was a moment of a unified process, a part of a whole. This whole might be a national literature, a genre or an author's *oeuvre*. To Friedrich Schlegel, Greek poetry appeared to be an 'independent, complete, perfect whole . . . in which even the smallest part is necessarily determined by the laws and purpose of the whole and yet is free and exists for itself . . . The greatest as well as the smallest advance develops as if of itself from the preceding one, and contains the complete germ of the following phase' (*Kritische Ausgabe*, I: 305–6).

To know the past we must of course read and study, but by itself this is not enough. With the past as with everything else, a principle of Romantic hermeneutics was sympathy, that is, imaginative participation in the life represented. One must, says Herder, 'step into their time, their land, their circle of thoughts and feelings, see how they live? how they are brought up? what objects they see? what things they passionately love? what their air, their sky, the structure of their organs, their dance, their music may be. All this one must learn to know not as a stranger or a foe but as their brother and contemporary' (*Sämmtliche Werke*, XI: 226). 'Every sound criticism in the whole world says that in order to understand and explain a work of literature, one must put oneself into the spirit of its author, of his public, of his nation, and of his piece' (VI: 34). 'One must place oneself in the midst of their epoch and nation', said A. W. Schlegel, 'in order from that point to share their view of the world, which, however, cannot happen unless one divests oneself of personal inclinations and habits' (*Vorlesungen über schöne Literatur*, p. 482). The more an author has given his works individuality and particularity, the more the reader must negate his own identity.

Because of the concepts of organic development and sympathetic participation, the dilemma of critical relativism presented itself. If, as Friedrich Schlegel argued, 'the old Hellenic epic is . . . an entirely individual form that could only originate and ripen in this state of culture, in this place, in this time' (*Geschichte der Poesie der Griechen und Römer* (1798), *Kritische Ausgabe*, I: 442), and if every literary work is similarly determined in its time and place by historical necessities, most especially if each work is a moment in the world progress of the human spirit, how can one criticize it? In 'Also a philosophy of history towards the formation of humanity' (1794), Herder famously stated that 'nothing in the whole kingdom of God . . . is a means only – everything is a means and an end at the same time' (*Sämmtliche Werke*, V: 527). Each work, author, century is justified by history. If the writings of every age are to be entered and grasped by sympathetic identification, where is the standpoint from which an objective, universally valid criticism could be pronounced? Herder castigated those who 'believe that the taste of the present is the only taste' (XXXII: 28). But was this – the canonization of whatever temporary and local taste happens to be ours – in fact the only alternative to critical relativism? This may help explain why Romantic criticism was more oriented to appreciation than evaluation.

On the whole, even the most historically minded of the Romantics were not relativists. The strategy most commonly followed was to concede the impact of the 'age' on the author, and, if necessary, to condemn the age. In the latter step, Romantic critics differed in taste and in tone but not in principle from those of the Enlightenment. A writer might be of his or her time and nevertheless – or therefore – condemnable. On this principle an earlier generation had confidently dismissed the rude and barbarous Middle Ages. Thomas Campbell, in whom the Enlightened mentality survived, had read the commentaries of Richard Hurd 'and others, who forbid us to judge of the "Fairy Queen" by the test of classical unity, and who compare it to a gothic church, or a gothic garden'. But this comparison is 'nothing to the purpose' of criticism. Whether the poem is gothic or not, its plot is 'too intricate and too diffuse' ('An essay on English poetry', p. 110). In 1801–2 A. W. Schlegel had no doubt that 'one people or age may be more poetic than another' (*Vorlesungen über schöne Literatur*, p. 191). Friedrich Schlegel argued that every generation had its 'particular advantages and disadvantages, of which the cause lay mostly in external factors and in the age itself. One must keep this in mind, in order not to require qualities from a writer that, in his situation, he probably could not have had, or to reproach him with faults that actually belong not so much to him as to his age as a whole.'[28] Working toward a passage quoted earlier, Herder remarked that 'it is usually necessary to subtract from an author what belongs to his time . . . He bears the fetters of his epoch' (*Sämmtliche Werke*, II: 265). Such language suggests that there is a standard by which faults and limitations can be recognized and judgment pronounced. The Romantic historical sense might bring critical charity or justice to the individual writer without redeeming his age.

III

What is the purpose of literary history? Obviously the Romantics did not think, as some persons now do, that literary history should be written in

---

[28] Friedrich Schlegel, *Kritische Ausgabe*, vol. VI: *Geschichte der alten und neuen Literatur*, Hans Eichner (ed.), Paderborn: Schöningh, 1961, p. 377.

order to intervene in present-day politics. They did not approach texts suspiciously as bags of ideological poison. But they were highly curious about the overt and unconscious beliefs literature expresses. They supposed that as compared with other historical documents, literature gives a more complex insight into the mentality of an age, into the morality and wisdom, as Francis Jeffrey put it, that were 'then current among the people' (*Contributions*, II: 256). In the new attention to medieval and Renaissance literature, they saw works restored to the canon that ignorance or prejudice had lost. This, they thought, was also a function of literary history. Before the attacks of aesthetes and later of the New Critics, it used also to be assumed that historical knowledge enables one to perceive, understand and appreciate literature more deeply and correctly. Romantic literary historians took this for granted, but they also had other purposes for literary history that are now no longer pursued.

We know what poetry is from its γενεσις, says Herder, spelling the word in Greek for emphasis (*Sämmtliche Werke*, v: 380). The origin 'holds the whole nature of its product, just as the complete plant with all its parts lies covered in the seed' (XXXII: 86–7). Thus we know what the lyric is by studying its folk origins in ancient Greece and Palestine; we know Greek culture and art by tracing their origins back to Egypt and Phoenicia. Already the Romantics confronted the difficulty that every origin has its origin, every source its source, in a recession without a beginning. As A. W. Schlegel put it, 'until I know the cause of its cause, the immediate cause seems accidental to me, and thus in an infinite series backward. Hence history can never achieve insight into necessity, because it can cite no absolutely first cause' (*Vorlesungen über schöne Literatur*, p. 188).

Or we can know what a genre is, or a national literature, by inferring not from its origin but from its end. We can know modern poetry from its history, says Friedrich Schlegel, because its history shows a tendency, reveals where it is going. 'Perhaps from the spirit of its previous history we will succeed in discovering also the *meaning* of its present striving, the direction of its further course, and its future goal.' 'When the direction and the goal of its career make apprehensible the *purpose of its strivings*, the meaning of its whole mass will be completely clarified' (*Kritische Ausgabe*, I: 224, 229).

One object, then, of Romantic literary history was the underlying form, indwelling principle, essence, *Geist* or idea. Of what? Of works, authors, genres, traditions, national cultures and humanity. This view bestowed a deep, ultimately metaphysical purpose to an activity that all literary historians must perform. The subjects of literary history are expressed in general terms – 'the spirit of the age', 'Greek tragedy' – if only for the practical reason that we cannot mention separately every particular item that we have in mind. The question then concerns the ontological status of such collective references. The mind of England, said Friedrich Schlegel, is inclined to paradox and scepticism (*Geschichte der alten und neuen Literatur*, p. 336), but this was only a German way of remarking that English thinkers were steeped in the empirical philosophy and psychology of their country. To them generalizing terms and names of types seemed necessarily inadequate to the particularity and variability of our precepts. Still worse, the meaning of terms such as 'the lyric' varied from mind to mind, depending on the associations with which they happened to be linked. Such terms lacked a real, objective referent. In the different intellectual traditions of Germany, such terms signified collective individuals, ideal subjects, or *Geister* – entities that in some sense were real. Hence literary history had in Germany an intellectual status it could not easily attain in England. Idealistic philosophy was conducive to literary history, and is surely another reason, along with the prevalence of universities, why the discipline flourished more in Germany than in Great Britain or France.

To Friedrich Schlegel, for example, the *Geist* of modern poetry is an organic part of a larger whole or *Geist*, which is that of all western poetry. But this *Geist*, as with Hegel, is part of a still deeper, more comprehensive spirit coming to realization through history. The whole of history assigns meaning to each moment, gives the 'plot', so to speak, that determines the significance of each event. This whole is known by philosophy and religion, and without these 'history is only a dead heap of useless materials, without inner unity, without its own final purpose, and without result' (p. 339). History is ultimately the history of the formation of humanity. Literary history is a current in the larger stream, but one that especially reveals the direction of the whole. To write a literary history is to trace the progress of the human spirit.

With this concept we are far indeed from modern historiography. It would be quite mistaken to associate this view only with German thinkers, for essentially the same purpose had motivated the histories of learning in the Enlightenment, and it was present in histories of literature wherever they were written. John Colin Dunlop, a bright lawyer and sheriff in Edinburgh, argued that his history of prose fiction gives a 'successive delineation' of 'prevalent modes of thinking'. It offers 'interesting facts' for the philosophical study of the human mind, 'retrieves from oblivion a number of individuals', and helps us to avoid 'the errors into which our predecessors have fallen'. Above all, it depicts 'the advance of the human mind' (*History*, 1: 35).

Of literary historians in the early nineteenth century, the one who most resembles a modern historian – this is not necessarily a compliment – is Gervinus, and for him the purpose of literary history was somewhat different. Since the beginning of the new literary history in the eighteenth century there had been an endemic scepticism about the possibility of historical knowledge. Gervinus sought the more immediate causes of events rather than the deep-lying, ever-working ones that are disclosed to the philosophy of history. In Hayden White's typology of historians, Gervinus would belong more to the ideographic kind, that seeks less embracing syntheses.[29] Gervinus's method is more sociological than that of the Schlegels. He believed, for example, that literary history should pay close attention to the material and institutional determinants of literature and of its reception. Moreover, in contrast to the Schlegels, Gervinus wished to notice minor authors and works, for the 'history of literature, like political history, has to do with masses', and it is by the common soldiers that the wars of literature are won. No one can read everything, but thus far 'the historians of our literature have read infinitely too little' and hence have 'plowed in the air' ('Prinzipien', p. 28).

Though not himself a sceptic, Gervinus thought that an uncommitted, impartial attitude was necessary to historical understanding. In other words, he was committed to the requirements of his profession as he perceived them. 'In general whoever is trapped in a philosophical system, anxious over a moral principle, or imprisoned in a certain taste', mistakes his vocation as a historian, and 'will never accomplish anything. For the historian must be completely free and able to take any point of view' (p. 61).

Moreover, Gervinus stressed that contrasting points of view might be equally justifiable. A literary history must of course have a plot, for otherwise it is not history, does not exhibit an inner connection of events. But the same events can be emplotted in contradictory ways with equal plausibility. Take, for example, 'our last period' of German literature. It could be correlated 'with the general revolution of the European spirit' or it could stand in opposition to this. The historian could 'show it as completing what the Reformation began to effect for spiritual freedom, or as the beginning' of the political movement for civil freedom. No historian 'could represent all the points of view from which a material so rich and many-sided might be treated.' 'He can win a thousand sides from history and must choose one . . . He must just begin' (pp. 63, 61).

On the other hand, Gervinus cautions against projecting arbitrary ideas into the historical material. The initial choice of a point of view should be regarded only as tentative and preliminary. It will be confirmed by research or shown to be untenable. Ultimately Gervinus cherished the same purpose for literary history as other Romantic historians. A history of German literature would show it freeing itself from repressive influences –

---

[29] Hayden White, *Tropics of discourse: essays in cultural criticism*, Baltimore, MD: The Johns Hopkins University Press, 1978, pp. 64–5.

monkish, scholastic, mercantile, foreign and learned. It becomes first independent and then hegemonic among European literatures, a narrative of progress that 'cannot yet be proved on the basis of the political history of Germany' (p. 64).

IV

But if progress is the providential plan of history, it was easier to see this plan fulfilling itself in the history of learning and culture than specifically in *belles lettres*. How could one glorify either Greek or medieval literature and also maintain the general progress of the human mind? In dialectical squirming, the literature of the present or near future might be assigned the role of returning to those former summits or surpassing them. This was Friedrich Schlegel's solution, with which he hoped to reconcile the quarrel of the ancients against the moderns.[30] In Great Britain, however, such optimism shipwrecked on the set of ideas we call primitivism. Literature and the arts were seen to decline as civilization advanced, and, moreover, because civilization advanced. Literature fosters refinement – this was a large piece of the argument – and civilized refinement erodes creative power.

In the *ur* ages – Homeric, Ossianic or chivalric – everything was conducive to poetry. Why? Because human beings caught their ideas from nature and experience rather than from books; because their emotions were unrepressed and strong; because they expressed themselves spontaneously, uttering their joy and grief just as it arose within them; because their language was more concrete and figured; because they lived amid the sublime scenery of untamed nature; because their lives were more adventurous and their social institutions more colourful; because their work was not yet specialized, overdeveloping some of their mental faculties and suppressing the rest; because their imagination was not yet regularized and subdued to ego-reality, but projected itself into the vast, gloomy forests and mountains, peopling them with nymphs, oreads, dragons and witches; because the first poets rendered what is most basic and important in life, and thus, since an artist must offer some originality, confined succeeding poets to the nuanced and secondary; because the greatness of the first writers undermined the self-confidence of later ones, who could not hope to emulate their predecessors; because the arts were not yet divided, so that poetry, dance and song merged in a *Gesamtkunst*, or, more generally, because poetry then comprised all the genres – legislation, literature,

[30] Ernst Behler, Introduction to Friedrich Schlegel, *Kritische Ausgabe*, vol. I: *Studien des klassischen Altertums*, p. clxiii.

history, philosophy, theology – that later separated, and was therefore prized and honoured to a degree that is no longer conceivable; because in the first ages there were no critics or connoisseurs to browse like asses on the shoots of poetry. All these theories were worked out in detail. They were made highly sophisticated and plausible. As René Wellek says, they amounted to the first conceptions of a 'purely deductive, general, speculative history of poetry, which could be constructed from a knowledge of human nature, without regard to particular times and places' (*Rise of English literary history*, p. 74).

Summarizing as I must, it is impossible to convey the wholly admirable ingenuity and sometimes startling sagacity of these arguments. Among the authors and titles I have in mind are Thomas Blackwell, *An Enquiry into the life and writings of Homer* (1735), David Hume, 'On the rise and progress of the arts and sciences' (1742), Richard Hurd, 'A discourse concerning poetical imitation' (1751), Joseph Warton, 'Essay on Pope' (1756), John Brown, *The history of the rise and progress of poetry* (1764), and William Duff, *An essay on original genius in philosophy and the fine arts, particularly in poetry* (1767). By the end of the eighteenth century ideas developed in these and other essays appear in one British writer after another, as part of the stock of literary insight. Hazlitt, for example, wrote an essay to explain 'Why the arts are not progressive', and argued elsewhere that great dramatic tragedy cannot be produced in the modern world of theatre goers. The patterns of tragedy

must be drawn from the living models within the breast, from feeling or from observation; and the materials of Tragedy cannot be found among a people, who are the habitual spectators of Tragedy, whose interests and passions are not their own, but ideal, remote, sentimental, and abstracted. It is for this reason, chiefly, we conceive, that the highest efforts of the Tragic Muse are in general the earliest.

(Hazlitt, *Complete works*, v: 13)

Francis Jeffrey believed that 'the first writers naturally took possession of what was most striking, and most capable of producing effect, in nature and in incident'. Their successors were therefore obliged, 'for the credit of their originality, to produce something which should be different', and the relentless pressure of this, accumulating as each generation left the next confronting more predecessors, forced literature to take up subjects and methods in which nature was increasingly secondary to novelty. 'The early Greeks . . . wrote down whatever struck them as just and impressive, without fear of finding that they had been stealing from a predecessor' (*Contributions*, I: 109). Thomas De Quincey argued similarly that 'in the earliest stages of literature men deal with the great elementary grandeurs of passion, of conscience, of the will in self-conflict . . . We then have an Iliad, a Jerusalem Delivered, a Paradise Lost.' But as the times become modern, 'expanding social intercourse in towns . . . banishes these gloomier and grander phases of human history from literature'. This happens, De Quincey typically adds, 'spontaneously in every people, and by a necessity that moulds the progress of civilization' (*Collected writings*, XI: 60–1).

It seemed, then, that for houses, candles and carriages, for the abolition of slavery and the relative emancipation of women, for politeness in social intercourse, for precision and abstraction in language and thought, for the accumulation and diffusion of knowledge in books, in short, for refinement, utility and science a price had to be paid, was paid, in the arts. This paradox is a theme of Hegel's speculative history of the arts in his *Aesthetics*, though he puts the 'idea' into the slot usually occupied by advancing civilization. It is equally the theme of Thomas Love Peacock's sprightly 'Four ages of poetry' (1820), in which, perhaps with his tongue in his cheek, Peacock also regards poetry as outdated. 'As reason gains the ascendency', poetry can no longer accompany it, and leaves it 'to advance alone'. 'Mr. Scott digs up the poachers and cattle-stealers of the ancient border. Lord Byron cruizes for thieves and pirates . . . among the Greek Islands'. Poetry once fulfilled a civilizing function, but is now irrelevant to 'the progress of useful art and science, and of moral and political knowledge'.[31]

These arguments were naturally resisted. Pessimism about the direction of art's history was reinforced in Germany by Winckelmann, whose greatly influential book taught that Greek sculpture represented the norm of beauty for all times and nations. But the history of art, said A. W. Schlegel, 'should not be an elegy to lost and unrecoverable golden ages'. 'Since infinite progress is required in all things, we can expect' that the genius of humanity will produce a greater art from and because of the heterogeneity and multiplicity that it must harmonize in the modern world (*Vorlesungen über schöne Literatur*, p. 193). As for the primitivists, Friedrich Schlegel warns against confusing the 'general requirement of representation and manifestation with a special form of figuration'. The essence of poetry does not lie in specific qualities of mind or speech, such as 'mighty outbursts of fearful passions in wild, natural people'. Sensation and imagination are inherent in human nature and cannot be refined away (*Kritische Ausgabe*, I: 268).

How to interpret history's plot deeply troubled Keats. I cite him to emphasize that such questions had practical meaning for writers. 'The antients', such as Milton and Shakespeare, 'were Emperors of vast Provinces', Keats thought, while the modern poet was like an 'Elector of Hanover', fussily ruling his petty kingdom. Poetry has declined, then, and yet a modern poet such as Wordsworth seems deeper than Milton. He sees

---

[31] Thomas Love Peacock, 'The four ages of poetry', in *English Romantic writers*, David Perkins (ed.), New York: Harcourt, Brace, and World, 1967, pp. 761, 763, 765.

more into the human heart and explores its dark passages. If this is so, the reason is certainly not that Wordsworth's individual abilities are greater than Milton's, but there has been a collective progress or 'grand march' of intellect since Milton's time. The question Keats pondered was whether the poet could transcend his age, or should even aim to do so, to become a writer of epic totality, or a dramatist of Shakespearean range, or whether he should, or must, 'martyr himself to the human heart', becoming a writer of lyric introspection, like Wordsworth, and whether this would be advance or decline in comparison with the poetry of the past.[32]

We have been considering the patterns or plots that Romantics discerned in literary history. No one, so far as I know, took the typically modern view that history fluctuates without a direction, goes nowhere. The nearest approach to this scheme of meaninglessness comes in theories of historical oscillation between poles. In his 1837 history of English literature, Robert Chambers, for example, thought there was a 'fixed law that an age of vigorous original writing, and an age of imitation and repetition, should regularly follow each other'. As Chambers develops this scheme, it has affinities with the later one of the Russian Formalists. For the Formalists, literature defamiliarizes its subject matter and style by new devices, and then, in the next phase, these novelties are widely adopted, becoming automatic and predictable; a new movement of defamiliarization must then ensue. For Chambers a 'vigorous original writing' makes 'so great an impression on public taste . . . that for some time there is an intolerance of every thing else'. Eventually, however, 'men begin to tire of a constant reproduction of the same imagery and the same modes of composition', and 'a fresh class of inventive minds is allowed to come into operation – who, in their turn, exercise the same control over those who are to succeed them'.[33] As with the Formalists, Chamber's scheme would not determine the particular qualities or characteristics of the dominant style or the order in which styles appear. With the sole reservation that each age must differ from the last, the movement of literary history could be random.

For the most part, to sum up, Romantic speculation imposed on literary history a career of either progress or decline. It created narratives of self-fulfilment, homecoming, heroic conquest, in short, of comedy or romance. Or, alternatively, it emplotted literary history as an ironical and tragic story in which the arts declined because civilization advanced. The prospect of progress opened more gloriously if the subject of literary history was human thought in general, the *historia litterarum*, rather than

---

[32] John Keats, *Letters*, Hyder E. Rollins (ed.), 2 vols., Cambridge, MA: Harvard University Press, 1958, vol. I, pp. 224, 282.

[33] Robert Chambers, *History of the English language and literature*, Edinburgh: William and Robert Chambers, 1837, pp. 190–1.

belles lettres. Explanations of why progress must take place might be either metaphysical or mechanical. In the former case the actual course of events was conflated with a logical imperative, but this was a difficult reconciliation. As Friedrich Schlegel phrased the dilemma, 'nothing is generally so illuminating as the theory of perfectibility. The pure sentence of reason concerning the necessary infinite perfecting of mankind is without all difficulty. But its application to history can occasion the worst misunderstandings if the *eye* fails to find the proper point of view, to observe the right moment, from which to look out over the whole' (*Kritische Ausgabe,* I: 263). For a mechanical theory of progress one could turn to Condorcet's *Sketch of a historical tableau of the progress of the human spirit* (1794). Condorcet maintained that literature improves because each author builds on the discoveries of previous ones.

V

According to William Hazlitt, the '*nucleus* of the prevailing system of German criticism' lies in the distinction between the classical, on the one hand, and the romantic or modern, on the other hand (*Complete works,* XVI: 63). Along with schemes of progress or of progress-with-decline, this was the third of the grand plans of Romantic literary history. Friedrich Schlegel worked out the distinction in 'On the study of Greek poetry' (1795). He maintained that though ancient and modern poetry have the same essence – for both are poetry – they are opposite in spirit. By the modern or romantic was meant literature written since the end of the classical world. Dante, Cervantes and Shakespeare were exemplars. At this time Schlegel favoured the classical, but he soon switched allegiance to the romantic. The purposes of the distinction gradually changed as it was redeployed by one critic after another. For Romantic readers in general its service was to overcome the hegemony of the classical while still preserving the classical as an ideal. One could fully share the fervent enthusiasm of the age for ancient Greece (as opposed to the vision of Rome that had inspired the last generation), and yet one could equally admire the medieval and early modern. As A. W. Schlegel explained in 1809–11, in 'a period not far back . . . several inquiring minds, chiefly German, endeavoured to . . . give the ancients their due, without being insensible to the merits of the moderns, although of a totally different kind' (*Lectures,* p. 21). The distinction was propagated in numerous writings of the Schlegel brothers, especially A. W. Schlegel's *Lectures on dramatic art and literature* (1809–11), and was also spread throughout European cultural criticism by Madame de Staël's *On Germany* (1810). The terms classic and romantic ambiguously named both perennial types and historical periods of culture. A hundred years after the Schlegels, T. S. Eliot and others revived the distinction in Modernist polemics. They allied the Modern with the Classical against the Romantic, which, by this time, had shifted its meaning, and now applied to the ethos of poetry in the nineteenth century.

Romantic critics correlated the key terms of the distinction with others to create a grid of critical associations. The classic was ancient, non-Christian, southern, French, linear or sculpturesque, objective, homogeneous, natural and naive; antithetically, the romantic was medieval or early modern, Christian, northern, Germanic, painterly, subjective, heterogeneous, spiritual and sentimental. Laying this grid over works of art, linear style became southern and classical, while the painterly was contrastingly northern, as in Wölfflin's famous dichotomy. Some of these categories might be switched in particular cases without disabling the general usefulness of the system. Though neither Christian nor northern, the art of India is romantic, said Jean Paul, because in it 'religion breaks down the barriers of the world of sense'.[34]

According to Friedrich Schlegel in his 1795 'On the study of Greek poetry', Greek cultural development was guided throughout by nature and never seriously subjected to foreign influences. It was, therefore, organic and homogeneous. Moreover, it was complete. Its inner spirit was able fully to evolve and manifest itself. In Greek art a maximum of beauty was reached, for though the constituents of beauty are separately capable of infinite progression, in a beautiful object they must be in proportion, and the harmony of the whole limits the development of each part. Of the homogeneous, unified, and teleological, one can easily write the history.

On the other hand, modern or romantic poetry, Schlegel continues, is an infinite striving. There is no moment of completion or perfection, no moment when the spirit of modern poetry is fully developed and present. Its essence must be inferred from its origins, from its manifestations in Dante, Cervantes, Shakespeare and others, from the genres it evolves, such as the romance and the novel, and from the apparent direction of its evolution. Thus its essence can be known only through its history, and yet Schlegel endows romantic literature with characteristics that would seem to make the writing of its history impossible.

While Greek poetry was a product of nature, modern poetry, Schlegel argues, has been fostered and guided through its whole course by theory. The intellect can build its theory by abstract reasoning or by enshrining an already existing work of art as the realization of its programme. The latter case accounts for the importance of classical imitation in the modern theory

[34] Heinrich Wölfflin, *Principles of art history: the problem of development of style in later art*, M. D. Hottinger (trans.), New York: Dover, 1950; Jean Paul Richter, *Horn of Oberon: Jean Paul Richter's school for aesthetics*, Margaret R. Hale (trans.), Detroit, MI: Wayne State University Press, 1973, pp. 61–2.

and practice of art. The purpose of theory is to 'restore its lost lawfulness to corrupted taste and its true direction to art that has wandered from its way' (*Kritische Ausgabe*, I: 237). But as abstract principle or theoretical stricture intervenes, the development of literature ceases to be natural and organic. At some time in the future a valid theory of art will be achieved, a theory capable of fulfilling its function as a guide to art and taste. In the past, however, theory has possessed only inadequate, inconsistent, ungrounded concepts, so that the productions and course of modern literature have been arbitrary. But history, in Friedrich Schlegel's philosophical understanding of it, is determined by inner necessity or law. It cannot be arbitrary.

Other traits of modern poetry are a 'restless, unappeasable striving for the new', and a preponderance of 'the characteristic, individual, and interesting' (p. 228). With the latter set of terms Schlegel again draws a sharp contrast with Greek poetry, which is objective – in other words, its representations preserve a 'lawful relation of the general and the individual' (p. 291). The overbalance of modern poetry toward the individual appears not only in its representations but also in its poets. In Greece even those poems that 'betray little artistic wisdom and invention' display the same spirit that 'we can read in Homer and other poets of the first rank'. In modern poetry, however, 'the few common features are very indefinite, and actually each artist exists by himself, an *isolated egoist* in the midst of his age and his people' (pp. 282, 239). Schlegel's criticism is not mitigated by his assertion that modern poetry also pursues the characteristic, for this term, as he uses it, does not refer to the typical but to the interest of modern poetry in characterizing. To characterize a person, an age or a nation is to describe him, her or it as a particular, unified, organic individual. But a poetry that is restlessly in pursuit of the new cannot both fulfil its aim and have a history, since each work would be a new beginning. And a poetry that is devoted to the individual and characteristic cannot easily supply the schools, genres and other groupings that are indispensable to the organizing of the past and the writing of literary history. To list the traits and define the 'spirit' of a collection of works that are radically individual is paradoxical. Schlegel is perfectly aware of this and expresses the difficulty forcefully. However, the paradox is to him only a challenge, since he is confident that within the apparent 'anarchy', 'lawlessness', 'purposelessness', and 'chaos' of the history of modern poetry, there is a *Leitfaden*, a guiding thread. Following it, he will discover the meaning, direction and goal of modern poetry (pp. 221–4).

The division of western culture into the classical and the romantic does not of itself provide a narrative plot or meaning for history. In this respect it differs from the Romantic schemes of progress or of decline. Like every periodization, it fulfils formal needs in writing literary history, which requires, as Friedrich Schlegel said, 'clear divisions into parts and a satisfying unity of the whole'. It must present a 'quality that continues through a succession of poets and . . . a correlation' in the spirit of works produced at the same time (pp. 221–2). And like every classification in literary history, this one is vulnerable to empirical exceptions. In his *School for aesthetics* Jean Paul pointed out that one can find romantic passages in Homer and 'Greek islands' in Shakespeare. 'Every century is differently romantic', and so is every nation. Romanticism is not the same in southern and northern countries and has a different character, among southern ones, in Italy and Spain (pp. 60, 68, 63–4). The *locus classicus* of such arguments is Arthur Lovejoy's famous 1924 essay 'On the discrimination of Romanticisms', where Lovejoy argues that the term 'Romanticism' should either be used in the plural or dropped.[35] Jean Paul also powerfully raises objections that we might now more identify with Croce. Works have countless aspects, can be interrelated in innumerable configurations. The classifications of literary history are merely conventions or, at best, practical conveniences, and have little correspondence to reality. 'How pointless to take a people, even more so an era . . . in other words, to take a great various life, ever flowering in a different form, and nail it to a pair of broad generalities' (*School for aesthetics*, pp. 58–9).

Nevertheless, Jean Paul adopted the distinction, like many critics of his time. We must ask why a distinction with all the conceptual arbitrariness Schlegel criticized in modern theory, utterly vulnerable to empirical and scholarly demolition, nevertheless flourished and became one of the accepted premises of the age. Why was this dubious set of concepts felt to be a truly enlightening discovery? The answer can only be found in the uses to which it was put. One was to overthrow the hegemony of French neoclassic culture, of what in England was called the 'French taste' – the taste that, as Romantic critics asserted, had been dominant in the eighteenth century. In every country the distinction of the romantic from the classical helped to justify the new appreciation of medieval and early modern literature in the national language. This was modelled as the national literature, as the bearer of a tradition from which the 'French taste' had deviated. With a glowing sense of rediscovery, readers took up 'our older and great school of poetry',[36] contemplating in it the character or *Geist* of their people. A similar use of literary history continues to the present day, especially with marginal social groups, such as blacks, gays and women. They turn to the past literature of their own group in search of tradition and self-understanding, and they find their own present situation reflected in this literature.

[35] Arthur O. Lovejoy, *Essays in the history of ideas*, New York: Putnam's Sons, 1960.
[36] Leigh Hunt, Preface [to *Foliage*], including cursory observations on poetry and cheerfulness, in *Literary criticism*, Lawrence Huston Houtchens and Carolyn Washburn Houtchens (eds.), New York: Columbia University Press, 1965, p. 129.

In its defence of the medieval and early modern, its polemic against universal neoclassic (or French) cultural norms, and its alliance with nationalist sentiment, the distinction between the classical and the romantic served main goals of Romantic literary history. Furthermore, the distinction also helped to make literary history possible. It resolved a fundamental dilemma, reconciled history with aesthetics, by showing how beauty could have a history. If one could say that there are different kinds of beauty, different manifestations of the same essence, one could write literary history. If the grand question, to go back to Carlyle, was of the essence or nature of poetry, one could say that the essence could be known through its historical manifestations, perhaps only through them.

17
Literature and the other arts

HERBERT LINDENBERGER

I believe it may be considered as a general rule, that no Art can be engrafted with success on another art. For though they all profess the same origin, and to proceed from the same stock, yet each has its own peculiar modes both of imitating nature, and of deviating from it, each for the accomplishment of its own particular purpose. These deviations, more especially, will not bear transplantation to another soil.[1]

It is a necessary and natural consequence of their perfection that, without any shifting of their objective boundaries, the different art forms are becoming increasingly similar to one another *in their effect on the mind* [*Gemüt*]. Music in its highest ennoblement must become form and move us with the quiet power of antiquity; plastic art in its highest perfection must become music and move us by means of its direct sensuous presence; poetry in its most perfect development must, like music, grip us powerfully but at the same time, like sculpture, surround us with quiet clarity. The perfect style belonging to each of the various art forms is shown in its ability to eliminate their specific limits without giving up their specific advantages.[2]

Consider these statements written within ten years of one another. Each emanates from a figure who is at once a major theorist of art and a practitioner whose work retains its classical status today. Yet no two statements could be less alike in the circumstances under which they were voiced or in the roles we assign them within intellectual history. Sir Joshua Reynolds's warning to keep the various forms independent of one another was delivered in his capacity as president of the Royal Academy, and its recipients were art students assembled in 1786 for the annual distribution of prizes. Friedrich Schiller's words were written in the private study as part of a treatise in epistolary form that sought to establish a new rationale for art amid the political turmoil about which all Europe, and this author in particular, was fretting in 1793.

---

[1] Sir Joshua Reynolds, *Discourses on art*, Robert R. Wark (ed.), San Marino, CA: Huntington Library, 1959, p. 240.
[2] Friedrich Schiller, *Über die ästhetische Erziehung des Menschen* (22nd letter), in *Theoretische Schriften*, Rolf-Peter Janz (ed.), Frankfurt am Main: Deutscher Klassiker Verlag, 1992, pp. 640–1. Translation mine; unless otherwise indicated, translations throughout this chapter are my own. Emphases indicated in quotations throughout the chapter are in the original.

The first statement, like the various pronouncements about decorum and pictorialism in the annual prize-awarding addresses that make up what we call Reynolds's *Discourses*, represents an aesthetic that goes back to Renaissance humanism and that had not changed substantially in several centuries. The second statement, like many of the other observations in the *Aesthetic letters* about the value and function of art, expresses a utopian vision about a possible union of the arts that achieves significance for us by dint of historical hindsight through our awareness of Wagner's notion of a *Gesamtkunstwerk* and, even more conspicuously, in our own, postmodern time, through our routine use of the term *multimedia* as a generic category. Not that the author of these prophetic words ever put them into practice: indeed, in his varying roles as philosopher, historian, dramatist and lyric poet, Schiller observed the boundaries between genres and media as rigorously as Reynolds had done in his painting.

In fact, in a kind of 'saving' clause at the start of this statement, 'without any shifting of their objective boundaries', Schiller protects his readers from any immediate threat to the traditional borderlines separating the arts. Yet the relationship between artwork and audience that emerges from this passage, unlike the one suggested by Reynolds, points to the future, for Schiller projects his union of the arts as something located, as he puts it with typographical emphases, 'in their effect on the mind'. The very title of Schiller's treatise, *On the aesthetic education of man*, indicates that his is an affective theory of art concerned with the ways that consumers can experience art as a means of moral growth. Reynolds's defence of the separateness of the arts is based on the predominantly mimetic theory (note the phrase 'modes of imitating nature') that dominates not only his own aesthetic but also most of the critical thought of the preceding centuries. Moreover, Schiller's repeated use of the words *perfect* and *perfection* to characterize the mission of art suggests that by the end of the eighteenth century the various arts were coming to occupy an ideal, autonomous, more privileged space transcending other forms of human activity.

The radically different ways in which the arts are related to one another in these two passages (as well as the distinctive theories of aesthetics that stand behind each statement) help confirm our contemporary notion that in numerous forms of discourse – political, economic, philosophical – the late eighteenth century constitutes a watershed in the history of western thought. This chapter will centre around some questions about the ways that the various arts came to be understood in relation to one another. How can the move towards affective and expressive theories of art be connected with the breaking down of barriers that traditionally separated the various art forms? How can the diverse arts be said to function together as a system similar to other systems of thought? How were the arts classified and evaluated in relationship to one another? What new hierarchies emerged among the genres constituting a single art form? Was there really a move from the autonomy of individual arts to a union, as my juxtaposition of these statements may imply, or did this shift also imply a dominance of one or more arts within this supposed union?

Disparities among the arts

Despite the traditional autonomy of the various arts that Reynolds reiterated in his *Discourses*, two media, poetry and painting, had been linked together steadily since the Renaissance.[3] This relationship was based upon what we today recognize as a misreading of Horace's dictum, in the *Art of poetry*, that poetry is akin to painting.[4] Horace referred simply to the differing degrees of scrutiny one gave the two so-called 'sister arts' according to the distance from which one viewed a painting or to the degree of attention a particular literary or rhetorical genre demanded. For the Renaissance, however, his phrase '*ut pictura poesis*' provided not only a rationale for mutual imitation between the two art forms, but it also propagated what Rensselaer W. Lee has called 'the theory of the learned painter',[5] by means of which painting could lay claim to the high prestige that literature had traditionally enjoyed. It is significant that until well into the nineteenth century the most illustrious visual genre was history painting, which included not only what we label history today but virtually any form of public narrative, whether drawn from the Bible, mythology or political history. 'Je suis peintre d'histoire, je ne suis pas portraitiste', Ingres protested during the early years of the nineteenth century when a prospective sitter asked to see 'M. Ingres le portraitiste'.[6] 'The great work of the painter is the "historia" ', Leon Battista Alberti had written in 1435 in his influential treatise *On painting*, adding that the function of 'literary men' [*litterati*] was to 'assist in preparing the composition of a "historia" '.[7]

[3] For a classic account of the relations between poetry and painting from antiquity through the eighteenth century, see Jean Hagstrum, *The sister arts: the tradition of literary pictorialism and English poetry from Dryden to Gray*, Chicago, IL: University of Chicago Press, 1958.
[4] For a convincing demonstration of what Horace actually meant in the passage, see Wesley Trimpi, 'The meaning of Horace's *ut pictura poesis*', *Journal of the Warburg and Courtauld Institutes* 37 (1973), pp. 1–34.
[5] See Rensselaer W. Lee, *Ut pictura poesis: the humanistic theory of painting*, New York: Norton, 1967, pp. 41–8.
[6] See Walter Friedlander, *David to Delacroix*, Robert Goldwater (trans.), New York: Schocken, 1968, p. 80.
[7] Leon Battista Alberti, *On painting and on sculpture: the Latin texts of 'de pictura' and 'de statua'*, Cecil Grayson (ed. and trans.), London: Phaidon Press, 1972, pp. 71, 95, respectively.

From the Renaissance onward painting thus became a highly textualized art dependent upon literary precedents.

The sisterhood claimed by poetry and painting did not exist for poetry and music, even though the latter two were sometimes linked in ancient Greece.[8] As long as both poetry and painting were treated as imitative arts that represented actions or objects in the external world, they shared a common aim with one another. Music was treated as an imitative art only to the extent that composers sought sounds reflecting the words of a poem they were setting; otherwise, discussions of music concerned themselves with the effects that music could exert upon its listeners. The relative prestige of literature is revealed by the fact that at the inception and reformation, respectively, of opera such major composers as Monteverdi and Gluck both insisted on the primacy of poetry over music.

The disparities evident between literature and the other arts on a theoretical level also manifest themselves on the social scale. For most of western history practitioners of the visual and aural arts counted as craftspeople. A large number of painters and musicians were themselves the children of practitioners who taught them their own crafts, or they came from backgrounds too modest to assure them the degree of literacy – often including years spent studying classical languages – demanded of those who would call themselves poets. The disparity between music and poetry, even as late as the eighteenth century, was especially strong: whereas Bach, Mozart, Beethoven and Rossini were all sons of musicians, Handel the son of a barber-surgeon, Haydn of a wheelwright, and Gluck of a forester, writers ordinarily came from more socially elevated backgrounds or practised occupations demanding a high degree of literacy: Voltaire's father, for instance, was a notary; Johnson's, a bookseller; Wordsworth's, a legal agent for a landowner, Goethe's, a prominent official with the rank of 'imperial counsellor'. Even the exceptions, when examined closely, affirm the relatively higher status of those calling themselves 'writer'. Thus, as the orphaned and haphazardly educated son of a watchmaker, Rousseau made his role of outsider within the literary world central to his persona; indeed, early in his career the public acknowledged him more readily as the composer of a popular opera than as the writer of a provocative pamphlet. If Sir Joshua Reynolds, as the son of a clergyman–schoolmaster, came from a more literate background than did painters such as Gainsborough and David, both of whom were sons of cloth merchants, this fact also helps explain the respect he commanded as a man of letters.

The disparity between literature and the other arts is evident as well in the relative success with which writing was transmitted over the ages. How much, after all, would we know of classical antiquity if its literary

---

[8] See Hagstrum, *The sister arts*, pp. 8–9.

remains, fragmentary though they may be, had not come down to us? The music of antiquity has never been adequately reconstructed; the buildings, with rare exceptions, are in ruins; all but a few works of the legendary Greek sculptors are known only by later copies. Moreover, whereas the writings of authors deemed of classical status were easily available to literate persons from the Renaissance onward, most famous paintings could not be viewed directly but, until the recent development of public museums, solely by means of prints. Difficulties in the transmission of musical texts, together with constant changes in performing techniques, prevented the understanding and the revival of the musical past until quite recent times. Gregorian chant, institutionalized as it was within Roman Catholic liturgy, was the only musical form to maintain its canonical status over many centuries. Individual composers were often viewed more as performers (even of their own compositions) than as creators in the manner of poets. With the exception of Palestrina, whose compositions, like Gregorian chant, were performed in church, no composer achieved long-term canonical status until the rise of a movement in late eighteenth-century England to perpetuate the work of earlier composers, above all of Purcell and Handel.[9] When William Cowper in *The task* celebrated Handel as 'the more than Homer of his age',[10] he signalled the beginning of an attitude that would allow a composer of the past to be revered similarly to a classical writer.

The traditional primacy of literature, together with the relative autonomy of the various arts, is manifest as well in the academic study of the arts. Literature was the first of the arts to become a subject for formal investigation in the university, for it developed during the nineteenth century from the study of the history of the individual modern languages. The national, in fact nationalist orientation that resulted from the nineteenth-century biases within literary study established differing schemes of periodization in particular countries for the period that is the subject of the present volume: for example, whereas the term *Romanticism* generally encompasses the period 1798–1824 in England, what the French name with this term does not begin for some literary historians until 1830, while in Germany the term refers to writing between 1796 and the 1820s and has often been used so narrowly that it could not be applied to some of the most famous authors of the age.[11] Art history and music history

---

[9] For a detailed account of this canonization process, see William Weber, *The rise of musical classics in eighteenth-century England: a study in canon, ritual, and ideology*, Oxford: Clarendon Press, 1992.

[10] William Cowper, *Poetical works*, H. S. Milford (ed.), 4th edn, Oxford University Press, 1934, p. 233 (book VI, line 647).

[11] For a survey of classification schemes in different countries, see René Wellek, 'The concept of romanticism in literary history', in *Concepts of criticism*, Stephen G. Nichols, Jr (ed.), New Haven, CT: Yale University Press, 1963, pp. 128–98.

were relatively late and also quite separate developments within the university, and their period classifications are as independent of one another as those among the various national literary disciplines. Art historians classify painters from the late-eighteenth to the mid-nineteenth centuries largely according to formal criteria, for example the 'Classic' David, Ingres and Canova or the 'Romantic' Delacroix, Friedrich, Turner and Constable. Musicology, whose classifications derive from the development of German music, projects a Classical style from Haydn through Beethoven and a relatively late-blooming Romantic style that starts with Schubert and for some historians goes on as late as the end of the century.

No departmentally based academic discipline exists for the study of the various arts in relation to one another. In recent years the discipline calling itself comparative literature has encouraged university courses and symposia, as well as the compilation of bibliographies, on the subject it names 'literature and the other arts'. This term also happens to be the title assigned to the present chapter. It goes without saying that the term perpetuates the primacy that literature has enjoyed for much of history over its various sister arts.

The arts as system: treatises of aesthetics

Though not an independent academic discipline, that branch of philosophy known by the term *aesthetics* has, since its inception in the mid-eighteenth century, dedicated itself to theorizing the nature of art and the relation of the various arts to one another. Both the term and the discourse that it generated emerged from Alexander Baumgarten's treatise in Latin, *Aesthetica* (1750–8). Down to our own time the treatise of aesthetics has been a recognizable and continuing genre with its own set of conventions and with later examples building self-consciously on their predecessors. In many instances the treatise has served as a means of filling out a larger philosophical system, as it did for Schelling and Hegel. Often the title by which we know a treatise contains the term originally used by Baumgarten (Jean Paul, Solger, Hegel, Croce), or the title may simply include the term *art* (Schelling, A. W. Schlegel, Nelson Goodman) to alert us at once to its genre and to the fact that its subject matter occupies a realm distinct from that treated in other modes of discourse.

Though it is to the full-blown aesthetic treatise – complete with definitions of the nature of art, justifications for its significance and compendia of the various media and genres that make up the aesthetic realm – that we generally refer when we speak of a thinker's philosophy of art, many texts of more limited focus have contributed to the continuing discourse. For example, Burke's *Philosophical enquiry into the origin of our ideas of the sublime and the beautiful* (1757), though centred upon the terms indicated by its title, quickly made its way into the new aesthetic discourse, with an application of these terms forming a major component of Kant's own aesthetic inquiry. (The latter's *Critique of Judgement* [1790], though not overtly a philosophy of art but rather, like his earlier critiques, an examination of what can properly be stated about its particular area of investigation, still contains most of the elements to be found within aesthetic treatises.) Similarly, the terms in the title of Schiller's *On naive and sentimental poetry* (1795) helped shape many later systems through their usefulness in distinguishing older, more 'original', 'immediate' examples of art from later, more self-conscious and imitative examples.

Shelley's 'Defence of poetry' (1821), to the extent that the term *poetry* is extended to include art in general, indeed, even to the institutions of ancient Rome,[12] could be called a miniature aesthetic treatise. Some of the most telling contributions to aesthetic discourse have taken the even more miniature form of single paragraphs and sentences, most notably the so-called fragments that members of the early German school scribbled as part of their intense, ongoing discussions on art and its relation to other modes of knowledge. For example, Novalis's brief sentence, 'When one sets certain poems to music, why not set them to poetry [*Poesie*]?',[13] at once rethinks the relations of aesthetic forms to one another and expands the conventional definition of what constitutes poetry. Even travel guides such as Thomas West's *Guide to the lakes* (1778), to the extent that they instruct tourists at precisely which points to station themselves in order to experience 'picturesque' scenery as though it were landscape painting, participate in and advance the new discourse of aesthetics.

Within the formal and larger treatises the various art forms and their particular genres form a family whose network of interrelationships, however much these may differ from one treatise to another, is necessary to assure the cohesiveness of the system. Before the eighteenth century that whole spectrum which we today classify as the various 'arts' was not customarily discussed either systematically or in a comparative manner. During the Middle Ages, for instance, music, which was treated as one of the four mathematical arts called the quadrivium, belonged to a category different from the three verbal arts making up the trivium;[14] the visual

[12] *Shelley's poetry and prose*, Donald H. Reiman and Sharon B. Powers (eds.), New York: Norton, 1977, p. 494.

[13] Novalis, *Das philosophische Werk*, Richard Samuel (ed.), Darmstadt: Wissenschaftliche Buchgesellschaft, 1968, II: 360.

[14] See Ernst Robert Curtius, *European literature and the Latin middle ages*, Willard R. Trask (trans.), New York: Pantheon, 1953, pp. 36–9. For a comprehensive history of how those activities that, by the eighteenth century, came to be called the 'fine arts' were classified during earlier periods, see Paul Oskar Kristeller, 'The modern system of the arts', in *Renaissance thought and the arts: collected essays*, 2nd edn, Princeton, NJ: Princeton University Press, 1990, pp. 163–227.

arts, moreover, did not qualify for the title 'liberal' that was attached to the seven making up the trivium and quadrivium. To be sure, in his post-humously entitled *Paragone* (circa 1490), literally 'comparison', Leonardo da Vinci had briefly surveyed most of the arts contained within the formal aesthetic treatises that emerged four centuries later. But his purpose was not, like that of the latter, a justification and explanation of the larger cat-egory of art, but rather a defence of his particular art, painting, which had usually been belittled as a mechanical craft in comparison with those arts that seemingly demanded more learning. To justify the superiority of paint-ing against the other arts, Leonardo depreciates music for 'fad[ing] away as soon as it is born'; poetry for being 'often not understood, and requir[ing] many explanations'; sculpture for not 'requir[ing] the same supreme ingenu-ity as the art of painting'.[15]

Leonardo's remarks, brief though they may be, are notable at once for treating the arts as a group and for arguing, quite in contrast to theorists both before and after, for the superiority of painting. Even Sir Joshua Reynolds, despite his own professional stake in painting and in teaching young painters, maintains the traditional literary bias, with poetry being praised for its ability to engage the mind longer and more powerfully than painting (*Discourses*, pp. 145–6).

It was by means of the major aesthetic treatises of the last two hundred years that art received its legitimation, its identity, its aura. To assure art of its autonomy, these treatises were also forced to draw borderlines. A central method for creating these borders was to establish a transition zone between art and what are clearly non-artistic activities. Thus, Kant distinguishes between the 'purposive' and 'non-purposive' arts, with the former belonging to that transition zone and, as a result, certifying the impregnability of the non-purposive arts. The verbal arts, for example, divide between non-purposive poetry and purposive oratory; the plastic arts between sculpture and architecture; painting between painting proper and the purposive art of landscape gardening.[16] However different the particular systems of individual theorists, the more practically oriented arts play a similar role to insure the purity of the impractical ones. For example, Schopenhauer, in his long section on aesthetics in *The world as will and representation* (1818), places within his transition zone what he calls 'hydraulics as a fine art', namely the artificial waterfalls and foun-tains in the gardens of great houses, and, even lower in the zone, 'artistic

---

[15] See Leonardo da Vinci, *Paragone: a comparison of the arts*, Irma A. Richter (trans.), Oxford University Press, 1959, pp. 74, 60, 77, respectively. For a description of the relatively low status of the visual arts before Leonardo's time, see Richter's introduction, pp. 12–14.

[16] See Immanuel Kant, *Critique of judgment*, Werner S. Pluhar (trans.), Indianapolis, IN: Hackett, 1987, pp. 190–3.

horticulture' or landscaping.[17] August Wilhelm Schlegel, in contrast to most aesthetic theorists, seeks to raise the status of landscape gardening, which, in its finest examples, he compares to the art of major landscape painters; yet Schlegel also sets up his own lower forms, for example, Hogarth's art of caricature, to help validate the higher forms.[18]

Within the major treatises of aesthetics, a certain plenitude prevails by means of which art comes to constitute a world composed of a panoply of individual forms. Like the larger philosophical systems of which these treatises are sometimes a part, one notes an often elaborate array of categories parallel to and corresponding with another, together with subcategories that are themselves subdivided into further categories. Sometimes these categories take the form of concepts such as symbol and allegory (central, for example, to the systems of Schelling and Solger[19]) the beautiful and the sublime (note, for instance, Kant's division of the latter into its 'mathematical' and the 'dynamic' phases[20]), and sometimes these categories are simply the media (as well as the genres within a particular medium) that, taken together, are made to constitute the total world of art. 'Niemand klassifiziert so gern als der Mensch, besonders der deutsche' (nobody is so inclined to classify as man, especially a German), Jean Paul wrote in his own quite elaborate, though also witty, treatise, *Primer of aesthetics.*[21]

If concepts such as symbol and allegory, or beautiful and sublime, often come in twos within aesthetic systems, genres and media tend to appear in triplicate or quadruplicate. Since these genres and media are, in effect, the populace out of which the world of art is constituted, their presence in groupings larger than two serves to give this world a substantive grounding. By the end of the eighteenth century, literature had generally come to divide itself into the threefold pattern of epic, lyric and dramatic. Solger's treatise (finished before 1819), for example, divides the literary kinds into these three while dividing the other arts, namely sculpture, painting, architecture and music, into four (*Vorlesungen*, pp. 257–67). Herder, in his early aesthetic treatise, *The Critical Woodlands of Aesthetics* (1769), suggests three senses, hearing, seeing, feeling, as central to aesthetic experience to replace an earlier model that included only the first two of these

---

[17] See Arthur Schopenhauer, *The world as will and representation*, E. F. J. Payne (trans.), (New York: Dover, 1966), I: 218.
[18] See A. W. Schlegel, *Vorlesungen über schöne Litteratur und Kunst*, Heilbronn: Henninger, 1884, pp. 207–13 and 236–7, respectively.
[19] See F. W. J. Schelling, *The philosophy of art*, Douglas W. Stott (ed. and trans.), Minneapolis, MN: University of Minnesota Press, 1989, for example, pp. 45–50 and 147–52, and K. W. F. Solger, *Vorlesungen über Ästhetik*, K. W. L. Heyse (ed.), Darmstadt: Wissenschaftliche Buchgesellschaft, 1962, for example, pp. 129–45 and 260–1.
[20] See Kant, *Critique of judgement*, pp. 103–23.
[21] Jean Paul Richter, *Vorschule der Ästhetik*, in *Werke*, Munich: Carl Hanser, 1963, V: 67.

senses.[22] Hegel, for whom thinking in triads was second nature, in his lectures of the 1820s proposed a distinct ordering of the arts for each of three periods of history – the symbolic (or prehistoric), the classical and the romantic.[23] Wagner, in *The artwork of the future*, a work which, like the other aesthetic essays he wrote around 1850, serves at once to continue the theorizing of earlier treatises and to prepare the way for his own later practice as music–dramatist, derives art from precisely three forms – dance, music and literature.[24] But Wagner's tie to dance is perhaps more motivated by a desire for theoretical completeness than by his practical needs as an artist: though he names dance as 'the most real among all art forms' (p. 78)[25] and seeks to redefine it as gesture and movement, the degeneration into which he sees dance as having fallen on the modern stage prevented his giving this art much of a role in his own *Gesamtkunstwerke*, its role, in fact, being limited to the urban folk dances in *Die Meistersinger* and the formal ballet he felt forced to add to *Tannhäuser* to get this early work performed by the Paris Opéra.

Within the major aesthetic treatises the various art forms often come to shape a universe of their own by means of mutual correspondences and by the fact that they combine with one another to create new forms or to renew older ones. Rousseau, though he left no systematic treatise on aesthetics, made many suggestive remarks on the interrelationship of the arts, for example, 'The role of melody in music is precisely that of drawing in a painting.'[26] In Schelling's tightly argued treatise, music, painting and the plastic arts (the last in their most general sense) correspond, within the more limited realm of the plastic arts themselves, to architecture, bas-relief, and sculpture, respectively (*Philosophy of art*, p. 163). To illustrate this correspondence, Schelling, in an analogy apparently drawn from August Wilhelm Schlegel's theory and that achieved later notoriety, referred to architecture as 'frozen music' (p. 165).[27] Jean Paul, in turn, called music 'romantic poetry through the ear' (*Vorschule*, p. 466). Two arts are sometimes fused together to create a new one. Thus, for Wagner the Haydn symphony represents a fusion of dance with music, and Beethoven's

[22] Johann Gottfried Herder, *Die kritischen Wälder der Ästhetik*, in *Schriften zur Ästhetik und Literatur: 1767–1781*, Gunter E. Grimm (ed.), Frankfurt am Main: Deutscher Klassiker Verlag, 1993, pp. 289–99.
[23] G. W. F. Hegel, *Aesthetics: lectures on fine art*, T. M. Knox (trans.), Oxford: Clarendon Press, 1975, I: 76–81.
[24] Richard Wagner, *Gesammelte Schriften*, Julius Kapp (ed.), Leipzig: Hesse & Becker, 1914, X: 74–124.
[25] By 'real' Wagner means that dance is closer than other arts to the body.
[26] Jean-Jacques Rousseau and J. G. Herder, *On the origin of language*, John H. Moran and Alexander Gode (trans.), New York: Frederick Ungar, 1966, p. 53.
[27] On the history of the analogy, see Ernst Behler, 'Schellings Ästhetik in der Überlieferung von Henry Crabb Robinson', *Philosophisches Jahrbuch* 83 (1976), pp. 138, 146.

seventh symphony, in what has since become a cliché in music criticism, represents the 'apotheosis of the dance' (*Gesammelte Schriften*, x: 98, 101). Sometimes analogies are drawn between contemporary works within different media, as when August Wilhelm Schlegel briefly suggests a relationship between the *Divine comedy* and the gothic cathedral (*Vorlesungen über schöne Litteratur*, p. 182).

The complex relationships among the arts projected within these treatises include what are often highly evaluative judgments about how these arts and their various genres rank among one another. The bias in favour of literature discussed in the preceding section remains prevalent among most theorists, with some notable exceptions to be discussed later in this section. 'Poetry [*die poesie*] is the universal art', Solger writes at one point, though he later acknowledges that even the most universal art might not be able to exercise as powerful an influence as music or architecture within the intellectual climate in which he was writing (*Vorlesungen über Ästhetik*, pp. 259, 267). For Schelling poetry 'can be viewed as the *essence* of all art, similar to the way the soul is viewed as the *essence* of the body' (*Philosophy of art*, p. 202). But poetry during the Romantic period often means something more than that genre which we exemplify by a body of texts such as Shakespeare's sonnets and Keats's odes or even by literature as a whole. To the extent that it counts as the 'universal' or model art form, it often seems to swallow up other art forms within its boundaries, as in the Novalis fragment quoted earlier about setting poems not to music but to poetry. As Lothario, one of the voices in Friedrich Schlegel's *Dialogue on poetry* (1800) puts it, 'Every art and every science that operates by means of discourse, if it is practised for its own sake as art, and if it achieves the highest summit, is poetry [*Poesie*]'. But one of Schlegel's other characters, Ludoviko, immediately expands the definition to encompass the non-verbal arts within the domain of poetry: 'And every art that does not exercise its being in words has an invisible spirit [*Geist*], and this is poetry'.[28] John Stuart Mill, distinguishing a 'higher' form he calls 'poetry' from a 'lower' manifestation he calls 'oratory', lumped together instances from all the major arts – Mozart's aria 'Dove sono', Guido's madonnas, Greek statues of the gods, as well as a 'real' poem, Burns's 'My heart's in the highlands' – to exemplify the more prestigious term.[29] The word *poetry* became so all-encompassing that by mid-century John Ruskin, writing a book supposedly devoted to the understanding,

---

[28] Friedrich Schlegel, *Gespräch über die Poesie*, in *Charakteristiken und Kritiken I (1796–1801)*, Hans Eichner (ed.), Munich: Schöningh, 1967, p. 304.

[29] John Stuart Mill, 'What is poetry?' (1833), in *Essays on poetry*, F. Parvin Sharpless (ed.), Columbia, SC: University of South Carolina Press, 1976, pp. 14–15, 17.

indeed validation of painting among the arts, subordinated painting to the higher term: 'Painting is properly to be opposed to *speaking* or *writing*, but not to *poetry*. Both painting and speaking are methods of expression. Poetry is the employment of either for the noblest purposes.'[30]

However narrow or all-encompassing the particular definition of poetry or literature in particular systems, the world of art that an individual theorist projects generally contains its own chain of being by means of which various art forms exist in distinct hierarchical relations to one another. It is remarkable not only how long literature kept its place at or near the top of the hierarchy but also how persistently architecture and other 'purposive' arts were kept near the bottom. When August Wilhelm Schlegel sought to raise the status of architecture, he did so by downplaying its practical uses and stressing instead its imitation of human and natural forms (*Vorlesungen*, pp. 169–80). Still, one of the central facts about the relationships of the various arts between the mid-eighteenth and mid-nineteenth centuries is the rise in the status of music. As M. H. Abrams has pointed out, the ascent of music in the hierarchy was made possible by the shift from mimetic to expressive (and I might also add, affective) theories of art.[31] As early as 1769, Herder, asking what the lost music of the ancient world was 'expressing', called the poetry and music of antiquity the 'inseparable sister arts' that once worked together to exert their effects (*Die kritischen Wälder*, pp. 363–4). Both here and in his essay on the origin of language (1772) Herder described song and speech as inextricably mixed in the sounds uttered by early man (pp. 360–1);[32] to the extent that origins help determine the stature of phenomena, music could claim a centrality in the history of culture that it had not known before. Precisely the same year that Herder declared the sisterhood of poetry and music, Daniel Webb, in a treatise entitled *Observations on the correspondence between poetry and music*, cited sonorous passages from the *Aeneid* and *Paradise lost* to point out the affinities between the two arts in arousing the passions.[33] Yet the groundwork that allowed a new significance to music was laid not so much in formal treatises as in the less formal essays and fragments of the early German Romantics, for instance, in the praise heaped by Wackenroder (in the guise of his alter-ego, the art-obsessed Josef Berglinger) upon that new genre, the symphony, for its ability to create 'a beautifully developed

---

[30] John Ruskin, *Modern painters*, London: George Allen, 1911, III: 13.

[31] See Abrams's discussion appropriately subtitled 'ut musica poesis' in *The mirror and the lamp: Romantic theory and the critical tradition*, New York: Oxford University Press, 1953, pp. 88–94.

[32] See also Rousseau and Herder, *Origin of language*, pp. 87–91.

[33] Daniel Webb, *Observations on the correspondence between poetry and music*, London: Dodsley, 1769.

drama' that remains a 'pure poetic world' without the encumbrances of plot and character.[34] To the extent that Wackenroder resorts to literary analogy, indeed to a representational poetics, to make his point, the power of the literary model is still evident here; yet he insists that music does the job better than literature. Indeed, one can cite Wackenroder as the first in a long line of German writers who idealized music as being truer to their artistic perceptions than any other medium, including the literary medium within which they themselves were forced to work.

The first major treatise to treat music unambiguously as the highest of the arts was that of Schopenhauer, who ranked the arts according to their ability to objectify the will, that central principle within his system from whose 'restlessness and impetuosity' art supposedly protects the individual (*World as will*, p. 219). Although Schopenhauer gives a relatively high place to tragedy (since it accords with his bias towards the renunciation of the world), no art can emulate music, which 'expresses the profoundest wisdom in a language that [the composer's] reasoning faculty does not understand' (pp. 253, 260); one of the central attributes that had long been used to argue for literature's superiority – namely its ability to provide a rational meaning to life – in Schopenhauer's anti-rational philosophy becomes the means for its dethronement in favour of music. But Schopenhauer's work remained unknown for a whole generation after it was published in 1819. Wagner's major aesthetic writings, completed before his discovery of the philosopher in 1854, still give priority to the verbal element in opera; only later, by means of his own musical practice and his (and Schopenhauer's) influence on his sometime disciple Nietzsche in *The birth of tragedy*, does music emerge as the supreme art.[35]

Within most treatises of aesthetics, even though illustrative examples of artworks may be drawn from different eras, the system, with its hierarchies and inward correspondences, exists in some timeless realm; indeed, the illusion of timelessness helps confirm the substantiality and autonomy that art possesses among human endeavours. It was of course Hegel's

---

[34] Wilhelm Heinrich Wackenroder, *Sämtliche Werke und Briefe*, Silvio Vietta and Richard Littlejohns (eds.), Heidelberg: Winter, 1991, I: 244. For a searching study of the role played by instrumental music in Romantic theories of art, see Carl Dahlhaus, *Die Idee der absoluten Musik*, Kassel: Bärenreiter, 1978.

[35] For the early Nietzsche's use of Schopenhauer, as well as of the later Wagner, to argue for the supremacy of music, see *The birth of tragedy*, Walter Kaufmann (trans.), New York: Vintage, 1967, pp. 100–3; for an extreme statement by Nietzsche not only about the supremacy of music but about its independence from the texts that it purports to be setting, see his essay 'On music and words', Walter Kaufmann (trans.), in Carl Dahlhaus, *Between Romanticism and Modernism*, Berkeley, CA: University of California Press, 1980, pp. 106–19. For a late statement by Wagner that revises the theory in his early aesthetic essays by stressing the role of symphonic music (above all Beethoven's) in shaping his music–dramas, see 'Über die Anwendung der Musik auf das Drama' (1879) in *Gesammelte Schriften*, XIII: 282–98.

achievement among theorists of art to historicize the categories – with the result that the hierarchy of media and individual genres became relative to a particular age. Not that Hegel was the first to suggest the relativity of artistic value to a particular historical context: more than a half century before, Herder, whose anticipations of what later generations could take for granted often seem uncanny, had written: 'There exists an ideal of beauty for every art, for every science, for good taste altogether, and it is to be found in peoples and eras and subjects and productions' (*Die kritischen Wälder*, p. 286). It was left to Hegel to work out the detailed historicization of the arts. Thus, architecture, relegated to the bottom of most systems, for Hegel landed at the top of the hierarchy during the symbolic or prehistoric period, in which the construction of massive buildings such as the tower of Babel and Egyptian temples becomes the means of bonding a people who have not yet reached the stage of self-consciousness (*Aesthetics*, II: 638–9, 644–8). Sculpture, above all in Greek examples as mediated to German aesthetics by Winckelmann, becomes central to the next, the Classical age, which demands a form such as statues of the gods that objectify spirit but that can 'still ignore the subjectivity of the inner life' (p. 718). As self-consciousness (for Hegel the defining characteristic of historical progress) increases, literary genres move up the hierarchy. During the last of his eras, the romantic (which encompasses the whole post-classical period), we move from painting to music to the literary genres, with epic, lyric and dramatic in ascending order. Since Hegel associates drama with 'those epochs in which individual self-consciousness has reached a high stage of development', it is not surprising, in view of the value that he places upon self-consciousness, that this genre represents for him 'the highest stage of poetry and of art generally' in the modern world (pp. 1179, 1158). For most readers today Hegel's historical method of ordering the arts doubtless makes his treatise appear more modern (however much these readers may differ with his ratings of particular art forms) than the more universalizing treatises of his time. Yet the historical perspective he introduced into European thought still so shapes our own thinking that it is difficult to treat these other treatises with the same seriousness we accord Hegel's.

The canons of particular artists from which the various treatises draw their examples vary considerably in the time-span that they cover. The problems of musical transmission were so great, as I indicated earlier, that most treatises can go back at most a generation to illustrate their points, though many speculate about what the music of antiquity might have been like. Mozart and Rossini provide a surprisingly large proportion of the examples used, though earlier religious music (for example, Handel's), which generally had a longer performance life than that of secular composers, receives attention as well. Schopenhauer, who usually avoids commending individual composers, was so taken by his contemporary Rossini's ability to use music to calm the unrelenting will that he claimed his operatic music 'requires no words at all' but 'produces its full effect even when rendered by instruments alone' (*World as will*, p. 262).

The time-span for the visual arts in these treatises is obviously much longer than that for music. Ancient sculpture, presented usually by way of Winckelmann's interpretations, plays a central role in the treatises to a degree that painting does not. Indeed, the canon of painting in these treatises often starts with what we have since come to call the high Renaissance, with a surprisingly limited number of artists' names recurring from one analyst to the next. Michelangelo and Raphael count as the ultimate painters for most theorists of the period with little if any mention of their *quattrocento* predecessors. When Hazlitt writes of the great painters of the past, 'We are abstracted to another sphere . . . we enter into the minds of Raphael, of Titian, of Poussin, of the Caracci [*sic*], and look at nature with their eyes',[36] his citation of the Carracci reminds us to what an extent tastes have changed since his time. At least as surprising as the presence of the Carracci brothers (whose centrality in the foundation of Baroque style is still acknowledged in histories of art) is that of Correggio, whose name appears in an uncommon number of discussions of painting and whom Schelling, in a judgment quite typical of his time, calls 'the painter of all painters', a statement that was followed, also quite typically, with the reminder that 'the highest and genuinely absolute essence of art appeared only in Raphael' (*Philosophy of art*, p. 140).

By contrast with that of music and painting, the canon of literature extends through the whole of western culture. The disparity in time-span between literature and painting is evident in Hazlitt's list of what he called the 'giant-sons of genius', whose literary exemplars go back to Homer but in which painting starts only some three centuries before: 'Homer, Chaucer, Spenser, Shakspeare, Dante, and Ariosto, (Milton alone was of a later age, and not the worse for it) – Raphael, Titian, Michael Angelo, Correggio, Cervantes, and Boccaccio, the Greek sculptors and tragedians, – all lived near the beginning of their arts – perfected, and all but created them' (*Complete works*, v (1930): 45). As reshaped during the Romantic period, the literary canon to be found in aesthetic treatises of the time, as Hazlitt's list makes clear, is pretty much what it has remained to the present day, with Homer, the Greek dramatists (though with a certain disparagement of Euripides among German critics), Virgil, Dante, Ariosto, Cervantes and Shakespeare looming as giants. If Calderón (and distinctly not Lope de Vega) plays an unexpectedly large role in German aesthetics, this is due to the recent rediscovery (and translation) he had undergone in

[36] William Hazlitt, *Complete works*, ed. P. P. Howe (London: Dent), x (1932), 7.

the work of the early Romantics.[37] Although the canon remains largely western, it is not accidental, in view of the interest among the romantics in Indo-European philology, that references to Sanskrit literature, for example, the play *Shakuntala*, often appear.[38] And it is scarcely surprising that when recent writers are cited on the continent, these tend to be Goethe, Schiller, Byron and Scott, while the other English poets, indeed most contemporary foreign writers, are notably missing in continental accounts.

Interchanges and encroachments

The late eighteenth and early nineteenth centuries mark not only the first sustained attempt to theorize the arts as a whole but also a systematic effort, continuing to our own day, to break down long-established borders between the various arts as well as borders between the individual genres constituting each art form. The power of *ut pictura poesis* was so great from the Renaissance onward that one might easily assume that borders – at least those between painting and poetry – were regularly broken throughout this earlier period. Yet in retrospect one can interpret the pictorialist tradition, by means of which each art form claimed to be drawing upon the resources of the other, as a means of securing rather than destroying the borders between them. As a recent student of the tradition has put it, 'At the same time as it affirms what painters and poets have in common, *ut pictura* masks how far their respective arts are finally antithetical, locked in a contest from which neither escapes because neither can by itself ground or resolve it.'[39] Once we see pictorialism as a means of guarding the integrity of individual art forms, we can read Lessing's *Laocoon* as an attempt to keep painters and poets from taking the doctrine so literally that they misunderstand the peculiar limits of their respective media. Thus, for Lessing the recent poet Haller, in his long poem describing the Alps, had attempted a form of detailed, overly meticulous description suitable to painting but not to a temporally based verbal art form such as poetry.[40] Lessing of course was working out of a mimetic theory of

[37] See, for example, the discussions of Calderón in Schelling, *Philosophy of art*, pp. 273–6; Solger, *Vorlesungen*, pp. 319–20; and Hegel, *Aesthetics*, I: 405–7. Schelling and Hegel refer particularly to *La devoción de la cruz*, which counted as the exemplary Spanish play. But word of Calderón's special relevance also spread beyond Germany: note the reference to Calderón's sacred plays in Shelley's 'Defence of poetry', in *Shelley's poetry and prose*, p. 490.

[38] See, for example, Schelling, *Philosophy of art*, p. 57, and Hegel, *Aesthetics*, I: 339, and II: 1176.

[39] Christopher Braider, *Refiguring the real: picture and modernity in word and image, 1400–1700*, Princeton, NJ: Princeton University Press, 1992, pp. 221–2.

[40] Gotthold Ephraim Lessing, *Werke: 1766–1769*, Wilfried Barner (ed.), Frankfurt am Main: Deutscher Klassiker Verlag, 1990, pp. 125–6 (*Laocoon*, chap. 17).

art,[41] a theory that was little different from the one motivating Reynolds's stricture, quoted at the start of this chapter, that 'no art be engrafted . . . on another art'.

Once the mimetic mode gave way to expressive and affective theories, the barriers separating the arts could be challenged or ignored. If art was to be seen as the expression of genius, the major creators of the various arts were virtually interchangeable, as one notes in the following lines from Delacroix's journal, in which, advocating the importance of dispro-portion, the painter carefully includes representatives of all three major arts: 'If we admire Mozart, Cimarosa, and Racine less because of the admirable proportion in their works, do not Shakespeare, Michelangelo and Beethoven owe something of their effect to the opposite quality?'[42] For Delacroix those who count as geniuses in the various arts constitute a community more vital than that between a major artist and lesser practi-tioners within the same medium.

With music, according to M. H. Abrams, 'the first of the arts to be sev-ered from the mimetic principle by a critical consensus' (*Mirror and the lamp*, p. 92), the interchanges between music and the other arts, above all literature, became a central concern for artists seeking new ways to prac-tise their media. Beginning with the German Romantics, writers system-atically sought to make language render the effects of music upon them. Wackenroder's character Berglinger not only describes these effects in dis-cursive terms, as when, invoking the discourse of the sublime, he speaks of music 'penetrating his nerves with quiet terror [*Schauer*]', but he also resorts repeatedly to similes to translate his experience into literary terms, for example, when he describes the progress of a melody as similar to that of 'a brook . . . rushing through wild crags with frightening noise' (*Sämtliche Werke und Briefe*, pp. 132, 134).[43] Wackenroder's attempt to make literature aspire to the condition of music stands at the beginning of a tradition that ultimately leads to Thomas Mann's detailed recreations of his composer–hero Adrian Leverkühn's compositions in *Doctor Faustus* (1947). It is especially appropriate that some of the model attempts to render music in verbal discourse should come from E. T. A. Hoffmann, whose own vocational affiliations encompassed musical composition, lit-erary and music criticism (not to speak of his role as bureaucrat), and, most distinguished of all from our present-day point of view, the writing

---

[41] On the representational model common to Lessing and his predecessors Baumgarten and Mendelssohn, see David Wellbery, *Lessing's 'Laocoon': semiotics and aesthetics in the age of reason*, Cambridge University Press, 1984, pp. 49–54.

[42] Eugène Delacroix, *Journal*, André Joubin (ed.), Paris: Plon, 1932, II: 42 (entry of 9 May 1853).

[43] For a detailed analysis of Wackenroder's method of achieving 'verbal music', see Steven Paul Scher, *Verbal music in German literature*, New Haven, CT: Yale University Press, 1968, pp. 13–35.

of fiction. In his celebrated review of the Beethoven fifth symphony (1810), Hoffmann's contrast of Haydn and Mozart with Beethoven builds on Wackenroder's attempt at once to describe the effect of music and to suggest metaphorical equivalents for this effect. Whereas Haydn's symphonies 'lead us into unbounded green woodlands, into a jolly, colourful crowd of happy people', in Beethoven's work 'glowing rays shoot through the deep night of this realm, and we become aware of giant shadows that sway up and down, enclose us within increasingly narrow confines and destroy everything within us except for the pain of infinite longing [*Sehnsucht*]'.[44] Hoffmann's analysis is notable not only for its attempt to find verbal equivalents for music but, in the very process of discovering this language, for demonstrating that a listener's experience with Beethoven is something different in kind from that with earlier composers.

By the end of the eighteenth century, above all in Germany, music was fast coming to displace painting as the central model or at least analogy for literature. Hoffmann's claim to find romantic *Sehnsucht* in Beethoven's symphonic writing suggests the affinities a writer could feel with what a composer had accomplished. When Jean Paul labels chapters of his aesthetic treatise with such terms from church music as 'Jubilate lecture' and 'cantata lecture' (*Vorschule*, pp. 398–456), he signals this shift, which he also illustrated in descriptions in his novels of the effects of hearing music. But the musical analogy also manifested itself in less overt but also more fundamental ways in certain formal experiments, for example in Hölderlin's use of terms drawn from music to find a new mode of poetic organization by means of what he called 'the alternation of tones',[45] or in the volatile rhythmic and emotional shifts that mark the lyrics embedded in Tieck's narrative 'Love story of the lovely Magelone' (1797), whose overtly musical style is foregrounded in the 'real' music that Brahms later supplied in his Magelone song cycle (1861).[46]

The interchange between music and literature also worked in the opposite direction. Franz Liszt, in an essay (1855) on Berlioz's *Harold in Italy*, an instrumental work for viola and orchestra inspired by Byron's *Childe Harold*, suggested the role that literature was playing for composers of his time with the words, 'The masterpieces of music are increasingly

---

[44] E. T. A. Hoffmann, *Werke*, Georg Ellinger (ed.), Berlin: Deutsches Verlagshaus Bong, 1900, XIII: 42. For a detailed study of musical description after Hoffmann, see Thomas Grey, 'Metaphorical modes in nineteenth-century music criticism: image, narrative, and idea', in Steven Paul Scher (ed.), *Music and text: critical inquiries*, Cambridge University Press, 1991, pp. 93–117.

[45] See Lawrence Ryan, *Hölderlins Lehre vom Wechsel der Töne*, Stuttgart: Kohlhammer, 1960.

[46] On the musical character of these poems and their relation to Brahms's settings, see Manfred Frank, *Einführung in die frühromantische Ästhetik*, Frankfurt am Main: Suhrkamp, 1989, pp. 385–428.

appropriating the masterworks of literature.'[47] Music, one might say, was aspiring to the condition of a literature that was itself aspiring to the condition of music.

To be sure, the musical mimesis of texts goes back to earlier centuries, for example, to Monteverdi's distinctions between the 'agitated', 'soft' and 'moderate' styles suitable to particular passages of poetry being set by a composer.[48] But imitations of this sort are local, often quite literal-minded attempts to make vocal music mimic writing. By contrast, that Romantic instrumental genre calling itself 'tone poem', which continued to flourish until well into the twentieth century and which combines both art forms in its very name, is dedicated to recreating the larger idea of a literary work, sometimes even seeking, through the immediacy of musical effect, to outdo the famed literary original to which it feigns obeisance. The celebrated examples of musicalized literature – for instance, symphonies bearing titles such as *Harold in Italy*, the *Faust* and *Dante* of Liszt, or the *Manfred* of Tchaikovsky; tone poems such as Strauss's *Macbeth*, *Don Juan* and *Don Quixote*, or the settings of *Pelléas et Mélisande* variously by Fauré, Sibelius and Schoenberg, not to speak of innumerable concert overtures with titles the likes of *King Lear* and *Rob Roy* (Berlioz), *Faust* (Wagner), *Francesca da Rimini*, *Romeo and Juliet* and *Hamlet* (Tchaikovsky), or even, one might add, the not-so-celebrated *Manfred Meditation* for four-handed piano by that sometime-composer, Friedrich Nietzsche – give ample testimony about the prevailing literary canon at the times they were created. But composers did not simply go to established literary works to inspire and shape their works: they sometimes wrote programmes of their own – Beethoven, for instance, in his *Pastoral* symphony, Berlioz in his *Fantastic* symphony, Mahler (who even kept rewriting his programme after the completion of the work) in his *Resurrection* symphony. In each of these instances one suspects a need to 'textualize' these instrumental compositions, as though the music needed the written word to be legitimized.

If I have concentrated thus far on mutual encroachments between music and literature, this does not mean that painting lost its tie to literature with the decline of the *ut pictura poesis* doctrine. Indeed, the imputed

---

[47] Franz Liszt, 'Berlioz und seine Harold-Symphonie', in *Gesammelte Schriften*, L. Ramann (ed.), Leipzig: Breitkopf & Härtel, v (1882): 58.

[48] Claudio Monteverdi, *Tutte le opere*, G. Francesco Malipiero (ed.), Asolo: n. p., 1929, vol. VIII unnumbered page before p. 1. On the relation of Monteverdi's three styles to ancient Greek theories of musical imitation, see Barbara Russano Hanning, 'Monteverdi's three genera: a study in terminology', in Nancy Kovaleff Baker and Barbara Russano Hanning (eds.), *Musical humanism and its legacy: essays in honor of Claude V. Palisca*, Stuyvesant, NY: Pendragon Press, 1992, pp. 145–70. See also the analysis of passages by Monteverdi embodying these styles in Gary Tomlinson, *Monteverdi and the end of the Renaissance*, Berkeley, CA: University of California Press, 1987, pp. 202–10.

directive that one art should resemble the other may well have limited the possibilities of mutual interchange to surface imitation during earlier centuries. Yet when Keats, in 'Ode on a Grecian Urn', and Mörike, in 'Auf eine Lampe', write ecphrases on visual artifacts, they do not simply describe what they see, but they use these descriptions as a means to emulate the great aesthetic treatises of their time in acclaiming the autonomy of art.[49] Ruskin's attempt to communicate the nature and magnitude of Turner's achievement led him to develop a mode of composition as strikingly innovative as that of German writers such as Wackenroder and Hoffmann who had earlier sought to account for the effects of music. In a sentence such as the following, Ruskin, while discussing a Turner seascape, goes beyond traditional pictorialist description to stress the effect of the work upon the viewer beyond what the picture actually shows, much as Romantic musical descriptions had sought to suggest what the listener could be imagining: 'But the surges roll and plunge with such prostration and hurling of their mass against the shore, that we feel the rocks are shaking under them' (*Modern painters*, I: 399). Just as Liszt had boasted that music was appropriating literature, and just as Hoffmann in his role of author was appropriating music, so Ruskin, in innumerable passages of his art criticism, seeks to make his prose affect his reader in a mode analogous to those of the visual media he is describing.

But Turner was himself appropriating literature to the art of painting. As Ronald Paulson writes in a book on Turner and Constable significantly entitled *Literary landscape*, 'The art of Turner and Constable, however visual at the core . . . persists in asking verbal questions, and is incomprehensible without a consideration of its verbal aspect'.[50] What Paulson argues in the course of his book is not that these two painters were 'illustrating' literature in the pictorialist tradition (though Turner, unlike Constable, did his share of history paintings) but that, in their landscape painting, both created symbol systems that worked *like* literature without actually using or imitating literature. Indeed, as Paulson shows, the earnestness and largeness of scale that had traditionally marked history painting became transformed in differing ways by Turner and Constable

---

[49] For classic interpretations of these poems as at once ecphrases and statements about art, see Leo Spitzer, 'The "Ode on a Grecian urn" or content *vs* metagrammar', in Anna Hatcher (ed.), *Essays on English and American literature*, Princeton, NJ: Princeton University Press, 1962, pp. 67–97, and 'Once again on Mörike's poem "Auf eine Lampe"', Berel Lang and Christine Ebel (trans.), *PMLA* 105 (1990), pp. 427–34. See also Ian Jack, *Keats and the mirror of art*, Oxford: Clarendon Press, 1967, for an exhaustive investigation of how deeply Keats's poetry is suffused with his experiences viewing visual objects of art.
[50] Ronald Paulson, *Literary landscape: Turner and Constable*, New Haven, CT: Yale University Press, 1982, p. 5.

into the previously more circumscribed genre of landscape;[51] the epic quality of Constable's work is evident, for example, in the term 'six-footer' given to his large later paintings of seemingly simple scenes within the Stour valley.

Even history painting (which retained its hold to the point that an artist as late as Degas practised it in his youth) went through a certain transformation. Despite Ingres's boasting of his vocation of history painter, some of his most ambitious historical canvases are not actually scenes illustrating classic texts (though he also painted a number of these) but are primarily tributes to the power of artistic genius, as one notes from such titles as *The apotheosis of Homer, Virgil reading the Aeneid, Louis XIV and Molière, Luigi Cherubini and the muse of lyric poetry*; as such they participate in a programme similar to that of the aesthetic treatises of his time in demarcating a zone in which art achieves a quasi-religious status. Delacroix included a large number of scenes from literature among his subjects, and in this sense he continued the pictorialist tradition that had fed on literary texts (above all on the epic poems of Ariosto and Tasso) ever since the sixteenth century. Indeed, both Ingres and Delacroix left famous canvases depicting Ariosto's heroine Angelica.[52] Yet if one notes the large range of literary scenes that Delacroix reproduced – from texts as varied as the *Divine comedy, Hamlet* (both Ophelia's death and the gravedigger scene), *Othello* (the last-named mediated by Rossini's opera), Byron's *Don Juan, Marino Faliero* and *Sardanapalus*, Scott's *Ivanhoe* – one realizes that Delacroix sought something more than his pictorialist predecessors, that he aimed to replicate the literary canon in visual terms and, like Ingres (though more successfully), to make a larger statement about what he took to be the transcendent character of great texts.

The interchangeability of art forms is embodied in a rhetorical device, synaesthesia, by means of which the sense organ we use to experience a particular medium (for instance, hearing chords) is switched to a deliberately inappropriate medium (smelling colours). Although this device, like many others, goes back to Homer and the Bible, it was neither named nor used with great frequency until the nineteenth century. A brief passage from one of Hoffmann's musical writings proved seminal in literary history: the author's alter-ego, the bizarre musician Johannes Kreisler, in a reverie after listening to 'much music', finds 'colours, sounds, and odours coming together', with the smell of dark-red carnations mixing with the distant sound of a basset horn ('Kreisleriana', *Werke*, 1: 56). Baudelaire

---

[51] See Paulson, *Literary landscape*, pp. 63–73, 108–9, 133–9. Though Paulson limits his inquiry to these two British painters, much the same could be said of the way that German painters such as Caspar David Friedrich and Phillip Otto Runge reshaped the landscape genre.

[52] For a study of Angelica paintings from Mannerist through Romantic artists, see Rensselaer W. Lee, *Names on trees: Ariosto into art*, Princeton, NJ: Princeton University Press, 1977.

quotes this passage in his Salon of 1846 after complaining of the 'lack of melody' in younger painters and praising the 'plaintive colours' of Delacroix.[53] The passage further generated two programmatic sonnets – first, Baudelaire's own 'Correspondences', which not only echoes Hoffmann's images but adds its own synaesthetic image with the 'oboes green as meadows', and, second, Rimbaud's 'Vowels', which confounds sense experience even further than the earlier sonnet by assigning colours to vowels, creating a velvet jacket of flies, and endowing glaciers with lances.[54] In the wake of Baudelaire's and Rimbaud's experiments literary language has come to assert its autonomy over whatever objects it earlier claimed to imitate. Moreover, by means of synaesthesia literature again asserts its hegemony over the other arts, for, with the arbitrary signs it has at its command, it can scramble words associated with different media with an imperiousness that these other media cannot emulate.

The interchanges among art forms, indeed the encroachments of one art form upon another, during the Romantic period were mirrored by similar interchanges and encroachments among the various genres comprising each art form. As the Classical system in place since the Renaissance broke down, transgressing the boundaries that had long separated the poetic genres became a practice analogous to crossing the boundaries between art forms. Within German Romantic theory, for instance, the novel emerged as the privileged site on which genres that had long gone their separate ways could mingle together at ease. 'A novel [Roman] is a romantic book', as one of the characters in Friedrich Schlegel's Dialogue on poetry puts it, adding, 'I cannot imagine a novel being anything other than a mixture of narrative, song, and other forms' (Charakteristiken und Kritiken, pp. 335, 336). Not only did new generic combinations emerge, but the traditional hierarchy of genres underwent certain fundamental displacements. One can speak, for instance, of an elevation of lower genres to higher status. Thus, landscape painting, as I indicated above, assumed some of the functions, scope and earnestness long associated with history painting, the noblest genre within its medium. A similar process of what one might call 'heroicization' is evident within other art forms around 1800. The once lowly genre of the folk ballad took on massive proportions, both in length and philosophical scope, during the year

[53] Charles Baudelaire, Oeuvres complètes, Y.-G. le Dantec (ed.), Paris: Gallimard, 1951, pp. 606–7.
[54] See Baudelaire, Oeuvres complètes, p. 85, and Arthur Rimbaud, Oeuvres complètes, Roland de Renéville and Jules Mouquet (eds.), Paris: Gallimard, 1951, p. 103. Baudelaire quotes the octave of 'Correspondences' in his essay 'Richard Wagner and Tannhäuser in Paris' as a means of introducing the visual images set off in his mind by the music of Wagner and Liszt (p. 1043). Writing of Delacroix both in a review of his paintings (p. 700) and in his poem 'The beacons' (p. 87), he compares the effects of the painter's colour to the composer Weber's fanfares.

1798 in Goethe's and Schiller's ballads and in Coleridge's 'Rime of the Ancient Mariner'. Declaring his long poem *The prelude* to be 'in truth heroic argument',[55] Wordsworth adapted the organization, the verse form and the seriousness of tone associated with epic, the loftiest of literary genres, to package a landscape-obsessed autobiographical narrative. The symphony, previously taken to be a musical entertainment more unassuming in scope than, say, oratorio or *opera seria*, became heroicized literally at a single stroke by Beethoven's composition of the *Eroica* in 1803.

The myth of union

Behind the displacements and interchanges among genres and art forms there lurks a frequently articulated dream of union among the various arts. Schiller, in the quotation near the start of this chapter, expressed this desire without, of course, any design to put it into practice himself. A decade later, at the end of the university lectures posthumously published as his *Philosophy of art*, Schelling projected a union of the arts that could conceivably come together in concrete form by means of theatrical performance: 'The most perfect composition of all the arts, the unification of poesy and music through song, of poesy and painting through dance, both in turn synthesised together, is the most complex theatre manifestation, such as was the drama of antiquity' (p. 280). Despite his nostalgia for that union purportedly represented by Greek drama, he quickly recognizes the still-thriving descendant of this form: 'Only a caricature has remained for us, the *opera*, which in a higher and nobler style both from the side of poesy as well as from that of the other competing arts, might sooner guide us back to the performance of that ancient drama combined with music and song.'

Though Wagner likely did not know these lectures, which had not yet been published when he theorized his so-called *Gesamtkunstwerk* around 1850, the task he set up for himself was to return that multimedia form which Schelling had termed a 'caricature', namely opera, to the dignity it had supposedly known during its ancient days. Yet as one reads Wagner's aesthetic it is unmistakably clear that his projected union of the arts is above all a union focussed upon a single medium, drama. In *The artwork of the future*, while describing the procedures that the ideal future artist will use to create his work, Wagner writes: 'The space in which this marvellous process is achieved is the *theatre stage*, and the total art work [*das künstlerische Gesamtwerk*] that it brings to light is the *drama*' (*Gesammelte Schriften*, X: 167). Wagner's theory can be seen above all as a theory

---

[55] William Wordsworth, *The prelude*, Jonathan Wordsworth, M. H. Abrams and Stephen Gill (eds.), New York: Norton, 1979, p. 100 (1805 version, book III, line 182).

of drama, more precisely of dramatic performance, in which the possibilities of various art forms are utilized to establish a particular relationship between audience and the dramatic action enacted onstage. To the extent that Wagner favours a single genre, his theory is not wholly different from that of Lessing, whose attempt to establish a rigorous separation of the arts rose from his desire to privilege the dramatic element latent in the two art forms, poetry and painting, upon which he focusses: Lessing's demands that the painter construct his scene around the 'most pregnant moment' of his narrative (Laocoon, ch. 16; *Werke*, p. 117), and that the poet avoid excessive description in the interest of economy, attempt, like Wagner's theory, to create what is essentially a dramatic encounter between audience and work. It is no accident, moreover, that these two theorists both sought success as practitioners of the theatre.

I stress these underlying affinities between two theories that normally count as diametrical opposites as a means of questioning whether the watershed in the relations between the arts at the turn of the eighteenth century was as extreme as it was taken to be during succeeding generations. Once we look back from our present vantage point, the disruptions that have occurred within our own century both among art forms and in the definition of art seem considerably more radical than what, despite the boasts of individual artists and theorists, took place earlier. However much Berlioz may have tried to appropriate Shakespeare or Scott within his *King Lear* and *Rob Roy*, listeners who do not take their programme notes too earnestly are likely to experience each of these pieces above all as the sort of concert overture with which an evening at the symphony often begins. However distinct and difficult Wagner's style, the four works comprising *Der Ring des Nibelungen* belong recognizably to the same genre as, say, a work he much disdained, Meyerbeer's *Le prophète*, which, with its ice-skaters' ballet, even included an additional art form that Wagner subjected to his own generic transformation in the athletic feats of his gyrating Rhine maidens and of his Valkyries guiding their steeds among jagged peaks.

By contrast with the nineteenth century, our own time has posed altogether new and fiercer questions about the relations between individual art forms and genres and about what properly belongs to the domain of art. Note such typical challenges as the following: Robert Smithson's relocation of the boundaries between art and the natural world in 'earthworks' such as the Great Salt lake *Spiral jetty* (1970); Merce Cunningham's refusal to integrate his dance with its 'accompanying' music; John Cage's rethinking of the role of the creating artist in the 'chance operations' he used to generate his music, his graphic art and his written texts; the continuing textual invasions of visual art forms from Picasso's and Braque's collages to Jasper Johns's number paintings down to Jenny Holzer's shifting electronic displays of her own writing; the introduction into the visual arts of new technologies – photography, film, video, neon signs, often mixed with one another, with traditional visual materials, or with elements of other media such as music and poetry – that flagrantly defy the classifications by means of which art once sought to claim stability.[56] If the changes in the theory and practice of the arts that occurred nearly two hundred years ago no longer seem quite as revolutionary as they once did, this may well be simply that recent revolutions strike us as more provocative than earlier ones. But with the hindsight of another few generations, we (or, more precisely, others) may also come to view these so-called postmodernist developments as predictable outgrowths of the dislocations that the early Romantics initiated.

[56] For the historical significance of some of these developments, see Marjorie Perloff, *The futurist moment: avant-garde, avant guerre, and the language of rupture*, Chicago, IL: University of Chicago Press, 1986, and *Radical artifice: writing poetry in the age of media*, Chicago, IL: University of Chicago Press, 1991.

Bibliography

1 Classical standards in the period

Primary sources

Blake, William, *The poetry and prose of William Blake*, David V. Erdman (ed.), Garden City, NY: Doubleday, 1970.

Coleridge, Samuel Taylor, *Biographia literaria*, George Watson (ed.), New York: Everyman, 1971.

Goethe, Johann Wolfgang, 'On German architecture', in *Essays on art and literature*, John Gearey (ed.), Ellen and Ernest von Nordhoff (trans.), New York: Suhrkamp, 1986.

Keats, John, *The poems of John Keats*, Jack Stillinger (ed.), Cambridge, MA: Harvard University Press, 1978.

Pfotenhauer, Helmut von and Peter Sprengel (eds.), *Klassik und Klassizismus*, Frankfurt am Main: Deutscher Klassiker Verlag, 1995.

Schiller, Friedrich, *On the aesthetic education of man*, Reginald Snell (trans.), New York: Ungar, 1965.

Schlegel, August Wilhelm, *A course of lectures on dramatic art and literature*, John Black (trans.), London: Bohn, 1846.

Schlegel, Friedrich, *Dialogue on poetry and literary aphorisms*, Ernst Behler and Roman Struc (trans.), Philadelphia, PA: University of Pennsylvania Press, 1968.

Shelley, Percy Bysshe, *The complete poetical works of Percy Bysshe Shelley*, Neville Rogers (ed.), vol. II, Oxford: Clarendon Press, 1975.

Shelley's poetry and prose, Donald Reiman and Sharon B. Powers (eds.), New York: Norton, 1977.

Southey, Robert (ed.), *Specimens of the later English poets*, 3 vols., London: Longman, 1807.

Staël, Madame de, *Germany*, 2 vols., London: John Murray, 1814.

Stendhal, *Racine et Shakespeare*, Henri Martineau (ed.), Paris: Le Divan, 1928 (trans. Guy Daniels, *Racine and Shakespeare*, New York: Crowell-Collier Press, 1962).

Wordsworth, William, *The prose works of William Wordsworth*, Alexander Balloch Grosart (ed.), rev. edn, vol. II, London: E. Moxon, 1967, 3 vols.

Wordsworth: poetical works, Thomas Hutchinson (ed.), Ernest de Selincourt (rev. edn), London: Oxford University Press, 1974.

Wordsworth, William and Dorothy, *The letters of William and Dorothy Wordsworth: the middle years, part I: 1806–11*, Ernest de Selincourt (ed.), Mary Moorman (rev.), Oxford: Clarendon Press, 1969.

The letters of William and Dorothy Wordsworth: the later years, part I: *1821–28*, Ernest de Selincourt (ed.), Alan G. Hill (rev.), 2nd edn, Oxford: Clarendon Press, 1978.

The letters of William and Dorothy Wordsworth: the later years, part II: *1829–34*, Ernest de Selincourt (ed.), Alan G. Hill (rev.), Oxford: Clarendon Press, 1979.

Wolf, F. A., *Prolegomena to Homer* (1795) (with introduction and notes) Anthony Grafton, Glenn W. Most and James E. G. Zetzel (trans.), Princeton, NJ: Princeton University Press, 1985.

Secondary sources

Abrams, M. H., *The mirror and the lamp: Romantic theory and the critical tradition*, New York: Oxford University Press, 1953.

Amarasinghe, Upali, *Dryden and Pope in the early nineteenth century*, Cambridge University Press, 1962.

Barzun, Jacques, *Classic, Romantic, and Modern*, New York: Doubleday, 1961.

Bate, Walter J., *From Classic to Romantic: premises of taste in eighteenth century England*, New York: Harper, 1946.

Bate, Walter J. (ed.), *Criticism: the major texts*, New York: Harcourt, Brace, 1970.

Behler, Ernst, 'The origins of Romantic literary theory', *Colloquia Germanica* 2 (1968), pp. 109–26.

'The impact of Classical antiquity on the formation of the Romantic literary theory of the Schlegel brothers', in *Classical models in literature*, Zoran Konstantinovic, Warren Anderson and Walter Dietze (eds.), (Proceedings of the IXth Congress of the International Comparative Literature Association), Innsbruck: Institut für Sprachwissenschaft der Universität Innsbruck, 1981, pp. 139–43.

'Problems of origin in literary history', in *Theoretical issues in literary history*, David Perkins (ed.), Cambridge, MA: Harvard University Press, 1991.

Bialostosky, Don H. and Lawrence D. Needham (eds.), *Rhetorical traditions and British Romantic literature*, Bloomington, IN: Indiana University Press, 1995.

Brown, Huntington, *The Classical tradition in English literature: a bibliography*, Cambridge, MA: Harvard University Press, 1935.

Bush, Douglas, 'Wordsworth and the classics', *University of Toronto quarterly* 2 (1933), pp. 359–79.

Mythology and the Romantic tradition in English poetry, Cambridge, MA: Harvard University Press, 1937.

Butler, E. M., *The tyranny of Greece over Germany: a study of the influence exercised by Greek art and poetry over the great German writers of the eighteenth, nineteenth and twentieth centuries*, Cambridge University Press, 1935.

Elistratova, A. and E. Rona, 'Romantic writers and the Classical literary heritage', in *European Romanticism*, I. Soter, I. Neupokoyeva and E. Rona (eds.), Budapest: Akadémiai Kiadó, 1977, pp. 91–126.

Emmersleben, August, *Die Antike in der romantischen Theorie: die Gebrüder Schlegel und die Antike*, Berlin: Ebering, 1937.

Engell, James, *Forming the critical mind: Dryden to Coleridge*, Cambridge, MA: Harvard University Press, 1989.

Erskine-Hill, Howard, *The Augustan idea in English literature*, London: Arnold, 1983.

Flagg, John S., 'Shelley and Aristotle: elements of the *Poetics* in Shelley's theory of poetry', *Studies in Romanticism* 9 (1970), pp. 44–67.

Foerster, Donald M., *Homer in English criticism: the historical approach in the eighteenth century*, New Haven, CT: Yale University Press, 1947.

Foster, Gretchen M. (ed.), *Pope versus Dryden: a controversy in letters to the Gentleman's magazine 1789–91*, Victoria, BC: English Literary Studies, 1989.

Gleckner, Robert F. and Gerald Enscoe (eds.), *Romanticism: points of view*, Englewood Cliffs, NJ: Prentice-Hall, 1962.

Goldberg, M. A., *The poetics of Romanticism: toward a reading of John Keats*, Yellow Springs, OH: Antioch Press, 1969.

Graver, Bruce, 'Wordsworth's georgic beginnings', *Texas studies in literature and language* 33 (1991), pp. 137–59.

Hartmann, Heinrich, *Lord Byrons Stellung zu den Klassizisten seiner Zeit*, Bottrop: Postberg, 1932.

Hayden, John O., *Polestar of the ancients: the Aristotelian tradition in Classical and English literary criticism*, Newark, DE: University of Delaware Press, 1979.

Hedge, Frederic Henry, 'Classic and Romantic', *Atlantic monthly* 57 (1886), pp. 309–16.

Heussler, Alexander, *Klassik und Klassizismus in der deutschen Literatur: Studie über zwei literarhistorische Begriffe*, Bern: Haupt, 1952.

Highet, Gilbert, *The Classical tradition: Greek and Roman influences on Western literature*, New York: Oxford University Press, 1957.

Körner, Josef, *Romantiker und Klassiker: die Brüder Schlegel in ihren Beziehungen zu Schiller und Goethe*, Berlin: Askanischer Verlag, 1924.

Lange, Victor, 'Friedrich Schlegel's literary criticism', *Comparative literature* 7 (1955), pp. 289–305.

Levin, Harry, *The broken column: a study in Romantic Hellenism*, Cambridge, MA: Harvard University Press, 1931.

Lovejoy, Arthur O., 'On the meaning of "Romantic" in early German Romanticism' *MLN* 31 (1916), pp. 385–96.

Essays in the history of ideas, Baltimore, MD: The Johns Hopkins University Press, 1948.

MacClintock, W. D., 'The Romantic and the Classical in English literature', *The Chautauquan* 14 (1891), pp. 187–91.

McKillop, Alan Dugald, *English literature from Dryden to Burns*, New York: Appleton Century Crofts, 1948.

Miles, Josephine, *The primary language of poetry in the 1740s and 1840s*, Berkeley, CA: University of California Press, 1950.

Montgomery, Marshall, *Friedrich Hölderlin and the German neo-Hellenic movement*, Oxford University Press, 1923.

Moreau, Pierre, *Le classicisme des romantiques*, Paris: Librairie Plon, 1932.

Nitchie, Elizabeth, 'Virgil and Romanticism', *Methodist review* 113 (1930), pp. 859–67.

Nottelmann-Feil, Mara, *Ludwig Tiecks Rezeption der Antike: literarische Kritik und Reflexion griechischer und römischer Dichtung im theoretischen und poetischen Werk Tiecks*, Frankfurt am Main: Peter Lang, 1996.

Parker, Mark, 'Measure and counter-measure: the Lovejoy-Wellek debate and Romantic periodization', in *Theoretical issues in literary history*, David Perkins (ed.), Cambridge, MA: Harvard University Press, 1991, pp. 227–47.

Paulson, Ronald, *Breaking and remaking: aesthetic practice in England 1700–1820*, New Brunswick, NJ: Rutgers University Press, 1989.

Richter, Helene, 'Byron: Klassizismus und Romantik', *Anglia* 48 (1924), pp. 209–57.

Schultz, Franz, *Klassik und Romantik der Deutschen. Erster Teil: die Grundlagen der klassisch-romantischen Literatur*, Stuttgart: Metzler, 1935.

Stephens, John C., ' "Classic" and "Romantic" ', *Emory University quarterly* 15 (1959), pp. 212–19.

Stern, Bernard S., *The rise of Romantic Hellenism in English literature 1732–86*, Menash, WI: George Banta, 1940.

Szondi, Peter, 'Antike und Moderne in der Ästhetik der Goethezeit', in *Poetik und Geschichtsphilosophie I*, Senta Metz and Hans-Hagen Hildebrandt (eds.), Frankfurt am Main: Suhrkamp, 1974, pp. 11–265.

Thayer, Mary R., *The influence of Horace on the chief English poets of the nineteenth century*, New Haven, CT: Yale University Press, 1916.

Van Rennes, Jacob Johan, *Bowles, Byron, and the Pope controversy*, Norwood, PA: Norwood Editions, 1927.

Vines, Sherard, *The course of English Classicism from the Tudor period to the Victorian age*, London: Hogarth Press, 1930.

Vogler, Thomas A., 'Romanticism and literary periods: the future of the past', *New German critique* 38 (1986), pp. 131–60.

Walzel, Oskar, *German Romanticism*, Alma Elise Lussky (trans.), New York: Putnam's Sons, 1932.

Webb, Timothy, 'Romantic Hellenism', in *The Cambridge companion to British Romanticism*, Stuart Curran (ed.), Cambridge University Press, 1993, pp. 148–76.

Weisinger, Herbert, 'English treatment of the Classical–Romantic problem', *Modern language quarterly* 7 (1946), pp. 477–88.

Wellek, René, *The rise of English literary history*, Chapel Hill, NC: University of North Carolina Press, 1941.

'The concept of "Romanticism" in literary history: the term "Romantic" and its derivatives', *Comparative literature* 1 (1949), pp. 1–23.

A history of modern criticism: 1750–1950, vol. II: *The Romantic age*, New Haven, CT: Yale University Press, 1955, 8 vols.

'German and English Romanticism', *Studies in Romanticism* 4 (1964), pp. 35–56.

Wood, Paul S., 'The opposition to neo-Classicism in England between 1660 and 1700', *PMLA* 43 (1928), pp. 182–97.

2   Innovation and modernity

Primary sources

Baudelaire, Charles, *Baudelaire as a literary critic: selected essays*, Lois Boe Hyslop and Francis E. Hyslop, Jr (trans.), University Park, PA: Pennsylvania State University Press, 1964.
Oeuvres complètes, Claude Pichois (ed.), 2 vols., Paris: Gallimard, 1976, vol. II.
La Fanfarlo, Greg Boyd (trans.), Kendall E. Lappin (ed.), Berkeley: Donald S. Ellis, 1986.
Chateaubriand, François-René de, *Génie du christianisme, ou, beautés de la religion chrétienne*, Paris: Migneret, 1802 (trans. Frederic Shoberl, *The beauties of Christianity*, Philadelphia, PA: Carey, 1815).
Delacroix, Eugène, *The journal of Eugène Delacroix*, Walter Pach (trans.), New York: Crown, 1948.
Du Bos, Jean-Baptiste, *Critical reflections on poetry, painting, and music*, New York: AMS Press, 1978.
Foscolo, Ugo, *Ugo Foscolo's 'Ultime lettere di Jacopo Ortis': a translation*, Douglas Radcliff-Umstead (trans.), Chapel Hill, NC: University of North Carolina Press, 1970.
Goethe, Johann Wolfgang von, *The sorrows of young Werther. The new Melusina. Novelle*, Victor Lange (trans.), New York: Holt, Rinehart and Winston, 1967.
Hegel, Georg Wilhelm Friedrich, *Aesthetics: lectures on fine art*, T. M. Knox (trans.), 2 vols., Oxford: Clarendon Press, 1975, vol. I.
Manzoni, Alessandro, *Scritti di teoria letteraria*, Adelaide Sozzi Casanova (ed.), Milan: Rizzoli, 1981.
Novalis, *Schriften: die Werke Friedrich von Hardenbergs*, Paul Kluckhohn and Richard H. Samuel (eds.), 5 vols., Stuttgart: Kohlhammer, 1960–88.
Novalis Werke, Gerhard Schulz (ed.), Munich: Beck, 1987.
Schlegel, Friedrich, *Kritische Friedrich-Schlegel-Ausgabe*, Ernst Behler (ed.), 35 vols., Paderborn: Schöningh, 1958–79.
Philosophical fragments, Peter Firchow (trans.), Minneapolis, MN: University of Minnesota Press, 1991.
Staël, Madame de, *De la littérature considérée dans ses rapports avec les institutions sociales*, Paris: Maradan, 1800 (trans. Daniel Boileau, *The influence of literature upon society*, Boston, MA: Wells & Wait, 1813).

Secondary sources

Behler, Ernst, *Studien zur Romantik und zur idealistischen Philosophie*, Paderborn: Schöningh, 1988.
Unendliche Perfektibilität: europäische Romantik und französische Revolution, Paderborn: Schöningh, 1989.
Frühromantik, Berlin: Walter de Gruyter, 1992.
Behler, Ernst and Jochen Hörisch, *Die Aktualität der Frühromantik*, Paderborn: Schöningh, 1987.

Benjamin, Walter, *Illuminations*, Hannah Arendt (ed.), Harry Zohn (trans.), New York: Schocken, 1969.
  The concept of criticism in German Romanticism, in *Selected writings*, vol. I: 1913–26, Marcus Paul Bullock and Michael W. Jennings (eds.), Cambridge, MA: Belknap Press, 1996, pp. 116–200.
Bloom, Harold, *Kabbalah and criticism*, New York: Seabury Press, 1975.
Brown, Marshall, *The shape of German romanticism*, Ithaca, NY: Cornell University Press, 1979.
  'Romanticism and enlightenment', in *The Cambridge companion to British Romanticism*, Stuart Curran (ed.), Cambridge University Press, 1993, pp. 25–47.
Castex, Pierre-Georges, *Baudelaire critique d'art*, Paris: Sedes, 1969.
De Paz, Alfredo, *Europa romantica: fondamenti e paradigmi della sensibilità moderna*, Naples: Liguori, 1994.
Dierkes, Hans, *Literaturgeschichte als Kritik: Untersuchungen zu Theorie und Praxis von Friedrich Schlegels frühromantischer Geschichtsschreibung*, Tübingen: Niemeyer, 1980.
Flitter, Derek, *Spanish Romantic literary theory and criticism*, Cambridge University Press, 1992.
Gusdorf, Georges, *Fondements du savoir romantique*, Paris: Payot, 1982.
Lacoue-Labarthe, Philippe and Jean-Luc Nancy, *L'absolu littéraire: théorie de la littérature du romantisme allemand*, Paris: Editions du Seuil, 1978 (trans. Philip Barnard and Cherel Lester, *The literary absolute: the theory of literature in German Romanticism*, Albany, NY: State University of New York Press, 1988).
Paz, Octavio, *La otra voz: poesía y fin de siglo*, Barcelona: Seix Barral, 1990 (trans. Helen Lane, *The other voice: essays on modern poetry*, New York: Harcourt Brace Jovanovich, 1991).
Rincé, Dominique, *Baudelaire et la modernité poétique*, Paris: Presses Universitaires de France, 1984.
Schaeffer, Jean-Marie, *La naissance de la littérature: la théorie esthétique du romantisme allemand*, Paris: Presses de l'Ecole Normale Supérieure, 1983.
Van Tieghem, Paul, *Le romantisme dans la littérature européenne*, Paris: Michel, 1948.
Wellek, René, *A history of modern criticism: 1750–1950*, vol. II: *The Romantic age*, New Haven, CT: Yale University Press, 1955, 8 vols.

3   The French Revolution

Primary sources

Armstrong, Nancy, *Desire and domestic fiction: a political history of the novel*, New York: Oxford University Press, 1987.
Blake, William, *The complete poetry and prose of William Blake*, rev. edn, David V. Erdman and Harold Bloom (eds.), Berkeley, CA: University of California Press, 1982.
Campbell, Thomas, *Specimens of the British poets: with biographical and critical notices, and an essay on English poetry*, 7 vols., London: John Murray, 1819.

Coleridge, Samuel Taylor, 'On the principles of genial criticism', in *Biographia literaria, edited with his aesthetical essays*, John Shawcross (ed.), 2 vols., Oxford University Press, 1962.

Lay sermons, Reginald James White (ed.), London: Routledge & Kegan Paul, 1972.

Biographia literaria, or, biographical sketches of my literary life and opinions, James Engell and Walter Jackson Bate (eds.), 2 vols., London: Routledge & Kegan Paul, 1983.

De Quincey, Thomas, *Collected Writings*, new edn, David Masson (ed.), 14 vols., Edinburgh: Adam & Charles Black, 1889–90.

Fichte, Johann Gottlieb, *Addresses to the German nation*, George Armstrong Kelly (ed.), New York & Evanston, IL: Harper & Row, 1968.

Gibbon, Edward, *An essay on the study of literature*, New York: Garland, 1970.

Hazlitt, William, *The complete works of William Hazlitt*, P. P. Howe (ed.), 21 vols., New York: AMS Press, 1967.

Hegel, Georg Wilhelm Friedrich, *Aesthetics: lectures on fine art*, T. M. Knox (trans.), 2 vols., Oxford: Clarendon Press, 1975, vol. I.

Heine, Heinrich, *The Romantic school and other essays*, Jost Hermand and Robert C. Holub (eds.), The German library 33, New York: Continuum, 1985.

Jeffrey, Francis, *Contributions to the Edinburgh Review*, Boston: J. C. Derby, 1854.

Lanson, Gustave, *Histoire de la littérature française, remaniée et complétée pour la période 1850–1950*, Paul Tuffray (ed.), Paris: Hachette, 1952.

Rutherford, Andrew (ed.), *Byron: the critical heritage*, New York: Barnes and Noble, 1970.

Sainte-Beuve, Charles Augustin, *Chateaubriand et son groupe littéraire sous l'empire: cours professé a Liège en 1848–1849*, Maurice Allem (ed.), 2 vols., Paris: Garnier, 1948.

Schelling, Friedrich Wilhelm Joseph, 'On Dante in relation to philosophy', and 'The philosophy of art', in David Simpson (ed.), *The origins of modern critical thought: German aesthetic and literary criticism from Lessing to Hegel*, Cambridge University Press, 1988, pp. 232–47.

Schiller, Friedrich, *On the aesthetic education of man*, Elizabeth M. Wilkinson and L. A. Willoughby (ed. and trans.), Oxford: Clarendon Press, 1967.

Schlegel, August Wilhelm von, *A course of lectures on dramatic art and literature*, John Black (trans.), Alexander James William Morrison (ed.), London: Bohn, 1846.

Schlegel, Friedrich von, *Lectures on the history of literature, ancient and modern*, John Frost (ed.), Philadelphia, PA: Moss & Co., 1863.

Friedrich Schlegel's 'Lucinde' and the fragments, Peter Firchow (trans.), Minneapolis, MN: University of Minnesota Press, 1971.

Shelley, Percy Bysshe, *Shelley's poetry and prose: authoritative texts, criticism*, Donald H. Reiman and Sharon B. Powers (eds.), New York: Norton, 1977.

Staël, Madame de, *The influence of literature upon society*, Daniel Boileau (trans.), 2nd ed., 2 vols., London: Henry Colburn, 1812.

Taine, Hippolyte, *History of English literature*, Henri van Laun (trans.), 4 vols., Philadelphia, PA: Altemus, 1908.

Tocqueville, Alexis de, *Democracy in America*, 2 vols., New York: Vintage Books, 1945.

Träger, Claus and Frauke Schaefer (ed.), *Die französische Revolution im Spiegel der deutschen Literatur*, Frankfurt am Main: Röderberg, 1979.

Wordsworth, William, *The prose works of William Wordsworth*, W. J. B. Owen and Jane Worthington Smyser (eds.), 3 vols., Oxford: Clarendon Press, 1974.

Secondary sources

Baer, Marc, *Theatre and disorder in late Georgian London*, Oxford: Clarendon Press, 1992.

Baldick, Chris, *The social mission of English criticism, 1848–1932*, Oxford: Clarendon Press, 1987.

Banks, Brenda, 'Rhetorical missiles and double-talk: Napoleon, Wordsworth, and the invasion scare of 1804', in *Romanticism, radicalism, and the press*, Stephen C. Behrendt (ed.), Detroit, MI: Wayne State University Press, 1997, pp. 103–19.

Behler, Ernst, 'Die Auffassung der Revolution in der deutschen Frühromantik', in *Essays on European literature in honor of Liselotte Dieckmann*, Peter Uwe Hohendahl, Herbert Lindenberger and Egon Schwarz (eds.), St Louis, MO: Washington University Press, 1972, pp. 191–215.

'Französische Revolution und Antikekult', in *Europäische Romantik I*, Karl Robert Mandelkow (ed.), Neues Handbuch der Literaturwissenschaft 14, Wiesbaden: Athenaion, 1982, pp. 83–112.

Unendliche Perfektibilität: europäische Romantik und französische Revolution, Paderborn: Schöningh, 1989.

Brooks, Peter, *The melodramatic imagination: Balzac, Henry James, melodrama, and the mode of excess*, New Haven, CT: Yale University Press, 1976.

Butler, Marilyn, *Romantics, rebels, and reactionaries: English literature and its background, 1760–1830*, New York: Oxford University Press, 1981.

Carlson, Julie A., *In the theatre of Romanticism: Coleridge, nationalism, women*, Cambridge University Press, 1994.

Dawson, P. M. S., 'Poetry in an age of revolution', in *The Cambridge companion to British Romanticism*, Stuart Curran (ed.), Cambridge University Press, 1993, pp. 48–73.

Deane, Seamus, *The French Revolution and Enlightenment in England, 1789–1832*, Cambridge, MA: Harvard University Press, 1988.

Eagleton, Terry, *The function of criticism*, London: Verso, 1984.

The ideology of the aesthetic, Oxford: Blackwell, 1990.

Fink, Gonthier-Louis, 'Die Revolution als Herausforderung in Literatur und Publizistik', in *Zwischen Revolution und Restauration: Klassik, Romantik 1786–1815*, Deutsche Literatur: eine Sozialgeschichte 5, Horst Albert Glaser (ed.), Reinbek: Rowohlt, 1980, pp. 110–29.

Fink, Gonthier-Louis (ed.), *Les romantiques allemands et la révolution française*, Strasbourg: Université des sciences humaines de Strasbourg, 1989.

Flitter, Derek, *Spanish Romantic literary theory and criticism*, Cambridge University Press, 1992.

Fort, Bernadette (ed.), *Fictions of the French Revolution*, Evanston, IL: Northwestern University Press, 1991.

Furet, François, *Interpreting the French Revolution*, Elborg Forster (trans.), Cambridge University Press, 1981.

Furet, François and Mona Ozouf (eds.), *A critical dictionary of the French Revolution*, Arthur Goldhammer (trans.), Cambridge, MA: Belknap Press, 1989.

Hanley, Keith and Ray Selden (eds.), *Revolution and English Romanticism: politics and rhetoric*, London: Harvester Wheatsheaf, 1990.

d'Hondt, Jacques, 'Lumières et romantisme: le choc de la révolution', *Bulletin de la société américaine de philosophie de langue française* 2 (1990–91), pp. 115–26.

Hunt, Lynn, *Politics, culture and class in the French Revolution*, Berkeley, CA: University of California Press, 1984.

Klancher, Jon, 'Romantic criticism and the meanings of the French Revolution', *Studies in Romanticism* 28 (1989), pp. 463–91.

Lacoue-Labarthe, Philippe and Jean-Luc Nancy, *The literary absolute: the theory of literature in German Romanticism*, Philip Barnard and Cherel Lester (trans.), Albany, NY: State University of New York Press, 1988.

Mellor, Horst, 'Die frühe Romantische Dichtung in England: die Geburt einer Romantik aus dem Geiste der Revolution', in *Europäische Romantik II*, Klaus Heitmann (ed.), Neues Handbuch der Literaturwissenschaft 15, Wiesbaden: Athenaion, 1982.

Ozouf, Mona, *Festivals and the French Revolution*, Alan Sheridan (trans.), Cambridge, MA: Harvard University Press, 1988.

Paulson, Ronald, *Representations of revolution, 1789–1820*, New Haven: Yale University Press, 1983.

Peers, E. Allison, *A history of the Romantic movement in Spain*, 2 vols., New York: Hafner, 1964.

Rutherford, Andrew (ed.), *Byron: the critical heritage*, New York: Barnes & Noble, 1970.

Sabin, Margery, *English Romanticism and the French tradition*, Cambridge, MA: Harvard University Press, 1976.

Sayre, Robert, 'The young Coleridge: Romantic utopianism and the French Revolution', *Studies in Romanticism* 28 (1989), pp. 397–415.

Simpson, David, *Wordsworth and the figurings of the real*, London: Macmillan, 1982.

  Wordsworth's historical imagination: the poetry of displacement, London and New York: Methuen, 1987.

  Romanticism, nationalism, and the revolt against theory, Chicago, IL: University of Chicago Press, 1993.

  The academic postmodern and the rule of literature: a report on half-knowledge, Chicago, IL: University of Chicago Press, 1995.

Wellek, René, 'The concept of Romanticism in literary history', in *Concepts of criticism*, New Haven, CT: Yale University Press, 1963, pp. 128–98.

  A history of modern criticism: 1750–1950, vol. II: *The Romantic age*, New Haven, CT: Yale University Press, 1955, 8 vols.

4 Transcendental philosophy and Romantic criticism

Primary sources

Alison, Archibald, *Essays on the nature and principles of taste*, 1790, rpt. Hildesheim: Georg Olms, 1968.

Arnold, Matthew, *The poems of Wordsworth*, London: Macmillan, 1879.

Blair, Hugh, *Lectures on rhetoric and belles lettres*, 1783, rpt. Philadelphia: Troutman & Hayes, 1853.

Coleridge, Samuel Taylor, *Biographia literaria, or, biographical sketches of my literary life and opinions*, James Engell and Walter Jackson Bate (eds.), 2 vols., London: Routledge & Kegan Paul, 1983.

Hazlitt, William, *The complete works of William Hazlitt*, P. P. Howe (ed.), 21 vols., 1930–4, rpt. New York: AMS Press, 1967.

Hegel, Georg Wilhelm Friedrich, *Aesthetics: lectures on fine art*, T. M. Knox (trans.), 2 vols., Oxford: Clarendon Press, 1975.

Lectures on the philosophy of history, J. Sibree (trans.), New York: Dover, 1956.

Herder, Johann Gottfried, *Reflections on the philosophy of the history of mankind*, 1784–91, Frank E. Manuel (ed.), Chicago, IL: University of Chicago Press, 1968.

Hume, David, *Essays moral, political and literary*, Eugene F. Miller (ed.), Indianapolis, IN: Liberty, 1985.

Kames, Henry Home, Lord, *Elements of criticism*, 1785, 2 vols., rpt. New York: Garland, 1978.

Kant, Immanuel, *The critique of judgement*, James Creed Meredith (trans.), Oxford: Clarendon Press, 1980.

Mill, John Stuart, *Autobiography*, John M. Robson (ed.), London: Penguin, 1989.

Nisbet, Hugh Barr (ed.), *German aesthetic and literary criticism: Winkelmann, Lessing, Hamann, Herder, Schiller, Goethe*, Cambridge University Press, 1985.

'The oldest system-program of German idealism', in *Friedrich Hölderlin: essays and letters on theory*, Thomas Pfau (trans. and ed.), Albany, NY: State University of New York Press, 1987, pp. 154–6.

Schelling, Friedrich Wilhelm Joseph, 'Concerning the relation of the plastic arts to nature', Michael Bullock (trans.), in *The true voice of feeling: studies in English Romantic poetry*, Herbert Read (ed.), London: Faber and Faber, 1968, pp. 323–58.

System of transcendental idealism, Peter Heath (ed.), Charlottesville, VA: University of Virginia Press, 1978.

The philosophy of art, Douglas W. Stott (ed. and trans.), Minneapolis, MN: University of Minnesota Press, 1989.

Schiller, Friedrich, 'On the use of the chorus in tragedy', in *The dramas of Friedrick von Schiller*, R. D. Boylan (trans.), London: Bell, 1920, pp. 517–23.

'The stage as a moral institution', *Friedrich Schiller: an anthology for our time*, New York: Ungar, 1959.

On the aesthetic education of man, in a series of letters, Elizabeth M. Wilkinson and L. A. Willoughby (ed. and trans.), Oxford: Clarendon Press, 1967.

Essays, Walter Hinderer and Daniel O. Dahlstrom (eds.), The German library 17, New York: Continuum, 1995.

Schlegel, Friedrich von, *Friedrich Schlegel's 'Lucinde' and the fragments*, Peter Firchow (trans.), Minneapolis, MN: University of Minnesota Press, 1971.

Über die Sprache und die Weisheit der Indier: ein Beitrag zur Begründung der Altertumskunde, Amsterdam: Benjamins, 1977 (trans. E. J. Millington, *The aesthetic and miscellaneous works of Frederick von Schlegel*, London: Bohn, 1849).

Schopenhauer, Arthur, *The world as will and representation*, E. F. J. Payne (trans.), 2 vols., New York: Dover, 1969.

Simpson, David (ed.), *German aesthetic and literary criticism: Kant, Fichte, Schelling, Schopenhauer, Hegel*, Cambridge University Press, 1984.

The origins of modern critical thought: German aesthetic and literary criticism from Lessing to Hegel, Cambridge University Press, 1988.

Staël, Madame de, *Germany*, 3 vols., London: John Murray, 1813.

Wheeler, Kathleen (ed.), *German aesthetic and literary criticism: the Romantic ironists and Goethe*, Cambridge University Press, 1984.

Wordsworth, William, *The prose works of William Wordsworth*, W. J. B. Owen and Jane Worthington Smyser (eds.), 3 vols., Oxford: Clarendon Press, 1974.

Secondary sources

Ashfield, Andrew and de Bolla, Peter (eds.), *The sublime: a reader in eighteenth-century British aesthetic theory*, Cambridge University Press, 1996.

Ashton, Rosemary, *The German idea: four English writers and the reception of German thought, 1800–1860*, Cambridge University Press, 1980.

Beck, Lewis White, 'German philosophy', in *The encyclopedia of philosophy*, Paul Edwards (ed.), 8 vols., New York: Macmillan, 1967, vol. III, pp. 291–309.

Beiser, Frederick C., *The fate of reason: German philosophy from Kant to Fichte*, Cambridge, MA: Harvard University Press, 1987.

Bowie, Andrew, *Aesthetics and subjectivity: from Kant to Nietzsche*, Manchester University Press, 1990.

Brown, Marshall, *The shape of German Romanticism*, Ithaca, NY: Cornell University Press, 1979.

Bubner, Rüdiger (ed.), *Das älteste Systemprogramm: Studien zur Frühgeschichte des deutschen Idealismus* (Hegel-Studien, suppl. no. 9), Bonn: Bouvier, 1973.

Butler, Marilyn, *Romantics, rebels, and reactionaries: English literature and its background, 1760–1830*, New York: Oxford University Press, 1982.

Butler, Marilyn (ed.), *Burke, Paine, Godwin, and the Revolution controversy*, Cambridge University Press, 1984.

Cassirer, Ernst, *The philosophy of the Enlightenment*, Fritz C. A. Koelln and James P. Pettegrove, Princeton, NJ: Princeton University Press, 1951.

Caygill, Howard, *Art of judgement*, Oxford: Blackwell, 1989.

A Kant dictionary, Oxford: Blackwell, 1995.

Cohen, Ted, and Paul Guyer (eds.), *Essays in Kant's aesthetics*, Chicago, IL: University of Chicago Press, 1982.

Crawford, Robert, *Devolving English literature*, Oxford: Clarendon Press, 1992.
Curran, Stuart (ed.), *The Cambridge companion to British Romanticism*, Cambridge University Press, 1993.
Deane, Seamus, *The French Revolution and Enlightenment in England, 1789–1832*, Cambridge, MA: Harvard University Press, 1988.
Eagleton, Terry, *The function of criticism*, London: Verso, 1984.
   The ideology of the aesthetic, Oxford: Blackwell, 1990.
Engell, James, *The creative imagination: Enlightenment to Romanticism*, Cambridge, MA: Harvard University Press, 1981.
Gadamer, Hans-Georg, *Truth and method*, New York: Seabury Press, 1975.
Guyer, Paul, *Kant and the claims of taste*, Cambridge, MA: Harvard University Press, 1979.
Guyer, Paul (ed.), *The Cambridge companion to Kant*, Cambridge University Press, 1992.
Henrich, Dieter, 'Beauty and freedom: Schiller's struggle with Kant's aesthetics', in *Essays in Kant's aesthetics*, Ted Cohen and Paul Guyer (eds.), Chicago, IL: University of Chicago Press, 1982, pp. 237–57.
Lacoue-Labarthe, Philippe and Jean-Luc Nancy, *The literary absolute: the theory of literature in German romanticism*, Philip Barnard and Cherel Lester (trans.), Albany, NY: State University of New York Press, 1988.
Lyotard, Jean-François, *Lessons on the analytic of the sublime*, Elizabeth Rottenberg (trans.), Stanford, CA: Stanford University Press, 1994.
Man, Paul de, *Aesthetic ideology*, Andrzej Warminski (ed.), Minneapolis, MN: University of Minnesota Press, 1996.
McCormick, Peter J., *Modernity, aesthetics and the bounds of art*, Ithaca, NY: Cornell University Press, 1990.
McFarland, Thomas, *Coleridge and the pantheist tradition*, Oxford: Clarendon Press, 1969.
Nancy, Jean-Luc (ed.), *Du sublime*, Paris: Berlin, 1992.
Orsini, Gian N. G., *Coleridge and German idealism: a study in the history of philosophy*, Carbondale, IL and Edwardsville, IL: University of Southern Illinois Press, 1969.
Sabin, Margery, *English Romanticism and the French tradition*, Cambridge, MA: Harvard University Press, 1976.
Schaper, Eva, *Studies in Kant's aesthetics*, Edinburgh University Press, 1979.
   'Taste, sublimity and genius: the aesthetics of nature and art', in *The Cambridge companion to Kant*, Paul Guyer (ed.), Cambridge University Press, 1992, pp. 367–93.
Simpson, David, Foreword, *The philosophy of art*, by Friedrich Wilhelm Joseph Schelling, Douglas W. Stott (ed. and trans.), Minneapolis, MN: University of Minnesota Press, 1989, pp. ix–xxiv.
   'Romanticism, criticism and theory', in *The Cambridge companion to British Romanticism*, Stuart Curran (ed.), Cambridge University Press, 1993, pp. 1–24.
   Romanticism, nationalism and the revolt against theory, Chicago, IL: University of Chicago Press, 1993.

Taine, Hippolyte, *History of English literature*, Henri van Laun (trans.), 4 vols., Philadelphia, PA: Altemus, 1908.

Thorslev, Peter, 'German Romantic idealism', in *The Cambridge companion to British Romanticism*, Stuart Curran (ed.), Cambridge University Press, 1993, pp. 74–94.

Wellek, René, *Immanuel Kant in England, 1793–1838*, Princeton, NJ: Princeton University Press, 1931.

A history of modern criticism: 1750–1950, vol. I: *The later eighteenth century*, New Haven, CT: Yale University Press, 1955, 8 vols.

A history of modern criticism: 1750–1950, vol. II: *The Romantic age*, New Haven: Yale University Press, 1955, 8 vols.

Zammito, John H., *The genesis of Kant's 'Critique of judgment'*, Chicago, IL: University of Chicago Press, 1992.

Žižek, Slavoj, *Tarrying with the negative: Kant, Hegel, and the critique of ideology*, Durham, NC: Duke University Press, 1993.

5   Nature

Primary sources

Blake, William, *Poetry and prose*, Geoffrey Keynes (ed.), Oxford University Press, 1946.

Burke, Edmund, *A philosophical inquiry into the origins of our ideas of the sublime and beautiful*, James T. Boulton (ed.), London: Routledge and Kegan Paul, 1958.

Hazlitt, William, *Selected writings*, Jon Cook (ed.), Oxford University Press, 1991.

Novalis, *Schriften: die Werke Friedrich von Hardenbergs*, Paul Kluckhohn and Richard H. Samuel (eds.), vols. I–III, Stuttgart: Kohlhammer, 1960–88, 5 vols.

Schiller, Friedrich von, 'Über naive und sentimentalische Dichtung', in *Sämtliche Werke*, Herbert G. Göpfert (ed.), vol. V, Munich: Carl Hanser, 1960, pp. 694–780 (trans. Julius A. Elias, *Naïve and sentimental poetry, On the sublime*, New York: Frederick Ungar, 1966).

Schlegel, Friedrich, 'Über das Studium der griechischen Poesie', in *Kritische Schriften und Fragmente: Studienausgabe in sechs Bänden*, Ernst Behler and Hans Eichner (eds.), 6 vols., Paderborn: Schöningh, 1988, I: 62–136.

Kritische Friedrich-Schlegel-Ausgabe, Ernst Behler (ed.), 35 vols., Paderborn: Schöningh, 1958–79.

Wordsworth, William, *The prelude 1799, 1805, 1850: authoritative texts, contexts and reception, recent critical essays*, Jonathan Wordsworth, M. H. Abrams and Stephen Charles Gill (eds.), New York: Norton, 1979.

Secondary sources

Adorno, Theodor W., and Max Horkheimer, *Dialectic of Enlightenment*, John Cumming (trans.), London: Verso, 1997.

Abrams, M. H., 'Structure and style in the greater romantic lyric', in *From sensibility to romanticism: essays presented to Frederick A. Pottle*, F. W. Hilles and Harold Bloom (eds.), Oxford University Press, 1965, pp. 527–60.

Natural supernaturalism: tradition and revolution in Romantic literature, New York: Norton, 1973.

Bloom, Harold, 'The internalization of quest romance', *The Yale review* 58 (1969), pp. 526–36.

Bolla, Peter de, *The discourse of the sublime: readings in history, aesthetics and the subject*, Oxford: Blackwell, 1989.

Frank, Manfred, 'Philosophische Grundlagen der Frühromantik', *Athenäum* 4 (1994), pp. 37–130.

Einführung in die frühromantische Ästhetik: Vorlesungen, Frankfurt am Main: Suhrkamp, 1989.

Frye, Northrop, *A study of English Romanticism*, Brighton: Harvester Press, 1983.

Furst, Lilian R., *Romanticism in perspective: a comparative study of the aspects of the Romantic movements in England, France and Germany*, London: Macmillan, 1969.

Garber, Frederick, 'Nature and the Romantic mind: egotism, empathy, irony', *Comparative literature* 29 (1977), pp. 193–212.

Hartman, Geoffrey H., *Wordsworth's poetry, 1787–1815*, New Haven, CT: Yale University Press, 1964.

Hirsch, E. D., *Wordsworth and Schelling: a typological study of Romanticism*, New Haven, CT: Yale University Press, 1960.

Lovejoy, Arthur, 'On the discrimination of Romanticisms', in *English Romantic poets: modern essays in criticism*, M. H. Abrams (ed.), New York: Oxford University Press, 1960, pp. 3–24.

Man, Paul de, *The rhetoric of Romanticism*, New York: Columbia University Press, 1984.

McFarland, Thomas, 'Wordsworth on man, on nature, and on human life', *Studies in Romanticism* 21 (1982), pp. 601–18.

Modiano, Raimonda, *Coleridge and the concept of nature*, London: Macmillan, 1985.

Monk, Samuel H., *The sublime: a study of the critical theories in eighteenth-century England*, Ann Arbor, MI: University of Michigan Press, 1960.

Pipkin, James (ed.), *English and German Romanticism: cross-currents and controversies*, Heidelberg: Winter, 1985.

Rutter, Joachim, 'Landschaft: zur Funktion des Ästhetischen in der modernen Gesellschaft', in *Subjektivität: sechs Aufsätze*, Frankfurt am Main: Suhrkamp Verlag, 1974.

Weiskel, Thomas, *The Romantic sublime: studies in the structure and psychology of transcendence*, Baltimore, MD: The Johns Hopkins University Press, 1976.

Wellek, René, *A history of modern criticism: 1750–1950*, vol. 1: *The later eighteenth century*, New Haven, CT: Yale University Press, 1955, 8 vols.

'Romanticism re-examined', in *Romanticism reconsidered*, Northrop Frye (ed.), New York: Columbia University Press, 1963, pp. 107–34.

Wimsatt, W. K., Jr, 'The structure of Romantic nature imagery', in *Romanticism and consciousness: essays in criticism*, Harold Bloom (ed.), New York: Norton, 1970, pp. 77–88.

6   Scientific models

Primary sources

Böhme, Jakob, *Sämmtliche Werke*, K. W. Schiebler (ed.), 7 vols., Leipzig: Barth, 1922.
Carus, Carl Gustav, *Psyche: zur Entwicklungsgeschichte der Seele*, Pforzheim: Flammer und Hoffmann, 1846.
Coleridge, Samuel Taylor, *Inquiring spirit: a new presentation of Coleridge from his published and unpublished prose writings*, Kathleen Coburn (ed.), London: Routledge & Paul, 1951.
The notebooks of Samuel Taylor Coleridge, Kathleen Coburn (ed.), Princeton, NJ: Princeton University Press, 1957.
Collected letters of Samuel Taylor Coleridge, E. L. Griggs (ed.), Oxford University Press, 1956–71.
The collected works of Samuel Taylor Coleridge, vol. V: *Lectures 1808–19 on literature*, R. H. Foakes (ed.), Princeton, NJ: Princeton University Press, 1987, 16 vols.
Freud, Sigmund, *The standard edition of the complete psychological works of Sigmund Freud*, James Strachey (trans.), London: The Hogarth Press, 1958.
Goethe, Johann Wolfgang, *Die Schriften zur Naturwissenschaft*, Leopoldina-Ausgabe, Gunther Schmid (ed.), Weimar: Hermann Böhlaus Nachfolger, 1947–.
Goethe's color theory, Herb Aach (ed. and trans.), New York: Van Nostrand Reinhold, 1971.
Scientific studies, Douglas Miller (ed. and trans.), New York: Suhrkamp, 1988.
Sämtliche Werke nach Epochen seines Schaffens, Karl Richter (ed.), 21 vols., Munich: Hanser, 1985–96.
Goethe's botanical writings, Bertha Mueller (trans.), Woodbridge, CT: Ox Bow Press, 1989.
Elective affinities: a novel, David Constantine (ed. and trans.), Oxford University Press, 1994.
Herder, Johann Gottfried, *Sämmtliche Werke*, Bernhard Ludwig Suphan (ed.), 33 vols., Hildesheim: Georg Olms, 1967–8.
Kant, Immanuel, *Gesammelte Schriften*, Berlin: de Gruyter, 1910–83.
Metaphysical foundations of natural science, James Ellington (trans.), Indianapolis, IN: Bobbs-Merrill, 1970.
Lectures on metaphysics, Karl Ameriks and Steve Naragon (eds. and trans.), Cambridge University Press, 1997.
Novalis, *Schriften: die Werke Friedrich von Hardenbergs*, Paul Kluckhohn and Richard H. Samuel (eds.), 5 vols., Stuttgart: Kohlhammer, 1960–88.
Philosophical writings, Margaret Mahony Stoljar (trans.), Albany, NY: State University of New York Press, 1997.
Schelling, Friedrich Wilhelm Joseph von, *Sämmtliche Werke*, Karl Friedrich August Schelling (ed.), 14 vols., Stuttgart: Cotta, 1856–61.
Schlegel, Friedrich, *Kritische Friedrich-Schlegel-Ausgabe*, Ernst Behler (ed.), 35 vols., Paderborn: Schöningh, 1958–79.
Schubert, Gotthilf Heinrich, *Ansichten von der Nachtseite der Naturwissenschaft*, Dresden: Arnold, 1808.

Shelley, Mary Wollstonecraft, *Frankenstein: the 1818 text, contexts, nineteenth-century responses, modern criticism*, J. Paul Hunter (ed.), New York: Norton, 1996.
Shelley, Percy Bysshe, 'Defence of poetry', in *Shelley's prose, or the trumpet of a prophecy*, David Lee Clark (ed.), New York: New Amsterdam Books, 1988, pp. 275-97.
Wordsworth, William, Preface to *Lyrical ballads*, in *The prose works of William Wordsworth*, W. J. B. Owen and Jane Worthington Smyser (eds.), 3 vols., Oxford: Clarendon Press, 1974, I: 118-59.
Vico, Giambattista, *The new science of Giambattista Vico*, Thomas Goddard Bergin and Max Harold Fisch (eds. and trans.), Ithaca, NY: Cornell University Press, 1984.

Secondary sources

Abrams, Meyer H., *The mirror and the lamp: Romantic theory and the critical tradition*, New York: Oxford University Press, 1953.
Amrine, Frederick, Francis J. Zucker and Harvey Wheeler (eds.), *Goethe and the sciences: a reappraisal*, Dordrecht: Reidel, 1987.
Almeida, Hermione de, *Romantic medicine and John Keats*, New York: Oxford University Press, 1991.
Anderson, Wilda C., *Between the library and the laboratory: the language of chemistry in eighteenth-century France*, Baltimore, MD: The Johns Hopkins University Press, 1984.
Ault, Donald, *Visionary physics: Blake's response to Newton*, Chicago, IL: University of Chicago Press, 1974.
Barfield, Owen, *Saving the appearances: a study in idolatry*, Middletown, CT: Wesleyan University Press, 1988.
Béguin, Albert, *L'ame romantique et le rêve: essai sur le romantisme allemand et la poésie française*, Paris: Corti, 1946.
Bietak, Wilhelm, *Romantische Wissenschaft*, Deutsche Literatur, ser. 17, vol. 13, Leipzig: Reclam, 1940.
Black, Max, *Models and metaphors: studies in language and philosophy*, Ithaca, NY: Cornell University Press, 1962.
Bohler, Michael, 'Naturwissenschaft und Dichtung bei Goethe', in Wolfgang Wittkowski (ed.), *Goethe im Kontext: Kunst und Humanität, Naturwissenschaft und Politik von der Aufklärung bis zur Restauration*, Tübingen: Niemeyer, 1984, pp. 313-35.
Bonfiglio, Thomas P., 'Electric affinities: Arnim and Schellings Naturphilosophie', *Euphorion* 81 (1987), pp. 217-39.
Bono, James J., 'Science, discourse, and literature: the role/rule of metaphor in science', in *Literature and science: theory and practice*, Stuart Peterfreund (ed.), Boston, MA: Northeastern University Press, 1990, pp. 59-89.
Brown, Marshall, *The shape of German Romanticism*, Ithaca, NY: Cornell University Press, 1979.

Bush, Douglas, *Science and English poetry: a historical sketch, 1590–1950*, New York: Oxford University Press, 1950.

Burwick, Frederick, 'Elektrizität und Optik: zu den Beziehungen zwischen wissenschaftlichen und literarischen Schriften Achim von Arnims', *Aurora* 46 (1986), pp. 19–47.

The damnation of Newton: Goethe's color theory and Romantic perception, Berlin: de Gruyter, 1986.

Burwick, Frederick (ed.), *Approaches to organic form: permutations in science and culture*, Dordrecht: Reidel, 1987.

Cunningham, Andrew and Nicholas Jardine (eds.), *Romanticism and the sciences*, Cambridge University Press, 1990.

Eichner, Hans, 'The rise of modern science and the genesis of Romanticism,' *PMLA* 97 (1982), pp. 8–30.

Ellenberger, Henri F., *The discovery of the unconscious: the history and evolution of dynamic psychiatry*, New York: Basic Books, 1970.

Fink, Karl J., *Goethe's history of science*, Cambridge University Press, 1991.

Gode, Alexander, *Natural science in German Romanticism*, New York: Columbia University Press, 1941.

Grabo, Carl Henry, *A Newton among poets: Shelley's use of science in 'Prometheus Unbound'*, Chapel Hill, NC: University of North Carolina Press, 1930.

Hall, Jason Y., 'Gall's phrenology; a Romantic psychology', *Studies in Romanticism* 16 (1977), pp. 305–17.

Kapitza, Peter, *Die frühromantische Theorie der Mischung: über den Zusammenhang von romantischer Dichtungstheorie und zeitgenössischer Chemie*, Munich: Hueber, 1968.

King-Hele, Desmond, *Erasmus Darwin and the Romantic poets*, London: Macmillan, 1986.

Knight, D. M., 'The physical sciences and the Romantic movement', *History of science* 9 (1970), pp. 54–75.

Lakoff, George and Mark Johnson, *Metaphors we live by*, Chicago, IL: University of Chicago Press, 1980.

Lenoir, Timothy, *The strategy of life: teleology and mechanics in nineteenth-century German biology*, Dordrecht: Reidel, 1982.

Levere, Trevor Harvey, *Poetry realized in nature: Samuel Taylor Coleridge and early nineteenth-century science*, Cambridge University Press, 1981.

Levine, George (ed.), *Realism and representation: essays on the problem of realism in relation to science, literature and culture*, Madison, WI: University of Wisconsin Press, 1993.

Lyon, Judson S., 'Romantic psychology and the inner senses: Coleridge', *PMLA* 81 (1966), pp. 246–60.

Modiano, Raimonda, *Coleridge and the concept of nature*, Tallahassee, FL: Florida State University Press, 1985.

Müller-Sievers, Helmut, *Self-generation: biology, philosophy and literature around 1800*, Stanford, CA: Stanford University Press, 1997.

Nisbet, Hugh Barr, *Goethe and the scientific tradition*, London: University of London, 1972.

Orsini, G. N. Giordano, *Organic unity in ancient and later poetics: the philosophical foundations of literary criticism*, Carbondale, IL: Southern Illinois University Press, 1975.
Ortony, Andrew (ed.), *Metaphor and thought*, Cambridge University Press, 1993.
Poggi, Stefano and Maurizio (eds.), *Romanticism in science: science in Europe, 1790–1840*, Dordrecht: Kluwer Academic, 1994.
Proffitt, Edward, 'Science and Romanticism', *The Georgia review* 34 (1980), pp. 55–80.
Puppo, Mario, 'Letteratura e scienza nell'età del romanticismo', in *Letteratura e scienza nella storia della cultura italiana: atti del IX congresso dell'Associazione internazionale per gli studi di lingua e letteratura italiana, 1976*, Palermo: Manfredi, 1978, pp. 193–211.
Saul, Nicholas (ed.), *Die deutsche literarische Romantik und die Wissenschaften*, Munich: Iudicium Verlag, 1991.
Snelders, H. A. M., 'Romanticism and Naturphilosophie and the inorganic natural sciences 1787–1840: an introductory survey', *Studies in Romanticism* 9 (1970), pp. 193–215.
Stephenson, R. H., *Goethe's conception of knowledge and science*, Edinburgh University Press, 1995.
Underwood, Ted, 'The science in Shelley's theory of poetry', *Modern language quarterly* 58 (1997), pp. 299–321.
Wessell, Leonard P., *The philosophical background to Friedrich Schiller's aesthetics of living form*, Frankfurt am Main: Peter Lang, 1982.
Wetzels, Walter D., 'Aspects of natural science in German Romanticism', *Studies in Romanticism* 10 (1971), 44–59.
Johann Wilhelm Ritter: Physik im Wirkungsfeld der deutschen Romantik, Berlin: de Gruyter, 1973.
Whitehead, Alfred North, *Science and the modern world*, New York: Macmillan, 1925.
Whyte, Lancelot Law, *The unconscious before Freud*, London: Freidmann, 1978.
Wimsatt, W. K., 'Organic form: some questions about a metaphor', in *Romanticism: vistas, instances, continuities*, David Thorburn and Geoffrey Hartman (eds.), Ithaca, NY: Cornell University Press, 1973, pp. 13–37.
Wyatt, John, *Wordsworth and the geologists*, Cambridge University Press, 1995.
Wylie, Ian, *Young Coleridge and the philosophers of nature*, Oxford: Clarendon Press, 1989.
Ziolkowski, Theodore, *German Romanticism and its institutions*, Princeton, NJ: Princeton University Press, 1990.

7   Religion and literature

Primary sources

Blake, William, *The poetry and prose of William Blake*, David V. Erdman (ed.), Garden City, NY: Doubleday, 1970.
Burke, Edmund, *A philosophical inquiry into the origins of our ideas of the sublime and beautiful*, James T. Boulton (ed.), London: Routledge and Kegan Paul, 1958.

Reflections on the Revolution in France, Conor Cruise O'Brien (ed.), Harmondsworth: Penguin, 1976.

Byron, George Gordon, Lord, *Poetical works*, Jerome J. McGann (ed.), 7 vols., Oxford: Clarendon Press, 1980–93.

Chateaubriand, François-René de, *Le Génie du christianisme, ou, beautés de la religion chrétienne*, Paris: Migneret, 1802 (trans. Frederic Shoberl, *The beauties of Christianity*, Philadelphia, PA: Carey, 1815).

Coleridge, Samuel Taylor, *Poetical works*, E. H. Coleridge (ed.), 2 vols., Oxford University Press, 1912.

The Notebooks of Samuel Taylor Coleridge, Kathleen Coburn (ed.), 5 vols., London: Routledge and Kegan Paul, 1957–.

The collected works of Samuel Taylor Coleridge, Kathleen Coburn (ed.), 16 vols., Princeton, NJ: Princeton University Press, 1969–.

On the constitution of the church and state according to the idea of each, John Barrell (ed.), London: Dent & Sons, 1972.

'Confessions of an inquiring spirit', in *Collected works*, vol. XI: *Shorter works and fragments*, J. R. de J. Jackson and H. T. Jackson (eds.), Princeton, NJ: Princeton University Press, 1995, pp. 1111–71.

Darwin, Erasmus, *The loves of the plants*, 1789, facsim., Oxford: Woodstock, 1991.

Dupuis, C. F., *Origines de tous les cultes, ou religion universelle*, 12 vols., Paris: 1791.

Feuerbach, Ludwig, *The essence of Christianity*, George Eliot (trans.), New York: Harper, 1957.

Gibbon, Edward, *The decline and fall of the Roman Empire*, David Womersley (ed.), London: Penguin Books, 1995.

Gide, André, Introduction, in James Hogg, *The private memoirs and confessions of a justified sinner*, London: Cresset, 1947, pp. ix–xv.

Godwin, William, *Caleb Williams*, David McCracken (ed.), Oxford University Press, 1970.

Hegel, Georg Wilhelm Friedrich, *Lectures on the philosophy of religion*, E. B. Speirs and J. Burdon Sanderson (trans.), 3 vols., London: Kegan Paul, 1895.

Early theological writings, T. M. Knox (trans.), Philadelphia, PA: University of Pennsylvania Press, 1971.

Aesthetics: lectures on fine art, T. M. Knox (trans.), 2 vols., Oxford: Clarendon Press, 1975.

Phenomenology of spirit, A. V. Miller (trans.), Oxford: Clarendon Press, 1977.

Herder, Johann Gottfried, *The spirit of Hebrew poetry*, James Marsh (trans.), Burlington, VT: E. Smith, 1833; rpt. Napierville, IL: Aleph Press, 1971. (Earlier trans.: *Dialogues, containing the conversation of Eugenius and Alciphron on the spirit and beauties of the sacred poetry of the Hebrews*, London: T. Cadell, Jr., and W. Davies, 1801.)

God: some conversations, Frederick H. Burkhardt (ed.), New York: Veritas Press, 1940.

Reflections on the philosophy of the history of mankind, 1800, T. O. Churchill (trans.), Frank E. Manuel (ed.), Chicago, IL: University of Chicago Press, 1968.

Hogg, James, *The private memoirs and confessions of a justified sinner*, John Carey (ed.), Oxford University Press, 1947.

Hume, David, 'Of miracles', in *Enquiries concerning the human understanding and concerning the principles of morals*, L. A. Selby-Bigge (ed.), Oxford: Clarendon Press, 1975, pp. 109–31.

Dialogues concerning natural religion; and, The natural history of religion, J. C. A. Gaskin (ed.), Oxford University Press, 1993.

Kant, Immanuel, *Critique of judgment*, 1790, J. H. Bernard (trans.), New York, 1951.

Foundations of the metaphysics of morals; and What is Enlightenment?, Lewis White Beck (trans.), Indianapolis, IN: Bobbs-Merrill, 1959.

Religion within the limits of reason alone, Theodore M. Greene and Hoyt H. Hudson (trans.), New York: Harper, 1960.

The critique of pure reason, Norman Kemp Smith (trans.), New York: Macmillan, 1961.

The critique of practical reason, Lewis White Beck (trans.), New York: Macmillan, 1985.

Cambridge edition of the works of Immanuel Kant, Cambridge University Press, 1992–.

The metaphysics of morals, Mary Gregor (trans.), Cambridge University Press, 1996.

Kierkegaard, Søren, *Either/Or*, Howard V. Hong and Edna H. Hong (eds. and trans.), Princeton, NJ: Princeton University Press, 1987.

The concept of dread, Walter Lowrie (trans.), Princeton, NJ: Princeton University Press, 1989.

The concept of irony, Howard V. Hong and Edna H. Hong (eds. and trans.), Princeton, NJ: Princeton University Press, 1989.

Fear and trembling, Walter Lowrie (trans.), London: Everyman's Library, 1994.

Papers and journals: a selection, Alastair Hannay (trans.), Harmondsworth: Penguin Books, 1996.

Lamennais, Félicité-Robert de, *Paroles d'un croyant*, Paris: Rendeul, 1834 (trans. *Words of a believer*, London: Cousins, 1834).

Lessing, Gotthold Ephraim, *Theological writings: selections in translation*, Henry Chadwick (ed.), London: Adam and Charles Black, 1956.

Lowth, Robert, *Isaiah: a new translation*, London: Nichols, Dodsley, and Cadell, 1778.

Lectures on the sacred poetry of the Hebrews, 1749; Eng. trans. 1752; Latin: *Praelectiones*, London: Johnson, 1787.

Milton, John, *The poems of John Milton*, Helen Darbishire (ed.), London: Oxford University Press, 1958.

Paley, William, *A view of the evidences of Christianity*, London: Faulder, 1794. *Natural theology*, Philadelphia, PA: Maxwell, 1802.

Schelling, Friedrich Wilhelm Joseph, *Of human freedom*, James Gutmann (trans. and ed.), Chicago, IL: Open Court Publishing, 1936.

Schiller, Friedrich, *On the aesthetic education of man*, Elizabeth M. Wilkinson and L. A. Willoughby (eds. and trans.), Oxford: Clarendon Press, 1967.

Schleiermacher, Friedrich, *A critical essay on the Gospel of Luke*, Connop Thirl-
wall (trans. with an introduction), London: John Taylor, 1825.
    On religion: speeches to its cultured despisers [1800], Richard Crouter (ed.),
    Cambridge University Press, 1996.
Shelley, Mary, *Frankenstein: or, the modern Prometheus*, M. K. Joseph (ed.),
    Oxford University Press, 1969.
Shelley, Percy Bysshe, *Shelley's Poetry and Prose*, Donald H. Reiman and Sharon
    B. Powers (eds.), New York: Norton, 1977.
    'Essay on Christianity', in *Shelley's prose, or the trumpet of a prophecy*, David
    Lee Clark (ed.), New York: New Amsterdam, 1988, pp. 196–214.
    The Poems of Shelley, vol. I, Geoffrey Matthews and Kelvin Everest (eds.),
    London: Longman, 1989.
Strauss, David Friedrich, *The life of Jesus, critically examined*, George Eliot
    (trans.), London: Chapman Brothers, 1846.
Swedenborg, Emanuel, *Swedenborg: essential readings*, Michael Stanley (ed.),
    Wellingborough: Crucible, 1988.
White, Gilbert, *The natural history of Selborne*, Paul G. M. Foster (ed.), Oxford
    University Press, 1993.
Wordsworth, William, *Poems*, Matthew Arnold (ed.), London: Macmillan, 1879.
    Prose works, W. J. B. Owen and Jane Worthington Smyser (eds.), 3 vols.,
    Oxford: Clarendon Press, 1974.
    The Cornell Wordsworth, Stephen Parrish (ed.), Ithaca, NY: Cornell University
    Press, 1975.
    The letters of William and Dorothy Wordsworth, Alan G. Hill (ed.), 8 vols.,
    Oxford: Clarendon Press, 1979–89.
    The prelude 1799, 1805, 1850, Jonathan Wordsworth, M. H. Abrams and
    Stephen Gill (eds.), New York: Norton, 1979.

Secondary sources

Abrams, M. H., *Natural supernaturalism: tradition and revolution in Romantic
    literature*, New York: Norton, 1971.
Barth, Karl, *Protestant theology in the nineteenth century: its background & his-
    tory*, Valley Forge, PA: Judson Press, 1973. Translation based on 2nd rev.
    German edn, Zurich: Zollikon, 1952.
Beer, John B., *Coleridge, the visionary*, London: Chatto & Windus, 1959.
Bloom, Harold, *The visionary company: a reading of English Romantic poetry*,
    rev. edn, Ithaca, NY: Cornell University Press, 1961; 1971.
    Introduction, *Mary Shelley*, New York: Chelsea House, 1985, pp. 1–10.
Boulger, James D., *Coleridge as religious thinker*, New Haven, CT: Yale University
    Press, 1961.
Bull, Malcolm (ed.), *Apocalypse theory and the ends of the world*, Oxford: Black-
    well, 1995.
Burke, Kenneth, *The rhetoric of religion: a study in logology*, Berkeley, CA: Uni-
    versity of California Press, 1970.
Cambridge history of the Bible, vol. III: *The West, from the Reformation to the
    present day*, S. L. Greenslade (ed.), Cambridge University Press, 1963, 3 vols.

Cantor, Paul A., *Creature and creator: myth-making and English Romanticism*, Cambridge University Press, 1984.

Charity, A. C., *Events and their afterlife: the dialectics of Christian typology in the Bible and Dante*, Cambridge University Press, 1966.

Damrosch, Leopold, Jr, 'God and man', in *Symbol and truth in Blake's myth*, Princeton, NJ: Princeton University Press, 1980, pp. 244–301.

Dewey, John, 'James Marsh and American philosophy', *Journal of the history of ideas*, 2 (1941), pp. 131–50.

Erdman, David V., *Blake, prophet against empire: a poet's interpretation of the history of his own times*, Princeton, NJ: Princeton University Press, 1954.

Erskine-Hill, Howard, *Poetry of opposition and revolution: Dryden to Wordsworth*, Oxford University Press, 1996.

Frei, Hans W., *The eclipse of Biblical narrative: a study in eighteenth- and nineteenth-century hermeneutics*, New Haven, CT: Yale University Press, 1974.

Frye, Northrop, *Fearful symmetry: a study of William Blake*, Princeton, NJ: Princeton University Press, 1947.

The great code: the Bible and literature, New York: Harcourt Brace Jovanovich, 1982.

Gillispie, Charles Coulston, *Genesis and geology: a study in the relations of scientific thought, natural theology, and social opinion in Great Britain, 1790–1850*, Cambridge, MA: Harvard University Press, 1951.

Harrison, J. F. C., *The second coming: popular millenarianism, 1780–1850*, London: Routledge & Kegan Paul, 1979.

Hartman, Geoffrey, *Wordsworth's poetry, 1787–1814*, New Haven, CT: Yale University Press, 1964.

Havens, Raymond Dexter, *The influence of Milton on English poetry*, Cambridge, MA: Harvard University Press, 1922.

Hill, Alan G., 'Wordsworth's "Grand Design"', *Proceedings of the British Academy* 72 (1986), pp. 187–204.

Hort, Fenton John Anthony, 'Coleridge', *Cambridge essays*, vol. II, Cambridge: Parker, 1856.

Kahler, Erich, 'The nature of the symbol', in *Symbolism in religion and literature*, Rollo May (ed.), New York: Braziller, 1960, pp. 50–74.

Leventhal, Robert S., *The disciplines of interpretation: Lessing, Herder, Schlegel and hermeneutics in Germany, 1750–1800*, Berlin: de Gruyter, 1994.

Low, Lisa and Anthony John Harding (eds.), *Milton, the Metaphysicals, and Romanticism*, Cambridge University Press, 1994.

McFarland, Thomas, 'The Spinozist crescendo', in *Coleridge and the pantheist tradition*, Oxford: Clarendon Press, 1969, pp. 53–106.

'Coleridge's anxiety', in *Coleridge's variety: bicentenary studies*, John Beer (ed.), London: Macmillan, 1974, pp. 134–65.

Romanticism and the forms of ruin: Wordsworth, Coleridge, and modalities of fragmentation, Princeton, NJ: Princeton University Press, 1981.

McGuire, J. E. and P. M. Rattansi, 'Newton and the pipes of Pan', *Notes and records of the Royal Society of London* 21 (1966), pp. 108–43.

Mee, Jonathan, 'Is there an antinomian in the house?: William Blake and the after-life of a heresy', in *Historicizing Blake*, Steve Clarke and David Worrall (eds.), London, New York: St Martin's Press, 1994, pp. 43–58.

Mill, John Stuart, *On Bentham and Coleridge*, Chatto & Windus, London: 1967.

Miner, Earl (ed.), *Literary uses of typology: from the late Middle Ages to the present*, Princeton, NJ: Princeton University Press, 1977.

Monk, Samuel H., *The sublime: a study in critical theories in eighteenth-century England*, New York: Modern Language Association of America, 1935.

Morton, A. L., *The everlasting gospel: a study in the sources of William Blake*, London: Lawrence & Wishart, 1958.

Muirhead, John H., *Coleridge as philosopher*, London: Macmillan, 1930.

Newlyn, Lucy, *'Paradise lost' and the Romantic reader*, Oxford University Press, 1992.

Nicolson, Marjorie H., 'James Marsh and the Vermont transcendentalists', *Philosophical review* 34 (1925), pp. 28–50.

Mountain gloom and mountain glory: the development of the aesthetics of the infinite, Ithaca, NY: Cornell University Press, 1959.

Notopoulos, James A., *The Platonism of Shelley: a study of Platonism and the poetic mind*, Durham, NC: Duke University Press, 1949.

Nuttall, A. D., *A common sky: philosophy and the literary imagination*, London: Chatto & Windus, 1974.

Paley, Morton D. (ed.), *Twentieth-century interpretations of 'Songs of innocence and experience'*, Englewood Cliffs, NJ: Prentice-Hall, 1968.

Energy and the imagination: a study of the development of Blake's thought, Oxford: Clarendon Press, 1970.

The apocalyptic sublime, New Haven, CT: Yale University Press, 1986.

' "These promised years": Coleridge's "Religious musings" and the millenarianism of the 1790s', in *Revolution and English Romanticism: politics and rhetoric*, Keith Hanley and Raman Selden (eds.), Hertfordshire: Harvester Wheatsheaf, 1990, pp. 49–65.

Pocock, J. G. A., 'Edmund Burke and the redefinition of enthusiasm: the context as counter-revolution', in *The French Revolution and the creation of modern political culture*, 4 vols., Oxford: Pergamon Press, 1987–89, vol. III: *The transformation of political culture, 1789–1848*, François Furet and Mona Ozouf (eds.), pp. 19–43.

Prickett, Stephen, *Romanticism and religion: the tradition of Wordsworth and Coleridge in the Victorian church*, Cambridge University Press, 1976.

Origins of narrative: the Romantic appropriation of the Bible, Cambridge University Press, 1996.

Reardon, Bernard M. G., *Religion in the age of Romanticism: studies in early nineteenth-century thought*, Cambridge University Press, 1985.

Roston, Murray, *Prophet and poet: the Bible and the growth of Romanticism*, London: Faber and Faber, 1965.

Sanders, Charles R., *Coleridge and the Broad Church movement*, Durham, NC: Duke University Press, 1942.

Schenk, Hans Georg Artur Viktor, *The mind of the European Romantics: an essay in cultural history*, London: Constable, 1966.

Shaffer, E. S., 'Metaphysics of culture: Kant and Coleridge's *Aids to reflection*', *Journal of the history of ideas* 31 (1970), pp. 199–218.

    'Kubla Khan' and 'The fall of Jerusalem': the mythological school in Biblical criticism and secular literature, 1770–1880, Cambridge University Press, 1975.

    'Coleridge and Schleiermacher: the hermeneutic community', in *The Coleridge connection*, Richard Gravil and Molly Lefebure (eds.), Basingstoke: Macmillan, 1990, pp. 200–32.

Smart, Ninian, John C. Clayton, Steven Katz and Patrick Sherry (eds.), *Nineteenth century religious thought in the West*, 3 vols., Cambridge University Press, 1985.

Stephen, Leslie, *History of English thought in the eighteenth century*, London: Smith, 1881.

Storr, Vernon F., *The development of English theology in the nineteenth century, 1800–1860*, London: Longmans, Green, 1913.

Swiatecka, M. Jadwiga, *The idea of the symbol: some nineteenth century comparisons with Coleridge*, Cambridge University Press, 1980.

Tannenbaum, Leslie, *Biblical tradition in Blake's early prophecies: the great code of art*, Princeton, NJ: Princeton University Press, 1982.

Taylor, Charles, *Sources of the self: the making of the modern identity*, Cambridge, MA: Harvard University Press, 1989.

Thompson, E. P., *The making of the English working class*, London: Gollancz, 1965.

Weiskel, Thomas, *The Romantic sublime: studies in the structure and psychology of transcendence*, Baltimore, MD: The Johns Hopkins University Press, 1976.

Welch, Claude, *Protestant thought in the nineteenth century*, vol. I: 1799–1870, New Haven, CT: Yale University Press, 1972.

Wellek, René, *Immanuel Kant in England, 1793–1838*, Princeton, NJ: Princeton University Press, 1931.

    A history of modern criticism, 1750–1950, vol. II: *The Romantic age*, New Haven, CT: Yale University Press, 1955, 8 vols.

    Confrontations: studies in the intellectual and literary relations between Germany, England, and the United States during the nineteenth century, Princeton, NJ: Princeton University Press, 1965.

Williams, Raymond, *Culture and society, 1780–1950*, London: Chatto & Windus, 1958.

Wittreich, Joseph Anthony, Jr, *Angel of apocalypse: Blake's idea of Milton*, Madison, WI: University of Wisconsin Press, 1975.

    Visionary poetics: Milton's tradition and his legacy, San Marino, CA: Huntington Library, 1979.

Wolfson, Susan J., 'The formings of simile', in *Formal charges: the shaping of poetry in British Romanticism*, Princeton, NJ: Princeton University Press, 1996, pp. 63–99.

Ziolkowski, Theodore, *German Romanticism and its institutions*, Princeton, NJ: Princeton University Press, 1990.

8   Language theory and the art of understanding

Primary

Bernhardi, August Ferdinand, *Anfangsgründe der Sprachwissenschaft*, Stuttgart-Bad Cannstatt: Frommann-Holzboog, 1990.

Sprachlehre, 2 vols., 2nd edn, Hildesheim: Georg Olms, 1973.

Fichte, Johann Gottlieb, 'Von der Sprachfähigkeit und dem Ursprung der Sprache', in *Gesamtausgabe I*, vol. III: *Werke 1794–1796*, Reinhard Lauth and Hans Jacob (eds.), Stuttgart-Bad Cannstatt: Frommann, 1966, pp. 97–127 (trans. Jere Paul Surber, *Language and German idealism: Fichte's linguistic philosophy*, Atlantic Highlands, NJ: Humanities Press, 1996).

Herder, Johann Gottfried, *Abhandlung über den Ursprung der Sprache*, in *Herders sämmtliche Werke*, Bernard Suphan (ed.), Berlin: Weidmann, 1891, V: 1–154 (trans. (abridged) John H. Moran and Alexander Gode, in *On the origin of language: two essays by Jean-Jacques Rousseau and Johann Gottfried Herder*, Chicago, IL: University of Chicago Press, 1986, pp. 87–166).

Humboldt, Wilhelm von, *Über die Verschiedenheit des menschlichen Sprachbaues und ihren Einfluß auf die geistige Entwicklung des Menschengeschlechts*, in *Gesammelte Schriften*, Albert Leitzmann (ed.), vol. VII, Berlin: de Gruyter, 1968, 17 vols. (trans. Peter Heath, *On language: the diversity of human language structure and its influence on the mental development of mankind*, Cambridge University Press, 1988).

Novalis, *Schriften: die Werke Friedrich von Hardenbergs*, vol. II: *Das philosophische Werk*, Richard H. Samuel, Hans-Joachim Mähl and G. Schulz (eds.), Darmstadt: Wissenschaftliche Buchgesellschaft, 1965.

Mueller-Vollmer, Kurt (ed.), *The hermeneutics reader: texts of the German tradition from the Enlightenment to the present*, New York: Continuum, 1994.

Ormiston, Gayle L. and Alan D. Schrift (eds.), *The hermeneutic tradition: from Ast to Ricoeur*, Albany, NY: State University of New York Press, 1990.

Schlegel, August Wilhelm, 'Briefe über Poesie, Silbenmass und Sprache', in *Kritische Schriften und Briefe*, vol. I: *Sprache und Poetik*, Edgar Lohner (ed.), Stuttgart: Kohlhammer, 1962, pp. 141–80.

Kritische Ausgabe der Vorlesungen, vol. I: *Vorlesungen über Ästhetik I (1798–1803)*, Ernst Behler (ed.), Paderborn: Schöningh, 1989.

Schlegel, Friedrich, 'Zur Philologie', in *Kritische Friedrich-Schlegel-Ausgabe*, vol. XVI: *Fragmente zur Poesie und Literatur I*, Hans Eichner (ed.), Paderborn: Schöningh, 1981, pp. 33–82.

Schleiermacher, Friedrich, *Hermeneutik und Kritik: mit einem Anhang sprachphilosophischer Texte*, Manfred Frank (ed.), Frankfurt: Suhrkamp, 1977 (trans. James Duke and Jack Forstman, *Hermeneutics: the handwritten manuscripts*, Heinz Kimmerle (ed.), Atlanta, GA: Scholar Press, 1977).

Schulte, Rainer and Biguenet, John (eds.), *Theories of translation: an anthology of essays from Dryden to Derrida*, Chicago, IL: University of Chicago Press, 1992.

Staël, Madame de, *De l'Allemagne*, Jean de Pange and Simone Balayé (eds.), new edn, 5 vols., Paris: Hachette, 1958–60 (trans. O. W. Wright, *Germany*, Boston, MA: Houghton Mifflin, 1859).

Secondary sources

Aarsleff, Hans, *The study of language in England 1780–1860*, Princeton, NJ: Princeton University Press, 1967.

'Wordsworth, language and Romanticism', *Essays in criticism* 30 (1980), pp. 215–26.

Berman, Antoine, *The experience of the foreign: culture and translation in Romantic Germany*, S. Heyvaert (trans.), Albany, NY: State University of New York Press, 1992.

Bruns, Gerald L., *Modern poetry and the idea of language*, New Haven, CT: Yale University Press, 1974.

'Wordsworth at the limits of romantic hermeneutics', *The centennial review* 33 (1989), pp. 393–418.

Curran, T. H., 'Schleiermacher: true interpreter', in *The interpretation of belief: Coleridge, Schleiermacher and Romanticism*, David Jasper (ed.), London: Macmillan, 1986, pp. 97–103.

Derrida, Jacques, *Of grammatology*, Gayatri Chakravorty Spivak (trans.), Baltimore, MD: The Johns Hopkins University Press, 1974.

Fiesel, Eva, *Die Sprachphilosophie der deutschen Romantik*, Tübingen: Mohr, 1927; rpt. Hildesheim: Georg Olms, 1973.

Formigari, Lia, *Signs, science and politics: philosophies of language in Europe 1700–1830*, Amsterdam: John Benjamin, 1993.

Gadamer, Hans Georg, *Truth and method*, Joel Weinsheimer and Donald G. Marshall (trans.), 2nd edn, New York: Crossroad, 1988.

Gipper, Helmut, 'Sprachphilosophie in der Romantik', in *Sprachphilosophie: ein internationales Handbuch zeitgenössicher Forschung*, Marcelo Dascal *et al.* (eds.), Berlin: de Gruyter 1992, I: 197–233.

Gipper, Helmut and Peter Schmitter, *Sprachwissenschaft und Sprachphilosophie im Zeitalter der Romantik*, Tübingen: Günter Narr Verlag, 1979.

Jeanrond, Werner G., 'The impact of Schleiermacher's hermeneutics on contemporary interpretation theory', in *The interpretation of belief: Coleridge, Schleiermacher and romanticism*, David Jasper (ed.), London: Macmillan, 1986, pp. 81–96.

Körner, Josef, 'Friedrich Schlegels "Philosophie der Philologie" ', *Logos* 17 (1928), 1–72.

McKusick, James C., *Coleridge's philosophy of language*, New Haven, CT: Yale University Press, 1986.

Mueller-Vollmer, Kurt, 'Fichte und die romantische Sprachtheorie', in *Der transzendentale Gedanke: die gegenwärtige Darstellung der Philosophie Fichtes*, Klaus Hammacher (ed.), Hamburg: Felix Meiner, 1981, pp. 442–59.

'From aesthetics to linguistics: Wilhelm von Humboldt and the Romantic idea of language', in *Le Groupe de Coppet: Actes et documents du deuxième Colloque de Coppet 10–13 juillet 1974*, Geneva: Slatkine, 1977, pp. 195–215.

Nüsse, Heinrich, *Die Sprachtheorie Friedrich Schlegels*, Heidelberg: Winter, 1962.

O'Brien, William Arctander, *Novalis: signs of revolution*, Durham, NC: Duke University Press, 1995.

Paulin, Roger, 'Die romantische Übersetzung: Theorie und Praxis', in *Die deutsche literarische Romantik und die Wissenschaften*, Nicholas Saul (ed.), Munich: Iudicium Verlag, 1991, pp. 250–64.

Reed, Arden (ed.), *Romanticism and language*, Ithaca, NY: Cornell University Press, 1984.

Schnur, Harald, *Schleiermachers Hermeneutik und ihre Vorgeschichte im 18. Jahrhundert: Studien zur Bibelauslegung, zu Hamann, Herder und F. Schlegel*, Stuttgart: Metzler, 1994.

Surber, Jere Paul, 'The historical and systematic place of Fichte's reflections on language', in *Fichte: historical contexts/contemporary controversies*, Daniel Breazeale and Tom Rockmore (eds.), Atlantic Highlands, NJ: Humanities Press, 1994, pp. 113–27.

Language and German idealism: Fichte's linguistic philosophy, Atlantic Highlands, NJ: Humanities Press, 1996.

Taylor, Charles, 'Language and human nature', in *Human agency and language: philosophical papers*, Cambridge University Press, 1985, I: 215–47.

Trabant, Jürgen, *Apeliotes oder der Sinn der Sprache: Wilhelm von Humboldts Sprach-Bild*, Munich: Wilhelm Fink, 1986.

9 The transformation of rhetoric

Primary sources

Blair, Hugh, *Lectures on rhetoric and belles lettres*, London: W. Tegg, 1879.

Coleridge, Samuel Taylor, *Biographia literaria*, J. Shawcross (ed.), Oxford University Press, 1907.

Fontanier, Pierre, *Les figures du discours*, Paris: Flammarion, 1968.

Herder, Johann Gottfried, *Sämmtliche Werke*, Bernhard Suphan (ed.), Berlin: Weidmann, 1877–1913.

Hölderlin, Friedrich, *Sämtliche Werke*, Große Stuttgarter Ausgabe, Friedrich Beißner (ed.), Stuttgart: Kohlhammer, 1943–85.

Essays and letters on theory, Thomas Pfau (trans.), Albany, NY: State University of New York Press, 1988.

Kant, Immanuel, *Critique of judgment*, J. H. Barnard (trans.), New York: Hafner, 1966.

Kritik der Urteilskraft, Werkausgabe, vol. X, Wilhelm Weischedel (ed.), Frankfurt am/Main: Suhrkamp, 1974.

Novalis, *Schriften: die Werke Friedrich von Hardenbergs*, Paul Kluckhohn and Richard Samuel in collaboration with Hans-Joachim Mähl and Gerhard Schulz (eds.), Stuttgart: Kohlhammer, 1960–8.

Schlegel, August Wilhelm, *A course of lectures on dramatic art and literature*, London: H. G. Bohn, 1846.

Sämmtliche Werke, Eduard Böcking (ed.), Leipzig: Weidmann'sche Buchhandlung, 1846.

Schlegel, Friedrich, *Literary notebooks*, Hans Eichner (ed.), University of London/Athlone Press, 1957.

Kritische Friedrich-Schlegel-Ausgabe, Ernst Behler with the collaboration of Jean-Jacques Anstett, Hans Eichner, *et al.* (eds.), Paderborn: Schöningh, 1958–.

A Dialogue on poetry and literary aphorisms, Ernst Behler and Roman Struc (trans.), University Park, PA: Pennsylvania State University Press, 1968.

Philosophical fragments, Peter Firchow (trans.), Minneapolis, MN: University of Minnesota Press, 1991.

Smith, Adam, *Lectures on rhetoric and belles lettres*, J. C. Bryce (ed.) Indianapolis, IN: Liberty Fund, 1985.

Wordsworth, William, *Prose Works*, J. B. O. Warwick and J. W. Smyser (eds.), Oxford: Clarendon Press, 1974.

Young, Edward, *The complete works*, Hildesheim: Georg Olms, 1968, reprint of the 1854 London edition.

Secondary sources

Abrams, M. H., *The mirror and the lamp: Romantic theory and the critical tradition*, New York: Norton, 1958.

Attridge, Derek, *Peculiar language*, London: Methuen, 1988.

Barilli, Renato, *Rhetoric*, Giuliana Menozzi (trans.), Minneapolis, MN: University of Minnesota Press, 1989.

Barthes, Roland, 'The old rhetoric: an aide-memoire', in *The semiotic challenge*, Richard Howard (trans.), New York: Hill and Wang, 1988, pp. 11–94.

Behler, Ernst, *Irony and the discourse of Modernity*, Seattle, WA: University of Washington Press, 1990.

German Romantic literary theory, Cambridge University Press, 1993.

Behler, Ernst, and Jochen Hörisch, *Die Aktualität der Frühromantik*, Paderborn: Schöningh, 1989.

Bender, John, and David E. Wellbery (eds.), *The ends of rhetoric: history – theory – practice*, Stanford, CA: Stanford University Press, 1990.

Bloom, Harold, *et al.* (eds.), *Deconstruction and criticism*, New York: Seabury, 1979.

Blumenberg, Hans, 'Anthropologische Annäherung an die Aktualität der Rhetorik', in *Wirklichkeiten in denen wir leben*, Stuttgart: Reclam, 1981, pp. 104–36.

Bosse, Heinrich, 'The marvellous and Romantic semiotics', *Studies in Romanticism* 14 (1975), pp. 211–34.

' "Dichter kann man nicht bilden": zur Veränderung der Schulrhetorik nach 1770', *Jahrbuch für internationale Germanistik* 2 (1976), pp. 81–125.

Campe, Rüdiger, *Affekt und Ausdruck: zur Umwandlung der literarischen Rede im 17. und 18. Jahrhundert*, Tübingen: Niemeyer, 1990.

'Die zwei Perioden des Stils', *Comparatio* 2 (1991), pp. 73–99.

Chase, Cynthia, *Decomposing figures: rhetorical readings in the Romantic tradition*, Baltimore, MD: The Johns Hopkins University Press, 1986.

Dockhorn, Klaus, *Macht und Wirkung der Rhetorik*, Bad Homburg, Berlin and Zurich: Gehlen, 1968.

Engelsing, Rolf, *Analphabetentum und Lektüre: zur Sozialgeschichte des Lesens in Deutschland zwischen feudaler und industrieller Gesellschaft*, Stuttgart: Metzler, 1973.

Frank, Manfred, *Einführung in die frühromantische Ästhetik*, Frankfurt am Main: Suhrkamp, 1989.

Garber, Frederick (ed.), *Romantic irony*, Budapest: Akadémiai Kiadó, 1988.

Gasché, Rodolphe, 'Überlegungen zum Begriff der Hypotypose bei Kant', in Christiaan L. Hart Nibbrig (ed.), *Was heißt 'Darstellen'?* Frankfurt am Main: Suhrkamp, 1994, pp. 152–74.

Hamlin, Cyrus, 'The Temporality of selfhood: metaphor and Romantic poetry', *New Literary History* 6 (1974), pp. 169–93.

Henrich, Dieter, *The course of remembrance and other essays on Hölderlin*, Eckart Förster (ed.), Stanford, CA: Stanford University Press, 1997.

Hodgson, John A., *Coleridge, Shelley, and transcendental inquiry: rhetoric, argument, metapsychology*, Lincoln, NE: University of Nebraska Press, 1989.

Lacoue-Labarthe, Philippe, and Jean-Luc Nancy, *The literary absolute: the theory of literature in early German Romanticism*, Albany, NY: State University of New York Press, 1988.

Lausberg, Heinrich, *Handbuch der literarischen Rhetorik: eine Grundlegung der Literaturwissenschaft*, 2 vols., Munich: Hueber, 1960.

Man, Paul de, *Allegories of reading*, New Haven, CT: Yale University Press, 1979.

Blindness and insight, expanded edition, Minneapolis, MN: University of Minnesota Press, 1983.

The rhetoric of Romanticism, New York: Columbia University Press, 1984.

Mellor, Anne K., *English Romantic irony*, Cambridge, MA: Harvard University Press, 1980.

Menninghaus, Winfried, *Unendliche Verdopplung: die frühromantische Grundlegung der Kunsttheorie im Begriff absoluter Selbstreflexion*, Frankfurt am Main: Suhrkamp, 1987.

Most, Glenn W., 'Rhetorik und Hermeneutik: zur Konstitution der Neuzeitlichkeit', *Antike und Abendland* 30 (1984), pp. 62–79.

O'Brien, William Arctander, *Novalis: signs of revolution*, Durham, NC: Duke University Press, 1995.

Pfau, Thomas, 'Rhetoric and the existential: Romantic studies and the question of the subject', *Studies in Romanticism* 26 (1987), pp. 487–512.

Rajan, Tilottama, 'Displacing post-structuralism: Romantic studies after Paul de Man', *Studies in Romanticism* 24 (1985), pp. 451–74.

Reed Arden (ed.), *Romanticism and language*, Ithaca, NY: Cornell University Press, 1984.

Schaeffer, Jean-Marie, 'Romantisme et langage poétique', *Poétique* 42 (1980), pp. 177–94.

Schanze, Helmut, *Rhetorik: Beiträge zu ihrer Geschichte in Deutschland vom 16.–20. Jahrhundert*, Frankfurt: Athenäum, 1974.

Schanze, Helmut (ed.), *Friedrich Schlegel und die Kunsttheorie seiner Zeit*, Darmstadt: Wissenschaftliche Buchgesellschaft, 1988.

Smith, John, *The spirit and the letter: traces of rhetoric in Hegel's philosophy of Bildung*, Ithaca, NY: Cornell University Press, 1988.

Todorov, Tzvetan, *Theories of the symbol*, Catherine Porter (trans.), Ithaca, NY: Cornell University Press, 1982.

Ueding, Gerd, *Schillers Rhetorik: Idealistische Wirkungsästhetik und rhetorische Tradition*, Tübingen: Niemeyer, 1971.

Gerd Ueding (ed.), *Historisches Wörterbuch der Rhetorik*, Tübingen: Niemeyer, 1992ff.

10   Romantic irony

Primary sources

Kierkegaard, Søren, *The concept of irony, with constant reference to Socrates*, Lee M. Capel (trans.), New York: Harper, 1965.

Novalis, *Schriften: die Werke Friedrich von Hardenbergs*, Paul Kluckhohn and Richard H. Samuel (eds.), 5 vols., Stuttgart: Kohlhammer, 1960–1988.

Philosophical writings, Margaret Mahony Stoljar (trans.), Albany, NY: State University of New York Press, 1997.

Richter, Jean Paul Friedrich, *Horn of Oberon: Jean Paul Richter's school for aesthetics*, Margaret R. Hale (trans.), Detroit, MI: Wayne State University Press, 1973.

Schlegel, Friedrich, *Literary notebooks (1797–1801)*, Hans Eichner (ed.), London: University of London, Athlone Press, 1957.

Philosophische Lehrjahre I (1796–1806), *Kritische Friedrich-Schlegel-Ausgabe*, Ernst Behler (ed.), vol. XVIII, Munich: Schöningh, 1963.

Philosophische Vorlesungen I (1800–1807), *Kritische Friedrich-Schlegel-Ausgabe*, Jean-Jacques Anstett (ed.), vol. XII, Munich: Schöningh, 1964.

Charakteristiken und Kritiken I (1796–1801), *Kritische Friedrich-Schlegel-Ausgabe*, Hans Eichner (ed.), vol. II, Munich: Schöningh, 1967.

Friedrich Schlegel's 'Lucinde' and the fragments, Peter Firchow (trans.), Minneapolis: University of Minnesota Press, 1971.

Charakteristiken und Kritiken II (1802–1829), *Kritische Friedrich-Schlegel-Ausgabe*, Hans Eichner (ed.), vol. III, Munich: Schöningh, 1975.

Fragmente zur Poesie und Literatur I, *Kritische Friedrich-Schlegel-Ausgabe*, Hans Eichner (ed.), vol. XVI, Munich: Schöningh, 1981.

Solger, Karl Wilhelm Ferdinand, *Erwin: vier Gespräche über das Schöne und die Kunst*, Wolfhart Henckmann (ed.), Munich: Fink, 1971.

Wheeler, Kathleen (ed.), *German aesthetic and literary criticism: the Romantic ironists and Goethe*, Cambridge University Press, 1984.

Secondary sources

Albert, Georgia, 'Understanding irony: three essays on Friedrich Schlegel', *MLN*, 108 (1993), pp. 825–48.

Alford, Steven, *Irony and the logic of the Romantic imagination*, New York: Lang, 1984.

Allemann, Beda, *Ironie und Dichtung*, Pfüllingen: Neske, 1956.

'Ironie als literarisches Prinzip', in *Ironie und Dichtung*, Albert Schaefer (ed.), Munich: Beck, 1970, pp. 11–37.

Behler, Ernst, *Klassische Ironie, romantische Ironie, tragische Ironie: zum Ursprung dieser Begriffe*, Darmstadt: Wissenschaftliche Buchgesellschaft, 1972.

Irony and the discourse of modernity, Seattle, WA: University of Washington Press, 1990.

Ironie und literarische Moderne, Paderborn: Schöningh, 1997.

Benjamin, Walter, *Der Begriff der Kunstkritik in der deutschen Romantik*, in *Gesammelte Schriften*, Rolf Tiedemann and Hermann Schweppenhäuser (eds.), Frankfurt am Main: Suhrkamp, 1974, vol. i, pp. 7–122.

Bishop, Lloyd, *Romantic irony in French literature: from Diderot to Beckett*, Nashville, TN: Vanderbilt University Press, 1989.

Booth, Wayne, *A rhetoric of irony*, Chicago, IL: University of Chicago Press, 1974.

Bourgeois, René, *L'ironie romantique: spectacle et jeu de Mme de Staël à Gérard de Nerval*, Grenoble: Presses Universitaires de Grenoble, 1974.

Brooks, Cleanth, 'Irony as a principle of structure', in *Critical theory since Plato*, Hazard Adams (ed.), New York: Harcourt Brace Jovanovich, 1971, pp. 968–74.

Brown, Marshall, *The shape of German Romanticism*, Ithaca, NY: Cornell University Press, 1979.

Comstock, Cathy, ' "Transcendental buffoonery": irony as process in Schlegel's "Über die Unverständlichkeit" ', *Studies in Romanticism*, 26 (1987), pp. 445–64.

Dane, Joseph, *The critical mythology of irony*, Athens, GA: University of Georgia Press, 1991.

Daverio, John, 'Schumann's systems of musical fragments and *Witz*', in *Nineteenth-century music and the German Romantic ideology*, New York: Schirmer Books, 1993, pp. 49–88.

Dierkes, Hans, 'Ironie und System: Friedrich Schlegels "Philosophische Lehrjahre" (1797–1799)', *Philosophisches Jahrbuch der Görres-Gesellschaft* 97 (1990), pp. 251–76.

Dyson, A. E., *The crazy fabric: essays in irony*, London: Macmillan, 1965.

Finlay, Marike, *The Romantic irony of semiotics: Friedrich Schlegel and the crisis of representation*, Berlin: Mouton de Gruyter, 1988.

Fetzer, John Francis, 'Romantic irony', in *European Romanticism: literary cross-currents, modes, and models*, Gerhart Hoffmeister (ed.), Detroit, MI: Wayne State University Press, 1990, pp. 19–36.

Furst, Lilian R., *Fictions of romantic irony*, Cambridge, MA: Harvard University Press, 1984.

Garber, Frederick, *Self, text, and romantic irony: the example of Byron*, Princeton, NJ: Princeton University Press, 1988.

Garber, Frederick (ed.), *Romantic irony*, Budapest: Akadémiai Kiadó, 1988.

Gillespie, Gerald (ed.), *Romantic drama*, Amsterdam: Benjamins, 1994.

Hamilton, Paul, 'Romantic irony and English literary history', in *The Romantic heritage: a collection of critical essays*, Karsten Engelberg (ed.), Copenhagen: University of Copenhagen, 1983, pp. 11–32.

Hamlin, Cyrus, 'Platonic dialogue and romantic irony: prolegomenon to a theory of Romantic narrative', *Canadian review of comparative literature* 3 (1976), pp. 5–26.

Handwerk, Gary, *Irony and ethics in narrative: from Schlegel to Lacan*, New Haven, CT: Yale University Press, 1985.

Immerwahr, Raymond, 'The subjectivity or objectivity of Friedrich Schlegel's poetic irony', *Germanic review* 26 (1951), pp. 173–91.

'Romantic irony and romantic arabesque prior to Romanticism', *German quarterly* 42 (1969), pp. 665–85.

Jankélévitch, Vladimir, *L'ironie, ou la bonne conscience*, Paris: Alcan, 1936.

Kálmán, Győrgy C., 'Romantic irony as an international phenomenon', *Neohelicon* 18 (1991), pp. 289–96.

Kapitza, Peter, 'Theorie der Mischung und Universalpoesie', *Die frühromantische Theorie der Mischung: über den Zusammenhang von romantischer Dichtungstheorie und zeitgenössischer Chemie*, Munich: Hueber, 1968, pp. 157–84.

Kipperman, Mark, 'Fichtean irony and some principles of Romantic quest', *Studies in Romanticism* 23 (1984), pp. 223–36.

Knox, Norman, *The word 'irony' and its context (1500–1755)*, Durham, NC: Duke University Press, 1961.

Lacoue-Labarthe, Philippe and Jean-Luc Nancy, *The literary absolute: the theory of literature in German Romanticism*, Philip Barnard and Cherel Lester (trans.), Albany, NY: State University of New York Press, 1988.

Lang, Candace D., *Irony/humor: critical paradigms*, Baltimore, MD: The Johns Hopkins University Press, 1988.

Lukács, Georg, 'Richness, chaos and form: a dialogue concerning Laurence Sterne', in *Soul and form*, Anna Bostock (trans.), Cambridge, MA: The MIT Press, 1974, pp. 124–51.

Man, Paul de, 'The rhetoric of temporality', in *Blindness and insight: essays in the rhetoric of contemporary criticism*, Theory and History of Literature 7, Minneapolis, MN: University of Minnesota Press, 1983, pp. 187–228.

Meitinger, Serge, 'Idéalisme et poétique', *Romantisme* 14, no. 45 (1984), pp. 3–24.

Mellor, Anne K., *English Romantic irony*, Cambridge, MA: Harvard University Press, 1980.

Muecke, Douglas C., *The compass of irony*, London: Methuen, 1969.

Prang, Helmut, *Die romantische Ironie*, Darmstadt: Wissenschaftliche Buchgesellschaft, 1972.

Preisendanz, Wolfgang, *Humor als dichterische Einbildungskraft: Studien zur Erzählkunst des poetischen Realismus*, Munich: Fink, 1976.

Preisendanz, Wolfgang and Rainer Warning (eds.), *Das Komische, das Satirische, und das Ironische*, Munich: Fink, 1976.

Ryals, Clyde de L., *A world of possibilities: romantic irony in Victorian literature*, Columbus, OH: Ohio University Press, 1990.

Shrayer, Maxim D., 'Rethinking romantic irony: Puškin, Byron, Schlegel and *The queen of spades*', *Slavic and East European journal* 36 (1992), pp. 397–414.

Simpson, David, *Irony and authority in Romantic poetry*, London: Macmillan, 1979.

Sperber, Daniel and Deirdre Wilson, 'Irony and the use–mention distinction', in *Radical pragmatics*, Peter Cole (ed.), New York: Academic Press, 1981, pp. 295–318.

Sperry, Stuart M., 'Toward a definition of romantic irony in English literature', in *Romantic and Modern: revaluations of literary tradition*, George Bornstein (ed.), Pittsburgh, PA: University of Pittsburgh Press, 1977, pp. 3–28.

Strohschneider-Kohrs, Ingrid, *Die romantische Ironie in Theorie und Gestaltung*, Tübingen: Niemeyer, 1960.

Szondi, Peter, 'Friedrich Schlegel and romantic irony, with some remarks on Tieck's comedies', in *On textual understanding and other essays*, Harvey Mendelsohn (trans.), Minneapolis, MN: University of Minnesota Press, 1986, pp. 57–73.

Verstraete, Ginette, 'Friedrich Schlegel's practice of literary theory', *The Germanic review* 69 (1994), pp. 28–35.

Vlastos, Gregory, *Socrates: ironist and moral philosopher*, Ithaca, NY: Cornell University Press, 1991.

White, Hayden, *Metahistory: the historical imagination in nineteenth-century Europe*, Baltimore, MD: The Johns Hopkins University Press, 1973.

11 Theories of genre

Primary sources

Blair, Hugh, *Lectures on rhetoric and belles lettres*, vol. III, New York: Garland, 1970, 3 vols.

Godwin, William, 'Of choice in reading', in *The enquirer: reflections on education, manners, and literature in a series of essays*, New York: Kelley, 1965, pp. 129–46.

'Of history and romance', in *Things as they are; or, the adventures of Caleb Williams*, Maurice Hindle (ed.), London: Penguin, 1988.

Hegel, Georg Wilhelm Friedrich, *Aesthetics: lectures on fine art*, T. M. Knox (trans.), vol. I, Oxford: Clarendon Press, 1975, 2 vols.

Herder, Johann Gottfried, *Selected early works, 1764–1767: addresses, essays, and drafts; fragments on recent German literature*, Ernest A. Menze and Karl Menges (eds.), Ernest A. Menze and Michael Palma (trans.), University Park, PA: Pennsylvania State University Press, 1992.

Hugo, Victor, Preface to *Cromwell*, Paris: Garnier-Flammarion, 1968.

Kierkegaard, Søren, *The concept of irony*, Lee M. Capel (trans.), Bloomington, IN: Indiana University Press, 1971.

Peacock, Thomas Love, *The four ages of poetry*, in Shelley and Peacock, '*A defence of poetry' and 'The four ages of poetry'*, Indianapolis, IN: Bobbs-Merrill, 1965, pp. 3–21.

Reeve, Clara, *The progress of romance through times, countries, and manners*, 1785, rpt. New York: Garland, 1970.

Schelling, Friedrich Wilhelm Joseph, *The philosophy of art*, Douglas W. Stott (ed. and trans.), Minneapolis, MN: University of Minnesota Press, 1989.

Schiller, Friedrich, *Naive and sentimental poetry*, in *Naive and sentimental poetry; and, On the sublime*, Julius A. Elias (trans.), New York: Ungar, 1966, pp. 81–190.

Schlegel, August Wilhelm, *A course of lectures on dramatic art and literature*, Alexander James William Morrison (ed.), John Black (trans.), London: Bohn, 1846.

Schlegel, Friedrich, *Literary notebooks, 1797–1801*, Hans Eichner (ed.), Toronto: University of Toronto Press, 1957.

'Dialogue on poetry', in Ernst Behler and Roman Struc (trans.), *Dialogue on poetry and literary aphorisms*, University Park, PA: Pennsylvania State University Press, 1968, pp. 51–117.

Philosophical fragments, Peter Firchow (trans.), Minneapolis, MN: University of Minnesota Press, 1991.

Schopenhauer, Arthur, *The world as will and representation*, E. F. J. Payne (trans.), vol. I, New York: Dover, 1969, 2 vols.

Shelley, Percy Bysshe, *A defence of poetry*, in *Shelley's poetry and prose: authoritative texts, criticism*, Donald H. Reiman and Sharon B. Powers (eds.), New York: Norton, 1977, pp. 478–508.

Secondary sources

Bahti, Timothy, 'Fate in the past: Peter Szondi's reading of German Romantic genre theory', *Boundary 2* 11 (1983), pp. 111–25.

Bakhtin, Mikhail Mikhailovich, *The dialogic imagination*, Caryl Emerson and Michael Holquist (trans.), Austin, TX: University of Texas Press, 1981.

Beebee, Thomas O., *The ideology of genre: a comparative study of generic instability*, University Park, PA: Pennsylvania State University Press, 1994.

Benjamin, Walter, 'The storyteller: reflections on the work of Nikolai Leskov', in *Illuminations*, Hannah Arendt (ed.), Harry Zohn (trans.), New York: Schocken, 1969, pp. 83–109.

The origin of German tragic drama, John Osborne (trans.), London: Verso, 1992.

Corngold, Stanley, 'Nietzsche's moods', *Studies in Romanticism* 29 (1990), pp. 67–90.

Curran, Stuart, *Poetic form and British Romanticism*, Oxford University Press, 1989.

Fishelov, David, *Metaphors of genre: the role of analogies in genre theory*, University Park, PA: Pennsylvania State University Press, 1993.

Fowler, Alastair, *Kinds of literature: an introduction to the theory of genres and modes*, Cambridge, MA: Harvard University Press, 1982.

Frank, Manfred, 'The infinite text', *Glyph: textual studies*, vol. VII, Samuel Weber (ed.), Baltimore, MD: The Johns Hopkins University Press, 1980, pp. 70–101.

Genette, Gérard, *The architext: an introduction*, Jane E. Lewin (ed.), Berkeley, CA: University of California Press, 1992.

Guillén, Claudio, *Literature as system: essays toward the theory of literary history*, Princeton, NJ: Princeton University Press, 1971.

Hamburger, Käte, *The logic of literature*, Marilynn J. Rose (trans.), 2nd edn, Bloomington, IN: Indiana University Press, 1973.

Hamlin, Cyrus, 'The origins of a philosophical genre theory in German Romanticism', *European Romantic review* 5 (1994), pp. 3–14.

Hartman, Geoffrey H., *Beyond formalism: literary essays 1958–1970*, New Haven, CT: Yale University Press, 1970.
  The fate of reading and other essays, Chicago, IL: University of Chicago Press, 1975.
Lukács, Georg, 'The ideology of modernism', in *The meaning of contemporary realism*, John and Necke Mander (trans.), London: Merlin Press, 1962, pp. 17–46.
  The theory of the novel: a historico–philosophical essay on the forms of great epic literature, Anna Bostock (trans.), Cambridge, MA: The MIT Press, 1971.
Man, Paul de, 'The rhetoric of temporality', in *Blindness and insight: essays in the rhetoric of contemporary criticism*, Theory and History of Literature 7, Minneapolis, MN: University of Minnesota Press, 1983, pp. 187–228.
Nietzsche, Friedrich, *The birth of tragedy*, in *The birth of tragedy; and The genealogy of morals*, Francis Golffing (trans.), New York: Anchor Books, 1956, pp. 1–146.
Rajan, Tilottama and Julia M. Wright, 'Introduction', in *Romanticism, history and the possibilities of genre: re-forming literature 1789–1837*, Cambridge University Press, 1998, pp. 1–18.
Staiger, Emil, *Basic concepts of poetics*, Marianne Burkhard and Luanne T. Frank (eds.), Janetta C. Hudson and Luanne T. Frank (trans.), University Park, PA: Pennsylvania State University Press, 1991.
Szondi, Peter, 'Friedrich Schlegel's theory of poetical genres: a reconstruction from the posthumous fragments', in *On textual understanding and other essays*, Harvey Mendelsohn (trans.), Minneapolis, MN: University of Minnesota Press, 1986, pp. 75–94.
Todorov, Tzvetan, *Genres in discourse*, Catherine Porter (trans.), Cambridge University Press, 1990.
Weissenberger, Klaus, 'A morphological genre theory: an answer to a pluralism of forms', in *Theories of literary genre*, Joseph P. Strelka (ed.), University Park, PA: Pennsylvania State University Press, 1978, pp. 229–53.
Wellek, René, 'Genre theory, the lyric, and *Erlebnis*', in *Discriminations: further concepts of criticism*, New Haven, CT: Yale University Press, 1970, pp. 225–52.
Worringer, Wilhelm, *Abstraction and empathy: a contribution to the psychology of style*, Michael Bullock (trans.), Cleveland: Meridian Books, 1967.

12   Theory of the novel

Primary sources

Balzac, Honoré de, Preface to *La comédie humaine*, Marcel Bouteron (ed.), vol. I, Paris: Gallimard, 1950–6, pp. 3–16 (trans. Ellen Marriage, *The works of Honoré de Balzac*, vol. I, Philadelphia, PA: Avil, 1901, pp. liii–lxix).
  'A study of M. Beyle', in *The charterhouse of Parma* by Stendhal, 2 vols., C. K. Scott Moncrieff (trans.), New York: Boni & Liveright, 1925, I: vii–lxxiii.
Barbauld, Anna Laetitia (ed.), 'On the origin and progress of novel-writing', in *The British novelists*, 50 vols., London: Rivington, 1810, I: 1–62.

Blanckenburg, Friedrich von, *Versuch über den Roman*, Eberhard Lämmert (ed.), Stuttgart: Metzler, 1965.

Dunlop, John Colin, *History of prose fiction*, Henry Wilson (ed.), new edn, New York: AMS Press, 1969.

Eichendorff, Joseph von, *Der deutsche Roman des achtzehnten Jahrhunderts in seinem Verhältniß zum Christentum*, in *Sämtliche Werke des Freiherrn Joseph von Eichendorff*, Historisch-Kritische Ausgabe, Wolfram Mauser (ed.), 18 vols., Regensburg: Josef Habbel, 1965, VIII: 5–245.

Fielding, Joseph, *Joseph Andrews*, Martin C. Battestin (ed.), The Wesleyan edition of the works of Henry Fielding, Oxford: Clarendon Press, 1967.

The history of Tom Jones, Fredson Bowers (ed.), Oxford: Wesleyan University Press, 1975.

Geißler, Rolf (ed.), *Romantheorie in der Aufklärung: Thesen und Texte zum Roman des 18. Jahrhunderts in Frankreich*, Berlin: Akademie-Verlag, 1984.

Godwin, William, 'Of history and romance', rpt. as 'Essay on history and romance', in *Political and philosophical writings of William Godwin*, Mark Philp (ed.), 7 vols., London: William Pickering, 1993, VII: 290–301.

Goethe, Johann Wolfgang von, *Wilhelm Meisters Lehrjahre* (Gesamtausgabe der Werke und Schriften in zweiundzwanzig Bänden), 22 vols., Stuttgart: Cotta, 1940–1963, VII: 9–708 (trans. Eric A. Blackall, *Wilhelm Meister's apprenticeship*, New York: Suhrkamp, 1989).

Hazlitt, William, 'Lectures on the English comic writers', in *The complete works of William Hazlitt*, P. P. Howe (ed.), 21 vols., New York: AMS Press, 1967, VI: 1–168.

'Sir Walter Scott, Racine, and Shakespear', in *The complete works of William Hazlitt*, P. P. Howe (ed.), 21 vols., New York: AMS Press, 1967, XII: 336–46.

'The spirit of the age; or contemporary portraits', in *The complete works of William Hazlitt*, P. P. Howe (ed.), 21 vols., New York: AMS Press, 1967, XI: 1–184.

'The Waverley notes', in *The complete works of William Hazlitt*, P. P. Howe (ed.), 21 vols., New York: AMS Press, 1967, XX: 231–3.

Huet, Pierre-Daniel, *Traité de l'origine des romans*, 1670, rpt. Stuttgart: Metzler, 1966 (trans. *A treatise of romances and their original*, London: Battersby, 1672).

Hurd, Richard, *Letters on chivalry and romance*, 1762, rpt. New York: Garland, 1971.

Jeffrey, Francis, *Contributions to The Edinburgh review*, The modern British essayists 6, Philadelphia, PA: Hart, 1853.

Lämmert, Eberhard (ed.), *Romantheorie 1620–1880: Dokumentation ihrer Geschichte in Deutschland*, Frankfurt am Main: Athenäum, 1988.

Manzoni, Alessandro, *On the historical novel*, Sandra Bermann (trans.), Lincoln, NE: University of Nebraska Press, 1996.

Marlinsky, Aleksandr, 'On Romanticism and the novel', in *Russian Romantic criticism: an anthology*, Lauren Gray Leighton (ed. and trans.), New York: Greenwood Press, 1987, pp. 137–60.

Murray, Hugh, *The morality of fiction; or, an inquiry into the tendency of fictitious narratives, with observations on some of the most eminent*, Norwood, PA: Norwood, 1977.

Reeve, Clara, *The progress of romance through times, countries, and manners*, 1785, rpt. New York: Garland, 1970.

Richter, Jean Paul Friedrich, *Vorschule der Ästhetik*, Norbert Miller (ed.), Hamburg: Meiner, 1990 (trans. Margaret R. Hale, *Horn of Oberon: Jean Paul Richter's school for aesthetics*, Detroit, MI: Wayne University Press, 1973, pp. 179–95).

Sade Marquis de, *Idée sur les romans*, Jean Glastier (ed.), Bordeaux: Ducros, 1970, (trans. Austryn Wainhouse and Richard Seaver, 'Reflections on the novel', in *The Marquis de Sade: the 120 days of Sodom and other writings*, New York: Grove Press, 1966, pp. 91–116).

Schlegel, Friedrich von, *Literary notebooks (1797–1801)*, Hans Eichner (ed.), University of London, Athlone Press, 1957.

'Goethes Werke nach der Cottaschen Ausgabe von 1806', in *Kritische Schriften*, Wolfdietrich Rasch (ed.), Munich: Hanser, 1964, pp. 288–322.

Dialogue on poetry and literary aphorisms, Ernst Behler and Roman Struc (eds. and trans.), University Park, PA: Pennsylvania State University Press, 1968.

Friedrich Schlegel's 'Lucinde' and the fragments, Peter Firchow (trans.), Minneapolis, MN: University of Minnesota Press, 1971.

'Letter about the novel,' in *German aesthetic and literary criticism: the Romantic ironists and Goethe*, Kathleen M. Wheeler (ed.), Cambridge University Press, 1984, pp. 73–80.

'On Goethe's Meister', in *German aesthetic and literary criticism: the Romantic ironists and Goethe*, Kathleen M. Wheeler (ed.), Cambridge University Press, 1984, pp. 59–73.

Schleiermacher, Friedrich, 'Roman', in *Ästhetik. Über den Begriff der Kunst*, Thomas Lehnerer (ed.), Hamburg: Meiner, 1984, pp. 142–7.

Scott, Walter, *Sir Walter Scott on novelists and fiction*, Ioan M. Williams (ed.), London: Routledge & Paul, 1968.

'Prefaces to the edition of 1829', in *Waverley; or, 'tis sixty years since*, Claire Lamont (ed.), Oxford: Clarendon Press, 1981.

Staël, Madame de, 'Essay on fictions', in *An extraordinary woman: selected writings of Germaine de Staël*, Vivian Folkenflik (trans.), New York: Columbia University Press, 1987, pp. 60–78.

Weber, Ernst (ed.), *Texte zur Romantheorie*, vol. II, Munich: Fink, 1981, 2 vols.

Williams, Ioan M. (ed.), *Novel and romance, 1700–1800: a documentary record*, New York: Barnes & Noble, 1970.

Wollstonecraft, Mary, *The works of Mary Wollstonecraft*, Janet Todd and Marilyn Butler (eds.), vol. VII: *On poetry: contributions to the Analytical review*, London: Pickering, 1989, 7 vols.

Secondary sources

Bator, Paul G., 'Rhetoric and the novel in the eighteenth-century British university curriculum', *Eighteenth-century studies* 30 (1996–7), pp. 173–95.

Bauer, Matthias, *Romantheorie*, Stuttgart: Metzler, 1997.

Becker, Eva D., *Der deutsche Roman um 1780*, Stuttgart: Metzler, 1964.

Behler, Diana, *The theory of the novel in early German Romanticism*, Berne: Peter Lang, 1978.

Behler, Ernst, 'Goethes *Wilhelm Meister* und die Romantheorie der Frühromantik', *Etudes germaniques* 44 (1989), pp. 409–28.

Behrendt, Stephen C., 'Questioning the Romantic novel', *Studies in the novel* 26 (1994), pp. 5–25.

Bell, Michael Davitt, *The development of American romance: the sacrifice of relation*, Chicago, IL: University of Chicago Press, 1980.

Blackall, Eric A., *Goethe and the novel*, Ithaca, NY: Cornell University Press, 1976.

Blin, Georges, *Stendhal et les problèmes du roman*, Paris: Corti, 1990.

Böckmann, Paul, 'Der Roman der Transzendentalpoesie in der Romantik', in *Geschichte, Deutung, Kritik: Literaturwissenschaftliche Beiträge dargebracht zum 65. Geburtstag Werner Kohlschmidts*, Maria Bindschedler and Paul Zinsli (eds.), Bern: Francke, 1969, pp. 165–85.

Brown, Jane K. 'The theatrical mission of the Lehrjahre', *Goethe's narrative fiction: the Irvine Goethe symposium*, William J. Lillyman (ed.), Berlin: de Gruyter, 1983, pp. 69–84.

Brown, Marshall, 'The logic of realism: a Hegelian approach', *PMLA* 96 (1981), pp. 224–41.

Butler, Marilyn, *Jane Austen and the war of ideas*, Oxford: Clarendon Press, 1975. *Romantics, rebels, and reactionaries: English literature and its background 1760–1830*, Oxford University Press, 1981.

Davidson, Cathy N., *The revolution of the word: the rise of the novel in America*, Oxford University Press, 1986.

Favret, Mary A., 'Telling tales about genre: poetry in the Romantic novel', *Studies in the novel* 26 (1994), pp. 153–72.

Ferris, Ina, *The achievement of literary authority: gender, history, and the Waverley novels*, Ithaca, NY: Cornell University Press, 1991.

Handwerk, Gary, 'Of Caleb's guilt and Godwin's truth: ideology and ethics in *Caleb Williams*', *ELH* 60 (1993), pp. 939–60.

Jauß, H. R. (ed.), *Nachahmung und Illusion* (Kolloquium Gießen Juni 1963), Munich: Eidos, 1964.

Kelly, Gary, *English fiction of the Romantic period 1789–1830*, London: Longman, 1989.
'The limits of genre and the institution of literature: Romanticism between fact and fiction', in *Romantic revolutions: criticism and theory*, Kenneth R. Johnston, Gilbert Chaitin, Karen Hanson and Herbert Marks (eds.), Bloomington, IN: Indiana University Press, 1990, pp. 158–75.

Klancher, Jon, 'Godwin and the republican romance: genre, politics, and contingency in cultural history', *Modern language quarterly* 56 (1995), pp. 145–65.

Laubriet, Pierre, *L'intelligence de l'art chez Balzac: d'une esthétique balzacienne*, Paris: Didier, 1961.

Levine, George L., *The realistic imagination: English fiction from Frankenstein to Lady Chatterley*, Chicago, IL: University of Chicago Press, 1981.

Lukács, Georg, *The theory of the novel: a historico–philosophical essay on the forms of great epic literature*, Anna Bostock (trans.), Cambridge, MA: The MIT Press, 1971.

Mayo, Robert D., *The English novel in the magazines, 1740–1815*, Evanston: Northwestern University Press, 1962.

Mellor, Anne K., 'A criticism of their own: Romantic women literary critics', in *Questioning Romanticism*, John Beer (ed.), Baltimore, MD: The Johns Hopkins University Press, 1995, pp. 29–48.

Rader, Ralph W., 'The emergence of the novel in England: genre in history vs history of genre', *Narrative* 1 (1993), pp. 69–83.

'From Richardson to Austen: "Johnson's rule" and the development of the eighteenth-century novel of moral action', in *Johnson and his age*, James Engell (ed.), Cambridge, MA: Harvard University Press, 1984, pp. 461–83.

Richter, David H., *The progress of romance: literary historiography and the gothic novel*, Columbus, OH: Ohio State University Press, 1996.

Taylor, John Tinnan, *Early opposition to the English novel: the popular reaction from 1760–1830*, New York: King's Crown Press, 1943.

Trumpener, Katie, *Bardic nationalism: the Romantic novel and the British Empire*, Princeton, NJ: Princeton University Press, 1997.

'National character, nationalist plots: national tale and historical novel in the age of Waverley, 1806–1830', *ELH* 60 (1993), pp. 685–731.

Wilt, Judith, *Secret leaves: the novels of Walter Scott*, Chicago, IL: Chicago University Press, 1985.

13 The impact of Shakespeare

Primary sources

Bate, Jonathan (ed.), *The Romantics on Shakespeare*, London: Penguin Books, 1992.

Carlyle, Thomas, *On heroes, hero-worship and the heroical in history*, Michael K. Goldberg (ed.), Berkeley, CA: University of California Press, 1993.

Coleridge, Samuel Taylor, *The notebooks of Samuel Taylor Coleridge*, Kathleen Coburn (ed.), 3 vols., Princeton, NJ: Princeton University Press, 1957.

Biographia literaria, or, biographical sketches of my literary life and opinions, James Engell and Walter Jackson Bate (eds.), 2 vols., London: Routledge & Kegan Paul, 1983.

The collected works of Samuel Taylor Coleridge, vol. v: *Lectures 1808–1819 on literature*, R. A. Foakes (ed.), Princeton, NJ: Princeton University Press, 1987, 16 vols.

Coleridge's criticism of Shakespeare, R. A. Foakes (ed.), Detroit, MI: Wayne State University Press, 1989.

Emerson, Ralph Waldo, *Representative men*, in *Essays and lectures*, New York: Viking Press, 1983, pp. 611–761.

Goethe, Johann Wolfgang, *Wilhelm Meister's apprenticeship*, Eric A. Blackall (ed. and trans.), New York: Suhrkamp, 1989.

'Shakespeare: a tribute', in *Essays on art and literature*, John Gearey (ed.), Ellen von Nardroff and Ernest H. von Nardroff (trans.), New York: Suhrkamp, 1986, pp. 163–5.

Hazlitt, William, 'Shakespeare and Milton', in *Lectures on the English poets and the English comic writers*, William Carew Hazlitt (ed.), London: Bell, 1894.

Characters of Shakespeare's plays, London: Oxford University Press, 1949.

Johnson, Samuel, *Samuel Johnson on Shakespeare*, W. K. Wimsatt, Jr (ed.), New York: Hill and Wang, 1960.

Keats, John, *The letters of John Keats: 1814–1821*, Hyder Edward Rollins (ed.), vol. I, Cambridge, MA: Harvard University Press, 1958, 2 vols.

Lamb, Charles, 'On the tragedies of Shakespeare, with reference to their fitness for stage representation', in *Complete works and letters*, New York: Random House, 1935, pp. 289–303.

LeWinter, Oswald (ed.), *Shakespeare in Europe*, New York: Meridian Books, 1963.

Melville, Herman, 'Hawthorne and his mosses', in *Moby-Dick*, Harrison Hayford and Hershel Parker (eds.), New York: Norton, 1967.

Schlegel, Friedrich von, *Philosophical fragments*, Peter Firchow (trans.), Minneapolis, MN: University of Minnesota Press, 1991.

Simpson, David (ed.), *The origins of modern critical thought: German aesthetic and literary criticism from Lessing to Hegel*, Cambridge University Press, 1988.

Stendhal, *Racine and Shakespeare*, Guy Daniels (trans.), New York: Crowell-Collier Press, 1962.

Wheeler, Kathleen M. (ed.), *German aesthetic and literary criticism: the Romantic ironists and Goethe*, Cambridge University Press, 1984.

Secondary sources

Abrams, Meyer H., *The mirror and the lamp: Romantic theory and the critical tradition*, New York: Oxford University Press, 1953.

Arac, Jonathan, 'The media of sublimity: Johnson and Lamb on *King Lear*', *Studies in Romanticism* 26 (1987), pp. 209–20.

'*Hamlet, Little Dorrit*, and the history of character', *South Atlantic quarterly* 87.2 (Spring 1988), pp. 311–28.

Bate, Jonathan, *Shakespeare and the English Romantic imagination*, Oxford: Clarendon Press, 1986.

Shakespearean constitutions: politics, theatre, criticism, 1730–1830, Oxford: Clarendon Press, 1989.

Bate, Walter Jackson, *John Keats*, Cambridge, MA: Harvard University Press, 1963.

Behler, Ernst, *German Romantic literary theory*, Cambridge University Press, 1993.

Bradley, A. C., 'Hegel's theory of tragedy', in *Oxford lectures on poetry*, London: Macmillan, 1909, pp. 69–95.

Crawford, John M., *Romantic criticism of Shakespearian drama*, Salzburg: Institut für Englische Sprache und Literatur, Universität Salzburg, 1978.

Dirk, Delabastita and Lievan D'hulst (eds.), *European Shakespeares: translating Shakespeare in the Romantic age*, Amsterdam: Benjamins, 1993.

Donohue, Joseph W., Jr, *Dramatic character in the English Romantic age*, Princeton, NJ: Princeton University Press, 1970.

Furst, Lilian R., 'Shakespeare and the formation of Romantic drama in Germany and France', in Gerald Gillespie (ed.), *Romantic drama*, Amsterdam: Benjamins, 1994, pp. 3–15.

Grazia, Margreta de, *Shakespeare verbatim: the reproduction of authenticity and the 1790 apparatus*, Oxford: Clarendon Press, 1991.

Gundolf, Friedrich, *Shakespeare und der deutsche Geist*, Berlin: Bondi, 1911.

Habicht, Werner, 'Romanticism, antiromanticism, and the German Shakespeare tradition', in Tetsuo Kishi, Roger Pringle, Stanley Wells (eds.), *Shakespeare and cultural traditions*, Newark, DE: University of Delaware Press, 1994, pp. 243–52.

Lacoue-Labarthe, Philippe and Jean-Luc Nancy, *The literary absolute: the theory of literature in German Romanticism*, Philip Barnard and Cherel Lester (trans.), Albany, NY: State University of New York Press, 1988.

Matthiessen, F. O., *American Renaissance: art and expression in the age of Emerson and Whitman*, Oxford University Press, 1941.

Odell, George C. D., *Shakespeare from Betterton to Irving*, New York: Scribner's Sons, 1920.

Sauer, Thomas G., *A. W. Schlegel's Shakespearean criticism in England, 1811–1846*, Bonn: Bouvier, 1981.

Schoenbaum, S., *Shakespeare's lives*, Oxford: Clarendon Press, 1970.

Taylor, Gary, *Reinventing Shakespeare: a cultural history from the Restoration to the present*, New York: Weidenfeld & Nicolson, 1989.

Wellek, René, *A history of modern criticism: 1750–1950*, vols. I–III, New Haven: Yale University Press, 1955, 8 vols.

14 The vocation of criticism and the crisis of the republic of letters

Primary sources

Baillie, Joanna, 'Preface' to *A series of plays*, 1798, rpt. London: Routledge, 1996, I: 1–72.

Barbauld, Anna Letitia (ed.), *The British novelists*, 50 vols., London: Rivington, 1810.

Beiser, Frederick (ed. and trans.), *The early political writings of the German Romantics*, Cambridge University Press, 1996.

Burke, Edmund, *Reflections on the Revolution in France*, Conor Cruise O'Brien (ed.), Baltimore, MD: Penguin Books, 1969.

Carlyle, Thomas, *Critical and miscellaneous essays*, Henry Duff Traill (ed.), London: Chapman & Hall, 1899.

On heroes, hero-worship and the heroic in history, New York: AMS Press, 1969.

[Christie, Thomas], 'To the public', *Analytical review* 1 (1788), pp. i–vi.

Coleridge, Samuel Taylor, *The collected works of Samuel Taylor Coleridge*, Princeton, NJ: Princeton University Press, 1969–.

De Quincey, Thomas, *The collected writings of Thomas de Quincey*, new edn, David Masson (ed.), 14 vols., Edinburgh: Adam & Charles Black, 1889–90.

D'Israeli, Isaac, *Curiosities of literature: consisting of anecdotes, characters, sketches and observations, literary, critical and historical*, London: Murray, 1791.

Fichte, Johann Gottlieb, *The characteristics of the present age*, in William Smith (trans.), *Popular works of Johann Gottlieb Fichte*, London: Trübner, 1889, II: 1–288.

Fichte: early philosophical writings, Daniel Breazeale (ed. and trans.), Ithaca, NY: Cornell University Press, 1988.

Godwin, William, *The enquirer: reflections on education, manners, and literature*, London: Robinson, 1797.

Goldsmith, Oliver, *Collected works of Oliver Goldsmith*, Arthur Friedman (ed.), Oxford: Clarendon Press, 1966, 5 vols.

Hazlitt, William, *The complete works of William Hazlitt*, P. P. Howe (ed.), 21 vols., New York: AMS Press, 1967.

Hunt, Leigh, *Leigh Hunt's literary criticism*, Lawrence Huston Houtchens and Carolyn Washburn Houtchens (eds.), New York: Columbia University Press, 1956.

Jeffrey, Francis, *Contributions to the 'Edinburgh review'*, London: Longman, Brown, Green & Longmans, 1854.

Johnson, Samuel, *The Yale edition of the works of Samuel Johnson*, W. J. Bate *et al.* (eds.), New Haven, CT: Yale University Press, 1958–, 20 vols.

Kant, Immanuel, *Critique of judgment*, Werner S. Pluhar (trans.), Indianapolis, IN: Hackett, 1987.

Perpetual peace, and other essays on politics, history, and morals, Ted Humphrey (trans.), Indianapolis, IN: Hackett, 1983.

Mathias, T[homas] J[ames], *The pursuits of literature: a satirical poem in four dialogues, with notes*, 12th edn, London: Becket, 1808.

Reeve, Clara, *The progress of romance through times, countries, and manners*, 1785, rpt. New York: Garland, 1970.

Schiller, Friedrich, *On the aesthetic education of man*, Elizabeth M. Wilkinson and L. A. Willoughby (trans.), Oxford: Clarendon Press, 1967.

Schlegel, Friedrich von, *Literary notebooks, 1797–1801*, Hans Eichner (ed.), Toronto: University of Toronto Press, 1957.

Kritische Friedrich-Schlegel-Ausgabe, Ernst Behler (ed.), Munich: Schöningh, 1958–.

Philosophical fragments, Peter Firchow (trans.), Minneapolis, MN: University of Minnesota Press, 1991.

Schulte-Sasse, Jochen *et al.* (eds.), *Theory as practice: a critical anthology of early German Romantic writings*, Minneapolis, MN: University of Minnesota Press, 1997.

Shelley, Percy Bysshe, *The prose works of Percy Bysshe Shelley*, E. B. Murray (ed.), Oxford: Clarendon Press, 1993.

Shelley's prose, or The trumpet of a prophecy, David Lee Clark (ed.), Albuquerque, NM: University of New Mexico Press, 1954.

Simpson, David (ed.), *The origins of modern critical thought: German aesthetics and literary criticism from Lessing to Hegel*, Cambridge University Press, 1988.

Staël, Madame de, *De la littérature considerée dans ses rapports avec les institutions sociales*, Paris: Maradan, 1800 (trans. *A treatise on ancient and modern literature*, London: George Cawthorn, 1803, 2 vols.).

Wollstonecraft, Mary, *A vindication of the rights of woman*, Miriam Brody Kramnick (ed.), Harmondsworth: Penguin Books, 1975.

Women critics, 1660–1820: an anthology, Folger Collective on Early Women Critics (ed.), Bloomington, IN: Indiana University Press, 1995.

Secondary sources

Abrams, Meyer H., *The mirror and the lamp: Romantic theory and the critical tradition*, New York: Oxford University Press, 1953.

Arac, Jonathan, *Critical genealogies: historical situations for postmodern literary studies*, New York: Columbia University Press, 1987.

Aske, Martin, 'Critical disfigurings; the "jealous leer malign" in Romantic criticism', in *Questioning Romanticism*, John Beer (ed.), Baltimore, MD: The Johns Hopkins University Press, 1995, pp. 49–70.

Barrell, John, *English literature in history, 1730–80: an equal, wide survey*, London: Hutchinson, 1983.

  The political theory of painting from Reynolds to Hazlitt: 'the body of the public', New Haven, CT: Yale University Press, 1986.

Behler, Ernst, *German Romantic literary theory*, Cambridge University Press, 1993.

Behrendt, Stephen C., *Shelley and his audiences*, Lincoln, NE: University of Nebraska Press, 1989.

Beiser, Frederick C., *Enlightenment, Revolution, and Romanticism: the genesis of modern German political thought, 1790–1820*, Cambridge, MA: Harvard University Press, 1992.

Berghahn, Klaus L., 'From Classicist to Classical literary criticism, 1730–1806', John R. Blazer (trans.), in Peter Uwe Hohendahl (ed.), *A history of German literary criticism, 1730–1980*, Lincoln, NE: University of Nebraska Press, 1988, pp. 13–98.

Bialostosky, Don H., *Wordsworth, dialogics, and the practice of criticism*, Cambridge University Press, 1992.

Bromwich, David, *Hazlitt: the mind of a critic*, Oxford University Press, 1983.

  'Romantic poetry and the Edinburgh ordinances', *Yearbook of English studies* 19 (1989), 1–16.

Butler, Marilyn, *Romantics, rebels, and reactionaries: English literature and its background, 1760–1830*, New York: Oxford University Press, 1981.

  'Culture's medium: the role of the review', in Stuart Curran (ed.), *The Cambridge companion to British Romanticism*, Cambridge University Press, 1993, pp. 120–47.

Bygrave, Stephen, 'Land of the giants: gaps, limits and audiences in Coleridge's *Biographia literaria*', in *Beyond Romanticism: new approaches to texts and contexts, 1780–1832*, London: Routledge, 1992, pp. 32–52.

Carlson, Julie A., *In the theatre of Romanticism: Coleridge, nationalism, women*, Cambridge University Press, 1994.

Chandler, James K., *Wordsworth's second nature: a study of the poetry and politics*, Chicago, IL: University of Chicago Press, 1984.

'Representative men, spirits of the age, and other Romantic types', in Kenneth R. Johnston *et al.* (eds.), *Romantic revolutions: criticism and theory*, Bloomington, IN: Indiana University Press, 1990, pp. 104–32.

Christensen, Jerome, *Coleridge's blessed machine of language*, Ithaca, NY: Cornell University Press, 1981.

Practicing enlightenment: Hume and the formation of a literary career, Madison, WI: University of Wisconsin Press, 1987.

Lord Byron's strength: Romantic writing and commercial society, Baltimore, MD: The Johns Hopkins University Press, 1993.

Eagleton, Terry, *The function of criticism: from 'The spectator' to post-structuralism*, London: Verso, 1984.

Engell, James, *The creative imagination: Enlightenment to Romanticism*, Cambridge, MA: Harvard University Press, 1981.

Friedrichsmeyer, Sara, 'Caroline Schlegel-Schelling: "a good woman, and no heroine" ', in Katherine R. Goodman and Edith Waldstein (eds.), *In the shadow of Olympus: German women writers around 1800*, Albany, NY: State University of New York Press, 1992.

Furniss, Tom, *Edmund Burke's aesthetic ideology: language, gender, and political economy in revolution*, Cambridge University Press, 1993.

Gilmartin, Kevin, *Print politics: the press and radical opposition in early nineteenth-century England*, Cambridge University Press, 1996.

Goodman, Dena, *The republic of letters: a cultural history of the French Enlightenment*, Ithaca, NY: Cornell University Press, 1994.

Gross, John, *The rise and fall of the man of letters: aspects of English literary life since 1800*, London: Weidenfeld & Nicolson, 1969.

Guillory, John, *Cultural capital: the problem of literary canon formation*, Chicago, IL: University of Chicago Press, 1993.

Habermas, Jürgen, *The structural transformation of the public sphere: an inquiry into a category of bourgeois society*, Thomas Burger (trans.), Cambridge, MA: The MIT Press, 1989.

Hamilton, Paul, *Coleridge's poetics*, Oxford: Blackwell, 1983.

Heyck, T[homas] W[illiam], *The transformation of intellectual life in Victorian England*, London: Croom Helm, 1982.

Hohendahl, Peter (ed.), *A history of German literary criticism, 1730–1980*, Lincoln, NE: University of Nebraska Press, 1988.

Hogle, Jerrold E., *Shelley's process: radical transference and the development of his major works*, New York: Oxford University Press, 1988.

Izenberg, Gerald N., *Impossible individuality: Romanticism, revolution, and the origins of modern selfhood, 1787–1802*, Princeton, NJ: Princeton University Press, 1992.

Jacobus, Mary, 'The art of managing books', in Arden Reed (ed.), *Romanticism and language*, Ithaca, NY: Cornell University Press, 1984, pp. 215–46.

Keen, Paul, 'Whispers in the state: Romanticism and the public sphere', diss. University of York, 1996.

Kinnaird, John, *William Hazlitt, critic of power*, New York: Columbia University Press, 1978.

Klancher, Jon P., *The making of English reading audiences, 1790–1832*, Madison, WI: University of Wisconsin Press, 1987.

Lacoue-Labarthe, Philippe and Jean-Luc Nancy, *The literary absolute: the theory of literature in German Romanticism*, Philip Barnard and Cherel Lester (trans.), Albany, NY: State University of New York Press, 1988.

Leask, Nigel, *The politics of imagination in Coleridge's critical thought*, New York: St Martin's Press, 1988.

Levine, Joseph M., *The battle of the books: history and literature in the Augustan age*, Ithaca, NY: Cornell University Press, 1991.

Marino, Adrian, 'Literature and ideology in the republic of letters', in François Jost (ed.), *Aesthetics and the literature of ideas: essays in honor of A. Owen Aldridge*, Newark, DE: University of Delaware Press, 1990, pp. 214–24.

McGann, Jerome J., *Social values and poetic acts: the historical judgment of literary work*, Cambridge, MA: Harvard University Press, 1988.

Mellor, Anne K., *Romanticism & gender*, New York: Routledge, 1993.

'A criticism of their own: Romantic women literary critics', in John Beer (ed.), *Questioning Romanticism*, Baltimore, MD: The Johns Hopkins University Press, 1995, pp. 29–48.

Park, Roy, *Hazlitt and the spirit of the age: abstraction and critical theory*, Oxford: Clarendon Press, 1971.

Pfau, Thomas, *Wordsworth's profession: form, class, and the logic of early Romantic cultural production*, Stanford, CA: Stanford University Press, 1997.

Poovey, Mary, *The proper lady and the woman writer: ideology and style in the works of Mary Wollstonecraft, Mary Shelley, and Jane Austen*, Chicago, IL: University of Chicago Press, 1984.

Reiss, Timothy J., *The meaning of literature*, Ithaca, NY: Cornell University Press, 1992.

Roper, Derek, *Reviewing before the 'Edinburgh', 1788–1802*, London: Methuen, 1978.

Rose, Mark, *Authors and owners: the invention of copyright*, Cambridge, MA: Harvard University Press, 1993.

Schoenfield, Mark, 'Regulating standards: the *Edinburgh review* and the circulations of judgement', *Wordsworth circle* 24 (1993), pp. 148–51.

The professional Wordsworth: law, labor, and the poet's contract, Athens, GA: University of Georgia Press, 1996.

Schulte-Sasse, Jochen, 'The concept of literary criticism in German Romanticism, 1795–1810', in Peter Uwe Hohendahl (ed.), *A history of German literary criticism, 1730–1980*, Lincoln, NE: University of Nebraska Press, 1988, pp. 99–177.

Seyhan, Azade, *Representation and its discontents: the critical legacy of German Romanticism*, Berkeley, CA: University of California Press, 1992.

Simpson, David, *Romanticism, nationalism and the revolt against theory*, Chicago, IL: University of Chicago Press, 1993.

Siskin, Clifford, *The work of writing: literature and social change in Britain, 1700–1830*, Baltimore, MD: The Johns Hopkins University Press, 1998.

Swann, Karen, 'Literary gentlemen and lovely ladies: the debate on the character of Christabel', *ELH* 52 (1985), pp. 397–418.

Wellek, René, *A history of modern criticism: 1750–1950*, New Haven, CT: Yale University Press, 1955, 8 vols.

Woodmansee, Martha, *The author, art, and the market: rereading the history of aesthetics*, New York: Columbia University Press, 1994.

Zionkowski, Linda, 'Territorial disputes in the republic of letters: canon formation and the literary profession', *The eighteenth century: theory and interpretation* 31 (1990), pp. 3–22.

15   Women, gender and literary criticism

Primary sources

Alcock, Mary, 'A receipt for writing a novel', in Joanna Hughes (ed.), *Poems*, London: Dilly, 1799, pp. 89–93.

Anon., 'The living poets of England. Mrs Hemans', *The literary magnet* 4 (March 1826), pp. 113–21.

'The poetry of Miss Landon', *The literary magnet* n.s. 1 (January 1827), pp. 3–5.

Arnim, Bettina von, *Die Günderode*, in Walter Schmitz and Sibylle von Steinsdorff (eds.), *Werke und Briefe*, 4 vols., Frankfurt am Main: Deutscher Klassiker Verlag, 1986, I: 295–746.

Goethes Briefwechsel mit einem Kinde, in Walter Schmitz and Sibylle von Steinsdorff (eds.), *Werke und Briefe*, vol. II, Frankfurt am Main: Deutscher Klassiker Verlag, 1992, 4 vols. (trans. *Goethe's correspondence with a child*, Boston: Houghton Mifflin, 1868).

Austen, Jane, *Jane Austen's letters to her sister Cassandra and others*, R. W. Chapman (ed.), London: Oxford University Press, 1952.

Persuasion, Patricia Ann Meyer Spacks (ed.), New York: Norton, 1995.

Northanger Abbey, Claire Grogan (ed.), Peterborough, Ont.: Broadview Press, 1996.

Baillie, Joanna, 'Introductory discourse', *A series of plays*, 1798, rpt. London: Routledge, 1996, I: 1–72.

Barbauld, Anna Letitia, *The works of Anna Lætitia Barbauld, with a memoir by Lucy Aikin*, 2 vols., London: Longman, 1825.

The poems of Anna Letitia Barbauld, William McCarthy and Elizabeth Kraft (eds.), Athens, GA: University of Georgia Press, 1994.

'On the pleasure derived from objects of terror, with Sir Bertrand, a fragment', Michael Gamer (ed.), http://www.english.upenn.edu/~mgamer/Romantic/barbauldessays.html.

Barbauld, Anna Letitia (ed.), *Poetical works of Mr. William Collins*, London: Cadell and Davies, 1802.

The correspondence of Samuel Richardson, London: Richard Phillips, 1804.

The British novelists, 50 vols., London: Rivington, 1810.

Burney, Fanny, *Diary and letters of Madame d'Arblay*, Charlotte Barrett (ed.), 7 vols., London: Henry Colburn, 1842–6.

Byron, George Gordon Lord, *The complete works*, Jerome J. McGann (ed.), 7 vols., Oxford University Press, 1986.

Coleridge, Samuel T., '*The mysteries of Udolpho*, by Ann Radcliffe', *The critical review* 24 (August 1794), pp. 361–72.

'*The Italian*, by Ann Radcliffe', *The critical review* 28 (June 1798), pp. 166–9.

'*Hubert de Sevrac*, by Mary Robinson', *The critical review* 28 (August 1798), p. 472.

The complete poetical works of Samuel Taylor Coleridge, Ernest Harley Coleridge (ed.), 2 vols., Princeton, NJ: Princeton University Press, 1912.

The notebooks of Samuel Taylor Coleridge, Kathleen Coburn (ed.), 3 vols., Princeton, NJ: Princeton University Press, 1957.

The friend, Barbara E. Rooke (ed.), 2 vols., Princeton, NJ: Princeton University Press, 1969.

Table-talk, Carl Woodring (ed.), 2 vols. Princeton: Princeton University Press, 1990.

Http://www.english.upenn.edu/~mgamer/Romantic/coleridge.reviews, Michael Gamer (ed.).

Edgeworth, Maria, *Letters for literary ladies*, London: Johnson, 1795.

Letters from England 1813–1844, Christina Colvin (ed.), Oxford: Clarendon Press, 1971.

Genlis, Stéphanie-Félicité, Comtesse de, 'Le femme auteur', *Nouveaux contes moraux et nouvelles historiques*, 3 vols., Paris: Maradin, 1802, III: 51–150.

De l'influence des femmes sur la littérature française, Paris: Lecointe et Durey, 1826.

Goethe, Johann Wolfang, *Faust*, Walter Arndt (trans.), New York: Norton, 1976.

Plays, Charles W. Passage (trans.), New York: Frederick Ungar, 1980.

Hays, Mary, *Female biography; or memoirs of illustrious and celebrated women, of all ages and countries*, London: Phillips, 1803.

Hazlitt, William, *Lectures on the English poets*, in *The complete works of William Hazlitt*, P. P. Howe (ed.), 21 vols., London: J. M. Dent, 1930–34, V: 1–168.

Hemans, Felicia, *Records of woman*, Donald H. Reiman (ed.), 1828, rpt. New York: Garland, 1978.

'Scenes and passages from the "Tasso" of Goethe', *New monthly magazine and literary journal* n.s. 3 (1834), pp. 1–5.

Hitchener, Elizabeth, *The weald of Sussex*, London: Barlow, 1821.

Letters of Elizabeth Hitchener to Percy Bysshe Shelley, Philadelphia, PA: West, 1926.

Inchbald, Elizabeth Simpson, *The British theatre*, 25 vols., London: Longman, 1808.

Jameson, Anna, *Characteristics of women, moral, poetical, and historical*, 2nd edn, New York: Wiley and Putnam, 1847.

Jeffrey, Francis, ' "Records of woman" and "The forest sanctuary" by Felicia Hemans', *Edinburgh review* 50 (October 1829), pp. 32–47.

Jewsbury, Maria Jane, *Phantasmagoria*, 2 vols., London: Hurst, 1825.
  The history of an enthusiast, in *The three histories*, London: Westley, 1830.
  Occasional papers, Eric W. Gillett (ed.), London: Oxford University Press, 1932.
Landon, Letitia Elizabeth, *The Venetian bracelet*, London: Longman, 1829.
  Critical writings, F. J. Sypher (ed.), Delmar, NY: Scholars' Facsimiles &
  Reprints, 1996.
  Letitia Elizabeth Landon: selected writings, Jerome J. McGann and Daniel Riess
  (eds.), Peterborough, Ont.: Broadview Press, 1997.
Lazarus, Rachel Mordecai, *The education of the heart: the correspondence of
  Rachel Mordecai Lazarus and Maria Edgeworth*, Edgar E. MacDonald (ed.),
  Chapel Hill, NC: University of North Carolina Press, 1977.
Mitford, Mary Russell, *Narrative poems on the female character in the various
  relations of human life*, London: Rivington, 1813.
  *The friendships of Mary Russell Mitford as recorded in letters from her literary
  correspondents*, A. G. L'Estrange (ed.), New York: Harper, 1882.
More, Hannah, *Hints towards forming the character of a young princess*, 2 vols.,
  London: Cadell and Davies, 1805.
  Strictures on the modern system of female education, 1799, rpt. New York:
  Garland, 1974.
Morgan, Sydney Owenson, Lady *Memoirs: autobiography, diaries and cor-
  respondence*, London: Allen, 1862.
Naubert, Benedikte, *'Sich rettend aus der kalten Würklichkeit': die Briefe Bene-
  dikte Nauberts*, Nikolaus Dorsch (ed.), Frankfurt am Main: Lang, 1986.
Owenson, Sydney, Lady Morgan, *Memoirs: autobiography, diaries and cor-
  respondence*, London: W. H. Allen, 1862.
Piozzi, Hester, *Autobiography, letters and literary remains of Mrs Piozzi*, A.
  Hayward (ed.), London: Longman, 1861.
Polwhele, Richard, *The unsex'd females: a poem*, London: Cadell and Davies,
  1798.
Radcliffe, Ann, 'On the supernatural in poetry', *The new monthly magazine* 16
  (1826), pp. 145–52.
Reeve, Clara, *The progress of romance through times, countries, and manners*,
  1785, rpt. New York: Garland, 1970.
Robinson, Mary, *Sappho and Phaon*, 1796, rpt. Delmar, NY: Scholars' Facsimiles
  & Reprints, 1995.
Rousseau, Jean-Jacques, *Julie, ou la nouvelle Héloise*, in *Oeuvres complètes*,
  vol. II, Paris: Gallimard, 1961 (trans. Philip Stewart and Jean Vache, *Julie, or
  the new Heloise*, in *The collected writings of Rousseau*, vol. VI, Roger D. Mas-
  ters and Christopher Kelly (eds.), Hanover, NH: University Press of New Eng-
  land, 1997).
Schelling, Karoline, *Caroline: Briefe aus der Frühromantik*, Erich Schmidt (ed.),
  2 vols., Leipzig: Insel, 1913.
Schiller, Friedrich von, *Naïve and sentimental poetry, On the sublime*, Julius A.
  Elias (trans.), New York: Ungar, 1966.
Schlegel, Dorothea Veit, *Florentin: Roman, Fragmente, Varianten*, Liliane Weissberg (ed.), Frankfurt am Main: Ullstein, 1987 (trans. Edwina Lawler and
  Ruth Richardson, *Florentin*, Lewiston, NY: Mellen, 1988).

Schlegel, Friedrich, 'Fragmente', in *Kritische Friedrich-Schlegel-Ausgabe*, 35 vols., Ernst Behler and Hans Eichner (eds.), Munich: Schöningh, 1958, II: 147–272.

Lucinde, in *Kritische Friedrich-Schlegel-Ausgabe*, vol. V: *Dichtungen*, Hans Eichner (ed.), Munich: Schöningh, 1962, 35 vols., pp. 1–92 (trans. Peter Firchow, *Friedrich Schlegel's 'Lucinde' and the fragments*, Minneapolis, MN: University of Minnesota Press, 1971).

Gespräch über die Poesie, in *Kritische Friedrich-Schlegel-Ausgabe*, vol. II: *Charakteristiken und Kritiken I (1796–1801)*, Hans Eichner (ed.), Munich: Schöningh, 1967, pp. 284–362 (trans. Ernst Behler and Roman Struc, *Dialogue on poetry and literary aphorisms*, University Park, PA: Pennsylvania State University Press, 1968, pp. 51–117).

'Fragments', in *German aesthetic and literary criticism: the Romantic ironists and Goethe*, Kathleen Wheeler (ed.), Cambridge University Press, 1984, pp. 40–80.

Schlegel-Schelling, Cardine, *Caroline: Briefe aus der Frühromantik*, Erich Schmidt (ed.), 2 vols., Leipzig: Insel, 1913.

Seward, Anna, *Poetical works of Anna Seward with extracts from her literary correspondence*, Walter Scott (ed.), 3 vols., London: Longman, 1810.

Shelley, Mary Wollstonecraft, *The journals of Mary Shelley, 1814–1844*, Paula Feldman and Diana Scott-Kilvert (eds.), 2 vols., Oxford: Clarendon Press, 1987.

Frankenstein, or, the modern Prometheus, David L. Macdonald and Kathleen Scherf (eds.), Peterborough, Ont.: Broadview Press, 1994.

Shelley, Percy Bysshe, *Shelley's poetry and prose: authoritative texts, criticism*, Donald H. Reiman and Sharon B. Powers (eds.), New York: Norton, 1979.

Smith, Charlotte, *Desmond*, 1792, rpt. New York: Garland, 1974.

Marchmont, 1796, rpt. Delmar, NY: Scholars' Facsimiles & Reprints, 1989.

The poems of Charlotte Smith, Stuart Curran (ed.), New York: Oxford University Press, 1993.

Staël, Anne-Louise-Germaine Necker de, *Corinne; ou, l'Italie*, Paris: Nicolle, 1807 (trans. Avriel H. Goldberger, *Corinne, or, Italy*, New Brunswick, NJ: Rutgers University Press, 1987).

De l'Allemagne, 3 vols. Paris: Nicolle, 1813 (*Germany*, 3 vols., London: John Murray, 1813).

De la littérature considerée dans ses rapports avec les institutions sociales, Paris: Charpentier, 1887.

Essai sur les fictions; De l'influence des passions sur le bonheur des individus et des nations, Michel Tournier (ed.), Paris: Editions Ramsay, 1979 (*A treatise on the influence of the passions upon the happiness of individuals and nations*, London: Cawthorn, 1798).

An extraordinary woman: selected writings of Germaine de Staël, Vivian Folkenflik (trans.), New York: Columbia University Press, 1987.

Delphine, Avriel H. Goldberger (trans.), DeKalb, IL: Northern Illinois University Press, 1995.

Varnhagen, Rahel, *Gesammelte Werke*, Konrad Feilchenfeldt, Uwe Schweikert, and Rahel E. Steiner (eds.), 10 vols., Munich: Mattes & Seitz, 1983.

Williams, Helen Maria, *Peru: a poem*, London: Cadell, 1784.
Julia, Gina Luria (ed.), 2 vols., 1790, rpt. New York: Garland, 1974.
Wollstonecraft, Mary, *Mary, a fiction and The wrongs of woman*, 1798, rpt. Gary
    Kelly (ed.), London: Oxford University Press, 1976.
The collected letters of Mary Wollstonecraft, Ralph M. Wardle (ed.), Ithaca, NY:
    Cornell University Press, 1979.
Vindication of the rights of woman, in *A vindication of the rights of men*, David
    L. MacDonald and Kathleen Scherf (eds.), Peterborough, Ont.: Broadview,
    1997.

Secondary sources

Armstrong, Isobel, 'The gush of the feminine: how can we read women's poetry of
    the Romantic period?' in Feldman and Kelley (eds.), *Romantic women writers*,
    Hanover, NH: University Press of New England, 1995, pp. 13–32.
Baumer, Konstanze, *Bettina, Psyche, Mignon: Bettina von Arnim und Goethe*,
    Stuttgart: Heinz, 1986.
Behler, Ernst, *Irony and the discourse of modernity*, Seattle, WA: University of
    Washington Press, 1990.
'Die Poesie in der frühromantischen Theorie der Brüder Schlegel', in Ernst
    Behler (ed.), *Athenäum: Jahrbuch für Romantik* (1991), pp. 13–40.
Behrendt, Stephen, 'Mary Shelley, *Frankenstein*, and the woman writer's fate', in
    Feldman and Kelley (eds.), *Romantic women writers*, Hanover, NH: Univer-
    sity Press of New England, 1995, pp. 69–87.
Besser, Gretchen R., *Germaine de Staël revisited*, New York: Twayne, 1994.
Bohls, Elizabeth, *Women travel writers and the language of aesthetics, 1716–
    1818*, Cambridge University Press, 1995.
Bovenschen, Silvia, *Die imaginierte Weiblichkeit: exemplarische Untersuchungen
    zu kulturgeschichtlichen und literarischen Präsentationsformen des Weiblichen*,
    Frankfurt am Main: Suhrkamp, 1979.
Brantner, Christina E., 'Frühromantische Frauengestalten in Dorothea Veits Roman
    Florentin (1801)', *Michigan Germanic studies* 17 (1991), pp. 51–70.
Brown, Chandos Michael, 'Mary Wollstonecraft, or, the female illuminati: the
    campaign against women and "modern philosophy" in the early republic',
    Journal of the early republic 15 (1995), pp. 389–424.
Brown, Nathaniel, *Sexuality and feminism in Shelley*, Cambridge, MA: Harvard
    University Press, 1979.
Burroughs, Catherine B., *Closet stages: Joanna Baillie and the theater theory of British
    Romantic women writers*, Philadelphia, PA: University of Pennsylvania, 1997.
Carlson, Julie A., *In the theatre of Romanticism: Coleridge, nationalism, women*,
    Cambridge University Press, 1994.
'Forever young: Master Betty and the queer stage of youth in English Romanti-
    cism', in Thomas Pfau and Rhonda Ray Kercsmar (eds.), *Rhetorical and cul-
    tural dissolution in Romanticism*, Special Issue, *South Atlantic quarterly* 95
    (1996), pp. 575–602.
Cohen, Paula M., 'Jane Austen's rejection of Rousseau: a novelistic and feminist
    initiation', *Papers on language and literature* 30 (1994), pp. 215–34.

Cole, Lucinda, '(Anti)feminist sympathies: the politics of relationship in Smith, Wollstonecraft, and More', *ELH* 58 (1991), pp. 107–40.

Curran, Stuart 'Romantic poetry: the I altered', in Mellor (ed.), *Romanticism and feminism*, Bloomington, IN: Indiana University Press, 1988, pp. 185–207.

DeJean, Joan, 'Portrait of the artist as Sappho', in Gutwirth, Goldberger and Szmurlo (eds.), *Germaine de Staël*, New Brunswick, NJ: Rutgers University Press, 1991, pp. 122–37.

Ellison, Julie, *Delicate subjects: Romanticism, gender, and the ethics of understanding*, Ithaca, NY: Cornell University Press, 1990.

Eubanks, Kevin, 'Minerva's veil: Hemans, critics, and the construction of gender', *European Romantic review* 8 (1997), pp. 341–59.

Favret, Mary A., 'A woman writes the fiction of science: the body in *Frankenstein*', *Genders* 14 (1992), pp. 50–65.

Romantic correspondence: women, politics, and the fiction of letters, Cambridge University Press, 1993.

Feldman, Paula R. and Theresa M. Kelley (eds.), *Romantic women writers: voices and countervoices*, Hanover, NH: University Press of New England, 1995.

Ferguson, Moira, *Subject to others: British women writers and colonial slavery, 1670–1834*, New York: Routledge, 1992.

'Janet Little and Robert Burns: the politics of the heart', in Feldman and Kelley (eds.), *Romantic women writers*, Hanover, NH: University Press of New England, 1995, pp. 207–22.

Fermon, Nicole, *Domesticating passions: Rousseau, woman, and the nation*, Hanover, NH: University Press of New England, 1997.

Fraiman, Susan, 'Jane Austen and Edward Said: gender, culture, and imperialism', *Critical inquiry* 21 (1995), pp. 805–21.

Franklin, Caroline, ' "At once above – beneath her sex": the heroine in Regency verse romance', *Modern language review* 84 (1989), pp. 273–88.

' "Quiet cruising o'er the ocean woman": Byron's *Don Juan* and the woman question', *Studies in Romanticism* 29 (1990), pp. 603–31.

Frederiksen, Elke P. and Katherine R. Goodman (eds.), *Bettina Brentano von Arnim: gender and politics*, Detroit, MI: Wayne State University Press, 1995.

Fredricks, Nancy, 'On the sublime and beautiful in Shelley's *Frankenstein*', *Essays in literature* 23 (1996), pp. 178–89.

Friedrichsmeyer, Sara, *The androgyne in German Romanticism: Friedrich Schlegel, Novalis and the metaphysics of love*, New York: Lang, 1983.

'Caroline Schlegel-Schelling: "a good woman and no heroine" ', in Goodman and Waldstein (eds.), *In the shadow of Olympus*, Albany, NY: State University of New York Press, 1992, pp. 115–36.

Furniss, Tom, 'Nasty tricks and tropes: sexuality and language in Mary Wollstonecraft's *Rights of woman*', *Studies in Romanticism* 32 (1993), pp. 177–209.

Furst, Lilian, *The contours of European Romanticism*, London: Macmillan, 1979.

Giuliano, Cheryl Fallon, 'Gulnare/Kaled's "untold" feminization of Byron's Oriental tales', *Studies in English literature, 1500–1900* 33 (1993), pp. 785–807.

Goodman, Dena, *The republic of letters: a cultural history of the French Enlightenment*, Ithaca, NY: Cornell University Press, 1994.

Goodman, Katherine R. and Edith Waldstein (eds.), 'Introduction', *In the shadow of Olympus: German women writers around 1800*, Albany, NY: State University of New York Press, 1992, pp. 1–27.

Goslee, Nancy, 'Witch or pawn: women in Scott's narrative poetry', in Mellor (ed.), *Romanticism and feminism*, Bloomington, IN: Indiana University Press, 1988, pp. 115–36.

Greenfield, Susan C., ' "Abroad and at home": sexual ambiguity, miscegenation, and colonial boundaries in Edgeworth's *Belinda*', *PMLA* 112 (1997), pp. 214–28.

Gubar, Susan, 'Feminist misogyny: Mary Wollstonecraft and the paradox of "it takes one to know one" ', *Feminist studies* 20 (1994), pp. 453–73.

Gutwirth, Madelyn, *Madame de Staël, novelist: the emergence of the artist as woman*, Urbana, IL: University of Illinois Press, 1978.

   The twilight of the goddesses: women and representation in the French Revolutionary era, New Brunswick, NJ: Rutgers University Press, 1992.

Gutwirth, Madelyn, Avriel Goldberger and Karyna Szmurlo (eds.), *Germaine de Staël: crossing the borders*, New Brunswick, NJ: Rutgers University Press, 1991.

Harding, Anthony J. 'Felicia Hemans and the effacement of woman', in Feldman and Kelley (eds.), *Romantic women writers*, Hanover, NH: University Press of New England, 1995, pp. 138–49.

Helfer, Martha B., 'Dorothea Veit-Schlegel's *Florentin*: constructing a feminist Romantic aesthetic', *German quarterly* 69 (1996), pp. 144–60.

Henderson, Andrea, 'Passion and fashion in Joanna Baillie's "Introductory discourse" ', *PMLA* 112 (1997), pp. 198–213.

Hofkosh, Sonia, 'Sexual politics and literary history: William Hazlitt's Keswick escapade and Sarah Hazlitt's *Journal*', in Mary A. Favret and Nicola J. Watson (eds.), *At the limits of Romanticism: essays in cultural, feminist, and materialist criticism*, Bloomington, IN: Indiana University Press, 1994, pp. 125–42.

Hohoff, Curt, 'Lucinde und die Theorie der Liebe', in *Schnittpunkte: gesammelte Aufsätze*, Stuttgart: Deutsche Verlags-Anstalt, 1963, pp. 123–32.

Homans, Margaret, *Women writers and poetic identity: Dorothy Wordsworth, Emily Brontë, and Emily Dickinson*, Princeton, NJ: Princeton University Press, 1980.

   'Keats reading women, women reading Keats', *Studies in Romanticism* 29 (1990), pp. 341–70.

Jacobus, Mary, *Romanticism and sexual difference: essays on 'The prelude'*, Oxford: Clarendon Press, 1989.

Kelley, Theresa M., *Reinventing allegory*, Cambridge University Press, 1997.

Kelsall, Malcolm, 'The slave-woman in the harem', *Studies in Romanticism* 31 (1992), pp. 315–31.

Kohn, Denise, 'Reading *Emma* as a lesson on "ladyhood": a study in the domestic "Bildungsroman" ', *Essays in literature* 22 (1995), pp. 45–58.

Kohlenbach, Margarete, 'Women and artists: E. T. A. Hoffmann's implicit critique of early Romanticism', *Modern language review* 89 (1994), pp. 659–73.

Kuzniar, Alice, 'Hearing woman's voices in *Heinrich von Ofterdingen*', *PMLA* 107 (1992), pp. 1196–1207.

Kuzniar, Alice (ed.), *Outing Goethe and his age*, Stanford University Press, 1996.

Langbauer, Laurie 'An early romance: motherhood and women's writing in Mary Wollstonecraft's novels', in Mellor (ed.), *Romanticism and feminism*, Bloomington, IN: Indiana University Press, 1988, pp. 208–19.

Levin, Susan M., *Dorothy Wordsworth and Romanticism*, New Brunswick, NJ: Rutgers University Press, 1987.

'The gypsy is a jewess: Harriet Abrams and theatrical Romanticism', in Feldman and Kelley (eds.), *Romantic women writers*, Hanover, NH: University Press of New England, 1995, pp. 236–51.

Linkin, Harriet Kramer, 'Romanticism and Mary Tighe's *Psyche*: peering at the hem of her blue stockings', *Studies in Romanticism* 35 (1996), pp. 55–72.

London, Beth, 'Mary Shelley, *Frankenstein*, and the spectacle of masculinity', *PMLA* 108 (1993), pp. 253–67.

Lonsdale, Roger (ed.), Introduction, *Eighteenth-century women poets*, Oxford University Press, 1990, pp. xxi–xlvii.

Lootens, Tricia, 'Hemans and home: Victorianism, feminine "internal enemies", and the domestication of national identity', *PMLA* 109 (1994), pp. 238–53.

Lukács, Georg, 'Richness, chaos and form: a dialogue concerning Laurence Sterne', in Anna Bostock (trans.), *Soul and form*, Cambridge, MA: The MIT Press, 1974, pp. 124–51.

Luther, Susan, 'A stranger minstrel: Coleridge's Mrs. Robinson', *Studies in Romanticism* 33 (1994), pp. 391–409.

Malraux, Clara, *Rahel, ma grande soeur: un salon littéraire à Berlin au temps du romantisme*, Paris: Ramsay, 1980.

Manning, Peter J., *Byron and his fictions*, Detroit, MI: Wayne State University Press, 1978.

Marso, Lori, *(Un)manly citizens: the subversive feminine presence in J. J. Rousseau and Germaine de Staël*, Baltimore, MD: The Johns Hopkins University Press, 1998.

Maurer, Shawn Lisa, 'The female (as) reader: sex, sensibility and the maternal in Wollstonecraft's fictions', *Essays in literature* 19 (Spring 1992), pp. 36–54.

McCarthy, William, '"We hoped the *woman* was going to appear": repression, desire and gender in Anna Letitia Barbauld's early poems', in Feldman and Kelley (eds.), *Romantic women writers*, Hanover, NH: University Press of New England, 1995, pp. 113–37.

McGann, Jerome J., *The poetics of sensibility: a revolution in literary style*, Oxford University Press, 1996.

McKee, Patricia, *Public and private: gender, class, and the British novel (1764–1878)*, Minneapolis, MN: University of Minnesota Press, 1997.

Mellor, Anne K., *Mary Shelley: her life, her fiction, her monsters*, New York: Routledge, 1988.

Romanticism and gender, New York: Routledge, 1993.

'A criticism of their own: Romantic women literary critics', in *Questioning Romanticism*, John Beer (ed.), Baltimore, MD: The Johns Hopkins University Press, 1995, pp. 29–48.

'Righting the wrongs of woman: Mary Wollstonecraft's *Maria*', *Nineteenth-century contexts* 19 (1996), pp. 413–24.

'Sex, violence, and slavery: Blake and Wollstonecraft', *Huntington Library quarterly* 58 (1996), pp. 345–70.

'The female poet and the poetess: two traditions of British women's poetry, 1780–1830', *Studies in Romanticism* 36 (1997), pp. 261–76.

Mellor, Anne K. (ed.), *Romanticism and feminism*, Bloomington, IN: Indiana University Press, 1988.

Mellor, Anne K. and Richard E. Matlak (eds.), *British literature, 1780–1830*, Fort Worth, TX: Harcourt Brace, 1996.

Moskal, Jeanne, 'Gender, nationality, and textual authority in Lady Morgan's travel books', in Feldman and Kelley (eds.), *Romantic women writers*, Hanover, NH: University Press of New England, 1995, pp. 171–93.

Myers, Mitzi, 'Sensibility and the "walk of reason": Mary Wollstonecraft's literary reviews as cultural critique', in Syndy McMillen Conger (ed.), *Sensibility in transformation: creative resistance to sentiment from the Augustans to the Romantics*, Rutherford, NJ: Fairleigh Dickinson University Press, 1990, pp. 120–46.

Pascoe, Judith, *Romantic theatricality: gender, poetry, and spectatorship*. Ithaca, NY: Cornell University Press, 1997.

Richardson, Alan, 'Romanticism and colonization of the feminine', in Mellor (ed.), *Romanticism and feminism*, Bloomington, IN: Indiana University Press, 1988, pp. 13–25.

Robinson, Daniel, 'Theodicy vs. feminist strategy in Mary Wollstonecraft's fiction', *Eighteenth-century fiction* 9 (1997), pp. 183–202.

Ross, Marlon B., *The contours of masculine desire: Romanticism and the rise of women's poetry*, New York: Oxford University Press, 1989.

Safran, Morri (ed.), 'Women of the Romantic period', http://www.cwrl.utexas.edu/~worp.

Schlick, Yael, 'Beyond the boundaries: Staël, Genlis, and the impossible "femme célèbre" ', *Symposium* 50 (1996), pp. 50–63.

Schor, Naomi, *George Sand and idealism*, New York: Columbia University Press, 1993.

Scurla, Herbert, *Begegnungen mit Rahel: der Salon der Rahel Levin*, Berlin: Verlag der Nation, 1978.

Setzer, Sharon, 'Mary Robinson's sylphid self: the end of feminine self-fashioning', *Philological quarterly* 75 (1996), pp. 501–20.

Sha, Richard C., *The visual and verbal sketch in British Romanticism*, Philadelphia, PA: University of Pennsylvania Press, 1998.

Stephan, Inge, 'Weibliche und männliche Autorschaft: zum "Florentin" von Dorothea Schlegel und zur "Lucinde" von Friedrich Schlegel', in *'Wen kümmert's, wer spricht?': zur Literatur und Kulturgeschichte von Frauen aus Ost und West*, Inge Stephan, Sigrid Weigel and Kerstin Wilhelms (eds.), Cologne: Böhlau, 1991, pp. 83–98.

Swann, Karen, 'Harrassing the Muse', in Mellor (ed.), *Romanticism and feminism*, Bloomington, IN: Indiana University Press, 1988, pp. 81–92.

Taylor, Irene and Gina Luria, 'Gender and genre: women in British Romantic literature', in Marlene Springer (ed.), *What manner of woman: essays on English and American life and literature*, New York: New York University Press, 1977, pp. 98–123.

Waldstein, Edith J., *Bettina von Arnim and the politics of Romantic conversation*, Columbia, SC: Camden House, 1988.

'Goethe and beyond: Bettina von Arnim's *Correspondenic with a child* and Günderrode', in Goodman and Waldstein (eds.), *In the shadow of Olympus*, Albany, NY: State University of New York Press, 1992, pp. 95–114.

Walzer, Arthur E., 'Rhetoric and gender in Jane Austen's *Persuasion*', *College English* 57 (1995), pp. 688–707.

Wang, Orrin N. C., 'The other reasons: female alterity and Enlightenment discourse in Mary Wollstonecraft's *A vindication of the rights of woman*', *Yale journal of criticism* 5 (1991), pp. 129–49.

Warhol, Robyn, 'The look, the body, and the heroine: a feminist–narratological reading of *Persuasion*', *Novel* 26 (Fall 1992), pp. 5–19.

Watson, Jean, 'Coleridge's androgynous ideal', *Prose studies* 6 (1983), pp. 36–56.

Weigel, Sigrid, 'Wider die romantische Mode: zur ästhetischen Funktion des Weiblichen in Friedrich Schlegels *Lucinde*', in *Die verborgene Frau: sechs Beiträge zu einer feministischen Literaturwissenschaft*, Berlin: Argument, 1983, pp. 67–82.

Weissberg, Liliane, 'Turns of emancipation: on Rahel Varnhagen's letters', in Goodman and Waldstein (eds.), *In the shadow of Olympus*, Albany, NY: State University of New York Press, 1992, pp. 53–70.

Wilson, Carol Shiner and Joel Haefner (eds.), *Re-visioning Romanticism: British women writers, 1776–1837*, Philadelphia, PA: University of Pennsylvania Press, 1994.

Wolfson, Susan J., 'Feminizing Keats', in *Critical essays on John Keats*, Hermione de Almeida (ed.), Boston, MA: Hall, 1990, pp. 317–56.

'The "domestic affections" and "the spear of Minerva": Felicia Hemans and "the dilemma of gender"', in Wilson and Haefner (eds.), *Re-visioning Romanticism*, Philadelphia, PA: University of Pennyslvania Press, 1994.

'"A problem few dare imitate": *Sardanapalus* and "effeminate character"', *ELH* 58 (1991), pp. 867–902.

'Gendering the soul' in Feldman and Kelley (eds.), *Romantic women writers*, Hanover, NH: University Press of New England, 1995, pp. 33–68.

'Romanticism and gender', in *A companion to Romanticism*, Duncan Wu (ed.), Oxford: Blackwell, 1998, pp. 385–96.

Women critics, 1660–1820: an anthology, Folger Collective on Early Women Critics (ed.), Bloomington, IN: Indiana University Press, 1995.

Zantop, Susanne, 'The beautiful soul writes herself: Friedrike Helene Unger and the "Grosse Göthe"', in Goodman and Waldstein (eds.), *In the shadow of Olympus*, Albany, NY: State University of New York Press, 1992, pp. 29–52.

16　Literary history and historicism

Primary sources

Campbell, Thomas, 'An essay on English poetry', in *Specimens of the British poets: with biographical and critical notices, and an essay on English poetry*, London: John Murray, 1819.

Carlyle, Thomas, *Critical and miscellaneous essays*, H. D. Traill (ed.), 5 vols., New York: AMS Press, 1969.

Chambers, Robert, *History of the English language and literature*, 4th edn, Edinburgh: Chambers 1837.

Chateaubriand, François-René de, *The genius of Christianity: or, the spirit and beauty of the Christian religion*, Charles I. White (trans.), New York: Fertig, 1976.

De Quincey, Thomas, *The collected writings of Thomas De Quincey*, new edn, David Masson (ed.), 14 vols., Edinburgh: Black, 1889–90.

Dunlop, John Colin, *History of prose fiction: a new edition revised with notes, appendices and index*, Henry Wilson (ed.), new edn, 2 vols., New York: AMS Press, 1969.

Gervinus, Georg Gottfried, *Geschichte der poetischen National-Literatur der Deutschen*, 5 vols., Leipzig: Engelmann, 1835–42.

'Prinzipien einer deutschen Literaturgeschichtsschreibung', in *Literaturwissenschaft und Literaturgeschichte: ein Lesebuch zur Fachgeschichte der Germanistik*, Thomas Cramer and Horst Wenzel (eds.), Munich: Fink, 1975, pp. 19–64.

Hallam, Henry, *Introduction to the literature of Europe in the fifteenth, sixteenth and seventeenth centuries*, Paris: Baudry, 1839.

Herder, Johann Gottfried, *Sämmtliche Werke*, Bernhard Ludwig Suphan (ed.), 33 vols., Hildesheim: Georg Olms, 1967–8.

Hurd, Richard, *Letters on chivalry and romance, with the third Elizabethan dialogue*, Edith J. Morley (ed.), London: Frowde, 1911.

Jeffrey, Francis, *Contributions to the 'Edinburgh review'*, 3 vols., London: Longman Borown, Green & Longmans, 1846.

Marsch, Edgar (ed.), *Über Literaturgeschichtsschreibung: die historisierende Methode des 19. Jahrhunderts in Programm und Kritik*, Darmstadt: Wissenschaftliche Buchgesellschaft, 1975.

Pushkin, Alexander, 'On classical and romantic poetry', in *The critical prose of Alexander Pushkin*, Carl R. Proffer (ed. and trans.), Bloomington, IN: Indiana University Press, 1969, pp. 35–8.

Schlegel, August Wilhelm von, *A course of lectures on dramatic art and literature*, Alexander James William Morrison (ed.), John Black (trans.), Bohn's Standard Library 46, London: Bell & Sons, 1886.

Schlegel, Friedrich von, *Geschichte der alten und neuen Literatur, Kritische Friedrich-Schlegel-Ausgabe*, Hans Eichner (ed.), vol. VI, Munich: Schöningh, 1961.

Studien des klassischen Altertums, Kritische Friedrich-Schlegel-Ausgabe, Ernst Behler (ed.), vol. I, Munich: Schöningh, 1979.

Shelley, Percy Bysshe, 'Defence of poetry', in *Complete works*, Roger Ingpen and Walter E. Peck (eds.), vol. VII, New York: Gordian Press, 1965, 10 vols.

Secondary sources

Ansel, Michael, 'Auf dem Weg zur Verwissenschaftlichung der Literaturgeschichtsschreibung: Heines Abhandlung *Zur Geschichte der Religion und*

Philosophie in Deutschland und *Die romantische Schule'*, *Internationales Archiv für Sozialgeschichte der deutschen Literatur* 17.2 (1992), pp. 61–94.

Behler, Ernst, 'Problems of origin in modern literary history', in *Theoretical issues in literary history*, David Perkins (ed.), Cambridge, MA: Harvard University Press, 1991, pp. 9–34.

'Concepts of literary history in the comparative literary history of the Schlegel brothers', in *Comparative literary history as discourse: in honor of Anna Balakian*, Mario J. Valdés, Daniel Javitch and A. Owen Aldridge (eds.), Bern: Peter Lang, 1992, pp. 23–40.

Brewer, Daniel, 'Political culture and literary history: La Harpe's *Lycée*', *Modern language quarterly* 58 (1997), pp. 163–84.

Dierkes, Hans, *Literaturgeschichte als Kritik: Untersuchungen zu Theorie und Praxis von Friedrich Schlegels frühromantischer Literaturgeschichtsschreibung*, Studien zur deutschen Literatur 63, Tübingen: Niemeyer, 1980.

Mandelkow, Karl Robert, 'Kunst- und Literaturtheorie der Klassik und Romantik', in *Europäische Romantik I*, Karl Robert Mandelkow (ed.), Neues Handbuch der Literaturwissenschaft 14, Wiesbaden: Athenaion, 1982, pp. 49–82.

Moody, Jane, ' "Fine word, legitimate!": toward a theatrical history of Romanticism', *Texas studies in literature and language* 38 (1996), pp. 223–44.

Niggl, Günter, 'Die Anfänge der romantischen Literaturgeschichtsschreibung: Friedrich und August Wilhelm Schlegel', in *Die deutsche literarische Romantik und die Wissenschaften*, Nicholas Saul (ed.), Munich: Iudicium Verlag, 1991, pp. 265–81.

Rosenberg, Rainer, *Zehn Kapitel zur Geschichte der Germanistik: Literaturgeschichtsschreibung*, Berlin: Akademie-Verlag, 1981.

Seyhan, Azade, 'Cannons against the canon: representations of tradition and modernity in Heine's literary history', *Deutsche Vierteljahrsschrift für Literaturwissenschaft und Geistesgeschichte* 63 (1989), pp. 494–520.

Szondi, Peter, 'Antike und Moderne in der Ästhetik der Goethezeit', in *Poetik und Geschichtsphilosophie I*, Senta Metz and Hans-Hagen Hildebrandt (eds.), Frankfurt am Main: Suhrkamp, 1974, pp. 11–265.

Wellek, René, *The rise of English literary history*, Chapel Hill, NC: University of North Carolina Press, 1941.

17 Literature and the other arts

Primary sources

Baudelaire, Charles, *Oeuvres complètes*, Yves-Gérard Le Dantec (ed.), Paris: Gallimard, 1951.

Delacroix, Eugène, *Journal de Eugène Delacroix*, André Joubin (ed.), 2 vols., Paris: Plon, 1932 (trans. Walter Pach, *The journal of Eugène Delacroix*, New York: Crown, 1948).

Eitner, Lorenz (ed.), *Neoclassicism and Romanticism, 1750–1850: sources and documents*, 2 vols., Englewood Cliffs, NJ: Prentice-Hall, 1970.

Hazlitt, William, *The complete works of William Hazlitt*, P. P. Howe (ed.), 21 vols., New York: AMS Press, 1967.

Hegel, Georg Wilhelm Friedrich, *Aesthetics: lectures on fine art*, T. M. Knox (trans.), vol. I, Oxford: Clarendon Press, 1975, 2 vols.

Herder, Johann Gottfried, 'Die kritischen Wälder', *Werke*, 10 vols., vol. II: *Schriften zur Ästhetik und Literatur: 1767–1781*, Gunter E. Grimm (ed.), Bibliothek deutscher Klassiker 95, Frankfurt am Main: Deutscher Klassiker Verlag, 1993, pp. 9–442.

Hoffmann, E. T. A., *Werke*, Georg Ellinger (ed.), 15 vols., Berlin: Deutsches Verlagshaus Bong, 1900.

Kant, Immanuel, *Critique of judgment*, Werner S. Pluhar (trans.), Indianapolis, IN: Hackett, 1987.

Lessing, Gotthold Ephraim, *Laocoön: an essay on the limits of painting and poetry*, Edward Allen McCormick (trans.), Baltimore, MD: The Johns Hopkins University Press, 1984.

Liszt, Franz, 'Berlioz und seine Harold-Symphonie', in *Gesammelte Schriften*, Lina Ramann (ed.), 6 vols., Leipzig: Breitkopf & Härtel, V: 58ff.

Mill, John Stuart, *Essays on poetry*, F. Parvin Sharpless (ed.), Columbia, SC: University of South Carolina Press, 1976.

Nietzsche, Friedrich, *The birth of tragedy*, Walter Kaufmann (trans.), New York: Vintage, 1967.

Novalis, *Schriften: die Werke Friedrich von Hardenbergs*, vol. III: *Das philosophische Werk II*, Richard H. Samuel (ed.), Darmstadt: Wissenschaftliche Buchgesellschaft, 1968, 5 vols.

Reynolds, Sir Joshua, *Discourses on art*, Robert R. Wark (ed.), San Marino, CA: Huntington Library, 1959.

Richter, Jean Paul Friedrich, *Vorschule der Ästhetik*, in *Werke*, vol. V, Munich: Carl Hanser, 1963.

Rousseau, Jean-Jacques, and Johann Gottfried Herder, *On the origin of language*, John H. Moran and Alexander Gode (trans.), New York: Ungar, 1966.

Ruskin, John, *Modern painters*, 6 vols., London: George Allen, 1911.

Schelling, Friedrich Wilhelm Joseph, *The philosophy of art*, Douglas W. Stott (ed. and trans.), Minneapolis, MN: University of Minnesota Press, 1989.

Schiller, Friedrich, 'Über die ästhetische Erziehung des Menschen', in *Werke und Briefe*, vol. VIII: *Theoretische Schriften*, Rolf-Peter Janz (ed.), 12 vols., Frankfurt am Main: Deutscher Klassiker Verlag, 1992, pp. 556–676 (trans. Elizabeth M. Wilkinson and L. A. Willoughby, *On the aesthetic education of man*, Oxford: Clarendon Press, 1967).

Schlegel, August Wilhelm, *Vorlesungen über schöne Litteratur und Kunst*, Jacob Minor (ed.), 3 vols., Heilbronn: Henninger, 1884.

Schlegel, Friedrich, *Gespräch über die Poesie*, in *Kritische Friedrich-Schlegel-Ausgabe*, vol. II: *Charakteristiken und Kritiken I (1796–1801)*, Hans Eichner (ed.), Munich: Schöningh, 1967, pp. 284–362.

Schopenhauer, Arthur, *The world as will and representation*, E. F. J. Payne (trans.), 2 vols., New York: Dover, 1969.

Shelley, Percy Bysshe, *Shelley's poetry and prose: authoritative texts, criticism*, Donald H. Reiman and Sharon B. Powers (eds.), New York: Norton, 1977.

Solger, Karl Wilhelm Ferdinand, *Vorlesungen über Ästhetik*, K. W. L. Heyse (ed.), Darmstadt: Wissenschaftliche Buchgesellschaft, 1962.

Wackenroder, Wilhelm Heinrich, *Sämtliche Werke und Briefe*, Silvio Vietta and Richard Littlejohns (eds.), 2 vols., Heidelberg: Winter, 1991.
Wagner, Richard, *Gesammelte Schriften*, Julius Kapp (ed.), 14 vols., Leipzig: Hesse & Becker, 1914.

Secondary sources

Abrams, M. H., *The mirror and the lamp: Romantic theory and the critical tradition*, New York: Oxford University Press, 1953.
Adams, Hazard, 'Revisiting Reynolds's *Discourses* and Blake's annotations', in Robert E. Essick and Donald Pearce (eds.), *Blake in his time*, Bloomington, IN: Indiana University Press, 1978, pp. 128–44.
Altick, Richard D., *Paintings from books: art and literature in Britain, 1760–1900*, Columbus, OH: Ohio State University Press, 1985.
Barrell, John, *The birth of Pandora and the division of knowledge*, Basingstoke: Macmillan, 1992.
Barry, Kevin, *Language, music, and the sign: a study in aesthetics, poetics and poetic practice from Collins to Coleridge*, Cambridge University Press, 1987.
Braider, Christopher, *Refiguring the real: picture and modernity in word and image, 1400–1700*, Princeton, NJ: Princeton University Press, 1992.
Brown, Barry S., 'Sturm und Drang and the Romantic period in music', *Studies in Romanticism* 9 (1970), pp. 269–84.
Brown, Marshall, *Turning points: essays in the history of cultural expressions*, Stanford, CA: Stanford University Press, 1997.
Bryson, Norman, *Word and image: French painting of the Ancien Régime*, Cambridge University Press, 1981.
Chapple, Gerald, Frederick Hall and Hans Schulte (eds.), *The Romantic tradition: German literature and music in the nineteenth century*, Lanham, MD: University Press of America, 1992.
Clark, Kenneth, *The gothic revival: an essay in the history of taste*, 3rd edn, New York: Holt, Rinehart & Winston, 1962.
Dahlhaus, Carl, *Esthetics of music*, William W. Austin (trans.), Cambridge University Press, 1982.
Daverio, John, 'Schumann's systems of musical fragments and *Witz*', in *Nineteenth-century music and the German Romantic ideology*, New York: Schirmer Books, 1993, pp. 49–88.
Eaves, Morris, *William Blake's theory of art*, Princeton, NJ: Princeton University Press, 1982.
   The counter-arts conspiracy: art and industry in the age of Blake, Ithaca, NY: Cornell University Press, 1992.
   'The sister arts in British Romanticism', in *The Cambridge companion to British Romanticism*, Stuart Curran (ed.), Cambridge University Press, 1993, pp. 236–69.
Flaherty, Gloria, *Opera in the development of German critical thought*, Princeton, NJ: Princeton University Press, 1978.
Frank, Manfred, *Einführung in die frühromantische Ästhetik: Vorlesungen*, Frankfurt am Main: Suhrkamp, 1989.

Fried, Michael, *Absorption and theatricality: painting and beholder in the age of Diderot*, Berkeley, CA: University of California Press, 1980.

Frye, Northrop, 'Poetry and design in William Blake', in *Blake: a collection of critical essays*, Englewood Cliffs, NJ: Prentice-Hall, 1966, pp. 119–26.

The stubborn structure: essays on criticism and society, Ithaca, NY: Cornell University Press, 1970.

Galperin, William H., *The return of the visible in British Romanticism*, Baltimore, MD: The Johns Hopkins University Press, 1993.

Grey, Thomas S., 'Metaphorical modes in nineteenth-century music criticism: image, narrative, and idea', in *Music and text: critical inquiries*, Steven Paul Scher (ed.), Cambridge University Press, 1992, pp. 93–117.

Wagner's musical prose: texts and contexts, Cambridge University Press, 1995.

'*Tableaux vivants*: landscape, history painting, and the visual imagination in Mendelssohn's orchestral music', *Nineteenth-century music* 31 (1997), pp. 38–76.

Hagstrum, Jean H., *The sister arts: the tradition of literary pictorialism and English poetry from Dryden to Gray*, Chicago, IL: University of Chicago Press, 1958.

William Blake, poet and painter: an introduction to the illuminated verse, Chicago, IL: University of Chicago Press, 1964.

Heffernan, James A. W., *The re-creation of landscape: a study of Wordsworth, Coleridge, Constable, and Turner*, Hanover, NH: University Press of New England, 1985.

Museum of words: the poetics of ekphrasis from Homer to Ashbery, Chicago, IL: University of Chicago Press, 1993.

Kramer, Lawrence, *Music and poetry, the nineteenth century and after*, Berkeley, CA: University of California Press, 1984.

Kroeber, Karl, *Romantic landscape vision: Constable and Wordsworth*, Madison, WI: University of Wisconsin Press, 1975.

British romantic art, Berkeley, CA: University of California Press, 1986.

Larrabee, Stephen A., *English bards and Grecian marbles: the relationship between sculpture and poetry, especially in the Romantic period*, New York: Columbia University Press, 1943.

Lindenberger, Herbert, *Opera in history: from Monteverdi to Cage*, Stanford, CA: Stanford University Press, 1998.

Lockspeiser, Edward, *Music and painting: a study in comparative ideas from Turner to Schoenberg*, London: Cassell, 1973.

Mitchell, W. J. Thomas, *Blake's composite art: a study of the illuminated poetry*, Princeton, NJ: Princeton University Press, 1978.

Munsters, Wil, *La poétique du pittoresque en France de 1700 à 1830*, Geneva: Droz, 1991.

Neubauer, John, *The emancipation of music from language: departure from mimesis in eighteenth-century aesthetics*, New Haven, CT: Yale University Press, 1986.

Park, Roy, 'Ut pictura poesis': the nineteenth-century aftermath', *Journal of aesthetics and art criticism* 28 (1969), pp. 155–64.

Paulson, Ronald, *Literary landscape: Turner and Constable*, New Haven, CT: Yale University Press, 1982.

Perloff, Marjorie, *The futurist moment: avant-garde, avant guerre, and the language of rupture*, Chicago, IL: University of Chicago Press, 1986.

Pfotenhauer, Helmut, *Um 1800: Konfigurationen der Literatur, Kunstliteratur und Ästhetik*, Tübingen: Niemeyer, 1991.

Rosen, Charles, *The Romantic generation*, Cambridge, MA: Harvard University Press, 1995.

The Classical style: Haydn, Mozart, Beethoven, New York: Norton, 1997.

Rosen, Charles and Henri Zerner, *Romanticism and Realism: the mythology of nineteenth-century art*, New York: Viking Press, 1984.

Rosenblum, Robert, *Transformations in late eighteenth-century art*, Princeton, NJ: Princeton University Press, 1969.

Schweizer, Niklaus Rudolf, *The ut pictura poesis controversy in eighteenth-century England and Germany*, Bern: Herbert Lang, 1972.

Scott, David, *Pictorialist poetics: poetry and the visual arts in nineteenth-century France*, Cambridge University Press, 1988.

Spaethling, Robert, *Music and Mozart in the life of Goethe*, Columbia, SC: Camden House, 1987.

Weber, William, *The rise of musical classics in eighteenth-century England: a study in canon, ritual, and ideology*, Oxford: Clarendon Press, 1992.

Wellek, René, 'The concept of Romanticism in literary history', *Concepts of criticism*, New Haven, CT: Yale University Press, 1963, pp. 128–98.

'The parallelism between literature and the arts', in *English Institute annual: 1941*, New York: AMS Press, 1965, pp. 29–63.

Winn, James A., *Unsuspected eloquence: a history of the relations between poetry and music*, New Haven, CT: Yale University Press, 1981.

Index